CU00794646

MALTA: THE HURRICANE YEARS 1940-41

MALTA: THE HURRICANE YEARS 1940-41

Christopher Shores and Brian Cull
with Nicola Malizia

GRUB STREET · LONDON

Published by
Grub Street
The Basement
10 Chivalry Road
London SW11 1HT

Copyright © 1987 Grub Street, London
Text copyright © Christopher Shores, Brian Cull, Nicola Malizia

Reprinted 1999

Maps by Graeme Andrew

Shores, Christopher
  Malta: the Hurricane years: 1940-41
  1. World War, 1939-1945 - Aerial operations
  2. World War, 1939-1945 - Malta
  I. Title II. Cull, Brian III. Malizia, Nicola
  940.54'21   D785

  ISBN 0 948817 06 2

All rights reserved. No part of this publication may be reproduced, stored in a retrieval system, or transmitted in any form or by any means, electronic, mechanical, photocopying, recording, or otherwise, without the prior permission of the copyright owner.

Printed by Biddles Ltd, Guildford and King's Lynn

NB: Due to demand from customers this book is now back in print. However, because of production difficulties (ie: loss of film) there may be a slight reduction in quality in some of the photographs.

CONTENTS

FOREWORD AND ACKNOWLEDGEMENTS

The collection of information for the story of the siege of Malta has been a cross between detective work and the assembly of a large and complicated jigsaw puzzle. For the 1940–41 period particularly, records normally used in such research were incomplete or missing altogether in the majority of cases. Research has already taken the two English authors in excess of ten years, and they have still only completed the period up to 31 December 1941, which is dealt with in this volume.

We have tracked down and obtained assistance from a large proportion of the survivors of the long siege, or of their relatives, and it is only due to their invaluable help that it has been possible to present so complete a picture as now emerges. Regrettably there are still a few gaps, and despite repeated efforts, these have not proved possible to resolve – in most cases because, sadly, those who could provide the answers are dead.

The only fair way to express our deep thanks to those who gave so generously of their time and memories, is to list them in the order in which they appear in the text. Amongst the 'Fighter Boys', the first were those of the Hal Far Fighter Flight; George Burges provided a great deal of detailed information and reminiscences, and we were also aided by Peter Hartley; the late John Waters' logbook was also studied by kind permission of his brother. Considerable aid was given by Gerald Bellamy, who flew in those early days with 3 A.A.C.U., and later with 261 Squadron. Amongst the first Hurricane reinforcements who flew across France, 'Jock' Hilton Barber, Dick Sugden and George Maycock were most generous with their aid – and with their hospitality when Brian Cull visited them in Rhodesia. After long searches the late 'Eric' Taylor's sister, Mrs. Roberta Hards was traced and is thanked for providing a photograph and reminiscences of her brother. Jim Pickering offered much assistance and encouragement and supplied details of 418 Flight; he was instrumental in helping to reconstruct the early period of 261 Squadron's history, as were John Greenhalgh, Duncan Balden and Harry Ayre. Another logbook of great value was that of the late Fred Robertson, for which we are deeply indebted to Miss Rose Coombes of the Imperial War Museum.

Some of the earliest Naval fighter operations over the Mediterranean Fleet were detailed for us by C.L. Keighley-Peach. Two members of the disastrous Operation 'White' of November 1940 were found, and both were most forthcoming; thanks here to 'Jock' Norwell and Cyril Bamberger. Extracts from the diary of the late J.A.F. MacLachlan, published in 'The Saturday Book' and kindly supplied by courtesy of Hutchinsons were also particularly helpful. Next to arrive in Malta were the Naval airmen of 806 Squadron, and here we owe a great debt of gratitude to Desmond Vincent-Jones. Thanks are also tendered to Stanley Orr for details from his logbook provided for Chris Shores many years ago during research for an earlier book; to Robert Henley, Denis Tribe and Harry Phillips for additional information on 806 Squadron, and to Freddy de Frias re 803 Squadron. Ken Sims of the T.A.G. Associations provided invaluable assistance, as did the Fleet Air Arm Officers Association.

Amongst those who flew in from the Middle East late in January 1941, we have been aided by the late John 'Tiger' Pain, A.H. Deacon, Len Davies, the late Spencer Peacock-Edwards, and David Thacker, plus the diary of the late C.D. Whittingham. Much help also came from Doug Whitney, who flew in from Africa in March, and from Charles Laubscher, who is the sole survivor of the ill-fated detachment from 274 Squadron.

A great wealth of aid also came from amongst the April reinforcement flights which brought the first Hurricane IIs to the island. Operation 'Winch' of 3 April gave us Innes Westmacott and J.V. Marshall, while Operation 'Dunlop' of 27th. included Pat Hancock and Peter Jordan – and F.G. Sheppard, for information on whom we are indebted to another old friend, Ian Primmer of Australia. The aircrew who took part in Operation 'Splice' on 21 May, when 249 Squadron reached Malta, brought us a wealth of information. Thanks to ex-249 Squadron pilots R.A. 'Butch' Barton, 'Ginger' Neil, Pat Wells, Fred Etchells, 'Tommy' Thompson and John Beazley. Thanks too to Geoffrey Hare, commander of 800X Squadron, whose Fulmars led them in – and also to Philip Vella for valuable details on one of the Fulmar pilots, Arthur Jopling, including details from his logbook. The next reinforcement flight brought 46 Squadron (later 126 Squadron) to the island, commanded by one of the greatest Malta pilots, the late 'Sandy' Rabagliati. Grateful thanks to his brother Francis for the loan of his logbook, and for the provision of photographs, and also to Noel MacGregor who served with these squadrons.

Two noteable personalities were flown in aboard a Blenheim, and both have provided valuable information, particularly of night fighting over the island. These were George Powell-Sheddon and Don Stones. The final carrier-borne reinforcement of 1941 brought 242 and 605 Squadrons to Malta on 12 November; thanks to Ron Noble of the latter unit for much help, and for photographs of this critical period. Thanks too, to W.A. Satchell, who arrived late in 1941 to lead the Takali squadrons.

Other personnel who saw service on Malta and who were most helpful should also be recalled. A great deal of information on the reconnaissance operations and personalities was unstintingly provided by the late 'Titch' Whiteley, while Air Commodore Carter Jonas, O.B.E., generously allowed us to quote widely from his unpublished manuscript, 'Malta, Island Fortress', and provided other reminiscences. Much help also came from one of the R.A.F.'s greatest and most famous Engineering Officers, A.E. Louks, while other assistance came from John Tipton, a Wellington navigator in 40 Squadron, from ex-ground crew John Alton, and from Wg.Cdr. Bill Craddock.

The greatest encouragement and advice was given by Philip Vella, one of the 'founding fathers' of the National War Museum of Malta. Philip read the manuscript, provided his own boyhood reminiscences, checked civil and Army details, place names, etc., and also provided details from taped interviews and copied logbooks not only of the late Arthur Joping but also of the 228 Squadron Sunderland crew members, L.G.M. Rees and D.A.J. Taylor. He also kindly interviewed Wg.Cdr. G.V.W. Davies (Malta's original reconnaissance pilot), supplied transcript of a talk by Wg.Cdr. Edward Hardie, the former A.S.R. launch commander, and supplied many photographs. His hospitality to Brian Cull and members of his family in Malta was wonderful, while he took the trouble to see both English authors whilst visiting the U.K. Special thanks are also due to the Museum's air historian, Frederick Galea, to Richard Caruana and to the Museum's photographic expert, Louis Tortell.

Others to be thanked for aid include our old friend Eric Turner, late of the Air Historical Branch, Air Commodore H. Probert and Mrs. P.J. Elderfield of Dept. A.R.9a(R.A.F.) and the personnel of Dept.A.R.8b(R.A.F.) of the Ministry of Defence; the staff of the Public Record Office, Kew, the Imperial War Museum, and of the Commonwealth War Graves Commission, Maidenhead. Much assistance in obtaining certain books required for this study has been provided by Mr. David Wallis and staff at the Bury St. Edmunds Library, to whom we are extremely grateful. The Editor of 'Air Mail' is to be thanked for including our pleas for help in his journal.

The participation of the Luftwaffe required aid from Germany, and as always considerable help was forthcoming from friends there. Our thanks in this respect go to Hans Ring, Winfried Bock and Heinrich Weiss, without whose invaluable help sections of the book could not have been completed. Thanks also to WAST of Berlin for details of Luftwaffe casualties. Chris Ehrengardt of Paris gave details of the French floatplanes and their crews which reached the island, while Bjorn Olsen of Norway provided information on the Heinkel He115 'spyplanes' used from Malta. Help also came from David Brown of the Naval Historical Branch – an old friend and colleague – with information and advice on Fleet Air Arm matters.

Fellow enthusiasts Mike Schoeman of South Africa, Pete Clausen of Alabama, U.S.A., Paul Sortehaug of Dunedin, New Zealand, Ian Primmer of Thornton, Australia, and Jack Foreman of London have provided much help and encouragement; and very special thanks to our old and respected friend Bruce Lander of Oldham, for his most generous help; and to Eddie Pearson.

For specifically photographic help we thank Chaz Bowyer – and through him Graham Leggett – Bill Hartill, J. Arthur Heath, K. Cox (the latter three ex-Malta ground crew), Denis Tribe and Ian Primmer. Most recent aid in tracking down kin of one of the deceased Malta pilots, and in providing important references, has come from Oliver Clutton-Brock, to whom our thanks.

Finally some personal thanks; Brian Cull acknowledges the help and encouragement received over the years of research from friends Dick Rees and Barry Baddock; from Val Bickel, to whom very special thanks are due, and much belated gratitude is reserved for Mr. Jack Lee – a credit to his profession. He also records his sadness that his parents and sister, all of whom greatly encouraged his research in many ways, have all departed this life before our work was complete. Chris Shores records his particular appreciation for the efforts of our Italian co-author, Nico Malizia, and for the warm friendship and hospitality given by his family during a memorable visit to his home in Rimini. He also thanks his ever-patient wife Marion for her help and support.

Clearly such a work as this required wide reading and reference to much already-published material, most of which is warmly recommended to readers. A bibliography is provided at the rear of the book.

C.F. Shores – Hendon, London
B.H. Cull – Bury St. Edmunds, Suffolk
N. Malizia – Rimini, Italy
1987

INTRODUCTION

The little island of Malta lies at the 'crossroads' of the Mediterranean Sea. Situated 60 miles (90 kilometres) South of Sicily, it sits astride the main north–south route from Italy to Tripoli, Benghazi and Tunisia, and the west–east route from Gibraltar to Alexandria and the Suez Canal. Only half the size of the Isle of Man, this little speck of rock was home to 220,000 Maltese in 1940, and had until recently been the main base of the British Mediterranean Fleet.

With the growing hospitality of Fascist Italy – previously a traditional ally of Britain – during the thirties, it had become abundantly clear that the security of the island as a major base could not be relied upon. A new home for the Mediterranean Fleet was therefore developed at Alexandria, and Malta's importance declined strategically. At the 1939 Committee of Imperial Defence meeting a long-term air defence programme was agreed upon, as the Admiralty was anxious to retain the island as a staging post and reconnaissance base at least for light forces. The Air Ministry did not believe that it could adequately be defended, but acquiesed in the planned build-up to include 170 anti-aircraft guns, radar, searchlights, and four squadrons of fighters.

The Franco–German armistice of June 1940, coming as it did a few days after Italy's entry into the war, greatly increased Malta's importance once more, as it now became the only piece of friendly territory between Gibraltar and Egypt for the British. The demands of other theatres, coupled with the Air Ministry's understandable reluctance to send precious fighters to a location which they considered a lost cause, meant that at this stage Malta's defences were still far below those envisaged a year earlier.

Apart from the Air Headquarters in Valetta and the naval base and dockyard close by, there was little else. Three airfields had been developed for use by military aircraft at Hal Far, Luqa and Takali – the latter used mainly as a civil airfield at this stage – but no units had been sent out to operate from them. The single flyingboat squadron at the base anchorage at Kalafrana had been moved in September 1939 to Gibraltar. However in March 1939 one of the first three radar sets to leave the United Kingdom had reached Malta, so that an early warning system did already exist. (The other two sets had gone to Alexandria and Aden.) This first set, 241 A.M.E.S. (Air Ministry Experimental Station) was set up at Dingli Cliffs in March 1939; it was joined in June 1940 by a second station, 242 A.M.E.S. Also established on the island were 34 heavy and eight light anti-aircraft guns, and 24 searchlights. It was at least a start.

The Regia Aeronautica

When Italy entered the war her Regia Aeronautica was considered to be a modern and formidable force. In the event much of the equipment available was already approaching obsolescence, and Italian industry was to prove slow in producing replacements, spares, or more modern equipment. As a result serviceability levels were not very good, and this reflected itself in the relatively limited number of sorties that would be made compared with the overall strength apparently available. Before embarking upon the main narrative, the organization of the Regia Aeronautica's operational units is set out to provide an understanding of the unit descriptions, terms and strengths referred to in the text.

Command of a particular geographic area was exercised by a Squadra Aerea, responsible directly to the Comando Supremo in Rome. The Squadra could vary in size considerably, both in area and establishment, and was a command structure rather than a unit with a formal specific establishment. It can be compared loosely with an R.A.F. Group or a Luftflotte (Air Fleet) of the German Luftwaffe. Within the Squadra would be a number of stormi each normally comprising of two gruppi, and usually equipped throughout with one specific type of aircraft. The Gruppo was the basic operating unit, and comprised two squadriglie in the case of multi-engined types, and three squadriglie for single-engined types – particularly fighters. Because the aircraft establishment of a fighter gruppo was therefore generally higher than that of a bomber gruppo, the fighters tended to operate in gruppo strength, whilst bombers frequently operated in full stormo strength.

It must be made clear here however, that the Italian squadriglia was not directly comparable with the British squadron. It was in fact substantially smaller, comparing more directly with an R.A.F. flight. The Gruppo therefore was not greatly dissimilar in strength from a large R.A.F. squadron. The Stormo was roughly comparable with a fair-sized R.A.F. wing, but of much more rigid establishment and organization than the latter. Thus these Italian units were more directly comparable with the German Staffel, Gruppe and Geschwader. In the Luftwaffe system three Staffeln, each operating nine aircraft, formed a Gruppe, as with the Italian fighter system – although clearly a three-Staffel bomber Gruppe was larger than a two-squadrigle Italian bomber gruppo. Thereafter three Gruppen formed a Geschwader, while only two gruppi formed a stormo.

However the Regia Aeronautica also included a number of autonomous gruppi and squadriglie which operated individually under direct Squadra command, and not as part of a stormo or gruppo, as appropriate. These were always indicated by the inclusion of the word Autonomo (Aut.) after their unit title, and before the letters indicating their function (i.e. 23° Gruppo Aut.C.T.). The small °, ª, or ᵉ applied to Italian unit numbers correspond to the appropriate st., nd., rd., or th., applied behind numbers etc. in English, (i.e. 2nd., 3rd., a.s.o.) The function letters also require explanation. These indicate the basic function of the unit and are abbreviations as follows:

C.T.   – Caccia Terrestre   (Fighters, Land based)
C.M.   – Caccia Marittima   (Fighters, Water based)
B.T.   – Bombardamento Terrestre   (Bombers, Land based)
B.M.   – Bombardamento Marittima   (Bombers, Water based)
B.a'T. – Bombardamento a Tuffo   (Dive Bombers)
R.M.   – Ricognizione Marittima   (Reconnaissance, Water based)
R.S.T. – Ricognizione Strategica Terrestre   (Strategic Reconnaissance, Land based)
O.A.   – Osservazione Aerea   (Tactical Reconnaissance)
A.S. or – Aerosiluranti   (Aerial Torpedo carrying)
Sil.

Italian ranks were more directly comparable with those of the R.A.F., and were as follows:

Generale di Squadra Aerea	Air Marshal (A.M.)
Generale di Divisione Aerea	Air Vice-Marshal (A.V.M.)
Generale di Brigata Aerea	Air Commodore (Air Cdr.)
Colonello (Col.)	Group Captain (Gp.Capt.)
Tenente Colonello (Ten.Col.)	Wing Commander (Wg.Cdr.)
Maggiore (Magg.)	Squadron Leader (Sqn.Ldr.)
Capitano (Cap.)	Flight Lieutenant (Flt.Lt.)
Tenente (Ten.)	Flying Officer (Flg.Off.)
Sottotenente (Sottoten.)	Pilot Officer (Plt.Off.)
Aiutante di Battaglia (A/B)	No direct equivalent
Maresciallo (1ª, 2ª & 3ª Classe) (Mar.)	Warrant Officer (Wt.Off.)
Sergente Maggiore (Serg.Magg.)	Flight Sergeant (F/Sgt.)
Sergente (Serg.)	Sergeant (Sgt.)
Aviere Scelto (Av.Sc.)	Corporal (Cpl.)
1ᵉ Aviere (1ᵉAv.)	Leading Aircraftsman (L.A.C.)
Aviere (Av.)	Aircraftsman 1 (A.C.1)

A full Order of Battle for the 2ª Squadra Aerea in Sicily on 10 June 1940, and for the commands based on Sardinia and on the Aegean Islands on the same date will be found in Appendix VIII, which also details the units operated by the Regia Aeronautica from Sicily during 1941, with approximate dates.

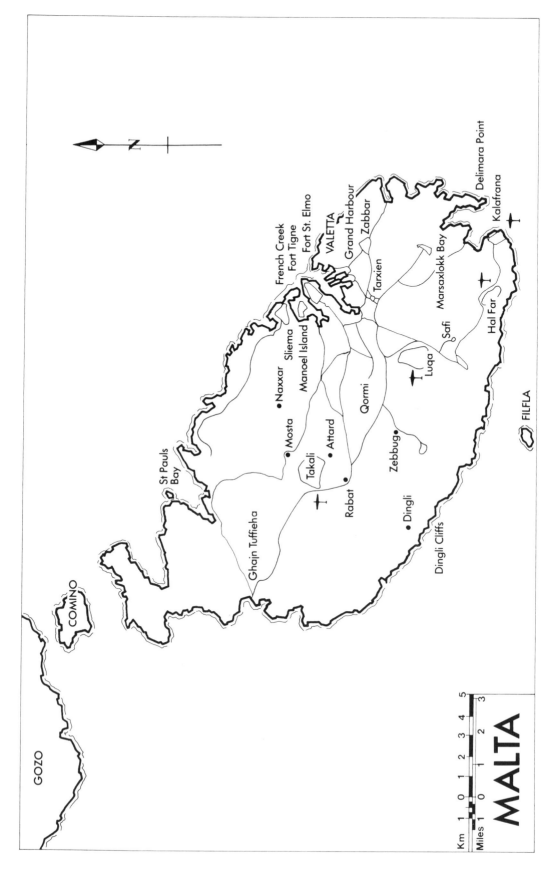

GOZO

COMINO

St Pauls
Bay

Ghajn Tuffieha

French Creek
Fort Tigne

Fort St. Elmo

VALETTA
Grand Harbour

Zabbar

Naxxar

Sliema

Manoel Island

Mosta

Tarxien

Marsaxlokk Bay

Delimara Point

Kalafrana

Attard

Qormi

Takali

Luqa

Safi

Hal Far

Rabat

Zebbug

Dingli

Dingli Cliffs

FILFLA

Km 1   0   1   2   3   4   5

Miles 1   0   1   2   3

MALTA

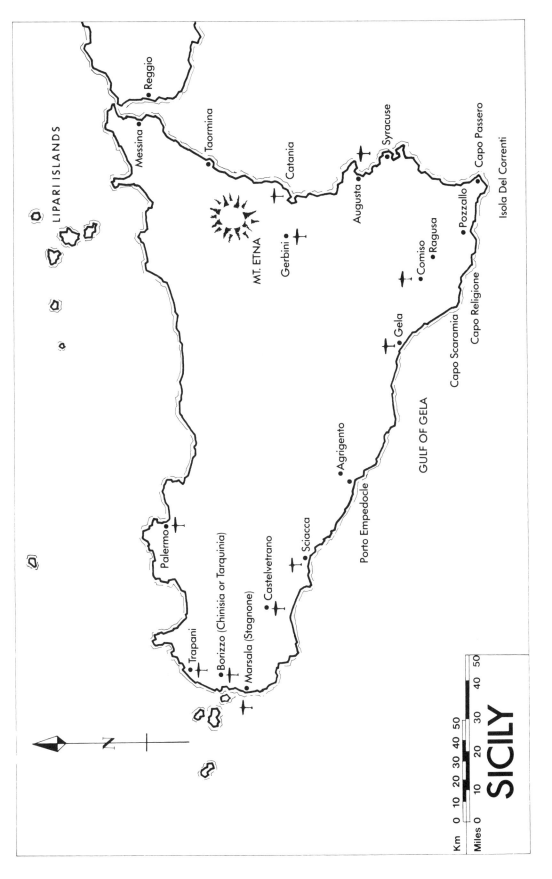

LIPARI ISLANDS

Reggio

Messina

Taormina

Catania

MT. ETNA

Gerbini

Augusta

Syracuse

Capo Passero

Pozzallo

Isola Del Correnti

Comiso

Ragusa

Capo Religione

Capo Scaramia

Gela

GULF OF GELA

Agrigento

Porto Empedocle

Sciacca

Castelvetrano

Marsala (Stagnone)

Borizzo (Chinisia or Tarquinia)

Trapani

Palermo

N

Km 0 10 20 30 40 50

Miles 0   10   20   30   40   50

SICILY

A Macchi C.200 of the 88ª Squadriglia, 6° Gruppo Autonomo C.T. passes over Hal Far airfield on the morning of 27 October, 1940, whilst engaged with others of the unit in escorting a photographic reconnaissance Savoia S.79. (*N. Malizia*)

Chapter 1

THE OPENING ROUND

The first day's attacks on 11 June 1940 included a raid by 15 Savoia S.79s of the 11° Stormo B.T. on the dockyards at Valetta. Here aircraft of the Stormo's 68ª Squadriglia, 34° Gruppo from Comiso, head for Malta. (*A.M.I. via N. Malizia*)

As the first grey light of dawn stole over Southern Sicily, shadowy figures could be seen in a state of great activity on the airfields at Comiso, Catania and Gela. An engine spluttered and burst into life, followed rapidly by another, and then a whole host. It was 0430 on 11 June 1940, and for Italy the war had begun. During the previous evening Benito Mussolini had announced his declaration of war on France and Britain, as the armies of these nations staggered beneath the violent blows of the German Wehrmacht's 'Blitzkrieg'. But this had been expected for some days – only the date had been uncertain. Indeed the units of the Regia Aeronautica's 2ª Squadra Aerea had moved to Sicily from Padua in great secrecy a full eight days earlier. From here their priority target was to be the island of Malta.

1

All units of the Squadra were to be involved in this first raid, the first off being thirty Savoia S.79 trimotor bombers of Colonello Umberto Mazzini's 34° Stormo B.T. from Catania. As the leading bombers lifted into the air, heading for Hal Far airfield, the time was noted at 0435. Fifteen minutes later fifteen more of these bombers from Col. Arnaldo Lubelli's 11° Stormo B.T. began leaving Comiso to attack the dockyards at Valetta, followed at 0500 by a final ten S.79s from Col. Enrico Pezzi's 41° Stormo B.T. from Gela, which headed for Kalafrana seaplane base. Allowing the bombers time to form up and set course for their targets, the fighter escort then began taking off from Comiso to provide cover over the target areas. These were Macchi C.200 monoplanes from Tenente Colonello Armando Francois' 6° Gruppo Autonomo C.T.; eighteen MC 200s, drawn equally from the 79ª and 88ª Squadriglia were ordered to undertake this mission, while three more from the 81ª Squadriglia were to maintain a protective patrol over the home airfields in case of any retaliatory attack on the returning bombers.

Malta's lone radar set soon recorded the incoming intruders – an event which had been expected for some time – and at Hal Far the readiness section of the Fighter Flight was ordered up. Led by Flt.Lt. George Burges, the three Gloster Gladiator biplanes clawed for altitude, but maintained a neat formation. Well before they had reached the level of the incoming bombers, the English pilots could see bombs falling on Valetta and Hal Far, but with so many possible targets to intercept they now became split up. Burges in N5531 saw nine bombers turning in a wide circle south of the island, obviously preparing to head back to Sicily. Cutting across the circle, he and one of the other pilots gave chase, and he was able to fire most of his ammunition at one bomber without apparent result. These were some of the 34° Stormo aircraft which had hit Hal Far, and the crews subsequently reported that the Gladiators fired from long range; one aircraft of the 52° Gruppo was hit in the fuselage, 1ᵉ Aviere Armiere Francesco Ferrara returning fire from the dorsal position with his 12.7mm Breda-SAFAT gun.

An escorting MC 200 from the 79ª Squadriglia spotted the third Gladiator, and Tenente Giuseppe Pesola blasted off 125 rounds at this without apparent result. His opponent, Flg.Off. 'Timber' Woods, had already been engaged with the bombers and gave a graphic account of the fight as it had appeared to him: "We sighted a formation of five S.79s approaching Valetta at a height of approximately 15,000 feet, and Red Two delivered an attack from astern. The enemy had turned out to sea. I delivered an attack from astern, and got in a good burst at a range of approximately 200 yards. My fire was returned. I then broke away and returned over the Island at approximately 11,000 feet south of Grand Harbour. While still climbing to gain height, I observed another formation of five enemy aircraft approaching. They were at about the same height as myself. I attacked from abeam at about 150 yards and got in one good burst. The enemy started firing at me long before I opened up. This formation broke slightly but left me well behind them when I tried to get in an attack from astern. Just after that, when again climbing to gain more height, I suddenly heard machine gun fire from behind me. I immediately went into a steep left-hand turn and saw a single engined fighter diving and firing at me. For quite three minutes I circled as tightly

2

Hal Far airfield received its first attack of the war on 11 June 1940 by S.79s of the Catania-based 34°
Stormo B.T. Here an aircraft of 216ª Squadriglia, 53° Gruppo is seen at its home airfield. (*C. Lucchini
via N. Malizia*)

Escort to the first day's raids was provided by the Macchi C.200 Series I fighters of the 6° Gruppo
Autonomo C.T. Aircraft of the 81ª Squadriglia, two of which are seen here about to take off, provided
a patrol over the Sicilian airfields to protect the returning bombers from a possible British counter-
strike. The pilot of the nearest Macchi appears to be ordering his dog to 'stay'. (*A.M.I. via N. Malizia*)

as possible and got the enemy in my sight. I got in a good burst, full deflection shot, and he went down in a steep dive with black smoke pouring from his tail. I could not follow him down, but he appeared to go into the sea." Woods was subsequently credited with probably shooting down the Macchi as the first victory for the defenders, but in fact Pesola's aircraft had not even been seriously damaged. Evasive action, and the black exhaust smoke from a hastily-opened throttle had obviously misled the British pilot.

First combat over the island was between an MC 200 and a Gladiator flown by Flg.Off. W.J. 'Timber' Woods, who was credited with a victory, although in fact the Italian aircraft returned safely to base. This is Woods, seen some months later in Greece. (*E.G. Jones Collection*)

Bombers of the 11° Stormo reported seeing a flyingboat identified as a Saro London, and fired on this, but then the raid was over. Thirty bombs of 250kg. and 112 more of 100kg. had been released on the three targets, achieving little concentration, but a wide spread of minor damage – mainly to surrounding civilian properties.

Five hours later a lone S.79 was sent out by the 34° Stormo to reconnoitre the results of the raid. Again Gladiators were 'scrambled', this time two going up to intercept the intruder. Flg.Off. John Waters in N5520 got within range and opened fire. He believed that he had shot down the Italian machine, but in fact it was merely driven away, making for Sicily without being able to complete its mission.

Despite the presence of the Gladiators, a further raid was despatched by 2ª Squadra during the afternoon, this time without fighter escort. Fifteen S.79s from the 11º Stormo went to Kalafrana and ten from the 41º Stormo to Valetta, while eight from the 34º returned to Hal Far and five more headed for Valetta's Grand Harbour. No Gladiators were able to intercept on this occasion, but the anti-aircraft defences put up a heavy and accurate barrage. Eight S.79s were hit, six of them from the 34º Stormo, and one crewmember was slightly wounded. 204 × 100kg., fifteen 250kg. and twenty 20kg. incendiaries were dropped, to complete the first day's hostilities over the island – the first day of a battle which was to last nearly two and a half years.

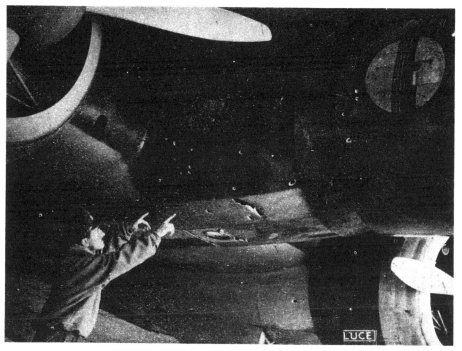

Damage to the Italians on 11 June 1940 was inflicted only by the anti-aircraft defences. An airman of the Regia Aeronautica points to splinter holes in the forward fuselage of his S.79. (*N. Malizia*)

Despite the inability of the Air Ministry to despatch viable fighter defences to the island, some measures at least were put in hand as the likelihood of an active and hostile participation in the war by Italy became more apparent. Earlier in the year the aircraft carrier H.M.S. 'Glorious' had served briefly in the Mediterranean before being rushed home to take part in the operations off Norway in April. On arrival she had offloaded eighteen Sea Gladiators (N5518–5535) which were to be held in reserve for her 802 Squadron, and were stored in crates at Kalafrana. As she headed homewards in great haste, she stopped long enough to embark

N5532, 5533 and 5534 on 12 April, but left the other fifteen behind. At that time no carrier remained with the Mediterranean Fleet, so there was no immediate call for these aircraft by the Fleet Air Arm, though immediately after the outbreak of war with Italy H.M.S. 'Eagle', having just been extensively refitted in Singapore, arrived at Alexandria to join the fleet. Although not normally carrying a fighter complement, she took on board four Sea Gladiators to supplement her 18 Swordfish to provide some degree of aerial protection; these fighters were issued from stocks held in Egypt. Of the fighters at Kalafrana, three were subsequently shipped to Egypt.

Flt.Lt. George Burges (left) was to become the first fighter pilot on Malta to receive a decoration. He had previously served as Personal Assistant to the A.O.C., Air Commodore F.H.M. Maynard, with whom he is seen here. (*G. Burges*)

Consequently during March 1940 measures were put in hand to provide a station Fighter Flight at Hal Far, then the main R.A.F. airfield and under the command of Wg.Cdr. G.R. O'Sullivan. No trained fighter pilots were available, but a number of volunteers were gathered from amongst those pilots on the island. Initially came Flt.Lt. P.G. Keeble and Flg.Off. W.J. Woods from the Hal Far Station Flight, and Flg.Off. P.W. Hartley, who had been flying Fairey Swordfish biplane floatplanes from Kalafrana with 3 Anti-Aircraft Cooperation Unit. They were joined during April by Sqn.Ldr. A.C. Martin, who had been commanding the other airfield at Luqa, Flt.Lt. G. Burges, who had been Personal

Assistant to the Air Officer Commanding on Malta, Air Commodore F.H.M. Maynard, and Flg.Off. J. Waters who had been serving with 3 A.A.C.U., but who during March had been sent aboard 'Glorious' for one week of fighter training with 802 Squadron. Somewhat later Flt.Off. P.B. Alexander would join this small team; he had been serving with an Experimental Flight which had been operating radio-controlled Queen Bee target 'drones'. Sgt. L.F. Ashbury was also attached to the flight for a short time. Six Sea Gladiators were made available to the R.A.F., four of which were initially erected and delivered to Hal Far on 19 April (N5519, 5520, 5524 and 5531). By the end of May the other two (N5523 and 5529) had been erected, while the six other crated aircraft were used for spares. Thus it can be seen that the Fighter Flight was no last minute panic organization, but had been in existence and equipped for nearly two months before the outbreak of hostilities. The assembled fighters were subsequently fitted with armour plate behind the pilots' seats and with variable-pitch three-blade airscrews.

Some of the stalwarts of the Hal Far Fighter Flight; l. to r. Flg.Off. John Waters and Flg.Off. Peter Hartley, both ex-No. 3 A.A.C.U., and Plt.Off. Peter Alexander from the Experimental Flight. (*Waters Collection*)

Also based at Malta at this time were the five Swordfish, mostly floatplane versions, useful only for air/sea rescue, together with a few Moths, Gordons and Magisters. 202 Squadron, which was equipped with Saro London flyingboats, had moved to Gibraltar in September 1939, but the aircraft would from time to time be detached to operate from the island, as would Short Sunderlands from 230 Squadron at Alexandria.

Swordfish floatplane of No. 3 Anti-Aircraft Co-operation Unit in flight over the Maltese coastline. After the outbreak of hostilities these aircraft were employed for air-sea rescue duties. (*Waters Collection*)

12–14/6/40

Following the initial day's onslaught, cloudy weather on 12 June brought a respite, while on 13th. bombers appeared singly during the day, doing little more than minimal damage and nuisance. One S.79 of the 60ª Squadriglia, 33° Gruppo, 11° Stormo B.T. was engaged by a number of Gladiators, but escaped. This would appear to have been the aircraft attacked by Flg.Off. Waters in N5520, who again believed that he had shot down his quarrie. The first loss sustained by the Italians was actually to occur on 14th., but in somewhat different circumstances. At dawn five S.79s from the 214ª Squadriglia, 52° Gruppo, 34° Stormo set off to bomb the dockyard and the Grand Harbour. Encountering bad weather two of the bombers aborted the mission and returned to base, but one of these crashed near Catania while coming in to land, and blew up; all the crew were killed.

15–16/6/40

The Gladiators were up again on 15th. when ten 11° Stormo bombers with nine escorting MC 200s appeared. Again interception could not be made until the bombing was complete. The intercepting pilots claimed damage to one bomber, reporting that it appeared to carry German markings – highly unlikely! The Italians reported damage to one machine, but attributed this to anti-aircraft fire, reporting that the Gladiators' assault was ineffective. Next day however another S.79, this time from 41° Stormo, was damaged by the fighters.

S.79s drone in over the North Malta coastline to bomb targets in the Grand Harbour. The geography of the target can be easily seen from the air. (*A.M.I. via N. Malizia*)

17–20/6/40

The island was to enjoy a number of days' respite after 16th., as 2ª Squadra turned its attentions to targets in the French protectorate of Tunisia. On 20 June came a welcome reinforcement. Two Royal Navy training squadrons, Nos. 767 and 769, had been based at the French Naval airfield at Olayvestre, near Hyères on the South coast. With the rapid German advance past Paris, these had been withdrawn to Algeria on 18th., and here they were split into two groups, each of twelve Swordfish aircraft. The best twelve with the most experienced crews became 830 Squadron under Lt.Cdr. F.D. Howie, and departed via Tunis for Malta. The other twelve went to Gibraltar. On arrival at Hal Far of 830 Squadron, the remainder of 3 A.A.C.U. was incorporated into the squadron to

9

provide an adequate ground echelon, and five R.A.F. gunners were taken on strength. Malta now possessed in these torpedo-bombers a limited anti-shipping strike arm. That very night however came the first Italian night raids on the island – against which little effective resistance could initially be offered. From Sicily six S.79s from the 34° Stormo and one from the Reparto Volo (Flying Detachment) of 3ª Divisione 'Centauro', were led off singly at intervals by the Squadra's commanding general, Ettore Lodi. Forty-two bombs of 100kg. were dropped during a four hour period.

21/6/40

Although these attacks did little damage, the events of 21 June were to be of more immediate concern. During the morning Sqn.Ldr. Martin crashed one of the precious Gladiators whilst taking off, while in the afternoon Flg.Off. Hartley damaged the undercarriage of his aircraft during take-off, and as a result crashed on landing. One Gladiator had sustained damage to the front of the fuselage while the other was damaged at the rear. The Command Engineering Officer, Sqn.Ldr. A.E. Louks, assessed the damage and considered one good aircraft could be constructed out of the two wrecks; to quote Louks: "... a hybrid was born out of two corpses."

22/6/40

The first concrete success occurred on 22 June when during the afternoon a lone S.79 from the 216ª Squadriglia, 53° Gruppo, 34° Stormo, approached the island on reconnaissance, flown by Ten. Francesco Solimena. George Burges recalls: "'Timber' Woods and I were on the 1600 hours to dusk watch when the alarm went off. We took off and climbed as hard as we could go, as was the custom. We did not attempt to maintain close formation because if one aircraft could climb faster than the other then the additional height gained might be an advantage. Ground Control as usual gave us the position and course of the enemy. The enemy turned out to be a single SM79 presumably on a photographic sortie. It came right down the centre of the island from Gozo, and on this occasion we were 2,000–3,000 feet above it. 'Timber' went in first but I did not see any results. I managed to get right behind it and shot off the port engine. I was told this happened right over Sliema and Valetta and caused quite a stir in the population. The aircraft caught fire and crashed in the sea off Kalafrana." The pilot and one other member of the crew of this Savoia (MM22068) survived to become prisoners. Some distance away, a patrolling Cant Z.506B floatplane made a radio intercept from the stricken bomber and subsequently reported to 2ª Squadra that it had been shot down by the anti-aircraft defences.

23/6/40

Burges was to achieve a success of similar importance next day when he and Woods again scrambled after an incoming raid. This time the raiders were from

11° Stormo B.T., accompanied by an escort of MC 200s. The two Gladiators attacked the bombers without obvious result, but Burges was then attacked by one of the escorting fighters, an aircraft of the 88ª Squadriglia flown by Serg.Magg. Lamberto Molinelli. Burges whirled N5519 round and a "real old W.W.I dogfight" began over the sea off Sliema. The faster Macchi had the initiative, but overshot the nimble Gladiator, allowing Burges to "belt him up the backside as he went past". After four or five such passes the Macchi suddenly caught fire and Molinelli baled out into the sea. (The Italians later recorded that he had been shot down by "one round of A.A."). Swiftly recovered from the water, Molinelli was taken to Imtarfa Hospital where Burges later visited him. He did not find his victim particularly friendly!

While landing from this action, 'Timber' Woods had collided with a Queen Bee target drone, causing damage to yet another Gladiator. Two days later the capitulation of France closed once and for all the overland reinforcement route. However aid had by this time already arrived – and in a very solid form. Hurricanes!

Reinforcements

The reinforcement of the Middle East with Hurricanes had already begun just before the entry of Italy into the war, but initially these were not intended for Malta, the defence of the main Fleet base at Alexandria enjoying a higher

One of the first Hurricanes to arrive in Malta on 13 June 1940 was flown by Flg.Off. F.F. 'Eric' Taylor. He remained on the island, becoming one of the most successful of the early fighter pilots. By the time of his death in action on 26 February 1941 he had been credited with at least seven victories and received the D.F.C. (*Mrs. R. Hards*)

priority. On 6 June 1940 six Hurricanes were assembled at 10 Maintenance Unit, Hullavington, together with a group of seven pilots: Sqn.Ldr. C. Ryley (i/c), Sqn.Ldr. C.W.M. Ling, Flt.Lt. T.M. Lockyer, Flg.Off. F.F. Taylor, Plt.Off. D.T. Saville, Plt.Off. H.A.R. Prowse and Plt.Off. T. Balmforth (reserve). On the same day two Hudsons were flown down from 233 Squadron at Leuchars, Scotland, to lead the Hurricanes during their long flight to the Middle East. Flg.Off. G.W.V. Davies would fly N7342, with Flt.Lt. L.F. Cooper as co-pilot, while Flg.Off. J.P. Stacey Smyth flew N7357, aided by Flg.Off. J.G.H. Potter. Two days later the two Hudsons and six Hurricanes left, via Tangmere, Rennes, Toulouse and Marseilles/Marignane, the reserve pilot, Balmforth, travelling in Davies' Hudson. While landing at Marignane Plt.Off. Prowse ran into a filled-in bomb crater; the undercarriage of P2644 sunk in and the port main wheel leg snapped off, the aircraft swinging to starboard and tipping onto its nose.

Flg.Off. G.W. Vincent Davies of 233 Squadron led some of Malta's initial complement of Hurricanes to the island in Hudson N7324. He and his aircraft and crew remained at Luqa, providing the island with its first effective long-range aerial reconnaissance facility, until the aircraft was shot down by mistake by a Royal Navy Fulmar. (*National War Museum Assoc.*)

The seven remaining aircraft reached Tunis/El Aouina airfield safely on 10th., but here more troubles manifested themselves. Next morning at 0630 Sqn.Ldr. Ryley signalled Air Ministry: "Due to defective auxilliary fuel pumps, Hurricanes can not fly non-stop from Tunis to Mersa Matruh..." It seems that two of the Hurricanes only were having pump trouble, for at 1635 H.Q. Malta signalled Air Ministry: "Following received from Bizerta... 'two Hurricanes and Hudson leaving for El Djem p.m. 11/6. Will fly to Mersa Matruh tomorrow if wind favourable. One Hudson and three Hurricanes request permission to arrive Malta today for servicing petrol pumps. Can not continue without this. Ends.' In view today's raids on Hal Far and absence of Merlin or Hurricane spares at Malta, also your specific instructions regarding alternative route in event hostilities with Italy, I have refused permission land Malta and have advised every effort to obtain local repairs in Tunisia." Clearly, a copy of Ryley's earlier signal had also been sent to H.Q. Malta. At 1810, Air Ministry sent: "If confident that auxilliary fuel pumps of three serviceable Hurricanes are functioning satisfactorily, these Hurricanes with one escorting Hudson should proceed on first following wind. If in doubt all Hurricanes should wait arrival of fitter from Hawkers who is leaving U.K. by air today, with twelve new auxilliary pumps, which will provide for all eventualities. The second escorting Hudson and remaining two Hurricanes are to proceed as soon as serviceable on first following wind. The fitter from Hawkers on return journey will land Marignane and make serviceable the auxilliary pump on the Hurricane which is now awaiting repair at this place."

Hurricane P2644 abandoned after losing the port undercarriage leg while landing at Marignane on 8th June 1940. These photographs of the aircraft, which still carries its underwing ferry-tanks, were taken by a German serviceman after the French capitulation. (*via J-L. Roba*)

12/6/40

Next day at 1432 Sir William Dobbie, Lieutenant-Governor of Malta, signalled the War Office: "Raids here yesterday show importance of fighter aircraft. The four Gladiators here, though successful in bringing one plane down, are too slow. There are five Hurricanes in Tunis en route to Egypt. A.O.C. has asked Air Ministry to let them be directed here. Wish strongly to support this request. Believe a few effective fighters would have far reaching deterrent effect and produce very encouraging results." It seems that War Office agreement was forthcoming, for at 1709 H.Q., R.A.F. Middle East signalled Air H.Q. Malta: "...I agree to proposal that five Hurricanes now at Tunis en route to Egypt be allotted Malta for the time being. Presume you will arrange with Admiralty for movement of stores understood to be now at Gibraltar." Stores were at once loaded onto the S.S. 'Palestinian Prince' which sailed from Gibraltar on 13 June, via the Cape of Good Hope.

13/6/40

Apparently by 13th. Sqn.Ldr. Ryley, Flt.Lt. Lockyer and Plt.Off. Saville had arrived at Luqa, led by Stacey Smyth's Hudson, for D.D.W.O. now signalled D.C.A.S.: "We have, as you know, sent six Hurricanes by air to the Middle East. At this moment two are in Tunis, three in Malta and one crashed Marseilles." These pilots did not remain however, leaving that same day for Mersa Matruh. On arrival here the formation almost suffered disaster, recalled by Flg.Off. Vernon Woodward, a Canadian fighter pilot serving with 33 Squadron, who was Duty Pilot at this airfield: "The Hurricanes with underwing long-range tanks, coming out of the sunset, with no advance warning were something we had not seen before. I was standing near one of our ground-to-air machine gun posts and ordered them to open fire – the Hudson was superficially damaged and the navigator wounded in one shoulder; the affair was 'laughed-off'". At Mersa Matruh Sqn.Ldr. Ryley was posted temporarily to command 230 Squadron on Sunderlands (having trained on Sunderlands pre-war), as the regular C.O., Wng.Cdr. G. Francis, was sick. Within a month he would hand the unit back to Francis, and would be posted to command 33 Squadron (Gladiators) at Helwan. The Hudson departed on 16th. on the first leg of the return flight to England.

21/6/40

Eventually the two remaining Hurricanes – P2641 and 2645 – reached Luqa with the second Hudson on 21 June, presumably after remedial works by the Hawker's fitter at El Aouina. Here Taylor (an ex-ferry pilot) and Balmforth, who had arrived in the Hudson, remained. 'Larry' Ling left by Sunderland for a training post at R.A.F. Habbaniya, Iraq. He would later play an active part in the defence of this base in May 1941, when he commanded one of the 'scratch' squadrons of training aircraft formed at that time.

15/6/40

In the meantime however, orders had been issued for twelve Blenheims and twelve Hurricanes to be flown to the Middle East as further reinforcements, before the route across France was lost. The Blenheims were drawn from 20 M.U. at Aston Down, while the Hurricanes came from 10 M.U., Hullavington (two), 20 M.U. (six) and 27 M.U., Shawbury (four). All twenty-four aircraft passed through Aston Down, where they were tested and handed over to the pilots as being in good flying condition. The Hurricanes had all been in the process of having extra fuel tanks removed on the previous night, prior to being disassembled and crated. Now that it was decided that they should be flown, the tanks had to be refitted late on 15th.

16/6/40

Sqn.Ldr. G.A.M. 'Scotty' Pryde, DFC, late of 21 Squadron, was placed in charge of the party, whilst four experienced navigators were posted in. The remainder of the personnel came from 4 Ferry Pilots' Pool, Kemble. Next day the pilots at Kemble – all volunteers for the flight – were flown to Aston Down in three Ansons, but arrived to find they were not expected, and were flown back. The flight was repeated in the afternoon, and this time they were introduced to Sqn.Ldr. Pryde.

It now transpired that Air Ministry had not allocated any gunners for the Blenheims and when enquiries were made, four gunners only were made available. Sqn.Ldr. Pryde informed Air Ministry that this was an insufficient number, but was told that only four could be spared; these were also trained W/T operators. When the O.C. 4 Ferry Pool, Sqn.Ldr. F.W.L. Wild, found out, he immediately – on his own initiative – instructed another eight gunners to be made available. Finally, all the Blenheims received a crew of three; four would have a pilot, navigator and W.O.P./A.G., the remainder a pilot, an air gunner and a fitter. It was decided to divide the aircraft into four flights, each consisting of three Blenheims and three Hurricanes; one Blenheim of each flight would contain a navigator and W.O.P./A.G. The formations and pilots were:

'A' Flight

Blenheims		*Hurricanes*	
L9351	Flt.Lt. J. Wilkinson-Bell	P2653	Plt.Off. R.H. Barber
L9314	Plt.Off. D.S. Johnson	P2584	Plt.Off. A.G. Maycock
L9315	Flg.Off. J. McCash	P2651	Plt.Off. C.R. Glen

'B' Flight

L9320	Flt.Lt. E.S.T. Cole*	P2544	Plt.Off. R.W.H. Carter
L9319	Flg.Off. B. Walker	P2642	Plt.Off. M.A. Sims
L9316	Sgt. R.T.M. Saunders	P2648	Plt.Off. J. Mansel-Lewis

'C' Flight

L9263	Sqn.Ldr. G.A.M. Pryde	P2623	Plt.Off. W.P. Collins

L9335	Wt.Off. F.W. Cook*	P2629	Plt.Off. W.R.C. Sugden
L9318	Sgt. M. Field	P2626	Flg.Off. J.C. Smyth

'D' Flight

L9300	Flg.Off. V.T.L. Wood*	P2625	Plt.Off. C. Haddon-Hall
L9317	Plt.Off. C.W. Handley	P2650	Plt.Off. G.D.H. Beardon
L9334	Plt.Off. S.J. Millen	P2614	Plt.Off. A.G. McAdam

(*Flt.Lt. Cole was a W.W.I fighter pilot who had been credited with 10 victories flying with 1 and 60 Squadrons during that conflict; Wt.Off. Cook had over 2,000 flying hours to his credit; Flg.Off. Wood had recently been a fighter pilot with 610 Squadron.)

All the guns were taken out of the Hurricanes and carried in the Blenheims. This was necessary partly because of the difficulties of fitting both tanks and guns, and partly owing to the question of load with the additional fuel aboard. It would have been possible to retain six guns but the fuel pipes to the outboard tanks would have passed very close to these, and if used, there might have been the chance of fire. The six guns with ammunition would have added another 250lbs. extra weight which, though possible, was highly undesirable.

17/6/40

Nine Blenheims and nine Hurricanes departed from Aston Down for Tangmere during the afternoon, followed by the remaining six aircraft during the evening. There was much congestion at Tangmere, for not only was there the normal station complement, but two additional fighter squadrons had arrived for a special operation. Besides the twelve Blenheims and twelve Hurricanes, there were eight additional ferry aircraft present. However, all crews found somewhere to sleep and all would be provided with a hot breakfast before they started next morning.

At about 2230 a change of route was necessitated as a result of information received from Bordeaux. This change was communicated to Tangmere by telephone at 2330 after most of the crews had gone to bed. Working out of the new course and alterations to the maps had therefore to be carried out before starting next morning. These last minute changes would result in a number of misunderstandings. The original written instructions had specified Cap Frehel–Nantes–Bordeaux–Castres–Marignane–Tunis–El Djem–Mersa Matruh. Now the route became Cap Frehel–Nantes–Bordeaux–Perpignan–Setif–Malta. Finally, at 2330, Sqn.Ldr. Pryde received a further call, changing the route to Cap Frehel–Marignane–Setif–Malta. It was the Air Ministry's intention that in flying to Marignane the aircraft would keep to the route laid down in the written orders i.e. via Nantes and Bordeaux, even though they were not to land at the latter for refuelling purposes. The Air Ministry again phoned Sqn.Ldr. Pryde at 0405 on the morning of 18th. to verify this. However, apparently Sqn.Ldr. Pryde understood the change to mean that Bordeaux should be cut out altogether, the aircraft flying direct from Cap Frehel to Marignane; this instruction was given to his flight commanders and further, that beyond Marignane the route was to be

16

Tunis–Malta. This course had two disadvantages; it passed over the Monts d' Auvergne, where weather conditions were likely to become more difficult than the route via Nantes and Bordeaux, which led along the coast and thence by the valley of the Gironde; secondly, it brought the formation nearer to the advancing Germans.

18/6/40

Orders had been given for the aircraft to be ready to start at 0430 and the majority were ready at this time. However, some of the Hurricanes had not arrived until late the previous evening and refuelling had not been completed, while further delay had been occasioned by the changes in route. As a result take-off commenced at 0630. An order had been issued to take-off in flights but this was not complied with. No attempt had been made to form up the aircraft on the ground so that they could take-off in correct order. In the case of 'D' Flight, Flg.Off. Wood found that his R/T was out of order and instructed the other two Blenheims to take-off with the rest of the formation, and for his three Hurricanes to remain behind with him. The three Hurricanes forming part of Sqn.Ldr. Pryde's flight were also delayed, partly because they were not refuelled in time and partly because they had formed up behind Flg.Off. Wood's Blenheim and could not get past. The result was that 11 Blenheims and six Hurricanes left at 0645.

The aircraft endeavoured to get into formation before they left Tangmere, but owing to the absence of those left on the ground, the formation was irregular and all aircraft flew in one big 'gaggle' although spread out fairly widely; generally the Blenheims led and the Hurricanes followed. The weather was excellent as far as the French coast and for some 50 miles beyond. Then it began to get hazy and the visibility deteriorated.

Some 70 miles south of the River Loire, when beginning to approach the Monts d'Auvergne, they encountered heavy and continuous cloud reaching from ground level up to 16,000 feet. Soon the cloud became so thick that it became impossible for the pilots to see their own wing tips; they broke formation altogether.

Four Blenheims (Sqn.Ldr. Pryde, Flg.Off. Walker, Wt.Off. Cook and Sgt. Saunders) and two Hurricanes (Plt.Off. Glen and Plt.Off. Carter) arrived separately at Marignane, at various times between 1145 and 1705. One of the Blenheims (L9316, Sgt. Saunders) had landed at Ruffec, 20 miles from Angouleme, and then at Montpelier L'or, refuelling at both locations. This party left the same day at 1745 for Calvi, Corsica. However Sqn.Ldr. Pryde's Blenheim suffered engine failure on take-off and ended up in the boundary fence, although no-one was hurt. The five remaining aircraft reached Calvi at 1900, where they stopped for the night.

Plt.Off. Millen in Blenheim L9334, after making attempts to fly eastwards round the clock to reach the Rhone valley, turned back and met a Hurricane flown by Plt.Off. Barber; both landed at Tangmere at about noon. These two took off again at about 1500, the official report stating "There is clear evidence that no pressure was brought to bear on either of these pilots to start off again from Tangmere against their will." Despite this notation, Roger Barber stated, when interviewed in 1976, that they "were ordered off again by an angry briefing officer, who implied that we were pretty useless". Plt.Off. Millen reached Marignane without further mishap that evening although he had again encountered bad weather; this time he flew 50 miles further south than before. On arrival, he was welcomed by Sqn.Ldr. Pryde and his crew.

Retracing his steps, Plt.Off. Barber reached the Alps in appalling conditions, low on fuel after a further four and a half hours in the air. With his wing tanks almost empty, and unable to transfer to them the remaining fuel in the long-range tanks, he looked for somewhere to land. Finally he spotted a small field on a mountainside, and after a couple of approaches dropped the Hurricane onto the ground; unfortunately the force of the landing broke off the tail wheel assembly, thereby causing damage to the underside of the rudder and rear fuselage. He landed close to the village of Monde, and was able to reach habitation on foot with ease. A curious crowd formed, none of them English-speaking. Fortunately there appeared to be a number of Belgian refugees present, and Barber, a South African, was able to understand their Flemish speech due to its similarity to Afrikaans. He befriended a young lad named Jan, who led him to shelter and a relatively riotous night with a crowd of refugees.

Another of the Hurricane pilots, George Maycock, had run into very bad weather which became worse as he flew further south. After climbing to 10,000 feet so that the formation would not lose sight of each other in the thickening haze, a sudden belt of solid cloud was met and Maycock lost contact with the others. "My aircraft then flew into a clearing in the clouds and I flew in a complete circle so as to give the other aircraft time to reappear. Almost immediately a Blenheim appeared, and I, now having no idea as to my exact position, altered course and flew towards him. I tried to contact him by R/T but was unable to do so owing to the electrical interference, and I took a quick look at my compass and realised that he was flying on an Easterly course, which was in the direction of enemy-occupied territory, and increasing my speed I flew alongside him in order to point out his error. Unfortunately, he was unable to understand my signals, and I broke formation with him."

Maycock finally found himself over the village of Loudun. He was about to land nearby when he noticed to his consternation that the village was being bombed! Next moment he spotted an aircraft closing on his tail. He tried to take evasive action, but the fighter (probably a Bf109) opened fire, a short burst hitting the tail and damaging the controls. He now had to land, but struck a hedge and the Hurricane flipped over on its back. Shaken but unhurt, he made his way to the local army commander, where he was advised that the Germans were only about 15km. away. After burning his wrecked aircraft, he managed to reach Bordeaux, sailing back to England in a cruiser on 21st.

The two remaining Hurricane pilots, Plt.Off. Mansel-Lewis and Sims, had landed at Angouleme where they spent the night. Meanwhile the Blenheims were faring much more badly. Flt.Lt. Cole was experiencing fuel supply problems; whilst his starboard tank was full, his port tank was emptying rapidly. He put the

Blenheim down on a sandy stretch of beach at Plage Des Blanc Sablonsfinisterre, where he and his crew were immediately arrested by French troops. After convincing the soldiers of their nationality, they found a garage from where they obtained some rubber tubing and two jugs, with which they transferred fuel from one tank to the other. They had just completed this task when the tide came in, leaving the Blenheim some 20 yards adrift. By 1900 the tide receded and after

Flg.Off. J.C. Smyth's Hurricane P2626 on its nose at Ussel on 18 June 1940 during the second delivery flight of Hurricanes across France to the Middle East. This aircraft was subsequently abandoned. Note that at this early date a Vokes tropical air filter is already fitted beneath the nose. (*W.R.C. Sugden*)

19

digging the aircraft out of the sand, they managed to take-off and landed back at Tangmere at 2300.

The remaining five Blenheims all crashed in France, with the loss of all fifteen men aboard. Sgt. Field crashed in L9318 at Crozon, near Brest, apparently totally lost; Plt.Off. Handley's L9317 came down at Charroux, Flg.Off. McCash's L9315 at La Tessone, Flt.Lt. Wilkinson-Bell's L9351 at Soulages and Plt.Off. Johnson's L9314 at Pruniers.

While this disastrous progression was underway, the remaining Blenheim (Wood) and the six Hurricanes which had been left behind at Tangmere, had also got off at 0930. Initially these too found the weather very good, but after crossing into France they encountered the same bad weather on approaching the Monts d'Auvergne. They turned back before entering the thick clouds and landed altogether at Ussel, an airfield situated about half way between Clermont-Ferrand and Brive. The field, although on high ground, was found to be boggy and the second Hurricane to put down, P2626 flown by Flg.Off. Smyth, tipped up on its nose; the other five landed safely.

After a brief conference with the French authorities, Flg.Off. Wood and Plt.Off. Haddon-Hall discovered that no food was available, so after a quick collection amongst the pilots, they went to a nearby village to obtain bread, ham and cheese for an impromptu lunch. Whilst awaiting their return the others righted Smyth's Hurricane, which proved to be little damaged and flyable. Following their meal the pilots sought to refuel their machines, Dick Sugden recorded: "It was a business too, as each machine had to be taxied to a pump, through what resembled a bog. As all the French machines were nosing in front of us, it was each man for himself. And, bless me, it started to rain in torrents. It was like a nightmare, pushing aircraft through mud nearly a foot deep, arguing in French and then having to unscrew the fairings off those infernal overload tanks. Just when my machine was being filled there was a cloudburst; everybody huddled together under the mainplanes, while I tried to shield the petrol tank with my body, whilst rain was pouring in cascades down the mainplanes. I don't know how much water got into the tanks, but it must have been a hell of a lot. I had long ceased to care, everything seemed so bloody awful. We knew that if the rain kept on, then we should never get those Hurricanes off the ground, let alone move them. At about 1700 the rain stopped. Everybody's machines had been more or less refuelled." It was now too late to fly on, and accomodation was found for the night.

19/6/40

At Marignane, following the arrival of Plt.Off. Millen's Blenheim the previous evening, Sqn.Ldr. Pryde now had means of catching up with his party. Detailing Millen and his crew to make their way back to England as best they could, Pryde awaited the arrival of other aircraft to make up a formation. The first to arrive was Plt.Off. Barber in P2653. He had set out from Monde with his new-found Belgian friends and a borrowed 12-volt battery. With power provided by the latter, fuel from the long-range tanks was pumped up into the wing tanks. The aircraft was turned in the direction of proposed take-off, and started by hand-cranking – no mean feat. Revving the engine hard against the brakes to raise the broken tail quickly, he got off safely. He now flew to Marseilles, landing at the civil airport, which caused further damage to the tail. No fuel was available here and he was advised to fly to the military base at Marignane. He landed at 1120.

At Ussel meanwhile Flg.Off. Wood's formation prepared to set out for Marignane. Due to the previous day's torrential rain the grass field was like a quagmire, and all aircraft were found to be bogged down. The Hurricanes were manhandled to firmer ground, but as the Blenheim taxied out it stuck fast and all efforts to free it were to no avail. Resolved to go on alone, the Hurricane pilots taxied into wind but Flg.Off. Smyth again stood his aircraft on its nose, this time causing serious damage to the propeller. Plt.Offs. Collins and McAdam got off, followed by Plt.Off. Sugden, but in taking off the latter lost his maps from the cockpit. He circled the airfield waiting for the others to join him, but not realising what had happened, Haddon-Hall called him over the R/T to land again. Meanwhile Collins and McAdam flew on to Marignane, arriving at 1210.

Hurricanes in a hangar at Marignane on 19 June 1940 whilst en route to Malta. In the foreground are, l. to r., Plt.Off. 'Jock' Barber, Plt.Off. C. Haddon-Hall, Plt.Off. W.R.C. Sugden and an unidentified pilot in shirtsleeves. (*R.H. Barber*)

Leaving Flg.Off. Smyth and Flg.Off. Wood and his crew to make their way back to England, the three Hurricane pilots took off for Marignane, but en route ran into heavy thunderstorms and were unable to find their destination. While circling in an effort to find the airfield, Plt.Off. Beardon became separated. Subsequently, Haddon-Hall and Sugden landed at Toulon – the first sizeable airfield they could find. After lunch they were taken round the base, seeing in one hangar an Italian CR42 biplane fighter, which had recently been brought down during a raid on the airfield. Both pilots were much impressed by the quality of the finish of the little aircraft – Dick Sudgen would soon come to know the type well! After getting separated, Plt.Off. Beardon had found Marignane alone, and had landed there shortly before the two Hurricanes of Mansel-Lewis and Sims had arrived from Angouleme, where it will be recalled, they had spent the night.

At about 1730 Sqn.Ldr. Pryde again set out for the North African coast, accompanied by the five Hurricanes flown by Beardon, Mansel-Lewis, Sims, McAdam and Collins. Under normal circumstances Pryde would probably have waited until the next morning. However, the French feared an air attack on Marignane if the Germans became aware of the presence of British aircraft, and he had been pressured by the authorities into leaving at the earliest possible opportunity.

Of the five Hurricanes, those flown by McAdam and Collins turned back after about an hour owing to trouble with the feed pumps on their extra fuel tanks – similar trouble to that experienced by the earlier reinforcement flight. The remainder of the formation continued on their flight south-eastwards, passed over Corsica and kept to the east of Sardinia. Dusk approached about half way across and it was quite dark before the African coast was reached. Bad weather was encountered soon after leaving Marignane, while over the African coast there was a thunderstorm in progress, whilst it also appeared that the Italians were bombing Bizerta or Tunis. Approaching the coast Sqn.Ldr. Pryde fired a Very light, presumably as a signal to the French. Quite shortly afterwards his aircraft crashed into the sea, turning over on its back. 'Scotty' Pryde and his gunner, Sgt. A. Scott, were killed instantly; Sgt. L. Hibbert, the navigator, died two days later. Mansel-Lewis attempted to 'pancake' near the Blenheim but his Hurricane turned up on its nose and sank at once. His parachute, which was still in its pack, kept him afloat until he could inflate his life-jacket. He swam in the direction of the Blenheim, where he found one body, and then set out for the coast which he reached three hours later. In the morning he was found by Arabs and was eventually taken to Bizerta. Meanwhile Plt.Off. Sims had reached the coast, only to be fired on by machine guns. Completely lost in the darkness, he baled out; he too was picked up by Arabs and joined with Mansel-Lewis in Bizerta. The third Hurricane crashed on the beach nearby; Plt.Off. Derek Beardon was killed. Both Mansel-Lewis and Sims were despatched to Casablanca, where they met some Fleet Air Arm officers from 'Ark Royal'. They were flown out to the carrier which took them to Gibraltar that same night. From there they would be shipped back to England.

Back at Marignane, 'Jock' Barber, who had been left behind due to his damaged Hurricane, had set out for the village of Estres to recruit the aid of the local blacksmith. A tail skid was swiftly fabricated from an old car spring and bolted to the rudder sternpost. A test flight resulted in the collapse of this lash-up on landing, but a new skid using double the number of spring leaves was made and fitted. Rather than risk a further collapse, he decided to await his next destination – Tunis – to make the test. He was joined by the returning Hurricanes of McAdam and Collins and later still by Haddon-Hall and Sugden, who arrived from Toulon. They decided to continue in the morning.

Plt.Off. R.H. 'Jock' Barber considers the temporary tailskid made for his damaged Hurricane out of old car springs at Marignane before continuing the flight to North Africa. The date is 19 June 1940. (*W.R.C. Sugden*)

The five Hurricanes left Marignane at 1400 and set course for Tunis. After half an hour they ran into a heavy rainstorm and became somewhat disorientated. Landfall was made after about three hours, but Haddon-Hall turned east along the coast instead of west. Realising that he was wrong, Barber flew ahead, waggling his wings, and turned west. The others followed and soon landed safely at El Aouina at about 1730. Here they were shocked to learn that Sqn.Ldr. Pryde's formation had not arrived. After a good night's sleep the five prepared to take-off to fly to Medjez-el-Bab, from where they would fly the final leg to Malta. First off was Haddon-Hall, but his engine cut and he crashed through the airfield fence. He was unhurt apart from some cuts to his face, but now had to be left behind. On landing at the dusty strip at Medjez the remaining four were delighted to find two more Hurricanes – those of Plt.Off. Carter and Plt.Off. Glen – and three Blenheims (Flg.Off. Walker, Wt.Off. Cook and Sgt. Saunders). Refuelling was very slow, taking about three hours due to inadequate equipment. Four tankers were used in succession but each either broke down or ran dry. Further, Hurricane P2544 (Carter) refused to start until further magneto adjustment had been made. By then it was too late to leave for Malta. No accomodation was available at Medjez, so they were driven into Tunis for the night. They returned to the airfield next morning, and at 1050 the Blenheims and two of the Hurricanes (Carter and Glen) set off for Malta, arriving at Luqa at 1300.

After refuelling, Collins and McAdam followed at 1230, but they turned back when Collins' aircraft developed fuel starvation. They were off again at 1445, landing safely at Luqa two and a quarter hours later. This left two Hurricanes at Medjez, where Plt.Off. Sugden could not get the engine of P2629 to start due to flat batteries. Plt.Off. Barber stayed behind to help him, and in blazing hot sun, with the temperature exceeding 100° Fahrenheit, they managed to get it started by hand cranking. At last they got away, landing at Luqa in darkness. The airfield was littered with old buses, cable drums and other obstacles, put there for anti-invasion precautions. As a complete anti-climax Dick Sugden struck one wing of his Hurricane against a bus, damaging both wing and bus.

These six Hurricanes had arrived the day following the two from the earlier flight, and the Hudson. Thus at this date – before the Gladiators had achieved their first actual success in combat – eight Hurricanes were on the island, although two of them were damaged (Sugden's P2629 and Barber's P2653) whilst P2623 had a hole in the petrol tank. Since Malta now had more Hurricanes than Alexandria (eight compared with three), three were to fly on after they had been serviced and refuelled. Thus on 24 June the three Blenheims and Hurricanes P2544 (Plt.Off. Carter), P2651 (Plt.Off. Glen) and P2641 (Plt.Off. Collins) departed for Mersa Matruh. The defences were thereby left with five Hurricanes and five additional pilots (Flg.Off. Taylor and Plt.Offs. Barber, McAdam, Balmforth and Sugden). The Hurricanes remaining on the island were P2614, 2623, 2629, 2645 and 2653. Flg.Off. Davies, Flt.Lt. Cooper, and their Hudson and crew were also retained on Malta, from where they were to undertake twenty-two reconnaissance sorties.

It will be recalled that Flg.Off. Wood and Flg.Off. Smyth had been left at Ussel with their respective aircraft. After the departure of the Hurricanes, Wood and his crew, with the help of Smyth, enlisted the assistance of six bullocks to try and free his aircraft. By 1900 it had been dragged clear of the bog and 45 minutes later the Blenheim was airborne. They landed at Montaudron, Toulouse, and next morning flew to Francazal, where they refuelled. From here they flew back to Kemble to eliminate the risk of losing the aircraft; Flg.Off. Smyth accompanied them as a passenger. Plt.Off. Millen, stranded at Marignane with his crew but without an aircraft, would be kept busy during the next few days, helping to evacuate aircraft to other airfields. On 20th. he flew a LeO451 to Perpignan; the next day another LeO to Algiers; after both flights he returned to Marignane as a passenger in another aircraft. On 22nd., accompanied by his crew, he flew another LeO451 to Oran, where he reported to the British Vice-Consul, thence by train to Casablanca, ship to Gibraltar and eventually to England in the same convoy as Mansel-Lewis and Sims. Millen, a New Zealander, was later posted to 1 P.R.U. on Spitfires, was promoted Flt.Lt., awarded the D.F.C., but was killed in action during December 1940.

26–30/6/40

By this time France had capitulated, allowing 2ª Squadra Aerea to turn its attentions once more upon Malta. On 26 June twenty-five bombers raided Hal Far and Valetta during the morning. Further raids followed, and on 28th. two S.79s of the 11° Stormo B.T. were intercepted by Flg.Off. Woods, who inflicted damage on an aircraft from the 33° Gruppo flown by Ten. Remo Maccagni. The pilot and two other members of the crew were wounded, while another crew member, 1ᵉ Aviere Motorista Angelo Alvisi, his sense reeling from the fumes from a punctured fuel tank, baled out into the sea and was lost. Woods received credit for the destruction of this bomber. At this stage the Italians suffered a small set-back to their activities when, following two fatal crashes, the MC200 fighters were grounded throughout the Regia Aeronautica by Stato Maggiore; for a time therefore the bombers were forced to operate without escort. At the end of the month Malta began hitting back, Swordfish of 830 Squadron undertaking their first sorties during the night of 30th. dive bombing, with little success, the oil refinery at Augusta (Sicily).

1–2/7/40

July saw the entry of the Hurricanes into the defence of Malta, but also saw the arrival in Sicily of replacement fighter escorts for the Italian bombers. From the 4° Stormo C.T. came the 9° Gruppo (73ª, 96ª and 97ª Squadriglia), equipped with the agile Fiat CR 42, eleven of these undertaking their first escort for the S.79s over Malta on 2nd. of the month. No British fighters appeared to do battle, but anti-aircraft fire damaged two 34° Stormo bombers.

25

First blood was to be drawn by both new types next day, when during the morning two S.79s approached on reconnaissance, covered by nine CR42s, three from each squadriglia, led by the Gruppo commander, a Spanish Civil War veteran with an artificial leg, Magg. Ernesto Botto. Flg.Off. John Waters flying one of the new Hurricanes (P2614), attacked the pair of bombers, which were from the 259ª Squadriglia, 109º Gruppo, 36º Stormo B.T., which unit had just arrived in Sicily. The fire from the Hurricane's eight guns proved devastating and the bomber fell into the sea five miles from Kalafrana, breaking up as it went. Tenente Mario Sguario's crew of five baled out, but none were ever found. As Waters returned to land, he was set upon by the CR 42s and his aircraft was badly shot up. As a result he crashed on landing and the aircraft was written off, although Waters survived unhurt. The 9º Gruppo submitted the first Italian fighter claim for an aircraft shot down over Malta, credit for this victory being given to Magg. Botto personally; initially the claim was recorded as a 'Spitfire'.

1ᵉ Aviere Motorista Giacomo Lucchini was a member of the crew of an S.79 of the newly-arrived 259ª Squadriglia, 109º Gruppo, 36º Stormo B.T. Their aircraft was shot down over Malta on 3 July 1940 by Flg.Off. John Waters in Hurricane P2614. Although the whole crew managed to bale out, they were never found. (C. *Lucchini via N. Malizia*)

4/7/40

Following this encounter, the Italian fighters attempted to 'beard the British fighters in their den' on 4 July. Early in the morning twenty-four CR 42s rose from Comiso airfield and headed for Malta. As they neared the island they divided into three sections; six fighters swept in to strafe Hal Far, while nine more provided close cover at 1,000 feet, the other nine remaining high above in case of fighter attack. The Italian pilots returned jubilantly, claiming seven fighters and one bomber destroyed on the ground; actual results of their attack were two of 830 Squadron's Swordfish damaged, but repairable.

5/7/40

Following the fall of France, numerous French aircraft were flown by their crews to British-held territory to continue the fight. Malta too was to receive one such reinforcement on 5 July when a Latecoere 298B torpedo-carrying floatplane flew in from Bizerta, Tunisia; the aircraft came from the Aeronavale's Escadrille 2HT, and carried the code HB2-5 on the fuselage. It was flown by Premiere-Maitre Rene Duvauchelle, with Quartier-Maitre Jacques Mehouas as radio operator/observer. The aircraft was subsequently to be put to good use. Meanwhile however the Italians reported a damaging raid on their airfield at Catania during the night of 5/6 July; this was an attack by nine Swordfish of 830 led by Lt.Cmdr. Howie. Thirty men were killed and ten wounded, while aircraft losses included an S.75 transport of the 601ª Squadriglia S.A.S. destroyed, two MC200s of the 88ª Squadriglia, 6° Gruppo, badly damaged and one S.79 of 214ª Squadriglia, 52° Gruppo, also damaged.

5 July 1940 saw the arrival of a Latecoere 298B torpedo-carrying floatplane, one of two which had absconded from the Aeronavale Escadrille 2HT at Bizerta, Tunisia. With its crew, it was attached to 230 Squadron at Kalafrana, and is seen here alongside one of the unit's Sunderland flyingboats. (*N.W.M.A.*)

6–7/7/40

Raids by the Regia Aeronautica on Malta were now becoming much more frequent. 30 bombers attacked Valetta, Hal Far and Takali on 6th., gunners at the dockyard claiming one shot down. Flg.Off. Woods and Plt.Off. Sugden (the latter in Hurricane P2645) scrambled just before dusk after a 'plot' in the vicinity of Filfla. Between here and the main island they spotted a floatplane flying about 100 feet above the sea. Woods made a quick firing pass, but as Sugden went in the aircraft waggled its wings, and both pilots pulled away in case it might be another French Late 298B. It was probably a Z.506B. 'Timber' Woods had more success next day when the fighters were scrambled during the morning to intercept two formations each of five S.79s, escorted by nine CR 42s. The dockyard was the target on this occasion, two Royal Navy personnel being killed and six injured, while nine civilians also died. Woods shot down one S.79 from the 233ª Squadriglia, 59° Gruppo, 41° Stormo, which was being flown by Ten. Pellegrino Zagnoli.

8/7/40

Great things were afoot at sea at this time. During 7 July the British Mediterranean Fleet had sailed from Alexandria in support of two convoys which were on their way through the Mediterranean. The naval force included the carrier 'Eagle' with Swordfish and three Sea Gladiators aboard, three battleships, five light cruisers and a number of destroyers. This force was soon spotted by Italian reconnaissance aircraft, and on 8 July air attacks began. By darkness twelve raids had been carried out, eleven of them by S.79s from the 10°, 14° and 15° Stormo B.T. in Libya, and the 34° and 41° Stormo which had moved to the Aegean Islands for this purpose from Sicily. A single S.79 from the 204ª Squadriglia, 41° Gruppo Autonomo B.T. was lost, Ten. Renato Torelli force-landing in Crete, where he and his crew were interned by the Greeks. An aircraft of 221ª Squadriglia scored a direct hit on the cruiser 'Gloucester'.

9/7/40

Next day R.A.F. flyingboats found Italian naval units which they had been seeking. However the two battleships, six heavy and eight light cruisers and twenty-four destroyers, were not out to attack the British convoys – they were returning from escorting an Italian convoy to Libya. During the mid part of the day action was joined as the Mediterranean Fleet sought to attack the Italian ships off the Calabrian coast of south-east Italy. Swordfish strikes gained no hits, but gunfire from H.M.S. 'Warspite' caused damage to the Italian battleship 'Giulio Cesare', and the heavy cruiser 'Bolzano'. Following this action the Italians withdrew. Tremendous efforts were made by the Regia Aeronautica bombers which put in no less than seventeen raids, claiming astronomical successes. From Puglie the 37° and 40° Stormo B.T. with S.81s and the 35° Stormo B.M. with Z. 506Bs attacked throughout the late afternoon and evening, joined by S.79s operating from Sicily with the 11°, 30°, 34°, 36° and 41° Stormo. Losses were light,

Sottoten. Luigi Ruggeri of the 257ª Squadriglia, 108° Gruppo, 36° Stormo B.T. having his S.79 shot down by fire from Italian destroyers (!) – the bombers reportedly bombed British and Italian vessels without discrimination! The returning Italian crews claimed hits on 'Ark Royal' (sic), the battleship 'Hood' and on two destroyers but only the destroyer 'Escort' sustained any damage and turned back towards Gibraltar.

During the day Malta had one alert, early in the morning; Flt.Lt. Burges and Flg.Off. Barber scrambled in Hurricanes to intercept. Climbing up into the beautifully clear morning sky, they were vectored by the controller onto a single S.79 of 192ª Squadriglia 87° Gruppo, 30° Stormo, flown by Cap. Valerio Scarabellotto, with an escort of four 9° Gruppo CR 42s. The Savoia was undertaking the usual daily reconnaissance over the island. By pre-arrangement, Burges was to attack the bomber whilst Barber kept the fighters at bay for as long as possible. Thus while the latter made an attack on the leading fighter from astern, Burges swung P2645 towards the bomber for a quick attack. Before being attacked by three CR42s, he got in a good burst of fire and believed that he had sent the S.79 down in flames to crash in the sea. Actually the crippled bomber, with pilot dead and one gunner mortally wounded, made the Sicilian coast where

When British ships were at sea, they were sought out by reconnaissance aircraft of the Italian water-based units, like this Cant Z.506B tri-motor floatplane of the 191ª Squadriglia R.M., seen in flight over the Mediterranean early in the war. (*A.M.I. via N. Malizia*)

it made an emergency landing at Comiso. Meanwhile 'Jock' Barber, having made his initial attack and convinced that he had hit the leading CR 42, flick-rolled and spun down to prevent any of the others getting on his tail. He then recovered height to attack the fighters again until his ammunition was exhausted, whereupon he stuck the nose down and dived away to safety. One of the Hurricanes was found to have suffered slight damage, but that evening Radio Rome reported that one of two intercepting 'Spitfires' had been shot down in flames.

8/7/40

On 8 July Wg.Cdr. R. Carter Jonas arrived by Sunderland to take over command of R.A.F. Luqa. Newly-promoted after commanding 80 Squadron in Egypt, Jonas discovered on taking over his duties at Luqa that several employees of Imperial Airways had been attached to the R.A.F. for controller duties. These included Messrs. Hood, Ryan and Tompkins, each of whom were performing invaluable service.

9/7/40

In support of the Mediterranean Fleet, a new battle squadron known as Force 'H', which was now based at Gibraltar under Vice-Admiral Sir James Somerville, had sortied on 8 July in an effort to create a diversion. Heavy air attacks by Sardinian-based aircraft during 9th. convinced the admiral that the risks did not justify the continuation of such a minor operation, and before the day was out the vessels turned back, losing the damaged H.M.S. 'Escort' to submarine torpedo attack. This brief operation brought action for the air group on H.M.S. 'Ark Royal' however. Having just completed their attacks on the French Fleet at Mers el Kebir, the aircrews were on top form. A shadowing Cant Z.506B floatplane of the 287^a Squadriglia R.M., flown by Cap. Domenico Oliva was caught by three Skuas of 800 Squadron at 1530 after it had been on patrol for three hours. Lt.R.M. Smeeton, the Commanding Officer, and his observer/gunner, Lt. E.S. Carver, in Skua A6A led Sub Lt. M.F. Fell/Naval Airman D.H. Lowndes (A6B) and Petty Officer (A) A.W. Sabey/Leading Airman J. Coles (A6C) in a determined attack, the stricken Cant falling into the sea. They continued to strafe it until it was totally destroyed, but during this sustained attack the observer and radio operator were mortally wounded. Subsequently S.79s of 38° Gruppo B.T. from Decimomannu attacked the carrier but were chased by Skuas of 803 Squadron, an aircraft of the 49^a Squadriglia being shot down. This S.79 fell to the Skua crewed by P.O.(A) A.W. Theobald and N/A Freddy de Frias, who recalls: "Theo and I were flying in L3017, as usual in Red Section led by Lt. Gibson. Throughout the day the Italians had pressed home medium level attacks on the Force; the Italians were pretty efficient and determined. They stayed in formation and were frighteningly good in their bombing. We took off at 1920, warned to expect a large formation. Fortunately we were able to get to 10–12,000 feet before they came in below us. Gibson led the Section down in a diving turn to get at them and for some reason Theo didn't get a decent burst in. But we ended up

30

flying straight and level with the enemy leader only forty to fifty feet on our starboard beam. I could hardly believe it was happening as I opened up with the Lewis on a simple no deflection shot using the nose of the enemy as an aiming point. After my first aiming burst the S.79 appeared to go nose down so I gave it the rest of the 100-round pan. Before I had finished, a side hatch opened and at least two people, perhaps three, baled out. The aircraft went into a dive and I caught a glimpse of it going into the sea before it went out of my vision behind the tailplane." De Frias would later be awarded the DSM mainly for this action. A second S.79 was badly damaged by the combined fire of the other two Skuas of Red Section – A7P crewed by Lt. D.C.E.F. Gibson/Sub Lt. M.P. Gordon-Smith and A7Q manned by P.O.(A) J.A. Gardner/N/A H. Pickering – and made an emergency landing on Majorca. Two others were claimed damaged by the Naval airmen, one by Midshipman(A) A.S. Griffith/N/A F.P. Dooley in A7G, and one by Lt. J.N. Christian/Sub Lt. A.H.S. Gore-Langton in A7F. In both these engagements the Italians incorrectly identified their opponents as Fulmars.

Next day the British fleets could not be found by air reconnaissance so no attacks materialized. At dusk 'Eagle' launched nine Swordfish of its resident 813 Squadron for a night attack on Augusta harbour (Sicily) where it was hoped to find the Italian Fleet; however only a few warships were present, the destroyer 'Leone Pancaldo' being sunk and an oiler damaged.

10/7/40

Malta again came under heavy attack, at least four formations totalling some twenty bombers appeared over the island, bombing Zabbar, Tarxien, the dock-yard and the submarine base on Manoel Island. On this occasion casualties were somewhat lighter and were listed as two military personnel slightly injured, one civilian killed and three injured. For the Italians it was to prove a costly raid. The main formation of fifteen S.79s drawn from the 87° and 90° Gruppo of the 30° Stormo at Sciacca, was led off by Col. Antonio Serra to meet covering CR 42s from the 9° Gruppo. The rendezvous was botched however, the bombers arriving 55 minutes later, and in consequence the twenty-one fighters were forced to return to base low on fuel. Over the target intercepting Hurricanes struck hard, Flg.Off. 'Eric' Taylor shooting down an S.79 of 195ª Squadriglia flown by Sottoten. Felice Filippi, which fell in flames, while 'Timber' Woods attacked a second flown by Sottoten. Luigi Illica Magnani of the 192ª Squadriglia which he initially claimed as a 'probable'. This bomber also fell in flames, and his claim was consequently upgraded to a 'confirmed'. Flg.Off. Peter Hartley (in P2614) at-tacked an aircraft of 194ª Squadriglia, which was badly damaged and force-landed on return to Comiso with one gunner mortally wounded. Ten more bombers were hit by anti-aircraft shrapnel and several crewmen were badly wounded. Gunners claimed four Hurricanes shot down, but British losses were in fact nil.

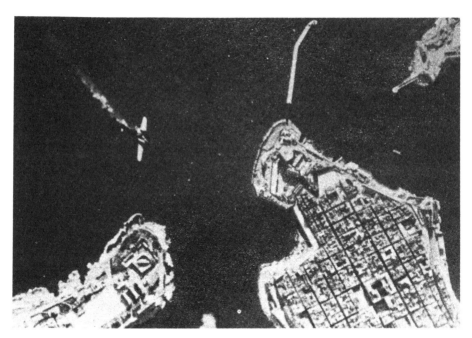

Caught without fighter escort on 10 July 1940, this 195ᵍ Squadriglia S.79 falls towards the sea at the entrance to Grand Harbour, one of two victims of R.A.F. Hurricanes. Ten. Felice Filippi and his crew of this 90° Gruppo, 30° Stormo B.T. aircraft, perished. ('*Interqest*' *via National War Museum Assoc.*)

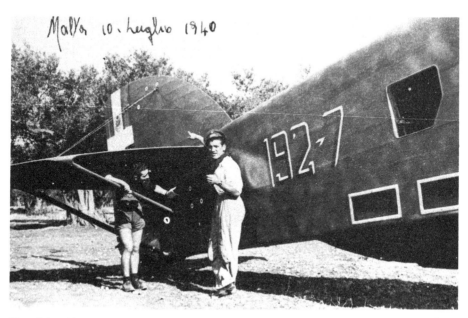

Men of the 192ª Squadriglia, 87° Gruppo, 30° Stormo B.T. at Sciacca, point to battle damage suffered by their S.79 over Malta on 10 July 1940. At the time it was customary to place a small red, white and green disc (the colours of the Italian flag) over each such scar. (*C. Rago via N. Malizia*)

11/7/40

Early on 11th. the Mediterranean Fleet was again discovered by a reconnoitring Cant Z.501 flyingboat from the Augusta-based 186ᵃ Squadriglia R.M. At once 2ᵃ Squadra Aerea sent out S.79s from the 30°, 34°, 36° and 41° Stormo and Z.506Bs from the 35° Stormo at Brindisi. These were joined in their attacks by Libyan-based S.79s of the 15° Stormo from Castel Benito and 33° Stormo from Bir el Bhera. Sixteen raids were made, one S.79 of the 195ᵃ Squadriglia, 90° Gruppo, 30° Stormo, claiming hits on a carrier – none were actually sustained. Again interceptions by Fulmars, together with Gladiators, were reported, but the defenders were in fact only 'Eagle's' tiny handful of Sea Gladiators, flown by Swordfish pilots. Cdr. C.L. Keighley-Peach in N5517 and Lt.(A) L.K. Keith in N5513 (the latter pilot a Canadian from Calgary) had been on patrol for about twenty minutes at 13,000 feet, when at 1415 they spotted a flight of five S.79s approaching 2,000 feet below. Keighley-Peach attacked the aircraft on the left of the formation, a 90° Gruppo machine from the 194ᵃ Squadriglia flown by Sottoten. Ciro Floreani, while Keith went for one on the right, both fighters diving vertically from above. Keighley-Peach made three dives, firing from 300 yards to 50 yards. The bomber dropped back and below the formation, emitting black smoke from the port wing. This soon turned to flames and the aircraft span into the sea, the crew being seen to bale out although they were never found.

Italian bombs hammer down on Luqa airfield during a raid in July 1940. (*N. Malizia*)

Return fire hit the Sea Gladiator, one bullet passing through the lower wing longeron to the starboard of the cockpit, going through the diagonal strut immediately above, and then breaking up, one fragment entering Keighley-Peach's leg (it was finally removed in 1976 when the old wound began to fester). Keith reported hits on his target, but did not see any result before A.A. fire from the Fleet forced the fighters to break away.

12–13/7/40

Raids continued against the fleet during the next two days as it headed back towards Alexandria, although after 11 July it was beyond the range of Sicily-based units. 14 attacks by Aegean and Libyan-based S.79s were put in on 12th., while on 13th. S.81s once again joined the assault. The fleet was again shadowed during the morning of this day by a Z.506B, and seven raids followed. Taking part were S.79s from the 34° Gruppo in the Aegean and the 15° Stormo in Libya, plus S.81s of the Aegean-based 39° Stormo. One aircraft from the latter unit, a machine of the 200ª Squadriglia, 92° Gruppo, flown by Sottoten. Enrico Carapezza, was lost, although defending gunners in the bombers optimistically claimed three fighters shot down. Again it was 'Eagle's' Sea Gladiator Flight involved – Cdr. Keighley-Peach in N5517 making first contact at 0750 when he reported sighting a lone S.79 ahead of the fleet. Making three diving attacks from out of the sun, he reported that flames issued from the port wing and the aircraft span into the sea, none of the crew being seen to bale out. At 1115, to the south of

On 12 July 1940 the autonomous 23° Gruppo C.T. arrived in Sicily to undertake bomber escort missions. Two Fiat CR 42 fighters from the unit's 75ª Squadriglia are seen heading for Malta. (*N. Malizia*)

Crete he and Lt.(A) Keith (in N5517 and N5513 respectively), saw three Savoias – identified again as S.79s – 5,000 feet below, approaching from the direction of Rhodes. Keith attacked first, firing on the left hand aircraft, and this was then attacked by Keighley-Peach, who made three more attacks on the same bomber, which fell into the sea in flames. Two men baled out, one being picked up by H.M.S. 'Hereward'. Keith attacked the other two without obvious results. Finally, at 1450 Keith – again in N5513 – saw five S.79s at 8,000 feet, making a beam attack followed by a stern chase on one. This finally caught fire, turned on its back and span into the sea, no-one being seen to bale out. One of the latter victories was obviously the S.81, but the identity of the other two bombers claimed has not been ascertained.

Claims do not tell the full story however, for the fighters had been most effective in breaking up the attacks of the bombers. Great controversy would break out in Italy between Navy and Air Force, the former casting grave doubts on the latter's claims to have reduced British naval power by 50% during the series of attacks, 8–13 July 1940. They were right too, for in fact only one hit on a cruiser had actually been scored, and this had in no way impaired the vessel's operating efficiency!

12–13/7/40

Over Malta meanwhile there had been more action. On 12 July the recently-arrived 9° Gruppo C.T. was ordered to fly on to Libya, to operate in the desert. To replace the unit two new gruppi of fighters flew in, the autonomous 23° and the 17° from 1° Stormo C.T. Both units flew their first sorties over the island on that same day, reporting an engagement with four British fighters. Ten. Gino Battaggion of the 23° Gruppo's 70ª Squadriglia claimed one shot down – identified as a Spitfire – while pilots of the 17° Gruppo (Maresciallo Magli and Serg. Abramo Lanzanari) claimed one more. No R.A.F. losses are recorded. The 23° returned next day, eleven CR 42s led by the unit commander, Magg. Tito Falconi, claiming two Hurricanes shot down on this occasion while on a reconnaissance of the island's principal ports; the successful pilots were in one case Cap. Guido Bobba, and in the other Cap. Ottorino Fargnoli and Cap. Antonio Chiodi with Serg.Magg. Celso Zemella and Serg.Magg. Renzo Bocconi. Their opponents had in fact been a single Hurricane (P2653, flown by Plt.Off. Dick Sugden) and a Gladiator with George Burges at the controls. Sugden recounted: "There were two of us standing by – George Burges and myself. It was one of those cloudless Med days, the horizon shimmering with heat and the edge of the cockpit burning hot if one's elbows touched it. We were about halfway through our readiness period – midday to 4p.m., and had been sitting cramped in our straps for two hours, reading and dozing. An instant and everything springs to life. The ground crews leap towards the starter batteries as the blare of the horn comes from the control tower. I hear the R/T crackle into 'Scramble – Scramble – Scramble!' A touch of the button and the engine roars to life. Within ten seconds George and I are tearing down the runway – pressure on the stick and I am airborne, snapping up the undercart and trying to tighten my helmet and straps, as we start a steep climbing turn. It hardly seems possible that in so short a time my brain has been roused from a gentle doze into a thing of concentration – concentrating on listening for the controller's orders and concentrating on trying to look at the whole sky at once. The engine is beating away perfectly, the aircraft is fine. The controller's voice comes through with terrific volume – 'Hello Visor, Banjo calling. Bandits 15 plus, ten miles North of Zebbug, angels 15.' If only I could climb quicker. It's a nasty feeling knowing they are above you, probably watching you stagger up to meet them. George's Gladiator has gone now, it climbs more steeply than the Hurricane."

"At last I am at 15,000 feet and I obey the controller and circle round Grand Harbour. I should be able to see them now, they are very close to me. Where the Hell are they? – hullo, there's the Flak – now where are they – THERE! A mile away I see two biplanes, diving slightly, going towards St. Paul's Bay, in line astern. The rear one is a CR 42 – is that George he's chasing? I just remember to scream 'Tally Ho!' over the radio, as I start to overhaul the little brute chasing George. Guns on 'Fire', reflector sight on, coming in fast from dead astern. Just before I fire I see that they are both CR 42s."

"The whole aircraft shakes as the eight guns rattle. I see the nose drop and hurriedly correct, but the Fiats turn steeply, right and left, then dive. I shove the nose down, the engine cuts and picks up again and I am just going to fire again when – what is this? Red sparks shooting past me, over each wing, coming from the sea. I hear a hiss and a crack and do a steep turn to the left. Oh, my God! There are about six little CR 42s dancing up and down behind me. They follow me easily on the turn, much more manoeuvreable than the Hurricane. There's only one thing to do and I half roll onto my back and go down vertically, leaving them standing. I curse myself bitterly for being such a fool as to (a) miss the bloke I was shooting at and (b) to be trapped so beautifully by his pals.

"At 4,000 feet I pull out, smack over Tigne, where the other chaps are probably bathing (they were, as it happens). Engine going O.K., everything seems alright. I start to climb again. Obviously they are up there watching me and I cannot see them, but what else can I do? I climb in a south-westerly direction, towards the sun and suddenly catch a glimpse of three of them circling about 5,000 feet above. I climb steadily, watching them hard and trying to watch my tail as well. As I do a climbing turn away from the sun, they gently start to dive towards me and then I see tracer going past again – there are their blasted friends again! This time I really dive, the controls almost solid but the engine has been hit; coolant starts to stream past, the cockpit fills with fumes and the windscreen smears with glycol. The engine merely splutters when I pull out of my dive at about 1,000 feet. Thank Heaven! There's no-one shooting at me now as I call up Banjo and tell them I may have to bale out. The air speed indicator is not working but I have tons of speed to make the aerodrome."

"I stagger on at the same height – with a terrific feeling of relief I see the aerodrome getting closer. I turn straight in, downwind along the long runway – down undercart and flaps – and come sailing in to make one of the best landings

I've ever made. The brakes are working and I leap thankfully out. The groundcrews come running out of their shelter (the raid is on) and I can remember a warning to them that the engine might go up. It didn't however, but continued to make noises like a steam engine. It felt good to be on solid ground again, after seeing all the holes in my aircraft." Plt.Off. Sugden was then called to the telephone in the control tower. The Air Officer Commanding (Air Commodore Maynard) was on the other end and the conversation went something like this – "Sugden, I told you before – I have told all the fighter boys – don't get mixed up with enemy fighters!" The telephone was then slammed down; within days he was posted. He made only three more sorties with the Fighter Flight – all on Gladiators – and then on 20 July joined what remained of 3 A.A.C.U. to fly Swordfish.

Untropicalized Hurricane I about to take off from Hal Far. (*R.H. Barber*)

13–16/7/40

On 13 July an S.79 of 36° Stormo B.T., one of eight engaged in a night raid on Valetta, was shot down by anti-aircraft fire. Ten. Pietro Ferri and his crew were lost. No further activity was noted until the morning of 16th., when a dozen CR42s from the 23° Gruppo again appeared over Malta on a reconnaissance. Flt.Lt. Peter Keeble in a Hurricane (P2623) and George Burges in a Gladiator had been scrambled, and dived on this formation, Keeble attacking one CR42, but being attacked himself by two more flown by Ten. Mario Pinna and Sottoten. Oscar Abello. After a long chase Keeble was hit and his aircraft dived into the ground and blew up. It was immediately followed by a CR42 flown by Ten. Mario Benedetti of the 74ª Squadriglia, which crashed within 100 yards of the Hurricane; both pilots were killed outright. Burges made no claim on this occasion, and it can only be assumed that Benedetti's aircraft had been hit by Keeble before he was shot down. The Italians claimed a second Hurricane (by Serg.Magg. Renzo Bocconi), but this was not allowed by 2ª Squadra intelligence staff. Keeble was the first of Malta's fighter pilots to lose his life in the defence of the island. Wg.Cdr. Carter Jonas had witnessed Keeble's fate, and recalls: "The sounds of firing and diving aircraft had almost ceased when Peter Keeble was killed, his Hurricane rocketting down out of a patch of blue sky, flattening out for a moment as if to attempt some sort of landing, and then diving into the ground to the right of the wireless masts at Rinella. . . . a day or two later, we buried him in the quiet little cemetary up at Bighi, with the wind sighing in the fir trees overhead."

19–21/7/40

At this time a Saro London flyingboat from 202 Squadron had returned to Malta and was engaged in carrying out anti-submarine patrols. On 19 July this aircraft reported bombing a submarine off Delimara Point, but three CR 42 pilots of 23° Gruppo saw the 'boat and attacked without obvious results. Two days later the aircraft was again involved in combat, this time one of these difficult-to-resolve mysteries which plague historians from time to time. During the morning of 21 July three S.79s and six escorting fighters appeared over the island, where one bomber of the 34° Stormo was hit by anti-aircraft fire, subsequently coming down in the sea 30 kilometres from Cap Pessaro. Believing that this was indeed the case, the R.A.F. sent out a Swordfish floatplane shortly after midday, but this failed to return. A second Swordfish which followed reported finding only a number of oily patches. Meanwhile however, London K5261 piloted by Plt.Off. E.C. Minchinton, a Canadian in the R.A.F., had found the wreckage of the S.79 floating in the sea 35 miles north of Malta, and took photographs of this. The aircraft was then attacked by two CR 42s while flying at only 300 feet, the gunners claiming one of these shot down.

This S.79 of 34° Stormo B.T. was hit by anti-aircraft fire over Malta on 21 July 1940, subsequently coming down in the sea near the Sicilian coast. It was photographed here by the crew of a 202 Squadron Saro London flyingboat (K5261) flown by Plt.Off. E.C. Minchinton. The London was claimed shot down by Italian fighters during this flight, but in fact returned undamaged. (*National War Museum Assoc.*)

The Italian version of events differs considerably. The crew of the S.79 were subsequently rescued, reporting that after landing in the sea they had been attacked by a Saro London, which had in turn been attacked by a CR42 of 72ª Squadriglia, 17° Gruppo, flown by Cap. Pietro Calistri, and shot down with ease. The pilot, reported as a 'Capt. Leslye', "survives – our prisoner". It is assumed that the aircraft shot down by Calistri was in fact the missing Swordfish seaplane, since even the name of the pilot differs completely from that of Minchinton, whose London returned undamaged. No CR 42 was reported missing.

24–28/7/40

Sunderland flyingboats from 230 Squadron also began to operate over the seas around Malta at this time, their first engagement with Sicily-based aircraft being reported on 24 July when Sqn.Ldr. Ryley's big aircraft was intercepted by a single MC200, but drove it off without damage. A much more violent series of clashes took place four days later however. Early on 28 July Sqn.Ldr. Ryley lifted L5804 off Kalafrana Bay to reconnoitre the Sicilian coastal areas. He arrived off Syracuse at 1048 and at 1105 was attacked by three MC200s of the 6° Gruppo Autonomo C.T. which, with the ban on their operational use now lifted, had taken off for a reconnaissance over Malta. The flyingboat crew reported being attacked by four fighters, and claimed that they had succeeded in shooting down one in flames and driven off the rest during a 57 minute running fight. No loss was actually sustained by the Italians, but the Sunderland did not escape unscathed on this occasion, suffering extensive damage, and with three of the gunners wounded. L.A.C. D.A. Campbell climbed into the wing to plug holes in the tanks, remaining there until he passed out due to petrol fumes. He was revived – by bullet splinters which struck him! A 'Daily Mail' correspondent, Alex Clifford, was also aboard and rendered considerable assistance, manning one of the guns after the gunner had been wounded; it was believed that he had gained hits on one of the attacking Macchis. The flyingboat limped back to Malta, put down on the water, and was at once beached by the pilot to prevent its sinking.

At 1550 Flt.Lt. Garside took off in Sunderland L2160, also heading for Sicily, where he bombed a submarine off Cap Spartivento, Calabria (not to be confused with Cap Spartivento, Sardinia). At 1640 this aircraft too was attacked by a trio of MC200s, but after their first pass one was reported to have broken away with smoke pouring from the engine. The other two attacked again, but this time the rear gunner thought he saw his fire striking one fighter, which appeared to break up and fall into the sea. Following this the third withdrew, and the Sunderland continued its patrol having suffered no damage. There does seem to have been a little wishful thinking on this occasion too, for once more the Macchis – again from the 6° Gruppo – all returned unscathed. During the day a third 'boat' flown by Flg.Off. A.M.G. Lywood was attacked by two CR 42s, but no damage was suffered. This series of running battles was widely publicised in the British Press shortly afterwards – mainly thanks to the opportune presence of the war correspondent in Ryley's aircraft. As a result the Sunderland received the popular – and very journalistic – nickname of 'The Flying Porcupine'.

Plt.Off. 'Jock' Barber (centre) with his ground crew and Hurricane in a sandbagged pen. (*R.H. Barber*)

The 157° Gruppo of the 1° Stormo C.T. at Trapani played only a minor part in the early Malta fighting. The CR 42 in the foreground was that flown by the Gruppo commander, Magg. Guido Nobili, and carries his personal emblem on the fuselage. (*G. Di Giorgio via N. Malizia*)

40

H.M.S. 'Eagle's' little band of fighters were again engaged on 29th. during a convoy escort sortie to Alexandria. Lt.(A) Keith and Lt.(A) P.W.V. Massy were on patrol when two flights each of three S.79s were seen at 15,000 feet. Keith attacked the left hand aircraft in one flight which broke formation at once and fled for home, apparently without dropping its bombs. He then attacked that on the right, this jettisoning its cargo and losing height rapidly to disappear in the clouds. Meanwhile Massy was after the right hand machine of the other flight; after five separate attacks it caught fire and dived into the sea, an explosion being seen in the rear fuselage just before it went into the water. Two members of the crew baled out, one of them was picked up alive by H.M.S. 'Capetown'. By now Massy was some way from the convoy and almost out of fuel; he was obliged to ditch near H.M.A.S. 'Stuart', one of the escorting destroyers, and was picked up safely.

Raids on Malta had continued sporadically during this period and it is possible that some claims were submitted by the A.A. defences on 28th. The last battle of the month occurred on 31st when nine 23° Gruppo CR 42s escorted a single reconnaissance S.79 over the island during the morning. Hardly any Hurricanes were now serviceable, and three Gladiators took off to intercept, flown by Flg.Offs. Hartley, Woods and Taylor. As they attacked the formation, the bomber turned away, but a dogfight at once began between the opposing fighters. A burst of fire from the guns of Serg. Manlio Tarantino's aircraft caused the fuel tank of Hartley's Gladiator (N5519) to explode, and he baled out suffering from severe burns. 'Timber' Woods shot down the commander of the Italian formation, Capitano Antonio Chiodi of the 75ª Squadriglia, his aircraft falling into the sea five miles East of Grand Harbour. He was subsequently awarded a posthumous Medaglia d'Oro (Gold Medal of Valour – Italy's highest military award).

Wg.Cdr. Jonas watched below: "... at about a height of 12,000 feet after a burst of fire in its petrol tank, the whole aeroplane appeared to blow up and dive vertically earthwards like a flaming torch, leaving a long trail of black smoke in the sky to mark its path. The pilot, fortunately, as the tank exploded in front of him, stood up in his seat and went headlong over the side. We watched him dangling on the end of his shroud lines until he disappeared below the cliffs at Hal Far where he was rescued from the water, more dead than alive, 45 minutes later. For many months afterwards Peter Hartley lay in Imtarfa Hospital, suffering from severe burns to his legs, hands and face, and I used to visit him at least once each week. For the first few weeks the doctors considered it to be extremely doubtful whether Peter would recover at all, after the long immersion in salt water following the shock of the burns. And I remember my first few visits to the hospital, with Peter lying rigid and motionless, speechless with pain; only his half-closed eyes moved, restless and frightened, beseeching relief. Youth, and a strong constitution, however, combined with devoted nursing, eventually won through, and many weeks later a somewhat scarred Peter was flown back to England by flyingboat, to complete his convalescence in a more suitable climate."

At the end of July Flt.Lt. George Burges was advised of the award to him of the Distinguished Flying Cross – the island's first decoration; the citation stated that he had shot down three Italian aircraft and probably three more. At the close of the month the defences were considered to have accounted for at least twelve attacking aircraft, but without spares for the Hurricanes, and with the Gladiators kept airworthy only by cannibalization, the strength of the Fighter Flight was diminishing rapidly. Help however, was immediately to hand.

Chapter 2

261 SQUADRON

Here they come again! 41° Stormo B.T. S.79s on their way to Malta in Summer 1940, escorted by CR 42s of 23° Gruppo C.T. (*N. Malizia*)

As soon as Italy became embroiled in the war it had become abundantly clear to the British authorities that if Malta was to be held, additional reinforcements organized on a more formal basis than a handful of Hurricanes flown across France, would be necessary. With the fall of France the direct flight route was in any event closed. Two possibilities remained; either to deliver aircraft to Africa – via Suez or West Africa and the long Saharan route to Egypt – or alternatively to fly them off a carrier from maximum range. The latter course was undoubtedly quicker, and offered a much better chance of the majority of aircraft despatched actually reaching their destination. Consequently during mid July 1940 a number of pilots were ordered to report in great secrecy to 418 Flight at Uxbridge. All but one were N.C.O.s and they were far from being a random selection, since most enjoyed a roughly similar past history – a relevant history which is well worth recounting here.

Early in 1939 a notice was sent to R.A.F. Volunteer Reserve Town Centres, inviting V.R. pilots to volunteer for a two week attachment to the Fleet Air Arm, to be spent on an aircraft carrier. Subsequently this was changed to a three month stint, and in consequence most of the volunteers in civilian occupations had to drop out. Upon mobilization in August of that year some forty R.A.F.V.R. pilots each of whom had a minimum of 100 hours flying training, and most of whom had previously volunteered for the two weeks' carrier trip, were posted to a Fleet Air Arm airfield at Donibristle on the Firth of Forth. At this stage the Fleet Air Arm had only recently been transferred from the R.A.F. to the Navy, and many of the pilots who had previously served in the Fleet squadrons had transferred back to the R.A.F. as soon as possible, despite advantageous transfer terms. The new arrivals at Donibristle were allocated wither to the Torpedo–Spotter–Reconnaissance Flight to fly Swordfish and Sharks, or to 769 Fighter Squadron (T) on Sea Gladiators and Skuas. Operational training was to include deck landings on H.M.S. 'Furious'. Indeed the first V.R. pilots to arrive were posted to the T/S/R unit, this being considered the best posting by the Navy, since it involved attack, while fighters were only defensive, and in the Naval view defence could not win victories. The later arrivals were 'admonished' for being too late for posting to T/S/R, but most were in fact pleased to have got onto fighters!

After six weeks at Donibristle 11 Sergeants were posted to 770 Squadron at Lee-on-Solent in company with eight F.A.A. pilots; here they went aboard the old training carrier 'Argus' to undertake deck landing training in the Western Meditarranean. On completion all were asked to transfer permanently to the F.A.A., but most were now disenchanted with Naval operations of aircraft, and with the obsolescent equipment available, and only two accepted the offer. The rest returned to the R.A.F. as staff pilots with No. 3 Bombing and Gunnery School, Aldergrove, Northern Ireland. On 4 May 1940 all were posted back to the F.A.A. in great haste, joining 759(T) Squadron at Eastleigh. After an intensive two week refresher course they were posted to Hatston in the Orkneys, being intended to fly Gladiators of 263 Squadron and Hurricanes of 46 Squadron onto H.M.S. 'Furious' for transfer to Norway, since the pilots of these units had not undertaken carrier landings. The pilots involved were Sgts. Ashton, Ayre, Bowerman, Kelsey, O'Donnel!, Pickering, Sturges and Timms. Their arrival was too late however, for the Hurricanes had been hoisted aboard from lighters, while the Gladiators had been flown on by F.A.A. Sea Gladiator pilots. Consequently the group was posted to 804 Squadron which had just been formed at Hatston, to fly Sea Gladiators on land-based defensive duties. Here Sturges was killed in a landing accident.

44

By now the Dunkirk evacuation was underway, and by mid-June it was the R.A.F. which was short of fighter pilots. The F.A.A. consequently provided about 40 pilots, including the seven remaining Sergeants. After a brief conversion course on Spitfires and Hurricanes at 7 Operational Training Unit, Hawarden, Cheshire, they were posted to various Fighter Command squadrons. Within a month came the order to report to Uxbridge, and the group found themselves together again, joined by Sgts. F.N. Robertson and R.J. Hyde, both of whom had been on the original Donibristle course, and who had in the meantime both seen action with 66 Squadron, flying Spitfires; Fred Robertson had already proved a most promising pilot with this unit, and had been credited with two confirmed victories.

From Uxbridge the group moved to Northolt, and were flown from there to Hullavington to collect Hurricanes from the Maintenance Unit there, and fly them up to Abbotsinch airfield, Glasgow. Several more Hurricanes were flown up by ferry pilots, one crashing on arrival. At Abbotsinch the Sergeants were ordered by a Naval officer to remove the wings from their aircraft for loading by barge onto 'Argus', which was then in dry dock. He was surprised and uncomplimentary to find the N.C.O.s possessed neither the tools nor the technical knowledge to perform this task!

Once aboard the carrier, the group – which had been led up to this point by Flt.Lt. Lambert, the only officer to join them at Uxbridge – were joined by a number of other officers; these were Flt.Lt. D.W. Balden, who assumed command of the Flight, Flt.Lts. A.J. Trumble and J. Greenhalgh, and Flg.Off. H.F.R. Bradbury. These officers were all regulars who had previously served with the F.A.A., but had preferred to remain with the R.A.F. on transfer of the service to the Navy. None had any recent fighter training; John Greenhalgh for instance, had just landed from a photo-reconnaissance sortie with 1 Special Duties Flight at Heston that same afternoon, when he was ordered to report to the R.T.O. at Euston station at once. From here he entrained for Greenock, having never previously flown a Hurricane! Thus the personnel of 418 Flight were brought together, and were at last advised that their destination was Malta, but they were ordered not to tell their families of this when writing home.

23–31/7/40

'Argus' sailed from Greenock on 23 July with twelve Hurricanes and two Skuas stowed between decks, arriving at Gibraltar a few days later. Here a quantity of spares for the Hurricanes were loaded into a Sunderland flyingboat, while the aircraft were re-assembled and ranged on deck. It had originally been proposed that two Blenheims should be carried to act as navigational aircraft following the fly-off, but this was considered impracticable, and the Skuas had been included for this duty instead. On 31 July the vessel set course for Malta, escorted by Force 'H', including the carrier 'Ark Royal', the battleships 'Hood', 'Valiant' and 'Resolution', two cruisers and ten destroyers. On 1 August the pilots were briefed by the Captain of 'Argus' that they were to fly off to Malta, but were incredulous of the proposed launch point, which they immediately realised was well beyond the Hurricane's flying range to reach the destination. Deadlock ensued until radio silence was broken to contact London, whereupon the pilots' assessment was confirmed. By evening the Italians had discovered the fleet, and a bombing attack from Sardinia was launched, but caused no damage.

Three Skuas, Red Section of 803 Squadron, from 'Ark Royal' claimed one of the attacking S.79s shot down, Lt. Gibson/Sub Lt. Gordon-Smith (A7P), P.O.(A) Gardner/N/A Pickering (A7Q) and P.O.(A) Theobald/N/A de Frias (A7L) making the claim at 1810. This was an aircraft of 18ª Squadriglia, 27° Gruppo, 8° Stormo B.T., part of a formation of three, which was lost while attacking the convoy. Aboard was Generale di Brigata Aerea Stefano Cagna and with him were Ten.Col. Nello Capanni and Magg. Spolverato, all of whom were killed together with the rest of the crew. Gen. Cagna, commander of Brigata Marto of the Aeronautica Sardegna, was later decorated posthumously with the Medaglia d'Oro.

S.79s of 18ª Squadriglia, 27° Gruppo, 8° Stormo B.T. at its home airfield of Viltacidro, at Cagliari. Sardinia. This unit's bombers were frequently engaged in operations against the ships of Force 'H', whenever the latter sailed into the Mediterranean from Gibraltar.

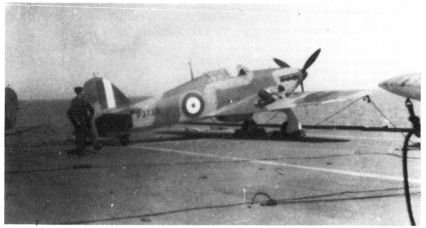

Hurricanes of 418 Flight aboard H.M.S. 'Argus' on the way to Malta on 1 August 1940. P3733 is being prepared for flight. (*J. Pickering*)

2/8/40

The vessels were now greatly at risk, as the Italians were fully aware of their presence, and the aircraft were got off as quickly as possible at dawn on 2 August. Each Skua was to lead half the Hurricanes, and each in the event was flown by an R.A.F. pilot. One Navy pilot who had been allocated to fly one of these aircraft had the courage to state that he felt he had insufficient experience on Skuas to take off from the carrier, and Sgt. Harry Ayre took his place, flying L2611. His navigation was undertaken by Capt. K.L. Ford, a Royal Marine. The other Skua was flown by Flg.Off. Bradbury, with Sub Lt. W.R. Nowell, a Naval pilot, acting as observer. With fourteen aircraft on the deck the area for the take off looked very small, and the first Skua dropped away below the level of the deck almost at stalling speed, finally building up enough momentum to keep going. With their greater power/weight ratio, the Hurricanes got off without any trouble, and the flight was soon underway, avoiding a direct overflight of Pantelleria. Malta was reached in two hours and 20 minutes after some 380 miles had been covered. Thus as the fighters came in to land at Luqa, Operation 'Hurry' had been almost a complete success – almost, because Sgt. Robertson in N2700 crashed on landing.

According to Robertson's logbook this was due to a faulty petrol gauge, but this was only part of the reason. 'Jock' Barber recalls: "Sgt. Robertson and two (other) Sergeant Pilots arrived in a vic formation over Luqa – very, very low and fast beat-up of the airfield, then a roll off the top. Robertson made a typical Naval 'split-arse' approach and as he made the final turn his motor cut. The aircraft turned upside down and went through three stone walls. However he only sustained minor concussion and was flying again within a few days." Obviously the offending gauge had led Robertson to believe that he had more fuel left than was in fact the case! Flg.Off. Bradbury's Skua also crashed when he stalled on landing, but while this aircraft, like Robertson's Hurricane, was badly damaged, no one was hurt.

The Hurricanes taking part in this operation were: N2484, N2622, N2672, N2673, N2700, N2701, N2715, N2716, N2717, P3730, P3731 and P3733. Pilots involved and their previous units were:

Flt.Lt. D.W. Balden (ex 266) Squadron	Flt.Lt. A.J. Trumble (ex 264 Squadron)
Flt.Lt. R.N. Lambert	Flt.Lt. J. Greenhalgh (ex 1 S.D. Flight)
Flg.Off. H.F.R. Bradbury	Sgt. F.N. Robertson (ex 66 Squadron)
Sgt. E.N. Kelsey (ex 611 Squadron)	Sgt. O.R. Bowerman (ex 222 Squadron)
Sgt. H.W. Ayre (ex 266 Squadron)	Sgt. R. O'Donnell (ex 19 Squadron)
Sgt. R.J. Hyde (ex 66 Squadron)	Sgt. W.J. Timms (ex 43 Squadron)
Sgt. D.K. Ashton (ex 32 Squadron)	Sgt. J. Pickering (ex 64 Squadron)

2–6/8/40

As an additional precaution two Sunderlands from a detachment of 10 Squadron, Royal Australian Air Force, which were based at Gibraltar, followed the flight in the hands of Flt.Lt. W.N. Gibson and Flg.Off. I.S. Podger, acting as airborne

Flt.Lt. (later Gp.Capt.) John Greenhalgh
(*J. Greenhalgh*)

Sgt. H.W. Ayre (*J.K. Norwell*)

Sgt. F.N. Robertson (*J.K. Norwell*)

Sgt. J. Pickering (*J. Pickering*)

Sgt. R.J. Hyde (*J. Pickering*)

Pilots of 418 Flight who flew from H.M.S. 'Argus' to Malta on 2 August 1940 – Operation 'Hurry'

Sgt. E.N. Kelsey (seen here with one of the old Fighter Flight Gladiators). (*J.K. Norwell*)

Flt.Lt. R.N. Lambert (r) and Sgt. O.R. Bowerman (*J.K. Norwell*)

'lifeboats' in the event of any of the pilots being obliged to ditch. They also carried twenty-three airmen who were to service the Hurricanes on Malta. Next day Podger flew back to Gibraltar carrying spares for the London flyingboats of 202 Squadron from the stores at Kalafrana, while Gibson flew on to Alexandria. He returned from there on 4th. carrying General Sir Archibald Wavell and his staff on a visit of inspection, while Podger returned with two tons of spares and ammunition for the fighters. Both aircraft left on 6 August to return to the 'Rock', and from there set course for their home base at Mount Batten, Cornwall, next day.

2/8/40

Meanwhile even as the fighters had been winging their way eastwards and the Fleet turned back towards Gibraltar, fighter patrols from 'Ark Royal' were in action on 2nd. against shadowers from Sardinia. Five Skuas from 800 Squadron flown by Lt. Smeeton/Lt. Carver, Lt. K.V.V. Spurway/P.O.(A) R.F. Hart, Sub Lt. Fell/N/A Lowndes, Sub Lt. B.H. Hurle-Hobbs/L/A E.E. Bell and P.O.(A) L.E. Burston/N/A R.H. Holmes, claimed one Z506B shot down, whilst another was claimed by another Section of 800 Squadron Skuas, crewed by Lt. G.R. Callingham/Mdspmn. H. Morris, Mdspmn., R.W. Kearsley/L/A L.V. Eccleshall and P.O.(A) W.J. Heard/N/A Hills. Italian records indicate that a Z.501

As Operation 'Hurry' was launched on 2 August 1940, Swordfish from H.M.S. 'Ark Royal' attacked Cagliari airfield, Sardinia. Here this aircraft (P4127) flown by Lt. G.R. Humphries was obliged to force-land due to damage suffered from anti-aircraft fire. (A.M.I. via N. Malizia)

flyingboat of the 146ª Squadriglia R.M. was attacked by seven fighters – obviously the five Skuas of Lt. Smeeton's patrol – limping back to Cagliari/Elmas with one dead and three wounded aboard. A Z.506B of the 198ª Squadriglia, flown by Sottoten. Sigfrido Marcaccini, was reported shot down by four more fighters, this clearly falling to Lt. Callingham's Section.

While these combats were taking place, fourteen Swordfish from the carrier attacked Cagliari airfield (Sardinia). One Swordfish – 2K of 810 Squadron – crashed into the sea on take-off having hit the forward pom-pom gun, Lt. J.R. Robins and his crew perishing. One Swordfish failed to return from the raid, Lt. G.R. Humphries of 820 Squadron force-landing his aircraft (P4127:4F) on the airfield following damage to its engine from A.A. fire; he and his crew were taken prisoners.

During a patrol off the Sardinian coast a Swordfish of 818 Squadron was attacked by two biplanes identified as CR32s. Lt. G.A.W. Goodwin managed to evade the attackers, his gunner – N/A F.W. Dodd – fighting back determinedly and believed he disabled one of the Fiats (thereby earning the nickname 'Killer' from his fellow TAGs).

6/8/40

On Malta it was to be a few days before the Hurricanes were fully ready for operations the rest of the spares and other equipment for them being delivered a couple of days later by the submarines 'Pandora' and 'Proteus'. Knowing of the presence of these reinforcements, the Italians launched a number of heavy raids, one of these wrecking two of the newly-arrived aircraft on the ground. The remaining aircraft of the Fighter Flight were incorporated, and on 6th. an initial squadron composition was put together under Sqn.Ldr. 'Jock' Martin on a three-flight basis. This initial arrangement was as follows:

'A' Flight	'B' Flight	'C' Flight
Flt.Lt. D.W. Balden	Flt.Lt. A.J. Trumble	Flt.Lt. J. Greenhalgh
Flt.Lt. G. Burges*	Flt.Lt. R.N. Lambert	Flg.Off. F.F. Taylor*
Flg.Off. R.H. Barber*	Plt.Off. T. Balmforth*	Plt.Off. A.G. McAdam*
Sgt. R.J. Hyde	Sgt. J. Pickering	Sgt. O.R. Bowerman
Sgt. E.N. Kelsey	Sgt. D.K. Ashton	Sgt. H.W. Ayre
Sgt. R. O'Donnell	Sgt. F.N. Robertson	Sgt. W.J. Timms

Flg.Off. H.F.R. Bradbury, Flg.Off. J.L. Waters* and Flg.Off. W.J. Woods* were held as reserves, while Plt.Off. P.B. Alexander* was posted to other duties at this stage. (N.B. those marked * were the original Fighter Flight pilots).

13/8/40

The first recorded engagement following the arrival of the new aircraft did not occur until the night of 13 August. Following several night raids, the arrival of the new Hurricanes had allowed an impromptu night fighter section to be formed, and Flg.Offs. Taylor and Barber had been selected for this duty. Between

2110 and 2302 hours a number of bombers came over singly and in pairs. Barber was ordered off in N2715, but at once the engine began overheating. To keep this within limits, he climbed with the propeller in coarse pitch, seeing an S.79 perfectly 'coned' by searchlights to the south of the island. By the time he had reached the level of the bomber it had passed beyond the range of the lights, but he then saw this (or another) aircraft in the moonlight. Pulling up underneath it, he kept firing into the belly until it stalled and fell away. He lost sight of it at this point, and after flying around without a further sighting, returned to base. Here he was advised that the radar 'plot' had faded, and he was credited with a 'probable'. His fire had indeed done its job better than he had realised; an S.79 of 259ᵃ Squadriglia, 109° Gruppo, 36° Stormo B.T. was badly hit and failed to make it home, coming down in the sea five miles from the Sicilian coast. Two members of the crew were drowned, the other three swimming ashore near Marina di Ragusa. This was the first aircraft shot down by a night fighter outside Western Europe during the war.

This same night nine Swordfish of 830 Squadron set out from Hal Far to carry out a further attack on Augusta harbour, three aircraft armed with torpedoes, the others with bombs. The torpedo-bombers went in low and were greeted by intense AA fire – Midspmn. D.S. Edmondson's aircraft was shot down and crashed on land, he and his TAG being killed; a second was hit and ditched in the harbour, Lt. D.W. Waters and his TAG taking to their dinghy but were promptly captured. The remaining torpedo-bomber, flown by Lt. A.F. Hall, was also hit but despite losing fuel managed to struggle back to Malta, finally ditching just off Hal Far. The crew were soon rescued from their dinghy.

S.79s of 194ᵃ Squadriglia, 90° Gruppo, 30° Stormo B.T. head for Malta. Note the two different styles of camouflage paint used on the third aircraft in the formation. (*N. Malizia*)

15/8/40

Two days later on 15th – one of the great days of the Battle of Britain – ten S.79s of 60° Gruppo, 41° Stormo in two equal formations approached Hal Far, escorted by eighteen CR 42s of the 17° Gruppo and one from the 23° Gruppo. Four Hurricanes attempted to intercept, but were engaged by the escort. Ten. Sartirana of the 72ª Squadriglia, 17° Gruppo, succeeded in shooting down Hurricane N2716 into the sea, the pilot – Sgt. Roy O'Donnell – being lost; his body was not recovered. Flt.Lt. Balden (in N2672), with Sgt. Kelsey on his wing, chased one straggling CR 42 which they had spotted to the north of the island. Balden fired one long burst whereupon the biplane looped and was lost to sight; it was claimed as damaged. On the ground bombs destroyed one Swordfish, and two personnel were wounded by splinters.

16/8/40

Next day 418 Flight and the remaining original Malta pilots formally became 261 Squadron, and a complete re-organization of the previous three-flight arrangement took place. Flt.Lt. Balden was promoted to take over command from 'Jock' Martin, and two flights were formed as follows:

'A' Flight	'B' Flight
Flt.Lt. Trumble	Flt.Lt. Greenhalgh
Flt.Lt. Lambert	Flt.Lt. Burges
Flg.Off. Waters	Flg.Off. Bradbury
Flg.Off. Taylor	Flg.Off. Woods
Flg.Off. Barber	Plt.Off. McAdam
Sgt. Robertson	Plt.Off. Balmforth
Sgt. Kelsey	Sgt. Hyde
Sgt. Bowerman	Sgt. Timms
Sgt. Ayre	Sgt. Ashton
	Sgt. Pickering

Hurricanes of the new 261 Squadron, one tropicalized and one not (the latter in the foreground) display totally different underside paint work. (*R.H. Barber*)

Thus in time-honoured R.A.F. peacetime manner command of the unit and of both flights had gone to the senior General Duties Branch officers in preference to both longer-serving Malta personnel and the more relevantly-experienced Sergeants. This would have been no problem had these career officers allowed the more experienced pilots to lead in the air, as would happen throughout the R.A.F. later in the war. At this stage however, not only did the A.O.C. insist on establishing procedure, but it was still natural for officers of their background to think it required of them. In the event it did not work well, and in due course pressure for changes in command were to come, initially from the original group – particularly the pilots who had ferried in the first Hurricanes. Indeed the pilots with 418 Flight had been under the impression that they were only ferrying the Hurricanes to the island, utilizing their carrier experience. They had expected to be flown out to Gibraltar by Sunderland immediately after their arrival, only

A 30° Stormo B.T. S.79 of the 87° Gruppo's 193ª Squadriglia in flight, showing its 'Electric Man' unit insignia.

learning that they were to stay on from Air Commodore Maynard on the day of their arrival.

20/8/40

The remainder of August was not to be unduly hectic however. Early on 20th. six S.79s from the newly-arrived 105° Gruppo Autonomo B.T., escorted by sixteen CR 42s from the 23° Gruppo, raided the airfields, four Hurricanes being despatched to intercept. The result was indecisive, but the formation was broken up and Sgt. Fred Robertson, on his first Malta sortie in N2715, was able to claim a CR 42 damaged; pilots of the 23° Gruppo claimed one Hurricane probably shot down. At Hal Far two Swordfish of 830 Squadron were slightly damaged, while three Blenheims in transit to Egypt were also hit, one being burnt out but the other two suffering only minor damage.

24/8/40

Four days later they were back, six S.79s of 192ª and 193ª Squadriglia, 87° Gruppo, 30° Stormo B.T., led by Ten.Col. Schiaretta and Cap. Verrascina, again raiding Hal Far and Kalafrana, escorted by seventeen CR 42s of the 23° Gruppo. Four Hurricanes were once more scrambled, led by George Burges, who attacked three of the bombers. He saw a few bits fly from one of these, which headed for Sicily losing height rapidly. He was then set upon by CR 42s and his aircraft was hit by fire from Ten. Mario Rigatti's aircraft (75ª Squadriglia). Visibility was poor and he managed to escape, but on landing the undercarriage of N2730 collapsed. Of the other British pilots, Flg.Off. Taylor claimed one CR 42 shot down and Plt.Off. Balmforth a second as a probable; Serg.Magg. Renzo Bocconi of the 75ª Squadriglia baled out of his stricken CR 42 and was rescued from the sea to become a prisoner. Ten. Rigatti was also hit after attacking Burges's Hurricane, returning to Comiso seriously wounded and with his aircraft badly damaged, claiming one British fighter shot down; he was later awarded the Medaglia d'Oro. It seems almost certain that he had been flying the aircraft attacked by Balmforth. At Hal Far another Swordfish was badly damaged during the bombing.

Tenente Mario Rigatti of the 23° Gruppo Aut. C.T. with his CR 42. On 24 August 1940 Rigatti was involved in a sharp battle with Hurricanes over Malta whilst escorting 30° Stormo B.T. S.79s. He returned to Comiso seriously wounded, claiming one Hurricane shot down; he was subsequently awarded the Medaglia d'Oro. (*Fam. Rigatti via N. Malizia*)

The tail of a CR 42 believed to be an aircraft of the 23° Gruppo Aut. C.T., shot down over Malta in Summer 1940 – possibly on 24 August. (*I.W.M.*)

29/8/40

The only other raid of note occurred on 29 August when ten newly-arrived Cant Z.1007bis trimotor bombers of the 106° Gruppo Autonomo B.T. raided Luqa from high level, escorted by eighteen CR 42s of 23° Gruppo and seven from 157° Gruppo, 1° Stormo C.T. Four Hurricanes reached altitude too late to catch the bombers, but were bounced from above by half a dozen of the CR 42s without result. However one Z.1007bis and one CR 42 were struck by single shell splinters from the A.A. barrage, whilst on landing at Trapani another Z.1007bis collided with a small building and was destroyed by fire, all the crew suffering injuries.

17–31/8/40

During the month the Mediterranean Fleet had carried out a raid on the port of Bardia, Libya. As the vessels headed back towards Alexandria on 17 August a series of bombing attacks were launched against them by the Regia Aeronautica. 'Eagle's' Fighter Flight of three Sea Gladiators had been flown to Sidi Barrani airfield in Libya, and from here patrolled over the Fleet. At 1040 five S.79s were seen at 12,000 feet, heading in from the north-east, and the fighters climbed to cut them of. Cdr Keighley-Peach in N5517 became separated, and realising the futility of chasing the fleeing bombers alone, headed back over the Fleet in time to see two more formations attacking. He made three attacks on one bomber, seeing numerous pieces fall off and it went into a shallow dive; one man baled out, but as the aircraft lost height rapidly, it disappeared into cloud. He attacked another twice but without result. The other two Sea Gladiators, N5513 (Lt. (A) Keith) and N5567 (Lt. A.N. Young) attacked several formations. Young attacked one in company with a 112 Squadron Gladiator (believed flown by either Flt.Lt. L.G. Schwab or Plt.Off. P.R.W. Wickham); Keith joined the attack and the port wing of the bomber burst into flames, two members of the crew baling out before the Savoia crashed into the sea. Other R.A.F. fighter pilots claimed five more, although actual Italian losses amounted to only four S.79s shot down and eight damaged (see 'Fighters over the Desert', pages 18–19). Five days later on 22nd. the Fleet put to sea again to support a new convoy and to look for the Italian Fleet. Nine days out, on 31st., Cdr. Keighley-Peach was scrambled from 'Eagle' in N5517, with Lt.(A) R.H.H.L. Oliphant in N5567, to intercept a 'shadower'. They found a Z.506B at 6,000 feet flying in the direction of Kythera Island. Keighley-Peach continues: "Again off Crete I came across a Cant Z.506B – I think the crew must have been asleep as I was offered no opposition and felt I was almost committing murder – it was so easy. The Cant ditched off the coast of Crete and I saw the crew descending via parachutes and they must have landed close enough to land to be able to swim ashore." This was the fifth confirmed claim to be credited to Cdr. Keighley-Peach, all gained whilst flying Sea Gladiator N5517.

Now great things were afoot again, for on 31 August the new armoured aircraft carrier H.M.S. 'Illustrious' entered the Mediterranean; joined by the battleship 'Valiant' from Force 'H', she was to become a part of Admiral Cunningham's Mediterranean Fleet. These two vessels brought to this fleet an added and precious advantage beyond the strength of their presence; both were fitted with R.D.F. (radar), a luxury previously denied to the vessels of this force. 'Illustrious' carried aboard two Swordfish squadrons, 815 and 819, each with twelve aircraft, and 806 Squadron – the first to be equipped with the new eight-gun Fairey Fulmar fighter. Commanded by the colourful and dashing Lt.Cdr. Charles 'Crash' Evans, the unit was well-trained and fully combat-worthy. The 32 year-old C.O. had already seen some seventeen years' R.N. service, and had been a pilot for ten of these; he had led the flight which shot down the first enemy aircraft of the war on 26 September 1939.

Cant Z. 501 flyingboats were much in evidence over the Mediterranean during Summer 1940, but they proved 'easy meat' for the carrier fighters of the British fleets. This is a 'Gabbiano' of the 146ª Squadriglia R.M., which was based on the Sicilian coast. (*A.M.I. via N. Malizia*)

It was intended that the two ships should be escorted as far as the Sicilian Narrows by Force 'H', and there would be met by the Mediterranian Fleet. Force 'H' was already at sea, and the fighters from 'Ark Royal' were swift in dealing with 'shadowers' from Sardinia. On the last day of the month Lt. Spurway was leading his section on patrol when he was directed to investigate a 'hostile' at 10,000 feet, which turned out to be a Z.506B of the 287ª Squadriglia R.M., and this was pursued for some 55 miles before Spurway was able to get in a telling burst; the Cant caught fire and fell into the sea. Two of Sottoten. Antonio Di Trapani's crew were seen to bale out, both men supported by the one parachute. Their fate is unrecorded. Three hours later a patrol of 803 Squadron Skuas –

57

Lt. J.M. Bruen, the commanding officer, leading Lt. C.W.R. Peever and Sub Lt. G.W. Brokensha, a South African – were ordered to intercept another 'shadower', this time a Z.501 in the markings of Ala Littoria, although flown by a crew from 188ª Squadriglia R.M., captained by Ten. Giovanni Riosa. It was shot down in flames from 500 feet, the wreckage burning furiously.

Regular victims of the 'Illustrious' Fulmars were the gaudily-painted Cant Z.506B floatplanes which tried to 'shadow' the carrier and her escorts. This is an aircraft of the 198ª Squadriglia R.M. (*A.M.I. via N. Malizia*)

1–2/9/40

Meanwhile other new reinforcements had been arriving in the area – but for the other side. Italy's home-produced dive-bomber, the twin-engined Savoia S.85 had proved to be a disastrous failure, and it had been necessary to acquire replacements from Germany – the notorious Ju87. These had been collected during August by the 236ª and 237ª Squadriglia of the 96º Gruppo B.a'T., which at once flew them to Comiso for operations. Fifteen were ready by the start of September.

As 'Illustrious' and her escort approached the Sicilian Narrows constant fighter patrols were maintained and during the early evening of the first day of the new month, patrolling Skuas were vectored on to an unidentified aircraft approaching from the south-east, some 18 miles distant. As the Skua leader closed in he recognised the intruder as a Hudson; this was Flg.Off. Davies' aircraft from Malta on a reconnaissance. The Skua leader and Davies exchanged signals when, without warning, three Fulmars appeared from below, the nearest aircraft opening fire on the unsuspecting Hudson, only breaking off its attack when recognition flares were fired from both Hudson and Skua, the attacking Fulmar pilot at the same time spotting the roundel on the fuselage. The Hudson was badly damaged, and Davies made for the Cap Bon Peninsula, Tunisia, the nearest landfall; here he crash-landed on El Aouina airfield at Tunis. Two of the crew, F/Sgt. Burnett and Sgt. Wright were both injured, and were removed to hospital, while Davies and Flt.Lt. Cooper were interned at Le Kef. They would later be moved to Algeria where they would remain until the Anglo–American landings of November 1942.

The Fulmar patrol – Blue Section of 806 Squadron led by the C.O., Lt.Cdr. Evans – had also been ordered to investigate the intruder and Blue 3, seeing the twin engines, assumed it was a Ju88 and attacked. The Fulmar was flown by 43 year-old Lt.Cdr. Robin Kilroy, former commanding officer of 815 (Swordfish) Squadron, who was on his way to Egypt to take command of the Royal Naval Air Station at Dekheila, just outside Alexandria. He had offered to assist with flying duties whilst en route.

That night Swordfish from 'Ark Royal' were engaged in a diversionary strike against Cagliari airfield to cover the passage of 'Illustrious' through the Narrows – codenamed Operation 'Smash', to be repeated the following night, Operation 'Grab'. The first raid was considered a success when bombs were observed hitting buildings and falling amidst dispersed aircraft; the second raid was marred by mist and low cloud. One Swordfish crashlanded on return to the carrier but Lt. Goodwin and his crew were unhurt.

By the morning of 2nd., 'Illustrious' and 'Valiant' were making progress eastwards for the rendezvous with the Mediterranean Fleet to the south of Malta, but 'shadowers' were about and the carrier was spotted by a searching Z.501 when still 35 miles to the west of the island. Fortunately Blue Section of 806

A new type to appear in Sicily in September 1940 was the German-built Junkers Ju87B dive-bomber. This is one of the first such aircraft of the 96° Gruppo B.a'T. to arrive at Comiso. (*G. Fiorin via N. Malizia*)

Squadron was already patrolling over the ships, and was directed onto the Cant by somewhat primitive morse code radio transmission at 1120. Lt.Cdr. Evans was again leading Lt.Cdr. Kilroy and Sub Lt. I.L.F. Lowe, the three Fulmars attacking the seaplane from astern, 500 feet above the sea, and shot it down in flames.

Despite its demise the Z.501 had managed to get off a sighting report. Nine Ju87s of the 96° Gruppo B.a'T. were also out during the morning, and these had also discovered the ships west of Malta, returning with their report so that a raid might be undertaken. First however at 1415 nine S.79s of the 36° Stormo, followed by nine from the 41° Stormo, were sent out. The former found nothing, but the 41° Stormo aircraft discovered 'Illustrious' and headed towards her. Fulmars were already up on patrol – Lt. W.L. Barnes with Yellow Section, Sub Lt. S.G. Orr leading White Section. At the first report of the bombers' approach, two more sections were catapulted off. The bombers suddenly found themselves faced by an attack by modern monoplanes, which they took to be sea-going versions of the Spitfire or Hurricane, instead of the usual one or two Sea Gladiators they were accustomed to meeting. Half at once jettisoned their bombs and turned for home, but the others continued the attack. Lt. Desmond Vincent-Jones, senior observer in 806 Squadron, was watching from the deck: "Barnes, as he always did, pressed home his attack until he appeared almost to ram the enemy bomber and Orr wasn't far behind. After a few moments parachutes appeared out of the two rear S.79s and they fell out of formation. The two leading Italians jettisoned their bombs and turned towards Sicily, hotly pursued by the Fulmars who claimed serious damage. Although made of laminated wooden construction the hump-backed S.79s somewhat resembling flying buffaloes, were much tougher to destroy than we imagined. This action, not lasting more than a few minutes, had been witnessed by the whole Fleet. As Admiral Cunningham said later 'seldom has a fleet had a greater boost to its morale, and from that moment on the whole picture changed'."

It seems that Vincent-Jones may have confused the memory of this raid with another which followed in the afternoon. At 1450 Lt. Barnes' section intercepted seven S.79s, Barnes attacking the far left-hand aircraft and shooting it down in flames, then claiming a second damaged, although experiencing strong return fire from the formation. One S.79 was indeed shot down and a second badly damaged, while in a third one member of the crew had been mortally wounded. 41° Stormo later put in a second attack, during which two more S.79s of the 235ᵃ Squadriglia, 59° Gruppo, were lost. Barnes' Yellow Section again intercepted six S.79s at 1915, Barnes himself making a quarter to stern attack on one which he shot down; he then damaged a second which was subsequently shot down by fire from the ships. The other two members of his Yellow Section also experienced successful combats – Yellow 3, Sub Lt. G.R. Golden and L/A Harry Phillips in N1874 claimed one S.79 shot down and a second damaged, whilst Yellow 2 – Sub Lt. A.J. Sewell and L/A D.J. Tribe put in claims for two more, as Denis Tribe recalls: "We claimed two shot down but in the action caught up with fire from the enemy (turret and single machine-guns). From the rear seat it was difficult to see except for tracers coming at us – a row of holes in my perspex cover; the glycol coolant pouring into my cockpit. Also the intercom was damaged and out of action. I thought I was badly hit as whenever I moved I could see blood. I was greatly relieved to find it was coming from a flesh wound under my right forearm. Although Jackie Sewell had armour-plated glass in front of him I thought he must have been hit because the plane seemed out of control. I could not communicate owing to the damage and I could not open my sliding cover. Fortunately he regained control and with damaged engine we made quite a good landing at Hal Far – guided by Lt. Barnes who also landed at Hal Far. I had first aid locally and in the early evening we were picked up by one of our Swordfish from 'Illustrious'."

Some two and a half hours after the first bombing attack, five Ju87s of the 96° Gruppo – three from 236ª and two from 237ª Squadriglia – appeared overhead at a moment when no fighters were aloft. Attacking in the face of heavy anti-aircraft fire, the dive-bombers, led by Magg. Ercolano Ercolani, dived on the ships, Ten. Brezzi claiming a hit on a cruiser. All the bombers returned, although Ten. Cumbat's aircraft was damaged.

Fast becoming a leading fighter pilot in early Autumn 1940 was the Fulmar pilot Sub Lt. Stanley Orr of 806 Squadron on H.M.S. 'Illustrious'. (*I.W.M.*)

Two hours later two more flights, each of four Ju87s were off separately. One quartette, escorted by MC200 fighters, attacked and claimed to have hit the bows of a cruiser, while the other four attacked a carrier and another large vessel, claiming hits on both – although the bomb on the carrier did not explode. They were then attacked by British fighters, but escaped. Naval A.A. gunners were highly optimistic as to the success they had gained, obviously assuming that many of the bombers' dives were terminal; they claimed five shot down!

4/9/40

The greatly-strengthened Mediterranean Fleet now headed eastwards to launch a dawn air strike with aircraft from both carriers against airfields on the Italian-occupied Aegean island of Rhodes. As dawn broke on 4 September, Swordfish from 'Illustrious's' 815 and 819 Squadrons hit Calato. However 'Eagle's' 813 and 824 Squadrons had been delayed in take off and the 13 Swordfish arrived over Maritza to find the defences alerted. The 163ª Squadriglia Autonoma was based here and scrambled a motely collection of CR 32s, CR 42s and Meridionali biplanes. One CR 32 and one CR 42 collided during take off and were destroyed, and another CR 32 flown by Serg. Aristodemo Morri failed to return. The rest however shot down four of the Swordfish (E4C, E4H, E4K, E4M), one falling to the commanding officer, Cap. D'Ajello. Two of the bombers came down in the sea, from where one was recovered, with its crew, by an Italian submarine; another (K8403 'E4M') force-landed on Scarpanto island. Of the twelve Naval aircrew lost, four were killed including Lt. D.R.H. Drummond and his crew, and the remainder taken prisoner. On the ground at Gadurra airfield considerable damage was done by the thirty high-explosive and twenty incendiary bombs dropped. Two S.79s of 39° Stormo were destroyed and three were damaged, together with two Cant Z.1007bis, an S.81 and an S.82 transport. Four men were badly wounded and twenty slightly hurt, while a quantity of fuel, oil and bombs were destroyed.

Off the island patrolling Fulmars enjoyed some success. At 1030 Lt. Barnes and Sub Lt. Sewell of Yellow Section engaged four S.79s, these escaping after each pilot had inflicted damage on them. The same pilots met two more of these aircraft at 1105, the pair attacking down to 80 yards, shooting one down in flames and damaging a second, while Sub Lt. Godfrey, flying as Yellow 3 in N1871 with L/A Phillips, hit another in its port engine. The first victim was an aircraft of 201ª Squadriglia flown by Ten. Nicola Dell'Olio. Three more S.79s of 92° Gruppo were hit, two of them severely, and they landed with two dead and five wounded aboard. Meanwhile at 1005 Lt. Cdr. Kilroy and Sub Lt. Orr had been vectored onto an aircraft which they identified as a Caproni Ca133 bomber-transport, as it was going in to land, and this was shot down into the sea. Two occupants were seen to bale out. The victim would seem in fact to have been an S.81 of 223ª Squadriglia. During the early afternoon, at 1345, Red Section met two S.79s at 7,000 feet 50 miles south of Castello Point. Lt. O.J. Nicolls leading the patrol closed to 100 yards and saw bits fly off the starboard wing of one he attacked but the bombers escaped serious damage.

On 4 September meanwhile, Malta suffered its first attack by the Ju87s, five of these coming over the island to bomb merchant ships in Valetta harbour, but attacking Fort Delimara instead when no sign of these vessels could be seen. The dive-bombers were escorted by CR 42s from the 23º Gruppo and MC200s from 6º Gruppo. Next day in the morning eight S.79s of the 34º Stormo appeared, escorted by ten 23º Gruppo CR 42s. This time Hurricanes intercepted and claimed three CR 42s shot down, one being reported to have been seen crashing into the sea five miles off Grand Harbour. It is believed that these claims were made by Flt.Lt. Greenhalgh, Plt.Off. Allan McAdam and Sgt. Reg Hyde; Sgt. Ayre also attacked a formation of CR 42s and fired one burst before diving away. His engine then 'blew up' and he force-landed at Luqa covered in oil; he was credited with one CR 42 probably destroyed. No Italian fighters were in fact reported lost on this day, but in recording the claims for three shot down, the 'Times of Malta' noted that one Italian pilot landed in a ditch and was taken prisoner, while a second was seen to crash into the sea by eyewitnesses. During the afternoon six Ju87s dive-bombed the island, but were not intercepted.

Ju87B of 96º Gruppo B.a'T. over Malta in September 1940. (*N. Malizia*)

7/9/40

The Italians returned on 7 September around midday, ten S.79s from the 36º Stormo with seventeen CR 42s of the 23º Gruppo raiding Valetta. Three Hurricanes and three Gladiators were up on this occasion, Flt.Lts. Greenhalgh and Lambert, and Flg.Off. Barber jointly shooting down a 258ª Squadriglia, 109° Gruppo S.79; a second was claimed probably damaged by the A.A. Ten.Col. Tito Falconi and Ten. Oscar Abello of the 23° attacked two of the Hurricanes, claiming one shot down each, but both British aircraft escaped with only minor damage.

Active throughout the latter half of 1940, the Swordfish of 830 Squadron were at this time Malta's main striking force. One of the unit's aircraft is seen here launching a practice torpedo off the island's coast. (*W.R.C. Sugden*)

10–13/9/40

During the night of 10/11 September the Latecoere 298B floatplane, crewed by Duvauchelle and Mehouas, landed a Commandant Robert, a supporter of General De Gaulle, on the Tunisian coast. The flight was accomplished in most adverse weather conditions, and took seven hours to complete. Throughout this period Malta remained a staging post for Blenheim and Wellington bombers flying through to Egypt. The Wellingtons came by night, flying right across France; the Blenheims did likewise, though often reaching Malta well after dawn. On 13th a Blenheim IV, N3589, landed in error on Pantelleria island, providing the Italians with an undamaged example of the R.A.F's main day bomber. Following the non-arrival of this aircraft at Malta a Swordfish of 830 Squadron was despatched to search for the missing crew, thought possibly to be down in the sea. In murky weather conditions the Swordfish, piloted by P.O.(A) C.H. Wines, suddenly encountered a Cant seaplane. He attempted a head-on attack and his gunner, L/A Pickles, managed to get in a short bursts from his Lewis gun but the Italian broke away and disappeared.

This Blenheim IV (N3589) landed in error on the island of Pantelleria during a delivery flight to the Middle East on 13 September 1940. It was painted with Italian markings and test flown by the Regia Aeronautica. (*'Intergest' via National War Museum Assoc.*)

14–15/9/40

Raids on Malta continued, seven of the 34° Stormo's bombers attacking Valetta and Kalafrana on 14th., while on 15th. the dive-bombers returned to bomb Hal Far. This raid was a bigger affair than before, including twelve Ju87s and a single S.86 – the prototype, flown by Mar. Elio Scarpini. Escort was provided by eighteen 23° Gruppo CR 42s and six 1° Stormo MC200s. Interception was reported by Hurricanes and Gladiators, and one fighter was claimed shot down by the gunner in Ten. Malvezzi's Ju87 but no losses were actually suffered on either side.

17/9/40

The Stukas returned again on 17th., this latter date giving rise to a bigger combat. Once more twelve Ju87s approached, seven from the 236ª Squadriglia, five from the 237ª. Twenty-one CR 42s from 23° Gruppo and six 6° Gruppo MC200s gave escort, Luqa being the target. After the bombing Ten. Malvezzi strafed the airfield, firing on a twin-engined aircraft, but a reported eight Hurricanes and five Gladiators – a gross overestimate of available strength – then attacked. Ten. Brezzi claimed one Gladiator shot down but his own Ju87 then came under attack and was badly damaged by two Hurricanes. On return to Sicily he counted eleven strikes and found the gunner, 1ᵉ Aviere Gianpiero Vio, dead. Another Ju87 from the 237ª Squadriglia, flown by Serg.Magg. Luigi Catani, failed to return, shot down by Flg.Off. 'Jock' Barber in N2484, who had also been responsible for the damage to Brezzi's aircraft. Reported Barber: "87s dive-bombed Luqa. Three or four Hurricanes scrambled. As we approached the

87s started to dive – I followed one down and opened fire. Pulled out to the south of the island and saw a single 87 near Filfla – as I approached it was obvious the rear gunner had spotted me as the 87 turned to face me – we both fired in three head-on attacks. During the last attack I ran out of ammunition but as I turned I saw the 87 losing height rapidly, streaming glycol, as it splashed into the sea but floated." A launch from the Marine Craft Section at Kalafrana picked up the pilot and the dead gunner, 1ᵉ Aviere Francesca Di Giorgi, eight miles north-west of Filfla. The escorting fighters made no claims, but a CR 42 of the 70ª Squadriglia was shot down by Flg.Off. Woods, the pilot Sottoten. Franco Cavalli, being taken prisoner. An eyewitness reported: "The end for the machine came quickly. It suddenly looped the loop and the pilot was seen struggling to free himself from the cockpit. Just as the machine started to nose-dive at a sharp angle, the pilot baled out, and his parachute opened not a second too soon, for no sooner was he clear than flames burst out. The aircraft crashed into a field and buried its nose some five feet deep into the red earth. A big explosion followed and flames leapt up two storeys high; it continued smouldering right into the night. Meanwhile its pilot was floating in the air, swinging dangerously. It took him six minutes to land ... everyone was still undecided whether it was a British or enemy pilot and as he landed there was a rush to the spot. There were some angry cries when some of the villagers discovered that he was an enemy, but the man was lying helpless on his back. He asked for a glass of water which was quickly brought to him; he asked whether his mother would be informed he was alive. He was placed on a stretcher and carried to the village where he was taken charge of by military personnel." ('Times of Malta' No. 1587).

Bomb-laden Ju87B of 237ª Squadriglia, 96º Gruppo B.a'T. on Comiso airfield (*R. Papini via N. Malizia*)

The dead gunner, Di Giorgi, was buried in St. Andrew's Cemetery on 18th. with full military honours. Following this raid the 96° Gruppo, which also claimed a second Gladiator shot down on this mission, was to make no further sorties over Malta before departing for Albania to participate in the pending invasion of Greece. 'Jock' Barber was later to visit the wounded Stuka pilot, Catani, in hospital on several occasions. "I visited him at Imtarfa and took him several beers, which he seemed to enjoy. A Maltese nurse acted as translator. He was a most brave and skilful pilot who put up a very good show."

During this raid a Wellington at Luqa was totally destroyed by fire – the aircraft fired on by Malvezzi. Two airmen, Cpt. Joe Davis and A.C.1 Tom McCann, with complete disregard for their own safety, went into the blazing aircraft despite exploding ammunition and the likelihood that the fuel tanks would blow up at any minute, and retrieved four Vickers machine guns and six magazines of ammunition. Both men were subsequently awarded the B.E.M.

Hal Far airfield disappears under a cloud of smoke and dust as Ju87Bs of 96° Gruppo B.a'T. climb away after a dive-bombing attack. (*N. Malizia*)

On this same day a Sunderland from 228 Squadron, which unit had recently arrived in the Mediterranean to join 230 Squadron, was making a reconnaissance from Malta to Aboukir, Egypt. En route a Z.501 flyingboat was seen, Sqn.Ldr. G.L. Menzies and his crew at once attacking and shooting this down. Another Z.501 was intercepted by three Fulmars of White Section/806 Squadron at 1100, Sub Lt. Orr shooting this down also. He described this colourful paintwork on the top wing ... "orange and red stripes like ... rising sun"; he attacked and the aircraft started to climb, but the pilot had obviously been killed and it slowly spun into the sea. It is possible these were both Libyan-based aircraft from the 5ª Squadra Aerea.

These actions presaged a few quieter days, during which a new unit came into being on Malta. Before its untimely despatch, the lone Hudson had demonstrated convincingly the value of a long-range reconnaissance facility based on the island, able to fly safely over areas too dangerous for the Sunderlands. In England 22 Squadron, Coastal Command, at North Coates, had been requested in mid-August to evaluate the American-built Glenn Martin 167F attack bomber. This aircraft had been supplied in numbers to the French, following the fall of that nation, the outstanding residue of the contracts had been at once taken over by the aircraft-hungry R.A.F. Although subsequently named Maryland, the inital aircraft were dubbed 'Bob Martins' by the 22 Squadron pilots – named after the famous dog condition powders!

Four leading fighter pilots of the 23° Gruppo Aut. C.T. in Summer 1940. L. to r. Serg. Luigi Bandini, Serg. William Dusi (rear), Serg. Celso Zemella and Serg. Fausto Albani at Comiso. (N. Malizia)

Much of the evaluation was done by Flt.Lt. 'Titch' Whiteley, who was impressed with the performance of the aircraft, which at certain altitudes could outrun a Hurricane. The aircraft was not only fast, but manoevreable and well-armed, with four fixed forward-firing machine guns in the wings, and a dorsal turret for rear defence, plus a hatch in the underside of the fuselage for a hand-held gun. After two weeks Whiteley was ordered to lead three of the new Martins to Malta, making the flight direct over France and Sardinia from Thorney Island.

All went well and the three aircraft, AR 705, AR 707 and AR 712, reached Luqa on 6 September. The crews were:

Flt.Lt. E.A. Whiteley; Plt.Off. P.S. Devine (Nav.); Cpl. J. Shephard (WOP/AG)
Plt.Off. J.H.T. Foxton; Plt.Off. A. Warburton (Nav.); Sgt. R.V. Gridley (WOP/AG)
F/Sgt. J. Bibby; Sgt. F. Bastard (Nav.); Sgt. D.J. Moren (WOP/AG)

'Paddy' Devine and Adrian Warburton were both General Reconaissance pilots, able to fly Avro Ansons, and it was Whiteley's intention that they should be available for conversion to fly the Martins if necessary.

In September 1940 Flt.Lt. E.A. 'Titch' Whiteley arrived on Malta with the first ex-French Martin 167F Maryland aircraft to form 431 Reconnaissance Flight. (*E.A. Whiteley*)

8/9/40

It had been intended that three more Martins would follow immediately, but in the event only one more – AR 713 – would arrive in the next four months. This particular aircraft was fitted with a non-standard Anson-type 'beehive' turret, which somewhat reduced its performance. The initial three on the island were joined by the lone Skua which had accompanied the 418 Flight Hurricanes (L2611, Sub Lt. W.R. Nowell and Capt. K.L. Ford, R.M.) to form 431 Flight under Whiteley's command. The first sortie was flown by Plt.Off. Foxton over Tripoli on 8 September, and soon the aircraft were regularly out on photographic and maritime reconnaissance sorties. The Skua quickly proved of little use for the work, but later two Blenheim IVs in transit were retained for about eight weeks (pilots – Flt. Lt. Tom Horgan and Flg.Off. Ferguson). After one sortie over Taranto it was decided that these latter aircraft were also unsuitable for photo-reconnaissance work, but they were used more successfully for maritime searches.

AR714, one of the early Martin 167F Marylands to arrive for the new 431 Flight, is seen here in a sandstone-walled blast pen at Luqa. (*R.H. Barber*)

Soon after arrival Foxton and Bibby both became indisposed temporarily with 'Malta Dog' – a local gastric upset – and the training of Warburton and Devine to fly the Martins was at once put in hand. Warburton nearly crashed the aircraft twice, and Whiteley was almost ready to give up. Eventually however he succeeded, ultimately becoming the unit's most outstanding and highly-decorated pilot – although during September he was to crash AR712 on landing and wipe off its undercarriage.

At this time Whiteley expended much effort in persuading the reluctant authorities that the racecourse at Gibraltar was suitable as an airfield for the use of aircraft in transit. Although resisted for some time, his suggestion was finally acceded to, and an important landing strip was subsequently developed here, making the ferry route for multi-engined aircraft flying out from England, much less fraught with dangers. He was also to suffer much frustration in obtaining spares. He recalls: "I was continually signalling to Air Ministry for much needed spares hoping that some day a Sunderland or a submarine would deliver some.

Nothing had arrived when A.M. replied saying that my unit had already received the tail wheels, etc. and *they held a receipt for them* signed by 'Sgt. Bowden 431 Flt.' I thus discovered that there were *two* 431 Flights in existence viz one in the U.K. happily receiving spares which I had ordered, but failing to deliver any Marylands or spares to Malta. I responded with a signal to A.M. saying '*431 Flight was formed in Malta on 6 September 1940. It has no connection with any other unit trading under the same name in U.K. etc., etc.*' I, and the A.O.C., were furious to be told that our spares demands 'had been satisfied' – but the spares embezzled by this U.K. unit!"

At this time the lone Latecoere 298B floatplane at Kalafrana was also still giving good service, flying the Gaullist agent into France as already described, and dropping leaflets on Bizerta and Tunis on another occasion, while it also undertook long anti-submarine patrols. When it finally became unserviceable, 'Titch' Whiteley would recruit the two French crewmen to fly in 431 Flight instead. Meanwhile 3 A.A.C.U. was disbanded on 19 September and its remaining aircraft transferred to 830 Squadron, while most of the personnel were posted to the new reconnaissance flight.

25/9/40

On 25 September three Hurricanes and two Gladiators were scrambled after an incoming raid, meeting MC200 fighters. The intruders, a formation of nine aircraft from the 6° Gruppo, were over Malta on a reconnaissance. Maresciallo Gino Lagi was shot down – it is believed by Flg.Off. 'Eric' Taylor – while Sgt. Robertson, who had become separated from the rest of the British formation, attacked two Macchis and claimed one probable. His target was probably the aircraft flown by Cap. Giuliano Giacomelli, which returned with heavy damage, while a third Macchi was hit in the right wing. Lagi, a member of the 79ª Squadriglia, was buried in St. Andrew's Cemetery.

Bombs burst on the edge of Hal Far airfield on 27 September 1940 as 34° Stormo B.T. S.79s pass overhead. (*N. Malizia*)

28/9/40

Towards the end of the month units of the Mediterranean Fleet were again engaged in operations. On 28 September the battleships 'Warspite' and 'Valiant', carrier 'Illustrious', cruisers 'Orion', 'Sydney' and 'York', together with 11 destroyers, put to sea to escort the cruisers 'Liverpool' and 'Gloucester' which were carrying troops and supplies to Malta. Numerous air attacks developed as they passed through the Eastern Mediterranean, but none were effective. The destroyer 'Stuart' suffered a burst steam pipe however, and had to turn back, but in so doing came upon the Italian submarine 'Gondar', and made a depth charge attack. The submarine was forced to the surface, and was sunk next morning by the bombs of a patrolling flyingboat.

29/9–1/10/40

Over the Fleet Fulmars were on patrol and were successful against 'shadowers' on 29th. At 1124 Blue Section intercepted a Z.501 at 8,000 feet, Sub Lt. Hogg attacking it and reporting that it spiralled down in flames. The No. 2 aircraft, flown by Sub Lt. Lowe, was hit by return fire and forced to ditch 5 miles astern of H.M.A.S. 'Stuart'. The destroyer turned about and raced to the vicinity of the ditching, rescuing both Lowe and his TAG, L/A P. Douet. Three hours later White Section caught another Z. 501, Sub Lt. Orr shooting this down in flames from 10,000 feet.

The cruisers 'Liverpool' and 'Gloucester' reached Malta safely, unloading swiftly and putting to sea again, as the Fleet headed back towards Alexandria. On the first day of the new month the Italian submarine 'Berille' was surprised on the surface, and after the crew had surrendered and been taken off, was sunk. During the day, at 1115, Blue Section caught yet another 'shadower' at 4,000 feet. "Standard red and white stripes on top mainplane, white rudder with green St. Andrew's cross" is how Lt. Cdr. Evans described it as he chased it down to sea level with the starboard engine on fire; it hit the sea and broke up. On 6th the body of an Italian airman, simply identified as A. Girandola, was picked up from the sea by H.M.S. 'Coral'. It seems likely that this was one of the crew of the floatplane.

4–8/10/40

261 Squadron's fighters again engaged MC200s over Malta on 4 October, Sgt. Robertson claiming one damaged, while one more was credited as destroyed to an unnamed pilot. Once again their opponents were aircraft of the 6° Gruppo on a photographic reconnaissance; on this occasion Ten. Mario Nasoni was shot down and killed, his aircraft being that carrying the camera. October was to prove a very quiet month however, with only one attack on the island during the first two weeks. This occurred on 8th., when five S.79s of 36° Stormo raided Kalafrana in the dark. Flg.Off. Taylor went up to intercept with the aid of searchlights, shooting down the bomber of 257ª Squadriglia, 108° Gruppo, flown by Ten. Adolfo Ferrari, in flames; he also damaged a second. The gunners in the

surviving bombers claimed one British fighter shot down, but Taylor's was the only interceptor in the air, and it is possible that they thought Ferrari's burning S.79 was their victim. On return the bombers landed at Comiso rather than at their own base at Castelvetrano; the damaged aircraft got down only with difficulty, with three of the crew having suffered wounds during the attack.

An S.79 is prepared for a raid on Malta on a Sicilian airfield. The bombs in the foreground are the classic Italian 250 kg. missiles. (*A.M.I. via N. Malizia*)

10/10/40

When dusk fell on 10 October a balance was drawn. In four months of war the island's fighter defences had recorded 72 interceptions by day and two by night. Claims totalled:

	S.79	CR 42	Ju87	MC200	Total
Confirmed	9*	7	2	4	22
Probables	5*	2	1	1	9
Damaged	5*	2	0	1	8

(*including one S.79 destroyed, one probable and one damaged at night).

Anti-aircraft defences claimed in addition three S.79s shot down, three probables and two damaged, a CR 42 probable and an MC200 damaged. Losses in the air had totalled two Hurricanes, one Gladiator, one Swordfish and the Hudson destroyed, while on the ground two Hurricanes (one of them N2717), one

Swordfish, one Blenheim and one Martin had been destroyed. Other aircraft had been damaged but were repairable, although in some cases had in fact been 'cannibalized' to keep others flying.

12/10/40

A further convoy, bound this time for Malta, brought out the Regia Aeronautica in force on 12th., units from Sicily launching eighty-four bomber and thirty-eight fighter sorties. H.M.S. 'Eagle' was near missed by a dozen bombs and suffered damage from the shock waves. 806 Squadron's Fulmars from 'Illustrious' were active however, Sub Lts. Sewell and J.M.L. Roberts catching a 'shadowing' Z.501 at 1145, chasing it from 3,000 feet to sea level where it ditched. They strafed it, but saw no signs of life. At 1230 Red Section, led by Lt. Nicolls in N1876, sighted twelve S.79s at 14,000 feet, Nicolls carrying out a beam attack on the second

'Sicilian fruit for Malta'! Regia Aeronautica armourers indulge in the favoured wartime propaganda exercise of painting messages for the enemy on bombs! (*N. Malizia*)

74

section of three and then a stern attack on lone aircraft. He saw white smoke pour from the starboard engine, and pieces flying off; it was considered unlikely that it could get home. Blue Section met five more Savoias at 1350, attacking these at 16,000 feet. Lt. Cdr. Evans led Sub Lts. Hogg and Lowe into beam attacks, shooting down one in flames and forcing a second to ditch.

2ª Squadra Aerea suffered quite heavily; the first attack by twelve S.79s of 34º Stormo escaped interception, but that following by ten 36º Stormo aircraft was savaged by the Fulmars, two S.79s flown by Ten. Alberto Soldati of the 108º Gruppo and Ten. Francesco Tempra of the 109º Gruppo being shot down, while a third returned badly damaged with one dead and two wounded aboard. A fourth, flown by Ten. Giorgio Pieri of the 109º Gruppo – possibly also damaged – flew into a mountainside on its return to Sicily and was totally destroyed. The third raid, by seven S.79s of 34º Stormo attacked Italian warships by mistake, while other S.79s from 105º Gruppo Aut. and fourteen Ju87s from the 96º Gruppo B.a'T. saw nothing. During one of the raids a civil S.73 airliner from Benghazi strayed into the thick of the action, landing later at Catania damaged by both A.A. fire and fighters, and with one passenger dead and two wounded. The Italian Navy meanwhile lost two destroyers sunk and one damaged, all in an action with the cruiser 'Ajax'.

12–15/10/40

A Maryland from 431 Flight had gone out early on a reconnaissance of the Taranto–Brindisi area, searching for Italian Fleet involvement. During the mission the aircraft was attacked by fighters, the crew (Plt.Off. Foxton, with Warburton and Gridley) claiming one badly damaged. While the Maryland was away a Sunderland flown by Flt.Lt. I.F. McCall of 228 Squadron, which unit was now fully based at Kalafrana, was sent out to find and rescue the crew of the Z.501 which 'Illustrious's' Fulmars had shot down; this was accomplished successfully. Such a rescue was again reported on 16 October, when a Sunderland also picked up the crew of a force-landed Swordfish, but this is believed to be a repeat report of the operation on 12th. Meanwhile at 1330 on 13th. one of 'Eagle's' Sea Gladiators (N5567) flown by Lt. (A) Oliphant engaged a single S.79 while on patrol, catching the aircraft after a twelve minute chase. After a first attack the bomber's port engine was hit and the aircraft lost height rapidly. It was last seen very low over the water when the British pilot was forced to break away due to shortage of ammunition. The flyingboats at Kalafrana were reinforced by the arrival of another French 'boat on 15th. This time it was a Loire 130 (No. 73) which had been based aboard the battleship 'Richelieu' for catapult launching. During a ferry flight from Bizerta, Tunisia to Dakar, French West Africa, the crews of two of these aircraft decided to make a bid for freedom, but only No. 73, flown by Deuzieme-Maitre Georges Blaize made it. The other Loire, manned by an inexperienced crew, ditched in Bizerta Lake where the aircraft was later destroyed; the crew were subsequently court-martialled. During 15th. the body of Giuseppe Granzoto, late of 257ª Squadriglia, was washed ashore on Malta. He was buried next day in St. Andrew's Cemetery.

16–27/10/40

On 16th Flt.Lt. Waters of 261 Squadron, flying Hurricane P2645, claimed an S.79 shot down, although no loss on this date has been discovered in Italian records. After this no further action was reported for over ten days, until 27th. On that date six Hurricanes and two Gladiators were scrambled at 1055, and engaged nine Italian fighters. The intruders were MC200s of 6° Gruppo, led by the commanding officer, Magg. Mezzetti. Two Hurricanes were claimed shot down by Cap. Ruspoli, but apparently Mar. Marasco's Macchi was badly damaged, for he subsequently baled out over his own airfield. He would appear to have been the victim of Flg.Off. Taylor, who claimed one MC200 probable; a second Macchi was claimed damaged, while no R.A.F. losses were recorded.

30/10/40

The last action of the month occurred on 30th. when a further reconnaissance of Taranto and Brindisi was made by a 431 Flight Maryland during the morning. This time Plt.Off. Warburton was at the controls, with Sgts. Strong and Moren as crew. They engaged a Z.506B floatplane and forced it down on the sea with one engine on fire. It was photographed after the crew had got out into their dinghy, and Warburton then broadcast a distress signal on their behalf, indicating their position.

Recently the fighters of 261 Squadron, while still based at Luqa, had started using the civil airfield at Takali for operations, hopping their aircraft over to this base daily. Now it was organized as a full R.A.F. station under the command of Wg.Cdr. G.R. O'Sullivan, and the unit was able to move in fully, leaving Luqa clear for multi-engined types.

Towards the end of October Wg.Cdr. Jonas, station commander at Luqa, had been informed that a dozen Wellingtons of 148 Squadron would be arriving from England for operations from Malta and would be stationed at Luqa. Wg.Cdr. Jonas later recorded his impressions of the arrival of the bombers, and of the earliest operations: "So there were to both bombers and fighters at Luqa. In breaking the news to my adjutant that afternoon I remarked that the station might be described as a kind of 'aerial liquorice allsorts'! As dawn was breaking two days later, after herculean efforts on the part of everyone preparing for their arrival, I stood on the tarmac once again and watched the dim shapes of the Wellingtons arriving after their long trip. But aeorplanes, particularly bombers, require a large number of men to maintain and service their thousand and one complicated parts; and here were a dozen Wellingtons with their crews alone, and a faint chance that their mechanics would follow by sea, some time in the future."

31/10/40

"It was all rather typical of those early wartime enterprises in our little island. Bricks were expected to be produced without the essential straw. But somehow the impossible was achieved, and our latest 'children' were provided with riggers and fitters, armourers and instrument makers, by the only solution of combing once again the manpower of Hal Far, Kalafrana and even Luqa itself. It was a great night when the Wellingtons set off on their first bombing raid (31 October), bound for Naples, 350-odd miles distant. Of course the immediate preliminaries of any bombing raid are characterised by an atmosphere of expectancy and hurried preparations. But although during the months that followed, I watched many raiding bombers throbbing away from Luqa into the night, it is always the preliminaries of that first Wellington raid that I vizualize when I think of night bombing from Malta."

"Naturally, being the first occasion that heavy bombers had ever operated from the island, it was regarded as somewhat of a special operation; and as I walked along the road through the camp towards the big wooden hut where the flying crews were assembled, I saw by the cars outside that both the Governor (Dobbie) and the A.O.C. (Maynard) had already arrived. Standing behind the A.O.C. I listened to the commanding officer (Sqn.Ldr. P.S. Foss) who was to lead the raid, 'briefing' the pilots, navigators, wireless operators and air-gunners, who stood in an irregular semicircle around him. There were references to positions on the target maps that they held, the route to be taken, the 'run in', bomb lead, petrol endurance, height of bombing and wireless signals. Looking round at the crews before us, a mixture of officers and sergeants, I was surprised to see how young most of them looked ... an hour later I stood by the control tower in the darkness, watching the looming black shapes of the bombers roaring past me down the runway. Watching the long orange flames from the exhausts, climbing away over the valley. Watching the red dot of light on the rudders, until they too had disappeared among the stars."

"But during the ensuing days, most of us learnt with consternation, that the aerodrome at Luqa was by no means large enough for the operation of heavy-laden bombers. The pilots themselves, or at least some of them who probably represented the experienced majority, were quite emphatic about this. Certainly, watching the take offs on that first Naples raid had been at times a nerve-racking experience for the spectators. 'Will they never lift?', we asked ourselves, as the dark forms thundered closer and closer to the far boundary; and we crouched low, watching for a glimpse of starlight below the red dot on the tail, that told us that they were off. One loquacious young pilot claimed to have cut things so fine, that he had hit some obstacle with his wheels, as he skimmed over the far wall; and a rather battered and overturned tar sprayer was discovered the following morning and proved to everyone how authentic his supposition had been. Obviously there were only two solutions to such a problem, the first being to lighten the bombload and the second to extend the runways; the former a temporary and immediate remedy, while the latter might be classed as a 'long term policy'. Certainly we could do nothing about the rarefied atmosphere of the island; a condition which from a flying point of view, is found in all hot places, all over the world."

3/11/40

"Not for long were we to escape disaster, and although the bombload had been reduced, tragedy and calamity came upon us. Looking back on that unhappy evening (3 November) I find that I am unable even to recollect the whereabouts of the target; remembering only that it was the second operational trip from Luqa that the Wellingtons had done. Apart from that conditions were similar to those of the first raid, and as the first bomber thundered past me, I remarked to the doctor who was standing beside me, that as far as the weather was concerned it might be considered an ideal night for the trip. And then number two roared towards us, materialised itself momentarily into a shapeless form, and was gone. Half blinded with dust and grit from the slipstream, we watched the little red tail light climbing up amongst the stars and heard the strange echo from the engines as the aircraft swept over the steep valley beyond the aerodrome. And then terrifying in its inevitability and steadiness, we watched the red dot of light sinking, sinking towards the ground. What could have happened? Had his motors failed? No, we could still hear them roaring at full throttle a mile or two away. Was he overloaded? Or was it that some fiendish eddy in the valley beneath had reached upwards, to pull him down? There was no answer ... instead, the pulsating beat of the distant motors ceased abruptly and a burst of livid red flame like a Guy Fawkes bonfire, appeared across the valley. The Wellington crashed and was burning, with a full load of petrol and bombs aboard. I looked round for my friend the doctor, but he was already in the ambulance, speeding away into the night, with his instruments and his thoughts. But, like the tradition of the theatre, the raid must go on; and with a beacon of burning petrol to use as a marker, the next bomber disappeared into the darkness."

Wreckage of a burnt-out Wellington, believed to be one of those which crashed on 3 November 1940 when taking off for a raid. (*P. Vella*)

"Then number four swept past, climbing slowly across the valley, and then commenced to turn gently to the right. Surely the red light was sinking now, sinking slowly towards Hamrun. The tragedy of number two was being repeated; disaster was inevitable. Lower and lower went the red dot, then the horrifying silence followed by the burst of orange-red flames. Even as I watched, wishfully hoping that some were left alive, there was a blinding flash away to the left, and a deep thunder rolled across the valley. The bombs had exploded!"

"Miraculously and unacccountably, even after the crashes themselves, followed by the fires and the bomb explosions, some were left alive. In fact in the first crash, all escaped except the second pilot who died later; from the second Wellington only one lived and recovered. However it was not until the following day that we learnt the full story of the accidents, and their aftermaths of courage and self sacrifice. Of the first Wellington that had crashed, Sgt. Lewin had been the pilot. He merely stated briefly that after a longer run than usual, he finally left the ground shortly before the far end of the runway, and climbed up rather slowly to a height of about 500 feet. At this point the aeroplane not only refused to gain more height, but in spite of all his efforts to prevent it, continued to sink, steadily downwards towards the ground. Just at the last moment with no time to jettison either bombs or petrol or for his crew to bale out, the starlit ground suddenly loomed up as a grey blur before him, and pulling back on everything, Lewin had contrived to make a reasonably safe landing. Here the pilot's story ended with a 'then we all got out, as the Wimpey caught fire as soon as we touched the ground.'"

"But the navigator and the rest of the crew related a very different story – a story of courage and 'guts' that ... I find hard to equal. Thrown from their positions in the crash and seeing the flames, they had scrambled to safety, fighting their way through the tangle of steel and canvas, out into the night air.... Then out of the flames Sgt. Lewin had come, his face bloody from cuts, limping from a smashed kneecap. 'Run for your lives boys, the bombs' he had shouted. And as they ran to safety they had looked back; in the firelight they had seen their captain going back, fighting his way into the flaming cockpit, dragging the unconscious second pilot out; 25 yards away Lewin dropped his burden and sank down beside it, covering his friend's body with his own. Just then there was a blinding shattering roar and the bombs exploded. When Sgt. Lewin had lifted his own injured body away ... he saw that his second pilot was dead."

"The pilot of the second Wellington that had crashed ... was dead, as were all but one sorely battered member of his crew. For this pilot had not had the good fortune of Sgt. Lewin ... instead Qormi village lay before, with its houses and churches and stone walls. Helplessly and inevitably had the bomber gone on, crashing and burning its patch through walls and houses; finally to break its back and hurl itself into a stone quarry. This time a Maltese policeman, peering down from the edge of the shaft, saw by the light of the flames that a body lay at the bottom, injured and motionless." A rope was found, but Sgt. A.T. Smith did not have sufficient remaining strength to hold on, so Police Constable Carmel Camilleri tied the rope round himself, and was lowered into the bomb-filled inferno to lift the sole survivor out. Subsequently he was awarded a George Medal, while Sgt. R.M. Lewin received a George Cross. Sadly, Sgt. Smith later died of his injuries; others killed that night included pilots Plt.Off. D.R. Allen and D.P. Rawlings, observer Sgt. T.R. Woor, and gunner Sgt. P.E. Forrester.

1/11/40

Generally the first days of November saw a resurgence of activity, initially centred over the sea between Sicily and Malta. During the morning of 1st two 228 Squadron Sunderlands set off from Kalafrana to search for survivors of a missing Wellington bomber. N9020, flown by Sqn.Ldr. Menzies and Flg.Off. S.M. Farries, searched the waters to the immediate East of Sicily, while L5806 'Q', piloted by Flt.Lt. E.M. Ware, set course further afield to the Southern Adriatic in the area of Zante, Cephalonia and Corfu. These missions were to prove ill-fated, for before the morning was out N9020 was caught near the Sicilian port of Augusta by two MC200s of the 6° Gruppo's 88ª Squadriglia, flown by Ten. Armanino and Serg.Magg. Stabile, and was shot down with the loss of the whole crew. In the afternoon, as L5806 returned from its long sortie, it too was intercepted when only 32 miles short of Malta. Two more 6° Gruppo Macchis in the hands of Ten. Pesola and Ten. Tomaselli, joined by a 23° Gruppo CR 42 flown by Ten. Ezio Monti, attacked the big boat but were unable to shoot it down, having to content themselves with a claim for a 'damaged'. The Sunderland had indeed been hit hard; two of the crew were wounded, while matresses, flares and other combustibles were set alight, and had to be hastily jettisoned. Despite severe damage, including a number of bullet holes in the fuselage and hull, Ware was able to land back at Kalafrana safely. No sign of the Wellington or its crew had been found. Ware later received the D.F.C. for this and other sorties, whilst one of the air gunners, L.A.C. R.J. Barton, received the D.F.M. Although wounded in the leg, Barton had continued to man his gun throughout.

On this day patrolling Fulmars from 'Illustrious' were vectored onto 'shadowers', Sub Lt. Sewell, with L/A Tribe in Fulmar 'Y', intercepted two Z.506Bs and shot one down in flames; the other escaped in a damaged condition.

2/11/40

Next morning, 2 November, Plt.Off. Warburton carried out a long reconnaissance over Taranto and Brindisi in one of the precious Marylands. The aircraft was intercepted by three CR 42s and a flyingboat of some description, but escaped after the turret gunner had reported that he had hit one fighter, possibly wounding the pilot and damaging the engine. A bullet had entered the nose of the Maryland however, just missing Sgt. Frank Bastard, smashing through the instrument panel and hitting Warburton in the chest. Fortunately it was almost spent by the time it struck him, and the wound was little more than skin deep. Nonetheless it hit with sufficient force to render him unconscious, and he fell forward over the controls. Bastard took over and flew the aircraft straight and level until Warburton recovered sufficiently to resume control. Bastard then helped him to carry out the landing; he was later awarded a D.F.M. for this and other activities. Warburton made a speedy recovery.

Meanwhile a raid in the other direction was underway. Twenty S.79s of the 34° Stormo attacked Valetta and Takali under the protection of a fairly strong fighter escort. Eleven MC200s from the 71ª and 72ª Squadriglia led by Magg.Bruno Brambilla, and five CR 42s of the 80ª Squadriglia led by Cap. Luigi Corsini undertook the mission, these squadriglie forming the 17° Gruppo of the 1° Stormo C.T. They reported being involved in a big dogfight with five Hurricanes, Mar. Carozzo claiming one shot down; Serg. Abramo Lanzarini of the 72ª Squadriglia was killed when his aircraft crashed on the island at Zeitun. 261 Squadron had in fact scrambled only two or three fighters, including Gladiator N5520 in the capable hands of George Burges. An unidentified pilot claimed the Macchi shot down, while Burges attacked a formation which he identified as comprising eight CR 42s. He thought he had shot one of these down but did not see it crash; he claimed a second damaged.

6–7/11/40

Three days' quiet followed this activity, at the end of which on 6 November a lone CR 42, believed to have come from the 23° Gruppo, made a surprise strafing attack on one of 228 Squadron's Sunderlands riding at anchor in Marsaxlokk Bay, succeeeding in damaging it. On 7th. Adrian Warburton undertook another of his seven hour reconnaissance flights over Taranto and Brindisi, during the course of which interception again took place. The gunner reported four MC 200s and thought he had damaged one. The attackers on this occasion were in fact seven strong and came from the 372ª Squadriglia Autonoma C.T. They pursued the intruder over Taranto, but were unable to catch it and all returned safely to base.

L. and r. Mar. Giovanni Carmello, a successful fighter pilot of the 75ª Squadriglia, 23° Gruppo Aut. C.T. with his CR 42 prior to a sortie over Malta. (*Fam. Carmello via N. Malizia*)

The reason for Warburton's sortie was about to become obvious, for further major naval operations were underway at both ends of the Mediterranean. A considerable force of troops had now been gathered on Gibraltar, intended to provide a more effective garrison for Malta. One infantry battalion, two field batteries of 25 pounder guns, a light tank troop, one light and two heavy anti-aircraft batteries comprised the force involved, and on 6 November 2,150 men from these units went aboard the battleship 'Barham', cruisers 'Berwick' and 'Glasgow', and three destroyers, and sailed for the island. Their heavy equipment was to be delivered by merchant vessels later in the month. One day out from Gibraltar on 7th, three Skuas from 800 Squadron sighted a Z.506B whilst on patrol. The leading Skua, crewed by Lt. Spurway and P.O.(A) Hart, opened fire at extreme range, hitting the floatplane which slowed down. Spurway pressed home his attack and the Cant alighted on the sea, one member of the crew being seen to wave a white cloth as the fighters circled overhead.

8/11/40

At the same time as the convoy had sailed from Gibraltar, another convoy of five cargo ships sailed from Alexandria for Malta under the codename MB.8, while other vessels headed for Greece and Crete. To provide cover for MB.8 directly, and for the other vessels indirectly, four Mediterranean Fleet battleships, two cruisers, 'Illustrious' and thirteen destroyers put to sea. Because considerable aerial reaction was expected, the carrier also embarked two or three of 'Eagle's' Sea Gladiators as reinforcements for 806 Squadron's Fulmars on this occasion. First action came on 8 November, and it was two of the biplanes which made the first 'kill', at 1230, Lt. Nicolls and Sub Lt. Sewell catching and shooting down a Cant Z.501 of the 186ª Squadriglia R.M. flown by Ten. Paolo Primatesta, which had left its base at Augusta at 0900. A contemporary British report noted: "It struck the water and two members of the crew of five were unable to extricate themselves; they were drowned. The other three, a Naval sottotenente, a sergente maggiore and a wireless operator, managed to scramble into the Cant's dinghy. The chance of survival was exceedingly remote as their dinghy quickly developed a leak. A Sunderland flyingboat on patrol spotted the tiny boat, and as it was far from land decided to investigate. Although there was a nasty swell at the time, the Sunderland alighted on the sea and rescued them."

Early in the afternoon two formations of S.79s from the 34° Stormo, totalling fifteen aircraft, took off from Catania to search for the vessels which were known to be approaching the area. 180 miles east of Malta one section made contact with 'Illustrious' fighters, directed to intercept them by the ship's radar. At 1620 the Fulmars – Blue Section (Lt.Cdr. Evans with Sub Lts. Hogg and Lowe) energetically attacked a formation of seven bombers, driving them off with three aircraft seriously damaged and six crewmen wounded. Evans claimed one S.79 shot down and that three parachutes were seen to come from a second aircraft attacked by all three, but on this occasion all regained Sicilian soil, although one of the damaged machines had to make an emergency landing at Reggio Calabria, on the toe of the mainland. The second formation returned to base having seen nothing.

9/11/40

Italian reconnaissance aircraft made further searches, the British ships being spotted several times, but without effect. A Z.506B floatplane from the 170ª Squadriglia R.M. from Augusta was caught by Sub Lt. Stan Orr in Fulmar N1881 at 1640, flying at 5,000 feet. He made two stern attacks and one from the beam, and the Cant crashed in flames, Sottoten. Tealdo Euria and his crew being lost. During this day convoy MB.8 reached Malta safely, followed next day by the troop-carrying warships from Gibraltar. During the early hours Maryland AR719 took off from Thorney Island, (Hampshire) crewed by Flg.Off. J.T. Burgess and Sgt. B.F. Hubbard, on posting to 431 Flight. The aircraft was due to arrive at Malta at 1100, but was not heard from again.

8/11/40

Malta had also received additional reinforcement by air during this period when 37 Squadron began moving to the Mediterranean from England. Six Wellingtons departed from Feltwell, Norfolk, during the early hours of 8 November, setting course for Malta. One was forced to turn back, but the other five approached the area as dawn broke. Passing close by Pantelleria, Flt.Lt. M.J. Baird-Smith's aircraft was attacked and damaged by Italian fighters, two members of the crew being wounded. Despite this, all five bombers landed safely at Luqa.

10/11/40

Reconnaissance by Malta's Marylands had indicated the presence in Taranto harbour of six battleships together with many cruisers and destroyers. As these had not put to sea to challenge the British fleets, a daring night torpedo attack was planned, and in consequence 'Illustrious' did not immediately head back to Alexandria. Searches and attacks by the units of 2ª Squadra Aerea in Sicily continued during 10th., 806 Squadron's Fulmars making further interceptions. At 1220 Lt. Barnes and Sub Lt. Sewell shot down a Z.501 of the 144ª Squadriglia R.M. from Stagnone, flown by Sottoten. Alfio Ferri, after chasing it down from 4,000 feet to sea level; it was then strafed. At 1310 Barnes' Yellow Section intercepted a raid by nine S.79s from the 30° and 36° Stormo; they attacked one which started losing height after being hit in the starboard engine, and claimed it as damaged. In fact Ten. Raffaele Brandi's aircraft failed to return.

8–9/11/40

Even as 'Illustrious's' air group prepared for their forthcoming attack, 'Ark Royal' launched her own aircraft for a diversionary strike on Cagliari once more, escorted to the target area by the main strength of Force 'H'. One of her Skua squadrons – 803 – had now been replaced by 808, the second Fulmar squadron to see service in the Mediterranean area. As the carrier and her escorts approached Sardinia on 8th. the Fulmars were to gain their first victory at 1800 when the commanding officer, Lt. Rupert Tillard shot down a lone S.79 at 3,000 feet some 50 miles South of Sardinia. Tillard's first attack appeared to kill the rear gunner, and he then shot the aircraft down into the sea. Swordfish from 810,

818 and 820 Squadrons then undertook their strike on 9th., while the fighters were also in action again. At 0950 Red Section of 808 Squadron intercepted a Z.506B of the 196ª Squadriglia R.M. flown by Ten. Silvano Donda at 6,500 feet, and this was shot down in flames by Lt. Tillard. Soon after 1100 a formation of some twenty-five to thirty S.79s from Decimomannu airfield were encountered some ten miles from the carrier, soon after they had left the Sardinian coast. Lt. Tillard and two other Fulmar pilots engaged at 1115, Tillard attacking the leader of one formation from 300 yards down to 50. This bomber was reported to have crashed into the sea by another pilot, and by watchers on H.M.S. 'Glasgow'. Now Skuas of 800 Squadron joined the fight, three attacking at 1130 and claiming hits to several bombers, but none shot down; 6K was twice hit by return fire, and 6M once. Three minutes later a further trio (6F, 6G and 6H) also attacked, claiming several hits. On this occasion none of the S.79s were in fact lost, but of the 20 taking part, 18 were hit, many members of the crews being wounded and some killed. The Skua crews involved were:

6K	L2908	Lt. Spurway/P.O.(A) Hart
6L	L3049	Sub Lt.(A) Hurle-Hobbs/P.O.(A) V.H. Cordwell
6M	L3007	P.O.(A) Burston/N/A Holmes
6F	L3015	Lt. J. A. Rooper/Sub Lt.(A) G.R. Woolston
6G	L2952	Lt. R.G. French/N/A G.J. Jones
6H	L3017	P.O.(A) A. Jopling/N/A J. Glen

11–13/11/40

Escaping further discovery by searching aircraft, 'Illustrious' was able to launch her Swordfish during the night of 11/12th for the now-famous attack on Taranto, which has been adequately and fully chronicled elsewhere. Immediately on recovery of the bombers, the carrier made all speed towards Alexandria, Fulmars keeping a steady patrol overhead from first light in the expectation of massive air searches, followed inevitably by fierce bombing attacks. In fact the combat air patrol proved spectacularly successful, catching several 'shadowers' before, apparently, they could send accurate sighting reports, and no attack developed. Sub Lts. Orr and W.H. Clisby were up on the first patrol, seeing a Z.501 at 5,000 feet at 1155, which they claimed shot down in flames. Ten minutes later Blue Section, led by Lt.Cdr. Evans, engaged another from astern, and this too was claimed shot down in flames by Evans and Sub Lt. Lowe. Within half an hour a Z.506B was sighted at 7,000 feet and following two attacks by Evans this also fell in flames. One of these 'shadowers' reportedly fell into the sea alongside the battleship 'Warspite', before the eyes of the Commander-in-Chief. Next day at 1530 Sub Lts. Orr and Hogg jointly attacked another Z.506B at sea level, leaving it in a badly damaged condition after using up all their ammunition; it was then seen to fall in flames. Italian records indicate the loss of two Z.506Bs on 12th., one of 184ª Squadriglia R.M., the other flown by Ten. Aldo Salvaneschi of the 170ª Squadriglia R.M. – both Sicily-based. The identity of the other aircraft claimed has not been definitely established.

12/11/40

As the Mediterranean Fleet headed away, 431 Flight completed the picture, having provided the invaluable pre-strike reconnaissance and photography during some dozen flights in which all members of the flight had taken part. Now on the morning of 12th. Flt.Lt. Whiteley himself set course for his eighth sortie over Taranto, approaching by way of the Gulf of Corinth and Corfu, still unaware that the attack had taken place. As he approached he found the defences more 'alive' than usual, but while making his photo pass was thrilled to see one battleship partly submerged and another which seemed to have been beached; general chaos obviously reigned! Trying to radio Malta in code, he found this gave no scope for the report he wished to make, so he reported the details of his sighting in self-evident code, ending "One battleship (BS) sinking." Further details had to await his arrival and the development of his photographs.

12–14/11/40

With the British fleets out of range again, 2ª Squadra Aerea now returned to the attack on Malta during 12th., twelve MC200s from the 6° Gruppo, which had now lost its autonomous status and become a part of 1° Stormo C.T., flying a reconnaissance over the island during the morning. AA fire split up the formation enabling Hurricanes to press home an attack, the aircraft of Ten. Giuseppe Volpe being shot down into the sea – it is believed by Plt.Off. Balmforth. Volpe's body was recovered by a trawler after the Hurricane pilot had indicated the position of the crash. Two days later five Hurricanes scrambled to meet two S.79s and eight escorting CR 42s north of Gozo. Flg.Off 'Jock' Barber's Hurricane suffered an overheated engine and he became separated from the others. Flying alone he saw the incoming Italian formation below him and made several diving attacks, claiming one CR 42 probably destroyed. No combat was recorded by the Italians on this occasion.

Old stalwarts and new, Winter 1940. This group of 261 Squadron pilots includes (l. to r.) Flg.Off. 'Jock' Barber, Sgt. C.S. Bamberger, Plt.Off. C.E. 'Hamish' Hamilton, Flt.Lt. J.A.F. MacLachlan (foreground), Flg.Off. 'Eric' Taylor and Sgt. R.J. Hyde. (*R.H. Barber*)

13–16/11/40

During the night of 12/13 November seven more Wellingtons from 37 Squadron reached Malta from England, and as darkness fell on 13th. four of this unit's aircraft flew their first operational sorties in the new theatre, attacking Taranto harbour. The squadron was not destined to remain long on the island however; on 15th. the first two flew on to Kabrit in Egypt. On the way an Italian seaplane was encountered, and this was claimed shot down by the crew of Plt.Off. D.F. Benbow's aircraft. Three further aircraft flew into Luqa from Feltwell on 19th., but on 21st. all remaining aircraft made the journey to Egypt. Meanwhile on 16th. 148 Squadron's Wellingtons attacked Bari on the Italian east coast, one of these bombers failing to return.

17/11/40

Following the successful delivery of 418 Flight with its Hurricanes during August, a repeat performance was now being readied. In mid-November the old carrier 'Argus' again sailed for Gibraltar, once more with twelve Hurricanes and two Skuas aboard, plus thirteen R.A.F. fighter pilots and two Naval crews. Escort this time was provided by the battleship 'Renown', carrier 'Ark Royal', three cruisers and seven destroyers. The Italian Fleet was reported to be at sea, and 'Argus's' captain was eager to be rid of his charges at the earliest possible moment. At dawn on 17th. therefore engines were started and at 0615 the first six Hurricanes took off, together with Skua L2882 (flown by Sub Lt. W.R. Nowell, who had been transported from Malta to Gibraltar especially for this flight, and Sub Lt. P.G. Smith). It was some 400 sea miles to Malta which should have meant that the Hurricanes, if flown at appropriate speed, revs and altitude, would reach the island with 45 minutes' fuel to spare. In the event it took 15 minutes to get all seven aircraft into the air and formed up, so that a third of their safety margin had already evaporated. At last they set off; the flight was led by newly-promoted Flt.Lt. J.A.F. MacLachlan, D.F.C., in V7474. MacLachlan was a 21 year-old of part Scottish, part New Zealand ancestry, who had been decorated for service in France earlier in the year when he had flown Fairey Battle light bombers; he had volunteered for a transfer to fighters at the start of the Battle of Britain. The other pilots were Plt.Offs. C.E. Hamilton (V7370) and H.W. Eliot (V7548), and Sgts. J.K. Norwell (V7346), R.A. Spyer (V7413) and W.G. Cunnington (V7374). They headed for Malta at 150 m.p.h. at a height of 2,000 feet – far from ideal, since the Hurricane's best cruise range was achieved at 10,000 feet and at a lower speed.

The second flight followed an hour later, upon which the vessels of Force 'H' turned for base with all speed. 'Argus' still had the 'spare' pilot, Sgt. C.S. Bamberger, aboard; he would reach the island on 28 November aboard the destroyer 'Hotspur'. The second flight meanwhile was led by Skua L2987 (Pty Off. (A) W.E.J. Stockwell and Sub Lt. R.C. Neil), and comprised Flg.Offs. E.G. Bidgood, P.W. Horton, J.R. Walker, R.W. Clarke and Plt.Offs. F.J. Boret and J.M. Horrox.

As the first flight headed on towards Malta it was noticed that the cloud shadows and sea patterns were changing. A smoke float was dropped from the

Skua, showing that the wind had veered from west-south-westerly to east-south-easterly, thereby presenting the aircraft with an almost direct headwind to fly into. Soon visibility worsened, but Nowell's navigating was as good as before, and the first landfall – Galite Island – was safely reached, although 25 minutes behind schedule. Here a Sunderland from 228 Squadron met the formation to lead them on to Malta. Now however, fuel was running very low. At 0908, when still some 30–40 miles from the island, Sgt. Spyer's V7413 ran out of fuel and fell towards the sea. The pilot was able to bale out and MacLachlan followed him down, calling in the Sunderland. The latter landed and picked up the very relieved pilot out of the sea. Taking off again, the flying boat joined formation with MacLachlan and they set off after the rest. Well ahead, the other four Hurricanes could be seen straggling after the Skua. They passed through some cloud, but on emerging from this, there were only three. Sgt. Cunnington too had run out of fuel; he waved farewell and baled out at 0912. By the time the Sunderland appeared there was no sign of him however, and he was never found.

Finally the four remaining Hurricanes and the Skua landed at 0920, MacLachlan with four gallons of fuel left and Norwell with only two. The engine of another aircraft cut before it could taxi off the runway, and the fourth had little more left than Norwell's.

The second flight was much more unlucky. Firstly the Sunderland which was supposed to escort them in had failed to take off from Gibraltar. Then they missed, their landfall at Galite Island, missed the bomber sent out to meet them, and became hopelessly lost. The Skua navigator radioed for help, but his receiver was faulty and he could not pick up the replies. As the crew searched desperately for somewhere to put down, one Hurricane after another fell from the formation until none were left. Finally, just before the Skua itself ran out of fuel, land was seen through a curtain of mist – it was south-western Sicily. Before the pilot could go down to land however, the aircraft was fired on by Italian anti-aircraft (known as Dicat – Difesa Contraerea Territoriale), and crash-landed in a damaged condition on the beach at Punta Palo on the Isola delle Correnti, near Syracuse. A Maryland was sent out from Malta with Sqn.Ldr. Whiteley at the controls, and he searched for five hours but found no sign of any survivors; it seems that all the Hurricane pilots perished in the sea.

Hopelessly lost and out of fuel, Skua L2987 was brought down on the coast of Sicily by Petty Officer W.E.J. Stockwell on 17 November 1940. It was the sole survivor of the flight it was leading; all the six Hurricanes had gone down in the sea. The engine has become completely detached, and lies alongside the aircraft. (*N. Malizia*)

Operation 'White', as the reinforcement mission had been codenamed, had been an unmitigated disaster. An official inquiry was held in great secrecy, the blame being put mainly on the missing aircrew. It was subsequently tacitly agreed that inadequate weather forecasting, lack of liaison between Navy and Air Force as to the Hurricane's true range, and over-cautious handling of the fleet had in fact played a much greater in the tragedy than had aircrew error. The loss of so many pilots was particularly damaging, since all had enjoyed the benefit of some operational experience with fighter squadrons in England during the Battle of Britain. Several already had some victories to their credit, including Horton with three and one shared, and Walker with two. Fortunately the most successful, Norwell, who had three individual and four shared victories listed in his logbook, had survived, as had Hugh 'Chubby' Eliot, who had three and two shared with 73 Squadron during the Battle of France. Bamberger, who arrived by sea, also had two victories, flying Spitfires with 41 Squadron, in which unit Norwell had also served. Much was learned from this experience which was put to good use in ensuring that future ferry flights of this nature were never again planned and executed in such a haphazard manner.

One of the survivors of the Operation 'White' delivery flight was Sgt. J.K. 'Jock' Norwell. He is seen here (centre) with earlier arrivals, Eric Kelsey (l) and Harry Ayre (r). (*J.K. Norwell*)

20/11/40

The four surviving Hurricanes and the five pilots – later increased to six when Bamberger arrived – went to 261 Squadron, while the Skua went to join the Marylands in 431 Flight for the time being. Three days later a Wellington carrying Air Marshal O.T. Boyd, C.B., O.B.E., M.C., A.F.C., to the Middle East to become Deputy Air Officer Commanding-in-Chief, was obliged to force-land in Sicily, the crew and their important passenger being taken prisoner. That night Wellingtons from Malta attacked Bari again – and again one was lost.

23/11/40

The new Hurricanes did allow a stronger reception to be offered to the next raid on the island, which came in during the morning of 23 November. Ten 34° Stormo S.79s escorted by 18 CR 42s of 23° Gruppo raided Takali, eight Hurricanes scrambling to intercept the raid as it came over Filfla at 16,000 feet. George Burges in Hurricane V7548 attacked five of the bombers in company with a couple of the fighters. He thought he hit one "pretty hard", and saw it going down, although he did not see it crash. He then shot pieces off another. Sgt. Robertson in V7474, which MacLachlan had flown to the island on 17th., also tried to attack the bombers, but was attacked himself by six CR 42s. He took evasive action, and fired at four, reporting that his fire tore the fabric from the top wing of one, which went into cloud. He claimed a 'probable', but was credited with a 'damaged'. Meanwhile the Italian pilots were after the Hurricanes, Cap. Guido Bobba, Ten. Claudio Solaro and Serg. Pardini each claiming one shot down, while all the pilots of the 75ᵃ Squadriglia claimed a fourth between them. Flt.Lt. H.F.R. Bradbury's aircraft was hit badly and he force-landed at Luqa; all the Italian fighters returned safely to their base.

Hurricanes of 261 Squadron lined up in unaccustomed numbers. The nearest is V7474, flown to the island from H.M.S. 'Argus' on 17 November 1940 by Flt.Lt. J.A.F. MacLachlan. (*R.H. Barber*)

Ten.Col. Galeazzo Ciano (centre), commander of the 105° Gruppo Autonomo B.T., confers with his pilots before a raid on Malta. (*N. Malizia*)

During the Autumn of 1940 the 105° Gruppo Autonomo B.T. operated over Malta without loss. Here S.79s of the 255ª Squadriglia, from this unit head out past Mount Etna for a raid.

S.79s of 254ª Squadriglia, 105º Gruppo, Autonomo B.T., escorted by 23º Gruppo Aut. C.T. CR 42s, approach Malta. Note the very different camouflage pattern applied to this stormo's aircraft. (*N. Malizia*)

With bomb aimer's periscope extended beneath the ventral 'bathtub', a 255ª Squadriglia, 105º Gruppo Autonomo B.T. S.79 makes its bombing run over Grand Harbour. (*A.M.I. via N. Malizia*)

On this same day an MC200 was scrambled from Pantelleria, where it was on detachment, Mar. Leonida Carrozzo reporting intercepting a Blenheim at around 0700 which he claimed shot down in flames; this was in all probability an aircraft on a delivery flight. The Macchi was now short of fuel and Carrozzo was unable to get back to Pantelleria; he force-landed near Agrigento in Sicily, suffering slight injuries, and his aircraft a small amount of damage.

24/11/40

Next day two CR 42 pilots from the 23° Gruppo's 75ª Squadriglia, Ten. Monti and Serg. Gasperoni, claimed a lone Wellington shot down into the sea some 40–50 kilometres from Malta. At sunset six more of the unit's fighters led by Magg. Falconi carried out a strafe of Luqa airfield, claiming three aircraft destroyed on the ground. One of 148 Squadron's Wellingtons was reported destroyed in this attack. As they headed home again, one of the CR 42s ran out of fuel and Ten. Ezio Monti was obliged to bale out into the sea just off the Sicilian coast near Marsala.

Serg. William Dusi of the 70ª Squadriglia, 23° Gruppo Aut. C.T. with his CR 42. (*W. Dusi via N. Malizia*)

26/11/40

This same unit was again engaged in combat on 26th. when three CR 42s appeared over Malta on a reconnaissance. They were intercepted by two Hurricanes and Sgt. Dennis Ashton, who had been informed on the previous day that he had just become a father, shot down the CR 42 flown by Ten. Giuseppe Beccaria in flames. At once his own aircraft, N2701, was attacked by Cap. Bobba, and fell into the sea to the south of the island; Ashton did not survive. Beccaria's body was recovered from the sea and buried in St. Andrew's Cemetery.

27/11/40

Following the recently highly successful attack on the Taranto fleet base, a further convoy into the Mediterranean had been swiftly organised by the British, codenamed Operation 'Collar'. By late November three cargo vessels carrying armoured vehicles and other munitions urgently required by Wavell's forces in Egypt, gathered at Gibraltar; 'Ark Royal', 'Renown', 'Sheffield', 'Despatch', 'Manchester' and 'Southampton', with ten destroyers were to provide the initial escort, to be joined south of Sardinia by 'Ramillies', 'Newcastle', 'Berwick', 'Coventry' and four more destroyers from Alexandria. Force 'H' sailed on 25th., while the vessels from the east (Force 'D') had already left a day earlier. However on 26th. the Italian Fleet sortied to attempt an interception. From Naples came the battleships 'Vittorio Veneto' and 'Giulio Cesare', together with three cruisers and 11 destroyers under the command of Admiral Inigo Campioni. They were joined by a second squadron comprising three more cruisers and three destroyers. At 0630 next morning a force of one battleship, one cruiser and one destroyer was sighted off Cape Spartivento, Southern Sardinia, by Malta-based reconnaissance aircraft, and then a little later by 'Ark's' Swordfish, the first report being received by the Fleet at 0920. Italian reconnaissance aircraft were also searching for the British ships, and at 0755 a Fulmar patrol from 808 Squadron, Blue Section led by Lt. E.W.T. Taylour, spotted a Z.506B approaching from Sardinia; after a long chase it was shot down in flames and blew up on hitting the sea about ten miles north of Bone (Algeria). The first Italian sighting was made at 0945 by the crew of a Meridionali Ro 43 floatplane, catapulted from the cruiser 'Bolzano'. Continued 'shadowing' by Swordfish and Malta Sunderlands of the Italian vessels caused air cover from Sardinia to be requested and three CR 42s from the 3° Gruppo C.T. were sent off, but failed to intercept eleven Swordfish from 810 Squadron which took off from 'Ark Royal' at 1125 led by Lt.Cdr. M. Johnstone to attack. An hour later these aircraft launched a torpedo strike against the two battleships, claiming a hit on 'Vittorio Veneto', although in fact all torpedoes missed.

At 1220 meanwhile, the leading British vessels opened fire at long range on a vessel believed to be a cruiser, which was thought to have been damaged as the Italians headed away from the vastly-superior strength of Somerville's squadron. In fact it was the destroyer 'Lanciere' which had been hit, return fire damaging the British cruiser 'Berwick'.

At 1407, just as nine more Swordfish from 820 Squadron were preparing to take off, an incoming raid was detected, seven Fulmars of 808 Squadron which were on patrol being diverted to intercept. In the meantime the Swordfish got off, led by Lt.Cdr. J.A. Stewart-Moore, to search for the cruiser believed damaged. They did not find it, but located the main force and attacked a cruiser here, two hits being claimed; none were actually achieved. Over Force 'H' ten S.79s of 32° Stormo B.T. and five escorting 3° Gruppo CR 42s approached. At 1430 the Fulmar pilots attacked, two or three of the bombers being claimed shot down, but they held their formation and bombed – missing. Lt. Tillard led his Green Section after a sub-flight of three S.79s and claimed one shot into the sea. As they went into the attack they caught sight of a number of biplane fighters but thought they were Sea Gladiators, consequently when the CR 42s bounced the Fulmars Sub Lt. R.M.S. Martin's aircraft (N1941) was shot down into the sea, he and his TAG, L/A A.L.M. Noble, losing their lives. By now Lt. Tillard and the other Fulmar pilot of his section had exhausted their ammunition and were unable to fight back. Eight of the S.79s were hit by the Fulmars and anti-aircraft fire, two being badly shot up, but all returned to their bases. However during the course of the air battle a Vichy French four-engined civil Farman 223.4 transport aircraft (F-AROA 'Le Verrier') carrying the newly-appointed Vichy High Commissioner to Lebanon and Syria, M. Jean Chiappe, strayed into the battle zone. The radio operator just had time to send out an SOS, stating that the aircraft was being machine-gunned, before it was shot down off Cape Spartivento. All on board – five crew and two passengers – were lost. It would appear that it had been hit by one or more of the Fulmars.

Within the hour seven 800 Squadron Skuas were led off by Lt. Smeeton to locate and dive-bomb the damaged Italian warship. Again 'Lanciere' was not found but three ships identified as cruisers were spotted off the south-west tip of Sardinia, and these were attacked, two near-misses being claimed. While returning to the carrier, the Skua crews sighted a lone Ro 43 – 'Vittorio Veneto's' spotter aircraft, short of fuel and trying to reach Sardinia. Lt. J.A. Rooper's sub flight was ordered to attack and the four Skuas – Lt. Rooper/Sub Lt. Woolston in L3015 '6F', P.O.(A) Sabey/L/A Coles (L2900 '6C'), P.O.(A) Burston/N/A Holmes (L3007 '6M') and P.O.(A) Jopling/N/A Glen (L3017 '6H') – promptly shot it down into the sea in flames.

At 1645 a final raid was made by ten more S.79s, this time unescorted; 'Ark Royal' was their target, and some very near misses were achieved, although no hits were made. A number of Fulmars and Skuas intercepted, fire from these and the ships hitting nine of the bombers and again two were badly damaged. Lt. Callingham in L3008 '6P' led the Skuas of Blue Section against three sections of five S.79s but was unable to catch the first section; attacked the next section but was unable to close to less than 400 yards although appeared to be hit in the starboard wing tank, then jettisoned its bombs. Sub Lt. A.M. Tritton in L3024 '6Q' was also unable to close the range but observed his target also jettison its bombs as he fired.

26–28/11/40

'Illustrious' meanwhile was making a diversionary attack on the Italian-occupied island bases in the Aegean, having taken aboard an extra six Fulmars of the newly-formed 805 Squadron, under Lt.Cdr. A.F. Black. On 26th. a Swordfish of 819 Squadron was lost during a strike on the island of Leros, the crew of Lt. R.W.V. Hamilton – who had taken part in the Taranto raid – being buried on the island. Two days later, with the carrier now off Malta, came warning of approaching hostile aircraft and six patrolling Fulmars, three each from 805 and 806 Squadrons, were directed to intercept, meeting six CR 42s, aircraft of 23° Gruppo, on a reconnaissance mission to Malta. The two Fulmar sections attacked but the operationally inexperienced 805 Squadron trio – Lt.Cdr. Black, Lt. R.A. Brabner and Sub Lt. R.F. Bryant – were unable to make contact. Even though the leader expended some 3200 rounds in four bursts, he found the Fiats far too manoeuvrable to gain any hits. His observer, Lt. John Shuttleworth, recalls: "During the engagement I fired 'smoke puffs' from the rear cockpit whenever CR 42s got on our tail! ... I certainly saw one if not two parachutes floating down." In fact the 806 Squadron section was achieving good results, the experienced Sub Lt. Orr shooting down Serg.Magg. Arnaldo Sala's aircraft into the sea 30 miles off the Sicilian coast, the pilot being killed, while Sub Lts. Golden and Clisby claimed damage to two more; the latter's Fulmar (N1935) was also hit in the fight, his TAG, L/A Phillips being wounded in the leg, hand and face by an explosive bullet, although not seriously hurt.

With the arrival of the further convoy, and with the ships of Force 'H' at sea, 2ª Squadra Aerea was not surprisingly very active over Malta on 28th., following a day of readiness, but no action, on 27th. Two S.79s of 34° Stormo made a long reconnaissance over the Sicilian Channel during the early morning, sighting the British ships after two hours. Following this sighting, six Ju87s of the 97° Gruppo B.a'T. (a unit which had recently replaced the 96° Gruppo in Sicily) headed out towards Malta and the ships, covered by sixteen CR 42s of the 23°. Over the target the pilots of these fighters claimed four Hurricanes shot down, two confirmed and two probables; six pilots of the 70ª Squadriglia claimed one of the former jointly, while the other was claimed by Serg.Magg. Raffaele Marzocca of the 74ª, the two probables being credited to Cap. Bobba and Ten. Lorenzoni of this unit. No British account of such an engagement has been found recorded although it is feasible there is some confusion between this action and that of 'Illustrious's' Fulmars already recorded, or the following engagement, for early in the afternoon two squadriglie of the 30° Stormo B.T. despatched ten S.79s over the ships near the harbours, an escort of twelve CR 42s from the 23° and ten MC200s of the 6° Gruppo being provided. The Macchis flew ahead of the main formation to 'lure and distract' the Malta Hurricanes – a ruse which did not come off, for after a brief skirmish, the British fighters made straight for the bombers. For once the Hurricanes were up in time and were able to dive from 5,000 feet above. Sgt. Robertson sprayed the CR 42s on his way through their formation, then made an attack on the bombers, firing at the whole formation before concentrating on the left rear aircraft into which he exhausted the rest of his ammunition. He broke away from the bomber when within 25 yards of it, climbing upwards with CR 42s on his tail. He claimed a probable, but this was upgraded to a confirmed success when two crewmembers were picked up from the sea. His victim had been flown by Sottoten. Gaio Del Cerro. Apart from this loss, 30° Stormo had a second bomber damaged, this landing on Linosa Island with a dead photographer on board. It is believed that Flt.Lt. Greenhalgh claimed a CR 42 shot down during this combat, while two more were claimed damaged by other 261 Squadron pilots, though possibly the first claim related to Serg.Magg. Sala's aircraft on the earlier sortie. On this occasion only one Hurricane was claimed shot down by the 23° Gruppo, Serg.Magg. Marzocca of the 74ª Squadriglia making the claim, while a second was claimed by the gunners of the 30° Stormo's bombers. Two more Hurricanes were claimed as 'probables' by the pilots of 23° Gruppo jointly. It seems that no British fighters were actually lost or damaged on this occasion. Later the body of an Italian airman, unit unknown, but identified as Ovidio Venanza, was picked up and brought ashore. He was duly laid to rest in St. Andrew's Cemetery.

During the day a Blenheim landed at Hal Far having been damaged by fighter attack. This aircraft, en route from Gibraltar, had been intercepted by three Vichy French Dewoitine 520s of GCII/7 from Sidi Ahmed as it passed the North African coast, being claimed shot down by Lt. Merle, Sgt. Hagi and Sgt. Carrere to the south-east of Porto Farina; no member of the crew was wounded.

29/11–10/12/40

Next day another delivery Blenheim was caught by Vichy fighters when Sous Lt. Georges Valentin, also of GCII/7, shot down the aircraft into the sea west of Sidi Ahmed, the pilot being killed while the other two members of the crew were picked up and interned by the French, one of them having been wounded. On this same date Sqn.Ldr. Whiteley in Maryland AR707 recorded a "particularly sticky trip" when he ran into fighters over Sardinia early in the sortie, and was then chased all the way back from Sicily by others on the later leg of his flight. Yet again a further Blenheim was claimed shot down off Pantelleria on December 2nd. by Sottoten. Sergio Morandi of the 17° Gruppo in an MC200. Morandi was part of a small detachment which had recorded the earlier interception. Again this morning engagement was probably with a delivery aircraft. Generally however December was to prove a much quieter month. On 7th. three Wellingtons of 148 Squadron were led by Sqn.Ldr. A. Golding to attack coastal areas near Tripoli, while three more led by Sqn.Ldr. Foss attacked Mellaha airfield, to the east of the city. A further five Wellingtons followed at 15 minute intervals to bomb Castel Benito airfield in an attempt to prevent interceptors taking off. However at least one CR42 got into the air, attacking and damaging Foss's aircraft, and wounding the rear gunner, Sgt. A. Hollingsworth; on return to Luqa with starboard wing and tailplane damaged, the aircraft suffered a burst tyre and swung off the runway. Flg.Off. P.W. de B. Forsyth's T2838 was also badly hit by the fighter and force-landed on return.

There were now some changes in command – Flt.Lt. Trumble was promoted to command 261 Squadron viz Sqn.Ldr. Balden, who was now posted to H.Q. Luqa as Sqn.Ldr. (Admin.) Flt. Lt. Greenhalgh also left 261 for duties at A.H.Q., while John Waters became flight commander, 'B' Flight; 'A' Flight was now led by Flt.Lt. Lambert. John Greenhalgh recorded a memory of his time with the

Pilots of 261 Squadron relax at dispersal while awaiting the call to action.

261 Squadron pilots fool around at dispersal, using a trolley starter as an impromptu conveyance (one man-power!). Sgt. 'Jock' Norwell lends encouragement as Sgt. Jim Pickering 'drives' an unidentified colleague. (*J.K. Norwell*)

squadron: "During the summer of 1940 there was an evening telephone call between our Intelligence staff and the Italians in Sicily to enquire about casualties and survivors. This would cease with the arrival of the Germans – the whole tempo then changed."

18/12/40

Night raids continued – mainly by single aircraft. Late on 18 December Sgt.Fred Robertson took off in P3731 for a defensive patrol. At 2350 while at 15,000 feet he saw below the searchlights concentrating on an aircraft between Grand Harbour and Kalafrana – it was an S.79 of 193^a Squadriglia, 87° Gruppo, 30° Stormo, with Ten. Giulio Molteni at the controls. Diving to 10,000 feet, Robertson approached the bomber, opened fire from dead astern at 200 yards range, and fired three bursts. Flames poured from the fuselage and then the wing roots, and the bomber dived straight into the sea two miles east of Kalafrana Bay. Robertson landed at Luqa immediately after the combat as his oil temperature was rising; here he received a message of congratulation from the A.O.C.

Already making a name for himself during the latter months of 1940, Sgt. Fred Robertson was well on his way towards his position as Malta's top scorer for the first year of the war. (*J.K. Norwell*)

12–21/12/40

Two days later on 20 December the command structure of 2^a Squadra Aerea was ordered to Padua, all operational units in Sicily coming under a new

Aeronautica della Sicilia. Next day the new command recorded its first combat – an S.79 of 30° Stormo damaged over the sea by an unidentified Hurricane. At this time however the 23° Gruppo Autonomo C.T. left Sicily, ordered to Libya where Wavell's First Libyan Offensive had the Italians – Regia Aeronautica included – in grave trouble. Elsewhere in the Mediterranean the carriers 'Illustrious' and 'Eagle' were on the rampage throughout December. On 12th. targets at Bardia were bombed, then on 16th raids were launched against the islands of Rhodes and Stampalia in the Aegean. On 21st. 'Illustrious's' Swordfish sank two cargo vessels off the eastern Tunisian coast near Sfax, while early next morning fifteen of these aircraft attacked Tripoli, in Western Libya. During the first of these attacks Lt. D.C. Garton-Stones' aircraft was reported missing – the only loss. The carriers finally returned to their base on Christmas Day.

29/12/40

The final engagements of the month for Malta-based aircraft both involved the Marylands of 431 Flight – now up to five in number following reinforcements from Egypt. On Christmas Eve Flg.Off. Warburton made a reconnaissance over Naples. He reported: "I was entering the Bay of Naples from the south-west at 1,500 feet when I saw an S.79 with brown mottled camouflage heading across my track. The clouds were at 2,000 feet in a solid bank so if fighters appeared I could retire. I therefore made a stern attack; some pieces of the tail flew off and my rounds started going into the fuselage. I closed the range and concentrated on the starboard engine which started to smoke and eventually stopped. My rear gunner wanted to try the new turret so I broke away and drew parallel to the S.79, slightly above and about 100 yards to his starboard. My rear gunner put in a burst of about 20 rounds which ignited the petrol and the S.79 burst into a mass of flames and dived into the sea from 1,000 feet, disappearing immediately. I then carried on with my recco of Naples and then returned to Luqa."

31/12/40

Taranto and Brindisi were again the targets for reconnaissance on the last day of the year. A Maryland flown by Flg.Off. John Boys-Stone, a newly-arrived member of 431 Flight, was chased by two CR 42s and an MC200, but escaped. An S.75 transport aircraft was then encountered, and damage to the port engine was claimed.

On a lighter note, a lone CR 42 appeared over Malta on Christmas Day, dropping a small metal cylinder. When retrieved and opened this proved to be a Christmas 'Greeting' to " ... the boys of Hal Far and Kalafrana". It showed a brawny pilot in a CR 42 reaching out from his cockpit to knock down several Hurricanes with his fists, one giant hand clutching the throat of the pilot of one of these. In the background a crowd of sad-looking R.A.F. pilots queued at the 'Pearly Gates' waiting for St. Peter to let them in! Copies of this became something of a collectors' item. It is believed that it was dropped by a pilot of the 72ª Squadriglia, 17° Gruppo, since this was the squadriglia number carried on the fuselage of the Fiat in the cartoon.

Christmas greetings from the Regia Aeronautica fighter 'boys'! The cartoon dropped from a CR 42 over the island on Christmas Day by the 72ª Squadriglia, 17º Gruppo, 1º Stormo C.T. (*J. Pickering*)

Active over Malta during December 1940 were the CR 42s of the 1º Stormo C.T.'s 17º Gruppo. An aircraft of this Gruppo's 80ª Squadriglia is seen here at that time on Trapani/Milo airfield. (*G. Di Giorgio via N. Malizia*)

At the end of 1940 the defenders could look back with some satisfaction on the previous six months. Malta remained a striking base, giving home to destroyers, submarines, flyingboats and Swordfish, as well as the still-few Wellington bombers. There had been 211 alerts, and 85 civilians had been killed by air attack – 66 of them during the first month; many more had been injured and damage to private property had been considerable. However, despite many attacks the Naval Dockyard remained fully operational, although steps had been taken to remove most machinery into tunnels beneath the rock. The floating dock, a 40,000 ton structure, had been sunk on 20 June, while the Admiralty tug 'Hellespont' had suffered a similar fate on 7 September. Notwithstanding these setbacks, the recent convoys had built up supplies, and a respectable number of Hurricanes remained available for continued defence.

At the end of the year the R.A.F. fighters had claimed thirteen S.79s, ten CR 42s, six MC200s and two Ju87s shot down, plus 11 probables and 20 damaged. Flg.Off. 'Timber' Woods received the award of the D.F.C. during December, the citation stating that he had been credited with five aircraft confirmed destroyed plus one probable. Flg.Off. 'Eric' Taylor of 261 Squadron and Flg.Off. Foxton of 431 Flight had both been Mentioned in Despatches. Admitted losses to the defenders by the Regia Aeronautica at this time amounted to 35 aircraft, as follows:

To British fighters	18 bombers	9 fighters
To anti-aircraft fire	5 bombers	3 fighters
Total	23 bombers	12 fighters

It will have been noted in the text that several of the aircraft believed by the Italian authorities to have been lost to anti-aircraft fire had in fact fallen to fighters, including at least one bomber and two fighters.

Already a veteran of the defences by the end of 1940, 261 Squadron's newly-decorated Flt.Lt. George Burges relaxes here in 'civvies'. (*G. Burges*)

101

Throughout this period, and thereafter, the fighters were involved in many more scrambles which have not been listed here because nothing came of them. Positioned as it was astride the main Axis reinforcement route to Africa, and close to Sicily, many plots appeared on the island's radar which did not develop either into raids, or into flights passing near enough to be intercepted. In each case however it was necessary to alert the defences and get fighters off in time, in case an attack was to develop. The constant wear and tear on aircraft which this caused remained one of the major factors in limiting the number of fighters that could be got into the air to meet any particular intrusion.

At 31 December 1940 strength available on the island was as follows:

261 Squadron	16 Hurricanes	(+four in reserve)
	4 Gladiators	(+some still in crates as spares)
148 Squadron	16 Wellingtons	(+four in reserve)
228 Squadron	4 Sunderlands	(+two in reserve)
830 Squadron	12 Swordfish	
431 Flight	4 Marylands	(+one in reserve)

Chapter 3

A NEW YEAR DAWNS

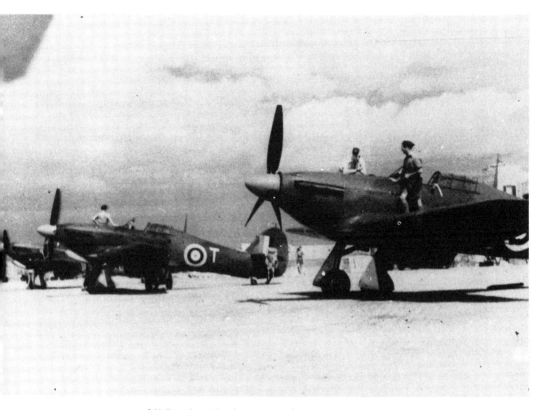

261 Squadron Hurricanes ready for action at Takali.

1941 began on quite a cheerful note for the British. The Battle of Britain seemed to have been won, and no German invasion of England had been forthcoming. The Blitz was underway by night it was true, but by day the news from North Africa was most heartening as Wavell's forces rolled across Libya. Here tens of thousands of demoralized prisoners and much equipment were taken as the small but efficient British force inflicted defeat after defeat on their numerically far larger opponent.

On Malta all seemed quiet, and for the first week of the new year nothing was to be seen. Rumour was rife however, and a disconcerting story was going the rounds that a German air fleet was on its way to the area from Northern Europe prior to a new invasion of Greece. Malta's main preoccupation now was reinforcement and supply. For this very reason a new convoy was due, the operation in which it was to play a part being codenamed 'Excess'.

'Excess' had begun badly. The vessels destined for the Mediterranean sailed with a major Atlantic convoy, but this suffered an attack by the German cruiser 'Hipper'. Elements of Force 'H' were despatched from Gibraltar to hunt the raider, and as a result, although the five ships due for the area reached Gibraltar, they were held there until the escort could be assembled once more. Four of the vessels were due to go direct to Piraeus with supplies for the Greek front, while the fifth, 'Essex', was to make for Malta. Included amongst the supplies aboard this ship were 4,000 tons of ammunition and a deck cargo of twelve crated Hurricanes, which would go far to making good the failure of the November reinforcement flight.

6/1/41

At Gibraltar one of the Greece-bound ships was forced ashore by bad weather, and was too badly damaged to continue, but early on 6 January 1941 the remaining four set sail with a small escort, the main body of Force 'H' following next morning. Included were the battleships 'Renown' and 'Malaya', the carrier 'Ark Royal', the cruiser 'Sheffield', and six destroyers. Because Admiral Somerville was short of smaller warships for this operation, Admiral Cunningham despatched the cruisers 'Gloucester' and 'Southampton' from Alexandria on 6th. to join Force 'H', together with two supporting destroyers, while three submarines were ordered to take up patrol station off the south of Sardinia in case of another sortie by the Italian fleet. The cruisers between them carried 500 more soldiers and airmen for Malta, who they landed early on 8th., sailing again a few hours later. They joined forces with Force 'H' at 0930 the next morning.

7–8/1/41

While this was going on, a major portion of the Mediterranean Fleet had put out from Alexandria on 7th., led by Cunningham in 'Warspite', joined by a second battleship, 'Valiant', and by 'Illustrious', together with a covering screen of seven destroyers. A force of cruisers provided distant cover against any Italian reaction from the Aegean, also providing escort for the auxilliary 'Breconshire' and the merchant vessel which were making the run from the east to Malta. Next day, as the vessels headed steadily westwards, 'Illustrious' landed-on its air group, including 806 Squadron at its strongest yet, and once again reinforced (for the fourth time) by Fulmars of 805 Squadron, three aircraft. With the rumour of imminent German intervention, every possible fighter aircraft had been gathered together. On this occasion however, the commanding officer, Charles Evans, was not present, as he had unfortunately been taken ill, and was in hospital.

Command of the squadron passed temporarily and slightly awkwardly into the hands of Lt. Vincent-Jones, the senior observer. "Being next in seniority the command of the squadron devolved on me; it is a somewhat invidious position to lead a squadron from an unarmed back seat. Shades of the 'Duke of Plaza Toro'. However in a team like ours it didn't seem to matter and I had wonderful support from Roger Nicolls, the Senior Pilot. To cause minimum disturbance and at the C.O.'s suggestion, I flew as Bill Barnes's observer."

As this conglomeration of warships and merchant vessels all headed for the centre of the Mediterranean, much was afoot in the Axis camp which had still not been observed by British reconnaissance or intelligence. Ready for the approaching Allied shipping, the 96° Gruppo B.a'T. despatched some of its Ju87Rs to Sicily again on 8th., these flying from Lecce to Comiso. Of more ominous portent however was the arrival at the same time of the first wave of a powerful German bomber contingent on the island.

Adolf Hitler had indeed proposed aid to Benito Mussolini as early as 20 November 1940, before things had started to go seriously wrong for the Italians either in Greece or North Africa. By early December the German offer was looking very attractive, and on 10th. of that month airfields were allocated to the Luftwaffe. The first priority to the Germans was to neutralize Malta and the British Fleet, thereby safeguarding the sea lanes to Libya. Consequently elements

The new enemy. A Junkers Ju87R of I/Stukageschwader 1, flying over Sicily shortly after arrival. This was one of the units involved in the attack on 'Illustrious'. (*Bundesarchiv*)

with anti-shipping experience were chosen for service in the new theatre, and the staff of Fliegerkorps X from Norway under Gen. Hans Ferdinand Giesler were ordered to Sicily, where they set up headquarters in the Hotel Domenico at Taormina. By 8 January 1941 ninety-six bombers – He111s, Ju88A–4s, and Ju87Bs and Rs – had reached the island; more followed over the next few days, including twenty-four Bf110 Zerstörer of III/ZG 26 and a force of Ju52/3ms for air transport support. Initial elements included I/Stukageschwader 1 and II/Stukageschwader 2 with fifty-four Ju87s, II/Kampfgeschwader 26 with thirty-two He111s, and Kampfgruppe z.b.V 9 with Ju52/3ms. They were followed later by II and III/Lehrgeschwader 1 with Ju88s and reconnaissance Staffel 1(F)/121 with ten Ju88Ds. Still later would come another similarly-equipped reconnaissance unit, 2(F)/123, a Staffel of He111s modified for torpedo-dropping, a Staffel of Bf110 night fighters, Seenotberichskommando X with He59 and Do24 waterborne aircraft for air/sea rescue duties, and ultimately a Staffel of single-engined fighters. By the end of January the number of Luftwaffe aircraft available in Sicily had risen to 141, and by May it would reach a peak of 243.

First of the German fighters in Sicily, this Messerschmitt Bf110C bears the unit markers and insignia of III/Zerstörerges Chwader 26 (*N. Malizia*)

9/1/41

As this dangerous new threat continued, early on 9 January 'Ark Royal' flew off a reinforcement of six Swordfish (821X Squadron) to Malta, where they were incorporated into 830 Squadron. At 1320 on that same date the first opposition

Hurricane Is with long range tanks on the deck of H.M.S. 'Furious', about to be flown off to Takoradi, West Africa, on 9 January 1941. A number of these aircraft were despatched to reinforce Malta after their arrival in Egypt. (*D. Whitney*)

Hurricane lifts off 'Furious' for Takoradi, 9 January 1941. (*D. Whitney*)

from Sardinian-based aircraft was encountered, when an incoming raid was plotted on the radar. Half an hour later ten S.79s of 32° Stormo B.T. swept in out of the sun, bombs falling close to 'Malaya' and 'Gloucester', but 808 Squadron's patrolling Fulmars were quickly amongst them. The C.O., Lt. Tillard, with Lt. Somerville as his observer, promptly shot down two of the bombers; the first caught fire and exploded, one member of the crew being picked up by H.M.S. 'Foxhound' after he had baled out, while the second crashed into the sea on fire, two of the crew being rescued by H.M.S. 'Forester'. Both Tillard and Somerville were subsequently awarded the D.S.C. for this action. During the day a trio of Skuas from the carrier's other fighter unit, 800 Squadron, became engaged with three CR 42s, managing to escape from these nimble fighters without damage – indeed Lt. Rooper was even able to claim hits on one of the biplanes.

Malta too saw its first action of the year on 9th. when during the morning sixteen MC200s from the 6° Gruppo (seven of 79ª, seven of 81ª and two of 88ª Squadriglia) were led to the island by Magg. Mezzetti to attack Luqa airfield, from where the Wellingtons of 148 Squadron had undertaken four raids on harbours at Tripoli, Naples and Palermo since the start of the year. Kalafrana meanwhile received a raid by nine of the 96° Gruppo's Ju87s, escorted by ten CR 42s of the 'Nucleo' 23° Gruppo (the residue of the unit still in Sicily). Six of the Macchis swooped on Luqa airfield at 1100, claiming damage to five aircraft on the ground – in fact three of 148 Squadron's Wellingtons were damaged – but were attacked by five 261 Squadron Hurricanes and came off worst. Two were claimed shot down by Flt.Lt. MacLachlan, one of which he pursued many miles out to sea, and one by Flg.Off. Taylor, while Flt.Lt. Waters in V7474 engaged in a "good fight" with one and claimed it badly damaged. Two Macchis were in fact lost, the pilots being Mar. Ettori Zanandrea in MM5787, who was killed, and Cap. Luigi Armanino, who baled out of MM4586 into the sea, wounded in the arm and thigh. The other fourteen Macchis returned to Sicily claiming a single Hurricane probably shot down. Armanino was clearly MacLachlan's second victim, and the latter was to get to know the Italian quite well, for when he himself was wounded the following month, he was to find himself in the next bed to his victim, who had previously flown CR 32 fighters in Spain during the Civil War.

10/1/41

By that evening Force 'H' had reached a point 25 miles north of Bizerta, and here Somerville's ships turned back for Gibraltar. The 'Excess' convoy headed on eastwards, led by 'Gloucester' and still with 'Southampton' in attendance. During the night the Mediterranean Fleet units made contact with the convoy and swung eastwards with it to pass south of Malta. Dawn on 10th. found the ships some 100 miles to the west of the island, having skirted Pantelleria. Here however the destroyer 'Gallant' struck a mine and had to be taken in tow. Two Italian torpedo boats appeared and attempted to attack but one – 'Verga' – was sunk by gunfire. As the vessels neared Malta, two separate groups of ships already at the island, left port to join the convoys and obtain protection from the Fleet units.

Two fast merchant ships, operating under the codename ME5$\frac{1}{2}$ were to sail with the three remaining 'Excess' vessels for Piraeus, while six slower ships, forming a separate convoy, MS.6, were to take a more southerly course, making for Alexandria. The Malta ships came out with an escort from the Light Force of four cruisers, an anti-aircraft cruiser, two destroyers and four corvettes. Before the day was out 'Essex' had slipped safely into Valetta, while ME.5$\frac{1}{2}$ had made contact with 'Excess', and both were safely on their way towards Greece.

All had not gone so well with the rest of the ships however. On Sicily reports of the British naval activity caused a major effort to be put in hand at once. Shortly after midday all available Luftwaffe dive-bombers, which had that very morning arrived at Trapani, were ordered to take part. I/St.G 1 under Hauptmann Werner Hozzel and II/St.G 2 led by Major Walter Enneccerus took off, accompanied according to some sources by a number of Ju88s. Torpedo-carrying S.79s of the 279^a Squadriglia Sil. also set out from the same base.

During the morning Swordfish from 'Illustrious' had carried out a bombing attack on an Italian convoy, but were now back aboard, while others were undertaking anti-submarine patrols in pairs. Two sections of Fulmars totalling five aircraft were on patrol, but the aircrew aboard ship were not entirely happy. Desmond Vincent-Jones explains: "'Illustrious' was stationed between the two battleships 'Warspite' and 'Valiant'. The Admiral may have had his reasons but we in 'Illustrious' felt it would have been tactically sounder if the carrier had been detached to act independently and at speed some 20 to 30 miles to the southward of the main fleet, thus keeping us further from the air threat in Sicily. The fighter C.A.P. (Combat Air Patrol) could be maintained over the fleet from a range of 20 miles with little greater difficulty than if the carrier were in company with the rest of the fleet."

One section of three Fulmars, led by Lt. R.S. Henley, reported that an aircraft which they identified as a Messerschmitt 109 attempted to join their formation, but did not attack. When it broke away the Fulmars proved too slow to pursue it. At 1030 a single S.79 was encountered, and this was claimed shot down by Henley and Sub Lt. Sewell jointly, but the latter's aircraft suffered slight damage from return fire and he was obliged to depart for the carrier. The remaining pair continued their patrol, engaging two more S.79s, both of which were claimed damaged by Henley. He recalled: "They made a low pass at the Fleet which drew us off at low altitude and high speed to the southeast, which allowed the Germans to come in on their attack. By the time I got back, without ammo, all I could do was to make dummy passes at them as they started their dive. We landed at Hal Far with virtually no gas after 3 hours 40 minutes, which speaks well for the endurance of the Fulmar." It was at this point that a pair of 279^a Squadriglia S.79s – possibly those attacked by Henley and his wingman – came in very low, beneath the radar, and made an extemely courageous attack with their torpedoes against 'Illustrious'. The torpedoes missed, and the other Fulmar section on patrol – Sub Lts. Orr and Hogg – were called down to give chase. A long stern chase followed during which Orr and Hogg fired off all their ammunition and claimed one of the S.79s shot down, but by this time were more than 50 miles from the carrier and getting low on fuel. It seems that only one of the two S.79s claimed was hard hit, and this managed to struggle back to Trapani where Ten. Angelo Caponetti crashed whilst attempting to land.

At 1235 four more Fulmars were scrambled just as an estimated twenty-four to thirty-six Ju87s commenced their attack; the fighters were unable to prevent the onslaught on the carrier. Denis Tribe, Sub Lt. Sewell's TAG in Fulmar 'Q' recalled: "We were at readiness on the flight deck and took off before 'Illustrious' was to wind. Before we were at 2,000 feet the first bomb from a Ju87 hit the ship. It went into the open lift well and exploded in the hangar – it was really horrific to watch as you realised how many would be blown to bits – also a very close escape. As we climbed to attack the Stukas were diving to bomb. When we reached height the air seemed full of aircraft. From the rear seat I saw one go down and another was damaged. It wasn't long before we were out of ammunition and landed at Hal Far." Another Fulmar, that crewed by Sub Lt. Lowe and L/A R.D. Kensett, was seen to shoot down one Ju87 when another got on its tail – a burst of machine-gun fire killed Kensett while Lowe was hit in the right shoulder. The Fulmar ditched near H.M.S. 'Nubian' and sank almost immediately but Lowe managed to extricate himself from the cockpit. When the destroyer arrived it could find no sign of the pilot but half an hour later another destroyer, H.M.S. 'Jaguar' sighted the bobbing figure quite by chance and picked him up. Apparently two more Ju87s were claimed by Sub Lts. Roberts and A.S. Griffith in this action.

Even as the dive-bombers wreaked their havoc at this moment of maximum vulnerability, further Fulmars were attempting to take off: Vincent-Jones continues: "There was no C.A.P. overhead and there were only six serviceable Fulmars in the hangar, two of which were brought up on the after lift. Barnes and I were leading the next section to take off and were on our way up to the bridge for briefing. I remember being told to get airborne as fast as possible as a huge formation was approaching from the northwards. There was no time for positioning us on the catapult and in any case the ship was steaming into wind so that we were free for a normal rolling take off."

"As Barnes and I arrived at our Fulmar, it had just come up on the after lift and was having its wings spread. As I leapt into the rear cockpit I remember seeing what looked like a gigantic swarm of bees approaching from astern of the ship. There were in fact well over 100 aircraft, the majority of which were Stukas. One section was already airborne but my own section was ranged on deck with our aircraft immediately behind the other aircraft in the section. His engine refused to start and I recall standing up in the cockpit and waving at the flight deck party to drag him over to the starboard side of the deck, out of the way. By now the 'swarm' was very close and beginning to fan out before starting to dive bomb, and there was no doubt which ship was to be the target. Barnes opened his throttle and we swerved round our unfortunate sectionmate. Soon we were away down the deck and starting to climb off the bow of the ship. When we had reached a few hundred feet we found ourselves surrounded by Ju87s as they were pulling out of their dives and some of them were very close, one hundred yards or so, and I could see clearly the rear gunners firing at us. Two bullets went through my plotting board and others lodged in my seat. I looked down and saw the poor 'Illustrious' passing through huge columns of water, her guns blazing and a fire and smoke coming from the after end of the flight deck. The first 500 kilo bomb had scored a direct hit on the Fulmar which had failed to start – no sign of it or its crew was ever seen again. The bomb went on down the after lift well and exploded on the maindeck killing about 30 of the maintenance crews of 806 Squadron who had been allocated the after end of the hangar. The blast went through the hangar and buckled the foremost lift, thus putting an end to any further chance of flying off other aircraft.'

"Meanwhile Barnes had no shortage of close range targets; he had in fact too many and contented himself with pumping bursts into Stuka after Stuka as they came through his sights – and there was no question of not being able to see the whites of their eyes! I had a cine camera with me and having nothing better to do, apart from being a terrified spectator, I thought this might be a heaven-sent opportunity to 'shoot' a classic film of the wounded 'Illustrious' and her assailants, which would make my fortune after the war. In the middle of my first 'take' a bullet tore into the canopy alongside me and I dropped the camera. Thereafter my thoughts of commercialism evaporated and I lost all interest in photography. From my rear seat I found it was difficult to see what was going on up front, but I saw one Stuka go down with smoke pouring out of its engine. Despite their slow speed Stukas did not respond easily to .303 bullets as they bounced off a sheet of armour fitted at the rear of the back seat to protect the air gunners."

"The next thing I remember was Bill Barnes telling me we were out of ammo. Shortly afterwards I received my first message from the ship, although looking down at her, with smoke and flames pouring out of the length of her hull, I marvelled that anyone was alive to press a morse key. She was however still manoeuvring at high speed. The message read 'All Fulmars proceed to Hal Far (Malta) to refuel and rearm before returning over ship at best speed.' I gave Bill a course to steer and within 20 minutes we passed over the perimeter of Hal Far airfield with our undercarriage down. We were greeted by a burst from one of the Maltese Bofors but luckily this missed astern and we were soon taxying in towards the control tower. Here we found the other four Fulmars who had landed just before us, after returning from the chase of the Italian S.79s. They were being refuelled and rearmed, and we soon joined them."

The Stukas had indeed pounded the carrier, diving from 12,000 feet down to 2,000 feet in a copy-book attack. Six bombs hit 'Illustrious', wrecking the flight deck, destroying nine Swordfish and five Fulmars and putting half the guns out of action; casualties were heavy. The captain pulled her out of line. He was ordered to make for Malta, but it was three hours before she was able to proceed, steering by main engines as her steering gear had been put out of order. Not only Barnes and Vincent-Jones had been amongst the attacking Ju87s; Lt. Charles Lamb of 815 Squadron had been about to land from an anti-submarine patrol when the attack began. After a desperate 'dice' to avoid being shot down by the dive-bombers as they completed their attacks on the ship, he drew off and flew around until fuel ran out, when he ditched the Swordfish in the sea close to H.M.S. 'Juno'. (Charles Lamb vividly recounts this episode in his book 'War in a Stringbag', Cassell & Co., 1977).

On Malta the first most personnel knew of the attack was when the first four

Fairey Fulmar I fighters of 806 Squadron aboard H.M.S. 'Illustrious', (*D.J. Tribe*)

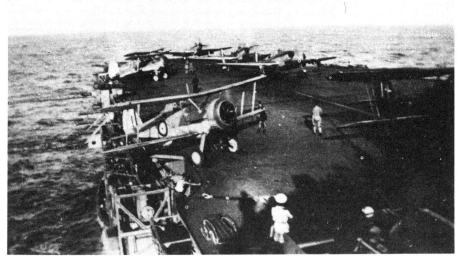

Gloster Sea Gladiators (left) of 'Eagle's' detached fighter flight, Fairey Fulmars of 806 Squadron, and in right foreground, a Fairey Swordfish, prepare to take off from the deck of H.M.S. 'Illustrious'.

(*D.J. Tribe*)

Fairey Fulmar I of 806 Squadron in flight over the Mediterranean late in 1940. (*D.J. Tribe*)

One of 'Eagle's' Sea Gladiators comes to grief against the island of H.M.S. 'Illustrious' whilst serving on detachment on that carrier late in 1940. (*D.J. Tribe*)

Lt. Cdr. Charles Evans (left) commanding officer of 806 Squadron, with Lt. Desmond Vincent-Jones, the senior observer. (*D.J. Tribe*)

Lt. W. L. Le C. 'Bill' Barnes, DSC, one of the most successful pilots of 806 Squadron, who was accidentally shot while based on Malta early in 1941. (*D.J. Tribe*)

Fulmars arrived at Hal Far, soon followed by two others. As soon as the Stukas returned to Sicily refuelling and rearming took place as quickly as possible to allow a second strike to be made. Meanwhile seven S.79s carried out a high-level attack but their bombs fell wide in the face of heavy A.A. fire. Three Ju87s of 236ª Squadriglia, led by Ten. Malvezzi, made a small contribution to the assault, one pilot claiming a hit on the carrier. Thirteen Luftwaffe Ju87s returned to the affray at 1715 and diving into the intense A.A. barrage hit her once more. It was whilst returning from this attack that the dive-bombers came up against a more telling attack by 806 Squadron, as Lt. Vincent-Jones recounts: "Refuelling and rearming, in particular, took much longer than usual as the ground crews at Hal Far were not familiar with Fulmars, neither did they have the right loading equipment. We waited with growing impatience as the fumbling went on and we heard reports of another big wave of enemy aircraft passing near Malta on its way to the fleet. After an hour or so six Fulmars were ready and Barnes and I got airborne with five others in company. We soon sighted 'Illustrious' on her way towards the Grand Harbour with smoke pouring out of her but still making a good 20 knots. She had parted company with the rest of the fleet. We were not in time to intercept before the attack developed but we caught up with the enemy on their way back to Sicily. Again there was no shortage of targets, but instead of being in the middle of them, this time it devolved into a stern chase and we came in for a lot of well-directed cross fire from the enemy rear gunners."

"We saw at least two Stukas drop out of formation but didn't have time to follow them down, moving as we did onto new targets. Ammunition expended, we returned to Hal Far and as we flew in over the coastline I got a glimpse of the poor old 'Illustrious' rounding the point only a few miles from the entrance to the Grand Harbour of Valetta. Smoke was still pouring out of her hull. Darkness was setting in and there was nothing more we could do. After a much needed bath, Barnes and I managed to get some transport and drove down to the ship which by now was safely berthed alongside Parlatorio Wharf. The scenes of carnage on board were beyond belief and have been well and accurately described by Nicholas Montsarrat in his book 'Kappillan of Malta' (Cassell & Co., 1973)."

"I was taken up to the Captain's cabin where I found Denis Boyd, sitting at his desk and I shall never forget the smile on his face as he said 'Well, we finally made it. Have a gin. Now tell me what your boys have been up to.' I gave him a very brief account of our day, as he was clearly in the last stages of exhaustion, and hurried off to see what I could find in the hangar. Barnes had already contacted the senior Flight Sergeant, who was fortunately still in one piece, and told him to round up a nucleus of ground crews from the 50 or so survivors, together with essential equipment and stores to maintain the seven remaining Fulmars, and that we'd come and collect them the following morning with transport from Hal Far, which was to be our base for the next three or four weeks. There was no shortage of volunteers as little doubt existed that the ship would be the main target of the Luftwaffe as long as she remained in harbour."

Thus according to Vincent-Jones' report, he had seen at least three Ju87s apparently badly hit by fire from Fulmars during the two raids, all of these falling from the formations. Reports, as indicated, are very sketchy, but seem to credit 806 Squadron with the two S.79s shot down in the late morning and five Ju87s destroyed, and others damaged, during the actual attack on 'Illustrious'. The A.A. Barrage was credited with bringing down a further three Stukas, with four more damaged. What of the actual losses? The official British war history mentions that the German figure for their losses on this date was six aircraft destroyed and one damaged, but a study of the loss returns for Fliegerkorps X lists only three Ju87s: Knights' Cross holder Lt. Gerhard Grenzel and his gunner in A5+DK of 2/St.G 1; Uffz. Karl Jägerman and gunner of 3/St.G 1 in A5+LL, and Lt. Helmut Leesch and gunner of 5/St. G 2 in T6+DN. One further aircraft of 4/St. G 2 crashlanded at Castelventrano with damage sustained from fighter attack.

Even as the carrier had reached Malta's coastline she was not free from attack, for more torpedo-carrying S.79s had attempted to attack at sunset when the vessel was only five miles off Valetta. They had been driven off by gunfire however, and she had docked at 2100 with 126 dead and 91 wounded aboard. Amongst the dead were the Fulmar crew whose aircraft had been hit at the start of the raid (Sub Lt. J. Marshall and Pty Off.(A) N.E. Tallack), while 815 and 819 Squadrons lost eight dead and two seriously injured – most of them men who had taken part in the Taranto raid the previous November. The three Fulmar crews of the 805 Squadron detachment survived although their aircraft were lost.

Further north on this same date, the Regia Aeronautica's 356ª Squadriglia, 21º Gruppo C.T., was warned of an intruder over the Bay of Naples. Serg. Giardano Migliavacca scrambled in an MC200 at 1245 and reported sighting a Blenheim at 16,000 feet. Initially this escaped him, but he then caught it as it returned southwards. After a brief fight, he claimed to have shot it down between the islands of Capri and Ventotene, no survivors being found.

Apart from the newly-arrived Fulmars, Malta's strength at this moment to face the onslaught that all knew must now come, stood at fourteen Hurricanes 'on strength', some of which were not serviceable, plus the twelve crated aircraft on 'Essex', which would take some days to offload and erect. There were twenty-three fighter pilots on hand; at about this time Flt.Lt. MacLachlan took over 'A' Flight from John Waters; 'Timber' Woods had been posted to Greece as a flight commander in 80 Squadron, while Flg.Off. Tom Balmforth was posted home to England due to ill health; he had been credited with one destroyed, one probable and one damaged over Malta. That night, as 'Illustrious' docked, an effort was made to hit back, six of 830 Squadron's Swordfish bombing the port of Palermo, Sicily.

11/1/41

Giesler was anxious for his men to have one more stab at the fleet before it was out of range, but after the heavy activities of 10th. bombs were scarce. Sufficient were scraped together to arm twelve Ju87s of II/St.G 2, and these were off early on 11 January, led by a 'pathfinder' He111, searching to the south-east of Malta. The Greek-bound convoy and its escorts were well away, as were the main units of the fleet, but the six slow vessels of MS.6 were still within range. With only the cruiser 'York' and four corvettes in attendance they had been joined by

'Gloucester' and 'Southampton' on the morning of the 11th. and were steaming steadily towards Alexandria.

None of these ships had the benefit of radar, and so it was that II/St.G 2 stole up upon them at extreme range from base for the Stukas (300 miles). The first that the sailors knew of their presence was when the dozen dive-bombers plunged down out of the sun towards them, planting two or three bombs directly onto 'Southampton' and one onto 'Gloucester'; they then made good their escape without loss or damage. The 250 kilo bomb which struck 'Gloucester', penetrated through five decks but failed to explode. 'Southampton' was badly hit however; attempts were made to get her to base, but at 2200 she had to be abandoned, following which the cruiser was sunk by three torpedoes fired from the cruiser 'Orion' which had come to the convoy's aid. During the attack one of 'Gloucester's' Walrus seaplanes (L2299) was airborne, the pilot being ordered to ditch alongside H.M.S. 'Diamond' as the parent ship was unable to slow down to make a recovery; the crew were picked up safely. A second Walrus (L2298) was damaged by shrapnel while stowed aboard 'Gloucester'.

12/1/41

Next day the battleship 'Barham' with 'Eagle' and the cruiser 'Perth', sortied from Alexandria to meet the incoming ships. It had been planned that the combined force should make a raid into the Aegean, and 'Eagle' had taken aboard a 'scratch' unit, 813 Fighter Flight, with three Sea Gladiators and two Skuas for this purpose. With 'Illustrious' out of action however, this operation was abandoned and the fleet made for harbour. Meanwhile the cruisers 'Orion' and 'Perth' sailed to Piraeus, where they took aboard a number of troops destined for Malta, who had been aboard other vessels of the 'Excess' convoy; they were transported safely to the island.

11/1/41

On Malta meanwhile the defenders were girding up their loins for the attacks which must soon come with the carrier present and under repair in the dockyard. At 0845 on 11th. a single S.79 appeared overhead at 23,000 feet, photographing the harbour. Six Hurricanes were scrambled to intercept, but failed to catch the intruder. Sgt. W.J. Timms took off on a solo sortie in N2622, but crashed and was killed in rather mysterious circumstances on which Jim Pickering was later to throw some light: " ... Bill Timms was scrambled solo from Takali with instructions to climb above the island with all haste. I would assume that radar had picked up a possible lone reconnaissance and the only hope of interception was to have a height advantage. I was on the Sergeants' Mess balcony, and watched part of the climb until I lost sight of the aircraft, and I would have expected it to be over 20,000 feet when the engine noise rose quickly to a scream and suddenly stopped."

"I think it is necessary to refer back to an incident in September or October 1940. Hurricanes at the time had two pitch airscrews – not constant speed. Take

116

off was in fine pitch, but to remain in this for the climb caused the engine to overheat. Change to coarse pitch increased the forward speed but reduced the rate of climb. The stops on the airscrews were changed to make the fine pitch a little coarser and although this slightly lengthened the take off run, the whole climb was made at the new less fine pitch setting, which gave a much better rate of climb than coarse pitch. If you were 'jumped' by hostile aircraft whilst climbing, the only action possible was to half roll and dive away, but if you forgot to change to coarse pitch, the engine would quickly over-rev and blow up, and this had happened on one occasion to Bill Timms in 1940. Then, having shaken off the bandits he glided back towards the island and decided he could reach Luqa for a force-landing, instead of baling out. As Malta terrain is impossible for force landings this decision was wrong. He was in fact undershooting the airfield, but although the engine had a conrod through the crankcase and other internal damage, he got a trickle of power out of it that just carried him in."

"I think the same thing happened on 11 January with regard to the engine blowing up, but the reason for it was different and lack of oxygen was suspected. He may have forgotten to turn his oxygen on during the climb, and have passed out, or there may have been a failure of the oxygen supply. We had the old rubber tubes connecting the oxygen bottle to the face mask and there was a suspicion that moisture could collect in a bend and freeze. Bill Timms had control of the aircraft when he passed over Takali at about 4,000 feet and was heading for Luqa with the obvious intention of force-landing there. When he was half way between Takali and Luqa, it was obvious that he could not reach either and I suspect that as in 1940 he tried unsuccessfully to get a burst of power from the engine to carry him in. He tried to bale out then when too low."

"Shortly after this, conversion of airscrews to constant speed units was completed and we were issued with a later design of oxygen supply, but this would have occurred in any event. Had there been bandits over the island, there would have been some Ack-Ack, but once you have heard a Merlin engine over-rev and blow up, you cannot mistake the sound, and whatever the cause, this is what had happened."

During the excitement of 10 January the vital 431 Flight was expanded into 69 Squadron, while news was received of the award of the D.F.C. to the unit's leading pilot, Flg.Off. Adrian Warburton. Next morning at 0700 one of the squadron's Marylands took off to check on the Italian fleet base at Taranto. As the aircraft (AR707) passed the coast of Sicily at about 10,000 feet near the port of Catania, having gone somewhat off its prescribed course which kept it further from hostile territory, intercepting MC200s led by Ten. Palazzeschi attacked and claimed an 'aircraft of the Blenheim type' shot down; F/Sgt. Rene Duvauchelle and his crew of Sgt. Mehauas and Sgt. G. Taylor, were reported missing; Duvauchelle and Mehauas were of course, the two Frenchmen who had brought the Latecoere 298AB to Malta.

Hurricane undergoing service in the open at Takali.

12/1/41

All remained quiet during the daylight hours of 12 January, but that night ten of 148 Squadron's Wellingtons were despatched to raid the airfields at Catania. It was a night for gallantry amongst the bomber crews; Flg.Off. C.M. Miller made four bombing runs over the target area despite a fierce concentration of small and large calibre Flak. On return to Luqa he offered to have his aircraft re-armed and to return to Catania for a second attack despite the fact that he had already seen Plt.Off. G.K. Noble's Wellington shot down with the loss of the whole crew. During his second sortie he again saw a Wellington going down, but carried out a successful bombing run himself. The navigator of another Wellington, Plt.Off. J.H.M. Davies, on return from his first sortie, discovered that a replacement navigator was required for one of the other bombers. He volunteered at once, and took off for his second raid almost at once.

The second bomber Miller had seen going down was that flown by Flg.Off. A.F.A. Osborn, who after bombing Catania, descended to 400 feet through the Flak and searchlights to machine gun the Flak sites and searchlight crews, managing to put several out of action. His Wellington was hit several times and the fuel tanks punctured, and after flying the bomber 140 miles out to sea he was compelled to ditch – fortunately near a naval vessel. One member of the crew had been seriously wounded and Osborn supported him in the water for half an hour until they were picked up. Sadly, the man later died of his wounds. Osborn,

118

Miller and Davies were all awarded D.F.Cs for their conduct on this night. A further Wellington crashed on return to Malta, possibly due to damage suffered during the raid; Sgt. G.C. Hall and two other members of his crew died of the injuries they sustained. Another pilot who took part in these raids was Flg.Off. G.D. Cox; he had originally served with 230 Squadron, and had been second pilot on the occasion when Sunderland L5804 had been badly damaged by MC200s during July 1940. He had then returned to the United Kingdom and at the end of October had ferried out a 148 Squadron Wellington to Malta. remaining on the island with this unit.

It was estimated by the authorities that the attack had destroyed nine Ju87s on the ground at Catania. Italian records show that ninety-two bombs hit the airfield, eleven of them failing to explode, while thirty-five more fell in the surrounding area. Five aircraft were destroyed, including a Ju88 of II/LG 1, two Ju52/3ms of KGr.z.b.V 9, an S.79 and a Ca133; six He111s of II/KG 26 and eleven MC200s were damaged. Three nights later nine Wellingtons repeated the attack, all returning safely on this occasion. It was estimated this time that about thirty-five Ju87s and 88s had been put out of action on this occasion. By now the squadron was being kept up to strength by replacement Wellingtons flown in from the Middle East as and when they became available.

13/1/41

Axis air reconnaissance had by now discovered the whereabouts of the damaged carrier, and on 13 January I/St.G 1 launched the first of a series of attacks, dropping superheavy 1,000 kilo bombs on the harbour, but on this occasion without scoring any hits. Three days later however a much larger effort was to be made, although this would be intercepted by three Fulmars and four Hurricanes. For the first few days after the arrival on the island of the Fulmars, they had been held on the ground while they were patched up and fitted with R/T 'voice' sets so that they could be controlled by the Malta Headquarters in the same way as the Hurricanes. Rear-view mirrors were not fitted to the Fulmars as standard, and to remedy this serious omission a number of mirrors from some of Hal Far Transport Section's older vehicles were commandeered and fitted to the pilots' cockpits. It now seemed merely unnecessary weight to carry the observers or TAGs, and at the request of the pilots these normally remained on the ground during fighter sorties from the island.

With so few fighters available it was clear that the guns would have to play a big part in the defence of the carrier. The vessel was in French Creek, across the Grand Harbour from Valetta, where she presented a relatively helpless target for the dive-bombers, if a rather difficult one to hit. An immediate conference was held, drawing on the experience against the earlier Italian dive-bomber raids, and on a report by Brigadier N.V. Sadler regarding methods employed in similar circumstances at Dover. Valetta's Fort Elmo was geared mainly for coastal defence, although it did have some Bofors for A.A. work, others being sighted on the bastions and around Valetta itself. However a chain of heavy batteries were deployed on the other side of the city from Runella to Marsa. Equipped with 5.25",

4.5″, 3.7″ and 3″ guns, these provided the backbone of the 'Grand Harbour Barrage'. With these a box barrage of great intensity was planned over the harbour such that every attacking aircraft had to fly through it to get to its target, just as they were taking aim. If any were actually shot down, this would be considered a bonus – to upset the aim and prevent attacks being pressed right home were the primary objectives. The plan also provided for the fighters to engage the Stukas as they approached and as they were coming out of their dives, when they were at their most vulnerable. The firing plans for the barrage were ready just in time – about an hour before the big attack of 16 January began! The unimpressive tally of aircraft shot down by the barrage must not therefore be allowed to detract from its great effectiveness. Whilst the fighters managed to shoot down some of the bombers, it was undoubtedly the barrage that was largely responsible for saving 'Illustrious'.

16/1/41

The raid on 16th. comprised 17 Ju88s escorted by 20 Bf110s, and 44 Ju87s escorted by ten MC200s and ten CR 42s. The rain of bombs from this force hid 'Illustrious' temporarily behind a wall of water columns thrown up by the explosions, whilst the carrier suffered two more direct hits which inflicted further

Two Gruppen of Junkers Ju88A bombers from Lehrgeschwader 1 operated over Malta during early 1941. One of these formidable bombers from one of these units, carrying the Geschwader badge, is seen here on Gela airfield. (*N. Malizia*)

damage. The seven defending fighters scrambled at 1455, and with the guns of the new barrage initially claimed ten victories, shared about equally between them; the total was subsequently whittled down to four Ju88s and one Ju87 destroyed, two Ju88s and two Ju87s probably destroyed, all by the fighters, while the guns received credit for three bombers of each type damaged. Sub Lt. Orr and Lt. Barnes of 806 Squadron each shot down a Ju88, and possibly Sub Lts. Sewell and Hogg claimed. It was recorded that one of the Fulmar pilots followed a Ju87 through the A.A. barrage as the aircraft dropped its bombs and tried to get away at very low level through the harbour entrance. It was so low that it had to rise to clear a breakwater, wobbling badly as it did so; this gave the pursuing Fulmar time to catch it and open fire, sending it into the sea. Landing, the pilot later sent a message to the A.A. command stating that he did not think much of the accuracy of the guns' fire, which had missed the bomber and badly damaged his own aircraft! LG. 1 had taken the brunt of the fighters' attack, one aircraft (L1+CT) flown by Oblt. Kurt Pichler, failed to return; three more from the Stab (H.Q. Flight), 5 and 6 Staffeln of II Gruppe all crash-landed at Catania due to damage; a fifth bomber from 8 Staffel force-landed at Pozzallo as a result of damage caused by anti-aircraft fire. Two more Ju88s of II/LG 1 were to be destroyed on the ground during the day when an Italian aircraft collided with them, and at Palermo a Bf110 of III/ZG 26 was also destroyed, though the cause in this case remains undisclosed.

A III/ZG 26 Bf110C carrying on its nose the emblem of the Gruppe's 9 Staffel. (*N. Malizia*)

The bombing on this date was like nothing the inhabitants of Malta had experienced before during the previous seven months of war. Philip Vella, now a luminary of the Malta War Museum, but then a boy of thirteen recalls: "During the raid on the 16th., I was at home in Valetta. When it became clear that this was no ordinary attack, my mother told me and my sister to run for it and take cover in the crypt of a nearby church; there were no rock shelters in the vicinity. It is difficult to describe the din; it sounded as if hell had been let loose. The noise of exploding bombs, flak of all calibres and the screaching wail of the diving Stukas was so scaring that people just stood where they were and froze. Suddenly we heard a terrific explosion; a row of houses two blocks away were flattened, some said by an aerial torpedo and others mentioned two bombs chained together. At that stage people panicked as they realised that the only shelter we had above our heads was a big empty dome. I do not remember how long the attack lasted, but it certainly seemed a long time. Our experience was insignificant compared to what people at Senglea went through – Willie Mizzi and eleven others were trapped for 48 hours under 40 feet of rubble."

Wreckage of a Ju87R of I/St.G 1 flown by Fw. Richard Zehetmair, which was shot down over Luqa by 261 Squadron Hurricanes on 18 January 1941. (*R.C. Jonas*)

18/1/41

The dive-bombers returned in force on 18th., on this occasion the airfields at Hal Far and Luqa being heavily attacked in an obvious attempt to cripple the defences before further efforts were made to finish off 'Illustrious'. Indeed, Luqa was for a time put out of action. Five Hurricanes and three Fulmars had become airborne again at 1515 and on this occasion these claimed seven Ju87s shot down with one more probable and two damaged; the guns claimed a further three Stukas shot down. Flt.Lt. George Burges was up four times during the day, flying three different Hurricanes. He claimed one Ju87 "almost certainly shot down" and two damaged. Sgt. Harry Ayre also put in at least two sorties, claiming a

122

Ju87 on the first of these and another as a probable on his next flight. Two more were credited to Flg.Off. 'Eric' Taylor, and one to Sgt. Cyril Bamberger. Only two losses were recorded by the Luftwaffe on this occasion, one Ju87R of I/St.G 1 coming down over Luqa, while a Ju88 of 7/LG 1 – L1 + ER flown by Lt. Horst Dunkel – force landed in the sea after a raid on Hal Far. The Stuka (A5 + JK) crashed near the airmens' married quarters, the pilot, Fw. Richard Zehetmair and his gunner both being killed. A second Ju87 returned to Sicily with a dead gunner aboard. MC200s of 6° Gruppo provided escorts for the Ju88s, and these too lost one of their number, Mar. Persani failing to return. One of 806 Squadron's Fulmars was shot down into the sea; Sub Lt. Griffith was not found.

Station Flight Swordfish, flown by Plt.Off. Dick Sugden, wrecked by bombs at Hal Far 18 January 1941. (*W.R.C. Sugden*)

19/1/41

This attack had been but a curtain-raiser for 19 January however. Raids came in throughout this latter day, all now aimed at Grand Harbour and 'Illustrious'. Six Hurricanes, one Fulmar and one Gladiator operated, most pilots flying at least four times between dawn and dusk. Major raids were made by Ju87s and Ju88s escorted by Bf110s, MC200s and CR 42s, while a smaller attack was made by seven He111s. The first assault came in at about 0830, comprising about forty Ju87s and Ju88s; amongst those intercepting was Sgt. Jim Pickering who claimed damage to both a Ju87 and a Ju88. He was back in the air at 0924 to investigate a suspicious plot which turned out to be a Z.506B with a single CR 42 as escort, which were circling to the north-east of the island. Pickering chased the float-plane half way to Sicily, finally making a long diving attack past the CR 42 towards the stern of the Cant. He saw some hits but did not stay to watch the results as the fighter was now between him and Malta, and he returned to base at low level and high speed.

'Illustrious' under attack in Grand Harbour, January 1941. (*J.K. Norwell*)

Sgt. Fred Robertson took off in V7474 with five others at 1005, intercepting about twenty Ju87s and twenty-four CR 42s north of Grand Harbour at 9,000 feet. Climbing into sun he saw A.A. bursts over the harbour as the bombers began their dives, and skirting the edge of the gun zone, he caught one Stuka as it came out at 2,000 feet and headed away north. One quick burst from astern and below, and it turned over and dived straight into the sea. He then saw a CR 42 coming at him head on and aimed a good burst at it. This too turned over and dived straight for the sea, but he was then attacked by others and had to break away. Credit; one Ju87 destroyed, one CR 42 'probable'.

At 1110 another Z.506B was seen circling the island, and two Hurricanes were sent off after this, flown by Flt.Lt. MacLachlan and Sgt. Bamberger. Vectored onto the floatplane, they found it to be an air-sea rescue aircraft, clearly marked with Red Crosses – an aircraft of 612^a Squadriglia – but in line with the RAF practice which had been established over the English Channel during the previous summer, MacLachlan shot it down. Robertson was off again at 1255 on his fourth sortie of the day, this time in P3731 as part of a formation of five. Some miles to the north of Valetta, while circling over St. Paul's Bay, he spotted six Ju87s and about a dozen CR 42s at 3,000 feet just as they were beginning their attack. Again he attacked a Stuka heading back for Sicily, but he was at once attacked by CR 42s and had to take evasive action. He turned after two Fiats and shot one down in flames, putting a solid burst into the second as well. The pilot of the first aircraft baled out, while the second went down towards the sea, smoking. Once more he had to turn away due to the presence of other fighters, and did not see the result. It would seem that he had been engaged with aircraft of the 23° Gruppo 'Nucleo'; ten aircraft from this unit and eight 6° Gruppo MC200s over the island lost Serg.Magg. Iacone of the 70ª Squadriglia, who baled out of his CR 42 north of Valetta during a fight. Credit; one CR 42 confirmed and one 'probable'.

Flt.Lt. J.A.F. MacLachlan one of 261 Squadron's most successful pilots during the early weeks of 1941. His culminating triumph came on 19 January, when he was credited with four confirmed and one probable victories in the single day. (I.W.M.)

George Burges also made four sorties; he claimed two Ju87s shot down which he saw crash into the sea off Grand Harbour. He knocked pieces off another but did not see it go down. On another sortie he sat behind a Ju88, using nearly all his ammunition on it. He last saw it heading for Sicily with the port engine on fire. During one of his flights a bullet hit the parachute harness buckle on his left shoulder, leaving a large bruise. Sgt. Bamberger was chased by two or three fighters which he took to be Messerschmitt 109s – possibly MC200s in fact. He evaded these by diving to low level and flying alongside a cliff edge along the coast. While so engaged he discovered a Ju87 doing the same and "blasted it".

Honours for the day undoubtedly went to Flt.Lt. MacLachlan however; apart from his victory over the Cant floatplane, he also claimed two Ju87s and one probable, and one Ju88. Total claims by the defenders included nine Ju87s, eight Ju88s, one CR 42 and the Z.506B. It is known therefore that six of the Ju87s, two of the Ju88s, the CR 42 and the floatplane were claimed by the fighters, and possibly two more bombers to unidentified pilots. Luftwaffe losses included three Ju87Rs, two of I/St.G 1 (Uffz. Rudolf Vater of 1 Staffel and Ofw. Kurt Zube of 2 Staffel, and their gunners, in A5 + EK and A5 + BK respectively) and one aircraft of II/St.G 2 (T6 + LP) flown by Ogefr. Hans Küsters. A further Ju87 of I/St.G 1 returned badly damaged. Two Ju88s of 8/LG 1 were lost – L1 + ES flown by the Staffel Kapitan, Hptm. Wilhelm Durbeck, and L1 + AS captained by Ofw. Hans Schneider; one of these two bombers came down near Kordin, just inland from Grand Harbour. Another Ju88 of the Stab III/LG 1 force-landed at Pozzallo with severe damage, while a Bf110D of III/ZG 26 crash-landed at Catania. The pilots of this latter unit claimed three Hurricanes shot down, one of them by Maj. Kaschka at 1050, while the Italians claimed two more destroyed and four damaged. Sgt. Eric Kelsey in P2629 was last seen chasing a Ju87 into the barrage and was not seen again, while four more Hurricanes were damaged during combats. Another of 806 Squadron's Fulmars was also lost, Lt. Robert Henley being shot down, possibly by the gunner of a Ju87, having first claimed a Ju88 shot down, a Ju87 probably so, and one of each type damaged. Henley: "I recall a fairly massive raid of Ju87s and J788s, with all available fighters scrambled – some four Fulmars – and we just graunced around, uncontrolled, shooting at anything which took our fancy/came within range. The poor old Fulmar had problems gaining height and in gaining speed against the Ju88s. My aircraft was hit – I think, of all degrading things, by a Ju87 – which stopped the engine some miles east-south-east of Hal Far, and I decided to glide as close to Malta as possible because (a) my T.A.G. – N/A Rush – told me, at this point, that he couldn't swim and (b) there seemed to be so many aircraft about and such chaos reigning that I doubted that two little parachutes five-ten miles out to sea would be noticed, much less noted as British, by the A.S.R. boys who were already having to face something of a racket – and ditched some one mile off Kalafrana. A very brave Maltese A.A. gunner who saw us go in, jumped into the sea and swam off to help us, and arrived even before the A.S.R. launch. Alas, I was never able to thank him." It will be noted that, although it had been decided not to carry T.A.G.s whilst land-based, on this occasion at least the rear seat in this Fulmar was filled by such a person.

During these attacks a 'glider bomb' was dropped, which landed within the Three Cities at Vittoriosa, demolishing a nunnery, although it failed to explode. It was later tackled by Sgt. R.C.M. Parker (later Major, George Medal) of the 24th. Company, Bomb Disposal Squad, Royal Engineers. He recalled: "I had great difficulty with it ... I know we got it out – steamed off the H.E. after defusing it – and it was flown back to the U.K. ... I know it was the only glider bomb we encountered and it was aimed at 'Illustrious'". Possibly this was an early experimental version of the glider bombs later used quite widely by the Luftwaffe against shipping targets.

Results of the January 'Blitz'; damaged hangar at Luqa. (*R.C. Jonas*)

Despite the danger, those on the ground watched with fascination as the attacks developed. Plt.Off. Peter Valachos, a Canadian Wellington pilot, was heard to say "A two million dollar show and we can't sell a seat!" Wg.Cdr. Jonas, with an eye for the ridiculous, recalls watching a Maltese sentry on duty at Luqa during the raids: "... sticks of bombs straddled the lonely little soldier, while shrapnel, stones and debris must have been falling around him like rain. He had, however, a rifle and twelve rounds of ammunition, and standing there in the open and entirely unprotected, he solemnly proceeded to fire at twelve separate dive-bombers as they roared over his head. One can only hope that his impulsive bravery was rewarded by some good deflection shooting. Pressing the trigger for the last time, instead of the customary kick on his shoulder, all that happened was a sharp metallic click. Now his rifle was merely a useless contraption of metal and wood. Here he found himself, unarmed and unprotected, in the centre of the target area, while enemy aircraft thundered above his head, and bombs exploded around him. Suddenly and without power to prevent it, blind panicky fear seized the soldier and, flinging his useless weapon across the tarmac, he ran as fast as his little legs would carry him to the nearest shelter, 25 yards away. Once safely below ground, breathless and incredulous of his escape, he flopped quietly down in a dead faint!"

During the three days of attacks on 'Illustrious' and the airfields – 16th., 18th. and 19th. – it was assessed that the defenders had accounted for 40 aircraft destroyed, five probables and 12 damaged, with A.A. being credited with sixteen of these destroyed plus a share of the probables and damaged. It is believed that Plt.Off. Hamilton, Plt.Off. McAdam, Sgt. Spyer and Sgt. Hyde all claimed during this period in addition to these pilots already mentioned. Despite the obvious high incidence of overclaiming in this very confused and desperate fighting, the interference with the bombers' attacks had been extremely effective. 'Illustrious' had been further damaged by a number of near misses, but not one further direct hit was achieved during the attacks on 19 January.

Remains of one of the Gladiators after bombing at Hal Far, 4th February 1941. This is believed to be N5531, 'Hope', the 'Six-gun' Gladiator (See Appendix III). (*National War Museum Assoc.*)

Another event of note on 19th. was the arrival on the island of – of all things – a Spitfire. Jim Pickering relates: " . . . 'Angus' Norwell was manning the Squadron 'phone at dispersal when the first Spitfire to arrive at Malta came into the circuit at Takali. This was a P.R.U. Spitfire that had left England for a recce of Turin (or somewhere else in Northern Italy). The pilot (Flt.Lt. P. Corbishley, D.F.C.) claimed that because of a westerly wind he didn't have enough fuel to return to England; so he diverted to Malta! However, we had no expectation of a Spitfire arriving and Norwell immediately phoned 'ops', where Gp.Capt. Sanderson answered the phone. Norwell simply said "There's a Spitfire in the circuit" and the S.A.S.O. said words to the effect that there was no Spitfire at Malta and didn't he know the difference between a Spitfire and a Hurricane, and in any case there were no aircraft airborne. Norwell, not knowing he was speaking to the S.A.S.O., passed some suitable comment. The S.A.S.O. turned to the Duty Officer at 'Ops' and said there was a bloody fool on the 'phone, this being overheard by Norwell, who said he entirely agreed but the bloody fool was not at his end of the line! We gathered that our amusement at this exchange was not shared by the S.A.S.O.!"

"Air Commodore Maynard immediately made use of the pilot and aircraft for recce from Malta, though I think these were restricted by unserviceability and lack of spares." The Spitfire in question was P9551, a P.R. Mark ID which was officially recorded as the "only one of its type and range in existence". The wings had been specially constructed, each containing a $57\frac{1}{2}$ gallon tank in the leading edge, in addition to a 29 gallon tank in the fuselage and the normal 85 gallon tank. Together these gave the aircraft a phenomenal range of 1,750 miles. A split pair of F-24 cameras were installed in the rear fuselage. Flt. Lt. Corbishley had been awarded an immediate D.F.C. in November 1940 for a flight in which he had obtained some excellent photographs over Southern France. Permission was granted from Air Ministry for the aircraft to be retained until wind conditions were favourable for it to return to England, and indeed Corbishley was to make his first sortie over Sicily with this aircraft on 21 January.

20/1/41

Following these few days of extremely heavy fighting, the assault tailed off – despite the presence of some 186 German aircraft in Sicily by this time. The S.A.S.O., Gp.Capt. A.C. Sanderson, attended a conference in Egypt on 20th., where his impassioned pleas for reinforcements for the defences brought immediate aid. This could now be spared, as the offensive in North Africa was virtually at an end. When the Sunderland carrying the Group Captain returned that evening, it carried aboard four fighter pilot reinforcements, the first members of a much larger batch that was to arrive over the next few days. These were Plt.Off. P.A. Worrall, ex 85 and 249 Squadrons, already with two and a half

One of the first reinforcement pilots to arrive in 1941, Plt.Off. Piers Worrall was flown to the island in a Sunderland on 20 January 1941.

129

victories to his credit, Plt.Off. P. Wyatt-Smith, a veteran of the Norwegian Campaign in which he had flown Gladiators with 263 Squadron, Plt.Off. J.J. Walsh, a Canadian from 615 Squadron, and Plt.Off. I.R. Currie, a Scot. Shortly after arrival Ian Currie developed cerebral malaria, which he had probably contracted at Takoradi on arrival in West Africa; he died on 31 January.

23–29/1/41

Three days later H.Q. Middle East signalled Malta: "Am despatching you six Hurricanes and seven Fulmars a.s.a.p. and about ten Brewsters (probably in cases) by next convoy." Owing to lack of spares and maintenance problems the offer of the Fulmars and Brewster Buffalos was declined, these aircraft being diverted to Alexandria, but the offer of six Hurricanes was accepted with alacrity. 261 Squadron did not have to wait too long, for on 29 January six Hurricanes and two navigating Wellingtons from 38 Squadron arrived, the latter carrying three additional fighter pilots, the kits of all nine pilots and the balance of the fighters' guns, which had been removed for lightness. Leading the Hurricanes was Flg.Off. C.D. Whittingham (ex 151 Squadron), and with him were Plt.Off. J.F. Pain, an Australian who had gained two victories during the Battle of Britain with 32 and 249 Squadrons, Sgt. A.H. Deacon (ex 85 and 111 Squadrons with three and one shared victories), and six other ex-Battle of Britain pilots – Plt.Off. P.J. Kearsey (ex 607 and 213 Squadrons); Plt.Off. D.J. Thacker (ex 32 Squadron); Plt.Off. D.J. Hammond (ex 54, 245 and 253 Squadrons); Plt.Off. C.E. Langdon (ex 43 and 145 Squadrons, a New Zealander with one victory); Sgt. C.W. McDougal (ex 111 Squadron) and Sgt. C.G. Hodson (ex 1 and 229 Squadrons). Whittingham, Pain, Deacon and Hodson had each been shot down during the Battle, both Pain and Hodson having been wounded.

29 January 1941 brought a reinforcement flight of six Hurricanes to Malta from the Middle East. One of the new pilots arriving on that day was Plt.Off. John 'Tiger' Pain, a Battle of Britain veteran.

(*J.F. Pain*)

To explain the arrival of these pilots it is necessary to return to the point when the 'Excess' convoy had sailed from England. It will be recalled that the ships had initially accompanied a much larger convoy into the Atlantic, the escort for which included the aircraft carriers 'Furious' and 'Argus', the cruiser 'Berwick' and a number of destroyers. The carriers were transporting numbers of Hurricanes for the Middle East, many of which were stowed below decks in 'Furious' with the wings removed. After the brush with 'Hipper' on Christmas Day, the convoy – less the 'Excess' ships – reached West Africa where two Naval squadrons were flown off to Bathurst. The carriers sailed on Southwards as the Hurricanes were prepared for flight, and on 9 January they were flown off to Takoradi. One Hurricane (Plt.Off. Heath) crashed into the sea, the pilot being rescued by a destroyer, and a second was tipped onto its nose during the take off attempt by Plt.Off. P.A. Mortimer; it got off nonetheless, but crashed on landing; 40 others got ashore safely. From here the aircraft were to be flown over the old Imperial Airways route to Cairo, via Lagos, Kano, Maiudugari, El Geneina, El Fasher, Khartoum and Wadi Halfa. The first six, all whitewashed in case of a force-landing in the jungle, were led off on 10 January by a Blenheim, reaching Khartoum three days later. Deacon, whose aircraft had developed a faulty fuel pump, took off late and followed the rest alone.

This trans-Africa ferry route had been officially opened in October 1940, although the first military aircraft to follow it – four Blenheims and five Hurricanes – had left on 20 September, reaching Abu Sueir on 26th. The first operating party had arrived on 21 August, having first to build considerable workshop and other accomodation; refuelling and rest stations also had to be constructed en route. On 5 September the first 12 crated Hurricanes and Blenheims arrived by sea, while next day 30 Hurricanes were flown off 'Argus'. Late in November twenty-two Polish pilots commanded by Wg.Cdr. M. Izycki arrived, their sole duty to ferry aircraft along this route. Crated aircraft would arrive at Takoradi in ever-increasing numbers until by 1943, the total had passed 3,500. A typical trip from Takoradi to Cairo, over some 4,000 miles of swamps, jungle or barren desert, if fighters were included in the convoy and if the trip was uneventful, would be:

Day 1: Takoradi to Lagos, Nigeria (380 miles)
Day 2: Lagos to Kano, Nigeria (525 miles)
Day 3: Kano to El Geneina, Sudan, refuelling at Maiduguri, Nigeria, and Fort Lamy, French Equitorial Africa (960 miles)
Day 4: El Geneina to Khartoum, refuelling at El Fasher and El Obeid (1,060 miles)
Day 5: Khartoum to Wadi Halfa (520 miles)
Day 6: Wadi Halfa to Abu Sueir, Cairo, refuelling at Luxor (500 miles)

Towards the end of November, H.M.S. 'Furious' arrived off the Gold Coast, carrying the Hurricanes of 73 Squadron (see 'Fighters Over the Desert'), and these were flown off to Takoradi, with just one mishap. However, the first six Hurricanes, which set out for Egypt on 1 December in company with a Blenheim guide, all force-landed in darkness in the Sudanese desert when the Blenheim became lost. Two Hurricanes had been written off, and the other four all damaged. Nevertheless, by the end of 1940 107 aircraft had reached Egypt via this route.

Of this January contingent, 38 of the fighters eventually reached Egypt, where a proportion were earmarked for Malta. Eight flew up to Bardia on 19th., and from there to Tobruk via Gazala. Here some guns were removed to lighten the aircraft before their departure. John Pain provided his reminisence of this journey: "The long flight from Ismailia to Malta was almost a continuation of the long haul from the deck of H.M.S. 'Furious' via Takoradi. We delivered our aircraft to Abu Sueir, Egypt, on 16 January, were accomodated at Ismailia, and left that aerodrome for Fort Capuzzo on 23 January. Our call came at lunchtime in Choclat's Bar, French Club, Ismailia – a case of down your drinks, you're flying! We left, nine of us, that afternoon and arrived at Landing Ground 2, Fort Capuzzo, before sunset; here we spent an overly long and unexpected four days as guests of 73 Squadron."

"The 'First Benghazi Stakes' was in full swing and Bardia fell the day we arrived at the Fort. This was the first experience for any of us of being part of a land advance. Originally we were to fly to Malta from the Fort, but when Tobruk fell it was decided to shorten the flight by moving the rendezvous to Ain el Gazala, West of Tobruk. This shortened our water section by about 60 miles. However, having arrived at Gazala on 26th. the escorting 'Wimpey' (Wellington) landed and went u/s. We returned to the Fort where sandstorms pinned us down for two days. This time was spent exploring the battlefields and acquiring souvenirs. All told we made three trips from the Fort to Gazala before we finally got away. The mess at Gazala was in an old tomb with the mess bar supported at each end by a sarcophagus. Outside the 'drome was still dangerous with S-mines and booby traps, and shrapnel was a serious hazard. While our aircraft were equipped with non-jettisonable, unself-sealing long rang tanks, our guns were empty. It had been considered in Cairo that the weight of ammo might be decisive in achieving the range to Malta with a safety margin."

"A loose 'vic' was formed on the Wimpey and I was on the outer starboard. Whittingham was the appointed leader of the Hurricane flight. The first portion of the flight, in beautiful Mediterranean weather, was still within fighter range of the Italian air force. Derna, about 40 miles west of Gazala, only fell the day we took off. Consequently, in loose formation, we kept up a fairly constant weave which settled down as we got further out to sea. The majority of the over four-hour flight was uneventful, other than each of us listening to our engine note with considerable concentration. About 100 miles out we sighted a destroyer, a small speck with a white wake some 10,000 feet below us. It lay directly in our path and the Wimpey made no effort to avoid it. The next moment this fly speck erupted and the barrage burst about 2,000 feet below us. The Wimpey made a dignified concession and altered course to starboard by at least five degrees. The next burst was about 500 feet below us and slightly behind. It was quite astonishing how much muck came out of that little ship. We never did find out whether it was Royal Navy or Italian."

"The rest of the flight was uneventful until we got a few miles from Malta.

When we sighted Pantelleria away to port we commenced a light weave. Then we sighted the haze over Malta and shortly after the island, dun coloured and bare looking. As we approached the Grand Harbour Barrage opened up accompanied by more isolated groups of A.A. fire and we realised we had arrived in the middle of a raid. Rigid R/T silence had been maintained throughout the flight to that point. We were almost over Filfla when we sighted a formation of Me109s slightly below us flying round the island cliffs." (These were probably in fact Italian MC200s, for no Messerschmitt Bf109s had yet reached the Mediterranean area.) "They sighted us and attacked. There was no alternative but for us to attack even though we had no ammo. I am not sure of who did what at this stage. We went into them almost head on and they scattered then followed a short dogfight. Two Hurris stayed with the Wimpey which went hell for leather for Luqa and made it safely."

"I think there were fifteen e/a. It was highly unusual for German pilots to attack from an inferior position, but it is possible our head-on attack threw them off balance. The melee was sharp and intense with our continuing pressing the attack, but when they broke we left them to it. It was pointless pursuing them with no ammo, and fuel was getting low. We landed at Hal Far where, according to my diary, we were met by A.V.M. Maynard – the first and only time I saw the man – who was intrigued by our un-R.A.F. appearance. This included some six days' growth of beard and six days' accumulation of sand where the grit would be most irritating. Water in the desert was reserved for tea, not washing! From Hal Far we moved to Takali where we joined the remnants of 261 Squadron. Subsequently, Whittingham suggested to the A.O.C. that we merited a Mention in Despatches for our flight and fight, but he knocked it back."

The day following the arrival of the Hurricanes, a further batch of six pilots were brought in by Sunderland, and these included Flg.Off. S.R. Peacock-Edwards, a Rhodesian who like MacLachlan had flown Battles in the Battle of France. He had then become a Hurricane pilot in time for the Battle of Britain, flying with 615 and 253 Squadrons, gaining two victories with the latter unit. The other five were Plt.Off. A.J. Rippon (ex 601 Squadron); Plt.Off. C.F. Counter, and Sgts. L. Davies, A.G. Todd and L.J. Dexter; Davies had been wounded during the Battle of Britain whilst with 151 Squadron.

Final reinforcements of January 1941 arrived on 30th. by Sunderland. One of those who came in with this batch was Sgt. Len Davies, seen here in the cockpit of his Hurricane. (*L. Davies*)

At about this time Flt. Lt. Gerald Watson also joined 261 Squadron. A pilot from 148 Squadron, he had crashed his Wellington and was attached to the fighter unit while awaiting a replacement bomber. Flg.Off. James Foxton, one of 69 Squadron's original Maryland pilots, also transferred to the fighters at this time, but 261 bade farewell to one of the most successful and long-serving pilots when George Burges, one of the original Fighter Flight members, was posted to 69 Squadron. Late January also saw the award of two more decorations to the island's pilots, D.F.C.s being announced for Flt.Lt. James MacLachlan for six victories, and for Flg.Off. Frederic Taylor for seven and one probable. The Italians too noted one change in their dispositions in Sicily when the 23° Gruppo 'Nucleo' was formed into the 156° Gruppo Autonomo C.T. under Cap. Luigi Filippi, comprising the 379ª and 380ª Squadriglia with the same CR 42s. By the end of January A.H.Q. Malta was able to report a quite satisfactory strength as follows:

261 Squadron	28 Hurricanes (5 unserviceable)
	4 Gladiators*
806 Squadron	3 Fulmars (1 unserviceable)
Jointly, 43 fighter pilots	
69 Squadron	4 Marylands
	1 Spitfire
148 Squadron	19 Wellingtons
228 Squadron	5 Sunderlands

(*During the next few days the remaining Gladiators were transferred to 806 Squadron, where they were used mainly for meteorological reconnaissance duties.)

20/1/41

Following the raids of 18th. and 19 January, the Governor had received a message from the Prime Minister, Winston Churchill; "I send you, on behalf of the War Cabinet, heartfelt congratulations upon the magnificent and ever-memorable defence which your heroic garrison and citizens, assisted by the Royal Navy and, above all, the Royal Air Force, are making against the German and Italian attacks. The eyes of all Britain and, indeed, the whole British Empire, are watching Malta in her struggle, day by day, and we are sure that success as well as glory will reward your efforts." General Dobbie replied: "Your telegram greatly appreciated by the garrison and people of Malta. By God's help, Malta will not weaken. We are glad to make a contribution to the victory which we know is sure and certain."

20–23/1/41

Meanwhile as telegrams passed between London and Valetta, and as the reinforcements arrived, activities over the island continued on a lower key. During the night of 20/21st. seven Wellingtons bombed Catania airfield again, being credited with the estimated destruction of seven aircraft on the ground; two

MC200s and a Ca133 were in fact destroyed, three transport aircraft being damaged. Further attacks continued on subsequent nights on Naples, Catania and Comiso, while Axis attacks on Malta arrived sporadically until 23 January. By this date 'Illustrious' had been sufficiently patched up to allow her to sail quietly out of harbour and on towards Alexandria and safety. From here she was subsequently to go on to the United States for major repairs which were to keep her out of the war for a full year.

Sub Lt. A.J. Sewell, one of the successful Fulmar pilots of 806 Squadron, who flew to Malta after 'Illustrious' had been damaged. (*I.W.M.*)

23–25/1/41

From Catania six Ju88s of 8/LG 1 were despatched to search for 'Illustrious' following reconnaissance reports of her departure from Malta; these carried out a fruitless search and by nightfall Lt. Hermann Böhmer's sub flight of three had become lost. Short of fuel but believing to be close to the southern coastline of the mainland, Böhmer ordered his crew of Ll+KS to bale out, and ordered the other crews to do likewise. Only the pilot of Ll+CS, Ofw. Herbert Isachsen,

135

came down over terra firma when he landed near Cape Rizzutto, not far from Crotone; a number of corpses were later discovered on nearby beaches, while one body, believed to have been a member of Uffz. Reinhold Schumacher's crew of the third aircraft, L1+JS, was eventually washed up on the coast of Albania, over 150 miles to the east. Eleven of the twelve airmen were lost. Next day it was the turn of 4 Staffel of LG 1 to lose an aircraft when L1+HM, captained by Uffz. Gustav Ullrich failed to return from a sortie to Malta. This may possibly have fallen victim to one of the Gladiators, now serving with 806 Squadron, as about this time, Sub Lt. Sewell was up in a Gladiator on a meteorological flight when he noticed a string of tracer passing his starboard wings, followed a moment later by a Ju88 diving towards Hal Far. Sewell followed the intruder down and reportedly shot it down off the coast. Lt. Vincent-Jones, who witnessed the action, added: "From the ground it gave the impression of a terrier yapping at the heels of a mastiff!" On this same day a Z.506B floatplane from the 170ª Squadriglia R.M., which had left its base at Stagnone at 0900 for a patrol over the central Mediterranean, also failed to return. It was believed to have been shot down by Malta-based fighters, possibly by a pair of 806 Squadron Fulmars. Two Hurricanes (Flg.Off. Barber and Sgt. Robertson) were scrambled on the approach of unidentified aircraft, and sighted a single S.79, obviously on a photographic-reconnaissance sortie, with an escort of four CR 42s. While Robertson took on the fighters, Barber made a bee-line for the Savoia, seeing his tracer hitting the fuselage before he had to break away to avoid a collision. Both Hurricanes then returned to Takali, no positive results of their attacks being noted. Next day a scramble from Hal Far was recorded, two Fulmars and three Gladiators going up, but no contact with enemy aircraft resulted.

During the night of 25/26 January 1941 Ten. Aldo Bellenzier was tricked into landing this Cant Z.501 flyingboat on the sea North of Comino in the belief that he was off the Sicilian coast. He and his crew were captured, but the aircraft was destroyed by high seas before it could be towed ashore. (*P. Vella*)

That night however a Z.501 flyingboat suffered damage while landing near Capo Muero, Sicily. A second 'boat took off to go to the aid of the crew, but became lost and the pilot, Ten. Aldo Bellenzier, radioed base for a searchlight to be put on as a beacon. This message was intercepted by the British listening service on Malta, and at once a light was switched on on the north coast of the island, causing Bellenzier to land north of Comino. An R.A.F. pinnace raced to the scene and captured the crew. The aircraft was moored pending being towed in, but before this could be done it was wrecked by high seas.

Close-up of the main crew quarters in the Cant Z.501 flyingboat. Note the nose-gunner's 7.7mm Breda-SAFAT machine gun. (*N. Malizia*)

137

26/1/41

Yet a further Ju88 was reported missing over Malta on 26th., this time from the reconnaissance unit 1 (F)/121. This aircraft (7A + DH) flown by Lt. Helmut Fund was intercepted by two Hurricanes at 1630 when flying at 10,000 feet, and had been chased all the way back to the coast of Sicily. When last seen the rear gunner had been silenced and smoke was issuing from the port engine, but shortage of fuel forced the fighters to turn away; obviously the attack had been more effective than the Hurricane pilots realized.

27/1/41

Sunderland T9048 of 228 Squadron, out from Kalafrana, sighted an enemy convoy, identified as two freighters and an escorting destroyer, between Lampedusa and the Kerkenah islands. On receipt of this information a Swordfish strike force – six aircraft armed with torpedoes while Lt.Cdr. Howie's carried bombs – set off at 1130 escorted by two Fulmars of 806 Squadron. The convoy was located almost two hours later and a successful attack was carried out on what turned out to be three unescorted German armed-merchantmen – the 3950-ton 'Ingo' was sunk while the larger 'Duisburg' (7500 tons) was left enveloped in clouds of smoke, both these ships victims of torpedo attacks; the third vessel, the smaller 'Inza' was dive-bombed by the C.O.'s aircraft and near-missed.

28/1–1/2/41

Little was seen of the Axis air forces during the last days of January as the various reinforcements arrived, the only raid of note being that made during the early morning of 28 January when a single aircraft bombed Luqa, where four airmen were killed and nine wounded. February began with a renewal of activity however, during which some of the new arrivals were involved in their first operational sorties over the island. At 1140 on 1st. three Hurricanes took off, flown by Flg.Off. Whittingham, Sgt. Robertson and Sgt. Davies. Fred Robertson in V7116 saw five CR 42s and a lone S.79 at 19,000 feet, coming in over Gozo – the daily reconnaissance flight again! The bomber was from 193ª Squadriglia at Sciacca, and was in fact escorted by four rather than five Fiats from the 156° Gruppo. Robertson attacked the bomber at once and followed it down for about 15 seconds before the fighters were upon him. Turning into these, he gave one a good deflection burst and it turned away and fell into a spin. He saw it recover partially, lose height and then go in a spiral dive into the sea. His shooting would seem to have been very good, for the Savoia returned very badly damaged with 100 bullet holes in it; two of the crew were wounded and one engine stopped. Whittingham and Davies gave chase to the fighters as they headed back towards Sicily, catching one 15 miles out to sea. Davies attacked first, but the fighter evaded his approach; Whittingham then attacked and claimed that he had shot the fighter down into the sea. 156° Gruppo reported meeting eight or nine Hurricanes, and suffered one loss, Serg.Magg. Andrea Baudone being killed.

About ten minutes before dusk four sections of Ju88s with fighter escort attacked, passing through the Grand Harbour Barrage to attack one of the airfields. Hurricanes were scrambled and Flg.Off. Peacock-Edwards claimed one of the bombers shot down while Plt.Off. Pain (in P3731) attacked another off Gozo and last saw it disappearing into cloud with the starboard engine ablaze. One Ju88 from 6/LG 1 was damaged during the attack and crashlanded at Catania on return, being totally destroyed, while an He111 of 4/KG 26 force-landed at Trapani and was also written off, though the reported reason in this case was engine trouble.

2/2/41

Flt.Lt. Corbishley again took off in Spitfire P9551 bound for a sortie over the Gulf of Genoa. The aircraft did not return and it was later learned that the pilot had baled out over Viareggio and was taken prisoner after the Spitfire had been hit by A.A. fire. Elsewhere this day Force 'H' had again sortied from Gibraltar into the Mediterranean with the intention of 'Ark Royal's' aircraft attacking Genoa. Bad weather prevented the air strike finding its target, and instead eight torpedo-carrying Swordfish from 810 Squadron were diverted for a night strike on the hydro-electric plant at San Chiara Ula Dam on Lake Tirso, on the island of Sardinia. In the face of heavy A.A. fire, machine-gun fire, heavy rain and poor visibility, only four Swordfish managed to release their torpedoes and these claiming no success. Lt. O'Sullivan's aircraft ditched in the lake having hit a horizontal trip wire protecting the dam from just such an attack. A.A. gunners claimed his aircraft shot down. O'Sullivan and his crew survived to be taken prisoners.

3–4/2/41

On 3 February Wellington IC P9265 of 148 Squadron was destroyed on the ground at Luqa during a bombing attack, while next day another dusk raid was reported approaching at 1845, Hal Far, Luqa and Kalafrana being the targets for three formations of Ju88s. Eight Hurricanes and two Fulmars were scrambled, two Ju88s being claimed shot down with a third probable and a fourth damaged; the A.A. defences claimed one more destroyed. Fred Robertson and another pilot went after seven Junkers approaching Grand Harbour, Robertson chasing the leading pair of bombers and attacking one of them from astern, following it through some cloud. He then attacked the second at 8,000 feet, seeing both engines catch fire. He reported that this bomber crashed into the sea five miles east of Zonkor Point. The probable was credited to Plt.Off. Pain in N2715 and the damaged to Sgt. Davies in V7072, who attacked a Ju88 silhouetted against the sunset and left it with one engine smoking. The second confirmed claim went to the Fulmar pilots, believed to have been Sub Lt. Stanley Orr and Sub Lt Roberts. Once again Lt. Vincent-Jones provides an account, which in this case suggests that other types than the Ju88s were also present: "A raid of more than 100 aircraft was detected one evening, shortly before dusk, crossing the 60 mile channel separating Malta from Sicily. Orders came through to get all serviceable Fulmars into the air. I was in my bath at the time when Stan Orr gave me the news. Telling him to get down to dispersal and get the remaining Fulmars started

261 Squadron pilots at Takali in February 1941, by the old bus used by them as a dispersal hut. L. to r. Sgt. Fred Robertson, Sgt. Len Davies, Sgt. R.A. Spyer and Sgt. C.S. Bamberger. Other pilots not identified. (*J.K. Norwell*)

up. I dried myself and pulled on my jacket and trousers faster than ever previously. I rushed after him and leapt into the rear seat as the chocks were pulled away. I had no time to collect a parachute or 'Mae West' and apart from my uniform and a towel had nothing on except my flying helmet. Looking upwards the whole sky seemed covered with enemy aircraft, mostly Ju88s but also a fair number of Heinkel 111s and Dorniers. Cursing the slow rate of climb of the Fulmar, we proceeded out to sea to gain altitude to get on terms with the bombers which were coming in at about 5,000 feet. By this time it was beginning to get darkish but we could clearly distinguish the bombs pouring down on Luqa."

Dornier Do 17Z at Comiso airfield in early 1941. No full unit of these aircraft appears ever to have been based in Sicily, and it is surmised that this was a single reconnaissance or 'Hack' machine. (*N. Malizia*)

140

"As we turned back towards the island, Orr sighted a Dornier silhouetted against the sunset to the westward and gave chase. We made our approach from his port quarter, and another Fulmar came up opposite us (I believe Roberts was the pilot) and concentrated on his starboard engine. The enemy rear gunner did not seem to be able to see us and was firing directly behind him. What looked like a stream of pink golf balls passed between the two Fulmars without doing any damage. It was not long before the Dornier went down into a shallow dive with a fire breaking out in the cabin. The crew were clearly visible against the flames as by this time it was fairly dark. Moments later the Dornier hit the water which soon put the fire out. Orr was so intent on his gunnery that he only remembered to pull out in time otherwise we might have dived in beside the Dornier, which I wouldn't have fancied, being 'Mae West-less'. At least there was no doubt about this one."

Despite these two eyewitness reports of crashes, available German records note that three Ju88s, all from II/LG 1, were badly damaged during this action and that all three limped back to Catania where they crash-landed. A total of five crewmen were wounded. At Hal Far a Gladiator and a Swordfish had been destroyed during the raid, and a further Swordfish damaged.

7/2/41

The continued fighter activity over the island now caused the Germans to shift some of their effort to the hours of darkness, and as in 1940 the Hurricanes soon showed that they could cope with this with the aid of searchlights – and a lot of luck! To spread the risk a little of the attacks on airfields, eight Hurricanes were shifted to Hal Far from Luqa on 7th. Their departure was followed by the arrival next day of eight Whitleys from the United Kingdom. These elderly bombers had been converted for paratroop dropping and were to take part in Operation 'Colossus', whereby a picked force of men were to be dropped into Italy on a sabotage mission to destroy an important aqueduct.

8/2/41

As night fell on 8 February 261 Squadron prepared to try and intercept the nocturnal raiders. Just at dusk radar plotted an incoming raid, and Flt.Lt. MacLachlan led off six Hurricanes, which climbed to 16,000 feet in the darkening sky. Formation flying was impossible in these conditions, and the fighters split up to patrol separate zones as two or three raiders were reported approaching. At 1910 MacLachlan spotted one unidentified bomber over Rabat at 10,000 feet, held in the beams of the searchlights; it was in fact an He111H of 5/KG 26. Closing to short range he opened fire, but was met by bursts of return fire, while a sudden blaze of anti-aircraft fire momentarily blinded him. Closing again to only 50 yards, MacLachlan fired two more bursts into the bomber, whereupon it went down steadily and vanished. The desperate transmissions of the crew were being monitored, and Malta H.Q. was able to confirm that it had crashed into the sea.

Heinkel He111 of II/KG26 takes off from Comiso airfield, January 1941. (*N. Malizia*)

As soon as MacLachlan landed, Plt.Off. 'Chubby' Eliot took off, but saw nothing. On his return MacLachlan took off once more, and this time saw a Ju88 of II/LG 1 turning northwards in the searchlights. Intercepting over Luqa, he gave chase and fired two bursts, one short and one long. Clouds of smoke poured back, but the Hurricane was then coned by the searchlights, and MacLachlan lost his prey. This too was later confirmed after soldiers reported seeing an aircraft crash into the sea. In fact the bomber managed to reach home base at Catania, but had suffered 80% damage. After a further 30 minutes on patrol, MacLachlan landed and Eliot went up again. This time he too spotted a bomber, but had not got within range before it escaped from the lights and disappeared into the murk. Each pilot was to complete a third sortie before being stood down at 0300.

Ground crew of 261 Squadron with one of the unit's Hurricanes, early 1941. (*National War Museum Assoc.*)

142

Fred Robertson was also airborne during this night, taking off in V7102 and patrolling at 4,000 feet. At 0045 he too saw a Ju88 caught by the searchlights, but this was above him. He climbed as fast as possible, firing two bursts, one astern and one from head on, but these were fired at maximum range of 500 yards, and he could get no closer before losing sight of the bomber. He was credited with one damaged and in fact an aircraft of III/LG 1 returned to Catania 50% damaged.

9/2/41

During the night eight Swordfish of 830 Squadron left the island to attack targets at Tripoli on the Libyan coast; one failed to return. Next day, whilst aircraft of this unit were being loaded with torpedoes, one of these deadly missiles exploded, destroying the aircraft and killing eight men. At this stage A.H.Q. Malta again drew a balance of successes gained by the fighters for the period 11 October 1940 to 10 February 1941. This read as follows:

				Grand Total, 11 June 1940 to 10 February 1941		
Type	*Destroyed*	*Probable*	*Damaged*	*Destroyed*	*Probable*	*Damaged*
S.79	2	2	2	11	7	7
CR 42	6	2	4	13	4	6
Ju87	13	2	6	15	3	6
MC200	6	2	2	10	3	3
Ju88	12	2	5	12	2	5
Z.506B	2	0	0	2	0	0
Total	41	10	19	63	19	27

Adrian Warburton, the famous Malta reconnaissance pilot, who served with distinction in 431 Flight and 69 Squadron. He is seen here later in the war as a Flight Lieutenant, after being awarded the D.S.O., D.F.C. and Bar. (*I.W.M.*)

Chapter 4

MÜNCHEBERG'S GRIM SHADOW

Oblt. Joachim Müncheberg, outstanding commander of 7 Staffel, Jagdgeschwader 26, who led his little unit to Sicily in February 1941, to operate over Malta; these were the first Messerschmitt Bf109E fighters to operate anywhere in the Mediterranean war zone. Müncheberg, already credited with 23 victories before coming to Sicily, wears his recently-awarded Knights' Cross at the throat. His Messerschmitts all featured yellow-painted noses on which was superimposed a red heart; they also carried the script S emblem of the Geschwader. (*Bundesarchiv*)

9/2/41

Further naval action marked this day when Force 'H' attacked Genoa on the Italian north-west coast. While three Swordfish directed the gunfire of the ships (Italian sources reported 76 killed and 226 injured in this attack on Genoa), and

Fulmars and Skuas patrolled protectively above, sixteen more Swordfish bombed and mined Livorne and La Spezia; Italian Dicat gunners claimed one Swordfish shot down and in fact Midspmn. N.G. Attenborough and his crew were killed, although it was believed that they had flown into a balloon barrage. Italian maritime aircraft were soon out in force searching for the British Fleet, but not until after midday was it at last spotted. Sottoten. Diego Dobrilla of the 287ª Squadriglia R.M. had taken off from his base at Elmas with a Naval tenente aboard his Z.506B as observer. Flying north from the island they spotted the vessels at 1215, but almost at once were attacked by patrolling fighters, three Fulmars of 808 Squadron and three Skuas of 800, reporting one of each type on their tail, which remained there for some twenty minutes. P.O.(A) Jopling and his TAG, L/A Glen, were in the Skua (L3007), they and the Fulmar firing from long range but only achieving a single hit on the dorsal turret, but both then closed in and after further firing the much-damaged floatplane came down on the sea, the engineer breaking an arm during the crash-landing. Six fighters then passed over but made no attempt to strafe. The crew remained with their stricken aircraft until evening, when they were rescued by the motor torpedo boat 'La Marsa'.

Meanwhile a Cant Z.1007bis bomber of the 51° Stormo B.T. was in transit from Vicenza to Alghero in Sardinia. At Pisa, where they landed to refuel, the crew were ordered to undertake a reconnaissance patrol searching for the British ships. Landing briefly at Sarzana to take aboard a Regia Marina observer, they set off on their mission, but at 1520 were intercepted by seven fighters which they identified as Hurricanes, but were in fact Fulmars of 808 Squadron. Lt. Taylour's Blue Section attacked and the bomber was badly hit, and five of the six men aboard were wounded. A crash-landing on the surface of the sea was carried out, during which the one unwounded member of the crew was injured, but all were safely picked up by the destroyer 'Camicia Nere'.

For Malta however an event of much lesser magnitude was soon to have an effect infinitely greater on the immediate concern of the defenders. During the day 7 Staffel of Jagdgeschwader 26 'Schlageter' landed at Gela, Sicily, on completion of the long flight from Germany. Equipped with Messerschmitt Bf109E fighters, the unit was composed of battle-hardened veterans who had seen much action during the fighting over England during the previous summer. The unit commander, Oberleutnant Joachim Müncheberg, was one of the Luftwaffe's outstanding fighter pilots at this time. Already awarded the Ritterkreuz (Knights' Cross) during September 1940, he had twenty-three victories to his credit. His little unit – never more than nine aircraft strong – were to play a part quite disproportionate to its small size during the next four months.

Already however, the Luftwaffe had been reduced in strength in Sicily as units began moving over to Libya to support the new German Afrika Korps, which was being assembled in the Tripoli area. During late January and early February the Bf110s of III/ZG 26, Ju87s of I/St.G 1 and Ju88s of II and III/LG 1 and 1(F)/121, moved to this new area. Before February was out they would be joined by II/St.G 2, and by the whole of Stukageschwader 3 direct from North-West Europe.

Bf110 of 5/ZG26 visiting Palermo's Boccadifalco airfield in North-West Sicily (*N. Malizia*)

10/2/41

During the night of 10 February the eight Whitleys at Luqa took off to drop their paratroops over Italy for the 'Colossus' venture. This, the first such mission by Britain's new airborne units, was aimed to demolish one of two viaducts over the Tragino river in Southern Italy. Six of the Whitleys were to carry the men – thirty five paratroops of No. 2 Commando – and the other two to bomb Foggia to create a diversion. One was late starting, that carrying the officer in charge of demolitions. However those from the other five landed safely, but found that the viaduct chosen had its supports constructed of reinforced concrete, rather than masonry, as had been presumed. Explosives were therefore concentrated on one pier, while the balance were used to blow up a small bridge over the Ginestra, a tributary of the Tragino, over which repair traffic would have to come. Their mission completed the men divided into three parties to march to the coast, where it was planned that a submarine would pick them up. At daybreak they went into hiding, but were found due to their tracks being seen in the snow which lay about. To avoid the risk of injury to the many civilians who gathered, the force was obliged to surrender, together with their Italian-born guide, Fortunato Picchi. Picchi, having served in the Italian Army during the First War, settled in England about 1920. A former Soho waiter and later assistant banquetting manager at the Savoy Hotel, he was interned when the war with Italy broke out, but was later released to join the Pioneer Corps. He then trained as a parachutist and volunteered as guide for this ill-fated raid. After capture he was arraigned on a charge of sabotage, and was shot in Rome. One of the two bomber Whitleys, N1456 skippered by Plt.Off. Jack Wotherspoon, experienced

146

engine problems, the crew being ordered to bale-out but the pilot force-landing the aircraft at the mouth of the River Sele; all were captured.

During that same night Plt.Off. Eliot and Sgt. Bamberger of 261 Squadron were on a night readiness and were both ordered off. Bamberger orbitted over Filfla for some time. He was just beginning to worry about his fuel situation when he was called into the searchlight area, only to be fired on by A.A. He advised Control that he was coming in to land and requested that the flare path be lit, but was advised that there was still an alert in force and therefore no flare path could be employed. A second request brought a blank refusal, but fortunately for him it was a bright moonlit night, and he was able to make a perfect landing on a grass slope near Rabat.

12/2/41

Malta's Wellingtons were also out again during the night of 10/11th., seventeen H.E. bombs and thirty incendiaries hitting Comiso airfield where five of KG26's He11s were damaged. On 12th. Flg.Off. Warburton of 69 Squadron undertook a reconnaissance over Southern Italy to seek the results of Operation 'Colossus', but this day was marked by the first appearance over the island of 7/JG 26. During the afternoon 'B' Flight of 261 Squadron was ordered to scramble after three Ju88s reported approaching at 20,000 feet. As they climbed after their quarry the Hurricanes were suddenly 'bounced' by the Bf109Es, Oblt. Müncheberg, Lt. Klaus Mietusch and Fw. Johannsen claiming one shot down each in quick succession between 1641 and 1645. Flt.Lt. G. Watson in N2715 and Plt.Off. D.J. Thacker in P3733 were both shot down into the sea, while Flt.Lt. H.F.R. Bradbury in V7768 was badly shot up. Wounded, and with his aircraft riddled with cannon and machine gun fire which stripped all the fabric from one side of the fuselage and almost completely severed the rudder control, Bradbury managed to reach the airfield and force-land. Thacker, who had also been wounded, managed to bale out into St. Paul's Bay.

One of the first Hurricane pilots to fall victim to Müncheberg's 7/JG26 Bf109s was Plt.Off. D.J. Thacker. He was wounded on 12 February 1941, baling out of P3733 into the sea. (*J.V. Marshall*)

'Jock' Barber recalled: " ... Watson and Thacker shot down – informed that all was clear but continued weaving – just as well as I then saw a red spinner in my mirror. Couple of tight turns and had almost turned inside the 109 when it made off. I then circled over Thacker until he was picked up." John Pain also had vivid memories of this occasion: "Once again the loss of a pilot could be laid at the door of the A.V.M. He was still insisting that the most senior officer led the flight. Watson was a Wimpey pilot who had been press-ganged onto fighters while awaiting a replacement aircraft. He had little knowledge of Hurricanes and none of air fighting. He led us out to sea after four 88s in a long stern chase – always deadly, particularly over Malta – when I saw we were actually overtaking the 88s, I realised they were acting as decoys. I pulled out to starboard and went through the gate (boosted the engine to the maximum). Watson, Thacker and Bradbury maintained their position and speed. As I banked to port to make a full beam attack on the nearest 88 I sighted the 109s coming down on the other three. I shouted a warning over the R/T and raked my 88 from nose to tail. One 109 closed with Watson who made no effort to evade, despite further calls from me. Thacker and Bradbury broke away and into the attackers. Watson rolled straight over on his back and went straight in. Thacker was set on fire and I'm not sure what happened to Bradbury. I got the 109 which got Watson and he crashed into the drink about 200 yards from Watty. I got two more bursts into two other 109s before running out of ammunition and, thank God, targets. I have no idea what happened to the 88." (The aircraft, from 3(F)/121, got back to Sicily in damaged condition and with a mortally wounded gunner.) "Thacker, who was the sort of swimmer who needed a Mae West to stay afloat in his bath, battled his burning Hurricane back over the Maltese coast at about 6,000 feet, he then pulled his hood back, rolled her and baled out. I was in company, but not formation. I followed him down. Unfortunately for Thacker the wind was offshore and instead of drifting over the island he went the opposite direction out to sea. By now I was low on petrol and flew back to Takali after Thacker hit the water. I refuelled and re-armed and went back to keep an eye on Thacker who was about three miles out in the channel. To my surprise this man who could not swim a stroke had covered a quarter of a mile towards Malta, judging by the fluorescine trail."

David Thacker recalls a slightly different version: "When I was shot down it was my first encounter with the enemy. Details of the number of Hurricanes scrambled or my position in the formation escape me. Similarly, I don't recall any organised attack. About 15,000 feet presumably someone called 'Tally Ho!' because I suddenly saw three Ju88s, which were at the same height, slightly to my left, range about 1,000 yards, and heading away from Malta. I pulled the boost over-ride, but to my surprise was unable to close the range. The only other Hurricane of which I was aware at this time was flown by Hamish Hamilton, which was ahead and to my left. This aircraft was firing at the Ju88s from astern. I did not hear any calls warning of the presence of the 109s, and every soon after first sighting the Ju88s I became aware that my aircraft was being hit. I excecuted a hard right turn, but could not see any other aircraft in my vicinity. The instruments were shattered, but the controls and engine were functioning except the latter was spewing coolant vapour. I headed back to Malta, well throttled

148

back and losing height. About 5,000 feet, when over St. Paul's Bay, the engine cut; the vapour and smoke had now increased, so I baled out. Soon after hitting the water, I saw a Hurricane above me which I discovered later was Barber. I made violent splashes to attract his attention; he circled until a rescue launch picked me up, some 30 to 45 minutes later. Contrary to John Pain's comment, I have always been a reasonable swimmer, and was convinced I would be able to reach the coast which I could see. I suffered shrapnel wounds in the buttocks and one arm. I was in hospital and convalescent for about a month. In retrospect, the Luftwaffe's planning and execution of this combat is hard to fault, whereas the least said about our own efforts the better!"

A Sunderland of 228 Squadron had been sent out at once to search for Thacker and he was soon spotted, being fished out of the water an hour later by a speedboat from Kalafrana. Plt.Off. Pain was credited with a 'probable' for the German fighter he had claimed shot down, but in fact the Luftwaffe suffered no loss or serious damage to any of its fighters on this day.

One of 69 Squadron's Marylands on Takali airfield, with Hurricanes of 261 Squadron in the background. (via J.V. Marshall)

A further raid appeared next day, 'A' Flight making the scramble for 261 Squadron on this occasion. Flt.Lt. MacLachlan led the Hurricanes up to 22,000 feet to the South of Comino where four Messerschmitts were seen coming straight at them. These broke away sharply on seeing the British fighters which gave chase but were unable to catch them. During this day the A.A. defences claimed a Ju88 shot down, while on 14th. on another scramble, 7/JG 26 was again encountered, Sgt. Len Davies having his Hurricane, V7771, slightly damaged by the Messerschmitts.

The appearance of the dreaded 'One Oh Nines' had seriously affected the squadron's morale. Reported Wg.Cdr. Jonas: "Day after day the sirens would scream dismally, and already our Hurricanes would be wearily climbing their way up into the sun. And more often than not, out of the sun would come the yellow-nosed Messerschmitts, long before our fighters had had sufficient time in which to gain their best operational height. To anyone interested in psychology, the effect of the Messerschmitts on the Hurricane pilots was obvious. For here was an ordinary average crowd of Air Force youngsters, neither better nor worse than their compatriots in squadrons all over the world. Many of them by now had been in Malta for several months ... and ever since Italy had entered into the war, these boys, often in obsolete aircraft, had carried out bravely and un- questioning, any task that they had been called upon to perform. Then more Hurricanes had arrived, and encouraged by successes, morale had risen, firey and inspired, to almost unbelievable heights. By now, not only were many of the Hurricanes tired and scarred, but the pilots themselves were tired. No new fighters ever seemed to come now, no fresh and eager faces appeared in the Takali mess. Instead there were empty places at the table, empty beds, cars for sale and dogs that needed masters ... "

The diary kept by Flt.Lt. Whittingham also gives an insight into the lives of the fighter pilots at this time – and to some of their off-duty pursuits. "February 10 – I have been given a dog – a mongrel pup called 'Lady', and I have bought a wizard little pony and trap for £70 – a trim grey called 'Lucky'. He is one of the best ponies on the island. It's an excellent thing to have a hobby here. It's such a dangerous sort of life that one can't help thinking about it a bit. So it's a good thing to get one's mind off in one's spare time. February 15 – P. and I drove

LG1 Ju88A at Comiso. (*A. Mauri via N. Malizia*)

150

'Lucky' to Valetta this morning. An air raid took place when we got there. The people rushing to the shelters upset 'Lucky' a bit. We stopped with him. The A.A. guns did not worry him much, nor did a bit of shrapnel that whistled down near him. What with continual air raids (seven times a day) and the presence of 109's about the place it is a logical conclusion that our chances of survival are not very high. But one simply must not think about this; at any rate, I am enjoying myself while it lasts. February 18 – now that the risk of death is so much more increased I've been doing a spot of philosophising. My attitude is that somebody has to do the job and if I get bumped off, I have experienced much more than the average bloke. February 23 – I am to be made flight lieutenant and given command of 'B' flight. This will please mother."

15–16/2/41

7/LG 1 reported the loss of a Ju88 – L1+JR flown by Lt. Wilhelm Gretz – over the island on 15th., probably shot down by A.A. fire, and two others from 4th Staffel returned to Sicily badly damaged, but next day came another severe blow to the defenders. 'A' Flight Hurricanes scrambled at 0915, Flt.Lt. MacLachlan leading in V7731. Recorded MacLachlan in his diary: "As 'A' Flight were on the 9 o'clock watch John decided to have all the blood-thirsty pilots on, in the hopes of getting a 109. We arranged that if we were attacked we would break away and form a defensive circle." About half an hour later, when the formation was patrolling over Luqa at 20,000 feet, they were suddenly attacked from above and astern by six Bf109Es. The flight at once broke to the right and formed a defensive circle, the Messerschmitts overshooting them – and probably climbing back to higher altitude. Sgt. Bamberger then spotted four more coming down out of the sun (these were likely to have been four of the original six, making their second swoop). He warned MacLachlan, who recorded: "Just as I took my place in the circle I saw four more Messerschmitts coming down out of the sun. I turned back under them, and they all overshot me. I looked round very carefully but could see nothing, so I turned back on the tail of the nearest Hun, who was chasing some Hurricanes in front of him. We were all turning gently to port as I cut the corner and was slowly closing on the Hun. I was determined to get him, and must have been concentrating so intently on his movements that, like a fool, I forgot to look in the mirror until it was too late. Suddenly there was a crash in my cockpit – bits and pieces seemed to fly everywhere. Instinctively I went into a steep spiral dive, furiously angry that I had been beaten at my own game. My left arm was dripping with blood, and when I tried to raise it only the top part moved, the rest hung limply by my side. Everything happened so quickly that I have no very clear recollection of what actually took place. I remember opening my hood, disconnecting my oxygen and R/T connections and standing up in the cockpit. The next thing I saw was my kite diving away from me, the roar of its engine gradually fading as it plunged earthwards. It was a marvellous feeling to be safely out of it, everything seemed so quiet and peaceful. I could clearly hear the roar of engines above me, and distinctly heard one long burst of cannon fire. I could not see what was happening as I was falling upsidedown and my legs obscured all view of the aircraft above me. My arm was beginning to hurt pretty badly, so I decided to pull my chute straight away in case I fainted from loss of blood. I reached round for my ripcord but could not find it. For some unknown reason I thought my chute must have been torn off me while I was getting out of my kite, and almost gave up making any further efforts to save myself. I remember thinking that the whole process of being shot down and being killed seemed very much simpler and less horrible than I had always imagined. There was just going to be one big thud when I hit the deck and then all would be over – my arm would stop hurting and no more 109s could make dirty passes at me behind my back. I think I must have been gradually going off into a faint when I suddenly thought of mother reading the telegram saying that I had been killed in action. I made one last effort to see if my parachute was still there, and to my amazement and relief found it had not been torn off after all. With another supreme effort I reached round and pulled the ripcord. There was a sickening lurch as my chute opened and my harness tightened round me so that I could hardly breathe. I felt horribly ill and faint. Blood from my arm came streaming back into my face, in spite of the fact that I was holding the stump as tightly as I could. I was able to breathe only with the utmost difficulty, and my arm hurt like hell. I could see Malta spread out like a map 15,000 feet below me, and I longed to be down there – just to lie still and die peacefully. I was woken from this stupor by the roar of an engine, and naturally thought some bloodthirsty Jerry had come to finish me off. I don't think I really minded what happened, though certainly the thought of a few more cannon shells flying past me didn't exactly cheer me up. To my joy, however, I saw that my escort was a Hurricane, piloted, as I later learned, by 'Eric' Taylor. He had quite rightly decided that he could do no good by playing with the Huns at 20,000 feet, so came down to see that none of them got me." Meanwhile the other Hurricanes had all returned to base, although Plt.Off. McAdam's aircraft had been virtually shot to pieces during the combat, while Flg.Off. Peacock-Edwards landed V7072 with numerous shell and bullet holes and with starboard aileron shot away, but neither pilot was hurt.

It seems fairly certain that MacLachlan had been shot down by Oblt. Müncheberg, who claimed one Hurricane from which the pilot baled out at 0945 (1045 C.E.T.). In the first pass he had already claimed one at 0938, Uffz. Liebing claiming a second; it is likely that these were the two damaged Hurricanes. MacLachlan, victor of eight combats over the island, was fortunate to come down on Malta itself, rather than in the sea: "For what seemed like hours I hung there, apparently motionless, with Malta still as far away as ever. Once or twice I started swinging very badly, but as I was using my only hand to stop myself bleeding to death, I was unable to do anything about it. At approximately 1,500 feet I opened my eyes again and to my joy realised that I was very much lower down. For a little while I was afraid I was going to land in the middle of a town, but I mercifully drifted to the edge of this. For the last 100 feet I seemed to drop out of the sky – the flat roof of a house came rushing up at me, and just as I was about to land on it, it dodged to one side and I ended up in a little patch of green wheat. I hit the ground with a terrific thud, rolled over once or twice, and then lay back intending to die quietly. This, however, was not to be. Scarcely had I got myself fairly comfortable and closed my eyes when I heard the sound of people running. I hurriedly tried to think up some famous last words to give my public, but never had a chance to utter them. I was surrounded by a crowd of shouting, gesticulating Malts, who pulled at my parachute, lifted my head and drove me so furious that I had to give up the dying idea in order to concentrate completely on kicking every Malt who came within range. (From what the soldiers told me after, I believe I registered some rather effective shots.) Eventually two very dim stretcher bearers arrived with a first aid outfit. I told them to put a tourniquet on my arm and give me some morphia, whereupon one of them started to bandage my wrist and the other went off to ask what morphia was. In the end I got them to give me the first aid outfit and fixed myself up. At last a doctor arrived who actually knew what to do. He put me on a stretcher, had me carried about half a mile across fields to an ambulance, which in turn took me down to the local advanced dressing station. Here they filled me with morphia, gave me ether, and put my arm in a rough splint. When I came round they gave me a large tot of whisky, another injection of morphia and sent me off to Imtarfa, as drunk as a lord. When I eventually arrived at the hospital I was feeling in the best of spirits and apparently shook the sisters by asking them to bring on the dancing girls."

"They wasted no time in getting me up to the theatre, and after making the General promise not to take my arm off I gave a running commentary as the ether took effect. When I came round I was back in M.3 surrounded by screens, with Sister Dempsey sitting in a chair beside me. After a quick glance I was delighted to see that my arm was still there, so went off to sleep again, feeling very cheerful about the whole thing. The next two days were pretty average mental and physical hell – thank God I cannot remember very much about them. I was having a saline transfusion day and night, and unfortunately my blood kept clotting, which necessitated making fresh holes in my arm and legs. I remember watching the saline solution dripping down the glass tube from the container – terrified that the drips were becoming less frequent and would eventually stop again. Everyone was simply wizard to me, especially Sister Dempsey. She used to sit by my bed for hours when she was off duty. I got a lot of secret amusement telling her to leave me as I wanted to die. She would get really worried and stroke my forehead and plead with me not to talk about dying. Had she but known it I had already made up my mind to get better, and nothing in the world was further from my thoughts than death."

"As these first two days dragged on I began to realise that there was no hope of saving my arm. The blood circulation was alright, but my finger movement was scarcely visible, and I could hardly feel anything in my hand. My whole arm began to smell positively revolting, and the pain was almost unbearable. Davidson and the General kept hinting that I would be much better off without it, but I was terrified that without it I should never be able to fly again, so refused to let them touch it. By the third morning, however, I was so weak and the pain so unbearable that they had little difficulty in taking me up to the theatre and performing the necessary operation. When I came to I was in the cabin at the end of M.3 and still having a saline transfusion. As I can remember very little about the rest of the day I presume that I must have been unconscious most of the time."

"This morning (20 February) I was moved back into the ward as I am now off the danger list. Just before lunch today a Macchi pilot whom I shot down on 9 January was wheeled in, and is now in the next bed to me. His arm is still very bad though the bullet wound in his thigh has healed. I think he was even more surprised to see me than I was to see him. It certainly is a crazy war!" Despite the amputation, the indomitable 'Mac' was not out of the air for long. As soon as he was up and about he insisted on taking up a Magister and flying it one-handed, and before long he was back on operations with an artificial arm. He was to become a leading exponent of night intruding later in the war, bringing his personal score to $16\frac{1}{2}$ before being shot down over France by Flak, and dying of his injuries from the crash which followed, in July 1943. He was not to fly operationally on Malta again however, for on release from hospital in March, he was despatched to Middle East Headquarters in Cairo. He followed the wounded Flt.Lt. Bradbury, who had also been sent off to this destination on 24 February, in company with Sqn.Ldr. Trumble, who was being rested. However, in the event Trumble was posted to Crete as commanding officer of Heraklion, but was captured during the invasion in May. 261 Squadron was taken over by Sqn.Ldr. Lambert, whilst 'A' Flight passed to Flt.Lt. Peacock-Edwards and 'B' Flight to Flg.Off. Whittingham. Around this time Flg.Off. Gerald Bellamy was posted to the squadron, having previously served with 3 A.A.C.U. He recalls: "I was posted off to Takali and given cockpit drill in a Hurricane. The only monoplane I had flown was a few hours in the 3 A.A.C.U. Magister. This was supposed to make me fit to fly a Hurricane!" Sgt. Ashbury, who had been one of the early Gladiator pilots, was posted to 148 Squadron. However he remained with the Wellington unit only for a short time before being posted to Control Office duties at Luqa. By 16 February A.H.Q. Malta noted that 261 Squadron had thirty pilots available from forty-three on strength, with nineteen serviceable Hurricanes to hand, nine more being in repair.

The fate of all too many Malta aircraft in early 1941; a shattered Maryland of 69 Squadron. (*R.H. Barber*)

17–23/2/41

A Bf110D night fighter of the newly arrived 1/NJG 3 was lost over the island on 17th but it is uncertain whether this fell to the A.A. guns or was shot down by Plt.Off. Hamilton, who claimed an aircraft identified as a 'DO215' round about this time. However, few engagements were noted for the fighters for several days, although Sgt. Robertson saw three Bf109s above him on 20th., but was unable to reach their altitude. On this same day 148 Squadron was reinforced by the arrival at Luqa of two Wellingtons (T2816 and T2891) and their crews from 70 Squadron, on detachment from Kabrit.

Three days later, on 23rd., the Stukas returned to the skies over Malta, and on this occasion the defences were able to engage them without undue fighter interference, although Plt.Off. Hamilton claimed one shot down, probably the aircraft (J9+JH) of III/St.G 1 flown by Ofhr. Roman Heil, whilst a second aircraft from this Gruppe, Fw. Erwin Diekwisch's 9th. Staffel machine, was hit in the engine by A.A. shrapnel. He managed to reach the coast of Sicily before he and his gunner were forced to bale out. The guns claimed three Ju87s shot down.

24/2/41

The Messerschmitts were back on 24th., four of them attacking a flight of patrolling Hurricanes over Imtarfa. As they opened fire the British formation broke up, Sgt. Bamberger going into a spin as the 109s disappeared back up into the sun. Sgt. Davies's Hurricane became separated and one Messerschmitt closed to 50 yards before opening fire – and missed! No losses were suffered on this occasion, although that night one of nine 148 Squadron Wellingtons failed to return from a raid on Tripoli, Flg.Off. G.H. Green and his crew being reported missing in T2891, one of the attached 70 Squadron aircraft.

25/2/41

Frequently during this period the British fighter pilots recorded combats and claims against aircraft identified as Dorniers – usually Do215s, but occasionally also Do17s. The Do215 saw only extemely limited service with the Luftwaffe as a reconnaissance aircraft, and no Do17 units seem to have served in Sicily or Italy. It is surmised therefore that such claims generally relate to Bf110s, which were of generally similar appearance. Such seems to have been the case on 25 February when eight of the Hurricanes were sent up after four aircraft reported as Do215s at 6,000 feet over the St. Paul's Bay area.

One of the intruders was straggling some half mile behind the rest, so this was attacked by the newly-promoted Flt.Lt. Whittingham, who fired a three second burst from astern and then broke away. The rear gunner returned fire, but the aircraft then dived into the sea in flames, this being confirmed by A.A. gunners at a coastal battery. The other pilots all attacked the remaining three and a multiplicity of claims were made, Plt.Off. Hamilton and Flg.Off. 'Jock' Hilton Barber (in V7102) each claiming one shot down, while Plt.Off. Walsh and Sgt. Davies claimed one damaged between them, although Davies' V7771 was damaged by return fire. Sgt. Robertson in V7116 claimed a damaged, but identified

155

148 Squadron suffered such an attrition rate to its Wellingtons during attacks on Malta's airfields early in 1941, that immediately after the end of February the unit was withdrawn to Egypt. On 26 February six of the bombers were destroyed and seven badly damaged in a single day. This selection of photographs shows a number of this unit's aircraft wrecked, burning, or damaged at this time. (*R.C. Jonas and National War Museum Assoc.*)

his victim as a Do17, while Plt.Off. Pain in V7670* made a similar claim, but against a Bf110. Yet another claim for one damaged was submitted by the A.A. gunners. The British pilots reported that the German aircraft were accompanied by nine Bf109s, but these did not come down 'to play'. No German records relating to such a formation have so far been found, but it is possible that they were aircraft of III/ZG 26. If so, then it was a case of sweet revenge for Whittingham, who had been shot down by this unit over England during 1940! However, the reconnaissance unit, 2(F)/123, lost a Bf110 in this area, Fw. Karl Bernhard and his gunner posted missing. That afternoon 7/JG 26 was over St. Paul's Bay, Oblt. Müncheberg and Lt. Mietusch each claiming Hurricanes shot down at 1545. It is possible that they may have shot down Plt.Off. Walsh, who was in the air again on a high patrol with Sgt. Davies. John Pain wrote home to his mother: "I note that a Canadian (Walsh) sprang a glycol leak at 27,000 feet and he was forced to bale out. He landed about 300 yards from a destroyer and was picked up with a leg broken in four places and a broken arm. Presumably he had hit the tailplane. He died in hospital of pneumonia." (Presumably his fatal illness was brought on by severe shock.)

26/2/41

On the following day, 26 February, the Axis launched one of the biggest 'Blitzes' to date – certainly the heaviest raid since that of 19 January. The attack came in at around 1300, with Luqa as the main target, the attacking force being identified as comprising thirty-eight Ju87s, twelve Ju88s, ten Do17s or 215s ten He111s and twenty to thirty fighters. The latter included the Bf109Es of 7/JG 26 with MC200s of 6° Gruppo and 12 CR 42s of 156° Gruppo, led by Magg. Mezzetti and Cap. Filippi respectively. Flg.Off. Taylor led off eight Hurricanes in V7671, climbing to 28,000 feet, when many Ju87s were seen below at about 10,000 feet just as the A.A. barrage opened up against them. The Hurricanes dived on them, but at once the escorting fighters were on their tails; at least two 'convoys' were noted of Ju87, Hurricane, Bf109E in line astern, all firing.

Plt.Off. 'Chubby' Eliot made his first claim on Malta for one shot down – a Ju87 in flames – and a second of these as a probable. Flg.Off. 'Terry' Foxton also claimed one Ju87 and a probable, but his Hurricane was then hit by a fighter, and with the radiator destroyed his engine soon seized; he crash-landed the smoking aircraft safely. The main force of level bombers passed over to 6–8,000 feet virtually unchallenged, their bombs crashing down on Luqa where six Wellingtons were burnt out (R1247, 1381, 1382, 1383, 1384 of 148 Squadron, plus the sole remaining aircraft of 70 Squadron detachment, T2816) and seven more badly damaged, as were several Marylands. The devastation was tremendous, hangars and workshops being badly smashed. One bomber – reportedly a Ju88 – was seen to be hit by A.A. and went vertically into the sea with a great howl of engines. Losses amongst the defending fighters were severe; Plt.Off. Kearsey in

---

*V7670 was later flown to North Africa and was subsequently captured by the Germans and painted with Luftwaffe markings. In due course it was recaptured on a Libyan airfield by British troops.

V7121 and Plt.Off. Langdon in V7474 were both shot down and killed. 'Eric' Taylor, Malta's current leading 'ace' with over seven victories, was last seen on the tail of a Stuka with a Bf109E on his own tail; he did not return either, and was reported dead when his 'Mae West' was washed ashore with a cannon shell hole in the centre of the chest. Again it seems probable that this experienced pilot had fallen victim to Müncheberg, who claimed one Hurricane at 1306, reporting "the fighting spirit of the British pilot was fantastic; he tried, although very badly hit, to still attack a Ju88 (sic)." Müncheberg claimed a second Hurricane four minutes later, Uffz. Ehlen also claiming one at this time, while Fw.Kestel had opened the scoring with one at 1305. Four further claims for Hurricanes were made by all 12 pilots of the 156° Gruppo jointly, two confirmed and two probables. The authorities credited the missing Taylor with a Ju87 probable; Plt.Off. Pain in V7114 claimed a Do215 probable and a Bf109 damaged, while other pilots were credited with two more probables – a Do215 and a Ju88. Although reported that the A.A. crews had shot down a Ju88, their claims for the day were for five Ju87s shot down, four probables and one damaged. It may be that a further Hurricane was also lost, some sources recording R.A.F. fighter losses for this day as five Hurricanes and three pilots. After the fight had ended John Pain went out in a Magister to look for survivors and found two German aircrew hanging onto a lifebuoy off Ghajn Tuffieha. They were picked up by a Kalafrana H.S.L. (High Speed Launch) and proved to be the crew of a Ju87. Eyewitnesses stated that one Ju87 crashed at Ras Hanzir in the inner part of Grand Harbour, beneath Corradino Heights. Another came down near the Leprosy Hospital, St. Bartholomew's, and pieces of wreckage from these two aircraft are still currently on display in the Malta War Museum.

II/St.G 1 in fact lost three Ju87s, two 4th Staffel aircraft flown by Fw. Johannes Braun (6G+PR) and Uffz. Heinz Langreder (6G+ER) being reported missing, while Oblt. Kurt Reumann, commander of 6th. Staffel, was seen to be shot down in 6G+GT by Hurricanes. Another aircraft, this one from 5th. Staffel, was also hit and damaged by Hurricanes, the gunner, Uffz. Robert Kolland, being wounded. One Ju87 of III/St.G 1, flown by Hpt. Helmut Mahlke, was hit in the starboard wing by an A.A. burst, and only by luck and much skill was he able to regain Sicily and land safely.

28/2/ – 2/3/41

Few interceptions took place over the next few days as the R.A.F. licked its wounds. 'A' Flight encountered four Bf110s over the island on 28th., but despite a general mix-up, heavy cloud allowed any pilot who felt threatened a quick avenue of retreat, and no claims resulted. During this time, despite the rapidly deteriorating availability of Hurricanes, the few remaining Fulmars were taking a 'low key' role. The policy was for them to remain around the fringes of a raid and try and pick off stragglers, leaving the 'infighting' to the Hurricanes. Little success had been achieved as they were too slow to have much chance of catching a fleeing Ju88 or Bf110. On 2 March however, they were called upon to play a more central part in the defence, as Desmond Vincent-Jones relates: "The day started auspiciously when an Heinkel 111 suddenly appeared out of the dawn mist with undercarriage down and started to make an approach to the main runway, presumably mistaking Hal Far for its own base airfield in Sicily. The aircraft was just about to touch down when the pilot found himself in unfamiliar surroundings and opened his throttle in time for his wheels to clear the cliff-edge at the end of the runway. He had achieved total surprise and there was complete silence until the first Bofors opened up when he was out to sea and on his way back to the mainland."

"At about 1100 hours a smallish raid was detected leaving Sicily on course for Malta. For some good reason no Hurricanes were available and orders were telephoned through for the Fulmars to get airborne and gain altitude over Hal Far. Bill Barnes took off with two others, one I believe was Orr, and had climbed to about 2,000 feet after making contact with the Malta Tower who told them the raid was coming in low and very fast." Müncheberg and his Kette from 7/JG 26 were on their way out on another hunting expedition. "Most of us were standing by the control tower when the Fortress guns opened up to the Northward, and coming through the Flak we saw a series of black dots approaching directly towards us and as they closed we recognised them as yellow-nosed Me109s. The Fulmars above us continued to circle totally oblivious, and we on the ground were powerless to warn them. We watched in horror as the enemy opened fire and chunks of metal could be seen falling off the luckless victim's wings and fuselage. The Me109s swept away out to sea and made no attempt to turn for a further attack. When we looked upwards again, we were amazed to see all three Fulmars still flying but firing emergency landing signals. By some miracle all three aircraft landed safely and by an even greater miracle none of the three pilots were wounded. It had seemed to us like certain death from the beginning of this hideous drama we had just witnessed. It was the end of daylight flying over Malta for the Fulmars. Barnes was laughing as he climbed out of his cockpit, and pointed at the huge hole in one wing-root made by a cannon shell and another through the opposite wing. The other two aircraft had been damaged but got off with bullet holes only."

This does not tie up entirely with the records of Hal Far, which noted that three Fulmars went up, and that one was damaged and the pilot slightly wounded. It also seems that at least one Hurricane had got into the air, for Sgt. 'Jock' Norwell of 261 Squadron noted in his logbook that he too was attacked by a Messerschmitt on this date, and his aircraft was damaged. Müncheberg and Fw. Johannsen each claimed a Hurricane shot down at 1045, both in the same location – obviously the Fulmars. It seems that official confirmation may not have been forthcoming, for the German O.K.W. records noted only a single Hurricane shot down during this day, while Müncheberg's claim was apparently classed as a 'probable', although it remained on his personal list of successes.

Vincent-Jones continues: "We decided that some sort of celebration would not be out of order on the occasion of this remarkable escape. 'Ginger' Hale, who had led 819 Squadron into Taranto harbour and had recently been appointed to command the Naval Section at Hal Far, suggested he should drive some of us, including the three lucky pilots into Valetta for dinner at the Union Club. This

160

sounded a good idea. Malta was on short rations and the menu was sparse but we must have consumed most of the champagne remaining in the club cellars. At about midnight we set off on our way back to Hal Far. 'Ginger' Hale was driving and Barnes was sitting between Robert Henley and myself in the back seat. As we were crossing the plain of Birzebbugia nearing the air station, we were surprised to hear a sharp report. Someone said "We've had a blow-out rear tyre" and Hale pulled to the side of the road. My arm was along the top of the back seat and I felt Barnes's head fall back. I at once thought that the poor fellow had had a pretty rough day and had gone to sleep as he hadn't made a sound. There was a bright moon and on looking closer I saw a dark smear coming from his mouth. Getting alarmed I pushed my hand under his jacket and withdrew it covered with blood. He was stone dead. Seldom can fate have played a stranger trick. Having saved him from almost certain death in the morning at the hands of the enemy, fate had collected him the same evening by a stray bullet fired in error by a Maltese Army recruit. Barnes was undoubtedly one of the finest officers and most courageous aviators that the Royal Navy has ever produced."

"It was afterwards discovered that the young Maltese soldier was on his first night as a sentry, with instructions to stop any passing car with his lamp and if the car didn't stop to fire his rifle over the top of it. His lamp had gone out and while he was relighting it, our car must have passed and he fired his rifle vaguely in our direction. The bullet ricochetted off a stone in the road and then passed exactly through the centre of the rear seat.

5/3/41

The next sizeable raid occurred on 5 March, and on this occasion 7/JG 26 was to enjoy some reinforcement for the first of two occasions. Some Bf109Es from I/JG 27 had reached Sicily on their way to Libya, and while on the island undertook one or two flights over Malta in company with the resident unit. On this afternoon at about 1700 an estimated sixty bombers approached the island, Hurricanes being scrambled to intercept. Flt.Lt. Whittingham led the interceptors, attacking a Ju88 and a Ju87, but seeing no result to his fire. Returning towards the island he saw five Ju88s heading out to sea and although he now had little ammunition left, attacked and thought that he had managed to damage one. Shortly after this he was attacked by a Bf110, but as this approached to about 100 yards it received a direct hit from an anti-aircraft shell and blew up. Sgt. Fred Robertson had gone off with seven other Hurricanes in V7116. At 1735 he spotted about sixty to seventy Ju88s, Bf109s and other types to the south of Luqa at 10,000 feet. Selecting a Ju88 – an aircraft of 4/LG 1 (L1+CM) flown by Lt. Reinhold Krause – he attacked from astern with three burst, seeing the starboard wing and engine catch fire. He followed the bomber down until it dived into the sea off Filfla, three survivors being seen in the water. At that point he was attacked by twelve Bf109s, but evaded and got in a good burst at one that overshot him. He saw this diving towards Filfla trailing clouds of black and white smoke, but was then chased by another Messerschmitt and failed to see what happened to it. A.A. personnel reported seeing it crash, and Robertson was credited with its destruction.

Meanwhile Sgt. Harry Ayre recorded that he was shot down after ten minutes in the air, but crash-landed unhurt and was soon up again in a new aircraft. On this occasion he claimed a Ju88 shot down, then shared with Plt.Off. Rippon and Plt.Off. Pain in shooting down a Do215; Rippon also shot down a Ju87, while Sgt. McDougal was seen to get another of these, but was then shot down himself by a Bf109. His Hurricane, V7102, crashed on land and he was killed. Pain also claimed a Bf110 probably shot down, and other pilots claimed damage to three Ju87s. The anti-aircraft gunners kept up a steady fire, claiming nine aircraft shot down, including the Bf110 which crashed near Takali, and four other aircraft damaged.

Meanwhile the German fighter pilots were making their own claims; Lt.Willi Kothmann of 1/JG 27 claimed one Hurricane at 1700 (probably Ayre), the only claim to be made by pilots of this unit over Malta during 1941. 7/JG 26 then arrived and Fw. Wagner claimed one Hurricane at 1730, Oblt. Müncheberg getting another two minutes later, while Gefr. Laub claimed a third at 1735. A pair of Messerschmitts made a strafing attack on St. Paul's Bay where a Sunderland flyingboat and the Loire 130 were slightly damaged at their moorings.

Both sides had again overclaimed substantially; only two Hurricanes had been lost – probably at least one Messerschmitt pilot thought that he had shot down Fred Robertson's aircraft. On the other side 4/LG 1 lost the Ju88 while St.G 1

March 1941 brought more reinforcement Hurricanes for Malta. Five flew in on 6th., two of them piloted by Plt.Off. P.A. Mortimer (1) and Plt.Off. D.M. Whitney. (*D.M. Whitney*)

had two Ju87s brought down, one (J9+CH) from 7th. Staffel, flown by Uffz. Wilhelm Singer, going into the sea, while a 9th. Staffel aircraft (6G + KR), piloted by Fw. Georg Latzelberger, was destroyed in a forced-landing having been hit by both fighters and A.A. fire. A third aircraft from III Gruppe returned with a wounded gunner. The Stab/St.G 1 lost two Bf110Es in the Hal Far area, one (DB + NO) flown by the Geschwader Adjutant, Hptm. Erich Müller, was shot down by A.A. fire, the other (KB + NC), piloted by the Staffel Kapitan, Oblt. Rudolf Gunther, was shot down by fighters, this probably the 'Do215' claimed jointly by Rippon, Pain and Ayre. No Bf109s were lost. It is likely that the majority of the A.A. claims related to aircraft shot down by the fighters but also fired on by the guns – possibly including some of the Hurricanes! Flg. Off. Gerald Bellamy recalls a rather macabre incident following this raid. The two Bf110s had crashed nearby, and "... they were scattered over a wide area – we all went out to view the wrecks. At luncheon, Bradbury's Alsation dog was found to have retrieved a boot of a German airman and was chewing it under the table. Unfortunately it still contained the foot!"

261 Squadron received some welcome reinforcements next day when five Hurricanes flew in from Egypt, led by two 148 Squadron Wellingtons, which carried two additional fighter pilots as passengers. Most of these new arrivals had reached the area with the deliveries of Hurricanes by H.M.S. 'Furious' as already recounted, and had thus been languishing in the Pilots' Pool at Ismailia, awaiting posting to a unit. Of the five who flew in the Hurricanes, three officers had previously gained operational experience in England. Plt.Off. C.K. Gray from 43 Squadron already had two victories to his credit, while Plt.Off. P.A. Mortimer, ex 257 Squadron, had one and one shared; Plt.Off. D.M. Whitney, a New Zealander, had served with 17 Squadron. The other members of the group were Sgts. A. Livingston, a Scot, and F.J. Jessop; flying in the Wellingtons were Sgts. H.J. Kelly and J.T. Hitching.

Plt.Off. Doug Whitney, a New Zealand pilot with 261 Squadron. (*D.M. Whitney*)

For some the stay was to be very brief; next morning (7th.) Flg.Off. Boys-Stones took off in one of 69 Squadron's Marylands (AR706) for a reconnaissance over the Fliegerkorps X headquarters area at Taormina. He was chased by fighters, but escaped, and during his return flight attacked and damaged a Z.506B floatplane. As the Bf109s were known to be about, Hurricanes were sent up to cover its return to base, but one of these – P2645 flown by Sgt. Jessop on his first local flight – was shot down by Fw. Kestel of 7/JG 26, the pilot being wounded. At the same time Lt. Mietusch attacked the Maryland, mistaking it for a Blenheim. Wg.Cdr. Jonas recalls: "... just as the Maryland crossed the coast preparatory to landing at Luqa, it was set upon by six Messerschmitts. In spite of the fact that one brave Hurricane came to the rescue (Jessop), the Maryland was soon on fire in one engine, and the rear gunner (Sgt. J. Levy) killed by a cannon shell in the chest. The navigator (Sgt. Alexander), in spite of being wedged within the narrow confines of the glass nose, managed to scramble out, and descended safely by parachute. And at barely 250 feet (after holding the aircraft steady to allow Alexander to get out), the pilot himself went head first over the side. But to bale out at 250 feet was tempting Fate too much – and although the parachute had just time to spring out of its canvas cover before the pilot hit the ground, no time remained for the canopy to open and check his fall. Freddie Moore had

Sunderland L2164 of 228 Squadron was shot up on the water in St. Paul's Bay on 7 March by Bf109Es of 7/JG26. A second attack on 10th. set the aircraft on fire. She is seen here, well ablaze. (*National War Museum Assoc.*)

L2164 with the fire quenched. The aircraft sank when efforts were made to tow it ashore. (*National War Museum Assoc.*)

watched the attack by the fighters, and ten minutes later, after a hectic cross-country drive in his little sports car, he was kneeling beside the pilot. Incredible to believe, although he had fallen unchecked for over 200 feet, onto solid rock below, the pilot was still alive, although dying from multiple injuries. "I think I must have left things a bit late", was all he said. The flaming Maryland had crashed a mile or so North of Dingli.

During this combat a second Hurricane was claimed by Fw. Kühdorf, but this appears not to have been confirmed; 261 Squadron recorded however that several other Hurricanes were damaged during the engagement. Two Messerschmitts then again strafed St. Paul's Bay where Sunderland L2164 of 228 Squadron was badly damaged. Sgt. A.S. Jones got one of the Vickers 'K' guns into action from the midships position, but was killed at his post by the fire from the fighters. The anti-aircraft defences claimed one Bf109 shot down and an unidentified aircraft as a probable, but again the German fighters suffered no loss. On this same date Flg.Off. Adrian Warburton took another of 69 Squadron's Marylands out to photograph Taranto. He was chased out over the Adriatic by fighters and was obliged to come down at Tatoi airport near Athens. He flew back to Malta from Greece next day.

9/3/41

With few Luftwaffe bombers now left in Sicily, raids were desultory and of nuisance value during most of March, the main torment for the defenders remaining the ever-present Bf109Es of 7/JG 26. During 9 March numerous single aircraft appeared overhead to strafe Takali airfield. Here one Hurricane was burned out and two others slightly damaged during a morning attack by a single Ju88 escorted by four Bf110s. One of the Bf110s crashed at Nadur on Gozo Island, the crew being killed; the reason for this has not been discovered. During the afternoon a single reconnaissance Ju88 was intercepted by four Hurricanes flown by Plt.Off. Rippon, Sgt. Pickering and two others. Jim Pickering recorded: "... I pulled up underneath the e/a and gave him two bursts ... the e/a was last seen at sea level eight miles away heading towards Sicily with some speed but apparently little concern." Pickering's own aircraft was hit twice in the starboard mainplane by return fire.

10/3/41

Next day the Bf109s were back, strafing the flyingboat anchorage again, where Sunderlands T9046 and L2164 of 228 Squadron were both hit. L2164 was set on fire, having already been damaged during the previous attack on 7th., and was ultimately sunk after efforts had been made to tow it ashore. That night an unidentified pilot believed to be Plt.Off. Tony Rippon, claimed a Do215 shot down, and this was almost certainly a Bf110C night fighter of 1/NJG3 reported lost over Malta, Oblt. Horst von Weegmann and his gunner missing in L1+BH; a second aircraft was claimed damaged. On this date a Bf110E of III/ZG26 was also reported lost, having crashed on Pantelleria island, Lt. Arnold Hadlich and his gunner being killed. This may have been due to an accident, but two Ju88s of 5/LG 1 were badly damaged over Malta, presumably hit by A.A. fire and force-landed at Catania on their return.

Unusual visitor (1). A Focke-Wulf Fw200C of I/KG 40 lands at Comiso during a routine visit to Sicily from its base in Brittany. (*N. Malizia*)

166

The date was also marked by the announcement of the award of the D.F.M. to the veteran fighter pilot Sgt. Fred Robertson, whose personal score over the island now stood at eight. Away to the East the Mediterranean Fleet at Alexandria was greatly strengthened by the arrival of the Fleet carrier H.M.S. 'Formidable' as a replacement for 'Illustrious'. Aboard the vessel were the Fulmars of 803 Squadron and the Fairey Albacores – biplane torpedo-bombers of 826 and 829 Squadrons. Earlier in the month 806 Squadron's three remaining serviceable Fulmars had been flown from Malta to Egypt via El Adem, each aircraft carrying three aircrew; the ground party sailed for the same destination in a destroyer. Now the squadron, brought up to a strength of six Fulmars, went aboard 'Formidable' to reinforce that vessel's meagre fighter component.

Unusual visitor (2). A Dornier Do215 strategic reconnaissance aircraft seen at an airfield in Sicily, taxi-ing past a line of Savoia S.82 transports. (*Stato Maggiore*)

15–16/3/41

Reinforcement of the heavy bomber force in Egypt was still continuing during this period, and during the night of 14th/15th. four Wellingtons from the Reserve Flight, Stradishall (Suffolk), and a Maryland, were despatched from England, approaching the Malta zone early in the morning. One Wellington (W5644) did not arrive; a radio message was intercepted which stated merely "Being attacked", but nothing further was heard. The bomber had been caught a little to the North-West of Gozo by 7/JG 26 at 0750, and shot down by Oblt. Müncheberg; the crew were seen by him to be getting into a dinghy. Next day the Staffel was again over Malta, Gefr. Laub and Uffz. Leibing each claiming a Hurricane shot down, although apparently one was not confirmed, only one claim being recorded by

O.K.W. No Hurricanes were actually lost on this occasion, but A.H.Q. Malta confirmed that one Hurricane had been slightly damaged. This however would appear to have been in combat with Bf110s, rather than Bf109s. Flg. Off. Barber had led four Hurricanes off to patrol South of Malta, and these met four Bf110s head-on. Recalls 'Jock' Barber: "... I did three head-on attacks on four Bf110s – they just missed my radiator and shot away my controls. This happened South of the island at about 1,000 feet. However I managed to get back and land alright." Sgt. Robertson claimed one of the Messerschmitts damaged.

17/3/41

A convoy was safely escorted to the island from the Eastern Mediterranean during this period, following which 'Formidable's' air group launched an attack on Tripoli on 17th. During this operation Fulmars shot down two shadowers. Further efforts were made to strengthen the defences at this time by the despatch of one flight of Hurricanes from 274 Squadron in North Africa. This unit had played a major part in the successful First Libyan Campaign, and included a number of experienced fighter pilots in its ranks. Seven Hurricanes and eight pilots were to be sent, but at El Abqar, where refuelling took place, Plt.Off. T.B. Garland crashed and suffered slight burns. Against advice he continued the journey aboard the Wellington which navigated the aircraft in. The other pilots involved were Flg.Off. E.M. Mason, D.F.C., Flg.Offs. C.J. Laubscher (a South African from the Transvaal), J.S. Southwell, Plt.Off. D.F. Knight, and Sgts. T.A. Quinn, M.P. Davies and R.J. Goode. 'Imshi' Mason was at this time the leading

On 17 March 1941 a flight of Hurricanes were detached from 274 Squadron in the Western Desert to reinforce 261 Squadron on Malta. One of the pilots involved was Flg.Off. Charles Laubscher, a South African. He is seen here a year later with his Tomahawk fighter when once more serving in North Africa. (*C.J. Laubscher*)

'ace' of the Middle East theatre, having been credited with over 15 victories by the end of January 1941. Southwell and Davies were recent reinforcements, the former having gained two victories with 245 Squadron over Dunkirk, while the latter had served during the Battle of Britain with 1 and 213 Squadrons. These new reinforcements arrived only just before a resumption of activities which were swiftly to thin their ranks to an alarming extent.

Charles Laubscher recalls: "My feelings were mixed at this news (of the move to Malta). On the one hand there was at last the opportunity of some concentrated action and, with 'Imshi' leading us, one could feel reasonably confident. On the other there was the undoubted fact that we would be on the receiving end. The 'Illustrious' had been subjected to vicious bombing only a short time previously, and the defending fighters had been battered by swarms of Me109s and Macchis. There was one compensating factor, however. We were to fly across, which suited me, as I had a morbid fear of being torpedoed at sea. Long-range tanks were fitted and tested, guns were checked and the Hurricanes generally prepared for the flight from Benina (near Benghazi) to Malta. We set off from Amriyah on 13 March, and spent the night with 73 Squadron, as El Adem was unsafe due to the unfriendly attention it was receiving from enemy dive-bombers. Our escorting Wellington was delayed due to phenomenal sandstorms in the Delta area, and it was only on 18 March that it arrived and we set off for Benina to refuel before the sea leg to Malta. Micky Garland crashed on landing, and journeyed to Hal Far as a passenger aboard the Wimpey. It was a pity that he was not left with his aircraft, as he was put on standby as soon as we arrived at Takali, and killed on his first operation in Malta ... "

Another of the 274 Squadron pilots sent to Malta on 17 March 1941 was Flg.Off. Johnny Southwell. He was killed five days later when his Hurricane, V7799, was one of five shot down by 7/JG26. (*Mrs. Joy Strange via C.J. Laubscher*)

169

18/3/41

Meanwhile on 18th. the Hurricanes were scrambled again, this time meeting Italian fighters. John Pain (flying P3731): "This was a brawl with some 15 CR 42s in which the entire flight got mixed up some miles out to sea at about 18,000 feet between St. Paul's Bay and Sliema. This was the usual madhouse performance the Italians always seemed to put on – a real World War I-style dogfight. I got my first into the sea close off Sliema and the second was on the way out some miles further out and he went in without a top wing. The last one was not confirmed, but Whittingham, I think, confirmed the first." No details of any other claims by 261 Squadron pilots are available, but their opponents are believed to have been aircraft on the 23º Gruppo C.T., which had just returned from Libya. On arrival the 156º Gruppo Autonomo was disbanded to reinforce this unit. That night nine Swordfish from 830 Squadron raided Tripoli; K 5939 flown by Sub Lt. W.E. Grant failed to return, he and L/A W.E.J. Thompson being reported prisoners.

22/3/41

22 March was to prove a disastrous day for 261 Squadron. It began when four Hurricanes were scrambled at 0830 after a reported five Ju88s at 21,000 feet. Jim Pickering was one of the four: "I was Red 2 in company with Red 1 and Green Section when I saw a Ju88 engaged by A.A. about 1,000 feet above us ... he saw me at this height and turned in a circle onto my tail. I pulled round inside onto his tail and he dived away towards Sicily. I gave one deflection burst from port beam at about 350 yards and one careful stern burst from the same distance, but could not even keep pace with this shallow dive. Some of the A.A. was either poor shooting at the bandit or very accurate shooting at me!" However a He111 of 5/KG26 was hit over Valetta, the pilot and Staffelkapitän, Hptm. Teske and one of his crew being wounded.

Sgt. Richard Spyer, one of the pilots to survive the flight to Malta with the ill-fated Operation 'White' on 17 November, 1940, was lost on 22 March in Hurricane V7672, shot down by Bf109Es. (*via R. A. Spyer Senior*)

Ten more Ju88s were reported approaching Grand Harbour during the afternoon with an escort of twelve Bf109s, and eight Hurricanes were sent up in two formations. 'Jock' Hilton Barber was not flying on this date, and saw what happened from the ground: "I was swimming when a battle started overhead. Suddenly a Hurricane came down in a screaming dive and splashed into the sea. This turned out to be P2653, the aircraft I had ferried to Malta in June of the previous year. Terry Foxton was killed." Plt.Off. Doug Whitney was in the air and was credited with shooting down one Bf109 which had just shot down one of the Hurricanes. He adds: "I certainly recall Garland being shot down with Southwell. ... It was in fact on this very flight that they (the 109s) bagged five of our eight ... 'Chubby' Eliot and self had a bit of a dogfight for a while trying to get on each others' tails as we were not certain the other was not a 109 until we saw the roundels." Five Hurricanes had indeed gone down, one of them last being seen chasing a German aircraft out to sea. Apart from Flg.Off. Foxton, Plt.Off. Garland (V7493), Flg.Off. Southwell (V7799), Plt.Off. Knight (V7358) and Sgt. Spyer (V7672) were all reported missing. O.K.W. subsequently claimed that German fighters had shot down seven Hurricanes without loss, yet strangely only three claims can be found for 7/JG 26, one of which may not even have been confirmed. Fw. Kestel, Uffz. Ehlen and Fw. Kühdorf each claimed one Hurricane; again no Messerschmitts were actually lost. It is noteable that at this time R.A.F. Intelligence, which was frequently very accurate, reported the presence of *two* Staffeln of Bf109Es in Sicily, one from JG 26 and one from JG 3. It seems possible that such a latter unit may well have served briefly on the island at this time, and been involved in this particular combat. It was a sad and disillusioning blow for 261 Squadron, as John Pain relates: "This was the one day when we thought we had the edge. It was the first time we had managed to get eight aircraft into the air in one formation in the nearly two months I had been on the island. Of the eight pilots only three returned. Hamish Hamilton and I went on search for survivors but found nothing, except sea marks of crashed aircraft."

23/3/41

Next day – possibly anticipating that the fighter defences had been crippled by the attrition of the 22nd., the Axis appeared in force for the first time in some days as a further convoy reached the island. Just before 1500, Ju87s of III/St.G 1 left Sicily escorted by fifteen MC200s of the 6° Gruppo C.T. As they approached the island some 30 minutes later fourteen Hurricanes were scrambled and a savage melee developed over the island. Sqn. Ldr. Lambert who was leading on this occasion, ordered the formation to go into line astern for the attack. He attacked one Ju87 from behind, breaking away as the tail broke off his victim and it crashed into the sea. Sgt. Robertson, who was flying about fifth in the line of Hurricanes (in V7495), and who recorded that the success of the attack owed much to Lambert's leadership and positioning of the squadron, attacked another Stuka from astern, setting fire to the starboard wingroot. He then broke away as Lambert was also firing at this aircraft, and watched it crash into the sea. Robertson then attacked another Ju87 from dead ahead, a bullet from the dive-

171

bomber's forward guns hitting his aircraft and puncturing the main fuel tank in the port wing. He followed the dive-bomber round in a very tight turn and shot it down into the sea, but found that his own aircraft was by then burning fiercely. Climbing to 200 feet above the sea, he baled out about one mile south of Rabat, landing in a field between Zebbug and Luqa. Villagers from the former location soon reached him and carried him shoulder-high in a triumphal procession.

Meanwhile overhead the battle raged. Apart from Lambert's one and Robertson's two victories, Flt. Lt. Peacock-Edwards claimed two Ju87s shot down and one damaged, Plt.Off. Rippon two shot down, Plt.Off. Whitney and Sgt. Ayre one apiece, while others claimed one probable and one more damaged. Recorded Peacock-Edwards: "Very good sport. The Ju87s were picked off like flies." Blazing away below, the gunners claimed a further four shot down and one damaged. The escorting Macchi pilots attacked the Hurricanes, claiming four shot down, one by all the pilots jointly, and one each by Magg. Mezzetti, Mar. Daffarra and Serg.Magg. Stabile, but on this occasion Robertson's Hurricane was the only British casualty.

"Charles Laubscher and I were on standby," relates Gerald Bellamy, "and for some reason did not hear the scramble. Ju87s were dive-bombing the aerodrome. Charles dashed past my aircraft – I followed in haste but was too far from the slit trench to make it. I heard/saw a large bomb leave the Ju87 and was certain that it was coming straight at me. I threw myself flat and heard a 'whompf' and felt a mild warm blast of air. I was completely unharmed! Apparently I was on the edge of the crater and the main blast had gone over me. Had I been a few feet nearer the bomb I should have been blown to pieces – had I been a few feet further away I should have been cut to pieces by shrapnel. The only effect on me however, was a slight deafness for a few hours!"

Wg.Cdr. Jonas witnessed the whole attack from the ground at Luqa, and wrote: '.. and then we saw them: vic following vic of small grey forms, 15,000 feet, 16,000 feet, perhaps even higher. The guns were firing now ... little grey puffs miraculously appearing around the bombers, above, below, behind, before, rapidly increasing in size as the wind caught them. Still they came on ... the leaders were beginning to dive now. Sticks against the dashboards, diving, brakes on, down, down, down ... the more reckless pilots dived down through the barrage, but those with more vivid imaginations pulled out of their dives several hundred feet above the shellbursts. But the ground defences were already hitting ... a Ju87 disintegrated in front of us from a direct hit, while two others failed to pull out of their dives, disappearing vertically into the sea off the harbour entrance."

"Two eyes were not enough. There was so much to see. Quite clearly the bombs could be seen leaving the aircraft; sometimes one, sometimes two, sometimes even a salvo of four – small grey forms. Almost immediately, as they disappeared behind the buildings of Valetta, we saw the flash followed by the crump of bursting, and the black clouds of smoke rising vertically into the still air. Clustered in the doorway of the stone hut, intent and fascinated by the spectacle before us, we had forgotten our own fighters. Now was the time to attack the bombers, as they pulled out of their dives, snaking low over the water,

172

slow and cumbersome. Then they came, diving out of the sun to our right, each picking up a Ju87. Now they were firing; short rattling bursts. The rear gunner in the Ju87 just in front of us was also firing. One watched the tracer and wondered if bullets ever struck each other in the air."

"All our fighters were coming in now – the noise was tremendous – bombs, guns and engines mingled in discordant sound. Out to sea a Ju87 zig-zagged at 500 feet, followed by a relentless Hurricane. Suddenly, the Junkers belched a long tongue of red flame, straightened out for a moment and then spun down into the water. At the same time, a second Junkers glided past us, its airscrew slowly turning. It disappeared behind the rocky spur way to our left, to crash out of sight in some tiny stone-walled field. For a few minutes we slipped into the hut. The shrapnel and spent machine gun bullets pattered down among the cactus like rain. The strange medley of sounds continued outside – inviting and too exciting to miss."

"We clustered at the narrow doorway, resting our useless hands upon our heads as substitutes for steel helmets. There we watched the rout of the dive-bombers, but the shrapnel pattered down again, and we drew back into the doorway. But we soon emerged again, for curiosity overcame caution. A black pall of smoke hung over Valetta. The raid was over. How many bombers had been brought down? How many fighters had we lost? What damage had been done? We did not know the answers."

Actual German losses in fact seem to have been much lighter than were claimed; two Ju87Bs of the Gruppenstab were lost over Valetta, returning crews reporting that both Oblt. Walter Preis's aircraft (J9 + JK) and that of Lt. Leopold Jarosch (J9 + BH) had been shot down by fighters, while one Ju87R (J9 + YL) of 9/St.G 1 flown by Stfw. Hans Ries fell to A.A. fire. A further Ju87R of 8th Staffel was badly hit but got to within ten kilometres of the Sicilian coast before Uffz. Erich Kaubitzsch was forced to ditch in the sea. During the day a Cant Z.501 flyingboat of the 184ª Squadriglia R.M. was also lost, apparently to Malta fighters, and probably while searching for the downed German aircrew; the crew of this aircraft were rescued near the Sicilian coast.

A group of Italian fighter pilots of the 23º Gruppo Aut. C.T., all wearing kapok-filled life jackets. (*Longhi-Lucchini via N. Malizia*)

173

24–25/3/41

6° Gruppo was back over the island on 24th., this time seven MC200s escorting He111s of II/KG 26. Because the attack was a high level bombing raid the British identified all the raiders as Italian. Seven Hurricanes were sent off but made no contact. Despite this one Macchi of the 79ª Squadriglia was seen to go into the sea between Gozo and Cap Scalambria – possibly due to oxygen starvation of the pilot, Serg.Magg. Arnaldo Gandais, who was killed.

No fighter interceptions could be made again on 25th., but the A.A. was able to claim one Ju88 probable and two damaged – no actual losses being recorded by the Luftwaffe. On this date 228 Squadron left the island, which was no longer considered really safe for the flyingboats following the recent strafing. One of the aircrew leaving with the unit was Plt.Off. Nigel Maynard, son of the Malta A.O.C. The unit now moved to Alexandria, although a small servicing detachment was to be left at Kalafrana for several more weeks in order that Sunderlands might land there as a forward base.

28/3/41

The marauding Messerschmitts appeared over Malta again in the afternoon of 28 March, Lt. Mietusch claiming one Hurricane shot down at 1730, and Oblt. Müncheberg a second two minutes later, this crashing South of Gozo. Another of the 274 Squadron detachment, Sgt. Reg Goode, was shot down in V7340 and severely wounded, while Sgt. Livingston's aircraft was badly shot up, although he managed to force-land near Luqa.

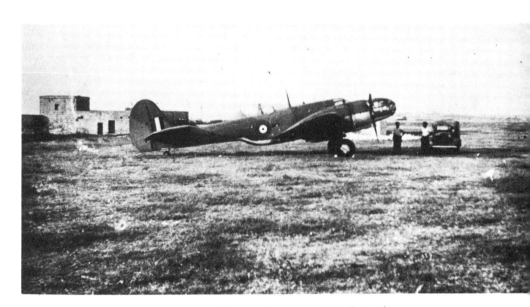

Maryland AR739 of 69 Squadron at Takali. (*J. Alton*)

During the previous day a major naval battle had ensued a few miles to the east, and had continued into the night – the 'Battle of Matapan'; a resounding defeat for the Italian Fleet. The first major victory for 'Ultra'. Although air units from Malta had not participated in the action, this day (29th.) a 69 Squadron Maryland was despatched from Luqa to reconnoitre the area. It failed to return. The then commanding officer of the reconnaissance unit recalled: "The naval battle off Cape Matapan occurred on 28th. In Malta the Navy knew little or nothing about what was happening – probably because of radio silence in the British Fleet. About midday on 29th. the Navy in Malta suddenly asked me whether I could search along the Greek coast for the remnants of the Italian Fleet which was believed to be escaping northwards. I despatched the standby crew – Flg.Off. F.R. Ainley with Sgt. G. Brown as navigator and Sgt. A.E. White as WOP/AG in AR727. They did not return."

"A few days later Athens advised that the aircraft had crashed in the sea close to an island – Zante. The pilot was killed. The navigator had survived with head injuries but the third crew member was O.K. I signalled to Athens asking them to designate the nearest airfield where I could pick up Brown and White in a Maryland. We never received a reply. By 6 April Greece was also being attacked by the Germans, and heavily blitzed. I was therefore delighted when one day in May they suddenly reported to me at Luqa. Brown still had some head bandages underneath a large Greek Air Force cap which, with reduced bandaging, lay

Pilots of 23° Gruppo Aut. C.T. at Comiso airfield in Spring 1941 in front of their CR 42s. L. to r. Serg. Felice Papini, Ten. Carlo Moruzzi, Mar. Augusto Brini. (*N. Malizia*)

almost around his neck. 'Sorry we are late back, Sir ... I expect you thought you had got rid of your two bad pennies!'"

"Apparently Ainley had told them he would try to force-land on a beach just after they flew near some naval ships. I assume the aircraft had been hit. It flipped over onto its back in shallow water. White had rescued Brown from the nose but Ainley was dead when they managed to get him out. The local Greek people were magnificent. They were taken to Athens, then to Southern Greece as the Germans advanced. Thence they escaped to Crete with White looking after Brown all the way. From Crete they escaped to Alexandria. Then they cadged a ride back to Malta on a ship – an ammuniton ship. They survived the bombing en route and reported to me as cheeky as ever. And of course wanting to be back on ops."

30/3/41

The end of March brought a fighter-bomber attack by aircraft of III/ZG 26. John Pain noted in his diary for 30th.: "First 110s bombed dispersal and lobbed three unexploded bombs between parked aircraft. Stones from one bomb damaged one Hurricane. Flg.Off. Bellamy, Flt.Lt. Peacock-Edwards and myself, all on tiptoe, moved the three Hurricanes to safety. Later the bomb disposal squad found that all three bombs were duds!" Despite such raids, A.H.Q. Malta was still able to record next day that 261 Squadron had 34 Hurricanes on strength.

Chapter 5

REINFORCEMENTS ARRIVE!

Operation 'Winch', 2–3 April 1941; the first Hurricane IIA aircraft to be delivered to Malta are seen here on the deck of H.M.S. 'Ark Royal', just about to depart from Gibraltar for the island. (*I.B. Westmacott*)

3/4/41

Early in April 'Ark Royal' again headed towards Malta, carrying aboard twelve new Hurricane IIAs which had been delivered to Gibraltar on 'Argus'. Operation 'Winch' was launched on 3 April when two Skuas led off the Hurricanes in two flights of six each. One flight was led by Flt.L.t. P.W.O. 'Boy' Mould, D.F.C., the other by Flg.Off. I.B. Westmacott (in Z3032). 'Boy' Mould had served in France with 1 Squadron in 1939/40, where he had shot down the first German aircraft to be claimed by R.A.F. fighters over the Western Front; he had over eight victories to his credit at this time. Innes Westmacott had flown with 56 Squadron during the Battle of Britain, claiming two and two shared victories before being shot down in flames and burned. The other ten pilots were Plt.Offs. H.F. Auger (French-Canadian), J.V. Marshall and P. Kennett, and Sgts. P.H. Waghorn, J.K. Pollard, E.R. Jessop, G. Lockwood, B.J. Vardy, H.H. Jennings and G.A. Walker. The flight was successfully undertaken to the area of Kerkenah Island, where two 228 Squadron Sunderlands met the Hurricanes and led them on the last leg to the island. Innes Westmacott recorded in his diary: "Was called at 0400 hrs. and got out of bed with great effort... "We eventually took off at about 0620 hrs. and everything went according to plan. The only snag was that Auger made a bad take-off and punctured one of his auxilliary tanks and broke off his tailwheel. He was very naturally scared stiff of using up all his remaining petrol and making a bad landing. However all was well. He landed at the first aerodrome he saw.... Most unfortunately, one of our Sgt. Pilots crashed on landing. He came in too fast and had to swing to avoid something at the end of his run – the undercarriage collapsed. It really is sickening to have an aeroplane, which is worth its weight in gold out here, broken through damned bad handling." This Hurricane was badly damaged, and ran into a parked aircraft; fortunately the latter suffered only minor damage. These first Mark IIs to reach Malta were a most welcome reinforcement, arriving at a time when Axis operations had fallen off, pending the German invasion of Yugoslavia and Greece. Soon after his arrival at Malta, Innes Westmacott confided his first impressions of his diary: "The main trouble here is transport. The bus service is not very convenient and there is a curfew at 2100, not that it worries us much! Only two private cars are allowd per squadron and motor bikes are scarce and expensive." More seriously, he noted: "From observations with one or two people I find that some of them are very scared of the 109s and morale could be better. I hope we shall be able to change all that."

During the day 'Ark Royal's' own fighters were active as the carriers headed back towards Gibraltar. At 0840 patrolling Yellow Section of 808 Squadron, led by Lt. Tillard, was advised of a 'shadower' in the heavily clouded skies, the three Fulmars separating to carry out individual searches. The Fulmar crewed by P.O.(A) D.E. Taylor/L/A G.C. O'Nion intercepted a Z.506B which made off on seeing the fighter and attempted to evade by making steep turns, but Taylor was quickly onto its tail and forced it down into the sea. The crew, with the exception of the apparently dead rear gunner, were seen inflating their dinghy and O'Nion took photographs of them and the sinking Cant as the Fulmar circled the scene. The Italians were later rescued by a Royal Navy destroyer. Twenty minutes after Taylor's combat the other two Fulmar pilots, Lts. Tillard and Royal Marine Lt. R.C. Hay, spotted another Z.506B as they were heading back towards the carrier, and attacked. This too made a number of very steep turns and made for nearby cloud, though its port engine was believed damaged, and possibly the rear gunner killed. The Fulmars continued searching for it and came across it (or the aircraft forced down by Taylor) floating on the sea; there were no signs of life. At least one Z.506B from the 287[a] Squadriglia was reported lost.

Hurricane IIAs ranged on 'Ark Royal' ready for take-off on 3 April 1941. (*I.B. Westmacott*)

6-9/4/41

7/JG 26 had left Sicily for Taranto during this period, operating over southern Yugoslavia on 6th., the day of the invasion of that country. Here Müncheberg shot down a Hawker Fury biplane of the Royal Yugoslav Air Force, destroying a second on the ground five minutes later. The Staffel returned to Sicily late on 8th.

69 Squadron's stripped photo-reconnaissance Hurricane I (V7101) in its pen ground crew. Although the tail of this aircraft is still camouflaged, the rest of it has already been painted blue overall. (*R.H. Barber*)

Meanwhile the arrival of the new Hurricanes and their pilots had allowed a number of the old 'workhorses' to be relieved. On 7th. Sgts. 'Jock' Norwell, Jim Pickering, Harry Ayre and 'Drac' Bowerman were flown from Luqa to Egypt in a Wellington piloted by newly-promoted and decorated Plt.Off. Lewin, G.C. Next day Flt.Lt. John Waters and Plt.Off. McAdam left for Gibraltar in a Sunderland on the first leg of the long journey home. On 9 April a Wellington on its way from Gibraltar was reported missing. This aircraft, W5677, flown by Plt.Off. J. Bridger, was carrying General Carton de Wiart, VC. newly-appointed head of the British Military Mission to Yugoslavia. The Wellington was obliged to ditch in the sea off the North African coast due to technical problems, the General and the crew being taken prisoners by the Italians.

During the night of 10/11 April Innes Westmacott undertook his first stint of night duty. He recorded: "Spent last night sleeping on a stretcher in the bus at dispersal point. There was no raid so we did not have to go up. Usually the two pilots who are on night duty sleep in the ambulance but the driver and medical orderly who also sleep in it had worked up a terrific 'fug' – 'Imshi' Mason and I felt we could not cope with the smell of unwashed feet, etc., so we dragged the two stretchers out."

11/4/41

A relatively strong force of fighters approached Malta on 11 April, apparently as cover for a Luftwaffe reconnaissance aircraft. Twelve MC200s of the 17° Gruppo under the command of Magg. Bruno Brambilla, covered by six CR 42s from the 23° Gruppo led by Ten.Col. Falconi, swept over the island, while the Bf109Es of 7/JG 26 also made for the same location. Numbers of Hurricanes were scrambled at various times during the mid-morning. Sgt. Deacon made his first sortie in V3978, seeing five CR 42s, but being unable to engage these. A little later two of the new Hurricane IIs, flown by Plt.Off. Peter Kennett and Sgt. Waghorn, intercepted a Ju88 and were reported to have shot it down. At that moment both were bounced by Bf109s, and were shot down. Their aircraft, Z3036 and Z2904, both crashed into the sea; Kennett got out and was seen by Sqn.Ldr. Lambert swimming and waving vigorously. However there was a long delay in sending out a rescue launch as the raid was still on, and he was dead when eventually picked up; Waghorn was also killed. Recorded Westmacott that evening: "Plt.Off. Kennett and Sgt. Waghorn killed.... It is the same old story – no one was looking behind. It is frightfully difficult to make inexperienced pilots realise the necessity of even so small a formation as two aircraft keeping one up above looking out while the other is attacking the Hun.... Not very long ago he (Kennett) told me he was sure he was going to be killed."

Meanwhile at 1130 eight more Hurricanes had taken off from Takali, Sgt. Deacon included, making his second sortie of the day in P3978. About ten minutes after take off Deacon had reached a position eight miles East of Filfla and a height of 10,000 feet. At that point he was attacked from behind and looking round, spotted two formations of Bf109s and MC200s, totalling an estimated twenty aircraft. Deacon had taken over the head of the formation as

On 11 April 1941 five Hurricanes were shot down in combat. Sgt. A.H. Deacon was shot-up by Bf109Es and stood P3978 on its nose when the undercarriage collapsed on landing. Note the 806 Squadron Fulmar in the background. (note panel in cockpit canopy smashed by a bullet.) (*A.H. Deacon*)

the leader's R/T was not working, and calling a warning to the other pilots, he swung into the attack on one Messerschmitt from the quarter position, breaking away to attack a second similarly, though in neither case did he observe any results. He then attacked a third which went down in a vertical dive, apparently into the sea. As he circled to watch this, he was attacked by two more Messerschmitts and his Hurricane was hit, the windscreen being smashed and the cockpit filling with smoke. Thinking that the aircraft was on fire, he tried to land at once at Takali, but was driven off by the ground defences, heading instead for Hal Far. Here, after running 50 yards, the undercarriage of his damaged aircraft collapsed and he was slightly injured in the resultant crash. Another of the Hurricane Is, V7116, was also badly shot-up and Plt.Off. Mortimer crash-landed this, also being slightly injured. Plt.Off. Doug Whitney also crash-landed in V7418, but was unhurt. He claimed one Bf109 shot down, but recorded of his own aircraft in his logbook: "Left me with one strand of rudder wire."

Plt. Off. P.A. Mortimer crash-landed V7116 after being badly shot-up by Bf109Es on 11 April 1941. (*I.B. Westmacott & D.M. Shitney*)

Wg.Cdr. J.E. Allen, the Hal Far station commander, reported seeing Deacon's combat and confirmed observing one Messerschmitt crash into the sea; Deacon was subsequently credited with one destroyed as a result. Again however, no Bf109Es were lost, although a reconnaissance Bf110C (4U + ZK of 2(F)/123 flown by Lt. Johann Scharringhausen, was reported shot down by fighters 40 kilometres from Gozo. This may well have been the aircraft seen to crash, and although Kennett and Waghorn were credited posthumously with a Ju88 probably destroyed, this could well have been their victim, no Ju88s being reported missing on this date. Other pilots were credited with two CR 42s probably shot down, and Deacon with two more Bf109s damaged. The Italians reported no losses, their pilots seeing three Hurricanes, but not engaging them. They strafed one of the airfields, claiming one bomber destroyed and several damaged.

The German fighters made three claims only, Joachim Müncheberg shooting down one Hurricane south-east of the island at 1130, and a second near St. Paul's Bay at 1153, while Fw. Johannsen also claimed one in the latter area at 1150. Münchenberg's second victim crashed near a crossroads at Wardia with the pilot apparently dead; this may have been Mortimer's aircraft. At the close of hostilities that evening A.H.Q. Malta issued a communique stating that since the beginning of the fighting over the island, Malta's defences had been credited with 132 destroyed, 44 probably destroyed and 58 damaged for the loss of 29 fighters, ten of the pilots having been saved.

11–12/4/41

During the night of 11th./12th. Plt.Off. Hamilton was scrambled soon after midnight, still wearing his pyjamas, and soon spotted a Ju87, an aircraft of 9/St.G 1 flown by Lt. Werner Zühlke, which he attacked and claimed shot down. A similar claim was submitted by the guns. Lt. Zühlke's aircraft (J9 + BL) crashed just behind the hangars at Takali, he and his gunner losing their lives. The next night it was the turn of 830 Squadron's Swordfish to strike at the enemy. During the day a Maryland of 69 Squadron, flown by Sqn.Ldr. Whiteley, had sighted a convoy of five freighters escorted by three destroyers to the south-west of Pantelleria. A Swordfish was despatched to shadow while seven others were readied and armed (six with torpedoes, one with bombs) in preparation for a night strike. Just before 2100 the attack commenced in the face of intense A.A. fire and two Swordfish (L7689 and P4065) were hit, both force-landing on the Tunisian coast near Hammamet. Sub Lt. R.N. Dawson, P.O.(A) C.H. Wines and their TAGs were captured.

13/4/41

Four raids were made on Malta on Sunday 13th., but the Hurricanes were involved in escorting four destroyers into harbour much of the day, and only two interceptions were made. On one of these Flt.Lt. 'Imshi' Mason was up in Z2838 with Flg.Off. Westmacott acting as 'weaver' above and behind to cover him. As Westmacott turned into one leg of his 'weave' Mason saw below him four Bf109s, and being well-positioned up-sun, dropped like a hawk onto them, his departure not being noticed by Westmacott, who remained aloft wondering where the other Hurricane had gone. Mason meanwhile attacked one Messerschmitt which at once went straight down, but the others attacked him and one got three hits on his aircraft, which shattered the windscreen and wounded him in the hand as he broke away. He was now 15 miles from land, so had to fight his way back. With instrument panel shattered and the cockpit full of bullet holes, he was forced down to sea level where the engine stopped and the aircraft started to burn on its left side. Unfortunately he made the mistake of undoing his straps before force-landing in the water and was thrown forward, breaking his nose on the remnants of the windscreen as one of the Messerschmitts passed low overhead. He started to swim, but was picked up 50 minutes later and returned to land and hospital. It was the end of his flying on Malta. Witnesses reported that both he and the Bf109 he had first attacked had been seen to come down, and he was credited with one victory. Another Bf109 was claimed shot down during this particular raid by Flt.Lt. Peacock-Edwards, but despite these two claims, again no Messerschmitts were lost. Peacock-Edwards' V7472 was badly hit and he crash-landed at Hal Far; the aircraft broke its back and was a write-off. Gefr. Laub and Fw. Wagner of 7:JG 26 both submitted claims for Hurricanes shot down, but O.K.W. recorded only one confirmed.

Leader of the 274 Squadron flight sent to Malta, Flg.Off. E.M. 'Imshi' Mason, D.F.C., was shot down on 13 April 1941 by a Bf109E, and forced to ditch into the sea. He is seen here after rescue and medical treatment, with a broken nose and bullet wound in his right hand. (*J.V. Marshall*)

This date also saw the departure from the Middle East of the old carrier 'Eagle', which left via the Suez Canal, whilst the headquarters of Fliegerkorps X moved from Sicily to direct operations over the Eastern Mediterranean and Aegean. However Malta welcomed the arrival of the 10th. Submarine Flotilla – the offensive striking power of the island was being gradually built up again.

14/4/41

Next morning, 14th, Flg.Off. Westmacott and Sgt. Deacon were scrambled before dawn as an unidentified 'plot' had appeared on the radar, approaching St. Paul's Bay fast and low. Westmacott saw tracer at low level in the direction of Luqa and thought it was fire from an enemy aircraft – in fact it was the airfield's own machine guns engaging the intruder. Deacon heard over the radio that a Bf110 was attacking Luqa, and going to investigate, shot at the aircraft without obvious effect. Westmacott had headed for Kalafrana where he saw a large twin-engined aircraft below and under fire, which appeared to be a Ju88. He fired, but at once saw that it was a Maryland, banking away as it dived vertically for the sea. It was a fact Adrian Warburton was out on an early air test prior to a sortie in AR735. He had to belly-land his aircraft on return to land, as it had been damaged in the starboard engine and undercarriage! However a Ju88 of 7/KG 30 was hit over Malta and crash-landed on return to Catania.

During the day Flg.Off. 'Jock' Barber left 261 Squadron on posting to A.H.Q. The last of the original Hurricane pilots still with the squadron, during his almost ten months of operations he had flown over 90 sorties, claimed three and one shared shot down and at least three damaged. After a brief rest he would join 69 Squadron and fly 28 reconnaissance sorties during the next three months.

15/4/41

Another 69 Squadron Maryland went out on 15 April, Sqn.Ldr. Whiteley at the controls. Leaving at midday he headed for the Tunisian coast in bad weather. As he approached the coastline he passed over a merchant ship. Having made landfall and fixed his position, he returned to the location, spotting a convoy of five merchant vessels and three escorting destroyers. Staying in the clouds, he radioed the position, course and speed, continuing to shadow the vessels until obliged to return, when Flg.Off. J.R. Bloxham took over. That night Capt. P.J. Mack's destroyer flotilla sailed from Malta, catching the Italian vessels and sinking them all, for the loss of H.M.S. 'Mohawk'. This latter vessel was hit by two torpedoes fired from the damaged Italian destroyer 'Tarigo', which had been taken over by Sottotenente di Vascello Ettore Bisagno, the only surviving officer, after the commander had been killed; the British ship went down near Kerkenah Island, but all the crew were rescued. Italian losses included the destroyers 'Tarigo', 'Lampo' and 'Baleno', and the merchant vessels 'Sabaudia', 'Aegina', 'Adana', 'Iserlohn' and 'Arta'. This was to be the last major action by the 14th. Destroyer Flotilla before the arrival on 29 April of the 5th. Destroyer Flotilla, which was commanded by Capt. Lord Louis Mountbatten in H.M.S. 'Kelly'.

There followed some weeks of relative quiet over the island, with only desulatory engagements, many of which can be listed briefly: On 17th. an unidentified Hurricane pilot claimed a Bf110 damaged; a Bf110C of 1/NJG 3 force-landed in the sea off Malta, Fw. Wolfgang Goldecker and his gunner being rescued by their own air/sea/rescue unit. A Ju88 of 7/KG 30 was lost over the island the same night, Uffz. Arthur Paproski and his crew in 4D+ER perishing. Two days later two Ju87s of III/St.G 1 flown by Lt. Klaus Steeg (J9+ZL) and Ofhr. Teutloff (J9+CK) were shot down by A.A. fire, the crews being reported missing. Other Stukas were successful in sinking the Panama-registered freighter 'Margit', which was caught in harbour.

20/4/41

On 20 April nine CR 42s of 23° Gruppo and 15 MC200s of 17° Gruppo escorted three S.79s of the 87° Gruppo B.T. over Valetta. Two Hurricanes intercepted, led by Flg.Off. Charles Laubscher, who recalls: "I was detailed with 'Tiger' Pain to give top cover to the squadron on the 20th. and we were allotted two of the new machines (Mark IIs). Operations reported that a big raid was building up over Sicily and shortly afterwards all aircraft were scrambled. We took off towards Rabat hill as usual and, as we wheeled to the south-west, it was evident how well the Mark IIs climbed. Although laterally we were little more than abreast of the squadron we were already six or seven hundred feet above them. We held our climb at full throttle, 'Tiger' on my starboard flank, and searched the sky for enemy fighters while trying to keep an eye on the squadron to port and soon well below us.'

"I think we had reached about 11,000 feet when the barrage opened up over Valetta and, against the white puffs, I saw seven biplanes heading directly towards us in a shallow vic formation. CR 42s! This was literally Manna from Heaven! For once we had height advantage, possibly only 300 or 400 feet, but sufficient, I believe, for their top mainplanes to conceal us from their pilots' sight. I wheeled left towards them and called 'Tiger' on the R/T to take the outside man on their port flank while I took the leader. We closed rapidly and I opened fire at about 800 yards sighting a little high at first to allow for the distance and then dropping my bead to centre on the machine. Things happen fast in a head-on attack and in two or three seconds we had passed directly over them. I immediately went into a steep turn to port to attack them again. I saw to my great satisfaction that the centre of the vic was empty and there were only two planes on their left, which probably meant that 'Tiger's' target had also gone down. At the same moment two Bf109s which had obviously stationed themselves too high to catch us in our initial attack, flashed past in a steep dive and then I was within range of the remaining Italian pilots once again."

"The five survivors in the CR 42 formation were swinging to their right towards and below me, which made it difficult to attack the three planes nearest me, so I chose the outer of the two planes on their left, laid off a deflection and opened fire again. My tracer passed in line with the machine but behind it, and rather than stop firing, I pulled back steadily on my control column until the tracers crept along the rear of the machine and into the cockpit. I knew immediately that the pilot was finished and stopped firing. The CR 42 hung on its side for a moment and then slipped gently into a dive. I did not watch him all the way but looked for another target. The sky now suddenly seemed clear except for a CR 42 going down in a spin ahead of me. I gave him a full deflection burst for good measure and then my ammunition ran out. It was time to return home so I jerked the machine into a spiral dive, just in case the remaining CR 42s or the two 109s were still in the vicinity, flattened out at about 800 feet and jinked my way back to Takali. It was a wonderful feeling to put up an affirmative two fingers as the mechanic helped me taxi in. That night Operations confirmed my claim for two CR 42s shot down. 'Tiger' also had his victory confirmed and the A.A. batteries claimed another – four out of seven destroyed – not a bad effort, we felt, particularly as the squadron had spent their time in a defensive circle!"

John Pain, who had flown Z3032, adds: "I got one confirmed and one unconfirmed. I was then attacked by six 109s and diced with them without anything firm being achieved other then preserving my own neck. When I got clear of them I went down almost to sea level and there were two holes in the water about where my two would have gone in. There was no other sign of wreckage of any other aircraft. I did not see Laubscher's two get hit, probably because I was busy myself. He said later he saw the 109s and took off for home. He was down and refuelled and re-armed when I got back." Italian records show only one CR 42 missing on this date, Serg. Giuseppe Sanguettoli of the 74ª Squadriglia being killed; the pilots of the 23° Gruppo claimed one Hurricane shot down between them. An MC200 pilot claimed one Hurricane damaged, and it is probable that it was these fighters, rather than Bf 109s, which attacked Laubscher and/or Pain subsequent to their fight with the biplanes.

261 Squadron Sergeant Pilots at Takali late in April 1941. L. to r., rear; T.A. Quinn, L.J. Dexter, P.L. Jordan; middle; L. Davies, M.P. Davies, R.J. Goode, E.R. Jessop, A. Livingston, E.L. Lawrence, A.W. Jolly; front; D.C. Smith. (*via P.L Jordan*)

There was a further skirmish between 261 Squadron and 7/JG26 this day during which a Hurricane pilot, believed to have been Sgt. Hyde, claimed a Bf109 shot down and one damaged. No losses were reported by the German unit, but Lt. Klaus Mietusch claimed one Hurricane shot down for his eighth victory. His victim was Flg.Off. Charles Laubscher, who remembers: "We were flying across the southern end of the island when Control came on the air with the warning that two bogeys were in our area. The R/T was bad and I thought he said 'below you' so I concentrated on that section of the sky almost exclusively, leaving it to Dick to watch above us. Suddenly he swung up close to my port side, waggling his wings frantically and pointing downwards. I thought he had seen the enemy aircraft and, as he winged over into a steep dive I followed him without question. Our speed built up rapidly and the inside of my cockpit started to mist up. I tried to pull the canopy back but it was impossible against the dive so I flattened out and throttled back. As my speed dropped I again tried to open the hood, fortunately with my left hand. Suddenly there was an ominous popping of cannon fire behind me and little white balls seemed to float past on both sides of the cockpit. I dropped my right wing suddenly as if I were turning into the cloud and immediately swung over into a steep left hand turn. There was a split second of violent clattering as cannon shells hit the machine and then I was clear, and in a 270° turn which took me back across my flight path and into the safety of that wonderful cloud. Even then I jinked from side to side as I pulled the hood back. I gave myself a minute or two to get my nerves under control and ventured outside the cloud, briefly at first then more confidently when it was apparent that the danger had passed, for the sky was clear of aircraft. I looked at my port wing to judge the extent of the damage and saw some nasty holes there while my instrument panel had also taken a slight hammering. It was obvious that my aircraft was not in a condition for any further fighting and I flew a zig-zag course back to the 'drome keeping a very watchful eye on the sky around me. When I landed and taxied to the dispersal point an awed group of aircraftsmen crowded around the machine to examine the damage. I was told later by the Flight Sergeant that they counted five cannon and thirty 7.62mm holes in the machine. One of the light calibre bullets had missed the top of my head by an inch and a half!!"

Also during this day as He111P bomber of 5/KG 4, one of several units passing through Sicily following action during the early stages of the Balkan Campaign, force-landed in the sea after a raid on Valetta. The crew were later rescued. A returning Heinkel of 6/KG 26 reported that its gunner had baled out over Malta for unknown reasons – there is no record of him landing safely. Next evening the Bf 109s of 7/JG 26 escorted a photo-reconnaissance aircraft over Malta, and here at 1807 Oblt. Müncheberg shot down Flg.Off. Auger in Hurricane Z3032 south-east of Hal Far. The pilot baled out into the sea, while the aircraft crashed some distance off Delimara Point. John Pain: "He landed safely in the drink between Filfla and the main island only a short distance from the cliff. He was seen to wave that he was O.K. to one of the other aircraft. He was not picked up by

A.S.R. largely due to the delay in allowing them to put to sea. We were given to understand that the A.S.R. boats did not put out on the express orders of the A.O.C. that they would be too vulnerable to air attack. This incident caused a very serious morale problem with all pilots and a number of letters were written to the A.O.C., stating our anger at the loss of Auger." Hurricanes subsequently searched until it was too dark to see, but no sign of the missing Auger could be found.

25 April: a night raid destroyed a Maryland (AR705) and a Magister at Luqa.
26 April: Plt.Off. Doug Whitney recorded in his logbook: "Takali blitzed. 44 bombs on 'drome. Took off at dawn, bomb craters and all!"
27 April: Sgt. Len Davies noted in his logbook: "Dawn patrol. Leading Sgt. Quinn. Had a slight argument with a Sunderland but left it O.K."
28 April: a Sunderland (P9600) of 10 R.A.A.F. Squadron on detachment at Gibraltar, flown to Malta by Sqn.Ldr. Podger to deliver maintenance crews for a Beaufighter unit.

27/4/41

Meanwhile on 27th. further welcome reinforcements were again on their way to the island. Under the codename Operation 'Dunlop' twenty-four Hurricanes and twenty-six pilots were carried towards the island on 'Ark Royal'. In charge of flying off on the carrier was Wg.Cdr. P.J.H. 'Bull' Halahan, D.F.C., a Battle of France veteran. He despatched the Hurricanes in three flights, each led by a Fulmar, while from Malta three Marylands and a Sunderland set out to meet the incoming formation and lead them in. A He111 appeared over the Fleet soon after the Hurricanes had departed and this was chased by the Fulmar patrol but managed to evade them and escape. Flg.Off. N.P.W. Hancock was leading the first seven Hurricanes, this flight meeting Sunderland L5807 of 228 Squadron as planned, and reaching the island without any problems. As they approached from the South, the pilots watched the flyingboat go down and land at Kalafrana, but at that moment Hancock saw two Bf109Es approaching, and thought for a moment that they were about to attack the Hurricanes. Instead the Kette, led by the intrepid Müncheberg, dived after the Sunderland strafing it as it taxied to its moorings, and sinking it. Flt.Lt. L.G.M. Rees, the pilot of the Sunderland reported: "My aircraft was launched at last light the evening before the sortie since it was dangerous at that time to leave an aircraft on moorings in daylight where it could be easy prey to enemy aircraft. I took off at the first light and made the rendezvous as planned and found the fighters had just become airborne. They formated on me and I led the formation back to the island. The Hurricanes were to land at Hal Far aerodrome and I circled that aerodrome until I had seen them all land safely. I then took my own aircraft to Kalafrana, landed and moored onto the slipway buoy. Almost before the mooring was completed the beaching party were towing out the beaching legs in order to get the aircraft into the hangar as soon as possible. I left the aircraft in order to go for de-briefing but I got as far only as the jetty when an attack was made on the Sunderland by three Me109 aircraft. They dived down from out of the sun to the south and in view of the short space of time that had elapsed since the aircraft had landed it is almost certain that the enemy aircraft must have seen the Sunderland in the air. A fuel tank in the port wingroot was holed by the attack and a fire started. This fire grew very rapidly and in a short time the port wing was burnt away. The fire spread to the rest of the aircraft and was only extinguished by the aircraft sinking."

"One member of my crew was hit between the legs and although he got ashore and was able to walk he was a very worried man until the M.O. assured him that his marriage prospects were in no way diminished". The Sunderland's midship gunner, L.A.C. D.A.J. Taylor (later a Sqn. Ldr.) continues: "When the Sunderland started to burn it started to drift towards a crane, which was, together with the surrounding area, the responsibility of the Royal Navy, and was used for torpedo storage. A power boat attempted to tow the burning wreck out into the bay but the flyingboat sunk before there was any further calamity." The reader will have noticed interesting and contradictory differences of detail between the accounts of Hancock and Rees, which have not been resolved – typical of the problems facing the latter-day historian!

This however, was the only unscheduled interruption, and twenty-three of the twenty-four Hurricanes landed safely on the island. The arrival of this strong reinforcement, following so soon on the heels of the 'Winch' arrivals on 3 April, now presented the beginnings of an overcrowding problem at Luqa and Hal Far. The decision was therefore taken to again begin basing some of the fighters on the third airfield at Takali on a permanent basis. The new pilots were:

Flt.Lt. C.G.St.D. Jeffries	Flg.Off. N.P.W. Hancock	Flg.Off. N.A.R. Doughty
Plt.Off. P.D. Thompson	Plt.Off. R.A. Innes	Plt.Off. P.J.A. Thompson
Plt.Off. B.M. Cavan	Plt.Off. R.C. Graves	Plt.Off. A.J. Reeves
Plt.Off. G.G. Bailey	Plt.Off. J.H.S. Haig	Plt.Off. D. Winton
Plt.Off. J.E. Hall	Plt.Off. D.C.B. Robertson	Plt.Off. A.S. Dredge
Plt.Off. R.T. Saunders	Sgt. H. Burton	Sgt. E.L. Lawrence
Sgt. R.A. Branson	Sgt. P.L. Jordan	Sgt. A.W. Jolly
Sgt. R. Ottey	Sgt. B.C. Walmsley	Sgt. D.C. Smith
Sgt. E.V. Wynne	Sgt. F.G. Sheppard	

Several of the new arrivals were experienced fighter pilots. Flt.Lt. Jeffries had gained some three victories with 3 Squadron in France; Flg.Off. Hancock had flown in France and the Battle of Britain with 1 Squadron, while Plt.Off. P.D. Thompson had flown in 32 and 605 Squadrons, claiming three and one shared victories. Innes, Dredge and Graves were all ex-253 Squadron, having gained respectively two and two shared, two and one shared, and one victory. Sgt. Sheppard was an Australian, while Sgt. Peter Jordan was from New Zealand. He provides further insight into Operation 'Dunlop': "In April Ted Lawrence and myself were flown to Hendon (from Elgin, Scotland, where 232 Squadron was based) and, under strict security arrangements, did 130 hours practising take offs before reaching a white line across the strip, seemingly only a few yards ahead of us. The Hurricanes were fitted with the (then) new-fangled 45 gal. long-range tanks, non-jettisonable and fitted under the mainplanes with auxilliary pumps to

onto the quarter deck and it was one of the latter which was rendered u/s during bad weather experienced in the Atlantic."

"On arrival in Gibraltar, the aircraft were off-loaded onto the quayside and the mainplanes and long-range tanks fitted by the ground staff, with the doubtful assistance of the pilots to whom the particular aircraft had been allocated. They were then hoisted by crane onto the after end of 'Ark Royal' and with little delay off we went into the Mediterranean. We were supposed to take off for Malta about 12

228 Squadron's Sunderland L5807 comes under fire at Kalafrana on 27 April 1941, bullet splashes from Oblt. Müncheberg's fire kicking up the water and gaining hits on the starboard inner engine. (N.W.M.A.)

pump fuel into the main tanks. We were told to use 15° of flap for take off, something completely new to us then."

"On 16 April we left Greenock on the old aircraft carrier 'Argus' with twenty-four Hurricanes, twenty-five pilots and an appropriate number of fitters and riggers for Gibraltar (although we did not know our precise destination at the time, of course. As far as I know, we were originally bound for Greece/Crete but it was too late for that. I remember that we were quite concerned that we might be expected to take off from 'Argus' as even the resident Swordfish seemed to have difficulty. Our aircraft (with mainplanes detached) overflowed from the hangar deck

The fire starts to get a hold, and the wing, weakened by cannon shell hits, begins to buckle. (N.W.M.A.)

With the fire now well-established in the starboard wing, L5807 lists to port. (All N.W.M.A.)

L5807 now well ablaze.

The fire is now totally out of control, and the stricken flyingboat is burnt out completely.

192

hours after leaving Gibraltar but, because of bad weather and (I think) intelligence reports about enemy activity around Sardinia and Sicily, we retraced our course and eventually took off about 36 hours from Gibraltar. We left in three flights, each led by a Fulmar for navigational purposes, some 500 nautical miles from Malta (my logbook shows the flight took three hours and 20 minutes). We passed Cap Bon (in the distance) and Pantelleria, the latter at sea level – which was just as well as it was raining at the time, otherwise we might have missed it and also because we were told afterwards that there was an airfield there with Bf110s. We were held off Malta for a while because of air raids (so what's new!) before landing at Hal Far. Later we flew to Takali where we joined 261 Squadron."

The Hurricanes were not the only reinforcements for the island to arrive on this date however. In London it had been decided to station detachments of Blenheim IV bombers from 2 Group, Bomber Command, on Malta. These could provide a day striking force for anti-shipping and coastal operations of a more flexible nature than the night-only Wellingtons. Consequently the remaining seven Wellingtons of 148 Squadron left for Egypt, making room for the first detachment of six Blenheims from 21 Squadron which arrived safely from England via Gibraltar.

The arrival of the substantial numbers of new fighter pilots allowed some more of the old stalwarts to be rested, notably Sgt. Robertson, D.F.M., and Sgt. Hyde. Fred Robertson's record was outstanding; he had taken part in 189 interception sorties, and been credited with ten confirmed, three probables and seven damaged while on the island; his assessment as a fighter pilot endorsed in his logbook by Sqn.Ldr. Lambert read 'Exceptional'. The New Zealander Reg Hyde is also believed to have done well. According to one source he was credited with five shot down and seven others damaged. More postings and changes followed. Sqn.Ldr. Lambert was now tired, and Flt.Lt. Whittingham was invited by the A.O.C. to take over 261 Squadron from him, which he did at the start of May. Lambert was then flown out to Gibraltar in Sqn.Ldr. Podger's 10 R.A.A.F. Squadron Sunderland, and later flew on to England. At the same time 261 Squadron's earlier C.O., Sqn.Ldr. Balden, was posted to Luqa as Station Commander.

28/4/41

Following Oblt. Müncheberg's successful strafe of the Sunderland at Kalafrana on 27th., O.K.W. claimed that fighters destroyed two more of these flying boats in similar circumstances next day. No record of such a loss has been found. On this date (28 April) however Flg.Off. Innes Westmacott and a Sergeant Pilot were scrambled, seeing a number of high flying Bf109s about. Two of these they spotted as the German pilots began diving onto the Hurricanes tails, and at the right moment Westmacott carried out a hard climbing turn, coming out behind one of the Messerschmitts as it began to pull up. He fired and believed that it had gone down. Looking around for his wingman, who had lost him in the manoeuvre and headed for base, he saw another Messerschmitt about to attack him, so repeated the same trick. This time the German fighter dived away and headed off north. Although he was credited with one Bf109 confirmed, again no loss was suffered by 7/JG 26.

29/4/41

This latter Staffel was back on 29th., providing escort for raiding Ju88s of LG 1 during another early evening attack. Lt. Mietusch reported engaging eight Hurricanes, one of which he claimed shot down at 1845, the pilot baling out. Two minutes later Müncheberg claimed another over St. Paul's Bay, the pilot of this also taking to his parachute. Finally at 1850 Uffz. Kühdorf claimed a third Hurricane in the same area, although this claim does not appear to have been confirmed. 9/LG 1 reported the loss of one Ju88 (L1 + BT) over Valetta, Fw. Rudolf Lenzner and his crew baling out to be taken prisoner when the bomber crashed at Bur Marrad. According to German records the aircraft fell victim to A.A. fire; it was in fact claimed as a probable by the guns, but was also attacked by Plt.Off. Rippon and newly-arrived Plt.Off. Hall, who were actually credited with its destruction. Baling out over Malta had now become a somewhat risky business, as Doug Whitney recalls: "They (the Maltese) were so bitter about the bombing that they inclined to treat anyone baling out as an enemy and this became so bad we all carried revolvers to protect ourselves until we could convince them otherwise. I remember a Rhodesian in our squadron writing a long letter to the 'Malta Times' about this very subject, but I don't think it was ever published."

30/4/41

On the last day of the month two flights of S.79s from the 87° Gruppo B.T., escorted by twenty-seven 1° Stormo C.T. MC200s, attacked Valetta. Hurricanes were seen by the Italian crews, but failed to intercept. However five bombers were damaged by shell splinters from the A.A. barrage. The gunners claimed two Ju88s shot down, one of which may in fact have been an He111H of 6/KG 26, which failed to return to base on this date.

1/5/41

The Messerschmitts were back in full cry early on 1 May, attacking Hurricanes over the Hal Far area. Oblt. Müncheberg fired at one at about 6,000 feet over St. Paul's Bay at 0753, his wingman – Fw. Johannsen – hitting a second at 0754 without observed results. Diving down to a few hundred feet over Hal Far, Müncheberg then claimed another at 0754 as it was landing, but having no witness of this was credited only with a probable, although it was subsequently included in his score. It seems likely that his victims were two Hurricane IIs of 'C' Flight, 261 Squadron, which were operating under Flt.Lt. Mould at Hal Far; on this date Plt.Off. R.A. Innes and Sgt. B.C. Walmsley were shot down in Z2900 and Z3061 respectively, and were both wounded.

Müncheberg's Staffel returned in the early evening as escorts to Italian bombers, engaging six Hurricanes over Luqa. Müncheberg shot one of these down at 1715, seeing the aircraft crash about a mile north-east of the airfield. German records reported that the pilot had been killed, and noted that one of Müncheberg's victims on this date was a Plt.Off. Ted Winters', on his 13th. sortie over the island. At 1720 Uffz. Kühdorf claimed another Hurricane over Luqa, but again this does not seem to have been confirmed. The identity of 'Ted Winters' has not been established, but despite the definite identification of only two of the Hurricanes claimed by 7/JG 26 in the period 28 April – 1 May, A.H.Q. Malta reported that actual R.A.F. losses in these four days amounted to six Hurricanes – closely in line with the claims – four by Müncheberg, one of which was not confirmed, one by Mietusch, two by Kühdorf – apparently neither of which were confirmed – and possibly one by Johannsen. On the credit side the A.H.Q. also announced that during April the fighters had claimed 11 destroyed, nine probables and three damaged.

1 May also saw the first operational sorties by the 21 Squadron Blenheims from Luqa, together with another claim for the Ju88 by the anti-aircraft defences. No loss is recorded. Further strengthening of both sides continued during this period. On 30 April 10° Stormo B.T.'s other Gruppo, the 32° (57ª and 58ª Squadriglia) arrived at Chinisia airfield near Trapani with S.79s, while on 1 May thirteen Bristol Beaufighter IFs of 252 Squadron reached Malta. Fifteen had left St. Eval, Cornwall, on 27 April led by Sqn.Ldr. R.G. Yaxley, M.C.; one (T3629), flown by Sub Lt. R.D.B. Hopkins, F.A.A., had force-landed at Casablanca on the way, and been interned. When the remaining fourteen left Gibraltar for Malta, the aircraft piloted by Flg.Off. J.B. Holgate had suffered engine trouble and been forced to return. A replacement Beaufighter (pilot Flg.Off. G.J. Lemar) was sent out from England, this reaching Malta in company with Holgate's aircraft two days later. The other pilots were Flt.Lt. W. Riley, Flt.Lt. R.E. Jay, and Flt.Lt. J.J. Lowe (flight commanders), Flg.Offs. J.W. Blennerhassett, C.S.H. MacDonald, N.E.H. Virgin, P.S. Hirst and H. Verity, Plt.Off. J.C. Davidson and three Fleet Air Arm Sub Lts., I.F. Fraser, V.B. Crane and K. Holme. The most colourful character amongst these was William Riley, who had a varied and successful operational career. During the Norwegian Campaign of early 1940 he had been a member of 263 Squadron flying Gladiators, and had claimed one victory and a share in another before being wounded. On recovery he had helped form 302 Polish Squadron during the Battle of Britain, claiming two victories and a third shared plus two probables while with this unit. By the end of the year he had converted to twin-engined fighters, joining 252 Squadron to fly Blenheim IVFs and Beaufighters. Shortly before the posting to Malta he had claimed the unit's first victory over a four-engined Fw200. His D.F.C. would follow shortly. It was of course, this unit for which the maintenance crews had been flown to the island by the 10 R.A.A.F. Squadron Sunderland a few days earlier. The specific reason for the arrival of 252 Squadron was to provide long-range protection for a fast merchant vessel – the S.S. 'Parracombe' – on its way from Gibraltar, unescorted, carrying 21 crated Hurricanes and much needed cargo for the island, and also for a convoy of five fast freighters for Alexandria ('Tiger' convoy) due to pass the island several days hence. Sadly the 'Parracombe' failed in its gallant attempt to

reach Malta when it struck a mine off Cap Bon.

Meanwhile the end of the German campaign in Yugoslavia and Greece meant that many of the Luftwaffe units employed there were now being posted elsewhere, some of these stopping off in Sicily for a few days on their way back to Germany and undertaking a few missions over Malta. Noteable amongst these units was III Gruppe of Jagdgeschwader 27, whose Bf109Es provided a welcome reinforcement for the busy pilots of 7/JG 26.

One of the first Bristol Beaufighters to operate from Malta, T3317 of 252 Squadron is seen here in early May 1941. (*J.A. Heath*)

2–3/5/41

On Malta two losses were suffered during early May which were not the result of enemy activity. On 2nd. Sgt. Ottey was killed when his Hurricane (Z3054) crashed from a great height – probably due to oxygen starvation. Next day one of 252 Squadron's newly-arrived Beaufighters (T3237) was mistaken for a Ju88 while on a local flight. It was attacked and badly damaged by a patrolling

Hurricane, Flt.Lt. Riley crash-landed on Luqa airfield having been slightly wounded.

5/5/41

The A.A. defences continued to take toll of attackers, 9/St.G 1 having a Ju87B so badly damaged over Valetta that the crew were forced to bale out on return to Sicily, while a second aircraft from this Staffel failed to return, Uffz. Heinrich Becker and his gunner perishing in J9 + CL. During the morning two Hurricanes flown by Flt.Lt. Jeffries and Plt.Off. Hall (Z2904) were patrolling over Kalafrana Bay at 29,000 feet when a Ju88 was spotted below. Hall reported: " ... when I saw a vapour trail and warned my Section Leader who manoeuvred for position, scanning the sky for enemy fighters. The section then dived down to attack, Yellow 1 (Jeffries) going in on the starboard quarter and I dived down and made a quarter-astern attack from below, opening fire at 400 yards and closing to 50 yards, giving the e/a three bursts of three seconds each. I then broke away because I saw two fighters above on the port side. On hearing "Go to it Rose Section – go to it" I decided it was Rose Section although the section was too far off to be identified definately. On turning back to finish my ammunition on the Ju88, which was pouring smoke from the starboard engine, my aircraft was hit by return fire from the e/a in both self-sealing tanks. During the engagement A.A. bursts were exploding all round me, my port plane received a near miss which made a large hole and spattered the aircraft with splinters, which injured my left elbow." Sgt. Jolly of Rose Section claimed a share in shooting down the Ju88, but his aircraft was also hit by A.A. splinters, whilst Jeffries' aircraft was hit in the port wing by return fire. The bomber attacked would seem to have been an aircraft (4D + CT) of 9/KG 30 which crashed on return, Lt. Albrecht Irion and all his crew being reported lost.

4 May also saw the first sortie by 69 Squadron's latest addition – a photo-reconnaissance Hurricane. This aircraft, V7101, had been stripped of all possible equipment and guns, and had been painted blue overall. In this condition, and with much-increased fuel tankage, it could usually reach at least 30,000 feet, and on one occasion was taken up to 36,000 feet by George Burges – although he reported that at this height it was very unstable.

6/5/41

The Mediterranean area sprung to life from end to end on 6 May. In Africa Rommel's forces had driven the weakened British units right back across Cyrenaica into Egypt, while the Balkans were firmly in German hands following the fall of Yugoslavia and Greece, and an invasion of Crete seemed imminent. To allow the army in Egypt to deliver an early riposte to the Axis forces facing them, before these could be built up to any really dangerous strength, a fast convoy carrying 295 tanks, 180 motor vehicles, and 53 crated Hurricanes had been despatched from England, leaving Gibraltar on the morning of 6th. with Force 'H' in attendance. To meet this Operation 'Tiger' convoy, the Mediterranean Fleet also steamed out of Alexandria, heading for a planned rendezvous south of

Malta. Meanwhile Malta's reconnaissance aircraft were out looking for Axis convoys bound for Tripoli or Benghazi so that the island's bombers might strike at them and disrupt the flow of supplies and reinforcements to Rommel's command.

At the same time a fairly substantial Luftwaffe attack was launched against Malta by the units briefly based in Sicily, and this led to some severe fighting over the island on 6 May. 7/JG 26 and elements of III/JG 27 escorted four He111s of II/KG 26 over the island at midday, this formation being intercepted by 'C' Flight Hurricane IIs from Hal Far. Flg.Off. Westmacott, although under fire from the Messerschmitts, attacked one Heinkel and shot it up. The bomber dropped from formation with smoke pouring from it and disappeared slowly out to sea. Westmacott could not follow as he was under attack by the Bf109s, but the Controller later reported that the bomber's 'plot' had disappeared from the radar screen halfway to Sicily, and Westmacott was awarded a probable. He subsequently received a personal letter from the A.O.C. congratulating him on his persistence in continuing to attack the bomber when under attack himself. II/KG 26 reported that one He111H of 4th. Staffel (1H+FM) crashed on return, reportedly due to engine trouble, and was destroyed, Lt. Eberhard Möller and his crew of four all being killed. This may well have been the aircraft attacked by Westmacott.

Meanwhile however, the rest of the Hurricanes had been suffering badly at the hands of the German fighters. Plt.Off. Dredge crashed Z3057 on the airfield in flames and suffered severe burns; Plt.Off. Gray baled out of his shattered Z3060, wounded in the left thigh; Sgt. Branson baled out of Z3059 with slight burns to the right leg, while Plt.Off. P.D. Thompson got the damaged Z3034 down safely, having suffered a minor splinter wound in his leg. This execution had been the work of just two pilots; Müncheberg shot down one Hurricane at 1222, this falling into the sea near Valetta, the pilot baling out. Four minutes later he claimed a second near Hal Far, but did not see it crash and had no witness, although he believed that the pilot of this aircraft also baled out. It seems likely that Gray was his first victim and Branson the second. Dredge's victor was probably III/JG 27's leading pilot, Oblt. Erbo Graf von Kageneck, who claimed one Hurricane over the Luqa area for his 14th. victory, and first over Malta. During the day a Beaufighter (T3294) was badly damaged on the ground at Luqa and was subsequently written-off; a further eight were slightly damaged during the same raid.

As darkness fell another raid developed, Sqn.Ldr. Whittingham and another pilot going up to intercept. Whittingham fired at four different aircraft during this sortie, being credited with one destroyed, one probable and one damaged; these would seem to have been an He111 and two Ju88s respectively. Actual German losses on this date were recorded as one Ju88A of 8/KG 30 (4D+FS) flown by Uffz. Werner Gerhardt, which was believed to have been the victim of A.A. fire by the Germans, but was probably shot down by Whittingham, and another He111 from 4/KG 26 which crash-landed on return with a dead gunner.

This same night saw three Swordfish of 830 Squadron out continuing a series

Plt.Off. A.S. Dredge was shot down in flames in Hurricane Z3057 on 6 May, only ten days after arriving on Malta; he baled out, badly burned, and was probably the first victim claimed over the island by Ritterkreuzträger Oblt. Erbo Graf von Kageneck of III/JG27. Dredge is seen here (I) later in the war with Flt.Lt. N.L.D. Kemp, D.F.C., who served on the island later in 1941 with 242 Squadron. (*National War Museum Assoc.*)

of mine-laying sorties to Tripoli harbour. However on this occasion a Swordfish (P4232 'A') was lost when Lt. N.K. Cambell's aircraft was hit by A.A. fire and he was forced to ditch just off the coast; he and his observer managed to swim ashore, and were subsequently captured, but the TAG, P.O.(A) W.G.T. Welsh succumbed to injuries sustained.

An Axis supply convoy was now spotted by a Maryland, and on 7 May an attack was laid on. Three of 252 Squadron's Beaufighters escorted five Blenheims of 21 Squadron to attack the ships near Lampedusa. While so engaged an Italian transport aircraft, variously identified as a Caproni Ca310 or a Savoia S.81, was intercepted and was shot down by the three Beaufighter pilots, Sqn.Ldr. Yaxley, Flt.Lt. Riley and Sub Lt. Fraser. Meanwhile one Blenheim flown by Plt.Off. D.F. Dennis attacked a merchant ship of some 5,000 tons, gaining hits as a result of which the vessel was believed to have foundered. Sgt. W. Mc.Osborne pressed home an attack on a destroyer, gaining a direct hit. Later reconnaissance indicated that this had sunk. Next day Dennis and Osborne participated in a further attack on another convoy. This time Dennis claimed hits on a destroyer while Osborne inflicted damage on a supply ship. A few days later they would both again be involved in an attack on a convoy, where one merchantman was seen to list and pour black smoke after suffering hits from Dennis' bombs. Both pilots received immediate decorations, a D.F.C. for Dennis and a D.F.M. for Osborne.

7/5/41

Over Malta on 7th. little had been seen, although the A.A. claimed two Ju88s shot down. On one patrol two of 261 Squadron's pilots collided, Hurricanes

V7365 and V7548 both being lost, while Sgt. Jennings was killed and Sgt. Walker slightly injured. More Italian bomber reinforcements reached Sicily, the 99° Gruppo (242ª and 243ª Squadriglia) of the 43° Stormo B.T. arriving at Gerbini under Ten.Co. Nello Brambilla, equipped with twin-engined Fiat BR 20Ms.

8/5/41

The 'Tiger' convoy came within range of air attack on 8th., and for the next four days most activity in the air tended to centre here. The convoy had escaped discovery until now due to bad weather and poor visibility, but this was not to continue, and a series of hard-fought combats now ensued. 'Ark Royal' had embarked a second squadron of Fulmars – 807 Squadron under Lt.Cdr. J. Sholto Douglas, replacing the low-performanced Skuas of 800 Squadron, and to assist the resident Fulmars of 808 Squadron (Lt. Tillard), but a total of only twelve aircraft were fully serviceable this morning. The early morning patrol had been vectored towards a 'shadower' and although spotted could not be intercepted, so all now knew that the assault would soon commence. The first incoming raid appeared on the radar screens at about 1345, still 32 miles from the ships. Two sections (four aircraft) of 807 Squadron were scrambled to join the four Fulmars of 808 Squadron on patrol, these latter aircraft intercepting sixteen S.79s of 38° Gruppo from Sardinia, but as Lt. Tillard led the attack they were themselves 'bounced' by a dozen escorting CR 42s of the 3° Gruppo C.T. Almost immediateiy Tillard's Fulmar was shot down, he and his observer, Lt. Somerviile, being killed. The three other Fulmars were also hit, the aircraft of both Lt. G.C. McE. Guthrie and P.O.(A) R.E. Dubber sustaining damage to their tail units, while in Lt. Taylour's aircraft the TAG, P.O.(A) L.G.J. Howard received a severe leg wound, an explosive bullet shattering both tibia and fibula. One CR 42 overshot their aircraft and Taylour managed to score hits on it, forcing it into a spin from which he considered it would not be able to recover. Having evaded the other Fiats, Taylour headed for the carrier with his wounded TAG, where only prompt and skilful action by the 'Ark's, surgeon prevented the loss of Howard's leg. The Italian pilots claimed five Fulmars shot down, one of these being credited to Cap. Giorgio Tugnoli.

By now the four 807 Squadron Fulmars had made contact with the S.79s, Lt. N.G. Hallett and his No. 2 – P.O.(A) A.G. Johnson – hitting one bomber but the gunner of which in return hit Hallett's engine, forcing him to ditch; both he and his Australian observer, Lt. V.A. Smith, managed to scramble out and were soon picked up by the destroyer 'Foresight'. Meanwhile the two Blue Section aircraft flown by Lt. R.E. Gardner and South African Lt. K. Firth attacked the same Savoia, flown by Cap. Armando Boetto, commanding officer of the 49ª Squadriglia, Blue 1 getting in the final burst before it disintegrated and fell into the sea. Eight of the bombers broke through the defences to launch torpedoes at the 'Ark' and at the battlecruiser 'Renown', but without obtaining hits. There followed a short lull, but from 1620 onwards a succession of attacks by small formations of S.79s commenced but all were successfully beaten off, mainly by the intense gunfire of the ships, although Yellow Section of 808 Squadron, two

Fulmars flown by Lt. A.T.J. Kindersley and Lt. Hay, R.M., caught one bomber at 1710 and claimed it shot down.

Just before dusk, at 1930, a further raid was detected when a full 70 miles distant. Three Fulmars were already up – Red Section of 807 Squadron – and four more (all that were now immediately available) were scrambled, the incoming attack proving to comprise twenty-eight Ju87s of I/St.G 1 from Cagliari, in two formations, with a top cover of six Bf110s of 9/ZG26, these led by Hpt. Thomas Steinberger. The three Fulmars of Red Section engaged the escort, while the other four, two each from 807 and 808, attacked the two formations of dive-bombers and broke them up. Lt.Cdr. Sholto Douglas engaged two Bf110s, but these turned on the Fulmar, gaining hits on both its wings which caused damage to the hydraulic system. Red 2, P.O.(A) R.T. Leggott, dived to attack a Ju87 but was himself attacked by a Bf110. He managed to turn inside his assailant and opened fire from 200 yards, seeing white vapour trail from the Messerschmitt as it pulled away. Lt. Taylour, flying as Yellow 1 and now with P.O.(A) F.A. Barnes in the rear seat, claimed one Ju87 shot down, but they too were then attacked by a Bf110, the starboard wing and hydraulic system therein being hit, with the result that the undercarriage leg on this side dropped down. Blue Leader, Lt. 'Jimmie' Gardner (who had previously flown on attachment to the RAF and had claimed five victories whilst with Sqn.Ldr. Douglas Bader's 242 Squadron) claimed another Ju87 shot down with a second as probably destroyed – the latter subsequently being confirmed by cine gun-camera. However the windscreen of his aircraft was shattered by crossfire from other Stukas, and with the radiator damaged, he crash-landed the badly-damaged Fulmar on the carrier's deck; neither he nor his TAG, P.O.(A) R. Carlisle, suffered injuries. One other Fulmar pilot, Sub Lt. R.F. Walker flying No. 2 to Gardner, reported seeing his fire hit a Bf110, following which he attacked a Ju87 which disappeared into cloud pouring smoke.

All seven Fulmars had landed back on the carrier by 2015 but two were again scrambled almost immediately on the approach of three more S.79s. Lts. Guthrie and Hay were unable to prevent the attack, two of the Savoias releasing torpedoes at 'Ark Royal' and 'Renown', narrowly missing the carrier.

The returning Zerstörer pilots of 9/ZG 26 claimed three of the Fulmars shot down, identifying their victims as 'Hurricanes', the first of these claims was made by Oblt. Bergfleth – probably Lt.Cdr. Sholto Douglas' aircraft – the subsequent two by Hptm. Steinberger. However the Messerschmitts did not get away unscathed – indeed Fw. Hans Hufnagel and his gunner were both wounded and crash-landed their badly damaged aircraft at Comiso, a second badly damaged Bf110 crash-landing at Trapani, whilst a third returned with minor damage. At least one Ju87 was damaged during the attack, both Lt. Neuberg and his gunner returning to Cagliari wounded.

At last darkness arrived and with it respite for the Fleet and convoy, and welcomed rest for the aircrews. However at midnight one of the convoy – the 'New Zealand Star' – was slightly damaged by a mine exploding in its paravane, then the 'Empire Song' hit two mines. A fire broke out in her ammunition hold and the crew were taken off by an attendant destroyer. At 0400 she blew up with the loss of fifty-seven of the precious tanks and ten of the even more precious Hurricanes. During the hours of darkness a lone torpedo-bomber attempted a daring attack on the battleship 'Queen Elizabeth', which was sailing with Force 'H' but was destined as reinforcement for the Mediterranean Fleet. The torpedo was only narrowly avoided.

To the east the Mediterranean Fleet had also come under air attack during 8th. from Rhodes-based Axis aircraft, and heavy air fighting had ensued with six of the attackers being claimed shot down by the defending Fulmars from the carrier 'Formidable'.

9/5/41

From Malta ten of 252 Squadron's Beaufighters were now able to provide good cover for the Fleet and convoy, and on one of these patrols Plt.Off. Davidson intercepted a Ju88 'snooper', Lt. Eduard Gessler and his crew of 4U + LK losing their lives when their 2(F)/123 aircraft went down between Lampedusa and Malta. At 0800 the 'Tiger' convoy was still some 90 miles to the west of Malta, while the Mediterranean Fleet was 120 miles to the south, but by 1515 the two west-bound Malta-destined convoys, for which the Mediterranean Fleet had also provided cover, had arrived at Malta. At this same time Force 'H' discharged its responsibilities for the 'Tiger' convoy to Admiral Cunningham's force, the two fleets meeting some 40 miles south of Malta. The poor weather, with many fog patches restricting visibility to less than two miles, prevented the warships and their respective convoys from being discovered, although another 'snooper', this time a Ju88 from 1(F)/121 was intercepted by a pair of Fulmars from 'Formidable's' 806 Squadron flown by Lts. Henley and P.D.J. Sparke, and claimed shot down. The badly damaged aircraft limped back to Sicily where it crashed whilst attempting to land and was destroyed. The crew survived but presumably they had not sighted the ships before being attacked as no attacks developed, to everyone's surprise. During this period three Fulmars, on patrol from 'Formidable', landed at Hal Far to refuel.

Meanwhile, Malta's fighters were in action during the day when Ju87s from both II and III Gruppe of St.G 1 carried out an attack on Grand Harbour, presumably the newly-arriving convoy having been spotted by reconnaissance aircraft. Two Hurricanes of 'B' Flight were on patrol and were vectored towards the Stukas, while other Hurricanes were hurriedly scrambled. Flg.Off. Laubscher, now in command of 'B' Flight, recalls: "I was leading Sgt. Peter Jordan on a patrol when we were vectored onto a flight of Ju87s which had attacked the Grand Harbour. They had turned back to Sicily and I couldn't see a formation but spotted a straggler who, curiously enough, was flying diagonally across our line of approach and not heading pell-mell for home. He was only 100 or so feet above the sea and we closed on him rapidly. I instructed Peter to keep a sharp lookout for enemy fighters and then to follow me. I started a quarter stern attack and had the unpleasant experience of flying down the middle of a cone of tracer from the rear gunner. I held my fire until the enemy was within range. When I pressed the button there was the ripping noise that was characteristic of the

Hurricane's eight guns and I saw strikes on the fuselage of the Stuka. The rear gunner was killed by that burst, as his gun swung up to a vertical position as he slumped down. I tried to turn in behind him but found that I was going to overshoot and pulled away to starboard. I swung in a wide circle around the machine climbing slightly to loose speed and came in at him again from dead ahead and slightly above. The pilot of the Stuka had plenty of courage and pulled up his nose to have a crack at me with his forward firing guns. I was so surprised that I involuntarily pulled up slightly and I passed over him before I could get him in my gunsight again. At that moment Peter came in from the port quarter, misjudged his deflection by a fraction and blew off the Stuka's tail. When I turned I saw a long patch of the fluorescent dye that the Germans carried staining the sea a light yellow-green but could not pick out the pilot. Nevertheless we circled the spot and radioed Control to get a radar fix on us and send out a crash boat. They never found him and I often wondered whether he went in with his machine and dead gunner or whether he managed to bale out and was picked up by the flyingboat they had stationed in Sicily for sea rescue work." Sgt. Peter Jordan added: "One of the crew baled out – nearly hitting me in the process – but I don't think his parachute would have opened properly from that height." His judgement of the situation would appear to have been correct, for this was undoubtedly Oblt. Ulrich Heinz's aircraft (J9+GL) of 9/St.G 1 lost with both members of the crew. A second Ju87 was claimed by Sgt. Len Davies (in Z4261), shared with an unidentified pilot, Davies recording: "Attempted raid on convoy by Ju87s. Ju87 shot down by Blue 1 – I finished it off." 4/St.G 1 reported that one of its Ju87s crash-landed at Comiso suffering 70% damage, and this may well have been the victim of their attack.

10/5/41

Throughout the day Axis reconnaissance aircraft searched for the convoy in variable visibility, Beaufighters from Malta continuing to provide cover and frequently heard making reports but experiencing difficulty in maintaining contact. Two Beaufighters were vectored onto one 'snooper' 70 kilometres south-west of the island, an aircraft of 2(F)/123. Following an exchange of fire the Ju88 flew back to Sicily in a damaged condition and with one crewman wounded, but one Beaufighter – T3239 'B' crewed by Flt.Lt. J.J. Lowe and F/Sgt. J.H. Tranter – failed to return, presumably shot down by return fire from the Junkers. Fulmars from 'Formidable' were also flying patrols and on one such sortie Lt. R. MacDonald-Hall, with L/A Harry Phillips in rear seat, sighted a He111 but were unable to catch it before it disappeared into the fog.

During this period single Sunderlands from the Australian squadron were regular visitors to the island, carrying supplies and personnel from Gibraltar. N9049, flown by Flg.Off. Thurston, had arrived with a load of ammunition for the Beaufighters on 7th, but had been delayed three days in leaving again due to a heavy swell on the sea. During the afternoon of 10th. a number of Bf109s from 7/JG 26 appeared and became engaged in a dogfight with intercepting Hurricanes. After five minutes or so, one Messerschmit – flown by 'Jochen'

Two Junkers Ju52/3m transports of the Luftwaffe destroyed at Comiso airport on 10 May 1941 by strafing Beaufighters of 252 Squadron. (*N. Malizia*)

Müncheberg – was seen suddenly to break away and dive out of the sun onto the moored Sunderland in Marsaxlokk Bay. He fired one short burst which at once set the port wing on fire, and although efforts were made to tow the flyingboat ashore, the flames spread rapidly and it sank, still blazing furiously. Fortunately no one was aboard at the time.

To reduce Axis activity, nine 252 Squadron Beaufighters made a low level strafing attack on Catania and Comiso airfields with some effect. At Catania Italian records show that an MC200, a Savoia S.82 transport, a Caproni Ca133 and a Ca164 were damaged, while at Comiso two Ju52/3ms were destroyed, two 23° Gruppo CR 42s badly damaged, one MC200, one S.81 and one Bf110 damaged. Six Italian servicemen, three Germans and three civilian workmen were killed. However at 2100 air attacks on the departing Fleet and convoy began and lasted for the next one and a half hours – torpedo-bombers attempted to attack down moon but were greeted by intense A.A. fire and were forced to turn away. No damage was caused to any of the warships or merchantmen. No further attacks developed but five escorting destroyers of Capt. Lord Louis Mountbatten's 5th Destroyer Flotilla were detached to carry out a bombardment of Benghazi just after midnight. They claimed a hit on a vessel in the harbour but were then attacked by Ju87s of II/St.G 2, which also machine-gunned the destroyers but without any serious effects. The Flotilla then returned to Malta. That night Swordfish from 830 Squadron laid mines in Tripoli harbour, while four Wellingtons from 148 Squadron, with three further Egypt-based aircraft, attacked the port as a diversion.

11/5/41

This was the last day during which the 'Tiger' convoy remained in reach of Axis air attack, and still bad visibility hampered both attackers and defenders. During the afternoon nine Ju88s appeared, and were intercepted by a patrolling Fulmar section, Lt. Henley chasing an aircraft of 5/LG 1, his fire wounding the gunner before the bomber disappeared into the murk. Meanwhile Lt. Sparke latched onto Ofw. Otto Engel's 7th Staffel aircraft (L1 + IR), but collided with it, he and his TAG, L/A A.S. Rush, and the crew of the Junkers all perishing.

12/5/41

The four remaining ships of the 'Tiger' convoy reached Alexandria safely this morning. 238 tanks and 43 crated Hurricanes would be an invaluable reinforcement for Wavell's forces. 'Formidable' was left with only four serviceable Fulmars, with no immediate replacements available. This would delay the carrier's involvement in the imminent air and sea battle for Crete. However the 'unsinkable aircraft carrier' Malta now had about 50 Hurricanes – mainly Mark IIa and IIb models – and some reorganization was due. Consequently on 12th. a new unit was formed at Hal Far to be known as 185 Squadron. This number had previously been given to a liaison unit with the R.A.F. contingent in France in early 1940, and before that to a Bomber Command training unit. The nucleus of the new squadron was provided mainly by 'C' Flight of 261 Squadron, the unit's ground component being provided by the latter unit and by 1430 Flight, an army co-operation unit which had been operating in Italian East Africa until the previous month, when the main campaign there had been satisfactorily completed. The pilots of 1430 Flight were currently flying with 112 Squadron in the defence of Crete. Command of the new squadron was vested in newly-promoted Sqn.Ldr. P.W.O. Mould, D.F.C., with as his flight commanders, Flt.Lts. C.G.St.D. Jeffries ('A' Flight) and I.B. Westmacott ('B' Flight). Other pilots were a mixture of new arrivals and seasoned veterans:

Flg.Off. H.W. Eliot	Flg.Off. N.P.W. Hancock	Plt.Off. P.D. Thompson
Plt.Off. D. Winton	Plt.Off. G.G. Bailey	Sgt. E.V. Wynne
Plt.Off. C.E. Hamilton	Plt.Off. J.E. Hall	Sgt. F.G. Sheppard
Sgt. C.S. Bamberger	Sgt. C.G. Hodson	Plt.Off. R.A. Innes*
Sgt. R.A. Branson	Sgt. B.J. Vardy	Plt.Off. A.S. Dredge*
Sgt. A.W. Jolly	Sgt. H. Burton	Llt.Off. C.K. Gray*
		Sgt. B.C. Walmsley*

*non-operational; wounded.

(at the same time Plt.Off. D.J. Hammond was posted from 261 Squadron to the Middle East due to ill health.)

185 Squadron was formed on 12 May 1941 from 'C' Flight of 261 Squadron and some spare pilots. Some of the squadron's initial complement of pilots are seen here: l. to r., back; Flt.Lt. C.G.St.D. Jeffries, Sgt. C.S. Bamberger, Plt.Off. C.E. 'Hamish' Hamilton, Plt.Off. H.W. 'Chubby' Eliot, Sgt. B.J. Vardy; front; Sgt. A.W. Jolly, Sgt. C.G. Hodson, Sgt. F.G. Sheppard. (*W. Hartill*)

More of 185 Squadron in May 1941: l. to r., back; Plt.Off. G.G. Bailey, Sqn.Ldr. P.W.O. 'Boy' Mould, Sgt. Bamberger (on wing), Sgt. Vardy, Sgt. Sheppard, Flg.Off. Eliot, Sgt. Hodson, L.A.C. W. Hartill; front; Sgt. Jolly and two groundcrew. (*W. Harthill*)

13/5/41

Initial operations by the new unit did not open an unauspicious note. Next day, 13th., four of the squadron's Hurricanes were led off at 1330 by Flt.Lt. Westmacott, climbing above other fighters from 261 Squadron. At 8,000 feet numerous Bf109s attacked but were evaded in cloud, and the section broke up. Westmacott then saw two 'red noses' coming up and thought they were from his own flight, as he called his pilots to rendezvous over Takali, going down through cloud to wait for them. Those behind him were not Hurricanes however – they were Bf109Es of III/JG 27. Suddenly he heard a clattering noise and his cockpit filled with smoke, the controls going dead – he had been shot down by Oblt. Graf von Kageneck. Out of control, the Hurricane (Z2837) went into a forward bunt, so he undid his seat straps, opened the hood and was thrown out. His parachute opened, but as he reached the ground a 25 m.p.h. wind pulled him over backwards and he was knocked out. He came round to find a hostile Maltese crowd around him, but when he made it clear that he was English the mood changed. He now discovered that he had been wounded in the elbow, and was taken to hospital where a piece of bullet casing was removed.

During the raid two Hurricanes were claimed by the Germans, the second victor not being identified; Plt.Off. P.J.A. Thompson of 261 Squadron was shot down and killed in V7115. On this occasion some of the Messerschmitts had

Several members of 185 Squadron were shot down immediately after formation of the unit by Oblt. Erbo Graf von Kageneck, the leading pilot of III/JG27, which was briefly operating over Malta at this time. (*August Graf von Kageneck via J. Roba*)

carried bombs for the first time – not a new role for III/JG 27, which had operated in this manner over the Balkans during the previous month.

14/5/41

Next afternoon at 1620 four 185 Squadron Hurricanes were again scrambled to provide top cover for 261 Squadron. Once again they were attacked by III/JG27 Messerschmitts, on this occasion the successful Plt.Off. Hamilton in Z2901 being shot down and critically wounded by Graf von Kageneck; he died shortly afterwards. Sgt. Wynne attacked one Bf109 from below, but without observed results. 'Hamish' Hamilton, a Scot, had already spent six months on the island but had volunteered to stay on until the new squadron (185) was settled in. Sqn.Ldr. Whittingham wrote of him: "One of the finest characters I have met. It was he who always took extra watches when things were hottest.... Dear old 'Hamish', you could almost smell the heather of Scotland when you spoke to him." John Pain adds:"Hamish's D.F.C. was reputed to have come through three days later." It is believed that before his death Claud 'Hamish' Hamilton had shot down at least five aircraft over Malta. Two more Hurricanes were claimed by O.K.W. on this date. Uffz. Kühdorf of 7/JG 26 claiming one which again seems not to have been confirmed. Z4087 of 261 Squadron was hit, and Plt.Off. B.M. Cavan was slightly injured. During the day's raid three Marylands were damaged on the ground at Luqa.

Oblt. Graf von Kageneck is helped into his parachute harness by his ground crew on a Sicilian airfield in May 1941. Note his Bf109E with victory bars on the rudder in the background. (*August Graf von Kageneck via J. Roba*)

15/5/41

Again on 15 May two 185 Squadron Hurricanes took off to cover 261 Squadron, Sgts. Bamberger and Wynne getting off at 1200 and climbing to 12,000 feet. As Bf109s were reported they stayed well above the other squadron, but to no avail. Suddenly Bf109s attacked and Wynne went down in Z3035 to crash at high speed to his death; his victor was Hpt. Max Dobislav of III/JG 27, claiming his ninth victory of the war in this combat. On landing the shattered Bamberger, who had now survived many weeks of combat, announced: "I'm not taking off from this bloody island again!" He did not fly operationally again with the squadron, being posted temporarily to A.H.Q. Malta at Safi as a test pilot until 12 June, when he was flown out to Gibraltar in a Sunderland. His 100 sorties over Malta had brought him two confirmed victories and three damaged. Later in the war he would return to action in Italy, becoming a flight commander with D.F.C. and Bar, and six confirmed victories to his credit.

Meanwhile three S.79s from 10° and 30° Stormo B.T. had also operated over Malta on 15th., one aircraft of 32° Gruppo being lost. Four more S.79s were sent out from Sicily to search for it but one ran out of fuel and had to ditch, the crew being picked up by an Italian hospital ship. The missing aircraft may possibly have fallen foul of Plt.Off. John Pain in Z4060, who claimed an aircraft shot down which he identified as an He111. "This was on the morning pre-dawn patrol when I was scrambled for an unusual low early morning recce. I chased him west along the south coast of the island and closed off Gozo. He went into the drink well out to sea off the island, by which time I was light on fuel and out of ammo. There was no doubt he crashed into the sea as I watched him hit, but I did not get a confirmation of this as there was no one else to see it and R.D.F. didn't seem to have much coverage up that way." The day's attacks resulted in one Wellington being hit and burnt out on the ground at Luqa, while three Beaufighters were damaged.

16/5/41

More changes were now taking place and further pilots were rested. Sgt. Deacon left on 13 May for Mersa Matruh in Hurricane V7771, the same aircraft he had flown to the island on 29 January. At Takali Gp. Capt. O'Sullivan, newly-promoted, was posted to Luqa, the new C.O. being Wg.Cdr. J. Warfield. Sqn.Ldr. Martin, one of the remaining 1940 Fighter Flight pilots, took command of Hal Far. 16 May saw the arrival of five Blenheims of 139 Squadron from England via Gibraltar, while five days later five more 82 Squadron aircraft arrived; one had been lost en route, Sgt. L.H. Wrightson and his crew perishing. Losses during the period 12–15 May had been rather heavy, the total of aircraft destroyed or damaged in the air or on the ground being recorded as:

Hurricanes	5 lost,	4 damaged
Wellingtons	1 lost,	1 damaged
Marylands	1 lost,	6 damaged
Beaufighters		3 damaged

German units were now leaving Sicily in a steady trickle as the Luftwaffe began regrouping for the forthcoming attack on Russia. The Regia Aeronautica was quick to reclaim its airfields on the island, and by mid May the force assembled there was once more quite impressive:

1° Stormo C.T.	6° Gruppo	6 CR 42s, 20 MC200s
	17° Gruppo	7 CR 42s, 21 MC200s
	23° Gruppo Autonomo C.T.	15 CR 42s, 4 Re 2000s*
43° Stormo B.T.	99° Gruppo	14 BR 20Ms
30° Stormo B.T.	87° Gruppo	7 S.79s
	90° Gruppo	7 S.79s
10° Stormo B.T.	30° Gruppo	7 S.79s
	32° Gruppo	12 S.79s

278ª Squadriglia Aerosiluranti	2 S.79sil
612ª Squadriglia Aerosoccorso	2 Z.506Bs
Reparto Volocaccia (Fighter Flt.)	1 CR 42

(*the Reggiane Re 2000s were a test batch of the first pre-production examples of this little monoplane fighter.)

16–17/5/41

On Malta meanwhile the Beaufighters of 252 Squadron were now fast approaching the need for major servicing. On 16th however eight of them were despatched to Maleme airfield, Crete, from where next morning they were to carry out a strafe of airfields in southern Greece at first light. These bases – Hassani, Argos and Molai – were in use by the Luftwaffe for attacks on Crete, which were reaching their climax at this time. Long lines of aircraft parked wingtip to wingtip were attacked, and much damage was believed to have been done; in fact many Bf110s and Ju52s were damaged, some seriously, but these attacks did little to stem the assault on the island. One Beaufighter, T3228 crewed by Flg.Off. Hirst and Sgt. E.R. Payton, failed to return and was shot down by the A.A. defences at Hassani. One more important duty awaited the Beaufighters on their return to Malta, as Sqn.Ldr. Whiteley, C.O. of 69 Squadron, recalled: "It was about this time that we were stood by to intercept transport aircraft proceeding from Italy to North Africa. A.H.Q. expected to detect these transports east of Malta at extreme range and by that time I could spare some Marylands while still meeting the P.R. tasks. I remember sitting in the cockpit and being cooked by the sun for a few hours, but we were never scrambled."

Further reinforcements were on the way aboard a big convoy sailing from Gibraltar. This included the carriers 'Ark Royal', 'Eagle' and 'Furious', two battleships and a strong force of cruisers and destroyers. Aboard the carriers were forty-eight Hurricanes and six Fulmars to be flown off, although on this occasion not all the fighters were for Malta. For the first time existing established squadrons were aboard. 213, 229 and 249 Squadrons had all been ordered to prepare for service in the Middle East, as was the special Fulmar flight which was to lead them, under the command of Lt.Cdr. G. Hare, D.S.C., who takes up the story of the preparations: "In mid April 1941 I was called to London for a secret verbal appointment and interviewed by Rear-Admiral Clement Moody, the Fifth Sea Lord (he had been my Captain in 'Eagle'). I was told that I was being sent as C.O. 800X Squadron which was then forming with Fulmars at Donibristle. Our job was to act as navigational escort for about seventy Hurricanes which would be transported to the Med in 'Furious' and flown off at maximum range as reinforcements for Malta which was under heavy air attack. I went straight to Donibristle where I found Lt. R.M. Smeeton (later Vice-Admiral Sir Richard) had already made great strides in equipping the new Fulmar IIs. I can't remember whether there were six or eight at this distance of time. I believe Smeeton was then serving at the Admiralty, he was not a member of 800X Squadron."

"About the beginning of May 800X flew to Speke R.A.F. station where the Hurricanes were being prepared for embarkation. Visibility was very poor and

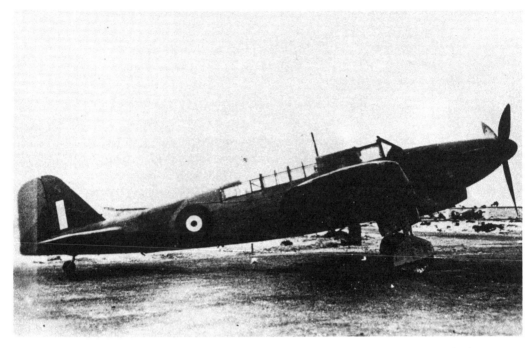

One of the 800X Squadron Fulmars which flew off H.M.S.'Furious' on 21 May 1941 to lead new Hurricanes to Malta. They then remained on the island to undertake night intruder sorties over Sicily. (*J.A. Heath*)

having been warned that barrage balloons were hoisted over the Liverpool area which had very recently suffered heavily in bombing raids, we went well out to sea before turning in to Speke, only to get entangled in a coastal convoy flying balloons. Luckily no Fulmar was lost. We were at Speke only three days or so before we got our orders for embarkation. One night the Mersey tunnel was closed to all traffic, approach roads sealed off so that the long column of Fulmars and Hurricanes could be towed to Gladstone Dock where 'Furious' was berthed. The Hurricanes had to be shorn of their wings to get through the tunnel but the Fulmars went through with wings folded. 'Furious' then sailed for Tail o' the Bank to pick up our Atlantic anti-submarine escort. The date must have been about 12 May."

The escort comprised a heterogenous collection of vessels including the old battleship 'Centurion' disguised with phoney wooden guns to look like H.M.S. 'King George V', the cruiser 'London' and a bevy of destroyers. Hare continues: "The passage was without incident. The Operations Officer of 'Furious' (Cdr. A.H.T. Fleming) and I carefully prepared diagrammatic charts for each Hurricane pilot of probable times, courses and distances to that they would not be lost should they become detached. This turned out to be a very wise precaution."

"The day before we arrived in Gibraltar we received a signal from Admiral Sir

212

James Somerville of Force 'H' who was in command of the operation, saying that on arrival in harbour we were to berth stern to stern to 'Ark Royal' so that some of our Hurricanes could be transferred to her and rolled off 'Furious' direct onto 'Ark Royal'. He also required all 800X Squadron's Fulmar IIs to be transferred to 'Ark' and they would be replaced as navigational escort to the Hurricanes by her Fulmar Is which were teased out and no longer suitable as fighters. I protested, as C.O. of 800X, to Cdr. Miles Cursham of 'Furious', the Commander Flying, that the object of the operation was the safe delivery of the Hurricanes to Malta but my protest went unheeded."

"During the night of 18–19 May 'Furious' arrived at Gib and the exchange of aircraft took place; then both ships sailed in company." It was the aircraft of 249 Squadron that had been transferred to 'Ark Royal'; meanwhile the groundcrews of all three squadrons were on their way round the Cape of Good Hope, bound via the Suez Canal for Egypt. "Next morning my senior pilot, Lt. P.J. Connolly, reported that the four Fulmar Is transferred to us were indeed in a very ropey condition but maintenance crews were working on them. He later reported that they were in worse condition than he had first thought and doubted whether they were fit for the job. I then went again to Cdr. Cursham and said I wished to report the fact to the Captain (A.G. Talbot). He advised me not to do so, as, he said, the Captain was a difficult man, and he had no intention of telling him himself. However, I insisted and he ushered me into the Captain's sea cabin. I didn't stay there long; I was told very forcibly that the job had to be done and to get the hell out of his cabin. I said I fully realised the job had to be done but I wished to protest against the shabby trick 'Ark Royal' had played on us. This incensed the Captain even more and out of that cabin I got!"

20–21/5/41

As the warships steadily ploughed eastwards, operations over Malta continued. On 20 May Oblt. Graf von Kageneck claimed III/JG 27's last victory over the island when he shot down Hurricane N2673 of 261 Squadron, Plt.Off. A.J. Reeves baling out with slight injuries. Flt. Lt. Hancock, who had taken over 'B' Flight of 185 Squadron after Innes Westmacott was wounded, crash-landed when his engine failed due to fuel starvation; a fault had prevented his being able to switch over tanks. Luqa was again hit, one Beaufighter being burnt out on the ground here. Next day in a further raid on this airfield another Beaufighter was to be slightly damaged, as was a Maryland, while a Wellington and a Blenheim were so badly hit that they had to be written off. It was on this day – 21 May – that Operation 'Splice' got underway – though with so many mishaps that disaster was only narrowly avoided. The aircraft were ranged on the decks before dawn, but on 'Furious' the first Fulmar failed to start and had to be put below. 213 Squadron was led off in sections, each headed by a Fulmar, but that leading Flt.Lt. Lockhart's flight became lost and returned to the carrier, then set off again with two hours' fuel already gone. Near Pantelleria the formation was fired on, so dived down to low level where Plt.Off. N.C. Downie's aircraft hit the sea and crashed. (He was later picked up by the Italians and made a prisoner.) The rest made Malta where on landing one aircraft's engine stopped at once as all its fuel had gone. Six 229 Squadron aircraft also reached Malta from 'Furious', but the remaining aircraft of this unit stayed aboard as the carriers had by then been as long in hostile water as was safe to allow.

Geoffrey Hare, who was incidentally an observer, not a pilot, was in one of the Fulmars which had got off. He continues: "Pat Connolly and I were in the third Fulmar (N1994) and we joined up our range of Hurricanes with some left from the second range which had returned. In all I expect we were about a dozen strong before taking departure for Malta from a point to the South of the Balearics. After going comfortably for nearly an hour Pat Connolly reported that he was losing engine pressure. At that time we were flying about 4,000 feet about 40 miles off the North African coast. A minute or two later Pat said he couldn't keep height for lack of power and we would have to ditch. I immediately gestured to the Hurricanes to carry on to Malta by themselves as we were ditching and we turned for the coast ourselves, losing height all the way. The morning was fine and the sea calm. Connolly told me over the intercom to stand clear as he was about to press the button of the destructor switch for the I.F.P. gear. Nothing happened. I then burrowed into the cockpit to wrench the gear from its housing but in so doing I became unplugged and did not hear the pilot shouting that we were about to ditch."

Hurricanes of 213, 229 and 238 Squadron aboard H.M.S. 'Furious' on 21 May 1941 ready to fly off to the Middle East via Malta on Operation 'Splice'. (*G.H. Westlake*)

"I struck the I.F.F. gear with my forehead with such force that my goggles, which I was wearing luckily, were shattered and my face badly bruised and bleeding profusely. I was scarcely conscious but Pat helped me out of the machine and as the dinghy hadn't emerged after the ditching we had to swim about 250 yards to the beach. Thank God for a Mae West! A reception party of Arabs and French gendarmes were there to greet us and put us under arrest. We were then taken by boat about ten miles to Bone where an armed Army escort awaited us for interrogation and we were kept in a locked room in the barracks. I can remember very little of what happened until we were transferred to Algiers. Pat Connolly was led away to incarceration and I was offered treatment for my facial injuries and an operation on my flattened nose. The French surgeon was very good. The U.S. Consul became responsible for our wellbeing but it was fourteen days or more before my parents got word of my survival after being reported missing on 21 May."

Meanwhile on Malta after a quick lunch the 213 and 229 Squadron aircraft took off again to fly on to Mersa Matruh, lead by four of 252 Squadron's Beaufighters. Seven of the 213 Squadron aircraft lost their Beaufighter and returned to the island. (The Beaufighter pilots reaching Africa were Wg.Cdr. Yaxley, Flg.Off. Virgin, Sub Lt. Fraser and Plt.Off Davidson). Four of 252's Beaufighters had been destroyed on the ground during air raids while on Malta and the remaining four left on the same day for Gibraltar on the first leg of the flight back to England, each carrying three aboard instead of the usual crew of two. On the second leg of the journey one Beaufighter force-landed in Eire, where Flg.Off. Holgate, Flg.Off. Verity and Sgt. Barnett were interned. A second crashed into the sea off Mount's Bay, Flg.Off. MacDonald, Flg.Off. Lemar and Sgt. Booth being rescued safely. Flt.Lt. Riley remained on the island – he was in hospital recovering from injuries.

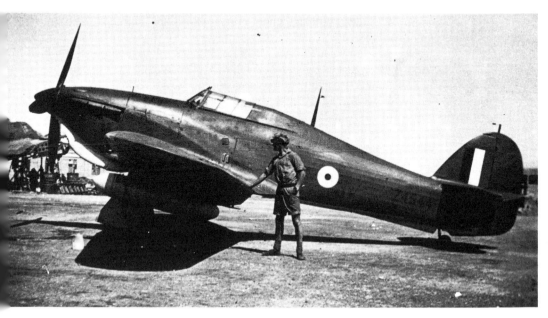

Newly-arrived tropicalized Hurricane IIA (Z4544) immediately after arrival on Malta. Note one of 252 Squadron's Beaufighters in the background undergoing major repair. (*J.A. Heath*)

215

While all this had been happening, 249 Squadron had also been launched from 'Ark Royal', also led by Fulmars. The first group, headed by Sqn.Ldr. R.A. Barton, had to turn back when the oil tank of the guiding Fulmar split. A relief guide was flown off and the flight reached Malta without further mishap. The second, with Flt.Lt. T.F. 'Ginger' Neil at its head, seemed doomed from the start. No sooner was Neil in the air than the left gun panel in the upper wing surface came loose and stuck up in the air. At the same time wind scooped all his maps out of the cockpit, which was still open. Finding that the aircraft would still fly, he formed up behind the Fulmar and they set course for Malta. After about an hour the Fulmar suddenly accelerated and climbed away. The Hurricane lost it and flew round for five minutes, going down to 400 feet above the water to avoid appearing on the radar screens on nearby Italian-occupied islands.

Finally in despair they turned back for the fleet, but on approaching this, the ships all scattered under the impression that an enemy torpedo raid was coming in. The Hurricanes flew around overhead for 15–20 minutes until their predicament became clear, when 'Ark Royal's' deck was cleared and another Fulmar sent off. They were now nearer to 550 miles from Malta than the 450 intended, and the Fulmar crew announced over the radio that they could not make it, breaking away to land on the carrier again. Neil did not hear this broadcast however, and headed for Malta with his followers, seeing a Ju88 and several other types of aircraft in the distance as they went. After five hours and 35 minutes in the air they were all desperately short of fuel, but at that moment Malta appeared dead ahead. They went straight in to land at Luqa, but as they approached saw bombs bursting on the runway – they had arrived in the middle of a raid! Opening up, most managed to complete a circuit, although several ran out of fuel at that point and went down to land at once, while others landed at Hal Far. Despite everything, all got down safely.

Another group was led by a Fulmar flown by Pty Off. (A) Albert Sabey with Sub Lt. Bernard Furlong as navigator. Immediately after take off they discovered that their undercarriage would not retract, and as this reduced speed and increased fuel consumption – due to the drag created – they led the flight back to the carrier, signalled their predicament, and again a further Fulmar was launched. Unfortunately for them, some of the Hurricane pilots failed to see this and stuck to their Fulmar, ignoring all signals to break away. Aware that it would be difficult and dangerous for the Hurricanes to attempt to land back aboard, Sabey set off towards Malta, hoping to meet one of the aircraft despatched from the island to lead in any lost aircraft, before their fuel ran out. This in fact transpired, and the Naval crew were further fortunate in being picked up safely after ditching in the sea; they were transported to the island.

Now it was that 249 Squadron received the news that it was to stay on the island. The pilots were dismayed, for they had no kit with them, all being aboard ship with the ground party, bound for Egypt. No kit or ground crew were seen again by the majority of the pilots. Worse was to follow, for they were taken by bus to Takali where 261 Squadron had been ordered to prepare for departure to the Middle East, 249 being the unit's relief – and they were ordered to take 249's new Hurricanes with them, leaving most of their own well-worn machines behind. 'Ginger' Neil was not impressed with what he saw, and described 261 as "the most motely crowd of goons you ever saw in your life – ferry pilots who had been formed into a squadron." The Hurricanes were "a poor crowd of battered Mark Is – no squadron markings, some with Vokes filters, some not. A variety of propellers, etc. Morale of the pilots dreadful." His description of the aircraft was not far out; John Pain reported: "By the time we left, aircraft were being repaired with dope-painted linen or cloth from anywhere and metal repairs were made with the aid of Players 50s tins. And of course, cannibalisation where practicable." One eyewitness noted seeing tailwheel tyres stuffed with straw due to lack of spares, and a pilot with the ripcord pull-ring on his parachute replaced with a piece of bent wire!

261 Squadron was indeed tired – it had taken a terrible beating from Müncheberg and his men. It had never been fully constituted or trained as a squadron, but it had achieved most creditable results nonetheless, with over 100 victories plus many more probables and damaged. The pilots were not sorry to go; Doug Whitney entered in his logbook of the flight out: "The finest sight of Malta I've seen ... " which, he adds, no doubt expressed his feelings at the time. (See Appendix IV for a summary of 261 Squadron's achievements, the subsequent careers of its pilots, etc.) On leaving the squadron did take at least two of its old Hurricane Is with it. P3731 (which had arrived from 'Argus' with 418 Flight in August 1940) and V7370 (which had arrived during the ill-fated second reinforcement flight in November of that year) reached Palestine, and were later taken on charge by the newly-formed 127 Squadron. Both were shot down over Syria by Vichy French Dewoitine 520s of GC III/6 on 5 July 1941.

249 Squadron was by contrast an experienced and successful team. It had a good record during the later stages of the Battle of Britain, where it had produced Fighter Command's only Victoria Cross of the war – Flt.Lt. J.B. Nicholson. Several of the pilots from that period were still with the squadron, including the tough Canadian C.O., Sqd.Ldr. 'Butch' Barton, D.F.C. ($8\frac{1}{2}$ victories and 6 damaged) and flight commander 'Ginger' Neil, D.F.C. and Bar (11 victories plus two shares). Others were:

Flg.Off. H.J.S. Beazley (2 victories and 2 shared)

Plt.Off. G.C.C. Palliser (2 and 2 shared)

Flg.Off. P.H.V. Wells (2 shared)

Plt.Off. A.R.F. Thompson (1 and 1 shared)

Plt.Off. J.P. Mills (3 and 1 shared)

The other flight commander was Flt.Lt. F.V. 'Tony' Morello, who had gained one shared victory with 501 Squadron. The balance of the squadron was made up as follows:

Flg.Off. E.J.F. Harrington	Flg.Off. E. Cassidy	Plt.Off. R.H. Matthews
Plt.Off. R.H.M. Munro	Plt.Off. J.T. Crossey	Sgt.G.A. Stroud
Sgt. D.C.H. Rex	Sgt. J.G. Parker	Sgt. M. Guest
Sgt. R.W. Lawson	Sgt. R. Rist	Sgt. C.A. MacVean
Sgt. F.A. Etchells	Sgt. J.G.K. Hulbert	Sgt. Cooper

To take 261 Squadron's place on Malta came 249 Squadron, which flew in from H.M.S. 'Ark Royal' on 21 May 1941. L. to r.; front; Flt.L. H.J.S. Beazley, Sqn.Ldr. R.A. Barton, D.F.C., Flg.Off. E.F.J. Harrington, Flg.Off. P.G. Leggett; *rear:* Plt.Off. D.A. Tedford, Plt.Off. G.C.C. Palliser, Sgt. R. Rist, Plt.Off. R.H. Matthews, Sgt. Branch, Sgt. J.G. Parker, Plt.Off. F.C. Hill, Sgt. D. Owen, Flg.Off. C.C.H. Davis; far rear: Sgt. Smith. (*R.A. Barton*)

Also arriving on the island at this time for Fighter Control duties was Wg.Cdr. Halahan, who had been despatcher aboard 'Ark Royal' during the previous flight. The remaining five Fulmars which had led the Hurricanes in were to stay on the island, although the original plan called for them to fly on to Maleme (Crete), where they were to assist the Fulmars of 805 Squadron in the defence of that island. However Crete was invaded the day before the arrival of 800X at Malta, where they were now to remain, attached to 830 Squadron, and were to play the role of night intruders, attacking airfields in Sicily with 20 lb. bombs. With few spares and no reserve aircraft, their service was not expected to be sustained. In the event it was to continue for longer than could possibly have been envisaged.

Next day 249 Squadron was split into two sections, one half commanded by Barton and one by Neil. Each half was to operate for half of each day, allowing 50% of the pilots to be off duty at any one time. 185 Squadron now moved to Takali alongside the newly-arrived unit with its own remaining ten Mark Is and two Mark IIs, leaving Luqa and Hal Far free for the time being for use as staging airfields to Egypt, and as bases for the bombers and reconnaissance aircraft. During 23rd. the remaining aircraft of 213 Squadron set off to complete their journey to the African mainland.

Pilots of 249 Squadron with one of their Hurricanes; rear: Sgt. Smith; on wing: Sgt. J.G. Parker, Plt.Off. F.C. Hill, Sgt. H. Moren, Sgt. R. Rist; standing in front: Plt.Off. G.C.C. Palliser. (*R.A. Barton*)

Commanding officer of 249 Squadron, Sqn.Ldr. R.A. 'Butch' Barton, D.F.C., who had $8\frac{1}{2}$ victories to his credit during the Battle of Britain. (*A.R.F. Thompson*)

For 249 Squadron the first introduction to real action on Malta came as something of a shock. About ten Hurricanes were gathered round the dispersal hut at Takali on the afternoon of 25 May when just before 1400 the sirens went, but the squadron was not ordered off, although the pilots were ready strapped into their cockpits. Suddenly Bf109Es of 7/JG/26 arrived with a crackle of gunfire, shooting-up the airfield. Flg.Off. Pat Wells was wounded in the leg, while Flg.Off. Harrington's aircraft was hit by a cannon shell in the forward fuel tank, another hitting his parachute pack; he was unhurt, but his Hurricane was a total write-off. Sgt. MacVean leapt from his cockpit in such a hurry that he broke both legs. The full results of the attack included two Hurricanes burnt out and three damaged, plus three groundcrew wounded. Pat Wells describes the attack: "This was our first readiness at Malta and whilst sitting in the crew room were astonished to hear the air-raid sirens howling – in the U.K. we had always been airborne *before* the sirens sounded. We rushed out to the aircraft and got ready for the scramble which never came. I noticed Flt.Lt. Neil get out of his aircraft obviously to go to the telephone. I am fundamentally lazy and decided that we would inevitably be scrambled so it was less effort to remain in my aircraft and wait for it, helmet on and listening to the R/T. The next thing I saw was people running – I still could not hear anything due to my helmet – and on looking round saw the 109s starting their dive on the field. I tried to start the engine but the airman on the starter battery trailer had fled so I could not do a thing except huddle in the cockpit, waiting for the sensation of being hit. The aircraft was burning well and this, plus exploding ammunition, drove me out. It was only when I got on the ground and tried to walk did I realise that I had a bullet through the top of my right ankle. The ambulance came and I was filled with delicious brandy but was instantly sick when I got to Imtarfa Hospital. Here I had the most devoted treatment from an Army Surgeon, Major C.S. Salisbury, an Australian who was ex-Chief Surgeon on the 'Queen Mary'. I can thank Charles Salisbury for still having that foot today."

Two of 249 Squadron's Hurricanes ablaze after being strafed by Müncheberg and his pilots at Takali on 25 May 1941. (*J. Alton & National War Museum Assoc.*)

Firefighters dowse the flames, but the aircraft is a total write-off. (*P.M.V. Wells*)

249 Squadron personnel glumly inspect the damage. (*National War Museum Assoc.*)

The German pilots involved in the attack claimed four Hurricanes destroyed, two by Müncheberg and one each by Lt. Johannsen and Obfw. Laub; they believed that six had been hit in all from an estimated fifteen. This debacle came as a great blow to the confident pilots of 249, epitomised by its effect on Flg.Off. Harrington. A few days later a 69 Squadron Maryland approached the airfield, looking for all the world like a Ju88. Harrington at once leapt into a slit trench in great haste, only to find it full of barbed wire which inflicted severe lacerations on him. Despite this bad start, this was to be the only meeting the unit was to have with Müncheberg's Messerschmitts, for their time in Sicily was almost at an end. It was a bad week for the British in the Middle East generally however, for in Crete evacuation was now beginning.

The first shock over, a member of the ground crew poses with his dog before one of 249 Squadron's shattered fighters. (*P.H.V. Wells*)

Luqa's battered control tower, partially protected by a wall of sandbags. The tower had just suffered further damage on 25 May 1941 when this photo was taken. (*J.A. Heath*)

27–29/5/41

On Malta the reduced Axis air activity as the last of the German aircraft departed Sicily allowed more offensive action to be put in hand. On 27 May, as 249 Squadron moved across to Hal Far for further operations, six Blenheims from 82 and 139 Squadrons were out attacking a convoy escorted by six destroyers. Heavy defensive fire sent two of the bombers into the water, Flt.Lt. G.M. Fairbairn ('H', V6427), Sgt. E.B. Inman ('J', V6460), and their crews being lost – a grim indicator of what lay ahead for the anti-shipping units. Their attack had however left the steamer 'Foscarini' on fire, and she was subsequently towed into Tripoli. By night Malta suffered its first raid by the recently-arrived **BR 20Ms** of the 43° Stormo B.T., ten of these bombers operating. Next day two more of 139 Squadron's Blenheims flew south to Sfax harbour, where they bombed a ship which was seen to blow up 12. BR20Ms returned that night to attack Valetta and Hal Far, but Hurricanes were up on this occasion, preventing half of the attacking force from reaching their targets and forcing them to return with their bombs. On 29 May anti-aircraft gunners submitted claims for a Ju88 probably destroyed, but it seems likely that they had in fact been firing at one of the Italian Fiats.

223

249 Squadron's top-scoring pilot when they arrived on Malta was Flt.Lt. T.F. 'Ginger' Neil, D.F.C. & Bar (r), who had been credited with shooting down 11 German aircraft and sharing in the destruction of two more. He is seen here with Flg.Off. J.T. Crossey (1) and Plt.Off. G.C.C. Palliser. (*P.C. Leggett via Chaz Bowyer*)

More Italian units were continuing to flow into Sicily, 7° Gruppo C.T. of the 54° Stormo arriving at Comiso with MC 200s. Commanded by Magg. Alberto Beneforti, this unit included the 76ª, 86ª and 98ª Squadriglia. It was followed by the 101° Gruppo Tuffatori (ex B.a'T) with the 208ª and 238ª Squadriglia, which flew their Ju87s in to Gerbini, while on 1 June the 85° Gruppo R.M. was formed at Stagnone, Marsala, from the 144ª and 197ª Squadriglia with Z.506B floatplanes. Eleven days later the other Gruppo of the 43° Stormo B.T., the 31° under Ten.Col. Giuseppe Bordin (65ª and 66ª Squadriglia) would reach Catania with more BR 20Ms.

Another 249 Squadron 'noteable' in May 1941 was Flg.Off. Pat Wells. He is seen here later in the year after posting to East Africa, with a Curtiss Mahawk in the background. (*P.H.V. Wells*)

224

1 June however saw the departure of 7/JG 26 for North Africa. During its four months in Sicily the little unit – and particularly its brilliant commanding officer – had been the scourge of Malta's Hurricanes. The Staffel had claimed at least 42 victories, of which 20 (including one over Yugoslavia) had been credited to Müncheberg, whose score now stood at 43. Substantial numbers of aircraft had also been claimed destroyed on the ground (or water). During this whole period not a single operational loss had been sustained; no better example of the supremacy of experience, good training, proper tactics, high morale and suitable equipment can be found anywhere. Yet despite their apparent invulnerability, few of the German pilots would survive the tribulations which would later confront the fighter pilots of the Luftwaffe. Müncheberg himself, promoted and highly-decorated, would fall in combat with American fighters over Tunisia during March 1943 after his 135th. victory. His second in command in 7 Staffel, Klaus Mietusch, was to rise to the rank of Major, gaining the Knights' Cross and a credited 72 victories before he too fell to U.S. fighter pilots in September 1944. Of the others, Hans Johannsen was killed in March 1942 with his score at eight; Karl-Heinz Ehlen died a month later with seven victories. Melchior Kestel was also killed in combat in June 1943, while Karl Laub, also with seven victories, was finally killed in December 1944. Karl Kühdorf survived, the only one of the more successful pilots to see the war out; his final score stood at 19 in April 1945, when he was shot down by Russian anti-aircraft fire and became a prisoner.

Soon to depart from Sicily, the Luftwaffe's most successful fighter pilots over Malta during the Spring of 1941 pose with Italian friends. L. to r. unidentified Italian pilot; Lt. Wenzel (JG27); Oblt. Joachim Müncheberg; the Italian base commander; Oblt. Erbo Graf von Kageneck; and unidentified Italian and German pilots. (*August Graf von Kageneck via J. Roba*)

For Malta's defenders the tide had turned. A new period was about to begin during which they would regain some of their earlier superiority over the base, and bend their efforts even more towards the offensive. This change was marked by the arrival on 1 June of Air Commodore Hugh Pughe Lloyd, M.C., D.F.C., to take over as A.O.C. from A.V.M. Maynard, A.F.C. Newly-promoted from the rank of Group Captain, Lloyd had been serving as Senior Air Staff Officer with No.2 Group of Bomber Command. Now with the recent arrival of detachments from his old Group on Malta, he arrived with a directive that his main task was to organise the offensive against the Axis supply shipping plying between Europe and Africa. His promotion to Air Vice-Marshal soon followed. His arrival coincided with a change of command at Luqa, Gp.Capt. C.A. Cahill, D.F.C., A.F.C., taking over from Gp.Capt. O'Sullivan.

Ju52/3ms in flight from Comiso–Catania in May 1941, beginning another supply mission to Tripoli. (*Fam. Carmello via N. Malizia*)

By now a number of Italian and German aircrew prisoners had accumulated on the island, the unwounded amongst them being housed at Kordin Military Detention Camp. The story goes that whilst the Governor General was paying a visit to the camp certain Luftwaffe officers complained of, amongst other grievances, inadequate seating – the lack of chairs. Within days a number of voluminous, ornately-carved armchairs arrived from His Excellency's residence!

Chapter 6

OFFENSIVE SUMMER

Third new squadron in a month! Hurricanes of 46 Squadron on board H.M.S. 'Ark Royal' prepare for take-off on 6 June 1941 during Operation 'Rocket'. (*W. Hartill*)

Summer 1941 was to be a period of growing confidence on the part of the Malta fighter squadrons – a period when activities moved from the purely defensive to an offensive of limited proportions as a supplement to the growing role of the island's bombing force. Early June saw the despatch from England of the first full squadron detachment of Blenheims to the island. The initial detachment from 21 Squadron had been a success, and apart from a single aircraft destroyed on the ground by bombs, all had returned safely on completion of their short stay. Now 82 Squadron prepared to increase its existing detachment to full unit strength of tropicalized aircraft. With the increase in the traffic of bomber aircraft to the Mediterranean area generally, the fighter detachments of the Regia Aeronautica

227

being maintained on Pantelleria became of more importance, both for intercepting these delivery flights, and for providing escort to the shipping convoys which now came under increasingly frequent air attack by day.

2/6/41

Five Blenheims from Malta were out on 2 June after a convoy of six ships which had been sighted by a Sunderland. Two CR 42s and a Z.501 were seen over the convoy, but the bombers kept their distance until these aircraft appeared to leave the area. It seems that the ships' crews had assumed the Blenheims to be friendly, since daylight attacks by the R.A.F. had not yet become common. At 1445 the bombers attacked, but one went into the sea during the run-in. It seems that this may well have fallen to a pair of CR 42 pilots from the 70ª Squadriglia, 23° Gruppo C.T.; Ten. Marco Marinone and Ten. Antonio Bizio reported seeing a lone Blenheim to the north-west of Lampedusa while they were escorting a convoy off the Italian coast, and they claimed this shot down between them. The attack by the other four Blenheims was successful; the steamer 'Montello', which was carrying ammunition, blew up and sank, whilst the 'Beatrice Costa', carrying a cargo of petrol in drums, caught fire. Her crew abandoned her, and she was sent to the bottom by her escort.

On Malta old faces continued to disappear as the existing healthy state of the defences allowed fighter pilots to be rested more regularly. On 4 June Sgt. R.J. Goode, one of the survivors of the 274 Squadron detachment who had been seriously wounded during the previous month, and Sgt. L.J. Dexter were sent to Home Establishment, followed next day by two noteable stalwarts from 69 Squadron – Sqn.Ldr. Whiteley, the commanding officer, and the ex-fighter pilot, George Burges, now also a Squadron Leader; the announcement of 'Titch' Whiteley's D.F.C. was made shortly after his departure. To replace him Sqn.Ldr. R.D. Welland arrived from England, having ferried out a new Maryland via Gibraltar.

3/6/41

On 3 June six Blenheims of 139 Squadron, led by Wg.Cdr. N.E.W. Pepper, D.F.C., were out on an offensive reconnaissance when they came upon a convoy of five merchant ships escorted by four destroyers and four Ju88s. The first section attacked with delayed-action bombs, but one of these exploded just as the second section came in at mast height, Flt.Lt. E. Sydney-Smith reporting that the bomb had struck an 8,000 ton ammunition ship. The Wing Commander's aircraft, 'J', V5860, caught the full blast and disintegrated, while a second Blenheim (Sqn.Ldr. J.R. Thompson) was damaged, but managed to limp back to Luqa.

3–6/6/41

For the fighters combats were sparse at this time; on 3rd. Sqn.Ldr. Barton recorded 249 Squadron's first claim over the island when he intercepted an S.79

of the 56ª Squadriglia, 30º Gruppo, 10º Stormo B.T. as it was flying from Sicily to Libya. Flying Hurricane Z4043, he recorded: "SM. 79 shot down into sea – on fire off Gozo – no crew known to have escaped." Two days later during an afternoon reconnaissance over the Greek coast, a 69 Squadron Maryland flown by Flg.Off. Roger Drew came upon a Z.506B floatplane over the island of Corfu. Drew attacked and inflicted damage on this aircraft, seeing the gunner bale out.

In the early hours of the next morning – 0140 on 6 June to be precise – Flt.Lt. Pat Hancock of 185 Squadron intercepted a bomber which he indentified as an He111: "Patrolling south-east of Grand Harbour to Kalafrana at 1600 feet – saw e/a illuminated south-west of Grand Harbour – attacked and observed tracer strikes – lost it but then found it again by moonlight – attacked again and saw further tracer strikes. Out of ammunition and returned to base." He claimed a probable. At this time 185 Squadron was redesignated as the island's night fighter unit, a move made possible by the arrival during the day of yet more reinforcements.

Even as 249 Squadron had been flying off 'Ark Royal' on 21 May, in England 46 Squadron's pilots and aircraft were loaded aboard the old 'Argus'. As with the former unit, the ground crews and even some of the pilots were sent by transport round the Cape to Egypt. After arrival at Gibraltar the unit joined the remaining elements of 229 Squadron there in being loaded aboard 'Ark Royal' and 'Furious' for delivery to Malta. Codenamed Operation 'Rocket' this new delivery sent off

Like 249 Squadron, 46 was commanded by a successful Battle of Britain 'ace', Sqn.Ldr. A.C. 'Sandy' Rabagliati, D.F.C., who would become one of Malta's greatest fighter pilots and leaders. (*F. Rabagliati*)

forty-three Hurricanes, one more returning with the carrier; the rest arriving safely, led in by nine Blenheims of 82 Squadron which were making their own delivery flight from Gibraltar on their way to join the rest of their unit. On this occasion there were few snags. Weather was perfect, and instead of tired Fulmars, the Blenheims proved more reliable. Sqn.Ldr. Fred Rosier led the first ten 229 Squadron aircraft, the remaining nine going off under the guidance of Flt.Lt. W.A. Smith. 46 Squadron sent its twenty-four fighters in similar flights during the morning, these landing at Hal Far after a four and a quarter hour flight.

This time the situation was reversed somewhat. On arrival 229 Squadron were required to exchange their Hurricane IIs for Malta's remaining Mark Is, and with the latter they flew on to Mersa Matruh next day, shepherded by a pair of the ubiquitous Blenheims, 46 Squadron was to stay however. Like 249 Squadron this was an experienced unit; like 249 it was not to see its ground party again! After service in Norway, 46 Squadron had lost most of its pilots and all its aircraft when H.M.S. 'Glorious' was sunk whilst carrying the air party back to England. Reformed, it had performed well throughout the Battle of Britain, and again several of the 1940 'noteables' were still with the unit. Commanding officer was Sqn.Ldr. A.C. 'Sandy' Rabagliati, D.F.C., a seven-victory 'ace' of distant Italian heritage, who hailed from Scotland, and who had been one of the few pilots to fly a cannon-armed Hurricane during the Battle of Britain. His flight commanders were Flt.Lt. P.W. 'Pip' Lefevre and Flt.Lt. N.W. Burnett. Lefevre was one of the original Norway pilots who had to date been credited with three shared victories; Burnett had one shared, and had also claimed a CR 42 as a probable when the squadron intercepted the first Italian air raid on England in November 1940.

Six other pilots had already been successful in combat, and these were:

Flg.Off. P.R. McGregor, another Norway veteran with one victory on that front;
Flg.Off. J.M.V. Carpenter, four victories flying Spitfires with 222 Squadron during 1940, but then shot down and wounded;
Plt.Off. L.D. Barnes, one and one shared with 257 Squadron;
Plt.Off. J.K. Kay, three victories and one shared with 257 Squadron;
Sgt. N. McD. Walker, a Scot, with one victory plus a share in a Fiat BR 20 during the Italian November 1940 raid.

The rest of the pilots were a fairly international bunch, and were as follows:

Plt.Off. C.A. Blackburn	Plt.Off. H.P. Lardner-Burke	Plt.Off. D.J. Steadman
Plt.Off. P. Rathie	(South African)	Plt.Off. A.G.S. Anderson
Plt.Off. J.G.M. Grant	Plt.Off. C.H. Baker	Sgt. A.N.C. MacGregor
(New Zealander)	Sgt. T. Hackston	(a Scot)
Sgt. A.S. Mackie	(a Scot)	Sgt. R.R. Carson
(a Scot)	Sgt. B.W. Main	Sgt. F.R. Emery
Sgt. J.H. Johnston	(Canadian)	
Sgt. J.D. McCracken	Sgt. W.E. Copp	
	(Canadian)	

On the following day Sgt. Jolly was loaned to 46 Squadron by 185 Squadron, while Plt.Off. Bailey, Sgt. Sheppard and Sgt. Livingston from this unit were loaned to 249 Squadron — mainly because of 185's current shortage of aircraft.

One of 46 Squadron's leading pilots in June 1941 was Flg.Off. J.M.V. Carpenter, an ex-Spitfire pilot.

7–8/6/41

Early on the morning of 7 June 14 MC200s of the 7° Gruppo C.T. carried out a strafe of Hal Far airfield, claiming a Wellington, two Swordfish or Albacores and two fighters destroyed on the ground. No details of actual losses are available. Some 20 hours later in the early hours of 8 June, Hurricanes of 249 Squadron undertook night patrols as 99° Gruppo B.T. BR 20Ms appeared overhead to bomb. Sqn.Ldr. Barton in Z3063 attacked Ten. Sergio Reggiani's aircraft and shot it down in flames; the pilot and co-pilot were rescued to become prisoners, but the rest of the crew perished. A second of the unit's bombers were attacked by Flg.Off. Beazley and Plt.Off. Palliser, and was believed to have gone down into the sea 40 miles from the island; the pair were credited with a 'probable', but in fact the seriously damaged bomber succeeded in limping home having been hit 50 times.

9/6/41

Four of 249 Squadron's aircraft were sent out on 9 June after a radar plot, catching four 193ª Squadriglia S.79s 50 miles out to sea. Sottoten. Marcello

231

Weber's aircraft went down in flames into the water, Sgt. Livingston claiming one of the bombers shot down while Flg. Off. Harrington, Sgt. Rex and Sgt. Lawson claimed damage to the other three; Sgt. Rex subsequently had to bale out, apparently due to a glycol leak, but he was later rescued as were the pilot and co-pilot of the downed Savoia. Although the confirmed victory was credited to Livingston, the account of the commander of the rescue launch, Flt. Lt. Edward Hardie, indicates that Rex may have claimed more than just a 'damaged': "...this morning the pilot had developed a glycol leak and he had to ditch in the sea. We had a very vague idea of where he was; we knew he was about 50 to 60 miles out ... visibility was poor and we went on and on and on – we did not see anything and I was about to give up in despair when I saw something on the horizon that looked like wreckage ... it was the wreckage of an Italian troopship. It was only the fact that I altered my course like that I came across the fighter pilot swimming like mad and, when I got him on board, I said "Where were you going?" and he said "I thought I would give you boys a helping hand in getting nearer to Malta". I told him that he had been heading for Benghazi! He told me before he did ditch he had shot down one of the Italian bombers and he did not know if any of the crew were still alive ... we looked around and came across one of the wings of the Italian bomber on which was the very badly burned pilot. When we got him on board, I had to restrain him because he wanted to shake hands with the boy who had shot him down ... I was nearer to Benghazi than I was to Malta and when I was on the way back I saw something else in the water – a dinghy with two F.A.A. officers in. They had ditched after running out of fuel whilst on a submarine patrol. So I went out for one and came back with four."

This combat had brought to a close the first full year of Malta's defence – and a further assessment of the victories claimed during that period. These now totalled 106:47:38 by the fighters (not including the Beaufighters of 252 Squadron), as follows:

Type	11/6/40–10/10/40	11/10/40–10/2/41	11/2/41–10/6/41	Totals
S.79	9:5:5	2: 2: 2	1: 1: 0	12: 8: 7
CR 42	7:2:2	6: 2: 4	3: 3: 0	16: 7: 6
Ju87	2:1:0	13: 2: 6	16: 6: 5	31: 9:11
MC200	4:1:1	6: 2: 2		10: 3: 3
Ju88		12: 2: 5	4: 7: 4	16: 9: 9
Z.506B		2: 0: 0	1: 1: 0	3: 1: 0
Bf109			6: 2: 1	6: 2: 1
Bf110			2: 0: 1	2: 0: 1
Do215			5: 3: 0	5: 3: 0
He111			2: 3: 0	2: 3: 0
BR 20			2: 2: 0	2: 2: 0
S.81			1: 0: 0	1: 0: 0
	22:9:8	41:10:19	43:28:11	106:47:38

232

The island had a most unusual arrival from Gibraltar during 9th. when the Cunliffe Owen OA Mk.I 'Flying Wing' (G-AFMB), an experimental civilian passenger aircraft piloted by Mr. Jim Mollison, landed to refuel. It left again next day destined for service with the Free French forces in Equatorial Africa.

With the departure of the Luftwaffe from Sicily, Regia Aeronautica Macchi C.200 fighters appeared once more, and would operate over Malta in considerable numbers throughout the Summer of 1941. (*A.M.I. via Raso-Malizia*)

11/6/41

For 46 Squadron the first clash with the Regia Aeronautica over Malta occurred during the early morning of 11 June. On that date one of the familiar reconnaissance S.79s approached the island with a heavy escort provided by 17 MC 200s from the 7° Gruppo. Seven Hurricanes were scrambled, the Italian formation being spotted 15 miles East of Valetta at 0900 at a height of about 8,000 feet. Sgt. Walker who was acting as 'weaver' above and behind the other Hurricanes, was the first to spot the S.79 when it was 2,000 feet above him, and climbing to attack, opened fire at 250 yards, closing to 50. Pieces fell off the starboard wing and port engine, but he was then forced to break away. By now the others were on the scene, Sqn.Ldr. Rabagliati in Z2680, Flg.Off. McGregor and Plt.Off. Grant all attacking. The port fuel cell in the bomber's wing now caught fire and it dived into the sea; four members of the crew were seen to bale out, but none were picked up, Ten. Giorgio Pozzalini and his crew from the 194ª Squadriglia all being reported killed. The escorting fighters rushed to the rescue. Ten. Cibin and Serg. Facchini each claiming one Hurricane shot down.

One Hurricane was actually lost, Flt.Lt. Norman Burnett being posted missing in Z2480. The rescue vessel 'Jade', a former Hull fishing trawler under Mr. William Fellowes, searched to within sight of the Sicilian coast but was unable to find any trace of the wreckage or pilot. Two E-boats came out to challenge 'Jade' and gunfire was exchanged, one crewman being mortally wounded but a hit also being registered on the larger of the two E-boats, which then broke off the action.

Malta's own bombers were out during the day too. A pair of Blenheims from 82 Squadron attacked a convoy of six merchant ships and three destroyers, but Sqn.Ldr. M.L. Watson's 'K', Z6426, was hit by machine gun fire from the motorship 'Tembien', struck the mast of this vessel, and crashed into the sea. The remaining Blenheim was attacked by fighters during its return flight, but escaped; the air gunner claimed one of the assailants probably shot down.

This heralded a busier day on 12 June, when two major engagements were fought over and around the island. At 0721 18 Hurricanes, nine each from 46 and 249 Squadrons, were scrambled to intercept another incoming reconnaissance flight. Again it was a lone S.79, this time from 67ª Squadriglia, 32° Gruppo, escorted by fifteen MC200s of the 7° Gruppo, while fifteen more from the 17° Gruppo provided indirect support. For some reason the British pilots – new to the island in every case – identified as six Macchis and six Bf109s, all flying at 16–17,000 feet. The Hurricanes waded in, Flt.Lt. Neil of 249 Squadron claiming a 'Messerschmitt' shot down, and Sgt. Livingston another probable; the pilot of the aircraft attacked by Neil was seen to bale out into the sea off Filfla. For 46 Squadron Plt.Off. Rathie and Sgt. Johnston both chased a fighter which they saw going down at 1,000 feet over Hal Far and both fired at what they identified tentatively as a "CR 42 or possibly a Macchi" with an orange ring painted around the engine cowling. The fighter did a half-roll and the pilot was seen to wave his hands above his head. Rathie fired again, hitting the rear fuel tanks which exploded into flames and the pilot baled out. Flt.Lt. Lefevre managed to climb up to 22,000 feet, seeing Macchis "and Fiats" below him heading for Sicily. Diving with two or three others, he closed on one MC200, firing a two second burst. He obtained hits, but then saw another Hurricane shoot the Italian fighter down when only about 100 feet above the sea. He then saw another Macchi at the same level and fired off all his ammunition into it, closing from 250 yards to 100 yards; he reported that this fighter went straight into the sea. He then spotted a third Macchi pouring smoke and being chased by three Hurricanes.

Despite these detailed claims it seems that there was a fair degree of double claiming; Sottoten. Umberto Curcio of the 7° Gruppo failed to return in MC200 MM5354, while Serg. Antonio Tirapelle force-landed near Agrigento on return – though possibly not as a result of combat damage. The S.79 was hit by A.A. as it passed over the island, while hits on the bomber were also claimed by Sgt. Noel

Serried ranks of 1° Stormo C.T. MC200s head for Malta on a fighter sweep. (*N. Malizia*)

McGregor of 46 Squadron, the middle engine being put out of action, resulting in the mission being terminated. The close escort 7° Gruppo pilots had less opportunity to engage in dogfighting than did those of 17° Gruppo, and were able only to claim two Hurricanes probably shot down. The 17° however submitted a plethora of claims for seven shot down and two probables; one Hurricane each were credited to Capt. Olizio Nioi, Ten. Talamini, Sottoten. Chellini, Sottoten. Ligugnana, Serg.Magg. Rossi, Serg.Magg. Romagna and Serg. Buogo. Three of 249 Squadron's aircraft were hit; Plt.Off. Saunders baled out wounded over the sea. Fortunately, he was located by Sgt. McGregor who called up the rescue launch; four Macchis circled overhead without attacking during the rescue. Plt.Off. Rioch Munro, a Rhodesian, was killed however, whilst Plt.Off. Winton was able to force-land his damaged aircraft at Safi.

During the early afternoon an air-sea rescue Cant Z.506B floatplane (MM45292) of the 612ª Squadriglia, marked with Red Crosses, left Syracuse seaplane base for the second time that day to repeat a search for the missing Curcio; it was escorted by two CR 42s from the 23° Gruppo. Hurricanes of 46 Squadron were again scrambled, intercepting the Cant and a reported three CR 42s 45 miles from Grand Harbour at an altitude of 200 feet. Sqn. Ldr. Rabagliati, this time flying Z2491, and Sgt. Hackston both fired at the Cant, but broke away when they saw the Red Crosses. Sgt. Main followed and got in three short bursts which set the port engine ablaze, only seeing the markings as the aircraft landed burning on the sea. He then climbed to 2,000 feet where he made a beam astern

235

attack on a CR 42, firing a three second burst which caused the engine to pour flames and the pilot to bale out as the biplane dived into the sea. He then reported seeing a second CR 42 being shot down. Rabagliati meanwhile had got one burst at one CR 42 and then attacked another head-on, firing until he saw it fall to pieces in the air. Looking round, he saw two other Italian aircraft shooting down a Hurricane, and then saw a CR 42 and an unidentified aircraft orbitting over the Cant, which was burning furiously on the water. Hackston, after his initial attack, was able only to watch as a CR 42, attacked by one of the others, went diving into the sea. Five minutes later he was 'jumped' by three MC200s when at sea level, and fought with these for eight minutes. Finally he got a long burst into one at close range, seeing black smoke pour out and pieces fall off. He did not see it crash as the other two attacked furiously, but he was then able to outdistance them and escape. He was credited with the Macchi destroyed.

Italian records show that Sottoten. Vittorio Bertoccini of the 74ª Squadriglia was shot down in CR 42 MM7046, while the second CR 42 was damaged, although the pilot, Mar. Germano Gasperoni, was able to shoot down one of the Hurricanes in return. This was undoubtedly the aircraft seen being brought down by Rabagliati, and was flown by Sgt. Norman Walker, who was killed. According to these records no other aircraft were involved at this time, the identity of the Macchis reported by Hackston remaining a mystery – as is the apparently larger number of fighters seen by the various British pilots at the scene of the initial fight. The Italians also reported that the Hurricanes had strafed the Z.506B after it had landed on the water, although this may well have been Main completing his initial attack as the floatplane touched down. On return Sqn.Ldr. Rabagliati was soon off again to search for Walker, but no trace of him was found.

MC200 of the 79ª Squadriglia, 6º Gruppo, 1º Stormo C.T. Note the white-painted tailcone – an unusual feature. (*N. Malizia*)

In Mid June 1941 the 1° Stormo C.T. Macchis were replaced in Sicily by those of 4° and 54° Stormo C.T. Here an aircraft of the latter unit's 86ª Squadriglia, 7° Gruppo is seen on Comiso airfield, with two Reggiane Re 2000 fighters of the Sezione Sperimentale of the 23° Gruppo Aut. C.T. in the background. (*C. Raso via N. Malizia*)

Another Italian rescue aircraft was also sent out when the first Cant and the CR 42 failed to return. A Z.506B carrying the civil registration I-POLA, set off escorted by nine CR 42s from the 23° Gruppo, while 15 MC200s from the 7° Gruppo gave indirect support and nine more 17° Gruppo fighters flew a sweep over the general area. Nothing was seen, and on return the escort left I-POLA some 10–15 kilometres south of the Sicilian coast, off Cap Passero. Here it was caught by seven Hurricanes of 249 Squadron which had been scrambled when the Italian formation appeared on the radar. Recalls Sgt. Fred Etchells: "On third scamble of day I shot down Cant Z.506 near Sicily, which had red crosses on wings, and was apparently an air-sea rescue aircraft – Sqn.Ldr. Barton disapproved but A.O.C. approved. I did not see crosses on wings at time and do not know if it would have made a difference had I done so." Again the Italians reported that the floatplane was strafed after coming down on the water, one man being killed and two wounded; on this occasion the survivors were successfully rescued.

During the day one of the 800X Squadron Fulmars force-landed in the sea, P.O.(A) Sabey and his observer (the unit's C.O.) Lt. J.S. Manning being picked up safely; their aircraft had suffered engine trouble.

Following these fights little was seen of the Regia Aeronautica for several days – a convenient gap for the defenders, for on 14 June yet another delivery of Hurricanes took place – Operation 'Tracer'. On this occasion 'Ark Royal' was joined by the new Fleet carrier 'Victorious', which had just taken part in the hunting and sinking of the German battleship 'Bismark'. On 'Victorious' were twenty-eight Hurricanes of 238 Squadron, desert-bound, while 'Ark Royal' carried twenty more such aircraft of 260 Squadron. On this occasion four Hudsons from 200 Squadron on Gibraltar joined the convoy at fly-off to navigate the 48 Hurricanes to the island in batches of twelve each. One Hurricane failed to take off; one suffered engine trouble en route and was last seen heading for the African coast; one crashed into the sea; one overshot the runway on arrival and crash-landed, and one spun-in on arrival, Sgt. R. MacPherson, the 260 Squadron pilot, being killed in the crash; forty-three landed safely. Following this flight, a signal was sent from H.Q., R.A.F. Middle East, to Air Ministry, stating: "Report that four Hudsons escorting Hurricanes were flown by completely inexperienced crews who were unable to look after themselves much less escort twelve Hurricanes. Some crews were apparently on their first service flight ex-O.T.U. Three out of four Hurricanes lost due entirely to faulty navigation by one Hudson. The squadron commanders (of 238 and 260 Squadrons) further state that Admiral Somerville was with difficulty dissuaded from sending off all aircraft at night despite the fact that Hurricane pilots had not operated from carier before, even by day. Consider it fortunate under circumstances that only four Hurricanes lost. The Hudson mentioned in this signal had first flown 60 miles north of Malta, then south, missing the island by ten miles. The pilot then asked for a course when 70 miles away south-east. On being given a course, the pilot still flew for 15 minutes on a reciprocal bearing until given direct orders over the R/T in clear to turn about. The Hudson pilot was put under arrest on arrival on the island. Meanwhile Fulmars, rescue boats and Hurricanes of 249 Squadron were sent out to search for the missing pilots, Flt.Lt. 'Ginger' Neil finding 238 Squadron's Sgt. Campbell in the sea 40 miles from Kalafrana, where he was safely picked up, as was Sgt.A.D. Saunders of 260 Squadron, the other missing pilot. The fatal crash on landing and the other accident were both due entirely to lack of fuel.

15/6/41

No sooner were the aircraft refuelled than the first left for Egypt, undertaking the seven hour flight to Landing Ground 07. Twenty-one left that day, eight more on 16th. and five on 17th. Only a handful remained as reinforcements for the island. During 15th. meanwhile a Wellington – R3293 of 15 O.T.U. – flying in from Gibraltar crashed in Kalafrana Bay, Sgts. E.B. Beattie and J.R. Bolton and their crew all being killed.

Around this time 249 Squadron became involved in a rather silly misadventure which had sad repercussions for the recently-arrived Wg.Cdr. 'Bull' Halahan. One evening all the squadron's pilots went out drinking, became somewhat riotous, and all ended in jail, Halahan included since he had accompanied them. Although they were released before morning, all hell broke loose and the Wing Commander nobly accepted responsibility completely and took the full brunt. He was gone, posted away, virtually within 24 hours, being carried to H.Q., R.A.F. Middle East in Cairo in one of the 10 R.A.A.F. Squadron Sunderlands – a sorry fate for such a noteable fighter leader.

In Sicily the increasing Regia Aeronautica presence was somewhat re-organised by the formation of the Comando Bombardamento della Sicilia to direct the operations of the six bomber gruppi, the dive-bomber gruppo, and the single torpedo-bomber squadriglia. Further reinforcements were on their way at this time, Ten.Col. Carlo Romagnoli leading the 10° Gruppo, from his MC200-equipped 4° Stormo C.T., to Catania on 16th., while the newly-formed 173ª Squadriglia Autonomo R.S.T. was preparing to move in with Fiat CR25 twin-engined long range fighters for the strategic reconnaissance role. With the arrival of the first 4° Stormo unit, the 1° Stormo C.T. (6° and 17° Gruppo) left Sicily on 17th. for Veneto-Campoformido in the North of Italy, while the 23° Gruppo Autonomo C.T. moved from Comiso to Trapani. A few days later the headquarters of the 54° Stormo and the 16° Gruppo C.T. moved into the vacant space at Comiso from Gela.

Serg. Mariotti, a Macchi pilot of the 54° Stormo C.T., seen in the cockpit of his aircraft. Note the unit's 'Tiger' emblem. (*A. Mauri via N. Malizia*)

18/6/41

On 18 June nine MC200s from the 16° Gruppo approached Malta during the early afternoon, Hurricanes of 249 Squadron being scrambled and intercepting 20 miles north of Grand Harbour. Plt.Off. Palliser and Sgt. Sheppard (in Z4070) claimed one Macchi shot down between them, and a second was claimed as a probable. During the fight Sgt. Alex Livingston's aircraft (Z4058) was hit. A particular friend of his amongst the ground staff, Cpl. John Alton (later Squadron Leader), recalls: "He desperately tried to bring his aircraft back with a glycol leak. When he was over Takali the aircraft caught fire and he abandoned it, alas too late – a couple of hundred feet cost him his life. I was always saddened when we lost a pilot but Jock's death affected me for quite a while." No claim appears to have been made by the Italian fighters on this occasion, but one MC200 was hit and Mar. Sigismondo was wounded in the arm; he carried out a crash-landing on his return to base.

18–24/6/41

After 69 Squadron's initial experience with the converted Hurricane I (V7101), a modified long-range Mark II (Z3053) was delivered to the unit at this time. Most reconnaissance work continued to be undertaken by the faithful Marylands however, and these were still on occasion put to an additional offensive use. The squadron had also received a single Beaufighter, but when on 18 June Flg.Off. Warburton was ordered to fly a special reconnaissance over Messina searching for a reported large convoy, he crashed this aircraft on take-off. It was a complete write-off, but fortunately he and his navigator were unhurt. On 20 June Warburton made a sortie over Tripoli in a Maryland, during which he machine-gunned Homs and Misurata landing grounds, claiming three S.79s set on fire. Over the same area in the early morning four days later, Flg.Off. Drew and his crew engaged in a fight with an intercepting CR 42, which was seen to fall away steeply.

22/6/41

Meanwhile on 22nd. 46 Squadron had again been engaged in a battle with the Italian fighters. During the early morning of this day 17 Hurricanes were sent off, Sqn.Ldr. Rabagliati in Z2526 leading six to patrol at 19,000 feet. Here Sing Sing Controller vectored them onto two 'bandits' which turned out to be a pair of MC200s – two stragglers from a formation of 30 10° Gruppo aircraft which Ten.Col. Romagnoli was leading as escort to a single reconnaissance Z.1007bis. Rabagliati dived onto their tails and attacked the fighter on the right, which half-rolled and dived away to 500 feet. After first losing sight of it, Rabagliati spotted it again and gave chase, firing from dead astern and closing to 100 yards at which point it was reported that the Macchi was seen to go into the sea. Italian records indicate that although the aircraft was damaged, the pilot – Mar. Bignami – was able to get it back to Sicily. Serg. Steppi claimed one Hurricane shot down.

Of increasing importance in Malta's striking power during the Summer of 1941 were the Bristol Blenheim IV bombers detached to the island by Bomber Command's No. 2 Group. L9336 is seen parked at Luqa. (*C.G. Jefford*)

22–24/6/41

During the day 82 Squadron undertook its first major operation since the arrival on the island of the rest of the unit. Six Blenheims went out to attack a convoy off Lampedusa, which turned out to have an escort of CR 42s. Flak from the ships was fierce and as Sqn.Ldr. J. Harrison-Broadley approached the port engine of his aircraft was hit and caught fire. He continued his approach, but the starboard engine was then also hit and began to burn. His flying speed allowed him to complete his bombing run, one of his bombs being seen to hit one of the vessels, but immediately after this he was obliged to ditch the stricken bomber (Z6422). He and his crew were picked up and made prisoners.

Flt.Lt. T.J. Watkins, a survivor of the terribly costly raids undertaken by the squadron during the Battle of France a year earlier, attacked a 6,000 ton merchant ship in UX–B, Z9545, but his aircraft too was hit as he pressed home his bombing run, and he was badly wounded in the legs. Despite this, hits were gained on the target vessel, but the Blenheim then came under attack by one of the fighters. Watkins manoeuvred to give Sgt. E.F. Chandler, the gunner, the best possible field of fire, and as the CR42 closed in he claimed to have shot it down. Watkins then lapsed into unconsciousness due to his wounds as the aircraft headed for home. The observer, Sgt. J.S. Sargent, removed him from his seat and took over the controls. Watkins recovered consciousness momentarily several times, but on finding that the aircraft was over Malta, insisted on taking over again, and despite pain and great weakness due to loss of blood, he made a successful landing. Subsequently Watkins was awarded a D.S.O., Harrison-Broadley a D.F.C., while Chandler and Sargent got a D.F.M. each. The attack had in fact caused serious damage to both the motorship 'Tembien', and the German vessel 'Wachtfels', although both later reached Tripoli with the assistance of tugs. The squadron was out again on 24th., attacking the convoy in Tripoli harbour after it had docked. Led by Wg.Cdr. Atkinson, the Blenheims claimed severe damage to a 20,000 ton liner and a 12,500 ton motor vessel.

19/6/41

Before this however 82 Squadron had suffered an earlier loss when Sgt. J. Harrison and crew were reported killed on 19 June in undisclosed circumstances. Towards the end of the month the Blenheims were reinforced when a detachment from 148 Squadron returned to the island from Egypt, Sqn.Ldr. R.J. Wells, D.F.C., leading in six of the unit's Wellingtons.

23–25/6/41

The last week of June was to prove a most active one for 46 Squadron, which was to be engaged five days out of eight. The first of these saw the start of the offensive for the fighters. In the early dawn of 23 June Sqn.Ldr. Rabagliati led four of his Hurricanes in a strafe of the Italian seaplane base at Syracuse, where six moored aircraft and other general facilities were shot-up. Early on 25 June a large incoming raid was plotted on the radar, nine Hurricanes each from 46 and 249 Squadrons taking off and climbing hard. Only 46 Squadron was to intercept the incoming formation which was reported as one S.79 and 24 MC200s at 21,000 feet, 15 miles south of Sicily. The force which had left the coast of that island included a lone S.79 of 58ª Squadriglia, 32º Gruppo B.T., flown by Col. Ranieri Cupini, the Stormo commander, with an escort of no less than forty-eight MC200s, ten from 10º Gruppo and 12 from 16º Gruppo in the lead. Twelve of these fighters were forced to return almost at once with various technical troubles, but the bomber and the remaining thirty-six fighters continued. Sqn.Ldr. Rabagliati (in Z2481) led the attack straight into the formation, concentrating his own fire on the Savoia. Several pilots saw the undercarriage fall into the 'down' position, and the bomber was last seen heading home, losing height and streaming oil; Rabagliati was credited with a 'probable'.

Plt.Off. Anderson, flying No.2 to Rabagliati, fired at one Macchi, then attacked two more, firing at them continually in a dive from 18,000 feet to sea level, where one crashed into the sea 20 miles south of Delimara Point. Sgt. Copp attacked an MC200 at 10,000 feet, hitting it with a four second burst from dead astern, and then a two second burst from the starboard beam. The fighter turned hard to port, pulling its nose up high. This allowed Copp to get in another good burst into the cockpit and it dropped "like a plummet, apparently out of control". It was seen to go into the sea 11 miles south of Cap Religione. Meanwhile newly-commissioned Plt.Off. Main, having fired at the Savoia briefly, dived on seven Macchis, firing many bursts from beam and astern at 250 yards' range into one. He was then attacked by a second, but turned on this and chased it to within ten miles of the Sicilian coast. He last saw it going down steeply towards land at 8,000 feet after he had fired four short bursts into it, and he was awarded a confirmed destroyed for this, bringing the number of Macchis believed to have been shot down to three.

Actually losses to the Italians amounted to two Macchis of the 16° Gruppo; Mar. Giovanni Bravin was killed, but Mar. Otello Simionato came down in the sea 20 miles from the coast, and was rescued by a Z.506B. Ten. Virgilio Vanzan of the 10° Gruppo claimed one 'Spitfire' shot down, while others claimed a single 'probable' between them. On this occasion no British losses were suffered.

During the afternoon 69 Squadron's long-range Hurricane II reported sighting four 20,000 ton merchant ships with an escort of seven destroyers, to the south–east of the island. At this time the Italians had just started using four 20,000 ton liners – 'Marco Polo', 'Neptunia', 'Oceania' and 'Vulcania' – to transport troops to Libya to relieve forward elements of the Afrika Korps. On receipt of news of the sighting, a Maryland was sent off to shadow, with Flg.Off. Bloxham at the controls and carrying Lt. H.E.H. Pain, Senior Observer from 830 Squadron, whilst a strike by Swordfish was planned and organized. But first all available Marylands were armed with two 500 lb. bombs apiece, and were sent out to attack. From this unsuccessful mission Sgt. B.P. Hanson and his crew of AR726 failed to return, last being heard on the R/T announcing they were bombing the ships. It seems very probable that they were shot down by a MC200 of the 10° Gruppo flown by Serg. Roberto Steppi, who claimed a Blenheim shot down and another damaged. At 1800 a Swordfish set out to shadow the convoy, followed by more armed with torpedoes. Just over an hour later the attack commenced, several hits being claimed and possibly a large transport was sunk; the liner 'Esperia' reached Tripoli having been slightly damaged by air attack, while a Swordfish crewed by Sub Lt. D.A.R. Holmes and L/A J.R. Smith was shot down by A.A. fire; both were killed.

27/6/41

On 27 June 46 Squadron reported intercepting two separate raids during the morning, although Italian records show only the second of these. From the details of the two fights, it will become clear that on this occasion these records were almost certainly incomplete. On the first occasion ten Hurricanes went off to intercept a reported one S.79 and twenty-four escorting MC200s which approached Grand Harbour at 20,000 feet at about 0945. Sgt. Copp claimed one MC200 probable, which went into a dive after he had fired a two second burst at it. He then attacked a second over the island at 12,000 feet, firing a three second burst from the beam which caused the pilot to bale out, although his parachute did not open. Plt.Off. Anderson got on the tail of one Macchi and fired several times, hitting the cockpit. The fighter did a stall turn and went into a spin, pouring smoke. Sgt. Hackston reported that he saw it crash. The body of the pilot shot down by Copp was found near Ta' Karac; he had been wounded in the face, but killed by the fall in which his parachute had not opened. His aircraft fell near Birzebbugia. This is the clue to the possible gap in Italian records, for no Regia Aeronautica fighter pilot appears to have been reported killed on this date.

243

Some two hours or so after this initial combat nine Hurricanes were again scrambled by 46 Squadron, again meeting one S.79 with an estimated twenty-nine MC200s in attendance between 20,000 and 25,000 feet over Takali. This seems to have been a formation composed of a Savoia of 193ª Squadriglia and twenty-two escorting Macchis. Twenty MC200s from 10º Gruppo, twelve from 7º Gruppo and nine from 16º Gruppo had originally set out, but nineteen had returned early.

Sqn.Ldr. Rabagliati (in Z2593) led the Hurricanes in a stern chase of the formation, firing a two second burst at the S.79, which he claimed damaged. He was then attacked by three MC200s, turned into one head-on and fired a short burst from 100 yards. This aircraft burst into flames and crashed into the sea ten miles east of the island. He reported that he saw two more Macchis crash, one on the island and one in the sea nearby. Meanwhile Plt.Off. Barnes, who was acting as 'weaver' 4,000 feet above the rest of the squadron, climbed to 27,000 feet and attacked the high escort. Diving from the beam on one Macchi, he closed to quarter astern and saw the aircraft go down in an inverted dive, watching it go straight into the sea as he circled down. He then attacked another at 23,000 feet head-on, seeing the pilot of this carry out a force-landing on the sea. Barnes radioed the position, and the pilot, at first thought to be a Sergente but who was in fact Sottoten. Neri De Benedetti, was picked up by a Swordfish floatplane from the Kalafrana Rescue Flight; Barnes later met his victim. Sgt. Jolly, on attachment from 185 Squadron, also claimed one MC200 shot down and one probable during this action.

A further claim also exists, made by Sgt. Hackston. This was dated 26 June, but on that date no Italian raids were apparently made over the island so far as Italian records are concerned. He reported going up with eight other Hurricanes during the late morning and intercepting a single S.79 with escorting Macchis at 20,000 feet over Valetta – a set of circumstances very similar to that pertaining on 27th. It is therefore very possible that his report was incorrectly dated by one day. He attacked one Macchi as it broke away from an attack on a Hurricane, and fired a five second deflection shot at it, closing from 250 to 50 yards. He saw his fire strike the cockpit area, causing the hood to fly off, whereupon the aircraft flicked over on its back and he saw it fall inverted into the sea.

In the event the Italians lost two MC200s during this combat, both from the 90ª Squadriglia of the 10º Gruppo. Serg. Alfredo Sclavo was killed while Sottoten. De Benedetti was a prisoner. A 612ª Squadriglia Z.506B reported picking up a British pilot near the Sicilian coast. The 10º Gruppo pilots claimed three Hurricanes shot down and five probables, the successful pilots being Cap. Guiducci, Cap. Lucchini, Ten. Soprana, Ten. Vanzan, the captured De Benedetti (obviously claimed on his behalf by a fellow pilot), the deceased Serg. Sclavo (likewise) and Serg. Contarini, all of 90ª Squadriglia, and Serg. Perdoni of the 84ª.

The R.A.F. pilot reportedly picked up by the Cant rescue floatplane was probably from the latest ferry flight, which reached Malta during that same morning. Under the title Operation 'Railway I', 'Ark Royal' had flown off twenty-two new Hurricanes to the island, including some Mark IICs with four 20mm cannon; one went missing en route (Z3554), Sgt. D.R. O'R. Sherburne later being reported a prisoner, while a second crashed on landing, although the pilot was not hurt.

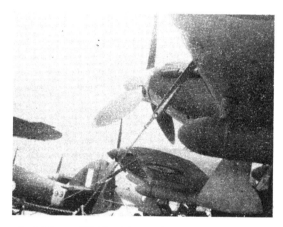

More new Hurricanes for Malta on H.M.S. 'Ark Royal'. Operation 'Railway I', 27 June, 1941. (*P.G. Leggett via Chaz Bowyer*)

28–29/6/41

Further raids were made over Malta by the Regia Aeronautica on 28 June, but details are not available. It is possible that the claim mentioned above which had been submitted by Sgt. Hackston, may have occurred on this date rather than 26th. or 27th. During the day Flg.Off. Bloxham led three 69 Squadron Marylands in an attack on a convoy which had been found off Tripoli. This was bombed and it was reported that at least one 15,000 ton troopship was left on fire. Next day another of 82 Squadron's Blenheims flown by Sgt. J.A. Cover failed to return.

'Railway I' brought a number of the new Hurricane IICs with the formidable armament of four 20mm Hispano cannons in the wings. One is seen here just after arrival, still with its long-range tanks in place under the wings. (*National War Museum Assoc.*)

245

Since it was intended that a new 46 Squadron should be built around the ground party in Egypt, on 28 June came orders that the unit on Malta should be renumbered 126 Squadron with effect from that date. On 30th. the unit moved from Hal Far to Takali, although for a period the aircraft were dispersed to nearby, newly-constructed Safi – a very narrow landing strip hewn out of rock and bordered by anti-invasion devices consisting of poles bedded into the ground, topped with explosive charges. Landing here in partial darkness after a day's operations, and taking off again before dawn for Takali each morning proved very hazardous, and in the first four days of July five of the unit's aircraft were to crash. The squadron's first interception under its new title was undertaken on the day of the move – 30 June – when at 1215 six Hurricanes were scrambled, including some of the new Mark IICs. On the Controller's orders Flg.Off. Carpenter led the section up to 17,000 feet to the north of the island, from which vantage point three MC200s were seen diving for home – apparently part of a formation from the 7° Gruppo. These could not be caught, but on turning Carpenter saw six more behind, one of which he chased down to sea level. Using emergency boost, he caught it and fired one three second burst from 250 yards, at which he reported the Macchi went straight into the sea. Sgt. Mackie meanwhile had chased one fighter to within 20 miles of Sicily, where he claimed shooting it down with a single burst. It spiralled down into the sea with smoke pouring from the engine and the starboard undercarriage leg extended about one foot from its recess in the wing. A third Macchi was claimed damaged by Sgt. McCracken, who pursued it for about 40 miles out to sea. 7° Gruppo reported the loss of Ten. Armando Cibin, who was shot down, but claimed two confirmed victories against Hurricanes by Cap. Saverio Gostini and Serg. Walter Omiccioli, plus three probables by Ten. Maurer, Mar De Mattia and Serg. Mauri.

On this date a further delivery of new aircraft arrived, 'Ark Royal' – this time accompanied by 'Furious' once more – undertaking Operation 'Railway II' to fly off forty-two more Hurricanes. Twenty-six went off the 'Ark' alright, but the second Hurricane (Sgt. M.T. Hare) of the first flight from 'Furious' swerved halfway along the deck and hit the navigating position, knocking off the long-range tanks which caused a large petrol fire, while the aircraft then crashed. Two Naval officers and one rating were killed, four more officers and ten ratings being seriously injured. Four R.A.F. officers, including Wg.Cdr. R.E. Bain, who was in charge of flying-off operations, and four Sergeant Pilots were also seriously injured; Sgt. Hare later died. Despite this serious mishap, the remaining eight Hurricanes of the first flight were all flown off safely. All pilots of the second flight of six were amongst the injured, and as a result no more could be launched. Of the thirty-five Hurricanes which got into the air, all reached Malta safely, together with six escorting Blenheims.

During June 830 Squadron had also been reinforced by the arrival of some more Swordfish from 'Ark Royal's' 825 Squadron; this unit had transferred to the carrier from 'Victorious' after the 14 June ferry run, 'Ark's' 820 Squadron going home to England for a rest with the former carrier. During the latter part of the month Wellingtons had again begun to use Malta as a base for their night raids, as already mentioned, while on 29th. seventeen Blenheims of 110 Squadron left England for this island on detachment, arriving in batches between 2nd. and 4 July. Another new arrival during June was an He115A-2 floatplane; carrying the R.A.F. serial BV185, this was an ex-Norwegian Naval Air Force machine (ex F-58) which had escaped to Britain in June 1940. Modified for clandestine secret intelligence and agent-dropping duties, much of the cockpit glazing had been removed and eight .303 in. Browning machine guns had been fitted in the wings, four of these firing rearwards. Its crew included a Norwegian volunteer pilot, Lt. Haakon Offerdal; the aircraft had been painted with spurious Luftwaffe markings. Its first mission was carried out during the night of 2/3 July, but the aircraft was plagued by engine trouble and was badly damaged during the night of 8/9 July when the hangar at Kalafrana in which it was installed was hit during an air raid. Lt. Offerdal returned to England on 15 July. Meanwhile other new arrivals at Kalafrana at this time were visiting Catalinas from 202 Squadron at Gibraltar.

July 1941 saw the continuation of a pattern which was to be followed for much of the rest of the year. Every week a steady flow of Blenheims and Wellingtons reached the island, a few to stay (some of them 'press-ganged'!) but most merely on refuelling stops before pressing on to the Middle East. Many of these aircraft were direct from the squadrons of Bomber Command, but were to be incorporated on arrival into Egypt's resident units.

185 Squadron at Hal Far, early July 1941, brought up to strength with pilots from recent reinforcement flights. L. to r. Front row; Flt.Lt. S.A.D. Pike, Flt.Off. C.G.St.D. Jeffries, Sqn.Ldr. P.W.O. Mould, D.F.C., Flt.Lt. N.P.W. Hancock, Plt.Off. P.D. Thompson; middle row; Plt.Off. B.J. Oliver, Sgt. T.H. Bates, Plt.Off. G.G. Bailey, Sgt. R.A. Cousens, Sgt. P. Lillywhite, Sgt. J.R. Sutherland, Plt.Off. A.J. Reeves, Sgt. W. Nurse, Sgt. B.J. Vardy; back row; Plt.Off. P.M. Allardice, Sgt. A.W. Jolly, Sgt. J. Ream, Sgt. C.L. Hunton, Sgt. J.R.R. Alderson, Sgt. A.J. Forth, Sgt. E.G. Knight, Sgt. B. Hayes, Sgt. J. Horsey. (K. Cox)

At the start of July 185 Squadron, strengthened by the arrival of new pilots from the delivery flights, moved back to Hal Far and resumed day operations, main responsibility for the night defence of the island being shifted temporarily onto 249 Squadron. However, within the next few days the Fulmars of 800X Squadron would be officially designated 'Independent Night Fighting Unit', under the command of the senior officer, Lt. Manning, the Senior Observer. Their main task would be to undertake intruder sorties over Sicily, when they would each carry four 20lb. bombs. 185 Squadron was still under the command of Sqn.Ldr. Mould, with 'A' Flight receiving a new commander, one of the recent reinforcements, Flt.Lt. S.A.D. Pike. 'B' Flight was still nominally commanded by Innes Westmacott, although he had not yet resumed flying after being wounded. In the air the flights continued to be led by Flt.Lts. Jeffries and Hancock. Other new arrivals with the squadron included Flg.Off. L.C. Murch, who had gained one and three shared victories flying with 253 Squadron in England, and:

Plt.Off. P.M. Allardice	Plt.Off. B.J. Oliver	Plt.Off. D.U. Barnwell
Plt.Off. P.J.B. Veitch	(New Zealander)	Sgt. R.J.F. Ellis
Sgt. J.R. Sutherland	Sgt. T.H. Bates	Sgt. P. Lillywhite
Sgt. B. Hayes	Sgt. J.R.R. Alderson	Sgt. R.A. Cousens
Sgt. J. Ream	Sgt. C.L. Hunton	Sgt. A.J. Forth
	Sgt. E.G. Knight	
	Sgt. J.A. Westcott	

126 amd 249 Squadrons had also received a number of reinforcements:

126 Squadron	249 Squadron
Plt.Off. E. Dickinson	Plt.Off. C.C.H. Davis
Sgt. A.H. Haley, R.A.A.F.	Plt.Off. P.G. Leggett
Sgt. T.C. Worrall	Plt.Off. J.M. Boyle
Sgt. W.D. Greenhalgh	Plt.Off. F.C. Hill
Sgt. J.F.E. Maltby	Plt.Off. G.V. Smith
Sgt. P.S. Simpson	Sgt. D. Owen
	Sgt. J. Kimberley
	Sgt. Carter

Hurricanes of 249 Squadron at 'readiness' at Takali, Summer 1941. (*P.G. Leggett via Chaz Bowyer*)

248

1–3/7/41

On the night of 1st/2nd. five Wellingtons of 148 Squadron carried out a bombing attack on Tripoli harbour, where a number of ships had been reported, and the crews returned believing they had hit an estimated 8,000 ton vessel. The Wellingtons returned to Tripoli again the following night whilst eight Swordfish of 830 Squadron also visited the port. Six of these carried mines which were sown inside the entrance, while two others bombed and set on fire the 1724-ton 'Sparta'. Reconnaissance next day indicated much congestion of shipping caused by the mines and four Blenheims of 82 Squadron were despatched on a daylight sortie to attack them. As a result of these attacks by the Wellingtons, Blenheims and Swordfish, further reconnaissance apparently confirmed an 8,000 ton vessel severely damaged, as was another of 3,000 tons, while a further ship of an estimated 5,000 tons was sinking. One of the Marylands operating in this area, that flown by Flg.Off. Drew, who was reconnoitring Tripoli, also attacked Zuara airfield where he strafed a number of Savoia S.81s, leaving one on fire.

4/7/41

Early in the morning of 4 July thirty-eight MC200s of the 54° Stormo set off to escort a Cant Z.1007bis of the Squadriglia R.S.T. from Palermo over Malta on reconnaissance. The bomber returned early with technical trouble, but the fighters continued to make a sweep. Four Hurricane IICs of 185 Squadron were scrambled, led by Flt.Lt. Jeffries, and these 'bounced' the Macchis, claiming two shot down and three damaged. Jeffries reported: "... saw e/as at 22,000 feet (north-east of Grand Harbour) ... attacked section of three, Nos. 2, 1 and 3 in that order. No. 2 dived away slowly and hood appeared to come off. No. 1 climbed away slowly. No. 3 turned on its back and started spinning down – I kept firing and at 8,000 feet it was spinning violently." He was credited with one destroyed and one damaged. Sgt. Jolly (back from 126 Squadron) reported: "I attacked a Macchi which was lagging – four second burst and he turned over and spun into the sea ten miles north of Grand Harbour ... circled oil patch ... saw another 200 spinning down apparently out of control." Sgt. Trevor Bates and Sgt. Sutherland claimed one damaged each. The Italians reported being attacked twice by formations of four Hurricanes and claimed one probably shot down on each occasion, one by 7° Gruppo and one by 10° Gruppo. One 7° Gruppo Macchi failed to return, Ten. Gian Paolo Mantovani being killed. One of the attacks on the Macchis may have been made by aircraft of 126 Squadron, for on this date it was reported that Sgt. Tom Hackston of that unit accidentally crashed into the sea and was killed, after taking off from Safi in Z3055 just before daybreak. Next day Blenheim Z9575 of 82 Squadron crashed on take-off from Luqa, two members of the crew being killed.

6/7/41

Shortly before midnight during the night of 6/7 July, Sub Lt. Mike Tritton and Lt. Manning set off on an intruder sortie in an 800X Squadron Fulmar. During the night twelve **BR** 20Ms from the 43° Stormo and five S.79s from the 10° Stormo raided Malta. Patrolling over Catania at 1,500 feet the Fulmar crew saw a large aircraft with navigation lights on; this was **BR** 20M MM21534, flown by Ten. Carlo Natalucci and Sottoten. Gianfranco Magrini, returning from Malta. Tritton attacked with a three second burst and the bomber crashed in flames into the sea at the mouth of the Simeto river. A second **BR** 20M force-landed on return.

Sub Lt. Mike Tritton (foreground) of 800X Squadron shot down a Fiat **BR** 20M bomber over Sicily in his Fulmar during the night of 6/7 July 1941. (*I.W.M.*)

7/7/41

Next morning a reconnaissance Z.1007bis from the 176ª Squadriglia carried out a sortie over Malta, escorted by 40 MC200s from the 7°, 10° and 16° Gruppo. The fighters reported a battle with Hurricanes over the target area, Ten. Maurer of the 7° Gruppo claiming one Hurricane shot down. The R.A.F. unit involved has not been discovered, and no loss is recorded.

F/Sgt. Fred Etchells of 249 Squadron, Takali, Summer 1941. (*F. Etchells*)

9/7/41

Another Italian raid during the night of 8/9 July preceded a more active day. Ten BR 20Ms from 43° Stormo and six S.79s from 10° Stormo took part, one Wellington being destroyed on the ground by bombs. Flg.Off. Cassidy of 249 Squadron was on patrol and caught one bomber to the south of the island, closing to very short range before opening fire, and seeing his victim go down in flames. He claimed a BR20, but in fact it was S.79 MM22594 which failed to return. Next morning four 185 Squadron Hurricanes were scrambled to investigate a radar plot near the island. They found four 54° Stormo MC200s and two floatplanes which were probably searching for survivors from the missing S.79. Flg.Off. Bailey claimed one Macchi damaged, while Sgt. Westcott claimed damage to one Z.506B. One Macchi was in fact hit, Sottoten. Giuseppe Avvico being slightly wounded; he crash-landed on return to base.

Four more Hurricanes were off in the early afternoon, Sqn.Ldrs. Mould and Rabagliati of 185 and 126 Squadrons, accompanied by Flt.Lt. Jeffries and Sgt. Mackie, making a strafing attack on Syracuse seaplane base, where they claimed six flyingboats destroyed and four damaged on the water. One Z.506B of the 612ª Squadriglia and one Z.501 of the Ricognizione Marittima were destroyed, and two more Z.506Bs were damaged; a number of vehicles were also hit, two of them being destroyed.

Meanwhile the Blenheims had gone out in force, seven 110 Squadron aircraft

251

attacking Tripoli harbour where direct hits were claimed on four merchant vessels, one of which was estimated to be 12,000 tons, two of 10,000 tons and one of 7,000 tons. Losses were heavy however, four Blenheims (Z6449, 9537, 9553, 9578) failing to return; Sqn.Ldr. W.T.C. Searle was seen to force-land in the sea, while Flt.Lt. M.E. Potier, Plt.Off. W.H. Lowe and their crews were reported missing; Sgt. W.H. Twist was shot down a few miles north of Tripoli, he and his crew becoming prisoners.

A little later two Marylands were sent out to check on the results of the two raids, one north and one south. The latter, flown by Flg.Off. Warburton, reached Tripoli, but was attacked and damaged by an MC200, which was claimed probably shot down by the gunner. The second sought to ascertain the effects of the Hurricanes' strafe at Syracuse, Flg.Off. P.R. Wylde himself strafing a number of floatplanes at this base. He claimed to have set fire to an He115, whilst his gunner believed he had inflicted damage on three more aircraft.

11/7/41

Two days later on 11 July the Regia Aeronautica launched a big fighter mission over Malta, eleven Macchis from the 54° Stormo attacking Hal Far airfield in three sections, while forty-two more gave cover. Twelve Hurricanes were scrambled by 185 Squadron, and possibly others from the other units on the island, for the Italians reported thirty Hurricanes intercepting, four of which were claimed shot down by pilots of the 10° Gruppo, Cap. Franco Lucchini and Mar Leonardo Ferrulli being amongst those credited with shares. Meanwhile the strafers claimed five Wellingtons destroyed on the ground and three Blenheims damaged. The Hurricanes waded in, Sqn.Ldr. Mould claiming one destroyed and two damaged, Flt.Lt. Jeffries one and another damaged, Plt.Off. Gray a further two damaged, other pilots claimed one more shot down – it is believed this credited to Plt.Off. Barnwell – and another three damaged. Jeffries reported: "... I fired short bursts at three different aircraft then attacked a fourth – five second burst – hits on fuselage." Cliff Gray added: "... opened fire from 150 yards – hits on fuselage from just behind the cockpit to tail ... attacked a second and saw pieces come off the fuselage." No losses were actually suffered by either side on this occasion, although five Macchis returned with damage – reportedly to all A.A. fire, but almost certainly in fact to the fire of the Hurricanes; the Italian pilots were probably too involved in their strafing attacks to notice what had hit them.

14/7/41

A 69 Squadron Maryland flown by Sgt. J.K. Hutt reconnoitred Taranto during the morning. It was attacked by an MC200 for 15 minutes but this was then apparently hit by the rear gunner and dived away vertically. Two Blenheims from 110 attacked Zuara airfield, near Tripoli, claiming to have set fire to a Ju52/3m seen there. On return to Luqa Z9551 crashed on landing but the crew survived.

15/7/41

The all-Australian crew of a 69 Squadron Maryland, AR729, flown by Sgt. C.F. Lee were lost when it failed to return from an afternoon reconnaissance over Tripolitania.

16/7/41

After dark Italian bombers raided Malta. Here S.79 (MM23897) of the 10° Stormo was shot down over the target, Ten. Mario Massini and his crew being lost. A 43° Stormo BR 20M was hit by fire from a night fighter, believed to have been a Fulmar of 800X Squadron flown by Sub Lt. Tritton; as a result it crashed while landing at Gerbini and was destroyed, one member of the crew being killed and two injured. Two Fulmars intruded over the Catania area during the night, dropping a number of bombs. One Fulmar, crewed by P.O.(A) Sabey and Sub Lt. Furlong, circled Gerbini aerodrome with their navigation lights on and were given the green to land! Flying low over the runway they released their 20 lb. bombs and believed they set an aircraft on fire. This may have been the crashed BR 20M.

This same night three Swordfish of 830 Squadron headed out in the opposite direction, their regular hunting ground at Tripoli, two armed with bombs while Lt. G.M.T. Osborn carried a torpedo. Gliding down over the harbour Osborn spotted a large tanker off the North Mole, released from 250 yards and scored a hit amidships. The 6,212 ton 'Panuco' was damaged sufficiently to make it impossible to unload her whole cargo and she was forced to return to Italy with 6,000 tons of fuel still on board.

17/7/41

During 17th. forty-nine MC200s drawn from the 7°, 10° and 16° Gruppo set off mid morning to escort one of the new reconnaissance Z.1007bis over Malta again. En route the 16° Gruppo fighters became separated and returned to base, but the rest of the formation reached the island where eight Hurricanes of 249 Squadron and eleven from 185 Squadron had been scrambled. The aircraft from the former unit made contact, Sqn.Ldr. Barton in Z3262 claiming one Macchi shot down in flames, while Plt.Off. Leggett claimed a second and Flg.Off. Davis one damaged. Two Macchis of 10° Gruppo were lost, Serg.Magg. Enrico Botti being killed, while Serg.Magg. Natale Finito was later rescued from the sea. In return Ten.Col. Romagnoli and Cap. Lucchini each claimed one Hurricane shot down and Serg.Magg. Miotto two; 'probables' were claimed by Mar. Ferrulli and Serg. Contarini. One Hurricane was actually lost, Sgt. Maurice Guest failing to return in Z2818. During the day 10° Gruppo submitted another claim, Serg. Bladelli reporting that he had shot down a Blenheim near Cap Passero.

18/7/41

Six Blenheims from 110 Squadron were led by Wg.Cdr. Theo M. Hunt, D.F.C., to attack a power station at Tripoli. Hunt was seen to obtain direct hits on the

253

target, but during the return flight the formation was attacked by an Italian fighter when ten miles out to sea from the African coast. The interceptor opened fire from long range, and Hunt's aircraft at once crashed into the sea.

19/7/41

Sgt. McCracken of 126 Squadron was killed in a take-off accident after dark. A new major convoy was now about to sail from Gibraltar for Malta, and a number of changes of disposition were made prior to this. In Egypt there were now elements of two Beaufighter squadrons that had been despatched by Coastal Command from England. 252 Squadron had already operated briefly from Malta during the previous convoy, but now it had been joined by 272 Squadron, although both units were considerably understrength. Most available Beaufighters were therefore concentrated in 252, while 272 flew the remaining eight from Edcu to Malta, where they were joined by eight new machines and crews flown directly from England. This raised both units to full strength. 148 Squadron flew its nine Wellingtons out to Egypt again to make room.

At the same time further deliveries of Blenheims arrived from Gibraltar on 19th. Of the six bombers flown in, four went on to Egypt, but two 105 Squadron machines were retained on the island. With these bombers – as passengers – had

In mid July 1941 Beaufighters returned to Malta, this time in the hands of 272 Squadron. Note the pen of limestone blocks, and the Bren Carrier towing a string of bomb trollies in the foreground. (*National War Museum Assoc.*)

come two experienced Battle of Britain fighter pilots, Sqn.Ldr. George Powell-Sheddon, who had three and one shared victories to his credit, and Flg.Off. D.W.A. Stones, D.F.C., who had nine and two shares, and six probables. The former had arrived with orders to form a new squadron, but finding that this had already been done, he left a few days later for Egypt. Don Stones meanwhile was posted to 249 Squadron, where he proved a most welcome addition. Plt.Off. Boyle from this unit and Plt.Off. Dredge – now partially recovered from his serious injuries – had been posted home a few days earlier. On his return to England Alan Dredge became one of the 'Guinea Pigs' at Mr. (later Sir) Archibald McIndoe's famous burns unit at East Grinstead. After plastic surgery Dredge returned to operational flying, being awarded the D.S.O. and D.F.C. before losing his life in May 1945. 249 Squadron also received a new Engineering Officer, Flg.Off. C.H. Jeffries. John Alton recalls: "He had a passion for clean aircraft and to this end pronounced that the rigger with the cleanest aircraft would be rewarded with a flight around the island in a Magister. As may be imagined, with CR 42s liable to drop in unannounced, to the airmen it was rather like an invitation to Russian roulette!" On Sicily meanwhile the test batch of Re 2000 fighters which had been serving with 23° Gruppo, were formed into an autonomous 377ª Squadriglia C.T. at Trapani under Cap. Pietro Calistri; (command later passed to Ten. Giorgio Solaroli).

Reggiane Re2000 fighters of a test batch were issued to a Sezione Sperimentale of the 23° Gruppo Aut. C.T. at Comiso during the early Summer of 1941, for operational tries. Two of these are seen here, with Serg.Magg. William Dusi of this unit in the foreground. (*Fam. Carmello via N. Malizia*)

During the night of 20 July Malta-based bombers carried out a raid on Naples. Two CR 42s from the 356ª Squadriglia, 21° Gruppo, were sent off in an attempt to intercept, but the night sky was not only dark, but foggy too. Nothing was seen, and on return Sotten. Marcelo Torreggiano crashed to his death near Marcianise, Caserta, when he got lost and ran out of fuel. On 21st. the new convoy sailed under the codename 'Substance'. Heading for the island were a troopship and six cargo vessels, while the Fleet auxiliary 'Breconshire' and six empty vessels currently in Grand Harbour were to come out and sail westwards to gain the protection of the incoming convoy's escorts on the return journey. The escort included 'Ark Royal', carrying 21 Fulmars and seven Swordfish, the latter reinforcements for Malta's strike force, 'Nelson', 'Edinburgh', 'Manchester', 'Arethusa' and a bevy of destroyers.

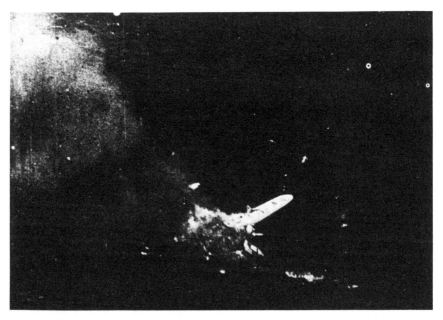

A Cant Z506B floatplane lies blazing and sinking on the water after it had been forced down East of Syracuse in a fight with a 69 Squadron Maryland flown by Flg.Off. Adrian Warburton, on 22 July 1941. (N.W.M.A.)

22–23/7/41

Reconnaissance aircraft were sent out by 69 Squadron to seek out the reaction of the Italian Fleet at Taranto on 22nd. On return from one such sortie during the morning Adrian Warburton encountered a Z.506B some 15 miles east of Syracuse. Attacking, he and the turret gunner forced it down on the sea, a second attack setting it on fire. The radio intercept unit on Malta subsequently reported that an Italian message indicated that two pilots had been killed in the aircraft.

Meanwhile the Blenheims and Swordfish kept after the supply convoys attempting to carry over the sustenance for the Axis North African armies. Following a sighting by a Maryland of 69 Squadron four Blenheims of 110 Squadron caught a force of four merchant ships and five destroyers about 17 miles off Pantelleria. In a dusk attack Sqn.Ldr. K.C. Forsythe and his flight scored direct hits on the German ammunition ship 'Preussen', which blew up, and set fire to the Italian 6996 ton tanker 'Brarena' which was prematurely abandoned by her crew. An escorting destroyer, the 'Fusiliere' picked the crew up and placed them back aboard, taking the freighter in tow. Following this successful attack the convoy was shadowed by another Maryland, carrying the observer C.O. of 800X Squadron, Lt. Manning, awaiting the next strike, this by five Swordfish of 830 Squadron. These took off as the Blenheims returned, led by Lt.Cdr. Howie (another observer C.O.) flying in Lt. R.W. Little's aircraft. The damaged tanker was sighted and received two torpedoes from Lts. Osborn and R.E. Bibby, while the towing destroyer was attacked and believed hit by a third fired by Sub Lt. D.B.A. Smith. The tanker was again abandoned and drifted onto Kerkenah Bank where she became a total loss.

A similar force of Blenheims was out again next day, this time to attack cargo ships in Trapani harbour. One Blenheim returned early but the other three pressed home their attack, claiming to have destroyed vessels of 7,000 and 3,000 tons respectively. An airfield between Trapani and Marsala was also bombed, but the leading Blenheim, Z7409 flown by Sgt. N.A.C. Cathles, was seen to hit the water twice close to the coastline, and then crash into the ground. It seems it was under attack by a CR 42 of the 23° Gruppo, which had scrambled with two MC200s. The Fiat pilot claimed the Blenheim shot down, the three crew being reported killed. The airfield strafe destroyed a Z.501 flyingboat of the 144ᵃ Squadriglia, moored by the shore.

During the evening of 22nd. nine S.79sil torpedo-bombers of the 283ᵃ Squadriglia from Sardinia, led by their commanding officer, Cap. Giorgio Grossi, had searched in vain for the approaching British convoy. At 0800 next morning they were off again, and this time were successful in their search. From now on the 'Substance' convoy could expect constant attack. At the same time as the torpedo-bombers approached, bomber S.79s of the Decimommanu-based 32° Stormo B.T. also appeared, together with a formation of five Cant Z.1007bis trimotors of 51° Gruppo. Seven of the available Fulmars were sent up to join four others on patrol, intercepting the incoming raiders which were moving very fast. The Fulmars attacked head-on, Red Section of 808 Squadron – led by the new C.O. Lt. E.D.G. Lewin, with Lt. Guthrie as his No. 2, splashed one of the torpedo-bombers, a second being claimed by the joint fire of the 807 Squadron pair, Lt.Cdr. Sholto Douglas and Lt. Hallett, and two more were believed badly damaged. Return fire and crossfire from the low-flying Savoias was accurate and intense, three of the now pursuing Fulmars taking hits in their engines and being unable to take alternative measures at this height were forced to ditch; all three crews were promptly picked up by the destroyers. Five Fulmars climbed to their maximum altitude after the Z.1007bis, but were unable to catch them. Meanwhile the surviving aerosiluranti S.79s, endeavouring to maintain formation, came in low in three sections on the warships, Ten. Bruno Pandolfi gaining a hit on the light cruiser 'Manchester' although return fire from the ship shot his aircraft into the sea; Pandolfi and his crew were picked up and made prisoners. The severely damaged cruiser had to be sent back to Gibraltar and would be non-operational for the next nine months, while the destroyer 'Fearless' was so badly damaged following an attack by two Savoias of the 280ᵃ Squadriglia that she had to be abandoned, and sent to the bottom by gunfire from other ships. 32° Gruppo reported losing one S.79 to the Fulmars during this action.

During the afternoon, at 1645, the four remaining serviceable torpedo-bombers of the 283ᵃ Squadriglia returned for a second attack, guided by a Z.506B, but were intercepted by Lt. Hay's Green Section of 808 Squadron while still some 22 miles from the convoy. Under a hail of fire from Hay, Sub Lt. A.P. Goodfellow and P.O.(A) Taylor, the aircraft of Ten. Dollfus was shot down into the sea with the loss of all the crew, while that of Ten. Cipriani was badly damaged, subsequently force-landing in the water off Cap Carbonara, from where the crew was later rescued. In another aircraft the C.O., Cap. Grossi, was wounded. The accompanying Z.506B was also claimed damaged.

By late afternoon the ships were coming within range of aircraft from Sicily and Malta. Five of 272 Squadron's Beaufighters were sent off to give escort at 1620, followed by six more at 1703, joining the convoy near Bizerta. Meanwhile from Sicily S.79sil torpedo-bombers of the 278ᵃ Squadriglia, escorted by 23° Gruppo CR 42s, were on their way, followed by S.79 bombers of the 10° and 30° Stormo, and Ju87s of the 101° Gruppo Tuff, plus 27 escorting MC200s from the 54° Stormo. The bombers gained one hit on the destroyer 'Firedrake', which was damaged, but it seems that the Beaufighters on patrol attacked both these and the torpedo-bombers. The CR 42 pilots reported that aircraft identified as Blenheims attacked the 278ᵃ Squadriglia aircraft near the Califfe islands, and one of these was claimed shot down by Ten. Giorgio Solaroli and Sottoten. Carlo Brigante Colonna – this was almost certainly the Beaufighter flown by Sgt. W.M.

Re 2000 after being moved to Trapani/Milo airfield with the 74ᵃ Squadriglia for operations. Ten. Giorgio Solaroli sits reading on the wing. (*G. Solaroli via N. Malizia*)

Deakin and Sgt. C.F. Jenkins, which failed to return. Another Beaufighter, piloted by Plt.Off. W.G. Snow, engaged an S.79 directly over the convoy, the bomber last being seen retreating with smoke pouring from it. The Macchis meanwhile reported intercepting a lone Blenheim – probably another Beaufighter – near Malta, apparently without effect, although one Macchi was lost, Ten. Folli being reported missing.

That evening Admiral Somerville turned Force 'H' back westwards, although the Fulmars continued to cover the cargo ships until the arrival of the Beaufighters from Malta. Three cruisers, 'Edinburgh', 'Hermione' and 'Arethusa', and eight destroyers continued with the convoy as Force 'X', commanded by Admiral Syfret. After dark Italian motor torpedo boats MAS532 and MAS533 attacked, hitting the cargo ship 'Sydney Star'. After troops and part of her crew had been taken off, she was able to continue to Malta under heavy escort.

24/7/41

Next morning the Sicily-based units were out again, a lone S.79 from the 278[a] Squadriglia claiming a cargo ship of 12,000 tons sunk, the empty Norwegian tanker 'Hoegh Hood' was torpedoed south of Sardinia, while fourteen 101° Gruppo Ju87s claimed one warship and one merchant ship sunk; no such losses were actually suffered. Patrolling Beaufighters engaged Ju87s on two occasions,

Junkers Ju87s were again over the Malta area during late July when the 101° Gruppo Tuffo arrived in Sicily to raid the island and British shipping in the Mediterranean. Here Ju87Rs of the 208[a] Squadriglia fly over Monte Erice to Trapani/Milo airfield on return from a sortie. (*A. Coppola via N. Malizia*)

259

Flt.Lt. G.L. Campbell alone attacking five over the convoy and driving them towards Sicily; he claimed two shot down, one of them in flames. Flg.Off. Davidson also attacked a number of the Stukas, but could not see the results of his fire. In fact all the Ju87s returned safely to their base. All the merchant vessels and the trooper had made harbour before the day was out.

25/7/41

During the early morning two sections of patrolling Fulmars were vectored onto 'shadowers', one Z.506B escaping after being damaged by a pair of 807 Squadron aircraft flown by Lt. Hallett and Sub Lt. K.G. Grant, but a second of the same species put up stiff resistance when attacked by the same pair, its gunner shooting down Sub Lt. Grant's aircraft, he and his TAG, L/A H. McLeod, being killed in the crash. By now the other Fulmar patrol had arrived on the scene and Lt. Guthrie joined Hallett in finishing off the Cant, which fell into the sea in full view of the Fleet.

Sardinian-based bombers were out hunting for the British ships, two sections of patrolling Fulmars from 808 Squadron attacking a formation of about twenty S.79sil at 1100, Lt. Kindersley's aircraft being shot down by return fire, he and his TAG, P.O.(A) Barnes being lost. The No.2 Fulmar, crewed by Sub Lt. R.C. Cockburn and P.O.(A) W.E. Curtriss, was also shot down, the crew surviving to report that the section had accounted for one S.79 for certain and a further one damaged. Red Section – Lts. Lewin and Guthrie – returned to the carrier making similar claims; records show that only one S.79sil was lost during this attack.

During Operation 'Substance' the two Fulmar squadrons had lost twelve of their twenty-four embarked aircraft, six of these having been shot down, but only two crews were lost. For their part in the operation four aircrew were decorated; Lt.Cdr. Sholto Douglas and Lt. Cockburn received D.S.O.s, Lt. Guthrie a D.S.C. and P.O.(A) Curtriss a D.S.M.

Over Malta on this date a lone reconnaissance Z.1007bis had appeared during the first half of the morning, escorted by twenty-six 10° Gruppo MC200s and twenty-one more of 54° Stormo. Twenty-two Hurricanes were scrambled by 185 and 249 Squadrons, reporting the formation included approximately four reconnaissance aircraft and a large force of fighters. This overestimate of the number of reconnaissance aircraft present would seem to stem from an unfamiliarity with the Cant Z.1007bis. Those approaching from the rear saw the twin tail fins and reported it as a BR 20 whilst those approaching from ahead saw the three engines and believed it to be an S.79.

Six pilots attacked the 'BR 20'; Flt.Lt. Pat Hancock: "...saw BR 20 being attacked by two Hurricanes – turned towards him and engaged – only fired two shells then cannons jammed ..."; Sgt. Alderson: "... six Hurricanes dived on BR 20 which flew almost immediately below me ... I fired from point blank range and hit e/a in fuselage ... I dived straight past the tail ..."; Sgt. Branson: "... closed to 50 yards ... starboard engine smoking ... last seen diving towards the sea smoking ..."; Sgt. Ellis: "... fired from 200 to 50 yards – hit starboard engine and wing... saw two other Hurricanes attacking same aircraft." Flg.Off. Don

Blenheim IVs go out on another mast-height anti-shipping strike. These are aircraft of 21 Squadron, passing Linosa Island. (*I.W.M.*)

Stones of 249 Squadron and Plt.Off. Barnwell also reported attacking this aircraft, which was last seen on fire at low level 20 miles north-east of Malta and was subsequently reported by Sgt. Branson to have crashed into the sea. It was credited jointly to the two squadrons, each pilot receiving a one sixth share in its destruction.

Four other 185 Squadron pilots had attacked the 'S.79', reported to have yellow-painted engine cowlings, and this was claimed shot down by Plt.Off. Thompson and Sgt. Forth, who reported: "...I was No. 2 to Plt.Off. Thompson, who attacked first and pieces came away...I attacked from 200 yards and silenced rear gunner and more pieces fell away..." Plt.Off. Barnwell, having lost sight of the 'BR 20' he had been attacking, saw a three-engined aircraft fall burning into the sea 20 miles from Malta, and one parachute descending, and was able to confirm Thompson's and Forth's claim. In fact all pilots had attacked the single unfortunate Z.1007bis, which was indeed shot down with the loss of most of the crew.

While this was going on the other 249 Squadron Hurricanes had become engaged with the fighters, Sqn.Ldr. Barton (in Z3492) and Plt.Off. Hill each claiming one Macchi shot down in the sea, while Plt.Off. Matthews shot one down which fell on Valetta, going down in Kingsway, near the La Valetta Band Club; the pilot baled out, but was killed. One wounded Italian pilot was subsequently rescued from the sea by the Kalafrana air-sea rescue service. The Italians reported that an initial attack by three Hurricanes was driven off, but that approximately 30 more attacked over Malta. Seven were claimed shot down, one by Serg. Cozzoli, the others by all the pilots jointly, but two Macchis from the 98ᵃ Squadriglia, 7° Gruppo were lost, Ten. Silvio Di Giorgio and Sottoten. Francesco Liberati both being seen to bale out. These pilots were both reported rescued by the Italians, but it is believed that this was merely because their parachutes had been seen to open. This would account for the fact that no mention was made of one being killed, because the dead pilot had indeed been able to bale out first.

On the ground Wg.Cdr. Jonas watched Matthews' victim come down: ".. out of the confusion of sound above us, something appeared, tangible and definite. It was a puff of white smoke. A little puff at first, but it grew rapidly and formed itself into a trail of white, like a comet. Then it faded away almost as rapidly as it had come. A moment later there was a new sound. Something terrifying which I could not describe. I had often wondered what a terminal velocity dive in an aircraft would be like. Now my wondering was to be answered. Just below where the white puff had first appeared was an aircraft ... diving vertically, earthwards ... I realized almost immediately that the aircraft would fall into Valetta. Also that it would fall very close to me. Probably fall on the very spot on which I was now standing. I argued to myself that it was too late to attempt to escape into the building, down the stairs to safety. I decided to stay and hope for the best, but now I realised also the meaning of the phrase 'rooted to the spot' ... it appeared to be coming straight for my eyes. As it flashed by, diving slightly over the vertical, I recognised it as a Macchi 200. A moment later, it hit the ground about 75 yards away ... three was a loud report, then silence, followed by the

A bomb-laden Re2000 heads out into the twilight for a night fighter-bomber attack on Malta, Ten. Giorgio Solaroli at the controls. (*G. Solaroli via N. Malizia*)

sound of running feet and excited shouts of the Maltese. I straightened up slowly ... I felt rather sick and looking around I saw my Engineer Officer friend, laughing. As he had been running to safety, one of the rotten staircase steps had given away. There he was, jammed between two of the treads – his head and shoulders above, and his body and legs swinging below. Apart from a deep graze on each shin, he was unhurt. The pilot had baled out but his parachute had failed to open. He had fallen from the vast Mediterranean sky – in memory of Icarus."

It was at this point, with all the vessels in Grand Harbour, that the Italians attempted an audacious raid by surface craft. This had in fact been in planning for several months – reconnaissances had been made and only a spell of bad weather had prevented the attempt being made a month earlier. The 1,568 ton sloop 'Diana' approached the Malta area before midnight on 25 July. It carried aboard nine explosive motor boats – barchini – known officially as MTMs, and their one-man crews, which formed part of the Tenth Light Flotilla. 'Diana' also towed a smaller electric-powered motor boat – an MTL – on which were two SLC human torpedoes and their four crewmen. Accompanying the vessels were two 60 foot motor torpedo boats (MAS 451 and 452), the latter towing a small motor boat (MTSM).

'Diana' hove-to 20 miles north of Malta. From here the MTSM would lead in the nine barchini to a point about a kilometre off the coast; MAS 452 would accompany them to a point five miles out, and there await the results of the raid. Meanwhile the MTL with the SLCs aboard would be towed by MAS 451 to the five mile point, from where it would continue to the launch point under its own power. From here it was proposed that SLC No.1, piloted by Magg. Teseo Tesei, would attempt to blow up the anti-torpedo net across the mole at the entrance to the main harbour, while SLC No. 2 would attack the submarine base at Manoel Island in Marsamxett Harbour, in the adjoining inlet. The barchini would then blow their way into the main harbour and attack targets of opportunity therein. It was anticipated that all the pilots would be captured – if they survived! It was also planned that BR 20Ms would bomb Luqa as a diversion with the hope that their engines would obscure the noise of the motor boats.

Quite unknown to the Italians at this time – or to very many other people on the Allied side – the British were receiving messages through 'Ultra' sources concerning most Axis naval movements in the Mediterranean – this was one of the main reasons why Malta's striking forces were enjoying such success in finding and attacking their convoys. A Special Liaison Unit had been established on Malta, responsible for receiving, distributing and ensuring the secrecy of 'Ultra' signals transmitted from England; the unit operated at the War H.Q. in Lascaris, situated beneath the Upper Barracca Gardens in Valetta. It was known therefore that a naval raid on the island was imminent, and all coastal gunners had been ordered to stand-by, sleeping at their guns. Thus when 'Diana' was picked up by the Malta radar on arrival at her station, the defences knew at once that something was in the offing, all elements of the defence being brought to full alert (Confirmation of this was given to Mr. Philip Vella of the Malta War Museum by Lt.Cdr. Charles Carnes, R.N.V.R., who was Decyphering Officer to the Office of the Vice Admiral, Malta, during the war, following the partial lifting of the Official Secrets Act in respect of 'Ultra').

26/7/41

The boats set off at 0200 on 26 July, reaching the kilometre mark at 0300 – behind schedule. Here it was found that SLC No.2 was defective, and Magg. Tesei ordered it back. He was due to blow the net at 0430, and pressed on. The diverting air raid came in 15 minutes early, and when an explosion was heard at 0425 it was assumed to be Tesei's SLC – it was in fact not, being caused by the bombing; Tesei was never seen again and his fate remains unknown. At once however, the barchini approached, and finding the net intact, Sottoten. di Vascello Carlo Bosio charged his explosive and leapt out. The boat, MTM No.1, hit the net and failed to explode. MTM No.2 was aimed at the net but hit the pier and blew up with the pilot still aboard, the force of the explosion bringing down the left-hand span of a steel bridge across the entrance to the harbour, which effectively blocked it. The defences now opened up and brought searchlights to bear; swiftly all the remaining MTMs were sunk by gunfire from the twin six-pounders of the Royal Malta Artillery, or deliberately by their pilots. Bosio climbed aboard MTM No.1 again and set the destruct mechanism, but this blew up before he could get clear.

Dawn was now breaking and Hurricanes were scrambled by 126 and 185 Squadrons, passing over the fight at the harbour entrance to attack the four motor boats offshore. 'Diana' was already well away on the way home; MAS 451 and 452, the latter towing the MTMS, were heading after her when the Hurricanes caught them. Flt.Lt. Lefevre of 126 Squadron attacked one with cannon fire, reporting that the crew signalled surrender, while other pilots from this unit shot up the other vessels with machine gun fire. Plt.Off. Bailey of 185 Squadron claimed one vessel sunk, while eight others from the same squadron attacked three vessels, all of which were claimed destroyed.

In fact MAS 451 was hit hard, the crew leaping overboard as she blew up and killed four seamen. The survivors were later picked up by a British vessel, claiming that they had shot down one Hurricane. MAS 452 was also hit (probably by Lefevre), Capitano de Fregata Moccagatta, Capitano di Corvetta Giobbe and six other members of the crew being killed. The eleven survivors transferred to the MTSM and escaped, subsequently rejoining the 'Diana'. It seems that the MTL was also sunk by the Hurricanes.

MC200s of the 7° Gruppo had been ordered off at dawn to escort the flotilla back, but arrived overhead to find the vessels already under attack by the Hurricanes. 'Bouncing' the latter, the Macchi pilots put in seven claims, which were apparently later reduced to three confirmed and two probables. Claiming pilots were Cap. Saverio Gostini, Sottoten. Giannoccarso (two), Serg. Magg. Facchini and Serg. Omiccioli; other claims were reduced to 'damaged'. Plt.Off. Denis Winton of 185 Squadron was shot down and baled out into the sea, but his aircraft was the only one lost.

As the Macchis attacked, Sgt. Haley of 126 Squadron, an Australian from

Sydney, broke away and dived to about 500 feet above the sea, getting behind one Italian fighter and putting four or five bursts into it before it dived into the sea ten miles from Sicily. At that point his own aircraft was hit several times, but he found that another Macchi was on his tail. Turning south, he was pursued for some five minutes, but at that point Plt.Off. Thompson of 185 Squadron saw Haley under attack and fired at the Macchi, believing that he had shot it down into the sea. Haley saw the second Hurricane put a burst across the nose of his pursuer which caused it to turn away, and swinging about, was able to get a short burst into the Macchi which then crashed into the sea about 15 miles from Sicily. Whether both pilots hit the MC200 or not is not certain, but each claimed its destruction so that total R.A.F. claims were for three Macchis shot down. Two Macchi pilots were indeed shot down during this combat, Mar. Avellino De Mattia of the 98ᵃ Squadriglia baling out and being rescued later, while Serg.Magg. Ruggero Gallina of the 76ᵃ Squadriglia was killed.

Denis Winton, after several hours in his dinghy, spotted the stationary MAS 452 nearby and swam to it, getting aboard to find it occupied only by the eight dead Italians. An Army rescue boat approached, but unsure of who was still aboard, contended itself to circle around; it was by then six hours since Winton had been shot down. Finally a Swordfish floatplane landed alongside, flying Winton and the flag from the vessel back to Malta. MAS 452 was taken in tow by the rescue vessel 'Jade' and brought into the harbour.

The raid had cost the Italians fifteen dead and eighteen captured (three officers and fifteen ratings) – brave men all. The second SLC had finally limped ashore after five hours in the water, the crew of two being included amongst those captured. It had been a gallant effort, but it had achieved nothing – defeated mainly by superior Intelligence information and the efficacy of the coastal radar. Later in the day a Blenheim was claimed shot down by a 7° Gruppo MC200 flown by Serg. Magg. Magnaghi, over the Mediterranean. A Blenheim (Z9605) of 105 Squadron was shot down off Lampedusa, reportedly by flak, but may have been Magnaghi's victim.

27/7/41

Next day – 27 July – 185 Squadron achieved a further success when four Hurricanes were scrambled after two 'hostiles' during the morning. A pair of S.79s were intercepted 50 miles from the island, and both were shot down, one by Plt.Off. Thompson and Plt.Off. Bailey, the other by Flt.Lt. Hancock and Sgt. Cousens. Pat Hancock recorded: "Plt.Off. Bailey saw the SM 79s first and attacked one ... I engaged the starboard aircraft firing from 300 to 50 yards ... port engine burst into flames and large pieces flew off ... it climbed then stall-turned into the sea ... own aircraft hit in starboard wing by a few bullets." Sgt. Cousens added: " ... Flt.Lt. Hancock attacked on the beam ... port engine on fire ... I opened at 300 yards with four second burst ... starboard engine caught fire ... e/a dived into the sea ... then attacked second SM 79 ... saw fire hitting forward of wing ... no visible result." The victims would appear to have been aircraft of 56ᵃ Squadriglia, 30° Gruppo, 10° Stormo B.T., the Stormo commander,

Something of a mystery; a Fiat CR 42 of the 98ª Squadriglia, 7º Gruppo, 54º Stormo C.T. – a unit mainly equipped with MC200s; this aircraft, flown by Serg. Arnaldo Mauri, has reportedly crashed on Pantelleria after suffering damage during a dogfight over Malta with Hurricanes. The date has not been ascertained. (*N. Malizia*)

Ten.Col. Roberto Liberi, being reported killed over the Mediterranean on this date. Intelligence later indicated that Air Generale Fedrighi, commander of the Regia Aeronautica in the Mediterranean, was also believed to have been lost with one of these aircraft. This information seems to have been wholly fallacious however, since no Generale of that name seems even to have served with the Regia Aeronautica!

28/7/41

As Force 'X' was due to return to Malta from Gibraltar again, carrying further soldiers, airmen and supplies for the garrison at the end of July, the Beaufighters stayed on the island for the time being. During the afternoon of 28 July these were sent out in pairs, escorted by Hurricanes, to strafe airfields on the Sicilian coast. At Catania Sqn.Ldr. Yaxley (who had previously led 252 Squadron from Malta) claimed the probable destruction of four MC200s, two S.79s and a Ju52/3m, while Flg.Off. R.O. Davenport claimed four S.79s as probables and damage to some MC200s and some training biplanes. The Italians, who took all the attacking Beaufighters to be Blenheims, recorded that this attack damaged eleven MC200s, three BR 20Ms and three CR 42s, while eleven men were wounded. At Marsala seaplane base Sgt. R.J.G. De Moulin, a Belgian, and Flg.Off. Clarke engaged a Z.501 in the air and strafed two more on the water; here according to the Italians four Z.501s were damaged and one civilian workman wounded. At the other seaplane base at Syracuse Flg.Off. Lemar and Sgt. J.F. Green attacked a number of Z.501s at anchor, claiming seven probably destroyed and two damaged; here four aircraft were actually damaged. Finally at Borizzo (Chinisia) Sqn.Ldr. A.W. Fletcher attacked six S.79s with yellow engine cowlings, claiming four destroyed, while Sgt. D.F. Touch claimed two more and a third badly damaged. Their attack in fact caused damage to six S.79s, four of which were very badly hit, and to a Ca 164 training biplane. Fletcher had also claimed two CR 42s destroyed, while he thought he had badly damaged two other aircraft; 4° Stormo C.T. records indicate that two CR 42s were in fact damaged. The pair then shot up troops, believing that they had killed about 25 of them, and then strafed a fishing boat during their return flight. Over Catania meanwhile three MC200s and an S.79 were seen in the air, one of the fighters attacking and damaging Flg.Off. Davenport's aircraft; it was driven off by Yaxley. 4° Stormo MC200 pilots claimed one Beaufighter shot down off Augusta and reported hits on a second.

29/7/41

Next morning a Maryland reconnoitred Borizzo and Marsala, reporting that at the former airfield thirteen S.79s were present, of which three were burnt out, three partly burnt and five damaged. At Marsala amongst fourteen Z.501s, one was seen to be without a tail and one partially burned.

Ju87Bs of 208ª Squadriglia on their way back from a raid, their bombs gone. (*N. Malizia*)

On 30 July six Beaufighters made the long flight to Sardinia where they strafed Elmas airfield. Sqn.Ldr. Fletcher claimed three more S.79s destroyed here and two damaged, while Flt.Lt. Campbell claimed damage to three more. Flg.Off. Davenport reported that he had caused a Z.506B on the water to catch fire, and had machine-gunned hangars, while Flg.Off. Davidson also claimed a floatplane destroyed and others damaged. Sqn.Ldr. Yaxley claimed four more floatplanes badly damaged, and Flg.Off. M.L.P. Bartlett claimed another damaged near a hangar. On the way back a lone four-engined transport aircraft was encountered and this was also attacked and claimed damaged.

At the close of July A.H.Q., Malta, issued its usual communique of results, crediting the fighters with twenty-one confirmed victories during the month, plus five probables and nine damaged, for the loss of three Hurricanes in combat, two of the pilots having been killed. At this time two pilots who had suffered wounds returned to flying duties, if not immediately to operational flying; these were Flt.Lt. Innes Westmacott of 185 Squadron and Flg.Off. Pat Wells of 249 Squadron.

Chapter 7

THE THORN IN ROMMEL'S SIDE

At the end of July 1941 the Malta Night Fighter Unit was formed. Sqn.Ldr. George Powell-Sheddon, D.F.C., was posted in to command this new formation. (*I.W.M.*)

The safe return to Malta of Force 'X' at the start of August 1941 carrying some 1,750 further officers and men, raised the strength of the garrison to over 22,000. These formed thirteen infantry battalions, three of them of the King's Own Malta Regiment. The anti-aircraft defences now possessed 112 heavy and 118 light guns, while there were an additional 104 pieces for ground and coastal defence. These were manned by two coastal, two heavy A.A. and two light A.A. regiments of the Royal Malta Artillery, and by a number of Royal Artillery regiments. This force was now backed up by a searchlight regiment, pioneers, service and other ancilliary troops, and by stores and equipment sufficient to last at least eight months. The fighter strength had risen to fifteen Hurricane Is and sixty Hurricane IIs, all in serviceable condition – a formidable strength when coupled with the bombers now on the island. On 28 July ten Blenheims had arrived from Gibraltar, representing the main strength of 105 Squadron. Twelve of these aircraft with ten key ground crew personnel aboard had departed England on 25th., led by their famous commanding officer, Wg.Cdr. Hughie Edwards, V.C., D.F.C. One bomber had to land in Portugal where it was interned, and one was delayed en route, following on 30th. The unit immediately took over from 110 Squadron, the remaining Blenheims of the latter unit being flown to Egypt for dispersal to the squadrons there.

Pilots of the M.N.F.U., l. to r., standing; Plt.Off. F.R.W. Palmer, Sgt. Reg Fowler, Flg.Off. Denis Winton, Flt.Lt. Don Stones, D.F.C., Flg.Off. A.R.F. Thompson; sitting; Plt.Off. P. Rathie, Plt.Off. Jack Grant, Plt.Off. J.P. Mills. (A.R.F. Thompson)

Sqn.Ldr. George Powell-Sheddon had now returned to the island with orders to form a special night fighter flight, and at the end of July the Malta Night Fighter Unit (M.N.F.U.) was formed with eight Hurricane IICs and four Mark IIBs. Don Stones and Ernest Cassidy were posted in from 249 Squadron as flight commanders, together with Flg.Off. Thompson and Mills, and Plt.Off. Robertson. From 126 Squadron came Plt.Off. Grant and Sgt. Mackie, while 185 Squadron

270

initially supplied Plt.Off. Barnwell. The unit was to be based at Takali. Sqn.Ldr. Powell-Sheddon initiated the idea of Hurricanes hunting in pairs in unison with the searchlights. There was a considerable problem in seeing the Italian night bombers as it was their practice to fly direct from Sicily to the south of Malta over the sea, then to sweep round and bomb as they made their way northwards back to Sicily. Now pairs of searchlights were stationed at each end of the island and Hurricanes would circle these. When the incoming raider was plotted by the radar 15 miles out the Hurricanes would increase height if necessary, so that they might find themselves at least 2,000 feet above the bombers. Then both fighters would turn inwards to approach the intruder from each side simultaneously. Very successful results would be achieved by using these tactics, although the Hurricanes usually flew with their tail lights on to avoid collision.

One of M.N.F.U.'s Hurricanes, Z2827, after a 'wheels up' landing. (*F. Etchells*)

31/7/41

Amongst the personnel brought in by Force 'X' had been a good number of R.A.F. Senior N.C.O.s and other ranks for aircraft servicing duties, a large proportion of these being posted to 126 Squadron, which had been much understaffed in this respect. At this time however two more time-expired fighter pilots left, Plt.Offs. Gray and Innes set off for home, while at Hal Far Lt.Cdr. Howie, recently awarded a D.S.O., relinquished command of 830 Squadron on posting to the A.O.C.'s staff. Temporary command of the squadron passed to Lt. Pain, in keeping with the squadron's tradition of appointing Observer commanding officers. Amongst the seven replacement Swordfish which had arrived from 'Ark Royal' during Operation 'Substance' were two equipped with 'Air to Surface

Vessel' (ASV) radar sets, the first so-fitted aircraft to be sent to Malta. Aircraft-borne ASV, combined with intelligence gathered from 'Ultra' sources and the island's own radar stations added to the daily reconnaissance sorties flown by the ever-vigilant 69 Squadron, threatened ominously for the numerous North Africa-bound Axis supply convoys. Malta now possessed the means of hitting back at the enemy with vengeance. In the coming months only the lack of sufficient numbers of Blenheim strike aircraft would frustrate the complete destruction of many of these convoys. But ultimately it would be the courage and daring of the Blenheim crews that mattered; many would make the supreme sacrifice; many already had. At this time the Regia Aeronautica added to their strength in Sicily when, on the last day of the month, the 282ª Squadriglia Autonomo Aerosiluranti arrived under Cap. Marino Marini, with new torpedo-carrying Savoia S.84sil bombers.

31/7/–1/8/41

On this last day of July Sgt. Hutt of 69 Squadron flew a morning reconnaissance to Tripoli in one of the Marylands, strafing Zuara airfield where he claimed one S.79 on fire and three damaged. During the day six of 105 Squadron's Blenheims went out on their first mission from Malta, an anti-shipping sweep. A convoy some 50 miles off Pantelleria was the target, but intense Flak and four CR 42s patrolling overhead dissuaded them, and the attack was not made. The presence of this convoy however presented 830 Squadron with its first opportunity of trying out the ASV aircraft and consequently, at 1000, Lt. A.S. Whitworth led off four torpedo-carrying Swordfish, he and Lt. Pain flying one of the ASV aircraft, to locate and hopefully decimate the convoy. Just over an hour later ships were detected some 20-odd miles ahead and an attack developed in poor visibility. Only one ship was believed hit and it was later confirmed that a 6000 ton freighter had been badly damaged. Next day three more Blenheims of 105

830 Squadron Swordfish in trouble. (*C.G. Jefford*)

Squadron were out and attacked merchant shipping in Lampedusa harbour, but here Z9605, flown by Flt.Lt. A.B. Broadley, DFC, was seen to be hit by machine gun fire from the ground, and to crash into the sea. On Malta on 31 July Sqn.Ldr. Barton of 249 Squadron recorded: "Engine failure on take-off. I crash-landed from 300 feet – almost impossible at Malta – my lucky day – only suffered second degree burns." He had been flying Z3492, and was admitted to Imtarfa Hospital.

272 Squadron Beaufighter at Luqa. (*C.G. Jefford*)

2–3/8/41

The first three weeks of August were to be devoid of major engagements, although activities continued with the accent on the increasing offensive involvement. On 2 August two Beaufighters from 272 Squadron made an early attack on Borizzo (Tarquinia) airfield. Here Plt.Off. Snow and Sgt. Touch claimed an S.79 destroyed and four damaged on the West side of the field, Touch then attacking and silencing an anti-aircraft position. The Italians again believed the attackers to be a pair of Blenheims, and reported that they had in fact managed to inflict only slight damage on two S.79s. Next day Flg.Off Davidson and Flg.Off. Lemar made a similar attack on Reggio Calabria airfield late in the afternoon. On this occasion Davidson attacked a long line of thirty MC200s, claiming to have hit at least ten of these, while Lemar strafed the same line and also some twin-engined aircraft. On completion of these sorties the Beaufighters returned to Egypt, but they were at once replaced by the Wellingtons of 38 Squadron, which flew in in batches between 5th. and 7th. from Shallufa. They undertook their first raid from the island against Tripoli after dark on 8 August.

5/8/41

The new M.N.F.U. enjoyed its first successes during the night of 5/6 August when eight BR 20Ms from the 43° Stormo raided Valetta. Flg.Off. Cassidy and Plt.Off.

Barnwell intercepted, Cassidy closing in on one bomber which he saw on the edge of a searchlight concentration. He got in several good bursts and saw pieces fly off after which his target lost height rapidly. It was later confirmed when a signal from Catania H.Q. to Syracuse was intercepted, this reporting the loss of the aircraft. Barnwell then attacked two bombers and claimed both shot down, one of them falling in flames. Only two BR 20Ms were actually lost, both falling soon after midnight. Ten.Col.Nello Brambilla, commander of the 99° Gruppo was killed in one, as was the other pilot, Sottoten. Antonio Romeo; some of crews from these aircraft survived and were rescued.

6–7/8/41

Next morning three MC200s flew a reconnaissance over Valetta. Apparently four Hurricanes intercepted and shot one of the Macchis down, but no further details of this combat are available. Next night the 43° Stormo tried again, but this time an aircraft flown by Cap. Bernadino Dalle Nogare, commander of the 65ª Squadriglia, 31° Gruppo, was lost, being reported shot down by A.A. fire; most of the crew were killed. British sources report; "Three bombers approach – one caught fire and crashed into the sea – no Hurricane involvement." George Powell-Sheddon notes that at this time some Italian bombers had trouble with their bomb release mechanisms – they would catch fire without being fired upon, and this would seem to have been the fate of this aircraft. The night also saw the first nocturnal sorties by Ju87s, five aircraft from the 101° Gruppo B a'T raiding Luqa. In the opposite direction Petty Off.(A) Jopling and Sub Lt. Furlong in Fulmar N4004 of 800X Squadron dropped 20lb. bombs on Gerbini airfield. Next night another Fulmar crewed by Petty Off.(A) Sabey and Lt. Manning strafed five bombers on this same airfield and claimed all badly damaged.

5–11/8/41

The crews of 105 Squadron were by now getting into the swing of their work. On 7th. they claimed four ships destroyed from a convoy of six. The 6813-ton freighters 'Nita' was sunk; one tanker was beached on Lampedusa, continuing to burn for eight days. On 11th. their targets were the Montecatini and Pertusola chemical works at Crotone in Calabria, Southern Italy; six bombers attacked, but lost that (Z7503) flown by Sqn.Ldr. G.E. Goode, D.F.C. The Swordfish were also very active, five dive-bombing the submarine depot. and oil storage tanks at Augusta on the night of 5th./6th., seven attacking a convoy between Lampedusa and Kerkenah Bank the next night. On this occasion both ASV-fitted aircraft were in use and it was claimed that an 8,000 ton freighter was left sinking and a smaller vessel damaged. The Swordfish were out again on the night of 10th./11th., one flare-dropper and three torpedo-carriers attacking a large ship anchored in Syracuse harbour. At least one success was scored on what was in fact the 13,060 ton 'California', a former liner-turned troopship, the ship sustaining severe damage, (and later sank) while the attacking Swordfish, flown by Sub Lt. M. Thorpe, returned to Hal Far badly damaged by A.A. shrapnel.

185 Squadron 'B' Flight's aircraft availability board, victory board (left) and the flag captured from one of the Italian motor launches (MAS 452) strafed outside Grand Harbour. Note that on the availability board, Mark IIC Hurricanes are indicated by a tiny ship's cannon emblem in front of the serial number.

8–10/8/41

During the morning of 8 August Hurricanes of 185 Squadron were scrambled but made no interception. 35 miles from the island Plt.Off. Oliver suffered an engine failure and had to bale out. He was safely picked up by a Swordfish floatplane. Also on this day Plt.Off. Saunders left 249 Squadron for the U.K. Two days later on 10 August Sqn. Ldr. Rabagliati of 126 Squadron was out on an evening test flight in Z3462 when he spotted a Z.506B which he at once attacked. The aircraft landed on the sea and he saw four members of the crew get out before it sank. During the day a 69 Squadron Maryland (AR739) crashed at Luqa, Flt.Lt. Wylde and his crew all being killed.

Hurricane II of 185 Squadron in full 'warpaint. (*Mrs. Davies via National War Museum Assoc.*)

11/8/41

After dark on 11th. BR 20Ms from 43° Stormo, together with five S.79s from the 10° and 30° Stormo, and a number of Ju87s, raided the island. Four Hurricanes were sent up by the M.N.F.U., and Sqn.Ldr. Powell-Sheddon made two attacks on one bomber in the searchlights, but was illuminated himself, losing his night vision and failing to see the results. Local police and intercepted Italian signals confirmed that an aircraft had crashed into the sea south of Malta, and indeed a BR20M flown by Ten. Livio Vercelli did fall to a night fighter, all the crew being killed. A few minutes later observers reported that an S.79 burst into flames and crashed; three parachutes were seen but no survivors were found. This is not confirmed from Italian records however, and it seems more likely that this was another sighting of the BR20M going down.

13/8/41

At 1400 on 13th. Sgt. D.L.J. Lawrence of 69 Squadron took off in Maryland AR741 for a leaflet-dropping sortie over Bizerta, Tunis, Sfax and Sousse. The aircraft was intercepted at 1515 by Dewoitine 520s of GC II/7; these had scrambled to meet British bombers, but finding none, were returning to Sidi Ahmed when they spotted "an unmarked Glenn Martin" dropping leaflets over their airfield. Sous Lt. Dussart got behind the Maryland but was shot at by the rear gunner, so he opened fire and shot it down between Bizerta and Cani Island. The crew baled out, but Lawrence was killed when his parachute failed to open.

Sgts. J.M. Alexander and F. Wilkins, the observer and air gunner, were rescued from the sea, one of them being reported by the French to have been wounded. During this day Walrus L2182, recently attached to the Kalafrana Seaplane Rescue Flight, crashed on take-off. The crew survived.

13–17/8/41

Malta's strike force – the Swordfish and Blenheims – were getting into the swing of sustained operations now and many targets were available. On the night of 13th./14th. Lt. Charles Lamb, now a flight commander with 830, led a further dive-bombing attack on the submarine depot at Augusta, while next night nine Swordfish – six armed with torpedoes, two carrying flares, the other controlling the operation with ASV – attacked a convoy of five merchantmen off Tripoli. Two of the ships were believed severely damaged by Lt. Osborn and Sub Lt. Taylor, while one of the attendant destroyers was also claimed hit by Lt. Whitworth's attack. On 15th. it was the turn of Blenheims of 105 Squadron, five of these, led by Flt.Lt. L.A. Lynn, attacking a convoy approaching Benghazi. Resistance was fierce; Plt.Off. Jack Buckley attacked one merchant ship estimated at 9,000 tons, passing through a curtain of fire to do so. He held his run although wounded, gaining hits on the vessel which was seen to be on fire. He subsequently received the DFC for this sortie. Altogether two schooners were claimed hit and a tanker was seen to explode, but one Blenheim hit the mast of this and spun into the sea, while a second bomber blew up in the air; Flg.Off. H.J. Roe and Plt. Off. P.H. Standfast and their crews failed to return. The following night five Swordfish carried out a dive-bombing attack on Catania harbour where reconnaissance had revealed a large supply ship unloading for the past two days. Dense smoke from burning stores on the quay made it impossible to establish whether the freighter was hit but did not prevent one of 830's more eccentric observers hurling empty beer bottles into the affray!

Yet again the Swordfish were out after a convoy on the night of 16th./17th., this time seven aircraft attacking six merchant ships, with an escort of six destroyers, to the west of Lampedusa. Four crews claimed hits, one 8,000 ton ship being claimed sunk and two others damaged. In fact daylight reconnaissance revealed that the 5479 ton 'Maddalena Odero' had beached on Lampedusa, and three Blenheims were despatched to destroy her; they returned having scored direct hits and the resultant fires burned for several days.

15–17/8/41

The fighters were now in such strength and their activities so curtailed, that during the day Plt.Off. G.D. Marshall and three sergeants were sent off with Hurricanes as reinforcements for the Middle East; a report subsequently received stated that three of these aircraft had failed to arrive at their destination. On 17th. Sqn.Ldr. Rabagliati and Plt.Off. Main each claimed a Z.506B destroyed on the water when Rabagliati led four Hurricanes on an early morning strafe of Syracuse seaplane base. Two such aircraft of the 612ª Squadriglia were indeed left in flames, and four more were damaged, all the latter hit by fire from Flt.Lt. McGregor's aircraft.

A welcome sight to shot-down aircrew; H.S.L. 107, one of the R.A.F. special air/sea rescue launches which operated from Kalafrana, seen here at speed in St. Paul's Bay. (*National War Museum Assoc.*)

That same day eleven Hurricanes were sent off by 249 Squadron to investigate a reported plot of six aircraft. When they were in the air this was revised downwards to two 'hostiles', and five of the fighters were ordered to return and land, while a further three came back with various mechanical troubles. The remaining trio were vectored onto a single aircraft 40 miles out, which was seen east of Zonkor Point, and was tentatively identified as a Ca312 floatplane. Sgt. Rex and Plt.Off. Hulbert expended all their ammunition into it, and it was last seen trailing much black smoke from the port engine. A subsequent reconnaissance by several more of the unit's Hurricanes found a trail of oil and wreckage, the destruction of the floatplane being confirmed on this evidence.

19/8/41

The first appearance of the Macchis during August was not recorded in any strength until 19th., when twelve Hurricanes were scrambled by 126 Squadron to intercept twelve Italian fighters near Cap Passero at 23,000 feet. The 'Tally Ho!' was given and the Hurricanes chased four of their opponents right in over the Sicilian coast, six MC200s being seen at the same height as the British formation and six more 2,000 feet higher. The lower flight was split up and Plt.Off. Lardner-Burke went for the rear aircraft of the second section of three. He fired a short burst, apparently hitting the pilot, upon which the aircraft turned over and spun down; this was seen to crash in flames by Sgt. Worrall. Climbing and turning, Lardner-Burke saw Flt.Lt. Pip Lefevre shoot down a Macchi which fell on land. Following Lefevre, he attacked another Macchi himself and this fell into the sea just off the coast. By now his own aircraft had been hit several times and slightly damaged in the wing and tail but he attacked a third MC200 from astern, seeing his fire hit the cockpit area. White smoke appeared, and this too went spinning down, whilst Sgt. MacGregor claimed another probably destroyed. 10° Gruppo recorded a fight with Hurricanes, Ten. Soprana claiming one shot down, Serg. Ceoletta and Cap. Lucchini sharing a second, while Ten. Alessandrini claimed a probable; no losses were noted.

Flt. Lt. H.P. Lardner-Burke, D.F.C., of 126 Squadron, one of the most successful Hurricane pilots against the Italian fighters during the summer and autumn months of 1941. (*via R.W. Oxspring*)

20–21/8/41

The policy of taking the fight to Sicily was continued on 20th. when Sqn.Ldr. Rabagliati again undertook a strafe, this time of Augusta. Shooting-up the harbour, he claimed a Z.506B damaged on the water, four small balloons shot down in flames, and also attacked petrol tanks without observing the results. Two Z.506Bs were reported slightly damaged in this attack by the Italians. Next day the Regia Aeronautica retaliated, ten 10° Gruppo MC200s providing cover for six drawn equally from the 7° and 16° Gruppo, which strafed Hal Far without great effect. That evening a convoy of four large troop ships, with an escort of seven destroyers, left Tripoli for Italy, as revealed by 'Ultra'. A patrolling submarine – 'Unique' – made the first strike when she torpedoed the 11398-ton 'Esperia' with only a small loss of life. It was too dark for a Blenheim strike but nine Swordfish were prepared and armed for another night attack. At 2230 the two ASV Swordfish set out to locate and shadow, to be followed an hour later by the strike aircraft. Although the convoy was found, heavy cloud and high winds prevented a co-ordinated attack and only three aircraft – two torpedo-carriers, one bomber – actually found targets, attacking the escorting destroyers, albeit without any known success.

Newly-arrived Hurricane II (Z3757) for 249 Squadron, which crashed on arrival at Takali in August 1941; note the second crash-landed fighter in the left background. (*F. Etchells*)

22–23/8/41

Force 'H' sailed into the Western Mediterranean once more on 22 August to make bombing attacks on Sardinia. The fleet then sailed off Valencia in an effort to draw out the Italian Fleet units to action. A strong force put out to sea – too strong for Force 'H' to take on other than by air torpedo attack, and no action resulted. On 23rd. however two of 807 Squadron's Fulmars from 'Ark Royal' caught a Ju52/3m on the route between North Africa and Italy, this being shot down in flames by Blue Section – Lt. Gardner/Sub Lt. L. Rowland and Sub Lt. J.F. Rankin/L/A M. Godfrey, whilst Lt. Taylour's Black Section found a 'shadowing' Z.506B. Although all three Fulmars attacked they were unable to shoot it down, the considered opinion being that the Italians were now adding armour-plating to their flyingboats and floatplanes in view of the catastrophic losses suffered in recent months. On the return flight to the carrier P.O.(A) Taylor, who had separated from the other two of his section during the action, became lost and was forced to ditch when he ran out of fuel. Fortunately for him and his TAG, L/A J. Rigby, they were spotted and rescued by a patrolling Sunderland.

26/8/41

Three days later on 26 August came the last engagement of note that month. Ten Hurricanes of 126 Squadron and eight from 185 Squadron were scrambled late in the afternoon to intercept fifteen incoming MC200s. The 126 Squadron aircraft engaged at 16,000 feet 25 miles south-east of Cap Scaramia, reporting seeing nine of the Italian fighters. Plt.Off. Lardner-Burke, seeing one break away, attacked it. After two bursts he saw the port wing drop down and the aircraft dived very steeply towards the Sicilian coast. He followed, firing a very long burst which caused the tailplane to break up, and it dived straight into the sea from 1,000 feet. Sgt. Greenhalgh also attacked one Macchi in the formation, getting in a three second burst with his cannons from dead astern. He also reported that one leg of the undercarriage dropped down and white smoke poured from the engine. By now he had come in very close and broke violently to avoid a collision; he was credited with a probable. Plt.Off. Dickinson saw a Macchi heading for the coast followed by a Hurricane which turned back. He dived after the Italian, catching him two miles from the coast near Pozzallo, and from dead astern gave it a two second burst from 100 yards. The pilot baled out and the aircraft hit the water. He was then attacked by another MC200, but when he turned into this, it dived for the sea and headed home. Sqn.Ldr. Rabagliati (in V7103) also claimed one MC200 shot down as did Sgt. MacGregor. Sgt. John Maltby failed to return. Italian sources indicate that only five MC200s were out undertaking an escort patrol south of Cap Scaramia. The pilots of these claimed two Hurricanes shot down (by Sottoten. Duca Gabriele Ferretti and Serg. Omiccioli of the 86ª Squadriglia) and one probable (Mar. De Mattia); Sottoten. Luigi Cantele was shot down, baling out and being picked up safely later. If he was indeed the only pilot shot down on this occasion then it would appear that all the R.A.F. pilots had attacked the same aircraft.

Sgt. A. Noel MacGregor of 126 Squadron. (*A.N.C. MacGregor*)

26–31/8/41

Two Blenheims of 105 Squadron went out during 26th. to photograph damaged cargo ships and to attack one, but Sgt. R.J. Scott's aircraft (Z7682) hit the mast of the target vessel and broke up, bursting into flames before going into the sea. That night Sqn.Ldr. Powell-Sheddon and Flg.Off. Cassidy patrolled together, both attacking one bomber which was seen losing height with smoke pouring from the starboard side. They then attacked another, shooting away half of the starboard engine. The wheels dropped down and the aircraft circled Gozo at 1,000 feet, last being seen heading for Sicily. Two BR 20s were claimed probably destroyed; in fact both got back, though both had been damaged. One crew reported that they had been attacked by fighters, while the other thought their aircraft had been hit by A.A. fire. The crew of one baled out near the coast, the pilot then making a force-landing, but the bomber caught fire and was destroyed. On 29 August Flt.Lt. Beazley and Flg.Off. Pat Wells of 249 Squadron flew a reconnaissance to Pozzallo, strafing a schooner in the Sicilian Narrows during their return flight. On the night of 31st. Flt.Lt. Westmacott went along as an observer in a 38 Squadron Wellington flown by Sqn.Ldr. Rollinson during a raid on Tripoli harbour, during which the 6,630 ton steamer 'Riva' was sunk. Rollinson's bomber was hit by light Flak, but returned and landed safely, despite a burst tyre. On the previous day meanwhile two CR 42s of the 23° Gruppo took off from Pantelleria during the afternoon to provide escort to a convoy. They reported that three Wellingtons attempted to attack the ships; Serg. Francesco Cuscuna attacked one which dived into the sea after he had hit the engines, while Sottoten. Wisdor Pederzoli claimed a second in flames; the third was claimed as a 'probable'. On this day a Wellington (W5559), of the Overseas Air Delivery Unit, flying from Gibraltar to Malta was shot down eight miles south of Lampedusa, presumably a victim of 23° Gruppo.

The last night of the month saw five Swordfish of 830 Squadron searching for a reported convoy off Lampedusa but only a small merchant vessel was found, the 861-ton 'Egadi' being torpedoed and sunk. The squadron was now short of torpedoes; it was necessary for these to be flown in by Sunderland or delivered by submarine.

CR 42s of the 75ᵃ Squadriglia, 23° Gruppo Aut. C.T. outside the famous underground hangar on Pantelleria island. Despite concentrated Allied bombing in 1943, this hangar remains intact to this day. (*N. Malizia*)

The end of August brought the usual communique; during the month the fighters were credited with twelve destroyed, three probables and one damaged for the loss of one Hurricane and pilot. Sqn.Ldr. Russell Welland was now posted from 69 Squadron to command 55 Squadron flying Blenheims in Egypt. He would be killed in action within two weeks. His position as leader of 69 Squadron was filled by newly-promoted Wg.Cdr. J.N. Dowland, GC; he had won the George Cross the previous year for twice removing unexploded bombs from ships. Within the squadron news was received of the award of a Bar to Adrian Warburton's D.F.C., and of a D.F.C. to Flg.Off. Roger Drew. D.F.Ms were also announced for Sgts. R.S. Mortimer and C. Clark, but these two N.C.O.s had been killed when their aircraft crashed at Luqa on 10th. of the month.

Wg.Cdr. Hughie Edwards was posted from 105 Squadron to the A.O.C.'s staff at this time, Wg.Cdr. D.W. Scivier being posted in from 110 Squadron as the new C.O. News also arrived that 107 Squadron in England was preparing to join 105 on Malta for a similar detachment. On Sicily the bomber force was also further strengthened by the arrival at Chinisia of the 9° Stormo headquarters section and the 33° Gruppo B.T., both equipped with Cant Z.1007bis bombers, under the command of Col. Alfredo Barbati. To make room for the new arrivals, the 10° Stormo with its 32° Gruppo moved from Chinisia to Sciacca, while from this latter base the 87° Gruppo of the 30° Stormo left the island for Forli.

New arrivals in Sicily at the end of August 1941 were the first Cant Z.1007bis bombers of the 33° Gruppo, 9° Stormo B.T. Here a formation of these aircraft from the unit's 60ª Squadriglia fly across Sicily on their way to the target. (*N. Malizia*)

1–2/9/41

September opened with a night attack on Comiso airfield by Fulmar N4001, Petty Off.(A) Jopling and Sub Lt. Furlong releasing four bombs amongst dispersed aircraft on the ground. Late the next night two Fulmars took off for another nocturnal visit to Sicily where the Gerbini–Catania area was this time the chosen area of search. Sub Lt. Tritton first flew to Gerbini aerodrome where he dropped two of his 20lb. bombs, then strafed dispersal points and machine-gun posts before flying on to Comiso and depositing his other two bombs on the airfield. P.O.(A) Sabey also arrived over Gerbini, having first witnessed a mammoth explosion many miles out to sea – obviously a ship blowing up. Once. over the airfield he saw an aircraft with its landing lights on, but this disappeared as he approached. Another was seen coming in to land, which he attacked with a short burst, but saw no results before the aircraft was down safely. Climbing to 4,000 feet, he chased a third aircraft out to sea, and saw another which he caught just south of Mount Etna. Putting in a long burst, he saw his target go down in flames to the north-east of the airfield, but he then spotted three Italian fighters climbing up, so he departed for Comiso. Here he released his bombs on the north dispersal area, but then he spotted another fighter so made his way home, landing at Hal Far at 2330.

The various targets of his attacks had been 43° Stormo **BR** 20Ms, returning from Malta. The Italians mistook the intruding Fulmars for Beaufighters, reporting the one bomber crashed a few miles from the airfield in flames. Three members of the crew baled out, but one was dead when found; the remainder went to their death in the crash. A second bomber was damaged – obviously that attacked by Sabey as it was landing.

The huge explosion Sabey and his observer, the C.O., had seen earlier in their flight over Sicily had been caused by an Italian ammunition ship blowing up as a result of another 830 Squadron strike. Nine Swordfish had gone out after a convoy of five merchantmen, with destroyer escort, reported off the toe of Italy and obviously making for Tripoli. Hits on various large vessels were claimed by Lts. Lamb and F.C. Nottingham, and by Sub Lts. P. Cotton and R.G. Lawson, while others claimed one probable and two possible hits. One victim was the 6338-ton 'Andrea Gritti' which had been carrying bombs, ammunition, a tank repair workshop, twenty-five Daimler Benz Bf109 engines, as well as tons of petrol and food – all now lost with her entire crew; the 6,330 ton freighter 'Pietro Barbara' was also badly damaged but she was towed to Messina, where she sank.

3–4/9/41

The bombers were back over Malta next night (3/4th.), **BR** 20Ms, Z.1007bis and Ju87s all undertaking sorties without interception. The morning of 4 September brought a day of heavy combat however, as the fighters clashed twice. At 0150 nineteen MC200s of the 10° Gruppo set off from Comiso to search an area of sea where returning Ju87 crews of 101° Gruppo claimed to have sunk a ship during the night. While returning towards Sicily, and when only some nine or ten miles from Malta, they were engaged by a reported thirty Hurricanes, and a big dogfight commenced. In fact twelve aircraft from 126 Squadron and nine from 185 Squadron had been scrambled, sighting the Italian formation at 22,500 feet in the Grand Harbour area. Sqn.Ldr. Rabagliati, flying Z4941, at once attacked two Macchis, one of which went down pouring smoke and was confirmed to have crashed by one of the 185 Squadron pilots. Flg.Off. Carpenter, who was acting as top 'weaver', some distance above the other Hurricanes, climbed after four Macchis giving similar high cover to their own formation. Accompanied by Plt.Off. Lardner-Burke, who was in a Mark IIC, Carpenter attacked one Macchi from below and to port, at which all four dived and went into line astern. His fire struck the starboard aileron of the leading fighter and pieces flew off the wing. The Italian pilot did a flick roll and turned to see what was going on, at which point Carpenter claimed to have shot him down. Lardner-Burke meanwhile was attacking the No. 2 aircraft and saw the wing disintegrate under the impact of the 20mm shells. At once the aircraft went into a spin and the pilot baled out. At this point his cannons jammed, but looking down he was able to count three parachutes and two crashing aircraft.

A Cant Z.1007bis of the 59ª Squadriglia, 33º Gruppo, 9º Stormo B.T. at Trapani/Milo airfield, beneath Monte Erice. All white paintwork on the aircraft has been daubed over in black to prepare it for night operations. (*N. Malizia*)

Below meanwhile Plt.Off. Blackburn attacked two MC200s, scoring hits on both and seeing one dive down; he claimed a probable and a damaged. Flt.Lt. Lefevre, Sgt. Simpson and Sgt. MacGregor each claimed a Macchi shot down, as did Sgt. Russell, who also claimed another damaged; MacGregor force-landed Z3498 at Takali due to a burst glycol tank. The pilots of 185 Squadron also joined in, Flt.Lt. Jeffries attacking one MC200 orbitting at 19,000 feet and getting

286

in a short burst at only 25 yards range. He saw hits around the cockpit and the Macchi dived vertically towards the sea. Unable to observe the crash, he did see a puff of smoke where he assumed it would crash, and was awarded a probable. Returning pilots reported seeing three parachutes and one pilot bale out but fall without his 'chute' opening.

The Italians actually lost Ten.Col. Carlo Romagnoli, a veteran of the Spanish Civil War, and one of the Regia Aeronautica's 'aces', who was commander of the 10º Gruppo. Sottoten. Andrea Della Pasqua was also lost, while two more pilots got back in damaged aircraft. Five Hurricanes were claimed shot down by all pilots jointly. In the afternoon twenty more MC200s from the 54º Stormo operating from Pantelleria, and ten 10º Gruppo aircraft covered a Z.506B of the 612ª Squadriglia Soccorso to search for the missing pilots. The formation was led by Magg. Francesco Beccaria and Cap. Valentino Festa of the 54º, and Cap. Franco Lucchini of the 10º.

Ten. Col. Carlo Romagnoli, commander of 10º Gruppo C.T., who was killed in action near Malta on 4th September 1941.

Eight Hurricanes were scrambled by 249 Squadron to intercept, meeting the Italians five miles off Cap Passero at 1546, diving on them and engaging in a fierce dogfight at 1,000 feet, Sqn.Ldr. Barton, flying Z2794, described it as the hardest fight of his career: "... we attacked, from above, a formation of Macchis, escorting what I believe was an air/sea rescue floatplane. We had the advantage but somehow the Italians reacted strongly and an unhappy dogfight ensued – all low down close to the water. I ordered disengage – I doubt if anyone heard – and we ran for home – a most dangerous situation hence our losses. We should have done better." Barton himself claimed one probable and one damaged, while Sgts. Owen and Carter each claimed one shot down, and Plt.Off. Matthews one damaged. A third Macchi was reportedly seen to go into the sea, but two Hurricanes were lost (Z3056 and Z3521); Plt.Off. George Smith and Sgt. James Kimberley both being reported missing, believed killed.

The Italians, obviously incensed by the loss of Romagnoli, thought they had been attacked by twenty-five Hurricanes, and also reported seeing some Beaufighters. They claimed no less than sixteen Hurricanes shot down – again apparently by all jointly, no individual credits being given – eight damaged and one probable; obviously everyone was firing at the two unfortunate machines which did go down. One 10° Gruppo Macchi flown by Serg. Luigi Contarini was lost, while two more piloted by Mar. Avellino De Mattia and Serg. Walter Omiccioli of the 54° Stormo, were damaged; the Cant floatplane was also hit in the fuselage, but suffered only minor damage. No sign of the missing pilots from the morning combat was found.

Frequently in the firing line, and subject of much heart-searching – both Italian and British – were the Red Cross-marked air-sea rescue Cant Z.506B floatplanes operated by the Regia Aeronautica from Sicily. Several were shot down or damaged during 1941 by British fighters. (*C. Raso via N. Malizia*)

The aircraft reported as Beaufighters may actually have been Blenheims of 105 Squadron, five of which were led by Sqn.Ldr. B.W. Smithers to visit Southern Italy during the day to attack shipping in Crotone harbour. One returned early, but the other four made the attack, Smithers gaining a hit on one 4,000-ton ship which was seen to blow up. However Sgt. W.H. Wallace's aircraft (Z7654) was seen to have one wing blown off by a direct Dicat hit and crashed into the harbour, all the crew being killed.

5-6/9/41

The day's battles seemed to cool the ardour of the Italian fighters for some days, but by night the bombers were soon back. A little before dawn on 5th. three 9° Stormo B.T. Z.1007bis attacked Hal Far, but were intercepted by two all-black M.N.F.U. Hurricanes which were sent up at 0520. Plt.Off. Barnwell in a Mark IIB and Flt.Lt. Stones in a IIC caught one of the trimotors well-illuminated by the searchlights and shot it down between them. Two of the crew were reported to have baled out, but the rescue launch sent out found only the pilot, who had been wounded in the chest, and who had to be rushed to hospital for an emergency operation on being brought ashore.

During the afternoon a Maryland returned from a sea reconnaissance reporting yet another convoy, this of three merchant ships and four escorting destroyers some 30 miles south of Pantelleria. By 2145 six Swordfish had located the convoy and were positioning for the attack. Sub Lt. C.R.J. Coxon scored a certain hit on one ship which stopped and gave off heavy black smoke; it was later seen in a wide pool of oil, still smoking heavily and being attended by two of the destroyers. Coxon was credited with the sinking. Others claimed a possible hit on a tanker, two pilots releasing at the same vessel. One aircraft returned having suffered damage from A.A. fire, and another reported seeing a lifeboat full of survivors from one of the stricken ships, presumably from Coxon's victim.

8/9/41

Two nights later at 2210 on 8 September another raid came in, five Ju87s attacking Valetta and one BR 20M Hal Far, while nine Z.1007bis also approached. Sqn.Ldr. Powell-Sheddon and Plt.Off. Barnwell were sent off, the latter again seeing one of the Cants caught in the searchlights. Closing from astern, he later reported: "I got into range just before he got out of the searchlights. I fired a few bullets – closed to about 50 yards. He was diving so I throttled back and went after him for he showed up as clear as daylight against the moonlight... I gave him a few more short bursts and I saw burning lumps falling off the port engine... gunners meanwhile firing at me. Finally he dived straight down, levelled off and made a perfect landing on the sea." The bomber came down 15 miles east of Malta, and at dawn a seaplane from Kalafrana saw four survivors in their dinghy paddling towards the island. They were subsequently picked up and Barnwell later met the pilot before he went to prison camp.

That same night Petty Off.(A) Jopling, this time with Sgt. G.R.I. Parker as observer, attacked Gerbini in Fulmar N4004 of 800X Squadron. They then bombed the seaplane slipway at Augusta. Parker, who had also flown as an observer in the Swordfish of 830 Squadron, later remustered as a pilot, and became quite a noteable night fighter 'ace' with victories over nine aircraft and six V-1s, gained flying Mosquitos with 219 Squadron. He also added a D.F.C. and Bar to the D.S.M. awarded to him by the Navy for his work on Malta. Three nights later Jopling, with Lt. Manning in the back seat, bombed a chemical works at Licata and machine-gunned harbour installations.

9–14/9/41

On 9 September meanwhile the island welcomed a new delivery flight from 'Ark Royal', but only fourteen Hurricanes landed on this occasion. Four Blenheims had been due to guide the fighters in, but only two of these actually left Gibraltar, and without sufficient guides for the whole delivery, the carrier returned with twelve Hurricanes still aboard. This had been Operation 'Status I'. The reinforcements were for Egypt however, and next day they flew on to their destination. This had been only the first run in any event, for the 'Ark' was back on 13th. with 'Furious', this time forty-six Hurricanes flying off; when taking-off from 'Furious' Z5218 hit the 'island', caught fire and was catapulted into the sea, the pilot – F/Sgt. W.R. Finlay – being killed. This time seven Blenheims arrived to guide the rest of the Hurricanes, and all forty-five reached the island safely. This was 'Status II', and again twenty-three of the aircraft flew on to Egypt. The rest stayed however, being posted to the squadrons to bring them up to strength, and release some more tour-expired pilots for rests. Four American pilots were included in this batch, the first of a growing number of U.S. citizens destined to fly with the R.A.F. on Malta. They were Plt.Offs. H.M. Coffin, D.A. Tedford, E.E. Steele and E.E. Streets, who were all posted to 126 Squadron, although Don Tedford was moved to 249 Squadron a few days later. Other new arrivals included: 126 Squadron; Plt.Offs. W.C.W. Hallett and J.M.S. Crichton, and F/Sgt. R.J. Fowler; 185 Squadron; Sgt. D.E. Eastman and D.W. Lintern. At the same time Flt.Lt. H.W. Eliot, D.F.C., was posted from 185 Squadron home to England.

The American, Howard Coffin was later to write a book based rather loosely on his experiences on Malta, but including some diary entries which appeared to give details of combats not recorded elsewhere. Of the arrival flight he wrote: "And then suddenly, out of a long, thin cloudbank, an Italian Z506 put in an appearance. I imagine he was as surprised as we were, finding himself abruptly in the midst of 200 (sic) British planes coming in over the sea. At any rate, he did not open fire, and neither did we. I caught a glimpse of his startled face as he slipped down below us; and only later did I remember those 100 rounds of ammo in my guns. He disappeared as abruptly as he had come. Everyone else experienced the same delayed reaction as myself. It was a good lesson, although I suppose none of us could be blamed; we were all green to combat, and just about out of gas." On 14 September, the day after arrival, Coffin reported that Plt.Off. Tedford was involved in a scramble flying a 126 Squadron Hurricane carrying the codes HA-S.

A Macchi dived on the British formation and was shot down by Tedford. That same afternoon Coffin flew the same aircraft in a scramble after an escorted bomber formation in which two Italian bombers and three fighters were allegedly claimed shot down, but one Hurricane blew up. Coffin was then chased by a number of Macchis and got into a spin from which he could not effect recovery; he baled out. These reports have been investigated, but no confirmation of their authenticity has been found-in either British or Italian records, which appear to make no mention of any such combats.

This Hurricane of 126 Squadron suffered a take off accident at Takali on 12 September 1941; the pilot fractured two ribs. (*F. Etchells*)

10-13/9/41

Meanwhile the British bombers from Malta were continuing to wage their war against the Axis shipping without respite. An attack on Messina on 10th, hit the cruiser 'Bolzano', which was damaged, twelve members of the crew being killed and thirty-four wounded. Next day Sqn.Ldr. Smithers led Blenheims from 105 Squadron to attack two ships off the Greek coast, one being reported as seen to be sinking as the formation retired. On 10th. meanwhile yet another Axis convoy of six merchant ships and six destroyers left Naples, making for Tripoli. By the following afternoon it had been sighted by a 69 Squadron Maryland when it was between Pantelleria and Lampedusa, and 830 Squadron prepared for another night strike. By 2115 five Swordfish armed with torpedoes followed an ASV aircraft to the Tunisian coast where the convoy was being shadowed by the other radar-equipped Swordfish, and shortly after midnight attacks commenced – one ship was claimed probably sunk, two others believed damaged, while one aircraft returned with Flak damage to its tail. One of the ships hit was the 6479-ton 'Caffaro', still afloat at daybreak when Sqn.Ldr. Smithers arrived leading eight 105 Squadron Blenheims, but soon ablaze following their low-level attack. Three MC200s and three CR 42s of 23° Gruppo then appeared, promptly shooting down three of the Blenheims (Z7357, 7423 and 7504), one seen falling in flames, while another ditched some twelve miles from the convoy, the crew luckily being picked up by a submarine, but on return to Luqa the crews of Sqn.Ldr. F.R. Charney, D.F.C., Sgt. F.B. Brandwood and Sgt. Q.E. Mortimer were posted missing; Sqn.Ldr. Smithers' aircraft had also been badly hit but he managed to nurse it back to the island. That night the Swordfish were ordered off again after the surviving ships of the convoy, now nearing the comparative safety of Tripoli harbour, and at 2100 six torpedo-carriers followed an ASV aircraft to the Tripolitanian coast. After two hours the convoy was sighted and the Swordfish went in; two hits were claimed and the 6003-ton 'Nicolo Odero' was crippled. To support the efforts of the torpedo-bombers seven Wellingtons of 38 Squadron from Luqa were despatched and these arrived off Tripoli at 0330 and bombed the ships; four hits were claimed and two ships were seen to be on fire. Shortly after the attack had started the damaged 'Nicolo Odero' blew up.

15–22/9/41

On 15 September the newly-arrived 107 Squadron commenced operations from Luqa, but it was 105 which continued to take the brunt of operations for the next week. On 17th. four Blenheims from the latter unit made a dawn attack on a large liner in Tripoli harbour, but Plt.Off. P.E.C. Robinson's Blenheim crashed into the deck of a schooner, while that flown by Sgt. J. Bendall also failed to return, all members of both crews being killed. A reconnaissance Maryland (again acting on 'Ultra'-supplied information) located the three 20,000-ton troopships 'Vulcania', 'Neptunia' and 'Oceania' east of Spartivento, but before Malta's strike force could be despatched patrolling submarines had been directed to the area, H.M.S. 'Upholder' sinking both 'Neptunia' and 'Oceania', fortunately with only a relatively small loss of life. However that night six Swordfish were after another convoy, this one located off Trapani, one ship being claimed probably sunk while a second was damaged. Two Blenheims visited Tripoli harbour on 19th, one from each of 105 and 107 Squadrons, where they attacked some destroyers and a cruiser from as low as ten feet, claiming bomb hits on the larger warships.

The two commanding officers, Wg.Cdr. Don Scivier, A.F.C., of 105 and Wg.Cdr. Harte of 107, attacked a large cargo ship and six escorting destroyers on 21st., Scivier's bomb hitting the big ship on the waterline. One engine of the Blenheim was set on fire by Flak, but both aircraft got back safely. Next day three bombers from each squadron attacked barracks and a dump at Homs in Libya. During the attack two Blenheims collided at 600 feet, and while one was not too badly damaged, the other had the tail cut right off and crashed into the sea. It was Wg.Cdr. Scivier's aircraft. A further loss occurred that night when two

Swordfish returned to Hal Far from a convoy strike with their torpedoes still intact. One aircraft, that piloted by Lt. L.F.E. Aldridge, crashed on landing; there followed an explosion and he was killed. His TAG, L/A A.K. Pimlott, died from his injuries later that day. The next night a Wellington of 38 Squadron failed to return from a sortie, the crew being posted missing. A highlight on 22nd. was the arrival of a PRU Spitfire at Takali following a $4\frac{1}{2}$ hour flight from England, piloted by Australian Flt.Lt. N.H.E. Messervy. The specific task of this aircraft was reconnaissance and surveillance of the Italian Fleet bases prior to the next major convoy operation, the imminent Operation 'Halberd' – the despatch of nine cargo ships from Gibraltar with 50,000 tons of urgently-required supplies for Malta. However, because of badly-worn tyres the Spitfire was not able to operate for almost three weeks on waiting the delivery of another set specially flown out from England!

Clandestine activities also continued. On 17th. Lt. Charles Lamb with Sub Lt. J.M. Robertson as his observer, flew a French agent to Tunisia in their Swordfish, landing on a dry salt lake near Sousse. In fact the 'dry' lake bed was only a crust, and the wheels went through, the aircraft tipping onto its nose. The agent escaped, but Lamb and Robertson were subsequently arrested by Vichy police, and would remain interned for nearly 18 months. It had been arranged that had anything gone wrong, they were to rendezvous over Hammamet Bay, near Sousse, with the He115 'spyplane', but this did not prove possible. Five days later on 22nd. this latter aircraft would itself be lost; taking off from Kalafrana at 0005 in the hands of F/Sgt. Georges Blaize, the French airman, it was forced to alight on the sea 20 miles from base, and here it was broken up by high waves. Blaize, his gunner and fellow-countryman F/Sgt. R. Gatien, and their F.A.A. observer Sub Lt. Reg Drake, all lost their lives, the bodies of the pilot and observer being recovered from the sea by a Swordfish floatplane next afternoon. The Heinkel had carried the identification '115PP1' but the significance of this code is not known. During the same night a Wellington off from Malta on the last stage of the delivery flight to Egypt, disappeared. It was not heard from again and was presumed lost in the sea. At this time however, three more Swordfish arrived at Takali on their way to join 830 Squadron.

24–26/9/41

On 24 September two of 107 Squadron's Blenheims attacked transport on the Misurata–Benghazi road, but one flown by Sqn.Ldr. T.J.S. Warren, D.F.C., failed to return. Undaunted, three more were out two days later to attack the Zuara area, where twelve single-engined biplanes were strafed on the ground.

About this time Sqn.Ldr. John Greenhalgh, one of the 1940 Hurricane pilots, was promoted Acting Wing Commander, having spent the previous few months at A.H.Q.; he was now put in command of the Blenheims. He writes: "...I was sent up to Luqa by A.V.M. Lloyd to command the Blenheims that were en route to the Middle East, but were held over in Malta. The appointment was more a liaison than a true command because I do not recall that the 'Wing' ever had an identity. The squadrons or flights suffered frightful casualties and acting promotions from

Pilot Officer to Squadron Leader in days were probably common ... I never flew a Blenheim but although I was instructed not to fly, I did make a few sorties as a navigator. One of these was to Argostoli when we were badly shot up, the gunner was killed and we were lucky to return to Malta. I think my association with the Blenheims was from autumn of 1941 until January 1942."

Other units were enjoying a much quieter time. 69 Squadron, which had now added a Blenheim and a Beaufort to its Marylands and Hurricanes, continued its reconnaissances. During these Adrian Warburton and his crew sought action whenever possible. An S.79 was claimed damaged by them on 7th., while on 24 September while on a morning patrol over the Eastern Ionian Sea, a Z.506B was seen above some ships and was forced to land on the water, where the crew indicated capitulation. Two men got into a dinghy and paddled off, whereupon Warburton strafed the Cant until it sank. During this attack he experienced some return fire from the rear turret, so the gunner had obviously remained aboard, laying an ambush for the Maryland.

King Vittorio Emmanuel III (hidden behind an Italian General) visits the 23° Gruppo Aut. C.T. at Trapani/Milo. In the background are one of the unit's CR 42s and an all black MC200 used as a night fighter in the defence of Palermo by Magg. Tito Falconi and Cap. Claudio Solaro of this unit. (*N. Malizia*)

Amongst the fighter squadrons there was little to report. Flt.Lt. Morello and Flg.Off. Pat Wells of 249 Squadron, together with Flt.Lt. Pat Hancock of 185 Squadron, ended their tours, leaving for Egypt aboard a Sunderland. About this time four of 249 Squadron's sergeant pilots were posted to the Middle East as reinforcements for the Fighter Pool. 185 Squadron's commanding officer, Sqn.Ldr. 'Boy' Mould learned of the award of a Bar to his D.F.C.

11–25/9/41

The period was equally quiet for the Regia Aeronautica. During the night of 10/11 September four Z.1007bis of the 33° Gruppo raided Hal Far, but on return the commanding officer, Col. Alfredo Barbati, became lost in fog and landed in the sea; all the crew were killed. On 17th. an S.79 crashed at Sciacca, and an MC200 on Pantelleria, both the results of accidents. Five Ju87s raided French Creek in Valetta Harbour during the night of 25/26 September, one of these also coming down in the sea with the loss of Sottoten. Brissolese and his gunner of 208ª Squadriglia.

19–20/9/41

A more active spell was afoot however, for a new convoy was now preparing to sail, codenamed Operation 'Halberd'. This operation was lucky to get underway however, for Force 'H' at Gibraltar had but narrowly escaped disaster a few days earlier on 19th. After dark the Italian submarine 'Scire' had sailed into Gibraltar Bay unobserved and settled on the sea bed preparatory to launching another daring attack, this time by the 'maiale' – manned torpedoes. At 0100 on 20 September three 'maiale' were launched, two to set explosives on the hull of the battleship 'Nelson', and one after 'Ark Royal'. Ten. Vesco got within 50 yards of 'Nelson', but was hindered by patrolling British light craft, so attached his charge to the oil lighter 'Fiona Shell', and swam ashore after scuttling his 'maiale'. Ten. Catalano was so much delayed in evading patrols that he selected instead the motorship 'Durham', which was at anchor in the roads.

The third 'maiale', in the hands of Ten. Visintini (brother of the top-scoring fighter pilot of the East African Campaign), got into the harbour via the southern entrance undetected, but surfaced too late to reach 'Ark Royal' before daybreak. Constantly avoiding patrols, he attached his charge to the oiler 'Denbydale', and escaped from the harbour the way he had come, scuttling his craft in the Bay and swimming ashore. The first explosion went off at 0749, 'Fiona Shell' blowing up and sinking, while the 'Durham' was subsequently towed into shallow water in a sinking condition. 'Denbydale' was badly damaged, but did not sink. On this occasion the all-important warships had been lucky in escaping attack, and were able to sail on 24th. to escort the new convoy. 'Scire' and her intrepid crew were to strike again with much greater success during the night of 18/19 December, when the 'maiale' attacked the Mediterranean Fleet at anchor in Alexandria harbour, severely damaging the battleships 'Queen Elizabeth' and 'Valiant'.

24/9/41

Now however, Force 'H' was able to sail out of Gibraltar at full strength, the nine merchant ships of 'Halberd' being supported by 'Ark Royal', with twenty-seven Fulmars of 807 and 808 Squadrons aboard, plus 'Nelson' and her sister battleships, 'Rodney' and 'Prince of Wales', five cruisers and eighteen destroyers. The cruisers and destroyers were again to form Force 'X' and continue with the convoy right into Grand Harbour. Even as the ships weighed anchor on 24 September, thirteen Beaufighters of 272 Squadron were again flown across to Malta from North Africa. While en route three of the pilots – all Belgians – saw two Ju52/3m transports over the Gulf of Bomba, and these were both claimed damaged. The pilots responsible were Flg.Off. C.L. Roman, Sgt. O.G. Le Jeune and Sgt. De Moulin.

27/9/41

As the ships came within range of Sardinian-based aircraft at dawn on 27 September, a strong force of torpedo-bombers had been gathered in Sardinia. The 36° Stormo Aerosiluranti at Decimommanu had arrived from Italy only on 16 September. The Stormo had previously been a standard bomber unit with S.79s, and had operated over Malta earlier in the war. The unit was now commanded by Col. Riccardo Zario Seidl, an ex-sailor who had led a fighter unit during the Spanish Civil War, where he had gained six aerial victories. The command in Sicily had despatched two S.79s of the 278ª Squadriglia Aut. A.S. and three S.84s of the 282ª Squadriglia Aut. A.S., together with five torpedoes loaded into an S.82 transport, as a last minute reinforcement.

The early morning 'snoopers', plotted on the British ships' radars, apparently failed to make any sightings for it was 1150 before the torpedo-bombers started leaving their bases. The first formation away from Elmas comprised eleven S.79s of the resident 130° Gruppo Aut. A.S. (280ª Squadriglia led by Cap. Giorgio Grossi and 283ª Squadriglia led by Cap. Franco Melley) and of the 278ª Squadriglia detachment, plus the three S.84s of the 282ª, these led by Cap. Marino Marini. A little later the 36° Stormo S.84s followed in two formations, six aircraft of the 108° Gruppo left first, five more from 109° Gruppo following 15 minutes later. The 108° Gruppo bombers, led by Magg. Arduino Buri, the gruppo commander, picked up an escort of eight CR 42s from the 24° Gruppo Aut. C.T.. The 109° Gruppo aircraft were led by Col. Seidl personally.

The weather was ideal for such an attack as they headed south, with considerable mist and cloud, but as they approached the target area a strong wind caused the sky to clear rapidly. The crews were under the impression that the Italian Fleet would follow them into the attack. Indeed two task forces had put to sea, one composed of two battleships and eight destroyers, the other of four cruisers and eight destroyers, but when the strength of the British force was disclosed by reconnaissance, no attempt was made to close and engage.

The leading crews of the 130° Gruppo first saw the British convoy near the Tunisian coast, north of Galite island, about an hour and a half after take-off, and at once went into attack. Eight Fulmars of 808 Squadron were already up on patrol when the raid was reported, and seven more were scrambled at once, the patrolling aircraft intercepting the S.79s and S.84s very low over the sea, 10 miles north of the convoy. The Fulmar pilots identified their quarries as BR 20s and Z.1007s, and were unaware of the CR 42s flying top cover, some 7,000 feet above.

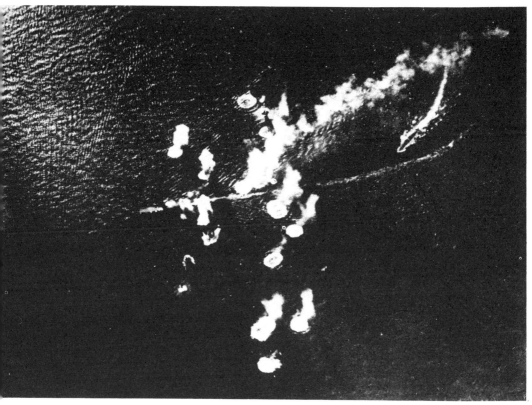

Royal Navy vessels, including an aircraft carrier, manoeuver to avoid the bombs of attacking Regia Aeronautica bombers. (*A.M.-. via N. Malizia*)

At 1303 Red Section (Lt. Lewin/Sub Lt. L.D. Urry and Lt. W.A. Medland/ P.O.(A) Sharp) gained position on the tail of Ten. Carlo Deslex's 280ª Squadriglia aircraft (MM24077) and jointly shot this down into the sea. Others were hit by the pursuing Fulmars but six of the S.79s crossed rthe barrier of A.A. gunfire raised by the destroyers, where two were claimed shot down by the guns.

One S.79 returned with a dead crewman and two others wounded, while gunners in the bombers believed they had shot one fighter down and claimed a second as probably destroyed – reported variously as Fulmars or Hurricanes; one gunner claimed a twin-engined Beaufort torpedo-bomber – it is probable that he was shooting at one of his own aircraft! In fact one Fulmar – Blue 1 crewed by Lt. M.W. Watson and Sub Lt. P.W.N. Couch failed to return; this aircraft was seen in combat with a number of CR 42s and was initially assumed to have been shot down by these. However it transpired that the Fulmar had in fact been tragically shot down by the guns of H.M.S. 'Prince of Wales'; the crew did not survive.

The returning Italian crews greatly overestimated the results of the torpedo attack, for two battleships, a cruiser and an unclassified ship were all claimed to have been sunk! In actual fact all torpedoes released at the ships had been avoided. By 1310 all was quiet again. But not for long! Five minutes later two sections of Fulmars – seven aircraft – were flown off and by the time a second raid was plotted some twelve minutes later a further seven, which had been rapidly refuelled and rearmed, were launched. At that point the 108° Gruppo S.84s approached, but were at once attacked by five Fulmars. The escorting CR 42s engaged these and drove them off, allowing the bombers to split into two sections of three aircraft each, and attack from each side. Those that went in on the left managed to drop their torpedoes accurately, and the leader, Magg. Buri, gained a hit on the bow of the battleship 'Nelson' causing serious damage. At this stage however, one of the aircraft in the other section was struck by A.A. fire, collided with another S.84, and both went into the sea; these were both claimed by the gunners aboard the ships. As Buri's trio headed away they were again attacked by Fulmars, and this time one of them was shot down. This fell to Black Section of 807 Squadron, a pair of Fulmars flown by Lt. Firth/Sub Lt. J.F. Turner and Sub Lt. J.E.G. Wardrop/L/A Barlow, who were jointly credited with one 'BR 20' shot down. A second was hit and claimed damaged by two aircraft of Yellow Section, those piloted by P.O.(A) Leggott and Sub Lt. G.P. Magwood. The crews of the two surviving S.84s of this section believed their gunners had accounted for two of the fighters in return. One CR 42 pilot, Serg. Luigi Valotti, attempted to divert the attention of A.A. gunners away from the bombers by flying over the ships. At first he was ignored, but then the guns turned their fire on this very courageous pilot, and his aircraft was shot down into the sea.

Some twenty-five minutes after the 108° Gruppo S.84s had appeared on the scene, those of the 109° arrived, but did not close range and only three were seen to release their torpedoes. Fulmars again attacked and one was immediately shot down, this probably falling to a trio of 808 Squadron pilots – Lt. Taylour's Black Section, himself and Sub Lts. Goodfellow and P. Constable. All the time the guns blazed away, gaining a vital success when they shot down one Savoia just as it was about to press home an attack on 'Ark Royal'; the crippled aircraft splashed into the sea just 1,000 yards away. The Fulmars pursued the torpedo-bombers at low-level through the gun barrage, two Yellow Section aircraft, those flown by Lt. Guthrie and Sub Lt. P. Guy caught yet another 'BR 20' and shot this down. However Yellow 2 flew too close to the guns of H.M.S. 'Rodney', the battleships' gunners mistaking it for hostile as it approached head-on and shot it down into the sea. Fortunately neither Percy Guy or his TAG, L/A Jones, were hurt and were quickly rescued by one of the destroyers, H.M.S. 'Duncan'. Whilst returning from a reconnaissance one of 'Ark's' Swordfish – 2H – blundered into seven CR 42s and was shot up and badly damaged, but the pilot succeeded in reaching the carrier safely with an uninjured crew.

The actions had brought success to the Fulmar crews – not only had they helped defend the convoy and the Fleet, but had accounted for four of the attackers, all identified as BR 20s, shot down. The Fulmar pilots, attacking mainly from astern and seeing the twin tails of the S.84s, had in all cases where claims were made, misidentified them as BR 20s, just as had the pilots on Malta earlier mistaken the Z.1007bis.

Thus the 36° Stormo had lost six of its eleven aircraft; thirty-eight crewmen did not return, thirty-seven of whom were dead, the sole survivor a prisoner. Col. Seidl, Cap. Alfonso Rotolo, commander of the 257ᵃ Squadriglia, Cap. Bartolomeo Tommasino, commander of the 258ᵃ Squadriglia, and Cap. Giuseppe Verna, commander of the 259ᵃ Squadriglia were all lost; all four pilots were later awarded the Medaglia d'Oro posthumously. Other aircraft lost were those flown by Ten. Danile Barro (257ᵃ Squadriglia) and Sottoten. Vincenzo Morelli (258ᵃ Squadriglia).

There was further action to ensue on this day however, when a 'shadowing' Z.506B of the 287ᵃ Squadriglia Autonomo R.M., flown by Sottoten. Giuseppe Majorana, was caught by Blue Section Fulmars of 807 Squadron at 1650. Lt. 'Jimmie' Gardner led his No. 2, Sub Lt. Rankin, into the attack and was joined by two more Fulmars, these from Green Section (Sub Lts. Walker and J.F. Underwood); between them they soon despatched the unfortunate Cant into the sea where it burst into flames and sank – no survivors were seen.

Torpedo-carrying Savoia S.79sil bombers of the Regia Aeronautica were active from Sicily in Summer 1941, achieving some noteable successes. (*N. Malizia*)

Under cover of darkness two S.79s from the 278ᵃ Squadriglia A.S. set out from Sicily as the convoy neared Malta, and the main bulk of Force 'H' turned back. At 2030 they launched a surprise attack, Cap. Dante Magagnoli succeeding in torpedoing the merchant ship 'Imperial Star' (12427 tons). Attempts to tow her having failed, and with her crew having been taken off, she was sent to the bottom with depth charges.

Italian fighter units in Sicily had provided covering patrols for their own naval units at sea during the day, but in doing so suffered considerable losses. A CR 42 of the 23° Gruppo was shot down by the destroyer 'Fusiliere' by mistake, although Cap. Pietro Serini was rescued from the sea at once. Ten MC200s of the 10° Gruppo ran out of fuel in bad weather and all had to ditch. Two pilots were killed and two injured (one of them Cap. Lucchini, whose face was badly hurt), but all those who survived were subsequently picked up safely. Other patrolling MC200s from 7° Gruppo, led by Ten. Maurer, engaged a single Blenheim which was claimed damaged by Serg.Magg. Magnagli of the 98ª Squadriglia.

Famous torpedo-bomber 'aces' of the Regia Aeronautica. Cap. Giuseppe Cimicchi (l) and Magg. Carlo Emanuele Buscaglia of the 132° Gruppo Aut. Sil. (r) with a naval armourer and torpedo. (*A.M.I. via N. Malizia*)

During the day Blenheims of 107 Squadron and Beaufighters from 272 Squadron strafed airfields in Sicily. At Catania two Z.1007bis were damaged slightly, as were two Z.501s at Stagnone (Marsala), but no other aircraft were hit. Meantime the Beaufighters had been reinforced by three Blenheim IVF fighters despatched from 113 Squadron in Egypt to provide convoy escorts and anti-submarine patrols.

The other side of the coin; an 830 Squadron Swordfish with torpedo, visits Takali from Hal Far. (*J. Alton*)

28/9/41

During the night the cruiser 'Hermione' shelled Pantelleria to discourage use of the airfield there on the morrow. Dawn on 28th. quickly brought an escort for the eight remaining ships of the convoy and those of the escorting Force 'X', composed of Beaufighters and a Fulmar of 800X Squadron. By noon all the ships were safely in harbour where unloading of supplies began in earnest.

As Force 'H' steadily headed westwards for Gibraltar Italian 'shadowers' followed and at 1148 one of these paid the penalty for being caught. Two sections of 808 Squadron Fulmars were up – Black Section comprising Lt. Taylour and Sub Lt. Constable, while Lt. Hay and Midspmn. R.H. Gardner made up Green Section. The four fighters shot down the Cant seaplane and again no survivors were seen.

Even as the ships approached harbour, Malta's aircraft were striking out in all directions. Six Hurricanes of 185 Squadron fitted temporarily with racks for four 40lb. bombs beneath each wing, were led by Sqn.Ldr. Mould to attack Comiso airfield, covered by six more led by Flg.Off. Thompson. On return they were refuelled and re-armed, 'Boy' Mould leading a further attack in similar strength, while Flg.Off. Murch led the escort. A third such mission was subsequently flown, led by Flt.Lt. Pike, by the end of which 5,140lbs. of bombs had been dropped. Most pilots in the squadron flew two sorties, one as fighter bomber and one as escort; Mould was the only pilot to bomb twice. During these attacks damage was inflicted on several buildings and a number of aircraft were left in flames.

Meanwhile six Beaufighters made the longer journey to Sardinia, to strafe

Cagliari airfield. Here Plt.Off. N.K. Lee engaged two S.79s in the air and claimed one probably destroyed. Sqn.Ldr. Fletcher gained hits on some moored seaplanes, and then also encountered two aircraft in flight, claiming both probably shot down. Units of the Italian Fleet were also seen and shadowed. On the previous date as the torpedo-bombers had gone out from Sardinia, CR42s from the 386ª Squadriglia, 21° Gruppo, had been despatched to the island on temporary duty from Caopdichino, Italy. Now these reportedly intercepted three strafing 'Blenheims' over Elmas, Cap. Bruno Mondini claiming one shot down. It was obviously the Beaufighters which they had met, although no loss was reported by the British formation. Nearer to Malta, two of 113 Squadron's Blenheim fighters patrolled near Pantelleria but the aircraft (T1821) flown by Sgt. H. Crossley failed to return. On another patrol by the two remaining aircraft of the detachment, flown by Sqn.Ldr. P.R.A. Ford and Plt.Off. Vic Cashmore, R.A.A.F., two fighters tentatively identified as Messerschmitts, attacked five miles south of Marsala. Ford's 'Z' was hit in the starboard wing and upper fuselage, and the pilot himself was wounded. Cashmore attacked one fighter and saw black smoke pour from its engine. During the day the 23° Gruppo scrambled a number of CR 42s and MC200s, (a few of which had now been received by the unit) on several occasions during the morning. Some Blenheims were encountered, Ten. Claudio Solaro claiming one shot down, which fell in the sea about 30 kilometres from the Sicilian coast, while Serg. Mario Mantelli claimed a second damaged. It seems probable that Solaro's victim was Crossley's aircraft, while Mantelli may have damaged Ford's Blenheim, unless the claim for a Blenheim damaged submitted by 7° Gruppo on the previous day was in fact wrongly dated and referred to this combat. Meanwhile, rather than continue to employ mass formations of fighters to escort a single bomber on reconnaissance over Malta, the Regia Aeronautica was now employing a few camera-equipped MC200s on these duties. During this day Sottoten. Ferretti of the 86ªSquadriglia, 7° Gruppo, made his fourth photo-reconnaissance sortie over Malta in a period of seven days, flying such an aircraft.

One of a small number of MC200s issued to the 23° Gruppo Aut. C.T. in Summer 1941 to supplement the unit's CR 42s at Trapani/Milo. (*N. Malizia*)

That night Petty Off.(A) Jopling with Sub Lt. Bland in the back of Fulmar N1958 of 800X Squadron was over Sicily again. He recorded: "Operated as night fighter over Sicily. Proceeded to Trapani where flare path was on. Saw aircraft signalling to land – gave chase but lost it in the dark. Machine gunned flare path and dropped four incendiaries, one causing minor explosions. Attacked A.A. battery of four guns with machine gun fire, silencing two. Proceeded to Marsala and machine gunned seaplanes and hangars without visible result. Drew heavy A.A. fire from Agrigento – caught napping here."

A 23° Gruppo Aut. C.T. CR 42 escorts an Italian navy cruiser. Note the Meridionali Ro44 floatplane on a catapult on the bow of this vessel. (*A. Brini via N. Malizia*)

29/9/41

Next morning early Flg.Off. Warburton was off again in a Maryland to patrol over the Marittimo area. Two MC200s were seen taking off from Cagliari airfield to intercept, and one of these was claimed shot down by the gunner, Sgt. Moren, D.F.M. This brought to ten the number of aircraft claimed by Warburton and his crew, five destroyed and two damaged in the air, and three on the ground. At the end of September they would be posted to H.Q., Middle East for a well-deserved rest from operations.

29–30/9/41

During this day, 29th., seven of the Beaufighters and the two surviving Blenheim IVFs returned to Africa. Of the remaining Beaufighters, two flown by Sgts. R.A. Haylock and N.A.J. Price went out on an anti-E-Boat patrol during the afternoon, attacking two of the gunboats without visible effect. They then encountered two Z.501 flyingboats, believing that they had inflicted heavy damage on these. Finally they fought an indecisive engagement with a pair of MC200s. Four Beaufighters were off again early on 30th., this time to strafe Cagliari airfield again. Here it was believed that five aircraft were destroyed or damaged; two seaplanes were also believed destroyed at their moorings. Later in the day the remaining Beaufighters once again returned to Egypt.

That same afternoon five of 185 Squadron's fighter-bomber Hurricanes again attacked Comiso, escorted by six more of the unit's aircraft. On the previous day the other unit of 4° Stormo C.T., the 9° Gruppo, had arrived in Sicily with the first operational examples of the new Macchi MC202 fighters, under the leadership of Col. Eugenio Leotta and Ten.Col. Marco Paulello. Three of these aircraft, which were fitted with the same model Daimler Benz 601 engine as the new Messerschmitt Bf109F which was just making its first appearance in North Africa, were scrambled by the 97ª Squadriglia, led by Ten. Frigerio. These intercepted the Hurricanes and Frigerio shot down Plt.Off. Lintern, who baled out of Z5265 just north of Gozo.

At the end of September 1941 the formidable new Macchi C.202 Folgore fighter made its debut in Sicily with the 4° Stormo C.T. This was one of the first of these aircraft to reach the unit. (*N. Malizia*)

After returning to base and refuelling, five of the Hurricanes set off again to escort a Fulmar of the Kalafrana Rescue Flight searching for Lintern five miles off Scalambria. A flyingboat may have followed them, for the Italians reported seeing a Sunderland and seven escorting Hurricanes searching for the downed pilot, who was not found. Again the MC202s attacked, but this time without result. Flt.Lt. Jeffries claimed one of the unidentified fighters as a probable, while Plt.Off. Veitch and Sgt. Jolly each claimed one damaged. However the rescue Fulmar was obliged to ditch, Lt.Eyres, the pilot, and Sub Lt. Furlong being picked up by one of the Flight's Swordfish floatplanes. It seems that their aircraft had been shot down by Ten. Luigi Tessari and Serg. Raffaello Novelli, who jointly claimed one fighter shot down into the sea, which they reported blew up ten kilometres south of Cap Scaramia. Tessari's MC202 received numerous hits in the fuselage from the Hurricanes. (During September the rescue Swordfish floatplanes had fished ten people out of the sea, including the crew of another Swordfish.)

A.H.Q.'s September resume listed eleven confirmed, one probable and five damaged for Malta's fighters during the month, but more importantly in three weeks of intensive operations against Axis convoys plying between Italy and North Africa eleven ships had been sunk, six by air attack, totalling 23,031 tons, with a loss of 28% of all cargoes shipped to Libya. But the cost was high – eight Blenheims and one Swordfish lost with the majority of the crews killed.

The loss of these ships and their cargoes was considered sufficiently severe as for Fliegerkorps X to be ordered to discontinue raids on Egypt and to provide more shipping protection, and to transfer one Gruppe of bombers and a Gruppe of Bf110s to Sicily.

A number of the island's aircrews were notified of awards of decorations, D.F.C.s going to Flt.Lts. Jeffries and Eliot of 185 Squadron, Plt.Off. Barnwell of M.N.F.U., Flg.Offs. Williams, Devine and Wells of 69 Squadron, whilst Sgt. A.J. Stripp of the same unit received the D.F.M. Lt.Cdr. J.G. Hunt arrived from the U.K. to take command of 830 Squadron viz Lt. Pain, while new aircraft arrivals included a detachment of 'special' Wellington VIIIs of 221 Squadron, three aircraft under the command of Flt.Lt. A. Spooner. These aircraft were also fitted with ASV radar and were to undertake night reconnaissance sorties in conjunction with the Swordfish of 830 Squadron, a number of which had just been fitted with special receivers for the purpose.

1/10/41

On the morning of the first day of the month the 9° Gruppo undertook its first sorties over Malta with its new aircraft, seven MC202s led by Cap. Mario Pluda taking part. At 1150 eight Hurricanes from 185 Squadron scrambled after the incoming 'bandits', climbing to 24,000 feet. At this height, 30 miles north-east of the island, they were jumped by the Macchis and Sqn.Ldr. 'Boy' Mould was shot down and killed. Cap. Carlos Ivaldi, Ten. Bonfatti and Serg.Magg. Dallari claimed two Hurricanes shot down and two probables between them in this first pass. Sgt. Knight got in a shot at the attackers, obtaining hits on Ivaldi's aircraft, which he claimed damaged. The Macchi had been hit in its main fuel tank, and with all fuel drained away, was obliged to force-land on a beach near Pozzallo, on regaining the Sicilian coast.

One of the first 4° Stormo C.T. MC202s in flight. (*A.M.I. via N. Malizia*)

Sicily received further reinforcements during the day with the arrival of Magg. Giovanni Buffa's 171° Gruppo Caccia Notturno (301ª and 302ª Squadriglia) equipped with modified CR 42CNs for night fighting. Five days later the 116° Gruppo (276ª and 277ª Squadriglia) of the 37° Stormo B.T. also arrived under Col. Giuseppe Scarlata, going first to Catania and then Gerbini with its **BR 20Ms**. On Malta meanwhile Pip Lefevre was posted from 126 Squadron to take over 185: John Carpenter was promoted flight commander in his place in his old unit.

Main enemy of the Malta night fighters during Summer and Autumn 1941 was the Fiat **BR 20M**. Here aircraft of the 277ª Squadriglia, 116° Gruppo, 37° Stormo B.T. prepare for a mission as dusk creeps over their airfield. This unit reached Sicily early in October. (*A.M.I. via N. Malizia*)

On 4th. 185 Squadron again scrambled eight Hurricanes after a reported six 'hostiles', but no interception took place. However, Plt.Off. Veitch failed to return, and was believed to have crashed after suffering oxygen failure, his aircraft (Z2518) being seen to dive into the sea off Benghaisa Point; he may well have fallen to one of the new Macchis – Serg. Teresio Martinoli apparently claiming to have shot down a Hurricane this day. Later in the day eight Blenheims from 107 Squadron were sent out to attack a 6,000-ton merchant vessel reported off the Tripolitanian coast. They could not find the target ship, so selected Zuara airfield as an alternative. As they approached they were met by intense Flak from destroyers in the harbour and from the shore, while four CR 42s were seen in the air. One of these followed the Blenheims 50 miles out to sea, gaining hits on Sgt. D.E. Hamlyn's aircraft and causing him to have to carry out a force-landing in the water near Tripoli. Two other bombers were damaged, but the gunners claimed to have damaged the fighter in return. Hamlyn and his crew were picked up when they were found floating in their dinghy near Djerba a few days later.

After dark that night Sub Lt. Tritton of 800X Squadron headed towards Sicily in his Fulmar. Over Trapani at 2328 he attacked an aircraft which he believed to be a Ju87. He chased this for 15 minutes during which time several of his guns jammed. No definite result to the engagement could be observed, the opponent last being seen leaving a trail of black smoke. Petty Off.(A) Jopling was also out in Fulmar N4004 over Marsala with Lt. Manning as observer. He stafed A.A. positions and seaplanes, claiming at least two of the latter severely damaged.

277ᵃ Squadriglia, 116° Gruppo, 37° Stormo B.T. Fiat **BR** 20M in flight. (*Zanetti-Lucchini via N. Malizia*)

Next day Mar. Diego Fiorentini of the 75ª Squadriglia, 23° Gruppo C.T., scrambled in an MC200 in the early afternoon, claiming a Hurricane shot down which was reported to have fallen into the bay off Porto Empedocle. No such loss has been discovered in British records, although it may have been a strafing aircraft from any of the squadrons. At this time fighter-bombing was becoming very much 'de rigeure', and on 7 October one flight of Hurricanes from 249 Squadron was led by 'Ginger' Neil to bomb Gela station, while by night Sqn.Ldr. Barton led the other flight to attack Comiso airfield. M.N.F.U. Hurricanes, each also carrying eight 40lb. bombs, raided a railway track at Scili in bright moonlight, while Fulmar N4004 of 800X Squadron operated over Eastern Sicily. Petty Off.(A) Jopling, who was again flying with Lt. Manning, reported: "Released four bombs on Catania, machine-gunned dispersed aircraft and A.A. positions. Attacked balloon barrage at Augusta and was hit by shell. Machine caught fire and was just able to make coast though engine was useless and about one mile east of Syracuse was compelled to land in the sea. Taken P.O.W. three hours later." (Arthur Jopling was to escape from prison camp on 9 September 1943, the day of the Italian capitulation; he managed to reach Allied lines safely.)

Operating regularly at night over Sicily in an 800X Squadron Fulmar was Petty Officer (A) Arthur Jopling. His aircraft was shot down by Flak during the night of 7/8 October 1941, and he became a prisoner of war. (*P. Vella*)

During the same night Blenheims from 105 and 107 Squadrons made their first night attacks from Malta, attacking a 2,000 ton vessel off Tripoli from 20 feet and claiming two hits on it. The Swordfish were also out again after a convoy of six cargo ships and escorting destroyers located east of Tripoli. They attacked just before 0200, three of the pilots reporting hits, Sub Lt. Taylor's target – the 6099 ton 'Rialto' exploding. Two lifeboats were seen leaving the ship and it was later reported sunk. The Regia Aeronautica was also active this night, two Cant Z.1007bis carried out a raid on Hal Far from which one failed to return, presumably shot down by the guns – or victim to the faulty bomb release mechanisms.

8–11/10/41

At this stage 'Sandy' Rabagliati left 126 Squadron on promotion to Wing Commander Flying at Takali. Pip Lefevre was posted back from 185 Squadron to replace him, and in the latter unit Flt.Lt. Pike became the new commanding officer. At Luqa Gp.Capt. Cahill handed over command of the airfield to Gp.Capt. S.H.V. Harris on 8 October. That same night one of the A.S.V. Wellingtons of 221 Squadron out on a 'Rooster' search, discovered an 8,000 ton merchant vessel. Flt.Lt. Spooner, the pilot, bombed it and left it on fire. A strike force of Swordfish was searching for a reported convoy off Lampedusa but was unable to locate it, so two bomb-carrying aircraft attacked their secondary target – Lampedusa harbour. In carrying out the attack Sub Lt. R.E.F. Kerrison's aircraft sustained damage to its fuselage and controls, but the pilot was able to coax it back to Hal Far. Four Blenheims from 107 Squadron made a shipping

Comiso airfield on the morning of 9 October 1941, following a night raid by British bombers. One of two MC200s of the 84ª Squadriglia, 10° Gruppo, 4° Stormo C.T. has been destroyed in its pen, and has burnt out. (*N. Malizia*)

309

sweep to the south of Italy on 9th., but two (Z7638 and 7644) failed to return. These were flown by the South African C.O., Wg.Cdr. F.A. Harte, and by Flg.Off. N. Whitford-Walders. Two days later the remains of the 105 Squadron detachment returned to England, but already fifteen more Blenheims from 18 Squadron were on their way to Malta to replace them. 107 Squadron continued to operate in the meantime, six Blenheims attacking shipping in the Gulf of Sirte on 11th. One cargo vessel was hit and left in flames, but Flg.Off. R.A. Greenhill's Blenheim was also seen to be hit in the belly and crashed into the sea. Sgt. A.D.M. Routh's bombs were observed to strike a corvette, which burst into flames, but his bomber then also went down.

That night seven Swordfish, led by the C.O. in Lt. Bibby's ASV aircraft, were on the tracks of another Maryland-reported convoy, this comrpising three cargo vessels, one tanker and five destroyers, and at 2100 it was found and attacked. Four hits were claimed and it was beleived one of these victims later sank. Flt.Lt. Spooner was about in his ASV Wellington and shadowed the same convoy whilst calling in six more Wellingtons from Luqa to carry out a second strike. These duly arrived and bombed but without apparent success. Meanwhile, back at Hal Far, the Swordfish were refuelled, rearmed and sent out again, but although they searched for two hours the tired crews were unable to relocate the convoy, but the ASV aircraft did detect more ships – four small and two large – which now became the target. Sub Lts. Lawson and Coxon claimed hits on the same vessel, which stopped, but then Coxon's aircraft received a burst of A.A. shrapnel through the mainwing.

11–13/10/41

Yet more bombers reached Sicily on 11th., the **BR 20Ms** of the 55° Gruppo (220ª and 221ª Squadriglia) commanded by Ten.Col. Renato Di Jorio arriving at Gerbini. Malta also received an unexpected visitor in the early hours of 13 October when a Sunderland of 230 Squadron carrying eight V.I.P.s landed at Kalafrana after losing an airscrew. Following repairs it took off again for Gibraltar – this time with thirty-three aboard! No such opportunity to utilize rare air transport was missed by the Malta command!

14/10/41

At 0535 on the morning of 14th. Luqa was strafed just before dawn by low-flying Macchis. Five all-black Hurricanes of the M.N.F.U. were led off by Flg.Off. Cassidy, followed by three Hurricanes each of 185 and 249 Squadrons. Plt.Off. Barnwell, the island's most successful night pilot, was lost in circumstances that at the time were not entirely clear. David Barnwell was the 19-year old youngest son of the late Captain Frank Barnwell, former Chief Designer at the Bristol Aircraft Company, who had himself been killed in an aircraft crash three years previously. David's two brothers had both already been killed flying with the R.A.F., one on bombers, the other on fighters. A contemporary report of his loss stated:

" ... engaged enemy aircraft attacking the island. The control room heard his voice saying 'Tally Ho! Tally Ho! Got one! Got one!' Five minutes later his voice sounded again, 'Baling out; engine cut; am coming down in the sea.' A rescue launch searched all day until dark, but found no trace of the pilot." At the time it was believed that his aircraft (Z3512) had suffered engine failure, but a squadron colleague, Flg.Off. Thompson, and available Italian records disprove that theory, as 'Tommy' Thompson noted: "My 21st. birthday! Dawn – scramble! Low flying attack on Luqa by six Macchi 202s. Plt.Off. Barnwell and myself jumped. Barnwell shot down one but failed to return himself." He later added: "The action took place about dawn and 249 Squadron were also scrambled – Plt.Off. Leggett fired at me over Grand Harbour – I seem to remember it cost him at least a couple of beers!" Barnwell was credited with one of the attacking Macchis shot down, taking his score to over five, and it seems probable that his final success was achieved over Sottoten. Emanuele Annoni, whose 9º Gruppo MC202 was hit in the fuselage by cannon shells, although he managed to fly it back to base. Claims for two Hurricanes shot down were made by Sottoten. Bruno Paolazzi and Mar. Manlio Olivetti – obviously one or both of these pilots were responsible for shooting down Barnwell; a probable was claimed jointly by Serg.Magg. Luigi Taroni and Serg. Gustavo Minelli.

MC202 in Sicily freshly painted with the unit's popular name and number – after Italy's top 'ace' of the First World War, Francesco Baracca – and pristine white spinner. (*A.M.I. via N. Malizia*)

16–17/10/41

During the night of 16/17 October Flt.Lt. Innes Westmacott again 'stowed away' on a Wellington, but this time it was on an event-marking sortie. The aircraft, piloted by Sqn.Ldr. L.H. Day, D.F.C., was carrying the first 4,000 lb. 'Cookie' bomb to be used in the area, and this was dropped near a factory in Naples. On return from this raid the Wellington flown by F/Sgt. P.S.G. Thornton, R.N.Z.A.F., crashed; the front gunner was killed, and all the rest of the crew suffered injuries. With daylight on 17th. six Blenheims of the newly-arrived 18 Squadron flew their first mission, an attack on Syracuse seaplane base, which they bombed from 12,500 feet – a change of tactics from the Blenheim's usual zero-level attacks. The bombers were escorted by Hurricanes of 249 Squadron on this occasion, and these engaged three MC202s of the 9° Gruppo which had been scrambled to intercept. One Blenheim was claimed shot down by Sottoten. Giuseppe Oblach, but his own aircraft was hit by return fire and he ditched in the sea, from where he was subsequently rescued by a motorboat; no bombers were actually lost during this attack.

Meanwhile six of 107 Squadron's Blenheims attacked in the opposite direction, bombing the Zuara-Sirte road in Tripolitania. An airfield was also bombed where one CR 42 was claimed destroyed and others damaged. A dozen more CR 42s were then seen on El Zuaia airfield, and these were also strafed. During the day a CR 42 failed to return from a convoy patrol, Serg. Guelfo Grancich being reported missing, fate uncertain.

17–18/10/41

'Ark Royal' was now once more on her way towards the island, this time bringing 828 Squadron, under Lt.Cdr. D.E. Langmore, equipped with eleven Albacores and two Swordfish to operate from Hal Far; the operation was codenamed 'Callboy' on this occasion. The day before the intended fly-off, a Sardinian-based Z.506B 'shadower' was intercepted by Yellow Section of 808 Squadron, a pair of Fulmars flown by Lt. Guthrie and Sub Lt. Guy, who proceeded to shoot out its port engine, then stopped the starboard engine, before sending it into the sea. Next day the Fulmars were again in action, Black Section of 807 Squadron being vectored onto a 'hostile', but only Sub Lt. Underwood, with L/A C. Coventry in the back, was able to make contact and then had difficulty in gaining on the intruder – a BR20M of 37° Stormo – as it fled towards Sicily. After pursuing it for some 45 miles with his engine at full throttle, Underwood managed to catch up with it and send it down into the sea, but having punished his engine in such a manner it now started to falter on the return flight to the carrier; it actually failed just as he landed back on!

Next day the thirteen biplane torpedo-bombers of 828 Squadron were flown off and headed for Hal Far, one Swordfish being lost en route. The new arrivals were greeted by the weary crews of 830 Squadron, whose activities had not lessened over the past few nights. An attack on the 7933 ton 'Bainsizza' south of Lampedusa, leaving her sinking, on the night of 13th./14th., was followed the very next night by the sinking of an already damaged cargo vessel, which had been torpedoed by a submarine and was now being towed to port. The crews were still resting from their latest strike – against a convoy of four merchantmen and four destroyers during which one attacking Swordfish (that flown by Lt. Nottingham) was damaged by the explosion of his target – when the new squadron flew in to Hal Far. Other new arrivals this same day, having flown in from Gibraltar to relieve 38 Squadron, were the Wellingtons of 104 Squadron, under Wg.Cdr. P.R. Beare. The new arrivals, as well as the residents, were treated to an air raid that evening, Z.1007bis attacking Luqa whilst a solitary BR 20M from the 37° Stormo bombed Hal Far. This aircraft was apparently hit and set on fire (or caught fire from the perennial bomb-release-fault), coming down in the sea near Gozo; two of the crew were rescued.

The arrival of the new aircraft and fresh crews did not prevent five Swordfish of 830 Squadron going out this same evening after another of the seemingly endless convoys of supply ships making for North African ports, this time four merchant vessels and four escorting destroyers being shadowed by Flt.Lt. Spooner's ASV Wellington, some 80 miles south-east of Lampedusa. The Swordfish attacked by the light of flares dropped by the Wellington, two of them (Sub Lts. Lawson and S. Campbell) releasing at the 4786 ton 'Caterina', which was apparently carrying ammunition. She blew up with such force that debris narrowly missed Campbell's aircraft at 2,000 feet as he completed his attack. Another pilot released his torpedo into the inferno, the ship sinking soon afterwards, whilst a second freighter was claimed damaged. The Wellingtons were also in action this night, six of the new arrivals joining eleven more from 38 Squadron to raid Tripoli, two of the 104 Squadron aircraft carrying 4,000 lb. bombs. Much damage was estimated to have been caused by these 'Cookie' bombs to the city, while in the harbour a 3,000 ton ship was reported to have received a direct hit from one of the smaller bombs.

19/10/41

On 19 October Sqn.Ldr. Barton and Plt.Off. Palliser of 249 Squadron were ordered to patrol to the south of Lampedusa Island. Barton, who flew Z3155 on this sortie, recalls: "Long-range patrol to try and intercept troop-carrying aircraft ferrying to North Africa. As I remember it we used 44 gallon external tanks (one under each wing) designed for ferrying only and quite unsuitable for combat." At 0805 while at 6,000 feet, they spotted a lone S.81 bomber-transport 1,000 feet below them, heading south. Both at once attacked from astern and fired several bursts. The central and starboard engines at once caught fire and it crashed into the sea where it blew up. Barton: "The SM 81 soon burned and there was little left by the time it hit the sea – not a pretty sight."

Sgt. G.W. Bates, flying a 69 Squadron Maryland on a similar patrol, encountered two Ju52/3m transports of III/KGzbV 1 some 45 miles south-west of Malta. Bates attacked, setting the port engine of '6305' alight; he was credited with its probable destruction but it survived to make a safe landing, although severely damaged. During the afternoon five Hurricanes attacked Comiso with bombs. As they returned to Malta five MC202s attacked the escort, which had been drawn from 126 Squadron, and managed to inflict damage on two of the Hurricanes. The Macchis were from 9° Gruppo, Serg. Martinoli claiming two Hurricanes shot down while two more were claimed damaged by Ten. Bussolin and Serg.Magg. Rossi.

20–22/10/41

Next morning two 185 Squadron Hurricanes flown by Flg.Off. Murch and Sgt. Lillywhite, patrolled over Lampedusa again, meeting six S.81s, one of which Lillywhite shot down in flames. At this same time a Maryland was patrolling in the Marittimo area where Plt.Off. H.J. Smaile engaged two Ju52/3ms, these also from III/KG.zbV 1, off the Sicilian coast. He hit one in the fuselage, causing heavy damage and wounding three of the crew, and was also credited with its probable destruction. Although the pilot managed to crash-land the transport it was a total loss. During the day four CR 42s were sent off by the 23° Gruppo to search for survivors from a German aircraft; four were found and rescued. Later six more CR 42s escorted Ju52/3ms flying between Pantelleria and Africa. This sudden upsurge in the appearance of transport aircraft on the route to North Africa had been occasioned by the recent heavy shipping losses. Two 185 Squadron aircraft again patrolled near Lampedusa on 22nd., but on this occasion were intercepted by five CR 42s, which they managed to evade.

21–24/10/41

The bombers continued to strike out during this period, twenty-four Wellingtons of 38 and 104 Squadrons attacking Naples on 20/21st. During this raid Sgt. F.M. Benitz, R.C.A.F., experienced engine trouble with his aircraft's port engine immediately after releasing the bombs. He set course for base, but discovered that some of the bombs had hung-up. Although steadily losing height, he changed course for the heavily-defended port of Palermo, where he managed to release the remaining missiles. By this time the engine had failed completely, but he managed to hold the bomber at 4,500 feet on its remaining engine and make a safe return to Malta. He was subsequently awarded the D.F.M. On 22nd. six 18 Squadron Blenheims raided the barracks at Homs, Tripolitania; the Blenheim flown by Sgt. J.D. Woodburn, D.F.M., R.C.A.F., failed to return. During the night of 23/24th. the 38 Squadron Wellingtons flew their last sorties from Malta before returning to Shallufa. Their place on the island was taken by a detachment of seven Wellingtons of 40 Squadron which arrived from England. The island's striking power was further augmented at this time by the arrival on 21 October of Force 'K' under Capt. W.G. Agnew. This force comprised the cruisers 'Aurora' and 'Penelope' from the Home Fleet, and two destroyers provided by Force 'H'.

Fighter activity was warming up again now however. During the afternoon of 22 October six 9° Gruppo MC202s, escorted by eight more, strafed Luqa twice. Nine Hurricanes of 249 Squadron were sent off to intercept, the Macchis diving on them as they were climbing up over St. Paul's Island. Sgt. Owen, who was flying 'Ginger' Neil's aircraft, 'R', was shot down in flames, but managed to bale out before the fighter hit the sea. Plt. Off. Matthews was also hit, the wing of his

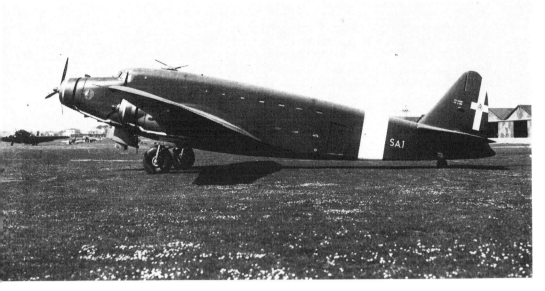

Italian transport aircraft frequently fell foul of Malta-based fighters whilst flying between Sicily and Tripoli. Many such flights were made by S.A.I. Savoia S.82s such as this one. (*A.M.I. via N. Malizia*)

aircraft and the fuselage near the glycol tank suffering damage. The Macchi pilots were from the 73ª Squadriglia, and they claimed heavily; two Hurricanes each were credited to Ten. Pietro Bonfatti and Sottoten. Alvaro Querci, and one each to Cap. Mario Pluda, Serg.Magg. Teresio Martinoli and Serg. Guerci, while probables went to Magg. Antonio Larismont Pergameni and Cap. Ivaldi; one Macchi was damaged in the fight.

It was the turn of Sardinian-based bombers to achieve success on the 24th., when four S.84s, equally drawn from the 256ª and 258ª Squadriglia, set out from Decimomannu to search for a lone British freighter. This was located some miles west of Galite island and Ten. Guido Focacci carried out a determined bombing attack on the 5720-ton 'Empire Guillemot'; the empty freighter later sank as a result of this attack.

25/10/41

On 25th. four Z.1007bis bombers from the 9° Stormo B.T. approached Grand Harbour around midday, escorted by MC200s of the 54° Stormo as close cover, with 20 MC202s of 9° Gruppo providing indirect support. 185 Squadron scrambled eight Hurricanes which dived to attack the bombers – again identified as **BR** 20s. One Cant was hit hard, the port engine being seen to stop, and it was classed as a probable. In fact the bomber managed to reach Sicily, where it crash-landed at Comiso with one dead and one wounded aboard. At this point the Hurricanes were bounced by the MC202s and Sgt. Ernest Knight was shot down, being listed as missing. Sgt. Hunton got a short burst into one Macchi which poured black smoke; he claimed a probable, but wreckage of

315

the fighter was later found floating in the sea. He had shot down the 4^0 Stormo's commander, Ten. Col. Eugenio Leotta, who was posthumously awarded the Medaglia d'Oro. Two fighters were claimed shot down by Ten.Col. Minio Paulello one by Magg. Larsimont Pergameni and one by Cap. Pluda and Ten. Bonfatti jointly, all on this occasion claimed as 'Spitfires'. 107 Squadron again sent six Blenheims south to Libya, these attacking along the Zuara-Benghazi road; one, flown by F/Sgt. W.T. Shaver, RCAF, failed to return.

28–29/10/41

Seven Albacores of 828 Squadron left Hal Far for their first operation from Malta, an attack on Comiso aerodrome. Bombs were seen falling on hangars and other buildings, and many fires were started, some burning furiously, indicating fuel dumps may have been hit. One hangar had indeed been badly damaged, whilst one CR 42 was destroyed and three others damaged. A.A. fire was intense, the Albacores coming under fire from gun positions all round the airfield, and consequently one aircraft was shot down. In the opposite direction six Wellingtons of 104 Squadron carried out an attack on Tripoli, from which they all returned safely.

With daylight on 29th. the first of the continually patrolling Marylands headed for its designated area, Lampedusa-Pantelleria-Gulf of Hammamet. Here Sgt. Bates again spotted a Ju52/3m which opened fire when he went to investigate. Opening an attack at once, he put the port engine out of action, and when last seen the transport was only ten feet above the water, apparently trying to land. Presumably this was also an aircraft of III/KG.zbV 1 but no loss has been discovered in the records; Bates was credited with its probable destruction. Two days later 69 Squadron moved with its seven Marylands and three Hurricanes from Luqa to Takali.

That night seventeen Wellingtons of 104 Squadron and 40 Squadron detachment continued the series of attacks on Tripoli, on this occasion the marshalling yards being the target. Many direct hits on the target area were claimed and all aircraft returned to Luqa in good order.

27/10/41

Meanwhile on 27 October a second He115, this time a B-2 model which had been captured from the Luftwaffe and carried the British serial BV187 (coded 'PP2') left Southampton for Malta, once more with Lt. Offerdal at the controls. After arriving safely, Offerdal and other pilots in BV187 undertook several missions to North Africa and these were later officially described as being of great importance to the war operations in the area. On one occasion the Heinkel is reputed to have landed in Tripoli harbour in daylight, painted in German colours, and picked up two Allied agents!

30/10/41

Italian fighters intercepted a delivery Blenheim IV on its way from Gibraltar to Malta, this aircraft from 22 OTU – 'G', Z7782 – crash-landing on the Sicilian coast, where the crew became prisoners.

This Blenheim IV, Z7782, on a delivery flight from 22 Operational Training Unit to Malta, was intercepted by Italian fighters en route on 30 October 1941, and crash-landed on the Sicilian coast, where the crew became prisoners. (*Intergest* via *National War Museum Assoc.*)

31/10/41

The final engagement of the month occurred during the night of 31 October/1 November, when night bombers again appeared over Malta – this time in the shape of four 116° Gruppo **BR** 20Ms. Plt.Off. Rathie and Sgt. Mackie of the M.N.F.U. intercepted, seeing one bomber in the searchlights at 11,000 feet. Mackie at first thought it was a Z.1007bis (misidentification the other way around for a change!) and diving, he made two attacks from 50 yards' range. He reported: "I was rather astonished not to be fired at as I made my first attack from astern at about 50 yards range and also to find that the aircraft did not make the slightest attempt at evasive action. I made another attack from astern and below, still without being fired at from the enemy aircraft which kept on its straight course. After the second burst it caught fire and went down. It was all rather too easy." The radio operator, 1ᵉ Aviere Tomaso Marcantonio, baled out as the bomber burst into flames; Ten. Francesco Toscano and the rest of his crew were killed.

That same night 828 Squadron was experiencing its second operation when seven Albacores penetrated into Sicily, attacking the railway junction at Canicatti, then bombing factories and warehouses on the coast at Licata on their way out. Spectacular fires were observed.

By the end of the month Flt.Lt. Messervy and his photo-reconnaissance Spitfire had departed for the U.K. During his brief spell on the island and following the arrival and fitting of the air-ferried new tyres, Messervy had carried out a number of long-range sorties over Italian ports and other military installations, often in very bad weather; sorties for which he would later receive a D.F.C.

The period of relative lull was nearing a close. After many months of stalemate the war in the Desert was nearing a major eruption, while for Malta the prospects were ominous. So effective had the anti-shipping campaign become, the Italians having now suspended all sailings to Tripoli, that sinkings in the Mediterranean during the preceding five months had been in excess of new construction. In the whole Mediterranean area during this period Axis shipping losses had totalled some 270,000 tons, but on the Italy-North Africa supply route alone forty vessels totalling 178,577 tons had been lost – the majority in the August-October period. Twenty-four of these ships – 101,894 tons – had fallen victim to aircraft, but at a cost to the Malta Blenheim units of at least thirty-five aircraft and most of their crews. Malta had become a festering sore in the Axis side which could not be allowed to remain so deadly where there to be any chance of a successful conclusion to the campaign in North Africa for them.

The month ended on Malta with another round of decorations. Wg.Cdr. Rabagliati and Sqn. Ldr. Barton of 249 Squadron were both notified of the award of Bars to their D.F.C.s, while D.F.C.s went to several of the 272 Squadron Beaufighter pilots for their recent activities, mainly while flying from Malta. Those decorated were Wg.Cdr. Yaxley, M.C., Flt.Lt. Riley and Flg.Off. Davidson; their observers, Sgts. D. Bowie and E. Buckley each received a D.F.M., while Sqn.Ldr. Fletcher gained a Bar to his D.F.C.

Chapter 8

THE GOING GETS TOUGHER

Hurricanes of 185 Squadron late in 1941. (*Mrs. Davies via National War Museum Assoc.*)

With almost no incoming raids by day, and only the nightly handful of raiders, whose attacks proved of little more than nuisance value, Malta had become wholly a base for offensive operations during the Autumn of 1941. From its harbours and airfields, submarines, surface raiders and bombers went out daily to harrass the Axis supply lines. Every day small formations of Blenheims sought out convoys, or attacked the coastal roads in Tripolitania, whilst the Swordfish and newly-arrived Albacores kept after the shipping by night and day. The Wellingtons, temporarily reinforced during October by detachments from 221 Squadron, concentrated on Tripoli as their main target, but also attacked other ports such as Naples, Palermo and Brindisi. The Hurricanes too were involved to an ever-growing extent in fighter-bomber and strafing attacks on targets in Sicily, only occasionally being called upon for interception duties.

In North Africa a long period of static warfare was drawing to a close. Since the advance of Rommel's newly-arrived units to the Egyptian borders the previous March, there had been little change in the respective positions. After the failure of two British offensives, main efforts had been expended by both sides around the beleaguered port of Tobruk, which held out against the Axis forces throughout the Summer (see 'Fighters over the Desert' for the detailed story of the air fighting in North Africa during this period). The demands of the fighting here slowed the build-up of supplies and reinforcements for a major offensive for both sides, and it had been to ensure that the British build-up was ready first that the efforts of Malta's units had been mainly directed.

In fact both sides were nearing readiness for large-scale action at much the same rate. Rommel was planning an all-out assault to take Tobruk during late November, while the British command planned their biggest offensive of the war for much the same period, aiming to link with the Tobruk garrison and end the siege. This would be only the first objective, which if successful, would be followed by the ejection of the Axis from Cyrenaica as a prelude to the capture of all Libya and the clearing of the North African coastline completely.

It was against this pending backcloth of mighty conflict that November opened. On Malta all seemed well; there were plenty of fighters and pilots, adequate supplies of fuel, ammunition, food, etc., and no indication that any enemy other than the Regia Aeronautica would be faced for some time. In the Soviet Union the Russians continued to hold on, while the onset of the Autumnal rains there were slowing down the German advance. Due to a rapid R.A.F. build-up, the Axis forces in Africa were already outnumbered, and any available reinforcements would surely be sent here in the first instance – if they could be spared from the Eastern Front.

1/11/41

November started quite auspiciously for the R.A.F. when six Blenheims, three each from 18 and 107 Squadrons, attacked another convoy. Twelve MC202s of the 9° Gruppo, led by the 4° Stormo's new temporary commander, Ten.Col. Marco Minio Paulello, intercepted the bombers, Serg. Martinoli claiming one shot down while Serg. Guerci claimed a second, which he reported fell with one engine on fire. In fact the Blenheims' crews saw only six of the Macchis, which carried on a running fight with them, but did not really press home their attacks. One Blenheim flown by Sgt. H.R. Leven was damaged, and the observer, Sgt. M.J. Nolan, was wounded, but one of the gunners was able to claim an attacking fighter probably destroyed. His victim was Ten. Felice Bussolin, who did in fact fail to return. However, the Italians recorded this combat as occurring the previous day.

By now 800X Squadron was reduced to just two serviceable Fulmars and night intruder sorties over Sicily ceased. They were now delegated the task of sending out special daylight patrols to cover the Kuriat-Pantelleria-Lampedusa area, to hunt for any Axis transport aircraft which might attempt to fly supplies to North Africa along this route. The first pair off, Lt. Eyres and Sub Lt. Tritton, experienced an uneventful three hours patrolling the area, while next day, the first of the month, Tritton accompanied Sub Lt. Hurle-Hobbs. Events were more lively when CR 42s, presumably up from Pantelleria, attempted to intercept the Fulmars, but were seen in time, evaded and the Fulmars returned to Hal Far. A similar attempted interception of the Fulmars took place the following day but these too were spotted in time by P.O.(A) Sabey. However as it would be only a matter of time before the Fulmars' luck changed, and as no Axis transport aircraft had been reported let alone sighted, these patrols petered out.

2/11/41

Two elderly Whitleys from 138 Special Duties Squadron arrived at Luqa this day, having flown out from the U.K. via Gibraltar; they were to be used for dropping agents and supplies into Yugoslavia. A submarine would arrive with the special supplies to be dropped, while a Sunderland was due in with two Serbian pilots who knew the Yugoslavian terrain and who were to guide the Whitley pilots to the dropping zone. Two agents, who were to parachute into Yugoslavia, were also imminently due from Cairo.

During the night of 2nd./3rd., Wellingtons from both 40 and 104 Squadrons raided Castel Benito airfield, Tripoli. A New Zealand pilot with 40 Squadron, Sgt. C.A. Armstrong, pressed home his attack in such a determined manner that it gained him the award of a D.F.M., his citation stating: " ... he bombed the aerodrome at Castel Benito, setting aircraft on the ground on fire. He then descended to 200 feet and machine-gunned the airfield." X9763 of the same squadron, piloted by Sgt. G.D. Colville, failed to return, and Italian night fighters are known to have claimed one bomber shot down on this night, identified as a 'Whitley'.

Malta had also been raided during the night by BR 20Ms and Z.1007bis, while by day three MC202 from the 9° Gruppo were scrambled, but saw nothing and returned. As they approached to land the alarm was sounded again and two of the pilots, about to touch down, raised their wheels again and set off southwards heading for the Gela area. Here they sighted a bomber which was identified as a Wellington, and was in fact Z1040 of the OADU en route from Gibraltar to Malta, which they and a number of other pilots who had arrived on the scene, shot down into the sea; credit was subsequently given to Sottoten. Virgilio Vanzan of 10° Gruppo. Only one survivor of the Wellington's crew was rescued. It seems likely that two of these aircraft also attacked a Maryland of 69 Squadron, Wg.Cdr. Dowland reported being intercepted by 'two 109s', the starboard engine being shot up, when flying near the Sicilian coast. With a display of skilful airmanship, Dowland coaxed the damaged aircraft back to Luqa on one engine. During the day Blenheims searched for survivors of the 40 Squadron Wellington lost from the night raid on Castel Benito airfield, while others searched for the missing OADU aircraft.

Views of 185 Squadron Hurricanes at Hal Far during late 1941. By the end of the year it would be rare to see a dozen airworthy fighters of a single unit available at one time in this way. (*Mrs. Davies via National War Museum Assoc.*)

4/11/41

Meanwhile pairs of Hurricanes from 185 Squadron were being sent out daily to strafe railway targets in Sicily, these generally escaping interception. A similar sortie by Plt.Off. Palliser and F/Sgt. Etchells of 249 Squadron on 4 November was caught by six MC202s after the pair had strafed Gela airfield, but the British pilots managed to evade their pursuers in cloud. Two Hurricanes were also sent out by 126 Squadron on this date, their target the seaplane base at Syracuse. Plt.Offs. Anderson and Coffin claimed four Cant Z.506Bs damaged or sunk, and both returned safely, although Italian Dicat gunners reported seeing one of the Hurricanes fall into the sea as a result of their fire; one Z.506B was actually destroyed. Finally a 69 Squadron Maryland pilot attacked another Z.506B off Cap Passero and claimed to have inflicted severe damage. The British aircraft was then attacked by an MC200, but this was evaded, the Maryland returning safely to the island. During the day Blenheim T1853 of 105 Squadron was lost whilst en route to the Middle East, the circumstances not being known.

5/11/41

Six Blenheims of 18 Squadron attacked a convoy, which was being shadowed by an ASV Wellington, in the Gulf of Sirte. One of the two 3,000 ton cargo ships attacked was left sinking but two of the Blenheims, captained by Sgts. H. Vickers and R.J. Morris, failed to return, shot down by the escorting destroyers. That evening soon after darkness fell, ten Ju87s, four BR 20Ms and three Z.1007bis attacked Valetta and French Creek. Two of the Ju87s, aircraft of 238ª Squadriglia, failed to return; one of these, crewed by Serg. Armando Tosi and Av. Amleto Bruttini, was shot down by A.A. gunfire and crashed about 100 yards from the Sergeants' Mess at Luqa, where it caught fire; both members of the crew perished. The pilot of the other Stuka, also shot down by gunfire, Sottoten. Vittorio Bragadin, was killed but his gunner survived. With daylight came the arrival of another 10 R.A.A.F. Squadron Sunderland, this one ferrying in fourteen fighter pilot reinforcements, including the distinguished Wg.Cdr. M.H. 'Hilly' Brown, a very successful Canadian pilot who had served with the late Sqn.Ldr. 'Boy' Mould in France in 1940, and who had just received a Bar to his DFC for thirteen combat victories, plus four others shared. He had been posted to the island as Wing Leader, Takali, the post about to be vacated by Wg.Cdr. Rabagliati.

8/11/41

After a two-day lull, 8 November proved to be the most eventful day for some weeks. A force of about eighteen MC200s and 202s from the 4° Stormo escorted four Z.1007bis bombers over Malta at midday, four Hurricanes from 126 Squadron intercepting them. Again there was complete misidentification of the bombers, but this time the three engines were seen from above, and they were thought to be Cant Z.506B floatplanes! The British fighters, led by Flt.Lt. Carpenter, made for the bombers but were attacked by the MC202s (the pilots of which identified their opponents as 'Spitfires' on this occasion). Carpenter claimed one Macchi shot down while an unidentified Sergeant claimed another damaged. The Australian Sgt. Allan Haley, who was flying Z3033, reported:
"As we were going for the bombers the Macchis dived on us. I counted sixteen of them and as I went after one of them I could see the rest of the Hurricanes were having excitement of their own... I put a few squirts into the one I was after and it started to smoke. Then another attacked me from astern. I turned and saw this other chap and flew straight at him. Bits were flying off his machine as I fired at him. I expected him to turn away but he didn't. Maybe the pilot was killed. I flew right into him and the Macchi broke up in the air. There were pieces all over the place. I am told one of my wings and the tail broke off, but I don't know for I didn't see the Hurricane again. I was in a spin and opened the lid. I didn't need to jump. I just opened the lid and I was out. I was at about 20,000 feet at the time. I thought I might have a broken leg. As I came down over the island I saw that I was going to land on a village. I hit the wall of a house and landed on a flat roof right on top of a dog. The dog let out a terrific yelp and jumped off the roof and bolted up the road still yelling. For all I know he is still travelling!" Haley was credited with one Macchi destroyed and one damaged.
Meanwhile Plt.Off. Lardner-Burke had attacked another MC202, which he claimed shot down, but this own aircraft was hit and he was shot through the

back, " ... badly wounded as he was," stated the official report, "he flew his damaged aircraft back, coolly circled the aerodrome, landed and taxied to his dispersal point." He was at once removed to hospital. Two of the Macchis were actually lost, Cap. Mario Pluda, commander of the 73ª Squadriglia, and Serg.Magg. Luigi Taroni both being killed. On this occasion the Italian fighter pilots were able to claim only one victory, by the pilots of 96ª Squadriglia jointly, plus two damaged.

At 1640 a Maryland of 69 Squadron with Wg.Cdr. Dowland at the controls at last located an important convoy between Corfu and Cephalonia, which Malta-based aircraft had been searching for since the previous day. There were five cargo ships, the German 'Duisburg' and the Italian 'Maria', Rina Corrado', 'Sagitta' and 'San Marco', plus two tankers, with a close escort provided by six destroyers, while four more destroyers and the cruisers 'Trieste' and 'Trento' acted as cover. Flying directly back to Luqa, Dowland reported personally to the A.O.C., and within the hour Force 'K' was steaming out to intercept. Twelve Blenheims, six from each of 107 and 18 Squadrons, were also despatched towards Cape Spartivento, and just after 2000 they came across two freighters and a destroyer. 107 Squadron went into the attack while 18 Squadron circled above. During the run-in Sgt. W.A. Hopkinson's aircraft collided with the mast of the larger of the two vessels and careered into the sea where it blew up; the crew died. A second Blenheim was hit by A.A. fire from the destroyer, sustaining damage to its turret. When the six aircraft of 18 Squadron joined the attack Flt.Lt. G.C. Pryor's Z7801 was also shot into the sea. The small freighter received a direct hit during the course of these attacks and was left on fire. Shortly after midnight Capt. Agnew's Force 'K' ('Aurora', 'Penelope', 'Lance' and 'Lively') caught up with the major convoy and in a spirited and one-sided action sank all five of the freighters and the two tankers, totalling some 39,787 tons, adding for good measure the destroyer 'Fulmine' to the bag. A little later another destroyer was torpedoed by the patrolling submarine 'Upholder'.

On this night of action, 830 Squadron had sent out three of its Swordfish to search for Italian submarines reported to be a possible threat to the returning Force 'K', but none were sighted, although the previous night Sub Lt. Coxon had attacked one seen on the surface, this later being sunk by one of the Royal Navy submarines. Meanwhile five of 828 Squadron's Albacores headed out to attack the submarine depot. at Augusta, four of these carrying out dive-bombing attacks while the other mistakenly bombed Syracuse harbour. Wellingtons of 104 Squadron were active, three bombing Brindisi on the Adriatic heel of Italy, three others attacking the docks and marshalling yards at Naples, on the Tyrrhenian coast. Apart from the two Blenheim casualties there were no losses amongst these various air attacks, nor within Force 'K'. A very successful night's action for Malta's diminutive strike force.

Amidst all the excitement one of the Special Duties Whitleys – Z9159 flown by Plt.Off. Austin – slipped out of Luqa, and with one of the Serbians flying as second pilot and navigator, headed north-eastwards up the Adriatic coastline of Albania and Yugoslavia, then inland to the designated dropping zone where two special containers were parachuted to unseen but waiting Partisans. The mission was accomplished without interference from Flak or fighters. However, in the morning the two agents arrived by submarine but without parachute packs, and as there were no spares at Malta the planned drop for the following night was postponed. When one of the Whitleys went unserviceable to add to reports of severe weather conditions arriving over Yugoslavia, the whole operation was cancelled; the Whitleys were ordered to depart for the U.K. at the first opportunity.

9/11/41

Two Hurricanes of 185 Squadron were despatched to patrol over the returning Force 'K' early on the morning of 9th., and these intercepted torpedo-bombers attempting to attack the ships. Flg.Off. Graham Bailey did not return, and was believed to have been shot down by return fire, although it was also thought that he had destroyed one of the bombers before he fell. However on this date 4° Stormo MC202 pilots claimed one Hurricane and one Blenheim shot down over the British warships.

10 R.A.A.F. Squadron's detached Sunderland was back from Gibraltar again during the day, bringing fifteen more fighter pilots. That evening ten Italian bombers again appeared over Malta and the pilots of the M.N.F.U. were active. Between 1940 and 2038 Plt.Off. Mackie (newly-commissioned) was in the air, attacking a BR 20M in the searchlights at 16,000 feet. He closed to 200 yards and fired, seeing flashes on the aircraft and pieces falling off. It went into a dive which he attempted to follow, but lost it at 3,000 feet. Two hours later Flt.Lt. Cassidy and Flg.Off. Thompson attacked another bomber and this too was hit, and was last seen shedding debris and losing height. Flt.Lt. Don Stones was also up during the night, but suffered engine trouble and was forced to bale out at 500 feet – he landed safely.

11/11/41

November was to be a month during which 69 Squadron was extremely active. During the morning of 11th. Flt.Lt. R.J.S. Wootton patrolled over the Ionian Sea in the area Kalamata-Zante, where he attacked and damaged a Z.506B. That night Wellingtons from 40 and 104 Squadron raided Naples. From this raid X9765 of 40 Squadron (Sqn.Ldr. A.D. Greer, R.N.Z.A.F.) failed to return; he was probably shot down by two MC200s of the 376ª Squadriglia, 21° Gruppo, which were scrambled over the Bay of Naples. Serg.Magg. Gulla and Serg.Magg. Gavani jointly claimed a bomber shot down into the sea near Cape Palinuro, south of Naples, which they identified as a Blenheim. A much greater loss was suffered by a force of seven Swordfish of 830 Squadron (on this night, the first anniversary of the FAA's devastating attack on Taranto), when sent off after a convoy reported west of Pantelleria. The formation was led by the C.O. in Lt. Osborn's ASV aircraft and was due to make contact with the shadowing ASV Wellington. On the outward flight to the rendezvous point, three Swordfish were forced to turn back due to faltering engines. Providence indeed! For not one of the four remaining aircraft returned, nor did the ASV Wellington. Unable to find any sign of the convoy nor to make contact with the Wellington, the Swordfish continued searching until a change in wind direction made it impossible for them to reach Malta, and with fuel gauges registering the last few gallons when just off the northern coast of Sicily, Lt.Cdr. Hunt ordered all aircraft to ditch in the vicinity of Palermo; Lt. Osborn and Sub Lts. Taylor and Campbell achieved safe ditchings, they and their crews paddling ashore and all seven men were taken prisoner. Something went wrong with the ditching procedure with Lt. A.F. Wigram's aircraft, he and his TAG, L/A K.D. Griffiths, losing their lives.

12/11/41

At 0630 on 12th. four 249 Squadron Hurricanes set course for Sicily on a strafing attack. Two were flown by Wg.Cdr. Rabagliati and Wg.Cdr. Brown. One of the other fighters was flown by the American Plt.Off. Tedford; the fourth returned early. The three remaining Hurricanes swept in over Gela airfield, attacking a CR 42, an MC200 and a Ju87 on the ground. Rabagliati was just shooting up the CR 42, which caught fire, when he saw Brown's Hurricane apparently stall, break away and crash; it had been hit by Dicat fire, and Brown was killed; the gunners claimed two Hurricanes shot down. Rabagliati then saw a Ju87 in the air and shot it down, strafed some troops on horses, and then – with Tedford still on his wing – headed for home. The Italians later dropped a message over Malta stating that Brown had been buried with full military honours.

This little attack was only an opener however. Soon eleven bomb-carrying Hurricanes were in the air and on their way to attack Comiso. Six were drawn from 249 Squadron, the other five from 126 Squadron, while an additional four and six respectively provided the escort. As the twenty-one Hurricanes approached they were met by three MC202s of the 9° Gruppo which had been scrambled during the previous raid. Cap. Frigerio attacked one Hurricane without result, but this was then attacked by Sottoten. Giovanni Deanna and Serg.Magg. Massimo Salvatore who shot it down into the sea near the coast; this was one of the Hurribombers (Z3158), flown by Australian Sgt. Simpson of 126 Squadron. Sottoten. Virgilio Vanzan of the 10° Gruppo took off in a CR 42 to search for the downed pilot, who he spotted, and who was then picked up by a launch and taken prisoner. During the raid one MC202 was claimed shot down by Flt.Lt. Carpenter, but no Italian loss was recorded. Meanwhile six Blenheims flew south to carry out a strike against Mellaha airfield, Tripolitania, completing the raid without interception.

While these offensive operations were underway a further load of reinforcements were being flown off to the island. During the previous month a new Wing of three squadrons of Hurricanes had been formed in England for service in the Mediterranean area. 266 Wing comprised established and battle-tested units, the most famous of which was 242 Squadron, Douglas Bader's old unit from the Battle of Britain. 605 'County of Warwick' Squadron had also taken part in the Battle, though the third unit, 258 Squadron, was of somewhat more recent formation. The two former squadrons now had few of the original 1940 pilots still on strength, but nonetheless did have the advantage of recent operational experience.

242 and 605 Squadrons loaded their Hurricanes aboard the old training carrier 'Argus', which had carried the very first Hurricanes to Malta over a year earlier, while 258's aircraft were crated and went aboard the special transport H.M.S. 'Athene' (this aircraft transporter could carry up to forty Hurricanes with wings removed). The ground parties of all three squadrons, together with 242's and 605's spare pilots also went aboard this vessel. The ships docked at Gibraltar on 5th., and here a proportion of the Hurricanes were transferred to 'Ark Royal'. When the two carriers sailed a few days later they carried aboard all the aircraft of 242 Squadron and the larger part of those of 605 Squadron. At Gibraltar 258 Squadron's crated aircraft were being erected with all speed, to be delivered with the balance of 605's in a second sortie by the carriers after their return.

Pilots of 605 Squadron who arrived in Malta aboard H.M.S. 'Argus' and 'Ark Royal' on 12 November 1941 – Operation 'Perpetual', the last of the Hurricane reinforcement operations, which resulted in the sinking of the 'Ark Royal'. L. to r. Plt.Off. Peter Lowe, Plt.Off. George Allen, Plt.Off. Howard Lester, Plt.Off. Ian McKay and Plt.Off. Philip Wigley, (*R.F. Noble*)

Under the codename Operation 'Perpetual', thirty-seven Hurricanes were flown off under the direction of Wg.Cdr. W.B. Royce, D.F.C., on 12th. in two batches, each of which was met and escorted to Malta by four Blenheims which had taken off from Gibraltar. Three Hurricanes were lost en route, one reportedly crashing in Sicily, while the others came down in North Africa; these three, BE369, BE561 and BG712, were flown by Sgts. W.L. Massey, D.H. Jones and D. Gray, all of whom were later reported to be prisoners. A fourth Hurricane (BG765, Plt.Off. Tew) was landed wheels-up at Hal Far and damaged. During the take off Plt.Off. Peter Lowe of 605 Squadron swung violently to port and broke 'Argus's' flying – off flag, almost knocking off the tail wheel of his aircraft in the process. Fellow pilots expected to see his aircraft crash into the sea but somehow Lowe managed to regain control and reached Malta safely, although the tail wheel collapsed on landing. 'Argus's' flag was retrieved by another 605 Squadron pilot and secreted aboard his aircraft – it later became a mess souvenir. The new pilots arriving with this batch of aircraft were:

242 Squadron	605 Squadron
Sqn.Ldr. W.G. Wells	Sqn.Ldr. R. Reid
Flt.Lt. S.E. Andrews, D.F.M.	Flt.Lt. S.R. Bird
Flt.Lt. N.L.D. Kemp, D.F.C.	Plt.Off. P.W. Lowe
Plt.Off. C.F. Sluggett	Plt.Off. P. Wigley
Plt.Off. M.C. Blanchard, R.C.A.F.	Plt.Off. I. McKay, R.C.A.F.
Plt.Off. C.R. Morrison-Jones	Plt.Off. R.F. Noble
Plt.Off. E.H.C. Kee	Plt.Off. G. Allen
Plt.Off. T.B. MacNamara	Plt.Off. O.O. Ormrod
Plt.Off. W.B. Hay	Plt.Off. J. Beckitt
Plt.Off. J.D. Tew	Plt.Off. H.C. Lester, R.A.A.F.
Plt.Off. L.A. Hall	Sgt. D.J. Howe
Sgt. R.V. Harvey	Sgt. A.S. Wilson, R.N.Z.A.F.
Sgt. G.F.R. Mulloy	Sgt. J.W.S. Fletcher, R.C.A.F.
Sgt. D.T. Neale	Sgt. D.J. Robb, R.N.Z.A.F.
Sgt. R.B. Lawes	Sgt. C.V. Finlay
Sgt. H. Hale, R.C.A.F.	Sgt. A. Howell
Sgt. J.L. Boyd, R.A.A.F.	
Sgt. W.N. Gardner	

Plt.Off. Kee had flown with 253 Squadron during 1940, being credited with three shared victories; Flt.Lt. Andrews is believed to have flown Fairey Battle bombers in France in 1940; he later served with 257 Squadron, gaining a shared victory. Plt.Off. Tew was another American – a Harvard graduate from Florida.

Newly-kitted in tropical 'gear', Plt.Off. Ron Noble and Plt.Off. Howard Lester (*R.F. Noble*)

329

Next day as the carriers headed back for Gibraltar disaster struck. At last 'Ark Royal's' charmed life came to an end as she fell foul of a salvo of torpedoes fired by U-81. Listing badly, the gallant ship was abandoned with the loss of only one life (Able Seaman E. Mitchell), and sank shortly afterwards. The Swordfish in the air on patrol at the time flew on to land at Gibraltar, but her Fulmars and those Swordfish still aboard went down with her.

There was no question of the slow and vulnerable 'Argus' making a second run alone, and the remaining Hurricanes and personnel stayed on Gibraltar, waiting for the arrival of a replacement carrier. In the event they were never to reach Malta, for before a new vessel could arrive the war in the Far East had broken out, and it was to here that the rest of the party was redirected. On Malta 242 and 605 Squadrons' aircraft were to be serviced by ground crews of 185 and 249 Squadrons – and indeed the pilots were increasingly to fly as integral parts of these units. Subsequently the rest of 605 Squadron was to operate in its own right in the Far East, while the ground party of 242 Squadron, joined by the pilots and aircraft of another unit, formed a new 242 Squadron. Thus the strange situation arose where for a brief period these two units appeared to be operating in two widely-separated theatres of war at the same time! (The story of the Far Eastern operations of these units will be told in another book by C.F. Shores and B.H. Cull, currently in preparation.) 605 Squadron's commanding officer, Sqn.Ldr. R. Reid, and the only flight commander to reach the island, Flt.Lt. Bird, would shortly leave again; arrangements for the leadership of the unit on Malta therefore had to be made. Soon after arrival Plt.Off. Allen was promoted to serve as one of the flight commanders, while Flt.Lt. Andrews was posted in from 242 Squadron as the new commanding officer.

A trio of 605 Squadron pilots; l. to r. Plt.Off. Ian McKay, a Canadian, Plt.Off. Ron Noble, Plt.Off. Howard 'Chuck' Lester, an Australian. (*R.F. Noble*)

14/11/41

On this day S.79sil from Sardinia were again successful in their attacks on a British convoy located east of Galite island, when Ten. Camillo Baroglio of 279ᵃ Squadriglia sank the 5463 ton 'Empire Pelican'. Next day it was the turn of S.84sil of 108° Gruppo to score against the convoy, the Gruppo commander, Magg. Buri, sinking the 'Empire Defender' (5649 tons) in the same general area.

15/11/41

Activities during mid-November continued on a somewhat reduced scale. Three delivery Wellingtons of the OADU were attacked early on 15th. by five CR 42s of the 23° Gruppo from Pantelleria. The fighters were engaged in escorting some Ju52/3m transports when they spotted the bombers, Sottoten. Gino Martini shooting down Z8989 in flames to the south-west of the island, while Serg. Giuseppe Saracino claimed a second as a probable. In fact only the one aircraft was lost, the crew surviving and subsequently being picked up by a floatplane from Kalafrana. Later in the day more Pantelleria-based CR 42s intercepted a passing Blenheim, Mar. Gasperoni, Serg. Sacchi and Serg. Cuscuna claiming to have obtained hits on this. The damaged O.A.D.U. Blenheim crash-landed on arrival at Luqa.

Plt.Off. J. Beckitt (l) and Plt.Off. G. Allen display the flying-off flag which they 'liberated' from H.M.S. 'Argus' during the take-off for Malta on 12 November 1941. Plt.Off. P. Wigley smokes his pipe in the doorway, far left. (*R.F. Noble*)

That evening four Reggiane Re 2000s of the recently-formed 377ª Squadriglia Autonome C.T. took off for their first offensive operation of the war, all carrying small bombs beneath their wings. One pilot was obliged to return early due to technical difficulties, whilst another was attacked by a night fighter which he identified as a 'Defiant' – presumably an M.N.F.U. Hurricane or an 800X Squadron Fulmar. He released his bombs in the sea and also returned. The remaining pair, led by Ten. Solaroli, carried on and dropped their bombs on Luqa. Four nights later a quartette of these aircraft again headed for Luqa, led on this occasion by Ten.Col. Tito Falconi of the 23° Gruppo. Once more a night fighter intercepted, Falconi and one other having to jettison their bombs whilst evading. The two other pilots pressed home their attacks at low level, reporting that they found the airfield lit up; all four returned to Trapani/Milo airfield undamaged.

The 17th. found six Blenheims of 107 Squadron near the Greek island of Cephalonia, after a reported convoy consisting of two merchant ships and a destroyer. A CR 42 was patrolling overhead as the Blenheims swept in, Sgt. Ivor Broome strafing the larger of the two vessels as he did so, seeing flames ensue from her cargo of drums of fuel; the second aircraft came under attack from the Fiat, sustaining several hits, but the third aircraft, flown by Sgt. Ron Gillman, scored two direct hits on the same ship, which caught fire and was enveloped in thick black smoke. All three Blenheims returned full of holes, the other three of the flight not being able to participate in the action. That night the Wellingtons divided their numbers between raiding Naples and Brindisi on the Italian mainland, and Tripoli and Benghazi.

In North Africa at this time the British forces had at last launched their offensive during the night of 17th./18th., under the codename Operation 'Crusader'. General Rommel, who was on the point of launching his own new assault on Tobruk, was taken by surprise, and soon a fierce tank battle was raging around the Egyptian-Libyan frontier area. The efforts of Malta's bombers were redoubled against the Axis supply convoys and ports, formations of Blenheims going out every day, and sometimes twice a day, while the Wellingtons, Swordfish and Albacores hammered away by night. On 19th. six 18 Squadron Blenheims attacked a convoy but defensive fire from the escorting destroyers was intense – three of the bombers being shot down into the sea with the loss of Sgts. D.W. Buck, J.H. Woolman and H.L. Hanson and their respective crews. On this same day a BR 20M of 276ª Squadriglia from Catania, flown by the commanding officer, Magg. Cesare Toschi, was lost, while next night another BR 20M flown by Ten. Arrigo Cesolini failed to return from a raid on Malta. A third was reported down near Castelvetrano on its way to attack the island. In no case has the cause of these losses been ascertained, but possibly due to premature detonation of bombs.

BG753, a Hurricane IIB of 605 Squadron flown by Plt.Off. R.F. Noble to Malta from H.M.S. 'Ark Royal' on 12 November 1941. (*R.F. Noble*)

20–22/11/41

69 Squadron was also again busy at this time. During the month the unit was joined for a few days by a photo-reconnaissance Mosquito from Benson, home of 1 P.R.U. in England. This aircraft, a P.R.Mark I, W4055, had made the four and a half hour flight from England in the hands of Sqn.Ldr. R.F.H. Clerke, an ex-Battle of Britain Hurricane pilot; Clerke would later gain the first daylight victory with a fighter Mosquito while serving with 157 Squadron, before commanding 125 Squadron on night fighting with the same type. Flt.Lt. 'Ginger' Neil of 249 Squadron engaged the Mosquito in a mock dogfight during its brief stay, and discovered that it could outfight his Hurricane! Reconnaissance Spitfire IVs from Benson were also now being flown out from home to operate from Malta for a few days at a time. It was the Marylands which continued to carry the brunt of the work however. On the morning of 20 November Plt.Off. R.G. Fox patrolled over the Corfu-Cephalonia area, where he engaged a Z.506B floatplane, and attacked four or five times with the front guns. The Cant's port engine was seen to be on fire, but he then ran out of ammunition and had to break away, claiming a probable. Return fire had struck his aircraft however, and he was obliged to force-land on return, being slightly injured in so doing. Two days later Flt.Lt. Wootton was able to claim a Ju52/3m damaged in the same area, but in between, on 21 November, an aircraft was lost by the unit. Wg.Cdr. Dowland, the

commanding officer, had undertaken a photographic run over Sicily in Hurricane II Z3053 during the morning, when he was attacked by six fighters, which he identified as '109s', and was obliged to bale out into the sea from 12,000 feet. It seems clear that his interceptors were in fact 9° Gruppo MC202s, Serg. Alfredo Bombardini of this unit claiming a reconnaissance aircraft shot down in flames. Dowland was picked up by a Swordfish floatplane an hour later, having been spotted in the sea by Plt.Off. Oliver of 185 Squadron, out searching for him.

Meanwhile as Dowland had headed north towards Sicily, five MC200s of 54° Stormo and ten 9° Gruppo MC202s were strafing Hal Far. Seven Hurricanes were sent off to intercept by 185 Squadron, these attacking five Macchis initially (probably the MC200s), five more then jumping the British fighters (probably some of the MC202s). No firm claims were made by the Hurricane pilots, but it was believed that three of the Italian fighters had been damaged; Sgt. Nurse's Hurricane was badly hit in return. The Italians reported fighting twelve Hurricanes and 'Spitfires', and claimed two 'Spitfires' shot down, one by Ten. Frigerio, Serg. Novelli and Serg. Angelo Golino, and one by Sottoten. Barcaro and Serg. Salvatore, while two more were claimed as probables; four were claimed destroyed on the ground plus a Blenheim, damage to the latter being credited to Mar. Damiani. Two Macchis returned damaged.

Eighteen MC202s from the 9° Gruppo returned to strafe during the afternoon, meeting on their way four 185 Squadron Hurricanes which were engaged in a convoy patrol. The Italians reported meeting twelve, and claimed five of these shot down into the sea, one each by Mar. Larsimont Pergameni, Serg. Novelli, Mar. Damiani, Sottoten. Querci and Serg. Magg. Rossi, plus two probables by Sottoten. Bonfatti and Ten. Frigerio. They then carried on to complete their strafe, returning without loss. One Hurricane was in fact lost, Sgt. Dick Cousens failing to return. During the day Sqn.Ldr. George Powell-Sheddon of the M.N.F.U. crash-landed on the Attard-Rabat road, his Hurricane having suffered engine failure on take-off; he was shaken but unhurt.

On the night of 20th./21st., four Albacores of 828 Squadron and three Swordfish of 830 Squadron, all armed with torpedoes, were led off in the direction of Cape Spartivento by Lt. Garthwaite in an ASV aircraft, following an earlier sighting by a Sunderland of a heavily protected convoy heading southwards. The initial strength of this convoy was estimated to be two cruisers and four destroyers protecting four merchantmen. When contact was made with the shadowing ASV Wellington this estimate was revised to one or two cruisers and twelve destroyers escorting the four cargo ships. The three Swordfish went in first and came under fire from one of the cruisers, the 'Trieste', but by doing so gave away her position to a prowling submarine, H.M.S. 'Utmost', which promptly torpedoed her, the cruiser sinking. Meanwhile both Sub Lts. Kerrison and J.R.O. Stevenson unwittingly attacked the other cruiser, the 'Duca degli Abruzzi', each registering a hit; the badly damaged warship was later towed to port. The third Swordfish, flown by Lt. P.E.H. O'Brien, was shot down, he and his observer being lost. The Albacores, meanwhile, attacked the merchant vessels and believed they had secured hits on three of them, but there were no actual losses.

22/11/41

The Regia Aeronautica's attack was stepped up next afternoon, when ten Ju87s from the 101º Gruppo Tuffatori set out with an escort of 61 MC200s and 202s drawn from the 54º Stormo and 9º Gruppo once again. The close escort MC200s became unco-ordinated and returned early, but the MC202s, which were providing indirect cover, reported engaging forty English fighters (!) and claimed eight 'Spitfires' shot down plus three probables. In the initial clash two confirmed victories went to Ten. Fernando Malvezzi and one each to Cap. Viglione-Borghese, Sottoten. Annoni and Serg. Magg. Labanti; the probables were credited to Serg.Spitzl., Serg. Minelli and Serg.Magg. Parodi. Sottoten. Giovanni Barcaro then claimed a further fighter shot down in flames, chased a second and claimed this too; the eighth was claimed by all pilots of the 9º jointly. One Macchi 202 flown by Ten. Pietro Bonfatti was shot down, the pilot being killed.

Most successful MC202 pilot of the 9º Gruppo C.T. over Malta by the Autumn of 1941 was Serg. Teresio Martinoli.

Twenty-one Hurricanes had in fact scrambled, 126 Squadron, with Wg.Cdr. Rabagliati at the head, providing top cover for 249 Squadron. They saw a force of fighters north of Gozo at 26–30,000 feet, identified variously as fifteen MC202s, or twenty-four Bf109s and Macchis. Once more Flt.Lt. Carpenter of 126 Squadron was leading the very high cover, climbing with two wingmen as fast as possible. They remained at altitude until all the Macchis had dived on the main force below, and then went down themselves, Carpenter attacking the last of a flight of four with a five second burst at 200 yards. The cockpit hood fell off, together with an unidentified object, and the fighter carried out a slow roll and disappeared. Carpenter was unable to follow as he was now engaged in a very violent dogfight, and he was only able to claim a 'damaged'. Sgt. Copp attacked a Macchi in a steep climb, seeing smoke pour out, but he too could only claim a 'damaged', as could Flg.Off. Kay and Sgt. MacGregor; Plt.Off. Main claimed two probables, but so hard was the fight that none of the 126 Squadron pilots were able to make any confirmed claims. Rabagliati was himself attacked twice by flights of Macchis, but was able to evade their attacks, and all the Hurricanes were able to return unscathed. 249 Squadron, lower down, claimed three destroyed, one probable and one damaged; Sqn.Ldr. Barton, flying Z3764, claimed one MC202 eight miles north-east of Gozo, the pilot not being seen to bale out. It is believed that one of the two other confirmed claims was submitted by Flg.Off. Crossey. Pilots reported seeing wreckage from one Italian fighter flying through the air and amongst it an object swathed in white, as though the pilot had abandoned his aircraft and become enveloped in the folds of his parachute. One 249 Squadron Hurricane suffered slight damage to the tail.

23–24/11/41

No further attacks were made during the rest of the month, all further engagements occurring as a result of British offensive action. On 23 November Sgt. Bates flew a reconnaissance over Tripoli in one of 69 Squadron's Marylands. He was intercepted over Mellaha, but evaded his attacker; later he was attacked again – reportedly by a Bf109E – Sgt. Pugh, the gunner, claiming to have shot this down into the sea. That night a Z.1007bis bomber was lost by the Italians during a raid on Malta, but next day Maryland BJ427 flown by Sgt. Hutt did not return from a search south-east of Malta. It was a day for losses, for during a strafing attack on Comiso airfield by five Hurricanes of 126 Squadron, Sgt. Greenhalgh was brought down; he crash-landed Z2491 and became a prisoner. After dark, eight Wellingtons from 104 Squadron and six from 40 Squadron raided Benghazi, Sgt. T.W. Parker of the latter unit failing to return in Z1046. This bomber came down in the sea midway between the target and base, Parker at least surviving; he was picked up five days later by an Axis vessel and became a prisoner. 24th. was however, also marked by the successful interception of two small German supply ships by Force 'K'.

On 24 November 1941 Sgt. W.D. Greenhalgh of 126 Squadron was brought down in a crash-landing in Z2491, HA-D, while strafing Comiso airfield. His Hurricane was salvaged by the Italians, and is seen here in a hangar at this airfield. (*N. Malizia*)

Sgt. Greenhalgh's Hurricane HA-D, Z2491 of 126 Squadron at Comiso airfield after salvage, still with a smashed propeller. An MC202 of the 4° Stormo C.T. is immediately behind it. ('*Intergest via National War Museum Assoc.*)

28–30/11/41

Four Blenheims of 18 Squadron, accompanied by two from 107 Squadron, the formation led by New Zealander Flt.Lt. E.G. Edmunds, sortied into Navarino Bay, on the western coast of Greece, to attack shipping. Despite heavy rain, bad visibility, and intensive fire from shore batteries and escorting destroyers, Edmunds and two other pilots – Flg.Off. V. Allport, also a New Zealander, and

BE402, a Hurricane IICC of 242 Squadron following a slight landing accident.

Sgt. J.H. Walker – claimed hits on an estimated 6,000 ton vessel which was left in flames. Their badly damaged victim was in fact the smaller (3363 ton) tanker 'Volturno', which was forced to return to port. Flt.Lt. Edmunds received an immediate DFC for this raid.

This had been a crippling month for the Axis convoys; 63% of all cargoes intended for Libya was lost, mainly to Force 'K' but air attack had taken its toll. Seven Blenheims failed to return from these convoy strikes, with the loss of the majority of the crews, whilst five Swordfish had also been lost, four of these due to running out of fuel on the night of 11th./12th., as recorded.

The Albacores of 828 Squadron were by now getting into the routine of almost nightly sorties, mine-laying one night, hunting for convoys the next, or dive-bombing land targets in Sicily or Tripolitania, such as on the night of 28th./29th., when five aircraft attacked Castel Benito airfield, having struggled through appalling stormy weather conditions, only to have one of their aircraft shot down in flames over the target area during the dive-bombing attack. The Wellingtons of 104 and 40 Squadrons were out night after night attacking coastal targets on mainland Italy or on the North African coast. This night one of the targets was Naples and one aircraft was apparently shot down by two pilots, Sottoten. Amedeo Parmeggiani and Sottoten. Calafiore, from 376ª Squadriglia. Next morning Kalafrana rescue service reported rescuing the crew of Z8404 of 104 Squadron, which had ditched on approaching Luqa.

Early on 29th. Wg.Cdr. Rabagliati led another low-flying Hurricane strafing attack on Comiso airfield, but found a lack of aircraft. It was assumed they had just left on a raid, but it is possible that the base had just been vacated pending the arrival of new occupants.

With the opening of major fighting in North Africa, the Germans had decided to reinforce the Luftwaffe in the Mediterranean despite the fact that heavy fighting was still continuing in Russia. The onset of winter there would restrict air operations in any event, and consequently elements from that front were to be sent to the South instead, their first duty being the subjugation of Malta. Feldmarshal Albert Kesselring, commander of Luftflotte 2, was designated Commander-in-Chief South at the end of November, while before the month was out the World War I fighter 'ace', Bruno Loerzer, would be ordered to move his II Fliegerkorps headquarters from Luftflotte 2 on the Moscow Front, to Messina Sicily. Units drawn largely from this Luftflotte were also ordered to Sicily, although most of these had first to return to Germany for re-equipment to make good the wastage of the Eastern Front.

III/JG 53, led by Hpt. Wolf-Dietrich Wilcke, had already returned to Germany in October for conversion to the Bf109F, and on 6 December this unit would arrive in Libya, where it was followed a few days later by the similarly-equipped III/JG 27 (II/JG 27 had already brought the first Bf109Fs to the Mediterranean earlier in the summer, after brief service in Russia). The other two Gruppen of Maj. Günther von Maltzahn's JG53 had left Russia earlier in the autumn for service in Holland; they were now to go to Sicily after re-equipment, and would be joined there by II/JG 3. This latter unit had been serving in Luftflotte 4 in South Russia, and had been led by Hpt. Gordon Gollob, at the time one of the

Luftwaffe's rising 'stars'. However at the time of posting to the South, Gollob was sent to a test pilot job at Rechlin, his place being taken by Ritterkreuzträger Hpt. Karl-Heinz Krahl, who had been serving on the Western Front with I/JG 2.

Deadly new arrival. A Messerschmitt Bf109F of II/JG53, believed to be the aircraft flown by Oblt. Gerhard Michalski, an 'Experte' who already had 22 victories to his credit by December 1941, and who was destined during the following year to become the Luftwaffe's single most successful pilot of the war over Malta. (*I. Primmer*)

Also from Western Europe came the Ju88C-equipped I/NJG 2 – the Fernnachtjagdflieger who had been undertaking intruder missions over England by night with telling effect. The fighter strength was to be completed by III/ZG 26, which was to return with its Bf110Ds and Es from the Desert in due course. The bomber force was to be entirely Ju88A-equipped on this occasion. I/KG 54 would move to Gerbini and two Gruppen of KG 77 to Comiso, while two similarly-equipped coastal units, Kampfgruppen (formerly Küstenfliegergruppen) 606 and 806, would go to Catania. Not all these units would arrive at once, and in fact they were to 'dribble' in gradually during the next few weeks, led initially by I/NJG 2. To make room for the new arrivals the Italians moved 116° Gruppo B.T. from Catania to Gerbini, moving the smaller 282ª Squadriglia Aerosil. into Catania from the latter airfield, while the 278ª Squadriglia Aerosil. moved over to Pantelleria.

On Malta the impact of the return of the Luftwaffe would not seriously be felt for a little time yet, and operations continued as before. The island was now considered secure enough for B.O.A.C. flyingboats to use Kalafrana as a refuelling base by night on quite frequent occasions, as these craft were now carrying important personnel and urgent supplies through the Mediterranean to

Egypt. These flights would continue throughout much of December, but would cease again when the island came under serious attack once more. November did however see the end of 800X Squadron – or the 'Independent Night Fighting Unit' – as it was known on the island. The unit was down to only two Fulmars (N1931 and N4001) of doubtful serviceability. For work with the detachment while flying from Malta, Sub Lt. Tritton received the D.S.C. and P.O.(A) Sabey the DSM, while one of each award was announced for the two prisoners of war, Lt. Manning and P.O.(A) Jopling.

Two more well-deserved decorations for other island personnel had been announced at this time as well, both going to 126 Squadron. Sqn.Ldr. Lefevre and Flg.Off. Lardner-Burke both being awarded D.F.C.s. Lefevre would return to England towards the end of December, followed at the turn of the year by Lardner-Burke when he was released from hospital. The Italians also had their successful fighter pilots at this time, and it was reported at the end of November that Serg. Teresio Martinoli of the 9° Gruppo had been credited with four victories flying MC202s since 4 October.

30/11/–1/12/41

December 1941 found Malta with the following units available:-

Fighters		Bombers	
126 Squadron	Hurricanes	18 Squadron (Det.)	Blenheim IVs
185 Squadron	Hurricanes	107 Squadron (Det.)	Blenheim IVs
249 Squadron	Hurricanes	40 Squadron (Det.)	Wellington ICs
M.N.F.U.	Hurricanes	104 Squadron	Wellington IIs
		221 Squadron (Det.)	Wellington VIIIs
Reconnaissance		828 Squadron (F.A.A.)	Albacores
69 Squadron	Marylands and Hurricanes	830 Squadron (F.A.A.)	Swordfish

Additionally two Beaufighters from 252 Squadron had just arrived at Luqa from North Africa flown by Canadian Flg.Off. Doug Smith and Sgt. F.R. Wallis, R.N.Z.A.F., with Sgt. Triggs travelling in one of the aircraft as a spare pilot. Wallis and Triggs flew the first sortie on 30th., the day after arrival, flying south again to attack motor transport east of Misurata. Smith made a lone attack on similar targets to the east of Sirte on 1 December, then undertaking a second mission in company with Triggs. During the intervening night Flt.Lt. Spooner of 221 Squadron had again been out with his 'Rooster' Wellington and had found two small convoys, each consisting of one freighter and one destroyer. He shadowed them throughout the night until strikes could be launched in which all four vessels were claimed sunk. When he finally landed, he had been in the air 11 hours and 20 minutes. In fact the 3476 ton freighter 'Capo Faro' did sink following the attack by six Blenheims of 18 Squadron, while the smaller 'Iseo' was damaged. Elements of Force 'K' were in the area and they sank the small troopship 'Adriatico'.

341

1435 Flight pose formally in December 1941, ground crew included. The pilots sitting in the front row, are 1. to r., Sgt. Dickson, Sgt. J.E. Wood, Plt.Off. D. Winton, Flg.Off. D.C.B. Robertson, Flg.Off. A.R.F. Thompson, Flt.Lt. E. Cassidy, Sqn.Ldr. I.B. Westmacott, Flt.Lt. D.W.A. Stones, D.F.C., Plt.Off. P. Rathie, Plt.Off. A.S. Mackie, F/Sgt. R.J. Fowler, Plt.Off. J.G.M. Grant, Plt.Off. J.P. Mills. (*I.B. Westmacott*)

2/12/41

On 2 December the M.N.F.U. was re-named 1435 (Night Fighter) Flight, and command passed to Sqn.Ldr. Innes Westmacott, previously a flight commander in 185 Squadron. George Powell-Sheddon was promoted Wg.Cdr. and became airfield commander. At the same time 'Sandy' Rabagliati was posted to H.Q. Mediterranean – although he would soon be back on operations. During early December activity again continued on a fairly subdued note. At night on 1st. one of 40 Squadron's Wellington ICs was lost over Benghazi, while on 2nd. Flg.Off. Smith in one of the Beaufighters engaged an S.81 transport near Tripoli and claimed to have shot this down. This same day Blenheims caught another convoy 70 miles north of Tripoli and damaged the 'Iridio Mantovani' – the freighter was bombed again later and sank. Then Force 'K', now strengthened by the arrival of the light cruisers 'Ajax' and 'Neptune', and two additional destroyers, 'Kimberley' and 'Kingston', intercepted the Italian destroyer 'Da Mosto' and sent this to the bottom.

Leaders of 1435 Flight, December 1941; l. to r. Flt.Lt. E Cassidy, Sqn.Ldr. I.B. Westmacott, Flt.Lt. D.W.A. Stones, D.F.C. All-black Hurricane in background. (*I.B. Westmacott*)

4/12/41

On 4 December four Blenheims from 107 Squadron, two of them fitted with additional forward-firing guns for strafing, made a successful attack on ferryboats at Messina, on the north-east corner of Sicily – the point closest to the mainland. Marshalling yards at Villa San Giovanni, the mainland port opposite Messina, were also attacked, but Sgt. R.G. Kidby's Blenheim was seen to be under attack by three Macchis, and he did not return. At this time the 10,000 ton tanker 'Reichenfels' had taken on 7,000 tons of fuel at Naples, then sailed for Tripoli at the start of December, this being her maiden voyage. On 4th., as she arrived on the North African coast, she was spotted by a Maryland. Blenheims from 18 and 107 Squadrons were sent out and attacked in the face of an escort of destroyers and four Z.501 flyingboats. After the first attack the crew were seen to abandon ship, one hit being claimed by Sgt. D.T. Bone and his crew. One Blenheim was attacked by an Italian fighter and the navigator, Plt.Off. A.S. Aldridge, was wounded in the back.

343

Flt.Lt. E. Cassidy and Flg.Off. A.R.F. Thompson of 1435 Flight, December 1941. (*I.B. Westmacott*)

5–6/12/41

During the night of 4/5th. a lone Re2000 again attacked Malta, while during the 5/6th. twenty Wellingtons from 40 and 104 Squadrons attacked the Royal Arsenal at Naples. A CR 42 of 356ª Squadriglia, 21° Gruppo, had taken off from Capodichino airfield at the approach of the bombers in the hands of Mar. Vincenzo Patriarca, an Italian/American who had flown in the Spanish Civil War, gaining several victories there. At 2135 Patriarca spotted Wellington R1066 of 40 Squadron (Plt.Off. D.F. Hutt), and engaged it in a long fight, firing 408 rounds of 12.7mm ammunition before he finally shot it down; two members of the crew baled out near the port, Hutt included, but four others were killed. Patriarca landed at Capua almost out of fuel, and with the tail of his fighter damaged by return fire. In another of 40 Squadron's bombers Flt. Lt. S. Storey, who had already been credited with shooting down four aircraft during the Battle of France, successfully drove off another night fighter. He was subsequently awarded the D.F.C. Over Malta on this night Flt.Lt. Don Stones of 1435 Flight attempted to intercept an intruder caught in the searchlights, which he identified as a Ju88 – possibly an aircraft of I/NJG 2 – but his guns failed to fire.

During 5th. the two Beaufighters had been on patrol to cover the arrival of Blenheims heading for the Middle East via Malta. 23 miles south-west of Pantelleria Flg.Off. Smith (with Sgt. D.J. Ashcroft as navigator) had intercepted an aircraft identified as a BR 20 (possibly an S.84), and had shot this down, one member of the crew being seen to bale out before the aircraft crashed into the sea. Next day the Beaufighters returned to Africa. During their brief stay they had been credited with the destruction of two aircraft in the air and three CR 42s severely damaged on the ground at Temet airfield, Tripolitania, together with eight petrol tankers destroyed and two damaged, one trailer destroyed and one damaged, and two trucks damaged. Sgts. Wallis and Ashcroft were to be lost over Tripoli three days later, whilst Flg.Off. Smith was killed soon after. Meanwhile on 5th. Sottoten. Duca Gabriele Ferretti, the photo-reconnaissance pilot, was killed on return from a sortie over Malta when his 86ª Squadriglia MC202 fell from a height of some 26,000 feet to crash on the tip of Sicily, cause unknown.

249 Squadron at Takali, Winter 1941; front, l. to r. Plt.Off. D.A. Tedford, Sgt. Branch, F/Sgt. D. Owen, Plt.Off. R.H. Matthews, Flt.Lt. H.J.S. Beazley, Sqn.Ldr. E.B.B. Mortimer-Rose, D.F.C., Flg.Off. C.C.H. Davis, unidentified Sgt., Flg.Off. E.J.F. Harrington; rear, Sgt. Phillips (?), Plt.Off. P.G. Leggett, Sgt.Davies. (*P.G. Leggett via Chaz Bowyer*)

The first two weeks of December saw several changes amongst personnel on Malta – and brought events elsewhere which were to affect the lives of those who remained. At the end of the first week Sqn.Ldr. E.B. Mortimer-Rose D.F.C., arrived from H.Q. Middle East, to take over 249 Squadron from Sqn.Ldr. Barton, who departed for that destination. During his six months on the island 'Butch' Barton had added five and one shared victories to his total, plus one probable and one shared. Mortimer-Rose was an ex-234 Squadron Battle of

Britain pilot, with seven and three shared victories to his credit. A week later another Battle of Britain pilot, Sqn.Ldr. S.C. Norris, D.F.C., arrived to take over 126 Squadron from the recently-decorated 'Pip' Lefevre. Norris also had seven victories, plus one shared, having flown with 610 and 485 (New Zealand) Squadrons in England. During the same period 249 Squadron was also joined by Sgt.G.E. Horricks, while Flg.Off. F.R.W. Palmer arrived from England to join 1435 Flight; Wg.Cdr. Powell-Sheddon, having now received the D.F.C., departed for the Middle East.

Sottoten. Duce Don Gabriele Ferretti di Castel Ferretto, the young nobleman fighter pilot turned photo-reconnaissance pilot, who was killed on 5 December 1941 when his 86ᵃ Squadriglia, 9º Stormo C.T. MC202 crashed on Sicily cause unknown. (*National War Museum Assoc.*)

In North Africa meanwhile, following a hard and costly fight, the Axis forces began to withdraw on 7 December, Tobruk being relieved next day. Even as this happened came news of the Japanese attack in the Far East, bringing new pressures and demands on the resources of Britain and her Empire, but also bringing the United States into the war on the Allied side.

8/12/41

The Malta bomber force continued its offensive on the Axis supply lines, but there was to be no slackening of losses. Eight Blenheims of 18 Squadron raided Catania on 8 December, but in bad weather conditions two of the bombers collided. During this attack one MC200 of the 6° Gruppo C.T. was destroyed and three slightly damaged on the ground. 18 Squadron lost a further aircraft next day during another raid.

11/12/41

The Blenheims were out again on 11 December, three of them attacking a 5,000 ton vessel in Argostoli harbour. The aircraft of Flt.Lt. Edmunds failed to return, and it would seem that this fell foul of two 23° Gruppo CR 42s flown by Mar. Germano Gasperoni and Serg. Leonzio Bicego who had taken off during the morning to escort some S.82 transport aircraft to Tripoli, and claimed a Blenheim shot down between them. Gasperoni returned with his aircraft damaged and a wound in his left arm. From Malta Flt.Lt. 'Ginger' Neil of 249 Squadron was sent off to escort a Wellington which was reported to be under attack whilst on its way to Malta from Gibraltar, carrying aboard his replacement, Flt.Lt. Sidney Brandt. The bomber had been intercepted by three 23° Gruppo CR 42s scrambled from Pantelleria, the pilots of which reported attacking four Wellingtons. One of these was claimed shot down into the sea by Serg. Luigi Sacchi, while Mar. Diego Fiorentini and Serg. Giuseppe Saracino attacked two others. Fiorentini (from the unit's 75ª Squadriglia) was shot down by one of the rear gunners; he baled out but his parachute did not open. It seems that two of the Wellingtons were lost, R1246 and R1250, both in transit from Gibraltar to the Middle East. One other aircraft lost on this day was a Hudson of 233 Squadron; F/Sgt. K.C. Brown and his crew were lost when making for Malta from Gibraltar.

12–13/12/41

While Hurricanes of 126 Squadron dropped bombs ineffectively on Comiso airfield on 12th., six 18 Squadron Blenheims returned to Argostoli harbour, but during this raid lost two of their number. It is likely that one fell to Lt. Herbert Haas of I/NJG 2, who claimed a Blenheim south of Malta – his unit's first victory in the Mediterranean area, and the first for Fliegerkorps II as well. Argostoli remained the target next day, five Blenheims from 18 Squadron and six from 107 Squadron attacking on this occasion. Opposition from all the ships in harbour was intense and a Macchi fighter also attacked the 107 Squadron formation, firing on all six bombers. The fighter was believed to have been hit by fire from Sgt. Crossley's Blenheim, but that of Sgt. A.J. Lee was seen to go into the sea, he and his crew surviving to become prisoners. Another Blenheim flown by Sgt. J.B. Drury (Z7858) was seen to crash into the sea as well. By night 40 Squadron despatched eight Wellingtons to Benghazi, but from this raid Plt.Off. G.H. Easton's X9993 failed to return. It is possible that the aircraft fell to a I/NJG 2 Ju88C, Lt. Peter Laufs of this Gruppe claiming a Wellington shot down south of Malta, although this was recorded as occurring the previous day. Alternatively his victim may have been another delivery Wellington – N2780 failed to arrive at Malta at this time. These two absentees brought the island's bomber losses to fourteen in two weeks – a staggering rate of attrition for the small force

347

employed. Transit crews flying Blenheims through to the Middle East now frequently found themselves 'press-ganged' as soon as they landed on Malta, to make good the losses suffered by 18 and 107 Squadrons. Swordfish of 830 Squadron were out this night following an ASV Wellington's detection of a tanker, the 1,235 ton 'Lina', heading southwards, the new C.O., Lt.Cdr. F.E.H. Hopkins, D.S.C., an observer, flying in Lt. Garthwaite's ASV Swordfish. At about 0100 the tanker was sighted and attacked, two hits being claimed by Sub Lts. Coxon and Kerrison and the vessel was seen to burn, and later sank. Next morning only a patch of oil and a ship's boat were to be seen in the area of the attack. Next night they were out again, this time after a reported tanker and a freighter, the tanker being claimed damaged.

Plt.Off. Graham Leggett and Plt.Off. Robert Matthews of 249 Squadron, Takali, December 1941. (*P.G. Leggett via Chaz Bowyer*)

17/12/41

On the 17th. two Blenheims from 107 Squadron attacked Sorman and Zuara on the Tripolitanian coast, but once again one was lost. Plt.Off. F.H.W. Keene's Blenheim was seen to be attacked and turn out to sea; Keene survived to become a P.O.W. Once more I/NJG 2 may have been responsible, Lt. Dieter Schleif claiming a Blenheim shot down in flames, but reportedly over Malta.

18/12/41

Next day Malta's fighters were in action for the first time in some days. Four Hurricanes of 185 Squadron were sent out to intercept a hostile radar plot, engaging three bombers 40 miles south-west of Filfla. These were identified as BR 20s, but were in fact S.84s of the 259ª Squadriglia, 109° Gruppo, 36° Stormo A.S., which were patrolling over a convoy. The Hurricanes attacked, Plt.Offs. Allardice and Oliver both claiming hits on the wings and fuselage of one bomber, although Allardice's Hurricane was hit in the tail by return fire. In fact their attack had been more effective than had been supposed, one S.84 (MM 22487) crashing into the sea where all but one member of the crew were killed. It seems that this aircraft was being flown by Sottoten. Antonio Galati, but that Magg. Goffredo Gastaldi was also aboard; both officers were lost. A second bomber returned with a mortally wounded man aboard and a second member of the crew less badly wounded. It was the Albacores turn to hunt the convoys this night, five aircraft off after yet another convoy making for Tripoli. One aircraft returned early but the others pressed on and found two supply ships. Lt.Cdr. Langmore, leading the attack, was shot down into the sea and lost with his crew; a second Albacore struggled back to Hal Far minus its port undercarriage, smashed when the aircraft touched the sea during its run in, and crashed while attempting a landing. Two hits were claimed on one of the ships.

Sqn.Ldr. E.B.B. Mortimer-Rose, D.F.C. (centre) with Flt.Lt. H.J.S. Beazley (r) and Flg.Off. C.C.H. Davis (l), 249 Squadron, Takali, December 1941. (*P.G. Leggett via Chaz Bowyer*)

19/12/41

Malta came under attack again on 19 December with the first real daylight attacks by elements of Fliegerkorps II. During the morning a reconnaissance Ju88 appeared over a convoy which was just arriving, including the faithful 'Breconshire'. Hurricanes intercepted and claimed that damage was inflicted. Somewhat later three Ju88s attempted to bomb the ships, and on this occasion four Hurricanes of 126 Squadron intercepted. Sqn.Ldr. Stan Norris made several attacks on one bomber which came down on Gozo. Two unidentified Sergeants attacked the other two, both of which were claimed damaged. Two members of the crew were removed from the wreckage of the aircraft shot down by Norris, both of them seriously injured; the third man was dead. One of the other two died later in hospital.

During the morning a Bf110 pilot of III/ZG 26, Lt. Scheid, claimed a Beaufighter shot down, but it seems possible that this was in fact a maritime-reconnaissance Blenheim IVF fighter from 203 Squadron operating from Egypt; one such was reported lost during the day. Flg.Off. A.T. Reed and his crew all being killed (see 'Fighters over the Desert'). Later in the day eighteen Hurricanes were scrambled in very bad weather to intercept thirteen incoming bombers and a fighter escort. The Hurricanes, from 126 Squadron again, were unable to see any decisive results of their attack, but Plt.Off. Edward 'Pete' Steele was shot down and killed. The first of the Americans to be lost over Malta, Steele was seen attacking a Ju88, and was believed to have been hit by return fire; allegedly, according to Howard Coffin, the Ju88 he had attacked also crashed into the sea, one member of the crew being seen to bale out. However two claims for Hurricanes were submitted by the Germans during this raid; one was made by Maj. von Maltzahn, Kommodore of JG 53 – his 52nd. victory – and one by Lt. Laufs, a pilot of one of I/NJG 2's night-fighter Ju88Cs, which were forming part of the escort on this occasion; this was his 12th. and last victory of the war, for he would be killed in action during the next month. During this fight 1/NJG 2 lost Ju88C Werk Nr.564, flown by Lt. Wilhelm Brauns. Brauns and his gunner were reported as prisoners, whilst the observer was killed. On the face of it, this would seem to have been the aircraft shot down by Stan Norris, but as two of the crew were reported to have survived it is possible that it may have been that seen by Coffin to crash following Steele's attack.

That night while Wellingtons of 40 Squadron were waiting to take off for a raid, an intruder – probably again from I/NJG 2 – strafed the airfield. Plt.Off. John Tipton, a navigator recalls: " ... our aircraft was hit ... and all the crew were casualties. I believe the explosion of the aircraft and its bomb load damaged all (the other) aircraft waiting to take off that night." Both X9912 and Z9029 were destroyed; others were damaged.

20/12/41

The real challenge to the Hurricanes came next day (20 December) when the Ju88s returned during the morning, but this time with a strong escort of single-engined fighters, including the newly-arrived Bf109Fs of I/JG 53. 11 of these from 1 Staffel and the Gruppenstab were escorting four bombers to attack shipping in Grand Harbour when twelve Hurricanes of 249 Squadron were scrambled at 1036 after the incoming formation, which was assessed to be 40 strong. Plt.Off. Palliser attacked one Ju88 head-on, opening fire when only a few yards away. He saw his bullets hit the starboard engine and the starboard wing then broke off. The bomber went straight down but he lost sight of it as it fell into cloud. Before he could follow he was attacked by a number of Macchis, but the bomber was seen to go into the sea by coastwatchers. Sgt. Howard Moren was believed to have collided with a Ju88 – presumably that which Palliser had attacked – and he was killed. Meanwhile three unidentified pilots, a Plt.Off. and two Sergeants, attacked several Ju88s, claiming four of them damaged. A Flg.Off. fired at a Macchi, hitting the starboard wing; he reported that it gave a "quick flick" and went straight down. Another Sergeant also attacked one of the Italian fighters which spun down apparently out of control, disappearing into cloud; they were credited with two Macchis probably destroyed. Oblt. Friedrich-Karl Müller of 1/JG53 dived on Flg.Off. Brian Cavan's Hurricane as it was flying at 20,000 feet, and shot it down. The Hurricane fell like a stone and crashed; Cavan was killed. This was Müller's 31st. victory. It is possible that other aircraft were destroyed on the ground during this attack, for eleven R.A.F. machines were recorded as lost on this date.

The return of the Luftwaffe soon made life harder for the Malta defences. In this evocative scene, ground crew rise from the cover to which they have rushed as a 242 Squadron Hurricane grinds to a halt on its belly, and the pilot leaps from the cockpit. (NWMA).

During the day Wg.Cdr. W.A.J. Satchell arrived to take over command of Takali following George Powell-Sheddon's departure. 'Bill' Satchell was a pre-war pilot of much experience who had commanded 302 Squadron, the first Polish fighter unit in the R.A.F., claiming three confirmed and three probable victories

351

with them during the Battle of Britain. He had been officer in charge of flying-off aboard H.M.S. 'Ark Royal' during Operations 'Status I' and 'Status II' earlier in the year.

21/12/41

During the late morning of 21 December a further raid approached, comprising four bombers and twenty escorting fighters – again both Bf109Fs and MC202s. Ten Hurricanes of 185 Squadron and eight of 249 Squadron were scrambled, led by Wg.Cdr. Rabagliati in Z4005. Rabagliati himself claimed one MC202 shot down, while a second was claimed as a probable and two Bf109s as damaged, the latter by Flt.Lt. Beazley and F/Sgt. Etchells of 249 Squadron. Sgt. Brian Hayes of 185 Squadron failed to return, his aircraft (Z2823) was observed falling into the sea some 5 miles out, while Plt.Off. Leggett of 249 Squadron was shot down, but survived and was taken to hospital with slight abrasions after baling out. In the early afternoon seven Hurricanes were again off after three reconnaissance aircraft, but on this occasion one was attacked and slightly damaged by a Bf109. O.K.W. recorded claims for four British fighters shot down on this date, one Hurricane being claimed by Maj. von Maltzahn of Stab/JG53.

22/12/41

A further O.K.W. report for 22nd. recorded two further victories by German fighters, again one by Maj. von Maltzahn. At least one of these was claimed when Bf109s were engaged in shooting up fishing boats off Grand Harbour. Plt.Off. Matthews of 249 Squadron was involved in attempting to intercept these when, according to Howard Coffin: "... another German was hard on his own tail, chasing him towards the shore ... Matthews was hit, and crashed into the sea wall at Valetta, where his aircraft exploded and started to burn." Sgt. Copp's aircraft was also damaged but he got down safely. The fighter units noted four alerts during the day, but were unable to make any claims. During one of these raids a Ju88C, R4+KK of 2/NJG 2 flown by Fw. Ernst Ziebarth, failed to return from a sortie over Malta, he and his crew being reported missing. It is assumed that their aircraft was hit by A.A. fire. A Blenheim of 18 Squadron also failed to return from a sea reconnaissance, F/Sgt. S.C. Griffiths and his crew later being reported killed; this may have been the second aircraft credited to Luftwaffe pilots on this date.

During the day a Sunderland (T9071) of 230 Squadron which was on its way to Kalafrana from Aboukir Bay, Egypt, carrying aboard Plt.Off. Easton, the 40 Squadron New Zealand pilot who had been shot down during the night of 13 December. The flyingboat, flown by another New Zealander, Flt.Lt. S.W.R. Hughes, was intercepted by two Bf110s of III/ZG 26 (one of which is believed to have been flown by Ofw. Helmut Haugk) when 50 miles north-east of Benghazi. During the fight one of the Zerstörer was claimed probably shot down by Sgt. Jacques Dupont, R.A.A.F., after two of the gunners had been wounded, but the Sunderland was badly damaged, both starboard engines being shot out of action. Hughes force-landed on the sea, coming to rest after two bounces. The crew had to spread themselves on the undamaged wing to keep the remaining float in the

Late 1941 brought many casualties in the air, and the destruction of a large part of the defence's force of fighters on the ground. Here a Hurricane has been thrown onto its belly and damaged by bomb blast, which had demolished this hangar at Takali. (*J. Alton*)

water, that on the starboard side having been smashed in the landing. In this way the aircraft drifted tail-first until it struck a reef just offshore at Ras Amt, and stuck there, beginning to break up as it was battered by heavy seas.

After two hours the crew and passengers – twenty in all – struggled ashore. Sgt. Dupont had helped one gunner, who had been mortally wounded, into a dinghy and swam alongside in the surging sea. The dinghy capsized, but he held onto his companion and finally got him ashore. Here a group of Italian soldiers approached and surrendered to them. More Italians then arrived and took the party prisoner, taking them to a Senussi village where the wounded gunner died and was buried. As it was uncertain whether the British had yet taken Benghazi or not, the parties split up next day. The group finally reached British lines having collected 130 voluntary Italian prisoners along the way! Sgt. Dupont was later awarded a D.F.M. for his gallantry on this date.

To return to the 22nd., meanwhile, both the Blenheims and Marylands were out during the day. Flg.Off. Roger Drew of 69 Squadron made a morning reconnaissance over Tripolitania. Over Chaddahia two Bf109s attacked, but one of these was seen to break away and dive towards the coast, leaving a trail of black smoke; Drew's gunner, Sgt. Moren, was credited with a probable. Six 107 Squadron Blenheims went out in pairs to attack the road west of Sirte, in the same general area. Transport and other such targets were attacked but after the bombing Sgt. R.F.J. Henley's aircraft was seen to turn away and crash into the sea.

23/12/41

The alerts sounded again on 23rd., as an estimated twenty-two raiders approached Grand Harbour once more. The attackers this time were apparently just two Ju88s escorted by Bf109s of II/JG 53, which had also now reached Sicily. Hurricanes of 126 Squadron were sent off to intercept, one Bf109F being claimed damaged; Lt. Hans-Jurgen Frohdies returned wounded. Two of the defending Hurricanes were also hit – Sqn.Ldr. Lefevre, imminently due to leave the island, force-landed at Hal Far with slight injuries, while newly-commissioned Plt.Off. Noel MacGregor force-landed Z5118, with a shrapnel wound in his foot, having been jumped by an aircraft he never even saw.

Immediately the raid was over a Maryland (BS766) was sent out by 69 Squadron to reconnoitre over Tripolitania again. It returned at 1600 flying on only one engine, and crashed as it attempted to land, Sgt. P.C. Wells and his crew all being killed. The observer's log book was recovered from the wreck and this indicated that the Maryland had been intercepted and damaged by fighters. On this date one of the 'Rooster' Wellingtons (Z8703) of 221 Squadron detachment, which was being flown by Sgt. W.D. Reason, failed to return from a special search.

24/12/41

Christmas Eve 1941 brought four alerts but only one interception. Wg.Cdr. Rabagliati led off seventeen Hurricanes of 126 and 185 Squadrons after four Ju88A-4s of II/KG 77 which dive-bombed Grand Harbour shortly after 0900; this was the twenty-fifth raid in seven days – an indication of the level of activity that the arrival of the Luftwaffe had brought. The Wing Leader was attacked by escorting Bf109s and driven off, but the rest attacked the bombers and claimed two shot down. One bomber from 5 Staffel (Werk Nr. 6575) was sent crashing down into the sea 20 miles east of Zonkor Point, Lt. Siegfried Tack and his crew all perishing, while a second, which it was believed had already been hit by the A.A. defences, was pounced upon and when last seen five miles north of Malta, was down below 1,000 feet, pouring smoke from both engines, and was classed as a probable. This was clearly Werk Nr. 4582, an aircraft of 4 Staffel flown by Fw. Otto Bude, which was hard hit and crashed on return to Catania, one member of the crew having been badly wounded during the combat. Aircraft of K.Gr.806 also took part in this attack, one of this unit's Ju88A-4s being lost when M7+HK flown by Uffz. Werner Lessner also failed to return. One Ju88 was credited to Sqn.Ldr. Mortimer-Rose, Flg.Off. Crossey and Flg.Off. Palliser, while the second was shared by F/Sgt. Etchells and two other pilots, one of whom is believed to have been Plt.Off. Coffin of 126 Squadron. One of 126's Hurricanes was shot down, F/Sgt. Frank Emery failing to return. During one of the day's raids the remaining He115 'Spy plane', BV187, was damaged by bombs at Kalafrana.

Shattered Swordfish of 830 Squadron, tossed over on its back by bomb blast at Hal Far. (*R.F. Noble*)

Meanwhile three Blenheims from 107 Squadron attacked schooners in Zuara harbour on this date, Two of the bombers were hit, Sgt. E. Crossley's aircraft crashing, while Plt.Off. I. Paul in the second aircraft was killed by a cannon shell (probably 20mm Flak).

25–26/12/41

Christmas Day proved peaceful, but on 26 December the Axis were back. Four alerts were sounded, and during one interception Sqn.Ldr. Mortimer-Rose's Hurricane was shot-up, and he crash-landed at Luqa with a bullet in his heel. Luqa itself was heavily attacked, a number of aircraft being destroyed or damaged on the ground here, including four bombers, one of which blew up and set fire to others, and a Maryland (BS763) and P.R. Hurricane (Z2332) of 69 Squadron, both of which were written off. According to O.K.W. two Hurricanes were claimed shot down by German fighters, one by Maj. von Maltzahn, while a bomber was also reported shot down. The latter claim would appear to relate to a Blenheim of 18 Squadron flown by Sgt. O.C. Summers, which failed to return from a patrol. The day also saw the departure for England of two time-expired stalwarts of 249 Squadron, Flt.Lt. Neil and Flg.Off. Harrington. With Sqn.Ldr. Mortimer-Rose now wounded, albeit slightly, command of 249 Squadron passed to Flt.Lt. Beazley. By night Ju88s were now attacking the island regularly. The all-black Hurricanes of 1435 Flight had moved over to Hal Far, as Takali was unserviceable due to heavy rain, and from here Sqn.Ldr. Westmacott and Flt.Lt. Stones attempted to intercept a lone Junkers which remained overhead for about two and a half hours. It proved a much more difficult opponent than had the Italian bombers, constantly changing height, speed and direction, but remaining at quite a low altitude. Westmacott opened fire, but was unable to gain any hits, and when Don Stones finally found himself in a perfect position to attack, his guns refused to fire!

27/12/41

A rather more successful interception took place during the morning of 27th. when Hurricanes led by Flt.Lt. Carpenter of 126 Squadron were ordered off in good time as the third alert of the day sounded. Climbing to 24,000 feet, the fighters patrolled for some forty minutes before being vectored onto a reported four or five Ju88s at 16,000 feet, five to ten miles east of Kalafrana. There were in fact just three bombers, aircraft of Stab II/KG 77, with an escort of twenty Bf109Fs above, but Carpenter was able to dive on the last Ju88 – Hptm. Eberhard Stahle's 3Z+BM – making a beam attack which he pressed to very close range. With an engine smoking, the bomber turned and dived for cloud cover, but Carpenter got in two more good attacks, setting fire to the damaged engine, and the bomber crashed into the sea. The rest of the Hurricanes were by now engaged with the escort, and Plt.Off. Main was able to attack one Bf109F from 50 yards and set it on fire. Although initially claimed as a probable, this was subsequently upgraded to confirmed; however, apparently the fire was extinguished and the pilot managed to get back to Sicily. Other pilots claimed damage to the other two Ju88s and another Messerschmitt. A Ju88 of KGr.806 flown by Uffz. Johann Krause returned from a sortie over Malta with the pilot and one other crewman wounded, but the damage reportedly caused by A.A. fire. Three victories were claimed by the returning JG53 pilots; Sgt. Copp, who had been shot up five days previously but had escaped without injury, was again involved, this time being shot down and baling out with slight wounds. The American Plt.Off. Coffin also had his Hurricane badly damaged but was able to land safely.

After dark a Ju88 again appeared over the island, but on this occasion Plt.Off. Winton of 1435 Flight was successful in intercepting it at 2020. Diving 4,000 feet to attack the bomber which had been picked up by the searchlights, he kept after it despite desperate evasive action by the pilot. Winton poured a stream of bullets into one engine, and moments later it burst into flames and fell like a ball of fire into the sea as watchers in the streets of Valetta below cheered furiously. As the aircraft hit the water there was a violent explosion and a sheet of white light lit up the sky. Howard Coffin noted in his diary: " ... it burst into flames and you could see the pilot bale out. The searchlights did a wonderful job of illumination. What a sight! And did the Maltese cheer! The lights followed him down until he landed in the water and then they snapped off. We have no more air/sea rescue boats." Earlier in the day he had noted: " ... they got the last of our air/sea rescue boats."

Two views of a very badly damaged Hurricane of 605 Squadron. The fabric on the rear fuselage and tail is ripped to shreds by splinters, but the remains of the code letters, UP, can just be seen. (*Mrs. Davies via National War Museum Assoc.*)

28/12/41

Several more scrambles occurred on 28 December, but only on one raid was an interception made. No claims resulted, but F/Sgt. Owen of 249 Squadron was shot down just after 1335. He came down in the sea wounded in the left arm, but was safely picked up by one of the Kalafrana Swordfish floatplanes. That night it was the turn of the guns to claim one of the intruder Ju88Cs from I/NJG 2 shot down; Lt. Wilfried Babinek and his navigator of 3rd. Staffel were both killed when R4+CL crashed into the sea.

29/12/41

29 December was to be the heaviest day of action since the return of the Luftwaffe to Sicily, and a costly one for the defenders. There were five scrambles during the day, three of them becoming major combats. The first of these occurred soon after 0945 when thirty-six raiders approached, sixteen Hurricanes being sent up, including seven from 185 Squadron and four from 242 Squadron. Two of the latter aircraft collided in mid-air, Plt.Off. Merton Blanchard being killed whilst Plt.Off. MacNamara baled out into the sea and was picked up safely. The raiders attacked two destroyers in harbour, and also bombed Luqa where two Blenheims were damaged. The remaining Hurricanes engaged two Ju88s and seven Bf109Fs, Flt.Lt. Thompson of 185 Squadron claiming one of the latter probably shot down (this claim may have been confirmed destroyed subsequently). Thompson's own aircraft was then hit by Bofors fire from the airfield, and he landed on one wheel. Sgts. Jolly and Vardy both had their fighters shot-up, but both managed to land back at base, while a fourth Hurricane was also damaged. Plt.Off. Oliver chased two Bf109s which were engaged in strafing aircraft on the ground, and claimed one of these damaged.

Eighteen Hurricanes were again sent up soon after 1430, to intercept twenty-four raiders. Sqn.Ldr. Pike of 185 Squadron attacked three Bf109s, and claimed all damaged, while Flg.Off. R.M. Lloyd attacked two more and claimed one shot down. The squadron had by now been completely broken up, and no one saw what happened to Sgt. Alfred Forth, whose Hurricane (Z4943) appeared over the airfield at 800 feet and then crashed, the pilot being killed. It was presumed that this was the result of enemy action. Lloyd's victim may have been an aircraft of Stab/JG 53 (Werke Nr. 7431) which apparently came down in the sea off the north coast of Malta, Lt. Joachim Louis being picked up wounded by a rescue craft.

An hour and a half later four Hurricanes were scrambled after five Bf109s which were attacking shipping and had set fire to the Gozo ferryboat, the schooner 'Marie Georgette'. One Messerschmitt was claimed as a probable by Plt.Off. J.R.A. Stuart but both Flt.Lt. Sid Brandt and Sgt. Roy Lawson were shot down into the sea. At the first opportunity a Swordfish of 830 Squadron slipped out to search for the missing pilots, but returned after a fruitless three hours. Twelve more Bf109Fs and a number of bombers swept in over Luqa where about fifteen aircraft were destroyed, including nine Wellingtons; 40 Squadron had three aircraft burnt out: X9889, 9907 and 9919, while six more from OADU were destroyed – Z8991, 9018, 9020, 9024, 9025 and 9041; others were damaged. Fires had broken out in an area where several bombed-up Wellingtons were dispersed, and where the bomb dump was situated. One of these bombers caught fire, and F/Sgt. A.J.M. MacDonald – in charge of the Luqa Fire Section – attempted to extinguish the flames with a portable fire hydrant. He was successful, thereby saving two other Wellingtons from destruction. For this, and other actions following raids on Luqa, he was later awarded the B.E.M.

Flt.Lt. Sid Brandt, newly-arrived on Malta as a Flight Commander in 249 Squadron, was shot down and killed by the Bf109Fs of Jagdgeschwader 53 on 29 December 1941. He was one of the last two R.A.F. fighter pilots to be lost over the island before the year ended. (*F. Margarson*)

Meanwhile, the ferryboat, which had a normal crew of ten, was carrying twelve passengers at the time it was attacked. The captain, Marcel Theuma, was mortally wounded and one other member of the crew was killed, but the other twenty people on board jumped into the sea and were all saved when rescuers formed a human chain to get them ashore. During the day's fighting O.K.W. reported that Luftwaffe fighters claimed five victories; whether any of these claims related to the 242 Squadron aircraft which had collided, or to the Hurricanes damaged in the first interception is not clear.

30/12/41

The last combat of the year occurred during the morning of 30th. Just before midday ten Hurricanes from 126 and 249 Squadrons – the Takali Wing – were sent off, led by Wg.Cdr. Satchell in Z3766. Bombers were attacking Luqa, Takali and the Dockyard on this occasion, the Hurricanes intercepting five Ju88s of KGr.806 near Luqa at between 4,500 and 15,000 feet. Bill Satchell attacked one bomber, using all his ammunition on it. He recalls: "... alone I pursued the Ju88 out to sea and unable to catch it, fired really well out of range but to my surprise immediately saw smoke pour from its starboard engine. Getting short of fuel then, I returned to Takali. Later the pilot of a P.R. aircraft reported seeing a Ju88 smoking from its starboard engine, in approximately the area where I had broken off the attack, crash into the sea. I was therefore credited with its destruction." This aircraft would appear to have been the one reported by the Luftwaffe to have crashed following engine failure, all but one of the crew being rescued. A second bomber – M7+AL, flown by Oblt. Georg Lust – was shot down over Luqa by Flg.Off. Barnes and Plt.Off. Anderson of 126 Squadron. Plt.Off. John Tipton, the 40 Squadron Wellington navigator recalls this particular combat clearly: "I was encouraged to see from my bedroom window two Hurricanes with a Ju88 at their mercy at very low level over Luqa. They were scissoring across its tail while the crew baled out – very low with little chance of survival. The pilot, a brave man, having seen them out did a pull off from the starboard wing. He may have been the one who that day was rescued from an angry bunch of Maltese by a member of 40 Squadron and hidden under a bed in a hut. By report he was more arrogant than grateful".

Other Hurricane pilots claimed one more Ju88 as a probable and one damaged, while the A.A. defences and Royal Navy gunners each claimed one more damaged. A patrolling Blenheim (Z9816) from 18 Squadron flown by Plt.Off. Wyatt was also lost on this date.

Even as the year drew to a close various changes and moves were underway. The survivors of 18 and 107 Squadrons learned that they would soon be relieved, for at the end of December the Blenheims of 21 Squadron left England on the first leg of the journey to the island. (15 Blenheims had been lost during December alone bringing total losses to over 57 aircraft.) For the detachment of 40 Squadron there was to be no such relief; on 31 December the parent unit in England received word that the remaining Wellingtons and crews of the Malta detachment would form the nucleus of a new unit, 156 Squadron. On Sicily the

Two views of a totally burnt-out Hurricane of 185 Squadron. (*Mrs. Davies via National War Museum Assoc.*)

Italians rested the long-serving 23° Gruppo Autonomo C.T., which – still mainly equipped with its obsolescent CR 42s, plus a few MC200s – was withdrawn to Northern Italy to re-equip. However the Luftwaffe had been reinforced by the arrival of III/JG 53 from Libya, following a few days' service there. This Gruppe does not seem to have seen any action over Malta prior to the turn of the year.

Since the arrival of JG53, R.A.F. claims for Bf109Fs totalled only two or three. Although several claims had been made in the February–June 1941 period when 7/JG26 and the elements of JG27 were present, no Bf109Es had actually been lost by these units. However, Luftwaffe loss figures for 1941 do indicate that two Bf109s were lost while operating from Sicily during the year, and these may well be related to these recent claims. At the close of December A.H.Q. Malta reported that during the month the fighters had been credited with nine confirmed destroyed, eight probables and eight damaged. Since the outbreak of hostilities in June 1940 the fighter pilots had in total been credited with the destruction of 199 aircraft, plus 78 probables and 79 damaged; the anti-aircraft defences were credited with an additional 50 more approximately. Fighter claim totals were as follows:

Type	Period 11 June 1941 to 31 December 1941			Period 11 June 1940 to 31 December 1941		
	Dest.	Prob.	Dam.	Dest.	Prob.	Dam.
CR 42	2	0	0	18	7	6
MC200	47	14	15	57	17	18
MC202	8	7	7	8	7	7
Ju87 (Italian)	3	0	0	5	1	0
S.79	4	1	1	16	9	8
BR 20	10	4	2	12	6	2
S.81	3	0	0	4	0	0
Z.1007bis	2	0	0	2	0	0
Ca 312	1	0	0	1	0	0
Z.506B	3	0	0	6	1	0
Bf109E	0	0	0	6	2	1
Bf109F	2	2	7	2	2	7
Bf110	0	0	0	2	0	1
Ju87 (German)	0	0	0	29	8	11
Ju88	8	2	9	24	11	18
Do215	0	0	0	5	3	0
He111	0	0	0	2	3	0
Ju52/3m	0	1	0	0	1	0
Total	93	31	41	199	78	79
Italian	83	26	25	129	48	41
German	10	5	16	70	30	38

Against these claims, a variety of figures were subsequently published for the Axis air forces which provide some measure of comparison, bearing in mind that the quoted Italian losses were to both fighters and anti-aircraft fire, while the Luftwaffe figures were to all operational causes.

Regia Aeronautica losses over Malta:

1 January 1941 – 31 December 1941			*11 June 1940 – 31 December 1941*
	Lost	Damaged	Lost
Bombers	27	25	54 (includes some dive-bombers)
Dive-Bombers	3	3	3
Torpedo-Bombers	2	16	2
Fighters	38	26	46
Total	70	70	105

Luftwaffe Losses operating from Sicily, 1941

Ju88	33
Ju87	29
He111	10
Bf110	4
Bf109	2
Ju52/3m	3
	81

On the debit side the defenders of Malta had suffered the loss of 47 fighter pilots killed in action (including one member of the Fleet Air Arm), six in accidents, one died through illness, and three pilots and one Fleet Air Arm Fulmar observer prisoners of war. Additionally about fifteen pilots had been lost whilst ferrying Hurricanes to Malta, including those lost during the first ferry flight way back in June 1940. Another twelve pilots had been seriously wounded. One Gladiator, at least 90 Hurricanes and three Fulmars had been lost in action, while many more had been destroyed on the ground. A further ten Hurricanes and two Fulmars had been destroyed in accidents.

The reconnaissance unit, initially numbered 431 Flight, later 69 Squadron, had suffered its share of casualties. At least eight Marylands, one Spitfire and one Hurricane II had been lost on operations, while again several more Marylands and at least one Hurricane were destroyed on the ground. Aircrew casualties amounted to at least twenty-one killed and one prisoner. Amongst the long-range fighter units, three Beaufighters had been lost, together with one Blenheim IVF fighter of 113 Squadron, whilst six aircrew personnel of 252 Squadron and three of 113 had lost their lives.

Not all the bomber losses have been recorded, for their records were frequently very incomplete. However their losses were perhaps the most severe. Well over 100 names of bomber aircrew are recorded on the Malta Memorial – and those are only the men who lost their lives flying from Malta and have no known resting place. Many more bomber aircrew were buried in Sicily, Italy, Greece and North Africa. As will have been noted, the Fleet Air Arm units had also borne a substantial share of the successes and losses, many of them in the vicinity of Malta. Their victories and losses while operating from the decks of the aircraft carriers of the Royal Navy are not included in the figures quoted above.

Victories claimed by the Luftwaffe over Malta during 1941 were:

Gladiators	2
Hurricanes	76
Blenheims	2
Wellingtons	1
Sunderlands	1
Others	2
	84

At about two minutes after 2355 on the night of 31 December 1941 a single Ju88 appeared over Takali airfield in bright moonlight and carried out half a dozen strafing attacks. Five minutes later a repeat attack was made – 1942 had begun. It would be a grim and costly year of great hardship, which culminated nonetheless in the raising of the siege finally and irrevocably. The story of that year of effort will be told in Volume 2, 'Malta – The Spitfire Year'.

Appendix I

FIGHTER UNITS BASED ON MALTA, 1940–1941

Unit and Base	Equipment	Service	Commanding Officer	Period of Command
Fighter Flight, Hal Far	Sea Gladiator Hurricane I	Apr. 40 – Aug. 40 Jun. 40 – Aug. 40	Sqn.Ldr. A.C. Martin	Apr. 40 – Aug. 40
418 Flight, Luqa	Hurricane I	Aug. 40	Sqn.Ldr. A.C. Martin/ Flt.Lt. D.W. Balden	Aug. 40
261 Squadron, Luqa, Takali	Hurricane I Sea Gladiator Hurricane IIA	Aug. 40 – May 41	Sqn.Ldr. D.W. Balden Sqn.Ldr. A.J. Trumble Sqn.Ldr. R.N. Lambert Sqn.Ldr. C.D. Whittingham	Aug. 40 – Dec. 40 Dec. 40 – Feb. 41 Feb. 41 – May 41 May 41
806 Squadron, Hal Far	Fulmar I	Jan. 41 – Mar. 41	Lt.D. Vincent-Jones, D.S.C.	Jan. 41 – Mar. 41
252 Squadron, (detachment) Luqa	Beaufighter	May 41	Sqn.Ldr. R.G. Yaxley, M.C.	Dec. 40 – May 41
185 Squadron, Hal Far, Takali, Hal Far	Hurricane I, IIA, B and C	May 41 –	Sqn.Ldr. P.W.O. Mould, D.F.C. (K.i.A. 1 Oct. 41) Sqn.Ldr. P.W. Lefevre Sqn.Ldr. S.A.D. Pike	May 41 – Oct. 41 Oct. 41 Oct. 41 – Jan. 42
249 Squadron, Takali	Hurricane I, IIA and B	May 41 –	Sqn.Ldr. R.A. Barton, D.F.C. Sqn.Ldr. E.B. Mortimer-Rose Sqn.Ldr. H.J.S. Beazley	Dec. 40 – Dec. 41 Dec. 41 Dec. 41 – Feb. 42
800X Squadron, Hal Far	Fulmar I	May 41-Nov. 41	Lt. J.S. Manning (P.O.W. 7/8 Sep. 41) Lt. D.E.C. Eyres	May 41 – Sep. 41 Sep. 41 – Nov. 41

Unit and Base	Equipment	Service	Commanding Officer	Period of Command
46 Squadron, Hal Far renumbered as:	Hurricane IIB	Jun. 41	Sqn.Ldr. A.C. Rabagliati, D.F.C.	Dec. 40 – Jun. 41
126 Squadron, Takali	Hurricane IIB and C	Jun. 41 –	Sqn.Ldr. A.C. Rabagliati, D.F.C.	Jun. 41 – Oct. 41
			Sqn.Ldr. P.W. Lefevre	Oct. 41 – Dec. 41
			Sqn.Ldr. S.C. Norris, D.F.C.	Dec. 41 – Mar. 42
M.N.F.U. renamed:	Hurricane IIB and IIC	Jul. 41 – Dec. 41	Sqn.Ldr. G.fl. Powell-Sheddon, D.F.C.	Jul. 41 – Dec. 41
1435 Flight	Hurricane IIB and IIC	Dec. 41 –	Sqn.Ldr. I.B. Westmacott	Dec. 41 – Mar. 42
252/272 Squadron, (detachment) Luqa	Beaufighter	Jul. 41 – Aug. 41	Sqn.Ldr. R.G. Yaxley, M.C./ Sqn.Ldr. A.W. Fletcher, D.F.C.	
272 Squadron, (detachment) Luqa	Beaufighter	Aug. 41 – Sep. 41	Sqn.Ldr. A.W. Fletcher, D.F.C.	Nov. 40 – Oct. 41
113 Squadron (detachment)	Blenheim IVF	Sep. 41	Sqn.Ldr. P.R.A. Ford	Sep. 41 (detachment)
242 Squadron, Hal Far, Luqa	Hurricane II	Nov. 41 –	Sqn.Ldr. W.G. Wells	Aug. 41 – Mar. 42
605 Squadron Hal Far, Luqa	Hurricane II	Nov. 41 –	Sqn.Ldr. R. Reid	Sep. 41 – Nov. 41
			Sqn.Ldr. S.E. Andrews, D.F.M.	Nov. 41 – Feb. 42
252 Squadron (detachment) Luqa	Beaufighter	Dec. 41	Flg.Off. D.A. Smith	Dec. 41 (detachment)

N.B. Ranks and decorations listed are those appertaining at the time.   K.i.A = Killed in Action.   P.O.W. = Prisoner of War.

Appendix II

BOMBER AND RECONNAISSANCE UNITS BASED ON MALTA, 1940–1941

Bomber Units, including Detachments – all Luqa-based

Squadron	Aircraft	Dates	Commander	Dates
148 Squadron	Wellington IC	Oct. 40 – Jul. 41	Sqn.Ldr. P.S. Foss	Nov. 40 – Dec. 40
			Wg.Cdr. F.F. Rainsford	Dec. 40 – Mar. 41
			Wg.Cdr. E.C. Lewis	Mar. 41 –
37 Squadron	Wellington IC	Nov. 40	Wg.Cdr. R.C.M. Collard	Nov. 40 –
21 Squadron	Blenheim IV	Apr. 41 – May 41	Sqn.Ldr. L.V.E. Atkinson	Apr. 41 – May 41
139 Squadron	Blenheim IV	May 41 – Jun. 41	Wg.Cdr. N.E.W. Pepper, D.F.C. (K.i.A. 3 Jun. 41)	May 41 – Jun. 41
82 Squadron	Blenheim IV	May 41 – Jul 41	Wg.Cdr. L.V.E. Atkinson	May 41 – Jul. 41
			Wg.Cdr. T.M. Hunt, D.F.C. (K.i.A. 18 Jul. 41)	– Jul. 41
110 Squadron	Blenheim IV	Jul. 41	Wg.Cdr. D.W. Scivier, A.F.C.	Jul. 41
105 Squadron	Blenheim IV	Jul. 41 – Oct. 41	Wg.Cdr. H.I. Edwards, V.C., D.F.C.	– Jul. 41
			Wg.Cdr. D.W. Scivier, A.F.C. (K.i.A. 21 Sep. 41)	Aug. 41 – Sep. 41
			Wg.Cdr. P.H.A. Simmons, D.F.C.	Oct. 41 –
38 Squadron	Wellington IIC	Aug. 41 – Oct. 41	Wg.Cdr. J.D. Rollinson. D.F.C.	Oct. 41 –
107 Squadron	Blenheim IV	Sep. 41 –	Wg.Cdr. F.A. Harte (K.i.A. 9 Oct. 41)	May 41 – Oct. 41
			Wg.Cdr. J.S. Dunlevie	Oct. 41 –
			Wg.Cdr. E.S. Barnes, D.F.C.	

Appendix II—Contd.
Bomber Units, including Detachments – all Luqa based

Unit	Aircraft		Commander	
221 Squadron (Special Flight)	Wellington VIII	Sep. 41 –	Flt.Lt. A. Spooner	Sep. 41 – (detachment)
104 Squadron	Wellington IIC	Oct. 41 –	Wg.Cdr. P.R. Beare, D.S.O., D.F.C.	Jul. 41 –
18 Squadron	Blenheim IV	Oct. 41 –	Wg.Cdr. A.H. Smythe	Jul. 41 –
40 Squadron	Wellington IC	Oct. 41 –	Wg.Cdr. L.J. Stickley, D.F.C.	Oct. 41 –

Reconnaissance Units – Luqa-based

Unit	Aircraft		Commander	
431 Flight became:	Maryland Skua, Blenheim IV	Sep. 40 – Jan. 41	Flt.Lt. E.W. Whiteley	Sep. 40 – Jan. 41
69 Squadron	Maryland Spitfire Hurricane I & II Blenheim Beaufort	Jan. 41 –	Sqn.Ldr. E.W. Whiteley Sqn.Ldr. R.D. Welland Wg.Cdr. J.N. Dowland, G.C.	Jan. 41 – Jun. 41 Jun. 41 – Sep. 41 Sep. 41 –

Fleet Air Arm Torpedo-Bomber Strike Units – Hal Far-based

Unit	Aircraft		Commander	
830 Squadron	Swordfish	Jun. 40 –	Lt.Cdr. F.D. Howie Lt. H.E.H. Pain Lt.Cdr. J.G. Hunt (P.O.W. 11/12 Nov. 41) Lt.Cdr. F.E.H. Hopkins, D.S.C.	Jun. 40 – Jul. 41 Jul. 41 – Oct. 41 Oct. 41 – Nov. 41 Nov. 41 –
828 Squadron	Albacore	Oct. 41 –	Lt.Cdr. D.E. Langmore (K.i.A. 18/19.12.41) Lt. G.M. Haynes	Jul. 41 – Dec. 41 Dec. 41 –

N.B. Ranks and decorations listed are those appertaining at the time.

Appendix III

"FAITH, HOPE AND CHARITY" –
THE LEGEND AND THE FACTS

Much has been written about the legendary "Faith, Hope and Charity", but this very title implies that only three Gladiators were involved in the defence of Malta. Readers will have noted in Chapter 1 that this was not the case. The authors feel it necessary to set out their findings on this particular contentious question in more detail than was desirable in the main text.

As already recorded, eighteen Sea Gladiators were in crates at Kalafrana by April 1940, of which three were allocated to H.M.S. 'Glorious'. By the time hostilities broke out in the Mediterranean area, six Sea Gladiators (N5519, 5520, 5523, 5524, 5529 and 5531) had been assembled for use by the Hal Far Fighter Flight. These six were flown regularly on operations during the ensuing months. One (N5519) was shot down on 31 July, when Flg.Off. Peter Hartley was severely burned, but this was the only recorded instance of a Malta-based Gladiator being totally destroyed in air combat. Obviously, others suffered varying degrees of combat and accidental damage; others, or the same aircraft, were damaged on the ground by bomb splinters, blast, fire etc.

It would appear that of the remaining nine 'unassembled' Gladiators, all but three were used as spares for those six which had been issued to the Fighter Flight. Records show that N5535 and two others were despatched, still crated, to Egypt. N5535 was later flown to 805 Squadron at Maleme, Crete; following operational sorties this particular aircraft was one of the few to survive the fighting, and it was flown back to Egypt on 11 May 1941. It will be seen therefore, that at least six Gladiators – not three – aided in the defence of Malta. Group Captain George Burges offers an explanation for the legend of the 'immortal trio':

"From time to time people refer to the story of 'Faith, Hope and Charity'. Reference to Admiralty records proves that there were quite a few other Gladiators on the island when hostilities with Italy started. We were certainly given four aircraft to set up the Hal Far Flight, and there were certainly some others at Kalafrana in crates and from time to time aircraft with other 'rudder numbers' appeared to replace casualties. Whether these other aircraft had been complete in their crates I do not know. An enormous amount of improvisation had to go on to keep aircraft operational and a 'new' fuselage would have 'second-hand' wings or engine. As the 'rudder number' was on the fuselage this would seem to be yet another new aircraft."

369

"Thus it was only during our training period, before the war started for us, and for only about the first week or ten days of the war period that the population ever saw three Gladiators in the air together – from then on it was two and sometimes only one. During this period none of us ever heard the aircraft referred to as 'Faith, Hope and Charity' and I do not know who first used the description. Nevertheless, the sentiment was appropriate because the civil population certainly prayed for us and displayed such photographs as they could get hold of. There is no doubt that the Gladiators did not 'wreak death and destruction' to many of the enemy, but equally they had a very profound effect on the morale of everybody in the island, and most likely stopped the Italians just using the island as a practice bombing range whenever they felt like it."

According to author Kenneth Poolman in his 1954 book entitled appropriately 'Faith, Hope and Charity', credit for the naming of the Gladiators as such should be accorded to Flg. Off. John Waters, although contemporaries of his have since denied knowledge of any such names at the time, attributing these names to journalists at a later date. From this distance one can only record recollections of those directly involved, however they may conflict. The following extracts are from notes recorded in early 1941 by a newly-arrived Hurricane pilot, the Australian John Pain: "All the hangars (at Hal Far) had been hit, but there were a few aircraft in them and in one was 'Hope' of the famous Malta trio. She was in the throes of becoming a six-gun Gladiator, the only one in the RAF, but she received a bomb smack through the centre section and that was the finish of her (this was probably N5531 destroyed in the raid on Hal Far on 4th. February – Ed.) 'Charity' had gone a little while before in a dogfight (Obviously Flg.Off. Peter Hartley's N5519 shot down the previous July – Ed.); 'Faith' was left."

John Pain's reference to 'Hope' being modified into a 'six-gun Gladiator' coincides with Kenneth Poolman's account: "However, there was one other Gladiator, crippled from continuous damage both in the air and on the ground, which had been written off as unserviceable. Louks (Sqn.Ldr. Louks, the Command Engineering Officer – Ed.) took this machine and had it patched up. He took a more efficient propeller from another unserviceable machine and fitted it to the Gladiator. Then he improved the armament. The four machine guns of the Gladiator had never really supplied enough fire power. If this machine was to shoot down Stukas he would have to increase its gun power. He did this by mounting two additional guns on the top wing, Great War fashion. When these modifications were finally complete the old Gladiator really looked like something from the old Western Front, as if Mannock or Ball or Bishop had flown in to help the Hurricanes of Malta. Looking at it in the half light of evening out on the grass in front of the hangar, with its biplane wings and guns mounted on the top plane, it looked a bit like a cross between a Nieuport Scout and a SE5A."

Air Commodore Carter Jonas, then Wg.Cdr. Commanding RAF Luqa, recorded in his 1943 unpublished manuscript: "But unique among the aircraft we possessed, and perhaps amongst aircraft produced during the last few years, yet typical of our constant shortages in Malta and our makeshift remedies, was the 'Bleariator'. The Bleariator owed its original conception and subsequent development, to an ingenious and capable Engineer Officer; who having a number of severely damaged aircraft in his workshops, and seeing no chance of ever obtaining any spares, decided to construct a fighter of his own design. The Bleariator originally started life as a Gladiator, but having been badly 'shot up' in combat, its engine was considerably damaged, and various portions of its mainplanes were practically unrepairable. A bomb blasted Blenheim and a damaged Swordfish, however, provided the missing components, and Bleariator was finally tested by the designer himself; powered with a Blenheim engine and Swordfish wingtips. The flight test was certainly encouraging as the performance as a whole, and particularly the climb, was considerably in advance of the more orthodox Gladiator. Before, however, the eagerly awaited day when the Bleariator should have gone into action for the first time, it was unfortunately destroyed on the ground by a near miss from an Italian bomb."

By the end of October 1940, A.H.Q. recorded that one Gladiator had been lost in combat and one badly damaged on the ground. By the end of December, four Gladiators were still reported as being on the strength of 261 Squadron, and indeed, three were scrambled in response to a radar plot on 25 January 1941. A.H.Q. subsequently recorded that four Gladiators were still with 261 Squadron at the end of January, and that these were then transferred to 806 Squadron, Fleet Air Arm. One of these was burnt out and two more were damaged during a raid on Hal Far on 4 February. The surviving Gladiator was then delegated to the less glamorous but equally important task of meteorological flights. Flt.Lt. Jim Pickering recalls: "I am not sure who flew that last surviving Gladiator on Met. flights – possibly F.A.A. pilots – but I can remember on one occasion when three 109s tried to shoot it down – the Gladiator pilot's R/T transmissions graphically described his distress at their attentions, which he evaded only by being able to turn inside each successive pass by the 109s." It is interesting to note that O.K.W. credited the Luftwaffe with shooting down two Gladiators during 1941, whilst operating over Malta.

This last surviving Gladiator is believed to have been N5520. However, mystery surrounds it's fate. In a recent publication, historian A. Coleman states that N5520 was last flown in June 1941, when Sgt. A.W. Jolly of 185 Squadron ground-looped this aircraft on landing from a Met. flight, and that "N5520 spent some time parked outside a hangar until a bomb hit the hangar, dealing the biplane the final blow with its blast." This was not strictly the case, as Sgt. F.G. Sheppard, also of 185 Squadron, has recorded in his logbook that he flew N5520 on Met. flights in January 1942! It is possible however, that N5520 was badly damaged during the 'Blitz' on Malta during 1942.

Sea Gladiator N5520 "Faith"

As any visitor to the National War Museum at Fort St. Elmo, Valetta, will see, N5520 "Faith" has been lovingly restored. The restoration was carried out in 1973 by an R.A.F. team from Luqa, headed by Chief Technician 'Curly' Alcock. The skeleton of N5520 was 'rediscovered' in 1943 in a disused quarry near Kalafrana and after being lightly repaired and decorated, was presented to the people of Malta on 3 September, 1943, by Air Vice-Marshal Sir Keith Park. For the next 22 years, N5520 was displayed in the Palace Armoury in Valetta, having been refurbished in 1961 by No.103 Maintenance Unit; here it remained until the opening of the National War Museum in May 1973.

There has been much discussion as to whether the Gladiator is really N5520. In 1957 author William Green published the following opinion: "The so-called 'Faith' presented to Malta, even assuming that one of the Sea Gladiators on the Island in 1940 was so named, displays no evidence of ever having been flown at all. The wing attachment points are still inhibited by the manufacturer's red lead, the stringers are in mint condition, and the engine has obviously been fitted afterwards. It shows no battle damage whatsoever, and the constructor's number which should appear on the fuselage frames and cabane struts has been carefully sandpapered off and painted over. According to the plaque accompanying the aircraft, this Sea Gladiator was N5520, but other sources have referred to 'Faith' as N5519, and yet the popularly accepted account states that 'Faith' was the last survivor of the trio." ('Famous Fighters of the Second World War', Macdonald, 1957)

However A. Coleman disagrees: "Some say that it is the remains of one of the spare aircraft that were cannibalized for spares and never flew. A closer inspection shows otherwise. Several modifications to the original airframe are apparent, mainly around the engine mounting, with additional frames probably indicating conversion to a Blenheim Mercury. Several expert airmen who inspected the Gladiator are all of the opinion that the airframe shows clear structural fatigue as well as indications of a heavy landing; one of the legs is cracked inside the fuselage. After a long search a serial number was found engraved on the rudder post on the front, hidden inside the fuselage, and this clearly reads N5520. Another serial not so clear and stencilled was found behind the plate underneath the elevators and lightly painted over in silver paint, and again on the inside of the fuselage. All other manufacturer's plates and markings had been rubbed off (wartime censorship?) except these two which are too well hidden anyway. The most interesting point about this relic is the armour behind the pilot's seat, taking us back to local modifications of May 1940, which was fitted only to the first four aircraft built and certainly not to the ones still crated. This proves without a shadow of doubt that the preserved aircraft is one of the four Gladiators originally assembled and which kept on flying well into 1941." ('Air Pictorial', July 1978)

It would appear conclusively that the aircraft on display at the National War Museum is N5520. However, whether this particular aircraft was originally named 'Faith' seems still in doubt.

Following the wide range of modifications and improvisations which have been in part referred to above, a report was submitted to A.H.Q. on 10 February 1941 from R.A.F. Hal Far, which stated; "All the Gladiators were fitted with variable pitch airscrews in addition to the armour plate and a marked increase in climb and a slight increase in speed was obtained. One was also fitted with six guns but this unfortunately was destroyed on the ground by enemy action the day it was completed." The Engineer Officer responsible was Sqn.Ldr. A.E. Louks.

Air combat claims

As far as can be determined, Malta's Gladiators claimed at least nine air combat victories, with at least another five enemy aircraft claimed as damaged. Of these claims at least three, possibly four, were claimed by pilots flying N5520.

Appendix IV

261 SQUADRON – A Brief History

The Squadron was formed in 1918 as a flyingboat unit at Felixstowe, but was disbanded shortly after. It was reformed officially on 16 August 1940 at Hal Far, Malta. However, in practical terms it had actually formed ten days previously, following the arrival of 418 Flight from the United Kingdom, and by amalgamation with the Fighter Flight at Hal Far. It would remain on Malta until 21 May 1941, on which date it was again disbanded and the majority of its pilots dispersed; some went to the newly-formed 185 Squadron at Hal Far, some to ferrying duties with the A.D.U. at Takoradi, others to non-flying duties elsewhere. Only a handful of pilots remained to be absorbed into the new 261 Squadron, which reformed at Habbaniya (Iraq), when 127 Squadron was renumbered as 261, on 12 July 1941.

During August 1941 the squadron moved to Shaibah (Iraq) for operational patrols over the oil ports of Abadan and Khorramshar, Iran. Then for a brief period, it was involved in the occupation of the Iranian oilfields, when an Iranian Air Force Audax was shot down by the C.O. Detachments were sent to Palestine and Cyprus and by early 1942 the squadron was fully based on Palestinian soil. It was here that it was learnt that the squadron would be despatched to Java, in company with other fighter units, in an effort to stem the Japanese invasion of South-East Asia. In company with 30 Squadron, 261 was embarked on H.M.S. 'Indomitable', but as this carrier was about to leave news was received that Java had been invaded, and their destination was changed to Ceylon. There now remained only five pilots who had served with the unit on Malta – Flt.Lt. J.V. Marshall, Flg.Off. C.F. Counter, F/Sgt. T.A. Quinn, Sgt. P.L. Jordan and Sgt. G. Lockwood.

By 8 March 1942 the squadron was based at China Bay, sharing the airfield with 273 Squadron. It was from here that they took part in interceptions of Japanese carrier aircraft attacking Ceylon on 9 April – the second such attack to be carried out by the Japanese in a four day period. Of sixteen Hurricanes flown by 261 Squadron pilots in this action, eight were either shot down or crash-landed, with another three damaged; two pilots were killed and four wounded, whilst claims submitted against the intruders totalled eight destroyed and 12 damaged.

After a period of training and re-equipment, the squadron returned to operations in February 1943, on the Burma Front, and would remain in this theatre until the end of the war. In June 1944 the squadron received Republic Thunderbolt fighter-bombers, and flew these until disbandment at Tanjore on 26 September 1945. During this period of operations over Burma, 261's main roles included ground strafing in support of the Army, and the provision of escorts to supply-dropping Dakota transports. Only on a few rare occasions were Japanese aircraft encountered in the air.

Air Combat Claims

Malta	August 1940 – May 1941	100+
Iran	August 1941	1
Ceylon	April 1942	8 plus 12 damaged
Burma	February 1943 – June 1945	5 plus 4 probables

Commanding Officers

Sqn.Ldr. D.W. Balden	August 1940 – December 1940
Sqn.Ldr. A.J. Trumble	December 1940 – February 1941
Sqn.Ldr. R.N. Lambert	February 1941 – May 1941
Sqn.Ldr. C.D. Whittingham	May 1941 – June 1941
Sqn.Ldr. E.M. Mason, D.F.C.	July 1941 – January 1942
Sqn.Ldr. D.R. Walker	January 1942 – March 1942
Sqn.Ldr. A.G. Lewis, D.F.C. & Bar	March 1942 – June 1942
Sqn.Ldr. R.T.P. Davidson	June 1942 – August 1942
Sqn.Ldr. E.R.G. Downey	August 1942 – July 1943
Sqn.Ldr. R.N.H. Courtney	July 1943 – December 1943
Sqn.Ldr. C.F. Counter, D.F.C.	December 1943 – March 1944
Sqn.Ldr. R.E.A. Mason	March 1944 – December 1944
Sqn.Ldr. R.H. Fletcher	December 1944 – June 1945
Sqn.Ldr. J.R. Graham	June 1945 – September 1945

Flying Personnel – Malta, August 1940 – May 1941
On formation an amalgamation of 418 Flight and the Hal Far Fighter Flight took place:

Sqn.Ldr. D.W. Balden	First C.O. – to H.Q. Luqa Dec. 40 – C.O. R.A.F. Luqa Feb. 41. To M.E.; C.O. 112 Sqn. Jun. 41 – Oct. 41 – then non-operational. Retired as Wg.Cdr. 1966.
Flt.Lt. A.J. Trumble	'A' Flt.cmdr. – C.O. Dec. 40 – Feb. 41 – H.Q., M.E. Feb. 41 – to Crete Apr. 41 – P.O.W. May 41. Retired as Gp.Capt. O.B.E., 1956.
Flt.Lt. J. Greenhalgh	'B' Flt.cmdr. – to A.H.Q. Dec. 40 – Wg.Cdr. i/c Blenheims, Oct. 41 – Jan. 42 – non-operational – retired as Gp.Capt. 1953.

Flt.Lt. R.N. Lambert	'A' Flt.cmdr. Dec. 40 – C.O. Feb. 41 – May 41 – to U.K. – Sqn.Ldr. in 236 Sqn. 1942; C.O. 143 Sqn. 1943; C.O. 272 Sqn. 1944 (wounded in action); Retired as Wg.Cdr., D.F.C.
Flt.Lt. G. Burges, D.F.C.	ex Fighter Flight – to 69 Sqn. Jan. 41 – Jun. 41 – non operational – retired as Gp. Capt., O.B.E., D.F.C.
Flg.Off. J. Waters	ex Fighter Flight – Flt.cmdr. Dec. 40 – to U.K. Apr. 41 – non operational – retired as Wg.Cdr., A.F.C. – killed in accident 18 Jan. 1971.
Flg.Off. F.F. Taylor, D.F.C.	ex Fighter Flight – K.i.A. 26 Feb. 41.
Flg.Off. W.J. Woods, D.F.C.	ex Fighter Flight – to 80 Sqn. in Greece, Jan. 41 (Here claimed a further 3 and 1 shared victories) – K.i.A. 20 Apr. 41.
Flg.Off. H.F.R. Bradbury	Wounded in action 12 Feb. 41 – to H.Q., M.E. – non operational – retired as Sqn.Ldr. 1957.
Flg.Off. R.H. Barber	ex Fighter Flight – to 69 Sqn. May 41 – Aug. 41 – to Rhodesia as instructor 41–44. Served 540 Sqn. (Mosquito P.R.XVI) 44–45 – Transferred R. Rhodesian A.F. – retired as Gp.Capt., D.F.C., A.F.C.
Plt.Off. A.G. McAdam	ex Fighter Flight – to U.K. Apr. 41 – 183 Sqn. 43–44 – K.i.A. 14 Jan. 44 in Typhoon IB as Flt.Lt., D.F.C., A.F.C.
Plt.Off. T. Balmforth	ex Fighter Flight – to U.K. Jan. 41 – 124 Sqn. 42–44 (C.O. June. 42 – Jan. 43 and Jun. 43 – Sep. 44) – claimed 1 further victory – retired as Gp.Capt., D.S.O., D.F.C., A.F.C., 1968.
Sgt. F.N. Robertson, D.F.M.	to U.K. Apr. 41 – commissioned – 60 O.T.U., 54 O.T.U., 219 Sqn. 153 Sqn., 96 Sqn. as night fighter. Killed in night collision with B-17 near Norwich 31 Aug. 43 as Flg.Off.
Sgt. E.N. Kelsey	K.i.A. 19 Jan. 41.
Sgt. O.R. Bowerman	to M.E. Apr. 41 – ferried Hurricane to Greece, then to A.D.U., Takoradi – 260 Sqn. W. Desert, Jul. 42 – 601 Sqn. Oct. 42 – K.i.A. 24 Oct. 42 as Wt.Off.
Sgt. H.W. Ayre	to M.E. Apr. 41 – ferried Hurricane to Greece, then A.D.U., Takoradi – Flt.Lt., A.F.C. later.

376

Sgt. J. Pickering	to M.E. Apr. 41 – ferried Hurricane to Greece, then to A.D.U., Takoradi (later ferried P-40s to A.V.G. in China) – 80 Sqn. 42 – 145 Sqn. 42–43 – C.O. 511 F.R.U., Belgium, 44–45 – retired as Flt.Lt., A.F.C.
Sgt. R. O'Donnell	K.i.A. 15 Aug. 40.
Sgt. R.J. Hyde	to U.K. Apr. 41 – 197 Sqn. 1942/43 as Flt.Lt. – retired as Sqn.Ldr., A.F.C.
Sgt. W.J. Timms	K.i.Accident 11 Jan. 41.
Sgt. D.K. Ashton	K.i.A. 26 Nov. 40.

Reinforcement Flight from 'Argus' 17 November 1940

Flt.Lt. J.A.F. MacLachlan, D.F.C.	'A' Flt.cmdr. Jan. 41 – wounded 16 Feb. 41 – to M.E. Mar. 41 – to U.K. and C.O. 1 Sqn. (where claimed 5 further victories) – to A.F.D.U. 43 (claimed further 3 and 1 shared victories, flying Mustang) Shot down and P.O.W. 18 Jul. 43, but died of injuries from crash 31 Jul. 43 as Sqn.Ldr., D.S.O., D.F.C. + +.
Plt.Off. C.E. Hamilton	attached to 185 Sqn. 12 May 41 – K.i.A. 14 May 41.
Plt.Off. H.W. Eliot	to 185 Sqn. May 41 (Flt.cmdr. Jul. 41) – to U.K. and 242 Sqn. Sep. 41, then 255 Sqn. 42. C.O. 255 Sqn. Aug. 43 – Feb. 44 (2 further victories) – C.O. 256 Sqn. Oct. 44 – Mar. 45 (2 further victories) – K.i.A. 4 Mar. 45 as Wg.Cdr., D.S.O., D.F.C.
Sgt. R.A. Spyer	K.i.A. 22 Mar. 41.
Sgt. J.K. Norwell	to M.E. Apr. 41 – ferried Hurricane to Greece, then to A.D.U., Takoradi – non operational – retired as Flt.Lt., A.F.C.
Sgt. C.S. Bamberger	to U.K. Jun. 41 – Central Gunnery School Jul. 41 – Apr. 42 – 93 Sqn. May 43 – Aug. 43 (1 further victory) – 243 Sqn. Aug. 43 – Aug. 44 (2 further victories) – Sqn.Ldr., D.F.C. – retired 1959.

Reinforcements from Middle East, 20 January 1941

Plt.Off. P.A. Worrall	to M.E. May 41 – to Burma 42 and Flt.cmdr. 136 Sqn. K.i.Flying accident May 42 as Flt.Lt.
Plt.Off. P. Wyatt-Smith	to M.E. May 41 – 73 Sqn. 41/42 (Flt.Lt.); killed as Flt.Lt. in flying acc at 20 M.U. 5 Jan. 45.

| Plt.Off. J.J. Walsh | died from injuries 25 Feb. 41. |
| Plt.Off. I.R. Currie | died from illness 31 Jan. 41. |

Reinforcement Flight from Middle East, 29 January 1941

Flg.Off. C.D. Whittingham	'B' Flt.cmdr. Feb. 41 – C.O. May 41 – to M.E. May 41 – non operational – retired as Sqn.Ldr. Died post-war.
Plt.Off. J.F. Pain	to M.E. May 41 – A.D.U., Takoradi – 73 Sqn 42 (1 further victory) – C.O. 26 A.A.C.U. 43 – 20 M.U. 43 – returned to Australia. Retired as Flt.Lt. Died 12 Sep. 80.
Plt.Off. P.J. Kearsey	K.i.A. 26 Feb. 41.
Plt.Off. D.J. Thacker	wounded 12 Feb. 41 – to M.E. – A.D.U., Takoradi – Flt.Lt., A.F.C. by mid-44. 151 Sqn. 44/45 (Sqn.Ldr.)
Plt.Off. D.J. Hammond	to M.E. due to ill health Apr. 41. Flt.Lt. by 1945. Sqn.Ldr. later.
Plt.Off. C.E. Langdon	K.i.A. 26 Feb. 41.
Sgt. A.H. Deacon	to M.E. – A.D.U., Takoradi 41–42 – to South Africa as instructor – 31 Sqn. as Flt.Lt. 45.
Sgt. C.W. McDougal	K.i.A. 5 Mar. 41.
Sgt. C.G. Hodson	attached 185 Sqn. May 41 – 242 Sqn. 42/43 as Plt.Off. (1 shared victory) – Flt.Lt. later.

Reinforcements from Middle East, 30 January 1941

Flg.Off. S.R. Peacock-Edwards	'A' Flt.cmdr. Feb. 41 – to M.E. May 41 – to South Africa 41 – 258 Sqn. Ceylon 42 (1 further victory) – C.O. 30 Sqn. Feb. 43 – May 44 – retired as Sqn.Ldr., D.F.C. 1958.
Plt.Off. A.J. Rippon	to M.E. May 41 – to A.D.U., Takoradi – 107 Sqn. (Mosquito F.B. VI) 44 – K.i.A. as Flt. Lt., D.F.C. 25 Aug. 44.
Plt.Off. C.F. Counter	to M.E. May 41 – to Iraq with reformed 261 Sqn. – Ceylon 42 (1 victory) – C.O. Dec. 43 – May 44 – retired 1958 as Wg.Cdr. D.F.C.
Sgt. L. Davies	to M.E. May 41 – to A.D.U., Takoradi.
Sgt. A.G. Todd	to M.E. May 41 – to 128 Sqn. 41–42 – to A.D.U., Takoradi – 164 Sqn. 44 (1 victory) as Flt.Lt., D.F.C. – retired as Wg.Cdr. 1958.
Sgt. L.J. Dexter	to U.K. Jun. 41. Flt.Lt. later.

Reinforcement pilots from Malta–based units

Flt.Lt. G. Watson	ex 148 Sqn. Wellington pilot – K.i.A. 12 Feb. 41.
Flg.Off. J.H.T. Foxton	ex 69 Sqn. Maryland pilot – K.i.A. 22 Mar. 41.
Flg.Off. G.H. Bellamy	ex 3 A.A.C.U. pilot – to M.E. May 41; 73 Sqn. 41/42 (Flt.Lt.) – to India 42–43 – Sqn.Ldr.

Reinforcement flight from Middle East, 6 March 1941

Plt.Off. C.K. Gray	wounded 6 May 41 – to U.K. Aug. 41 – 124 Sqn. 43 – retired as Wg.Cdr., D.F.C., 1963.
Plt.Off. P.A. Mortimer	to U.K. – instructor 42–43 – died of injuries in flying acc. as Flt.Lt. 7 Nov. 42.
Plt.Off. D.M. Whitney	to M.E. – to 128 Sqn. 41–42 – returned to New Zealand, 43; Fighter Instructor 2 Ftr. O.T.U., 2 F.T.S., 1 F.T.S.; Flt.Lt.
Sgt. A. Livingston	to 185 Sqn. May 41 – to 249 Sqn. Jun. 41 – K.i.A. 18 Jun. 41.
Sgt. F.J. Jessop	wounded 7 Mar. 41 – to U.K.
Sgt. H.J. Kelly	to M.E. May 41.
Sgt. J.T. Hitching	to M.E. May 41 – joined reformed 261 Sqn. Jul. 41. retired as Sqn.Ldr., A.F.C., 1958.

Detachment of 274 Squadron sent as reinforcements from Middle East, 17 March 1941

Flg.Off. E.M. Mason, D.F.C.	wounded 13 Apr. 41 – to M.E. – C.O. 261 Sqn. Jul. 41 – Jan. 42 (1 further victory) – C.O. 94 Sqn. Jan. 42 – Feb. 42 – K.i.A. 15 Feb. 42.
Flg.Off. C.J. Laubscher	to M.E. May 41 – rejoined reformed 261 Sqn. Jul. 41 – to 2 Sqn., S.A.A.F. as Flt.cmdr. Jan. 42 – Jun. 42 – instructor to Turkish Air Force – rejoined 2 Sqn., S.A.A.F. late 42 after transferring to S.A.A.F. (2 and 1 shared further victories with this squadron during two tours). C.O. 11 Sqn. S.A.A.F. 43–44 as Maj., D.F.C.
Flg.Off. J.S. Southwell	K.i.A. 22 Mar. 41.
Plt.Off. D.F. Knight	K.i.A. 22 Mar. 41.
Plt.Off. T.B. Garland	K.i.A. 22 Mar. 41.
Sgt. T.A. Quinn	to M.E. May 41 – joined reformed 261 Sqn. Jul. 41 – to Ceylon Mar. 42 – K.i.Flying acc. as F/Sgt. 7 Apr.42.

Sgt. M.P. Davies	to M.E. May 41 – to A.D.U., Takoradi – K.i.Accident.
Sgt. R.J. Goode	wounded 28 Mar. 41 – to U.K. – 65 Sqn. 42 – K.i.A. 29 Jun. 42.

Reinforcement flight from 'Ark Royal', 3 April 1941

Flt.Lt. P.W.O. Mould, D.F.C.	formed 185 Sqn. May 41 (C.O. until Oct. 41) – K.i.A. 1 Oct. 41 after 1 further victory, as Sqn.Ldr. D.F.C. +.
Flg.Off. I.B. Westmacott	to 185 Sqn. 'B' Flt.cmdr. May 41 – wounded 13 May 41 – C.O. 1435 Flt. Dec. 41 – Apr. 42 – O.C. R.A.F. Safi Mar. 43 – Nov. 43 – retired as Wg.Cdr., D.F.C., 1958.
Flg.Off. H.F. Auger	K.i.A. 23 Apr. 41.
Plt.Off. J.V. Marshall	to M.E. May 41 – joined reformed 261 Sqn. Jul. 41 – to Ceylon Mar. 42 as Flt.cmdr. – to Burma (1 victory) – C.O. 5 Sqn. Nov. 43 – Mar. 44 – C.O. 81 Sqn. Mar. 44 – Oct. 44. – retired as Gp.Capt., D.F.C., 1970.
Plt.Off. P. Kennett	K.i.A. 11 Apr. 41.
Sgt. J.K. Pollard	to M.E. May 41 – K.i.acc. as F/Sgt. 12 Dec. 41 (55 O.T.U.)
Sgt. E.R. Jessop	to M.E. May 41 – K.i.acc. 15 Nov. 41, Palestine.
Sgt. G. Lockwood	to M.E. May 41 – joined reformed 261 Sqn. Jul. 41 – to Ceylon Mar. 42.
Sgt. B.J. Vardy	to 185 Sqn. May 41 – Dec. 41.
Sgt. H.H. Jennings	K.i. acc. 7 May 41.
Sgt. G.A. Walker	to M.E. May 41.
Sgt. P.H. Waghorn	K.i.A. 11 Apr. 41.

Reinforcement flight from 'Ark Royal', 27 April 1941

Flt.Lt. C.G.St.D. Jeffries	to 185 Sqn. May 41 ('A' Flt.cmdr.) – claimed 2 victories with unit – to M.E. Oct. 41 – to Burma, C.O. 155 Sqn. Nov. 42 – Nov. 43 (1 further victory) – retired as Wg.Cdr., D.F.C. +, 1967.
Flg.Off. N.P.W. Hancock	to 185 Sqn. May 41 – 'B' Flt.cmdr. – to M.E. Sep. 41 – C.O. 250 Sqn. Nov. 42 – Feb. 43 (1 further victory, plus 4 on ground) – C.O. 2 Sqn. R. Egyptian A.F. 43 – Wg.Cdr., D.F.C. – retired 1958.
Flg.Off. N.A.R. Doughty	to M.E. May 41 – joined reformed 261 Sqn. Jul. 41 as Flt.cmdr. – retired as Sqn.Ldr. 1958.
Plt.Off. P.D. Thompson	to 185 Sqn. May 14 – Flt.cmdr. Sep. 41 (Claimed further victories)

	– 601 Sqn. 43 – 44 (Flt.cmdr. – claimed 2 e/a on ground) – C.O. 129 Sqn. Jul. 44 – Apr. 45 (claimed 5 V–1s shot down)– retired as Gp.Capt., D.F.C., 1975.
Plt.Off. R.A. Innes	wounded 1 May 41 – to U.K. Aug. 41 – retired as Sqn.Ldr. 1961.
Plt.Off. P.J.A. Thompson	K.i.A. 13 May 41.
Plt.Off. B.M. Cavan	to 185 Sqn. May 41 – to 249 Sqn. Jul. 41 – K.i.A. 20 Dec. 41 as Flg.Off.
Plt.Off. R.C. Graves	to M.E. May 41 – 30 Sqn. 41–42 as Flg.Off. in Ceylon. Flt.Lt. by 1945.
Plt.Off. A.J. Reeves	to 185 Sqn. May 41 – with 74 Sqn. 42–45 (C.O. Dec. 44 – May 45) – Sqn.Ldr., D.F.C.+.
Plt.Off. G.G. Bailey	to 185 Sqn. May 41 – to 249 Sqn. Jun. 41 – returned 185 Sqn. Jul. 41 – K.i.A. 9 Nov. 41 as Flg.Off.
Plt.Off. J.H.S. Haig	to M.E. May 41.
Plt.Off. D. Winton	to 185 Sqn. May 41 – to M.N.F.U. (claimed 1 victory) – to M.E. 42 – to Burma 43 (C.O. 155 Sqn. Nov. 43 – May 44) – Sqn.Ldr., D.F.C.
Plt.Off. J.E. Hall	wounded 4 May 41 – Controller duties whilst recovering; att. 185 Sqn. Oct. 41 – Dec. 41 (Flt. Lt.) – U.K. May 42.
Plt.Off. D.C.B. Robertson	to 185 Sqn. May 41 – to 249 Sqn. Jul. 41 – to M.N.F.U. Aug. 41.
Plt.Off. A.S. Dredge	wounded 6 May 41 – to U.K. – C.O. 3 Sqn. (5 V–1s) Oct. 43–Aug. 44–K.i. flying accident 18 May 45 as Wg.Cdr., D.S.O., D.F.C.
Plt.Off. R.T. Saunders	to 185 Sqn. May 41 – to 249 Sqn. Jun. 41 – wounded 12 Jun. 41 – to U.K. Aug. 41.
Sgt. H. Burton	to M.E. May 41. 501 Sqn. 44(2 V–1s). Flt.Lt.
Sgt. E.L. Lawrence	to M.E. May 41.
Sgt. R.A. Branson	to 185 Sqn. May 41 – retired as Flt.Lt., A.F.C., 1963.
Sgt. P.L. Jordan	to M.E. May 41 – joined reformed 261 Sqn. Jul. 41 – to Ceylon Mar. 42 – to Burma Feb. 43 as Flt.Lt. – returned to New Zealand.
Sgt. A.W. Jolly	to 185 Sqn. May 41 – loaned to 46 Sqn. Jun. 41 – returned to 185 Sqn. – 41 Sqn. 44 as Flt.Lt. – 610 Sqn. 45.
Sgt.R.Ottey	K.i. flying acc. 2 May 41.
Sgt. B.C. Walmsley	wounded 1 May 41 – to M.E. May 41.

Sgt. F.G. Sheppard	to 185 Sqn. May 41 – loaned to 249 Sqn. Jun. 41 – returned 185 Sqn. until early 42 – died post-war in Australia.
Sgt. D.C. Smith	to M.E. May 41.
Sgt. E.V. Wynne	to 185 Sqn. May 41 – K.i.A. 15 May 41.

Of the Fighter Flight pilots who did not join 261 Squadron, the following is known:

Sqn.Ldr. A.C. Martin	O.C. R.A.F. Hal Far May 41 – returned U.K. May 41 – 40 Sqn. as Flt.cmdr. – K.i.A. 26 Aug. 41.
Plt.Off. P.B. Alexander	to Gibraltar 40 and joined 202 Sqn. K.i.flying accident 21 Feb. 42 as Flt.Lt.
Plt.Off. W.R.C. Sugden	to 3 A.A.C.U. Jul. 40 – Sep. 40 – to Spotter Flight Oct. 40 – Feb. 41 – Station Flt., Hal Far Feb. 41 – Sep. 41 – to U.K. Sep. 41 – joined 464 Sqn, R.A.A.F. Sep. 42 – shot down and P.O.W. 19 Mar. 44 as Sqn.Ldr.
Sgt. L.F. Ashbury	to Station Flt., Hal Far, Jun, 40 – to 148 Sqn. Feb. 41 – to R.A.F. Luqa Mar. 41.

Below appears a reproduction of Pilots Routine Orders, 261 Squadron, August 1940. Programme, prior to forming two Flights:

Pilots' Routine

		'A' Flight	'B' Flight	'C' Flight
Blue	1	Flt.Lt. D.W. Balden	Flt.Lt. A.J. Trumble	Flt.Lt. J. Greenhalgh
	2	Flt.Lt. G. Burges	Flt.Lt. R.N. Lambert	Flg.Off. F.F. Taylor
Red	1	Plt.Off. R.H. Barber	Plt.Off. T. Balmforth	Sgt. H.W. Ayre
	2	Sgt. R.J. Hyde	Sgt. J. Pickering	Plt.Off. A.G. McAdam
Green	1	Sgt. E.N. Kelsey	Sgt. D.K. Ashton	Sgt. O.R. Bowerman
	2	Sgt. R. O'Donnell	Sgt. F.N. Robertson	Sgt. W.J. Timms

Reserves: Sqn.Ldr. A.C. Martin
Flt.Lt. H.F.R. Bradbury
Flg.Off. J. Waters
Flg.Off. W.J. Woods

Date	0430–0830	0830–1230	1230–1630	1630–2030
6 Aug.	A	B	A	B
7 Aug.	B	C	B	C
8 Aug.	C	A	C	A
9 Aug.	A	B	A	B
10 Aug.	B	C	B	C
11 Aug.	C	A	C	A

Important

Each Flight will report to the Operations Room 10 minutes before taking over its respective watch in order to receive any new instructions.

All microphones will be handed in to the Operations Room on the cessation of each watch by each Pilot.

Flying gear will be kept in the Look Out Tower above the Operations Room.

Each Pilot must ensure from the Signals Section that his microphone is serviceable prior to taking over watch from another Pilot.

Off Duty Crew

The crew who are off duty will notify the Control Officer in the Operations Room of all their movements when they leave the Camp. Telephone numbers must be made known if possible.

_____

N.B. In theory, this was for manning six aircraft at all times by day, two of which were Gladiators. It was quickly changed to include manning of one or two Hurricanes against night attacks.

Appendix V

R.A.F. PILOTS CLAIMING FIVE OR MORE VICTORIES
FLYING FROM MALTA, 1940–41

		Malta	*Total for War*
Sgt. F.N. Robertson, D.F.M.	261 Sqn.	10	12
Wg.Cdr. A.C. Rabagliati, D.F.C.+	46, 126 Sqns.	$8\frac{1}{4}$	$16\frac{1}{4}$
Flt.Lt. J.A.F. MacLachlan, D.F.C+	261 Sqn.	8	$16\frac{1}{2}$
Flt.Lt. G. Burges, D.F.C.	Ftr.Flt., 261 Sqn.	7	7
Flg.Off. F.F. Taylor, D.F.C.	Ftr.Flt., 261 Sqn.	7	7
Plt.Off. H.P. Lardner-Burke, D.F.C.	126 Sqn.	6	$8\frac{1}{2}$
Sqn.Ldr. R.A. Barton, D.F.C.+	249 Sqn.	$5\frac{1}{2}$	14
Plt.Off. D.U. Barnwell, D.F.C.	185 Sqn., M.N.F.U.	5+2 shares	5+2 shares
Flg.Off. W.J. Woods, D.F.C.	Ftr.Flt., 261 Sqn.	5	$8\frac{1}{2}$
Flt.Lt. J. Waters	Ftr.Flt., 261 Sqn.	5	5
Plt.Off. C.E. Hamilton	261 Sqn.	5	5
Sgt. R.J. Hyde	261 Sqn.	5	5
Plt.Off. A.J. Rippon	261 Sqn.	5	5

N.B. Plt.Off. J. Pain (261 Sqn.) claimed 6 victories and 5 probables over Malta but was apparently only credited with 3 of the 6 'confirmed'; his final total claims amounted to 6 confirmed and 9 probables.

N.B. Flg.Off. A. Warburton DFC+ and his Maryland crew of 431 Flt. and 69 Squadron claimed 5 in air combat plus 3 on the ground.

Ranks and decorations shown at time of serving with relevant designated squadrons.

ROYAL NAVY PILOTS CLAIMING FIVE OR MORE VICTORIES WHILST FLYING OVER THE MEDITERRANEAN 1940–41:

		Mediterranean	*Total for War*
Sub Lt. A.J. Sewell, D.S.C.	806 Sqn.	$9\frac{1}{2}$*	$9\frac{1}{2}$
Sub Lt. S.G. Orr, D.S.C.+	806 Sqn.	8	$8\frac{1}{2}$
Lt. R.C. Tillard, D.S.C.	808 Sqn.	$5\frac{5}{6}$	$5\frac{5}{6}$
Lt. W.L.LeC. Barnes, D.S.C.	806 Sqn.	$5\frac{1}{2}$	$5\frac{5}{6}$
Lt.Cdr. C.L.G. Evans, D.S.O., D.S.C.	806 Sqn.	$5\frac{1}{3}$	$6\frac{1}{3}$
Cdr. C.L. Keighley-Peach, D.S.O.	H.M.S. 'Eagle'	5	5
Lt. P.D.J. Sparke, D.S.C.++	806 Sqn.	5	5
Sub Lt. G.A. Hogg, D.S.C.+	806 Sqn.	5*	5

*N.B. These two pilots may have made additional claims whilst flying from Hal Far, January, 1941.

N.B. Lt. D. Vincent-Jones, D.S.C.+, Senior Observer of 806 Squadron, participated in at least 7 victories claimed by his pilots. Similarly, Lt. M.F. Somerville, D.S.C., Senior Observer of 808 Squadron participated in all of Lt. Tillard's claims.

N.B. The FAA claims totals compiled of mainly shared victories.

ROLL OF HONOUR; BRITISH AND COMMONWEALTH FIGHTER PILOTS WHO LOST THEIR LIVES FLYING FROM MALTA, 1940–41

"Propositi Insula Tenax Tenaces Viros Commemorat" (An Island Resolute of Purpose Remembers Resolute Men) – Latin epigram on the Malta Memorial.

1940

16 July	Flt.Lt. Peter Gardner KEEBLE	Fighter Flight
15 August	Sgt. Roy O'DONNELL	261 Squadron
26 November	Sgt. Dennis Kenneth ASHTON	261 Squadron

1941

11 January	Sgt. William John TIMMS	261 Squadron
18 January	Sub Lt. Arthur Stephen GRIFFITH	806 Squadron, F.A.A.
19 January	Sgt. Eric Norman KELSEY	261 Squadron
12 February	Flt.Lt. Gerald WATSON	261 Squadron
25 February	Flg.Off. John Joseph WALSH (Canadian)	261 Squadron
26 February	Flg.Off. Frederic Frank TAYLOR, D.F.C.	261 Squadron
	Plt.Off. Philip James KEARSEY	261 Squadron
	Plt.Off. Charles Edward LANGDON (New Zealander)	261 Squadron
5 March	Sgt. Charles White McDOUGAL	261 Squadron
22 March	Flg.Off. James Henry Terence FOXTON	261 Squadron
	Plt.Off. Dennis Frederick KNIGHT	261 Squadron
	Flg.Off. John Sydney SOUTHWELL	261 Squadron
	Plt.Off. Thomas Benjamin GARLAND	261 Squadron
	Sgt. Richard Alfred SPYER	261 Squadron
11 April	Plt.Off. Peter KENNETT	261 Squadron
	Sgt. Peter Harry WAGHORN	261 Squadron
23 April	Flg.Off. Henri Ferdinand AUGER (Canadian)	261 Squadron
2 May	Sgt. Raymond OTTEY	261 Squadron
7 May	Sgt. Henry Horace JENNINGS	261 Squadron

Date	Name	Unit
13 May	Plt.Off. Peter John Alfred THOMPSON	261 Squadron
14 May	Plt.Off. Claud Eric HAMILTON	185 Squadron
15 May	Sgt. Ernest Victor WYNNE	185 Squadron
11 June	Flt.Lt. Norman Whitmore BURNETT	46 Squadron
12 June	Plt.Off. Rioch Hamish McKenzie MUNRO (Rhodesian)	249 Squadron
	Sgt. Norman MacDonald WALKER	46 Squadron
18 June	Sgt. Alexander LIVINGSTON	249 Squadron
4 July	Sgt. Thomas HACKSTON	126 Squadron
17 July	Sgt. Maurice GUEST	249 Squadron
19 July	F/Sgt. John David McCRACKEN	126 Squadron
26 August	Sgt. John Francis Edgar MALTBY	126 Squadron
4 September	Plt.Off. George Vivian SMITH	249 Squadron
	Sgt. James Cecil KIMBERLEY	249 Squadron
29 September	Plt.Off. Donald William LINTERN	185 Squadron
1 October	Sqn.Ldr. Peter William Olber MOULD, D.F.C.+	185 Squadron
4 October	Plt.Off. Peter John Bryan VEITCH	185 Squadron
14 October	Plt.Off. David Usher BARNWELL, D.F.C.	M.N.F.U.
25 October	Sgt. Ernest George KNIGHT	185 Squadron
9 November	Flg.Off. Graham George BAILEY	185 Squadron
12 November	Wg.Cdr. Mark Henry BROWN, D.F.C.+ (Canadian)	
21 November	F/Sgt. Richard Allinson COUSENS	185 Squadron
19 December	Plt.Off. Edward Elmer STEELE (American)	126 Squadron
20 December	Flg.Off. Brian Moore CAVAN	249 Squadron
	Sgt. Howard MOREN	249 Squadron
21 December	F/Sgt. Brian HAYES	185 Squadron
22 December	Flg.Off. Robert Henry MATTHEWS	249 Squadron
24 December	F/Sgt. Francis Richard EMERY	126 Squadron
29 December	Plt.Off. Merton Campbell BLANCHARD (Canadian)	242 Squadron
	F/Sgt. Alfred James FORTH	185 Squadron
	Flt.Lt. Sidney BRANDT	249 Squadron
	F/Sgt. Roy William LAWSON	249 Squadron

AIRCRAFT DELIVERED TO MALTA BY AIRCRAFT CARRIER, 1940–41

Date	Operation	Carrier(s)	Aircraft Ferried	Aircraft Arriving
1940				
2 August	'Hurry'	'Argus'	12 Hurricanes	12 Hurricanes
17 November	'White'	'Argus'	12 Hurricanes	4 Hurricanes
1941				
3 April	'Winch'	'Ark Royal'	12 Hurricanes	12 Hurricanes
27 April	'Dunlop'	'Ark Royal'	24 Hurricanes	23 Hurricanes
21 May	'Splice'	'Ark Royal' 'Furious'	48 Hurricanes	46 Hurricanes
6 June	'Rocket'	'Ark Royal' 'Furious'	44 Hurricanes	43 Hurricanes
14 June	'Tracer'	'Ark Royal' 'Victorious'	48 Hurricanes	45 Hurricanes
27 June	'Railway I'	'Ark Royal'	22 Hurricanes	21 Hurricanes
30 June	'Railway II'	'Ark Royal' 'Furious'	42 Hurricanes	34 Hurricanes
25 July	'Substance'	'Ark Royal'	7 Swordfish	7 Swordfish
9 September	'Status I'	'Ark Royal'	14 Hurricanes	14 Hurricanes
13 September	'Status II'	'Ark Royal' 'Furious'	46 Hurricanes	45 Hurricanes
18 October	'Callboy'	'Ark Royal'	11 Albacores	11 Albacores
12 November	'Perpetual'	'Argus' 'Ark Royal'	2 Swordfish 37 Hurricanes	1 Swordfish 34 Hurricanes
	14 Operations		361 Hurricanes 9 Swordfish 11 Albacores	333 Hurricanes 8 Swordfish 11 Albacores

N.B. 150 approx. of the Hurricanes delivered flew on to North Africa; about 183, and all the torpedo-bombers remained on Malta.

Appendix VIII

REGIA AERONAUTICA ORDERS OF BATTLE, 1940–41

1. 10 June, 1940. On the outbreak of war, strength in Sicily was as follows:

2ᵘ Squadra Aerea, H.Q. Palermo; Generale S.A. Gennaro Tedeschini Lalli

Fighters

1ᵘ Div. Aerea C.T. 'Aquila', H.Q. Palermo; Gen. D.A. Vincenzo Velardi

1° Stormo C.T., H.Q. Trapani; Ten.Col. Mario Piccinini
17° Gruppo (71ᵃ, 72ᵃ, 80ᵃ Squadriglia)   26 Fiat CR 32   Magg. Bruno Brambilla   Palermo
157° Gruppo (384ᵃ, 385ᵃ, 386ᵃ Squadriglia)   17 Fiat CR 42   Magg. Guido Nobili   Trapani
6° Gruppo Auton. C.T.
(79ᵃ, 81ᵃ, 88ᵃ Squadriglia)   26 Macchi C.200   Ten.Col. Armando Francois
                                                                                            Catania

Bombers

3ᵃ Div. Aerea B.T. 'Centauro', H.Q. Catania; Gen. D.A. Ettore Lodi

11° Stormo B.T., H.Q. Comiso; Col. Arnaldo Lubelli
33° Gruppo (59ᵃ, 60ᵃ Squadriglia)   33 Savoia S.79   Ten.Col. Ferri Forte
34° Gruppo (67ᵃ, 68ᵃ Squadriglia)   Ten.Col. Vittorio Cannaviello

34° Stormo B.T., H.Q. Catania; Col. Umberto Mazzini
52° Gruppo (214ᵃ, 215ᵃ Squadriglia)   27 Savoia S.79   Magg. Paolo Maiorca*
53° Gruppo (216ᵃ, 217ᵃ Squadriglia)   Ten.Col. Luigi Rossetti

41° Stormo B.T., H.Q. Gela; Col. Enrico Pezzi
59° Gruppo (232ᵃ, 233ᵃ Squadriglia)†   18 Savoia S.79   Ten.Col. Emilio Draghelli
60° Gruppo (234ᵃ, 235ᵃ Squadriglia)   Ten.Col. Pasquale d'Ippolito

*On 16 June 53° Gruppo B.T. was taken over by Ten.Col. Renato Poli.
†At this time the 59° Gruppo B.T. was detached on the mainland at Bresso. It flew in to join the stormo on 30 June, bringing 15 more S.79s.

389

11ᵃ Div. Aerea B.T. 'Nibbio', H.Q. Castelvetrano; Gen. B.A. Giuseppe Barba

30° Stormo B.T., H.Q. Sciacca; Col. Antonio Serra
  87° Gruppo (192ª, 193ª Squadriglia)   27 Savoia S.79   Ten.Col. Vincenzo Tabocchini
  90° Gruppo (194ª, 195ª Squadriglia)   Ten.Col. Gennaro La Manna

36° Stormo B.T., H.Q. Castelvetrano; Col. Carlo Drago
  108° Gruppo (256ª, 257ª Squadriglia)   32 Savoia S.79   Ten.Col. Virgilio Silvestri
  109° Gruppo (258ª, 259ª Squadriglia)   Ten.Col. Ugo Vincenzi

96° Gruppo B.a.T., Pantelleria; Cap. Ercolano Ercolani
  236ª Squadriglia   4 Savoia S.85   Ten. Fernando Malvezzi
  237ª Squadriglia   Ten. Giovanni Santinoni

Other Types

83° Gruppo R.S.T.,
(184ª, 186ª Squadriglia) Augusta   21 Cant Z.501
(189ª Squadriglia) Syracuse
143ª Squadriglia R.S.T., Melenas   6 Cant Z.501
144ª Squadriglia R.S.T. Marsala   6 Cant Z.501
170ª Squadriglia R.S.T., Augusta   7 Cant Z.506B
Sezione (Idro), Marsala–Stagnone   3 Cant Z.506B

76° Gruppo Auton.O.A., Palermo—Boccadifalco
(30ª Squadriglia)   6 Meridionali Ro37bis

Additionally available for operations over the Mediterranean to East and West were two other air commands, the aircraft from which would on occasions be engaged by British carrier-based aircraft.

(a)

Sardinia

Aeronautica Della Sardegna, H.Q. Cagliari

8° Stormo B.T., H.Q. Villacidro
    27° Gruppo (18ª, 52ª Squadriglia)
    28° Gruppo (10ª, 19ª Squadriglia)   32 Savoia S.79

31° Stormo B.M., H.Q. Cagliari-Elmas
    93° Gruppo (196ª, 197ª Squadriglia)
    94° Gruppo (198ª Squadriglia)   24 Cant Z.506B

32° Stormo B.T., H.Q. Decimomannu
    38° Gruppo (49ª, 50ª Squadriglia)
    89° Gruppo (228ª, 229ª Squadriglia)   30 Savoia S.79

3° Gruppo Auton. C.T., H.Q. Monserrato
    (153ª, 154ª, 155ª Squadriglia)   27 Fiat CR 42

19° Gruppo Auton. Combattimento, H.Q. Alghero
    (100ª, 101ª, 102ª Squadriglia)   13 Breda Ba88

85° Gruppo Auton. R.S.T., H.Q. Cagliari-Elmas
    (146ª, 183ª, 188ª Squadriglia)   18 Cant Z.501
    148ª Squadriglia, Vigna di Valle   6 Cant Z.501
    199ª Squadriglia, Santa Giusta   7 Cant Z.506B
    124ª Squadriglia, Cagliari-Elmas   4 Meridionali Ro37
    5ª Sezione Costiera, Olbia   4 Cant Z.501
    613ª Sez.(Idro), Cagliari-Elmas   5 Savoia S.66

(b)

The Aegean Islands

Aeronautica dell'Egeo, H.Q. Rhodes

39° Stormo B.T.,
  56° Gruppo (222ª, 223ª Squadriglia), Gadurra   20 Savoia S.81
  92° Gruppo (200ª, 201ª Squadriglia), Maritza
84° Gruppo R.S.T.
  (147ª, 185ª Squadriglia), Leros   12 Cant Z.501
  163ª Squadriglia Auton. C.T., Maritza   11 Fiat CR 42
  161ª Squadriglia Auton. C.M., Leros   7 Meridionali Ro43 and Ro44
  Sezione (Idro), Rhodes   2 Cant Z.506B

2. By 1 January 1941 Italian air strength on Sicily had shrunk considerably, but was to be built up again as the year progressed. At 1 January the Order of Battle was as follows:

Comando Aeronautica Sicilia, H.Q. Palermo; Gen. D.A. Renato Mazzucco

Fighters

1° Stormo C.T., H.Q. Trapani; Col. Alfredo Reglieri
  6° Gruppo (79ª, 81ª, 88ª Squadriglia), Catania   Macchi C.200   Magg. Vezio Mezzetti
  17° Gruppo (71ª, 72ª, 80ª Squadriglia), Palermo   Fiat CR 32 and 42   Magg. Bruno Brambilla
Nucleo del 23° Gruppo C.T., Comiso.
  (70ª, 74ª, 75ª Squadriglia 'bis')   Fiat CR 42   Cap. Luigi Filippi

Bombers

30° Stormo B.T., H.Q. Palermo; Col. Arnaldo Lubelli
  87° Gruppo (192ª, 193ª Squadriglia)   Sciacca Savoia S.79   Ten.Col. Mario Giuliani
  90° Gruppo (194ª, 195ª Squadriglia)   Savoia S.79sil.   Ten.Col. Eugenio Cannarsa
  289ª Squadriglia Auton. A.S., Catania   Cap. Orazio Bernardini

Changes during 1941

Event	Aircraft	Commander
20 January 1941		
156° Gruppo C.T. (379ª, 380ª Squadriglia), Comiso; Cap. Luigi Filippi (formed from Nucleo del 23° Gruppo C.T., with Fiat CR 42s)		
2 February 1941 (Arrival)		
278ª Squadriglia Auton. A.S., Pantelleria	Savoia S.79sil.	Magg. Massimiliano Erasi
1 April 1941 (Change and Arrival)		
23° Gruppo C.T. returns to Comiso and absorbs 156° Gruppo C.T. and Squadriglie 'bis'.	CR 42	Magg. Tito Falconi
7 April 1941 (Departure)		
289ª Squadriglia Auton. A.S. leaves for Puglie		
21 April 1941 (Arrival)		
10° Stormo B.T., H.Q. Chinisia; Col. Ranieri Cupini	Savoia S.79	Ten.Col. Roberto Liberi
30° Gruppo (55ª, 56ª Squadriglia), Sciacca		
29 April 1941 (Arrival)		
32° Gruppo (57ª, 58ª Squadriglia) Chinisia (Part of 10° Stormo B.T.)	Savoia S.79	Ten.Col. Antonio Marcucci
7 May 1941 (Arrival)		
43° Stormo B.T., H.Q. Gerbini; Col. Sergio Lalatta	Fiat BR 20M	Ten.Col. Nello Brambilla
99° Gruppo (242ª, 243ª Squadriglia)		
25 May 1941 (Arrival)		
7° Gruppo C.T. (76ª, 86ª, 98ª Squadriglia), Comiso	Macchi C.200	Magg. Alberto Beneforti
29 May 1941 (Arrival)		
101° Gruppo B.a.T., Trapani (208ª, 238ª Squadriglia)	Junkers Ju87B	Magg. Giuseppe Donadio
11 June 1941 (Arrival)		
31° Gruppo (65ª, 66ª Squadriglia), Catania (Part of 43° Stormo B.T.)	Fiat BR 20M	Ten.Col. Giuseppe Bordin

12 June 1941 (Arrival)
54° Stormo C.T., H.Q. Gela; Col. Tarcisio Fagnani — Macchi C.200 — Magg. Francesco Beccaria
16° Gruppo (167ª, 168ª, 169ª Squadriglia)

16 June 1941 (Arrival)
10° Gruppo (84ª, 90ª, 91ª Squadriglia), Trapani — Macchi C.200 — Ten.Col. Carlo Romagnoli
(Part of 54° Stormo C.T. 91ª Squadriglia to Palermo)

21 June 1941 (Departure)
1° Stormo C.T. leaves for Italy.

20 July 1941 (Arrivals)
377ª Squadriglia C.T., Trapani — Reggiane Re2000bis — Cap. Pietro Calistri
173ª Squadriglia R.S.T., Palermo — Fiat CR 25 — Cap. Edoardo Agnello

31 July 1941 (Arrival)
282ª Squadriglia Auton. A.S., Gerbini — Savoia S.79sil. — Cap. Marino Marini

25 August 1941 (Departure)
30° Stormo B.T., 87° Gruppo leaves for Italy

29 August 1941 (Arrival)
9° Stormo B.T., H.Q. Chinisia; Col. Alfredo Barbati
33° Gruppo (59ª, 60ª Squadriglia), Trapani — Cant Z.1007bis — Magg. Ercole Savi

2 September 1941 (Arrival)
29° Gruppo (62ª, 63ª Squadriglia), Chinisia — Cant Z.1007bis — Magg. Cesare de Porto
(Part of 9° Stormo B.T.)

7 September 1941 (Departure)
90° Gruppo leaves for Italy (remaining part of 30° Stormo B.T.)

29 September 1941 (Arrival)
4° Stormo C.T., H.Q. Comiso; Col. Eugenio Leotta
9° Gruppo (73ª, 96ª, 97ª Squadriglia) — Macchi C.202 — Ten.Col. Marco Paulello

1 October 1941 (Arrival)
171° Gruppo C.N. (301ª, 302ª Squadriglia), Gela — Fiat CR42 — Magg. Giovanni Buffa

5 October 1941 (Arrival)
37° Stormo B.T., H.Q. Gerbini; Col. Giuseppe Scarlata
  116° Gruppo (276ª, 277ª Squadriglia), Catania   Fiat **BR** 20M
5 November 1941 (Arrival)
  55° Gruppo (220ª, 221ª Squadriglia), Gerbini   Fiat **BR** 20M
    (Part of 37° Stormo B.T.)

During December units were returned to Italy, or moved to North Africa to make room for the returning Luftwaffe. By 31 December 1941 the Order of Battle had shrunk again to:

Fighters

54° Stormo C.T.
  7° Gruppo
  16° Gruppo   Macchi C.200, C.202 and Fiat CR 42
  377ª Squadriglia Auton. C.T.   Reggiane Re2000bis
  Nuclei Caccia Notturna   Fiat CR 42

Bombers

9° Stormo B.T.
  29ª Gruppo
  33° Gruppo   Cant Z.1007bis
10° Stormo B.T.
  30° Gruppo
  32° Gruppo   Savoia S.79
  278ª Squadriglia Auton. A.S.   Savoia S.79sil.
  282ª Squadriglia Auton. A.S.   Savoia S.79sil.

Reconnaissance and Rescue

173ª Squadriglia Auton. R.S.T.   Fiat CR 25
612ª Squadriglia Auton. Soccorso   Cant Z.506

Magg. Cesare Toschi

Ten.Col. Renato Di Jorio

395

Appendix IX

AXIS AIRCRAFT AVAILABILITY, 1941

Month	Regia Aeronautica	Luftwaffe
January	63	141
February	70	160
March	92	209
April	105	222
May	130	243
June	161	22
July	155	—
August	150	—
September	180	—
October	198	6
November	198	6
December	141	76

(This listing is extracted from figures provided by Generale Giuseppe Santoro in L'Aeronautica Italiana nella Seconda Guerra Mondiale, Vol. II). The above figures include all types of aircraft.

Appendix X

R.A.F. HOURS FLOWN, 11 JUNE 1940–7 JUNE 1941

11 June – 11 October 1940

Flying hours of fighters	Gladiators and Hurricanes	343.50
Total reconnaissance hours	Sunderlands of 228 and 230 Squadrons; Swordfish of 830 Squadron and No.3 A.A.C.U. Marylands of 431 Flight; Hudson; Late 298B; London of 202 Squadron; Skua of F.A.A.	1,320.20

Average number of fighters available daily	6.5	
Average number of fighter pilots available daily	10	
Number of raids	161 alarms	
Number of fighter interceptions	Day	72
	Night	2

11 October 1940 – 10 February 1941

Flying hours of fighters	Hurricanes		440.35
	Gladiators		26.15
	Fulmars		25.45
			491.95

Marylands	69 Squadron	608.05
Sunderlands	228 Squadron	562.40
Blenheims	69 Squadron	139.35
Skuas	69 Squadron	48.30
Swordfish	830 Squadron	43.00
Late 298B	228 Squadron	41.20
Spitfire	69 Squadron	6.15
		1,448.45

Average number of fighters available daily		11
Average number of fighter pilots available daily		17
Number of raids		138 alarms
Number of fighter interceptions	Day	57
	Night	5

148 Squadron Wellingtons:
  flew 217 sorties, dropped

446,930 lb. G.P. bombs
103,650 lb. S.A.P. bombs
57,370 lb. Incendiaries

830 Squadron Swordfish:
  flew 41 sorties, dropped

14,840 lb. G.P. bombs
11,500 lb. S.A.P. bombs
11 'Cucumbers' (mines)
6 18 inch torpedoes

10 February – 7 June 1941

Flying hours of fighters	Hurricane I	1,719.30
	Hurricane IIs	69.10
	Fulmars	28.35
		1,816.75

Appendix XI

SUMMARY OF AIR RAID ALERTS
OVER MALTA, 1940–41

	1940	*1941*
January		57
February		107
March		105
April		92
May		98
June	53	68
July	51	73
August	22	30
September	25	31
October	10	57
November	32	76
December	18	169
	211	963

Figures supplied by the National War Museum Association.

Appendix XII

AIRCRAFT DESTROYED OR DAMAGED ON THE GROUND DURING RAIDS, 11 FEBRUARY – 11 JUNE, 1941

Hal Far	806 Squadron	2 Fulmars seriously damaged; 1 Fulmar slightly damaged; 1 Gladiator burnt out; 2 Gladiators damaged.
	830 Squadron	2 Swordfish burnt out; 12 Swordfish damaged.
	Station Flight	1 Seal burnt out; 1 Swordfish damaged
	Fulmar Flight	3 Fulmars damaged.
Luqa	148 Squadron	8 Wellingtons burnt out/written off; 7 Wellingtons badly damaged.
	69 Squadron	1 Maryland written off; 1 Maryland badly damaged; 8 Marylands slightly damaged.
	252 Squadron	2 Beaufighters burnt out/written off; 12 Beaufighters slightly damaged.
	139 Squadron	1 Blenheim written off.
	Station Flight	1 Magister written off.
Takali	261 Squadron	1 Hurricane written off; 2 Hurricanes damaged.
	249 Squadron	2 Hurricanes burnt out; 3 Hurricanes damaged.
Kalafrana		3 Sunderlands set on fire and sunk (one moored in Kalafrana Bay, one in St. Paul's Bay, one in Marsaxlokk Bay); 3 Sunderlands slightly damaged by machine-gun fire and shrapnel (two moored in St. Paul's Bay, one in Kalafrana Bay); 1 Loire 128 slightly damaged by shrapnel in Kalafrana Bay.

Appendix XIII

BRIEF BIOGRAPHIES OF MALTA'S AIR OFFICERS COMMANDING, 1940–41

(i) Air Vice-Marshal F.H.M. Maynard, C.B., A.F.C., Legion of Merit (U.S.)
Forster Herbert Martin Maynard was born at Waiku, Awitu, New Zealand, in 1893. He was educated in England at St. Johns School, Leatherhead, and University College, London. He saw service as an Engineer in the Royal Naval Division from September 1914–May 1915, rising from Sapper to Corporal. Commissioned as a Flight Sub-Lieutenant in the R.N.A.S., he served at Eastchurch, Dover and Dunkirk during the war, rising to the rank of Flight Commander before being commissioned as Captain 'A', Royal Air Force, in April 1918.

Awarded the A.F.C. in 1919 in recognition of his distinguished services during the war, he was granted a permanent commission that same year as a Flight Lieutenant. He served in the Middle East from 1921–23, being promoted Squadron Leader in the latter year. In 1929 he was appointed to command 12 (Bomber) Squadron, but after promotion to Wing Commander in 1931 he went to Headquarters, Iraq, for staff duties. His next command in 1935 was the University of London Air Squadron, and promotion to Group Captain followed in 1937. In 1938 he moved to the Air Ministry for staff duties until 1940, when he was promoted Air Commodore during January and appointed Air Officer Commanding, Mediterranean. Promotion to Air Vice-Marshal came in February 1941, and he was appointed Companion of the Most Honourable Order of the Bath (C.B.) the following June on his return from Malta. The next three years were spent in charge of Coastal Command administration, and his final year, before retiring in late 1945, was as A.O.C., 19 Group. He died in January 1976, aged 82.

(ii) Air Chief Marshal Sir Hugh P. Lloyd, C.B., C.B.E., M.C., D.F.C., Legion of Merit (U.S.)
Born at Leigh, Worcestershire, in 1894, Hugh Pughe Lloyd entered the Army during World War I, serving as a Private in the Royal Engineers from 1915–1917; he was wounded three times. Commissioned in the Royal Flying Corps in 1917, he was engaged in Army co-operation flying in France until the Armistice, being awarded an M.C. and D.F.C.

Air Chief Marshal Sir Hugh P. Lloyd (N.W.M.A.)

With peace came a permanent commission in the R.A.F., following which he served for ten years with bomber squadrons in India, operating over Waziristan, Mohmand and Tirah. He was mentioned in despatches on three occasions, and received four bars to his Indian General Service Medal. He returned to England in January 1939 and commanded a Wing in Bomber Command until December of that year. He was appointed Senior Air Staff Officer of No.2 Group in May 1941, a job which he held until posted to Malta to take over from Maynard. He was made a C.B. in January 1942, while still on the island. On leaving Malta in July 1942 he became S.A.S.O., H.Q. Middle East until 1943, then A.O.C. North-West African Coastal Air Force. Finally in 1945 he became A.O.C. of Tiger Force, destined for the Far East; with the end of the war in the East he served as Commander in Chief, Air Command, Far East, until 1949, and then as A.O.C. Bomber Command in the United Kingdom until his retirement in 1950.

Appendix XIV

SURVIVORS' IMPRESSIONS

Gp.Capt. G. Burges, O.B.E., D.F.C. Flt.Lt. J. Pickering, A.F.C.
Gp.Capt. E.W. Whiteley, C.B.E., D.F.C. Wg.Cdr. J. Tipton, D.F.C.
Wg.Cdr. A.E. Louks Sqn.Ldr. J. Alton

Gp.Capt. Burges (Fighter Flight, Hal Far, April–August 1940; 261 Squadron August 1940–January 1941; 69 Squadron January–June 1941)

After leaving Cranwell I went on a navigational and general reconnaissance course at Manston, and then on a flyingboat course at Calshot. I was posted to 202 (Flyingboat) Squadron early in 1937 and based at Kalafrana in Malta. In 1938 I became A.D.C. to the Air Officer Commanding, Mediterranean, who at that time was Air Commodore Paul Maltby. He was posted home during the year and his place was taken by Air Commodore Robert Leckie who had a great influence on the building of Luqa. When war was declared in September 1939 Air Commodore Leckie was sent to Canada to start the Empire Air Training Organisation, finally ending up as the Chief of the Royal Canadian Air Force.

For a time we did not have an A.O.C. and then early in 1940 Air Vice-Marshal Maynard was appointed and I stayed as his A.D.C. Before he actually arrived I was told to find him somewhere to live as there was no official residence for the A.O.C. on the island. One day I discussed this problem with Walter Starkie, who was Flag-Lieutenant to Sir Andrew Cunningham, and the next day he rang me to say that Sir Andrew would be only too pleased for Air Vice-Marshal Maynard and me to stay at Admiralty House until we found somewhere else. Our two 'masters' became great friends, and I think this resulted in our getting the Gladiators, despite Admiralty objections.

The largest flying unit in the island before the war had been 202 Squadron but it had moved to Gibraltar towards the end of 1939. This left a small Station Flight at Hal Far, and a small Anti-Aircraft Co-operation Unit, also at Hal Far. Thus, when it was decided to form the fighter flight we could only find six pilots. We decided to operate in two 'watches' of three pilots each – call them 'A' watch and 'B' watch. 'A' watch would cover the periods 0800 until 1200, and from 1600 until dusk. The next day we would exchange periods.

On the first day we went into action we realised that if we were to get into contact with the enemy we had to have height over him otherwise we would not be able to catch him as his aircraft were considerably faster than the Gladiators — the excess height would enable us to gain sufficient speed in a dive in order to intercept. We therefore decided to sit in our aircraft, all strapped in and ready to go, during the whole period of the 'watch'. It is damned hot in Malta during the summer and this technique was most wearing but we reckoned it was worth about 2000 feet. However, we started to get piles! The M.O. advised that instead of two 'watches' of three pilots we should have three 'watches' of two pilots.

It seems a pity now that more careful and detailed records were not kept of the early days of the war in Malta, and also that an official photographic record was not maintained. So far as I was aware none of us kept diaries and I think the reason for this was that we thought we would not last very long. We used to make a criptic note in our log-books of any combats, and make out a combat report which went to R.A.F. Headquarters in Valetta — whether these reports were ever written up in the Operations Record Book I do not know. In those days keeping official records was regarded as a bit of a bind, as most people had better things to do. I have little doubt that if detailed records were kept they were probably written up as and when the person responsible had time to do it. If they had realised at the time that many years later people would have regarded them as gospel truth, they would have had a fit!

During my 'fighter' period I still carried on my A.D.C. job and only turned up at the airfield for my 'watch' and so did not have much time to listen to the tales which must have been told in the Mess. I gave up the A.D.C. job and reverted to the trade for which I had originally been trained, that of general reconnaissance, and joined 69 Squadron on 26 January, 1941. The C.O. was an old friend of mine, Squadron Leader E.A. (Titch) Whiteley — he and I had been on the flying-boat course at Calshot at the same time. The unit was equipped with Martin 167s, later called the Maryland, which had been intended for the French Air Force and had been acquired in various ways — so we were some of the first people in the country to go metric — I seem to remember that we used to bring them in at 160 Km.p.h. I referred to the 'unit', the title of Squadron was a bit of an exaggeration as I think we had a total of about five aircraft! Our engineers went to the most extraordinary lengths to keep them serviceable — including getting the Dockyard to make spares of all sorts from bits of metal they had lying around!

Our Marylands were lovely aircraft to fly and had an exceptional performance up to about 10,000 feet then it fell off rather quickly so that we rarely flew above 15,000 feet. Unfortunately they were not built to take much punishment — there was little armour-plate and no self-sealing tanks — the wings were just full of petrol with nothing between it and the air outside except the duraluminium skin, in addition we carried a large overload tank inside the aircraft which put our range up to about 2,000 miles. Thus the last thing we wanted was an enemy fighter on our tails!

Our job was to keep a watch on the enemy airfields and harbours in order to provide photographs for the Royal Navy and for our own bomber force. For instance the reconnaissance for the Naval strike against the Italian fleet in Taranto was provided by the unit. In addition when intelligence suggested that an enemy convoy had sailed for North Africa we would go out and look for it and signal its position, course and speed, and hope that the Navy or our own Blenheim strike force would be able to intercept. The most successful of this type of operation took place on the 15th. April 1941. At that time there was a flotilla of destroyers in the Grand Harbour under Captain Mack whose task was to destroy enemy shipping taking supplies to North Africa. The enemy air activity was such that they mainly operated at night.

'Titch' Whiteley took off about mid-day on 15th. April in filthy weather and headed off towards the Tunisian coast hoping that the weather would improve so that he could fly higher and see further. It didn't, and on getting somewhere near the Tunisian coast he flew right over a merchant ship. He made a landfall on the coast to fix his position and returned to where he found the ship. He discovered that he had found a convoy of five merchant ships escorted by three destroyers. He stayed with them reporting their position, course and speed until he had to return to the Island. As a result of his report Captain Mack left Malta and in a night action sank all the merchant ships and destroyers. We lost H.M.S. 'Mohawk' which for sometime afterwards we could see lying on the bottom off Kerkenah Island. The crew were rescued by other ships in the flotilla.

Generally when we flew over a harbour or airfield the enemy would send up fighters after us. Very often we would see them climbing up to intercept and as we were at the most at only 15,000 feet we had to get our photographs and get out to sea quickly. If we did get chased we would put the aircraft into a shallow dive and open the throttles and revs, under which conditions we generally had the legs on the fighters. This was all very nice, but it meant that each target we had to photograph needed a separate sortie. This gave us the idea of putting cameras in a Hurricane, and I was given the job of sorting this out.

We were given Hurricane Mk.I V7101. We took out the guns, radio, armour plate, and anything else we could safely get rid of, and installed two cameras. Unfortunately we didn't have the facilities to install extra fuel tanks, and so we knew its range would be restricted to Sicily. What wouldn't we have given for one of the blue Spitfires the P.R. chaps were using in the U.K.! Incidentally we painted our Hurricane blue, mainly to enable our own gunners to recognise it! I actually got this aircraft up to 36,000 feet and I think by stripping so much out of it we had probably moved the centre of gravity too far back because at this height if one wasn't careful it whipped into a spin. I used to operate at about 30,000 feet and at this height could cover two or three targets in Sicily in one sortie.

In June 1941 Air Vice-Marshal Hugh Pughe Lloyd came out to take over from Air Vice-Marshal Maynard, who decided that I had been in Malta long enough and should go home with him. Two or three days before we were due to leave in a Sunderland I was asked if I would go along to Captain Caruana's Bar in Valetta for a farewell drink, in fact I think I must have been taken along there by one of my friends. When we arrived we found the bar absolutely packed with Maltese people – they gave me a silver cigarette case with my initials on the outside and an inscription inside "A small token of appreciation from a handful of Maltese". I still don't know who they were.

Flt.Lt. Pickering (Sergeant Pilot with 261 Squadron, August 1940 – April 1941)

There was obviously a total lack of operational experience at all levels at the beginning of the war in 1939. When hostilities commenced in Malta in June 1940, they had to start from scratch, and anyone who went from the U.K. to Malta – particularly from Battle of Britain squadrons, would find operations there still using methods that experience in the U.K. had outdated. On the other hand, local knowledge and flying in a different climate to that in the U.K. requires acclimatisation. This 'local knowledge' is equally important but is all too often discounted. From later experience in squadrons in the Far East and the Eighth Army, I saw far too many casualties amongst experienced fighter pilots who arrived full of enthusiasm and aggression, but who made no concessions to tactics evalued to take advantage of local conditions. When, for instance, Flg.Off. Mason, who was a splendid fighter leader from the Western Desert, arrived in Malta, he thought our local tactics were wrong and tried to use tactics he had developed in the Desert. He was shot down trying to use them, not long after his arrival in Malta, but fortunately survived this incident.

Losses amongst reinforcements were immediate and substantial. Although most were experienced fighter pilots, there was no time to obtain local knowledge and the arrival of 109s in Sicily in superior numbers was disastrous for Hurricanes. An analysis of casualties in Malta would, I think, show a trend that pilots who got through local familiarization had a better survival rate. There are many exceptions to this trend, but it was a substantial factor. Pilots arriving in Malta who went straight into action had a great disadvantage and I think that in the intensive air fighting later the low survival rate of fighter pilots is partly attributable to this factor.

The same considerations applied to Operations officers directing the flying. When they arrived in Malta, they would find that their experience was greater and more up to date than the staff they replaced and it is natural in those circumstances to regard what existed to be a shambles. Tactics however do not transplant quite as simply as this. They have to be evalued using local factors.

Within the limitations of the quantity and quality of aircraft available when I was in Malta and taking into account the fluctuating strength relative to the Italian and German opposition, I would now be less critical of the real or imagined shortcomings. Very occasionally, one had air superiority on single sorties, but usually the odds were heavily against Malta fighters, apart from tactical disadvantages of trying to gain height from below raids.

In reaching this later judgement, I do so in spite of the loss of personal friends. I was at school with Sgt. Timms. We joined the R.A.F.V.R. together in April 1937 and, except for three weeks, we were on the same units or squadrons from 1937 until he died in action. Sgt. Ashton similarly from September 1937 and Sgts. Kelsey and O'Donnell from 18 September 1939. I would not wish to associate myself with any recriminations on the leadership we had. If it fell short of what was possible, it still contained great courage, generosity and understanding and will stand comparison with any other theatre of operations.

I do not know what survives in the official records, but for propaganda purposes to encourage the Maltese, squadron difficulties and casualties were kept secret unless they occurred over the island. To avoid creating alarm and despondency amongst the Maltese, the opposition faced by the squadron was understated whenever possible. This inevitably understates the role of 261 Squadron in the defence of Malta. Lack of spares for aircraft often reduced the defence to three aircraft and until reinforcements arrived from North Africa early in 1941, whatever could be got into the air took on whatever attacked the island regardless of the odds, in the best R.A.F. traditions. When reinforcements arrived, casualties increased. This is the inevitable result of fighting against odds. 261 Squadron took on its role with quiet determination and knew what the cost would be. It was a heavy responsibility and a great cost to accept at such an early age amongst the pilots.

When Italy entered the war in 1940, there was no fighter defence for Malta. I think it might be assumed that the Overall War Strategy did not include plans for a fighter defence though an alternative theory might be that priorities elsewhere prevented the allocation of aircraft to Malta.

The first fighter defence was created by local initiative of the A.O.C. He found crated Gladiators and had them assembled. He commandeered three or four Hurricanes in transit to the Near East and he also utilised other aircraft whose presence in Malta was accidental in a reconnaissance unit, though I suspect that such a unit operated from Malta as a part of the O.W.S.

Early success by the scratch local pilots caused a change in the O.W.S. and a reinforcement flight of Hurricanes was despatched in July 1940 (418 Flight). This was a token gesture for the purpose of stiffening Maltese morale. There was some pro-Italian feeling in Malta at the time. A secondary benefit was that the presence of successful fighter aircraft in Malta compelled Italian bombers to use fighter escorts and direct some of their fighter strength away from Western Europe (the Balkans and Greece later).

The quality of Italian pilots was very good. The CR 42s came between the Gladiators and Hurricanes in performance, but their pilots were aggressive and skilled. A stern attack by a Hurricane on a CR 42 could result in the CR 42 pulling upwards sharply and at the top of a loop, opening head-on at the Hurricane whilst he was inverted. It was necessary for the Hurricanes to use air tactics for attacking CR 42s similar to those used by Bf109s against Hurricanes.

The original Macchis were faster than the CR 42s but less manoeuvrable. Their tactical handling was not good and one suspects that they were brought into service with insufficient practice combat experience. The S.79 bombers were operationally obsolete. I 'purloined' one at Castel Benito in 1943 and flew about 100 hours in it. Its speed was surprisingly high and it had a very good range, but its type of construction made it very vulnerable to damage from gunfire or shrapnel and its defensive armament left many blind spots. One can only admire the courage of pilots who flew it on offensive missions, because almost any hit could bring it down – usually in flames. From a pilot's point of view it was a very pleasant, safe and robust aircraft to fly, but it was an operational deathtrap.

The 'token' role of 261 Squadron meant that it operated between three and six aircraft at a time and these were invariably heavily outnumbered by both bombers and fighters. When the Luftwaffe arrived in Sicily early in 1941 it was up against astronomical odds and the Hurricanes were inferior in many performance aspects to the Bf109s and Ju88s. From its formation in August 1940 almost every flight was an operational one and there was little serviceability surplus to provide practice flying or to develop and try out fresh tactics. The loss or damage of a single aircraft was a most serious matter in trying to keep the token presence effective.

Early radar limitations and local operating problems – S.79 raids were made at between 15,000 feet and 18,000 feet (I think). There was insufficient warning for Hurricanes to climb to 20,000 feet before raiders were over the target. A long climb in low airscrew pitch created heating problems in the engine. Changes were made to airscrew stops (initially the Hurricanes were not fitted with constant speed units) to coarsen the fine pitch and this permitted a long climb in fine pitch. However, if one climbed up below a raid, the fighter escort of the raiders could pounce on the climbing Hurricanes when they were most vulnerable and unmanoeuvrable. If the Hurricanes climbed towards Sicily to intercept raiders on their return flight, they would be bounced by the second fighter escort (the relative speeds of CR 42s and S.79s and the range of CR 42s required this return flight 'back-up').

The main tactic became for Hurricanes to gain height in a climb to the South of the Island and then turn North to try and get to 20,000 feet over the raiders after they had turned for home. This would have been more effective with better radar, but vectoring and height information was not very accurate. On their homeward run, in a shallow dive towards Sicily, S.79s were almost as fast as maximum cruising speed of the Hurricanes and interceptions occurred more from luck than calculation. Without an initial height advantage Hurricanes could not catch Ju88s, which in any case operated above 18,000 feet.

There were insufficient aircraft for Hurricanes to put up regular patrols and in any case single aircraft would approach Malta without reaching the Island and until a positive raid developed, it was necessary to conserve flying time. In the early weeks of 261, aircraft on stand-by throughout daylight hours were manned by pilots in four hour shifts. They were strapped in ready to go so that they could start the engine and be airborne in seconds to gain precious time required for an interception.

The terrain of Malta was totally unsuitable for forced-landings and if it was not possible to force-land on an airfield with certainty, baling out or a landing in the sea was necessary in the event of damage in combat or engine failure.

One can advance any argument statistically, but 68 squadrons are listed as taking part in the Battle of Britain. Their normal strength was 18 aircraft with 12 operating as a squadron. Some of these squadrons were only active in the Battle of Britain for a short period. 3,080 pilots took part in the Battle of Britain – 520 were killed in action between 1 July and 31 October, 1940, or 17.2%. The total number of enemy aircraft shot down in the Battle of Britain is a matter of some doubt.

I have a note that between its formation on 16 August 1940 and its departure from Malta about June 1941, 261 Squadron had 115 confirmed aircraft shot down. I have no record of probables or damaged. These were obtained with the normal operating strength of less than six aircraft. Its own casualties are difficult to ascertain, but they were very much higher than 17.2% whilst I was on the Squadron. (In fact, 25.39% whilst Jim Pickering was with the Squadron – 22.77% overall when the Squadron left the Island – Shores and Cull).

The Squadron operated in Malta without respite for ten months. Battle of Britain squadrons had rest periods in their four months. Comparisons are invidious and I only wish to show that 261 Squadron had a long, hard stint that tested to the utmost its resolution against vastly superior numbers. It was much more successful than has been appreciated and in spite of its token role of maintaining a fighter presence on the Island.

Gp.Capt. Whiteley (Commanding Officer of 431 Flight, September 1940 – January 1941, and 69 Squadron, January 1941 – June 1941).

On the delivery flight (to Malta) all three aircraft exposed their full F42 camera magazines as we flew diagonally across Sardinia in the early morning.

Our first sortie from Malta was P.R. of Tripoli on 8 September 1940, perfect pictures being taken by Plt.Off. Foxton (Warburton navigating). After Tripoli it was Taranto, Naples, Brindisi, Palermo, the airfields of Sicily, Pantelleria and Sardinia. I photographed Taranto and Brindisi as early as 28 September (Warburton navigating) but I doubt whether that was the first visit by our unit. No Maryland took off from Malta without its camera(s). The unit photographic officer – one Adrian Warburton – saw to that.

Thanks to good Mediterranean weather, our success ratio was much higher than the figures for the U.K. P.R.U. If the clouds were low over the target, the navigators or wireless operators took oblique photographs with 35mm cameras – originally my Contax or one of two Leicas borrowed from the Marquis Scicluna. Reconnaissance of the nearby Sicilian ports was undertaken by a naval Skua which relied for its defence on cloud cover or the hope that enemy fighters would mistake for a cannon the puffs of smoke fired astern from a Very pistol.

Shortly after our arrival in Malta the other two pilots – Foxton and Bibby – suffered temporary indispositions. I therefore decided to train two navigators (Warburton and Devine) as pilots. Both had flown Ansons – but Warby not recently. Warby's first solo almost ended in disaster. He eventually landed cross wind with the top strands of the fence around his tail wheel – watched by an irate Wing Commander from H.Q. I was firmly reprimanded.

A few days later – still short of pilots – I sent Warby off again and all seemed well. Unfortunately the Bob Martins had one vice; in a cross wind they tended to swing into wind and then keep swinging. A pilot undergoing training in Malta had to be accompanied by a crew to provide warning (via W/T) of – and defence against – enemy aircraft. So on Warby's early flights, Sgts. Bastard and Moren lived through circular take-offs and zig-zag landings. I was tempted to give up but Bastard and Moren were always prepared – after high speed taxi-ing practice – to go off with Warby 'just once more'. Warby was greatly indebted to those two.

Admiral Cunningham's Mediterranean Fleet could not leave a convoy unprotected to bombard Benghazi or Tripoli, etc., unless he knew where the Italian battleships and cruisers were. The same restriction applied to Admiral Somerville based at Gibraltar. For all my time at Malta, the only aircraft capable of obtaining that vital information were my few Marylands. Without those convoys Malta was not going to survive. I therefore told my crews that their No.1 task was to bring back their photographs and their precious aircraft rather than risk it by engaging in aerial combat unnecessarily or trying to shoot down some of those training or communication aircraft we often saw while we were flying down the centre of Italy to approach, say, Taranto from the North. Admiral Cunningham went as far as to send me – a mere Flt.Lt. – a personal copy of his Operational Orders emphasising that I must have my aircraft serviceable.

A second consideration was our vulnerability to a single incendiary round. Unlike the Blenheims and Beauforts, those early Martins had no self sealing fuel tanks and no armour plate. On the other hand they had sufficient speed to avoid combat and by those tactics our few aircraft continued supplying the vital pictorial and other intelligence. The first principle of war in the old War Manual was "Maintenance of Aim". I thus survived fifty ops and did not in any of those sorties from Malta shoot down even one enemy aircraft. I was chased by every type of enemy fighter – I recall having 109s on my tail all the way from the Strait of Messina to Malta when I was getting short on fuel. But I did not try to fight them.

Notwithstanding my tactical policy, Adrian Warburton, while returning from a sortie, attacked and shot down his first victim – a Cant 506 – on 30 October. I have been told that I was mildly critical but he was over the sea, well away from any fighters and there was little risk to his aircraft – so I was really very pleased.

To encourage the U.K. assembly staff at Burtonwood (where Marylands were assembled) I sent the following (unofficial) cable to the Controller in terms which avoided a problem I had with the Malta censors – "Your friend Mr. Martin doing very nicely out here. Did some boxing yesterday and won by a knockout. Regards."

About the same time I cabled the manufacturers of our excellent engines – Pratt and Whitney – but in less diplomatic terms. P and W had declined to meet my requisition for a small engine tool on the grounds that 'If your engines are being properly operated in accordance with instructions in our handbook, you should have no occasion to change valve springs.' I replied via Air Ministry 'Messrs. Hitler and Mussolini do not appear to have studied the Pratt and Whitney handbooks. In any case they are not co-operating in ensuring proper treatment. Following damage from bombing and air combat etc. . . .'

The attack on Taranto on the night of 11/12 November 1940 was preceded not by one P.R. sortie but by many. The 10 or 12 aircrew of 431 Flight took their turn on operations – and most of them were involved in the P.R. watch on Taranto during September-November. I sent Warby (as pilot) to Taranto on the day preceding the night strike – 11 November. Photographically his sortie was abortive but he and his crew provided valuable last minute visual information about the disposition of the Italian battle fleet – and the cruisers.

The Taranto photographs sent to the 'Illustrious' men were, therefore, those taken the day before – 10 November. I did not fly on operations quite as frequently as the others, but I happened to be the pilot of the Martin which went to Taranto on 10 November. According to my log book it was my seventh P.R. cover of Taranto. John Gridley was in the rear cockpit. The standard of defences at Taranto had progressively improved, but competing with the enemy fighter screens around Malta on departure and return was probably a greater hazard.

I was again on the flying roster on 12 November and, with no expectations, allotted myself the sortie to Taranto – preceded en route as it had to be, by a reconnaissance from the Gulf of Corinth to Corfu. Our fleet was observing radio silence and, when I took off, I had no report of the attack. John Gridley was once more in the rear cockpit; in the nose was an attached Blenheim navigator whom I took for training and experience.

As I approached Taranto it became obvious that the F.A.A. had smartened up the naval and air defences. On this – my eighth visit – there was some pandemonium down below. The pilot of a Bob Martin had to concentrate on flying straight and level on his pre-planned photographic tracks, while maintaining a continuous scan for enemy fighters abeam and ahead. However, while executing a turn I was thrilled to see one battleship partially submerged. Another battleship appeared to have been beached; oil was pouring from other large ships and generally the place was in chaos. At last some real job satisfaction!

After making my getaway, I composed the expected radio sighting report in Naval Aircraft Code. But the code (as I had memorized it) provided no scope for reporting adequately what we had seen. So I reported sighting the battleships, cruisers, etc. in self evident code. At the end of the signal I cautiously added, in the understatement of the decade, 'One battleship (BS) sinking.' During the four hundred mile return journey I considered amplifying that report with some sort of compliment to the Navy, but I knew my cameras had been functioning and decided against it. Numerous photographs taken from 8,000 feet recorded the Navy's brilliant achievement.

The Fleet Air Arm success at Taranto boosted morale in 431 Flight because photographs which we had taken so often had at last put to real use. Our relations with the Navy were further improved by the attachment to 431 Flight of Lieutenant (later Vice-Admiral Sir Richard) Janvrin, R.N., who had taken part in the attack, and Lt. Walford, R.N.

Notwithstanding the lack of American spares in 1940 and occasional bomb damage, our Bob Martins were operating every day. We tried taking off with heavy rope around the tail wheel in lieu of tyre and tube – but the Command Engineer (Sqn.Ldr. A.E. Louks) soon produced a better solution. He had new hubs cast from melted-down enemy airscrews – hubs to fit our axle and Blenheim tyres.

But there seemed to be difficulty in operating this same aircraft in the U.K. Just before Christmas 1940 Air Ministry asked the A.O.C. whether he could spare a Glenn Martin crew to return to U.K. and do some trouble-shooting. Having promised to bring another aircraft back to Malta, I left with my original Wireless

Operator (Cpl. – later Flt.Lt. – J. Shephard) on the first transit Sunderland.

As from 1 January 1941 our establishment was to be increased from six Glenn Martins to 12 – plus ten Beauforts. 431 Flight was to be reconstituted as No. 69 Squadron. But that Whitehall decision in itself was not going to deliver any aircraft, personnel or spares to Malta.

My unofficial cargo on the return flight included London newspapers, gramophone records, tooth brushes and lipsticks. By about April 1941 the Squadron was again desperately short of hydraulic fluid. I knew now to dispense with this fluid provided I could obtain castor oil – but Command H.Q. reported, after an intensive search, nil supplies. Sqn.Ldr. George Burges therefore departed with a dozen lipsticks and visited matrons and nursing sisters. He returned with kegs of castor oil and so we were in business again. (Lipsticks can be powerful currency in a siege.) In at least one of the months which followed, 69 Squadron's operational flying hours were the highest of any squadron in Middle East Command.

In that first half of 1941 we watched the collapse of Yugoslavia, the invasion of Greece and, finally, the loss of Crete. But gradually Malta was building its strength – some Hurricanes, Wellingtons, Blenheims and Beaufighters arrived. Usually we were able to meet their P.R. and maritime reconnaissance requirements – and those of the Navy. Sqn.Ldr. Burges adapted a Hurricane for P.R. work over Sicily but after trying it, I preferred the Bob Martins.

In June 1941 I was recalled to engineering specialist duties – albeit on American aircraft – and my operational association with P.R. was terminated.

Wg.Cdr. Tipton (Wellington navigator in 40 Squadron, October 1941)

We left Wyton on 25 October 1941 (or rather Alconbury as 40 Squadron lived there). Wyton had no runways at the time and 15 Squadron (Stirlings) and 40 Squadron actually operated from Alconbury. We went to Hampstead Norris for briefing and take off. This was an unfamiliar airfield with a bump in the main runway and the pilots on their first night take-off from there (for Gibraltar) had the impression that they had run out of runway before the end. The aircraft were overloaded with ground crew and spares. The first three – we were the third – got off but the fourth failed to sustain height and crashed and burned out. Only three aircraft went to Gibraltar that night therefore, and on to Malta. The remainder of the Squadron flew direct to Malta a couple of nights later.

Perhaps the best picture I can give is by listing operations I flew in that time. They will be typical of the night bombing programme. We did not fly by day because of the vulnerability of aircraft out of their protective pens.

My only day flight was a sea search for a crew thought to be in the sea off Sicily.

5 November	Castel Benito airfield
6 November	Tripoli
8 November	Naples
10 November	Naples
14 November	Catania

18 November	Naples
19 November	Brindisi
21 November	Convoy attack
23 November	El Beica airfield
27 November	Naples
28 November	Benghazi
5 December	Naples
6 December	Naples
9 December	Tripoli
12 December	Patras
15 December	Taranto

Here I have to pause as our aircraft was hit by an intruder on 19 December and the crew were all casualties. The explosion of the aircraft and its bomb load also damaged, I believe, all aircraft awaiting take-off that night.

Our role was to prevent supplies reaching North Africa. Airfield attacks were against build-ups of transport aircraft – the most successful of these was against Castel Vetrano in Sicily during the period I was out of action. The Tripoli raids were against shipping which had arrived in the harbour and were often combined with a run up the coastal road to look for convoys. Other port attacks were similar except that the task at Naples and Brindisi were 'nuisance raids'. The purpose was mainly to fatigue workers and damage morale and so a single aircraft stayed over the port for two hours, the alert being maintained through the night. The purpose could be achieved by keeping the A.A. guns firing and when they paused a single bomb among the harbour shipping would start them up again. With luck some useful damage could be done. In this respect the Brindisi raid was particularly successful; I think we got the fuel tank going. Taranto was an attack on the Italian fleet.

It will be seen from the dates of operations when I was fully active that the Squadron must have been operating at high intensity. During our stay (the Squadron left Malta in February 1942 – Shores and Cull) the Squadron attacked more targets than the number of nights we were there – something over 160 I believe. In his farewell, Air Commodore (then) Lloyd said that he believed that no squadron had operated at such rates and under such conditions. Preservation of aircraft on the ground from the almost continuous raids was the major problem. Aircraft were kept in protected pens (made of sand-filled four gallon fuel cans) at Safi and were taxied up to Luqa at last light and back to their pens at first light each day.

Luqa runway was lined with hooded lights visible only from the approach and below 300 feet as a way of making life more difficult for intruders.

These were the difficulties for the night bombers. One may well ask how the Blenheims and Marylands operated at all. It was extremely difficult for them and with sometimes a standing patrol of Axis fighters circling the island they had to fight their way out of their base and again back into it on return. As if their shipping and harbour targets at mast height were not enough.

413

Sqn.Ldr. Alton (Corporal ground crew during 1941)

On an Autumn night in 1940 we left Uxbridge on a darkened train for an unknown destination overseas. None of us thought that the crescendo of exploding bombs and anti-aircraft fire was a foreboding of what the future held in store. The following morning we arrived at Devonport where, following breakfast as the R.N. barracks, we boarded the cruiser H.M.S. 'Newcastle'. Our draft numbered about 70, and without doubt our presence on board was an inconvenience to the ship's complement, who in any event were living in cramped conditions. To their eternal credit they treated us as very welcome guests, and even allowed us to touch their hallowed Walrus (the shipboard catapult-launched amphibian), which was credited with one enemy aircraft destroyed.

In darkness we slipped our moorings and headed West into a very inhospitable Atlantic, which very soon sorted out the airmen from the sailors. The next time we sighted land we were approaching Gibraltar, where R.A.F. uniforms were forbidden on deck. Ever resourceful, the R.A.F. borrowed the sailors' uniforms and confusion reigned. After a high speed dash, one sunny afternoon we sailed into Grand Harbour and for the first time we realised that we had reached our destination. A couple of days were spent at Kalafrana while we were being sorted out, then we were dispersed all over the island, I to Takali.

The first time I saw Takali it looked like a gigantic car park; there were cars everywhere with one clear gap straight down the middle. Amongst the cars were empty tar barrels. At the entry of Italy into the war an appeal went out for old cars to block airborne landings and this was the outcome. Some months later all obstructions were removed. The Italian Airways terminal building was in use as Station Headquarters and housed the Station Commander, Gp.Capt. O'Sullivan, known to his contemporaries as 'Ginger', and to the airmen for some obscure reason as 'Shem O'Sullivan'. Not far from this building a hangar was in the course of erection; the enemy awaited its completion before knocking it down again.

The Officers' Mess was in the town of Mosta just off the airfield. The Airmens' and Senior N.C.O.'s messes were on the airfield. In his book 'Briefed to Attack', Air Marshal Lloyd comments adversely on the airmen's accommodation and indeed this was justified. The Airmen's Mess was an old disused pottery. The brick ovens still existed and were designated 'air raid shelters'! The tall chimney towered over the whole building and remained standing until much later; it was deliberately demolished subsequently.

The upper floor was furnished with crude wooden bunk beds, these providing excellent habitation for the bed bugs which abounded; in time the wood became blackened and charred because the only means of obtaining a respite from the bugs was to go after them with a blowlamp. The ground floor contained the N.A.A.F.I., which dispensed Farsons 'Blue Label' and cigarettes; these commodities soon disappeared. The other facility on the ground floor was the dining area and cookhouse. Even today it nauseates me when I remember tinned Machonicie stew, tinned butter and fatty bacon, and corned beef which was served stewed, in fritters and every other way. I do not deny that in the early part of 1942 I would have welcomed any of these items. Also on the ground floor were the ablutions. Lavatories were wooden seated models and their use involved the risk of an infection of crab lice. Such hot water as was available was produced by a Heath Robinson device which caused drips of waste lubricating oil to fall on to a metal plate. Once the metal plate reached operating temperature, it was (at least in theory) self-sustaining. As the bombing progressed several near misses rendered the building unsafe and in 1942 it was finally demolished. The Senior N.C.O.'s Mess was a very unusual building and there was an interesting legend about it which now escapes me. It too suffered damage and was demolished in 1942.

As the first winter approached and the rains began, Takali airfield disclosed its one serious disadvantage, that of flooding. It is reputed to be the site of an ancient lake. For the ground crews this was a difficult time as the aircraft had to be towed to firm ground where they could take off and fly to Luqa. Until the airfield dried out operations were conducted from Luqa. This was very unpopular with both air and ground crew since it meant a cold and wet start in order to reach Luqa and prepare aircraft to be at dawn readiness. At the end of the day's operations there was a return journey with no prospect of hot baths or even a heated billet in which to relax.

Normally four aircraft were kept at readiness and in the early days this often represented full availability. When a convoy was due, the number was increased to six. For some strange reason, it gave a very satisfactory feeling to see all six scramble at once. It was usual for air and ground crew to work in shifts at Takali. Dawn to lunchtime, and lunchtime to stand-down. A Corporal (of which I was one of two) was responsible for aircraft turn-round between sorties and for dealing with defects.

Until about mid 1941, if my memory serves me right, we were comparatively free from daylight enemy action. I do recall that we fitted light bomb racks to the Hurricanes and sent them off at dawn to raid Catania in Sicily. Because the bombs were small I cannot think much damage was caused. However, I seem to recall that the enemy paid Takali a call and expressed his displeasure. Takali took the hint.

Once two Messerschmitt 110s sneaked in under the Radar at first light and strafed the aircraft at readiness; some two or three Hurricanes were burned out but although the air and ground crew shelters were in the line of fire, there were no casualties. Rumour had it that a Ju88 which was in company with the Messerschmitts crashed on high ground on Gozo. The camaraderie between the aircrew and ground crew was excellent and on return from a scramble there was a hearty welcome for the pilot. When, by 1941, the original pilots were replaced, some of the old spirit died out. If the whole squadron could have moved on as a complete unit morale would have been very high. I remember that several times it was rumoured that the whole squadron was to move to Tobruk in Egypt, but this never materialised.

In 1942 there were casualties amongst the ground crew at Takali, but in 1940 and 1941 we seemed to lead a charmed life. I earlier related the incident with the Me110s. Two other incidents come to mind. Once when operating from Luqa four Hurricanes were scrambled and as was customary the fitters and riggers sat around on the starter trollies awaiting the return of the aircraft. Four aircraft were seen approaching, which at a glance looked like our Hurricanes. This was a gross mistake, because they were Macchi 202s and before anyone could move, explosive bullets were churning up the ground, then just as quickly they were gone. Not a soul was so much as scratched. The other incident involved a visiting Blenheim taking off from Takali; when just airborne he had an engine failure and without further ado jettisoned his bombs. In theory they were dropped 'safe', but a couple of them did explode not very far from the aircraft and crews standing by. When the dust settled a quick check showed that we had once again 'got away with it'.

Wg. Cdr. A.E. Louks.

Wg.Cdr. A.E. Louks (Command Engineering Officer, 1940–41)

The Gladiator story began with their inability to intercept the Italian bombers, which came and went unescorted, so I suggested to the A.O.C. (Air Commodore 'Sammy' Maynard) that I should modify them to improve matters. We had a variety of crashed Blenheims – from being a staging post to the Middle East – and he gave me a free hand.

416

The Blenheims had two-pitch propellers and I calculated a revised pitch angle setting which would suffice to 12,000–14,000 feet for climb, and using a blend of 87 and 100 octane (the latter in very short supply) raised the boost by 21b/in. and I tested the first one – Sea Gladiator N5529 – to 10,000 feet in a shade under five minutes, so I left the calculated pitch setting as a norm for the next ones. I had also taken a template to the Dockyard for an armour plating shield behind the pilot, which they made from their lightest gauge material (used on exposed position light calibre weapons). That flight was at 1500 hrs. on 21.9.40. On 28.11.40 I have another entry when I flew another V.P. Gladiator – no number in my log book (it was N5520 – Ed.), but I was never a keen log book compiler. I must have missed out more flights then entered! Also I was testing Hurricanes to improve their performance, because as delivered they could not keep up with the revised Gladiators! Eventually, by utilizing the same principle with their two pitch propellers, brewing 92–94 octane fuel and raising the boost by 4 lb./in., they became very lively.

I reckoned it was better to risk engines rather than scramble a few impotent fighters. Unfortunately, my A.O.C., being a trifle euphoric from the successes we achieved, suggested I should tell the Middle East, to improve their potency. This I reluctantly did, and back came a signal from their A.O.A. (an Air Vice-Marshal) which said 'Restore aircraft to normal forthwith. Cease use of unauthorized modifications. No spare engines will be forwarded until they are restored to normal', or words to that effect. Maynard did not tell me to obey the order, he asked me what we should do. I suggested he should leave matters in my hands until after I had had words with Air Ministry. I signalled them giving details of the modifications, finishing with the statement that, reverting to standard would leave us without any fighter defences. After another blasting from Middle East – 'Why hadn't they been told when we complied with their previous signal?' – I wrote a mind-boggling letter, with more differentials and multiple integrals than any fair minded person should pen-plagiarize, I must add, from the Royal Aeronautical Society Journal on the cooling effect of multi-bladed propellers, including contrarotational effects, researched by an Italian Professore, no less, and sat back. After six weeks, I asked for a reply from Air Ministry and by return received 'concur all your modifications'. I sent this on to Middle East (for the attention of the A.O.A.) and subsequently learned that the day following he fell sick of the palsey – a heart attack – and I had unknowingly removed a minor stumbling block to the business of warmongering.

There were numerous developments I was fathering at this time, from conjuring up a mobile refuelling tanker, with home made pumps, adding to the fuel capacity of a marooned London flyingboat which could not reach either end of the Mediterranean on its normal fuel-load – stacks of Hurricane overload tanks inside the hull, plus jettisoning everything except the barest essentials, it staggered off after a marathon 'nearly-nearly' take-off, and was fully 20 feet up when it disappeared Westwards. It did reach Gibraltar with a 5% margin of fuel intact. Luck is the essential component of experiment.

Another Hurricane development was that of a P.R.U. version. Air Staff in Valetta wanted photographs of places the Marylands could not penetrate – and

417

return – so we set to, and using crashed Wellington fuel tanks, put an extra 150 gallons within their standard parameters, with an extra 25 gallon oil tank in the leading edge of one wing. Additional oxygen, and two cameras plus a one-piece windscreen and a perspex panel in the floor, completed the mods. The windscreen was half a Blenheim astro-dome, which looked about the right size. Again, we were lucky. It was. The range was now a maximum of 1500 miles, and the results so satisfactory, that subsequently we built several more to the same design (the original would have been V7101 – Ed.). In the middle of this unofficial exercise, the Inspector General arrived (Air Chief Marshal Sir Edgar Hewitt). I carefully arranged for the first model to be hidden whenever he visited Luqa. I was attached to his visiting entourage and one day, on our way back to H.Q. from Luqa, he stopped the car and told the driver to go back. When we reached the tarmac, there was the P.R.U. Hurricane standing alone. We got out and as he walked towards it, he asked me what it was. 'A Hurricane, Sir.' was the limit of my imagination. I explained we had removed the guns to make way for the extra tankage and gave details of the additional equipment. By then he was standing with one hand on the leading edge 'You've forgotten one thing' he said, 'with all that extra fuel, it needs extra oil.' I explained that he had his hand on the extra 25 gallon tank. 'Does it work?' he asked. 'All the photographs you have been looking at at H.Q. were taken by it'. These included Naples and other fairly distant targets. Then 'Have you told the Air Ministry about this?' 'No, Sir.' 'Well, if you haven't I wont!' End of episode.

The minor problems all had to be solved locally. The Marylands suffered from tail wheel shimmying and before we could make dampers, we were running out of tyres. I asked Air Ministry for more and was told to get them direct from the U.S.A.! We made a pattern which would fit a British tyre onto a hub that matched the American mounting, melted some crashed dural prop blades and after machining, fitted Blenheim tyres. Swordfish tyres could be used on Blenheims and we made up solid tyres (discs of scrapped outer covers, sandwiched between metal plates, and about $1\frac{1}{2}$ inches proud from pheuma). Additionally, we had provided the Swordfish with additional oil tanks – they were tending to lose oil with the hot weather – and all the pilot had to do was to turn the tap on after about an hour of flying, and using a not too large diameter feed pipe, they maintained their main tank oil level without creating other problems. Lucky again!

One day on take-off one Gladiator swung into the leader, with the two apparent 'write-offs'. I went out and surveyed the trouble and noticed that there was a good front and a good rear, so it was out with the hacksaws (metaphorically speaking) and a hybrid was born of the two corpses.

We had only one spare engine for the Marylands and my W.O. rang to say the supercharger had gone on one engine, could he have the spare. I asked him to let me check before saying yes and I went out and ran up the offending radial. There was no boost available. Something stirred in my subconscious and I banged open the throttle. The boost surged up to a respectable figure and then fell back with increasing revs. Another two bursts reproduced the symptoms, so I shut down and climbed out. I walked to the wing tip, accompanied by a slightly impatient W.O., where I asked him whether he had ever ridden a bicycle over the edge of a cliff. 'No, Sir' – very correctly! 'Neither have I, but I think it would be difficult to get much pressure on the pedals when airborne.' Pointing along the leading edge, I said 'Someone has had the prop dismantled and put it together with the blades flat!'

Then, a Sunderland on passage, but riding at anchor at St. Paul's Bay, attracted the attention of a marauding 109 and had a hole punched in the prop blade by a 20mm. shell. Off came the prop, the edges of the hole tapped flush and was plugged with a threaded plug, then given a half hour overspeeding on a test bench. I reasoned that one overstressed radial was a cheap insurance for a Sunderland. I told the pilot to get the prop changed if and when he reached Alexandria – he made it. Shortly after this, an 'expert' from the U.K. arrived and explained how dural prop blades could not be repaired if the hole exceeded $\frac{1}{2}$in. diameter, or was in the outer third of the blade. As our hole was nearly 1 in. diameter and in the outer third, I encouraged him to hurry to the Middle East, where they seem to be working to rule.

The island was fostering visiting squadrons of Blenheims for short periods of offensive forays, as well as acting as a staging post for aircraft in passage to the Middle East. Also a slightly protracted handing over from Sammy Maynard to Hugh Pughe Lloyd, which coincided with the visit of the Inspector General. Hugh Pughe brought his own choice of station commanders and heads of H.Q. departments, all except for my job of Command Engineer, and trouble started immediately. He addressed the new set up and told us that in future there would be no more enemy aircraft allowed over Malta! (My reaction was that he was either nutters or ignorant, or both.)

Within a few days, I was telephoned by a visiting Wimpey pilot from Luqa – en route to Middle East – that after flying about 80 miles towards Egypt, his oil temperature was rising over the top, so he turned round and reported the trouble. The new station commander did not believe him, ordered his second pilot to take over, demoted the captain, said the aircraft was serviceable and ordered them to continue their flight. I contacted the station engineer officer, placed the aircraft u/s and went out to inspect it. I found that the oil cooler elements for hot climates were wired in the 'off' position and decided that, if after a test flight, the original captain was satisfied, they could continue. When I returned to H.Q., the station commander and A.O.C. had already decided that I had usurped the station commander's authority. My reply was (a) the pilot had been telling the truth, (b) the station commander had no authority to override a report of unserviceability, and (c) if his orders had been followed we should have lost an aircraft and its crew. Strained relations from then on.

The Governor of the island had formed a Service Committee to advise him on the defence of the island, and I was R.A.F. member. He had agreed with all our recommendations, as indeed had the previous A.O.C. Without any reference to the Governor, Hugh Pughe refused to continue our previous practices and gave underground storage space for reserve fighters to the new Command Equipment Officer. He promptly stacked tins of aviation fuel on top of each other in the entrance to these excavated passages; the lower tins collapsed and the place became unapproachable for any purpose.

On a number of occasions I had to intervene – on behalf of the pilots – when

419

the A.O.C. made absurd requests of a technical nature without any reference to me. He told one squadron to fit Hurricanes with their discarded overload tanks, so that he could have a single aircraft patrolling 120 miles to the West of the island in the hope of intercepting enemy transport planes. I forbade a second use of the tanks, on the grounds that their pumps had been run dry for unknown periods and there was no test rig available to check their serviceability. The truth was slightly different, but it worked, specially coming after the Wimpey debacle.

On another occasion, I was summoned to his office and asked to investigate the possibility of fitting Hurricanes with bomb racks and to give an estimate of the time to equip half a dozen aircraft. I asked whether he wanted two 500lb. bombs and he said no Hurricane could carry such a load. I pointed out that the two 44 gallon overload tanks were nearly as heavy as 500lb. bombs and rather angrily he told me to go away and find out how long it would take. I said it would take a week. He said 'Stop guessing and go and find out.' I said 'I'm not guessing, I fitted a Hurricane with 250lb. bombs and dropped them on Filfla (a small rock offshore) six months before he came to Malta.' This really enraged him and nothing more was said about the proposed scheme.

Shortly afterwards, when I went into the ops room, the flight commander of the Marylands, a diminutive Aussie named Whiteley, was banging his fist on the table and telling the A.O.C. he wouldn't bloody well do it. Apparently Hugh Pughe had ordered him to carry out an 'op' which was plain suicide and Hugh Pughe said that Flt.Lt. Whiteley had put all his aircraft u/s to prevent this 'op', and would I go and put them serviceable. I said I would not dream of over-riding Whiteley's judgement on his own aircraft, and with that the 'op' was called off. (Actually at the time of A.V.M. Lloyd's arrival on the island 'Titch' Whiteley was a Sqn.Ldr., and his flight had become 69 Squadron – Ed.).

Later on, a similar situation arose when a suicide mission was ordered for a squadron of Blenheims, whose non-operational squadron commander was Wg.Cdr. Hughie Edwards, V.C., D.F.C. Edwards went to the ops room and told Hugh Pughe he would personally lead the attack if Hugh Pughe insisted on its performance. There was some eyeball to eyeball exchange of views and that 'op' was also called off.

In the late summer of '41 I went down with sandfly fever and dysentry. After a spell in hospital I returned to duty. After a decent interval I asked to see Hugh Pughe and asked for a home posting … after a few weeks my family and I embarked with a few others for a lengthy, tedious and occasionally dangerous trip, unescorted, in a 12,000 ton Blue Star ship for Gibraltar, followed by a 19 day winter epic in an 1100 ton coal-burning Polish ship, to Liverpool.

This rough and sketchy account of my job probably, like my log books, has more omissions than it deserves, but short of writing a book, at least it details some of the events for which I was solely to blame.

Appendix XV

REPORT BY R.A.F. LUQA TO A.O.C. REGARDING EARLY WELLINGTON OPERATIONS; DATED FEBRUARY 1941

At the end of October 1940 a detachment of Wellingtons from Stradishall and Marham were despatched to Malta to carry out four raids on Rome and Naples. The intention at that time was for each aircraft to do four sorties and then proceed to M.E., the aircraft being maintained and operated by a handling party at Luqa.

After carrying out one successful raid on Naples a series of accidents occurred which depressed morale and some time elapsed before the pilots regained their confidence in Luqa as an aerodrome suitable for Wellington aircraft. To this end the runways were extended and obstructions removed, including a church, while for the protection of the aircraft a number of stone pens were built, which have saved a number of aircraft from bombs and machine-gunning.

At first no maintenance crews with any knowledge of the Wellington were available and personnel were drawn from almost every unit in Malta. Subsequently, a small party came out by cruiser from Marham and this was supplemented gradually by drafts from convoys as they arrived.

The lack of senior officers and N.C.O.s soon became apparent with the detachment, having no entity, lacking 'espirit de corps'. A request was therefore made that the Wellington unit should receive an identity and as a result 148 Squadron was reformed.

The squadron consisted almost entirely of 'war weary' aircrews who required careful handling and watching, but who, nevertheless, were very expert in night bombing. Many of these aircrews have carried out more than 40 ops, and some as many as 50.

In January 1941 further difficulties, over and above the anxieties of finding the island and the size of Luqa, developed with the arrival of German aircraft in Sicily. Night raiders followed our aircraft back to Malta, the enemy A.A. became very accurate and intense, while Luqa became a primary target.

The loss of two aircraft on operations in one night, followed by a severe dive-bombing raid on Luqa, tended to shake morale again and it became necessary to rest a number of aircrews. Later both the Officers' and N.C.O.s' Messes were seriously damaged by bombing, as also were the Airmen's Quarters; some of the flying and maintenance crews being killed or injured. It became necessary to evacuate many of the flying personnel to other parts of the island.

These developments coupled with continuous enemy action by day and night, the difficulties of obtaining exercise and of securing a change of atmosphere and outlook, have considerably slowed down the rate and intensity of ops. Nevertheless, the Squadron is successfully countering the trials of a painful rebirth and has carried out some extremely successful and valuable operations.

N.B. Shortly after this report had been written the squadron was virtually wiped out on the ground, when, on 26 February, Luqa was again raided and six Wellingtons were burnt out, with another seven badly damaged. (Ed.)

CODE LETTERS ALLOCATED TO SQUADRONS OPERATING FROM MALTA (NOT ALWAYS APPLIED)

Fighters		*Bombers*	
46 Squadron	PO	18 Squadron	WV
126 Squadron	HA	21 Squadron	YH
185 Squadron	GL	37 Squadron	LF
242 Squadron	LE	38 Squadron	HD
249 Squadron	GN	40 Squadron	BL
261 Squadron	XJ	82 Squadron	UX
605 Squadron	UP	104 Squadron	EP
		105 Squadron	GB
		107 Squadron	OM
Beaufighters		110 Squadron	VE
252 Squadron	Nil	139 Squadron	XD
272 Squadron	Nil	148 Squadron	Nil
		221 Squadron	Nil

Reconnaissance	
69 Squadron	Nil

Appendix XVII

FORMATION OF THE NATIONAL WAR MUSEUM, MALTA G.C. BY PHILIP VELLA, SECRETARY TO THE NATIONAL WAR MUSEUM ASSOCIATION

A letter by Dr. E. Agius in the 'Times of Malta' of 29 October, 1943, when the streets of Malta were still littered with debris, seemed to have fallen on deaf ears, except for one or two other correspondents who supported the setting-up of a War Museum to house the many relics relating to Malta's role during the Second World War.

It took over 30 years for those correspondents to see their dream materialise when, on 29 July 1974, a group of volunteers formed the National War Museum Association. Although it soon transpired that many important and historic relics had by then been sold for scrap, co-operation and assistance were forthcoming from the Ministry responsible for Culture, the Department of Museums, the Armed Forces of Malta, the British Services and various individuals who helped the Association to open, on 30 May 1975, a War Relics Exhibition housed at Lower Fort St Elmo in Valetta, itself a historic site which had lived the days that the Exhibition meant to record. It was on the ramparts of this old Fort that six Maltese artillery men died in the defence of their homeland on the very first day of the war on 11 June 1940, while, 13 months later, on 26 July, 1941, their comrades foiled a daring attempt by the Italian Navy to penetrate into the Island's two main harbours.

The Exhibition soon out-grew itself into a virtual War Museum which on 5 November 1979 came to be officially recognised as the National War Museum.

The principal exhibits are the George Cross, awarded to Malta on 15 April 1942, and the fuselage of the legendary Gladiator N5520 'Faith', which was restored by the Royal Air Force soon after the Association was set up. These and all the other items evoke memories of Malta's struggle for survival as the most bombed spot on earth till the time when the Island became a springboard for the invasion of Sicily.

Other important exhibits include the front section of the fuselage, including the Merlin engine, of a Spitfire Mk. VC, which ditched in Marsalforn Bay at Gozo; a Junkers Jumo 211 engine hauled up from the seabed off Zonqor Point; the starboard wing, bearing the original markings, of a Bf 109 recovered from the Gozo Channel; the helm and name-board of the tanker 'Ohio'; the Ship's Bell of 'Port Chalmers', one of the five merchant ships which succeeded in making harbour during Operation 'Pedestal' in August 1942; an Italian Vickers Terni 75 mm field gun, the first captured by the 51st Highland Division during the Sicilian campaign; Willys jeep 'Husky', used by General Eisenhower during his short stay in Malta preparatory to the invasion of Sicily as well as the uniform jackets of the last British Flag Officer, General Officer Commanding Troops and Air Commander to serve in Malta.

Numerous photographic panels depict conditions prevailing in Malta during the crucial years from 1940 to 1943. They tell the story of a gallant people who withstood the long strain of bombing and siege to preserve their freedom.

Several important acquisitions have been made on the Association's initiative; the Earl Mountbatten of Burma presented one of his war-time uniforms worn in Malta in 1941 when commanding H.M.S. 'Kelly'; Air Chief Marshal Sir Hugh Pughe Lloyd, Malta's Air Officer Commanding during the height of the blitz, donated his battledress tunic; the uniform jacket of Flight Lieutenant George F. Beurling, Malta's top fighter ace, was donated by his family in Canada; the Trustees of the National Maritime Museum at Greenwich presented a replica of the battle-scarred Ship's Bell of H.M.S. 'Illustrious', while several British Regimental Museums sent items of militaria.

The part played by the Royal Navy, Army and Civilian Organisations is also recorded in the Museum.

The Association has also set up a Library and an Archive, besides a Photographic Collection. Although considerable progress has been achieved in this respect, the Association welcomes more material throwing light on Malta's role as a Fortress.

The National War Museum of Malta G.C. is instrumental in recording an important chapter in the History of the Island. It aims at perpetuating the heroic stand made by all Malta, civilians and servicemen alike, whose determination to stand up against a threat to their democratic way of life was heavily paid for in terms of lives.

Besides, it immortalizes the valorous effort made by British and Commonwealth airmen, soldiers, sailors and merchant seamen, whose dedication and devotion to duty, often paid at the supreme sacrifice, helped Malta to emerge from the war deeply scratched but unbeaten.

Let it be recorded that from 11 June 1940 to 28 August 1944, Malta experienced 3,340 alerts, totalling 2,357 hours and 6 minutes, claiming 1,581 civilian victims; their memory is recorded in Malta's National War Museum in a special section containing a Roll of Honour besides the original model of the War Memorial at Floriana, on the outskirts of Valetta.

A further 554 Maltese lost their life while serving with the Forces and in the Merchant Navy. This brings a total of 2,135, representing 1:126 of the population of Malta and Gozo, besides the much higher number of people injured through enemy action.

N.B. Philip Vella is a personal friend of both Brian Cull and Christopher Shores; he is a keen and conscientious researcher and recorder of Malta's valiant efforts in World War II, as shown in his own recent book: "MALTA: BLITZED BUT NOT BEATEN".

Bibliography

'*The Air Battle of Malta*' H.M.S.O.

'*2 Group, R.A.F.*' Michael J.F. Bowyer Faber

'*Faith, Hope and Charity*' Kenneth Poolman Kimber

'*Night Strike from Malta*' Kenneth Poolman Janes

'*Illustrious*' Kenneth Poolman Kimber

'*Ark Royal*' Kenneth Poolman Kimber

'*Ark Royal*' W. Jameson Hart-Davis

'*The Four Ark Royals*' Michael Apps Kimber

'*Send Her Victorious*' Michael Apps Kimber

'*Carrier Air Groups: H.M.S. Eagle*' David Brown Hylton Lacey

'*Carrier Operations in World War II*' David Brown Ian Allan

'*Carrier Fighters*' David Brown Macdonald & Janes

'*Royal Air Force, 1939–1945; Vol. 1. The Fight at Odds*' Dennis Richards H.M.S.O.

'*Briefed to Attack*' Air Marshal Sir Hugh P. Lloyd Hodder & Stoughton

'*Malta Story*' (*Based on the diaries and experiences of Flg.Off. H.M. Coffin*) W.L. River Dutton, N.Y.

'*The Battle for the Mediterranean*' Donald McIntyre Batsford

'*Red Duster, White Ensign*' Ian Cameron White Lion

'*The Shiphunters*' R.E. Gillman Murray

'*Taranto*' D. Newton & A.C. Hampshire Kimber

'*Fighter Squadrons of the R.A.F.*' J.D.R. Rawlings Macdonald

'*Bomber Squadrons of the R.A.F.*' P. Moyes Macdonald

'*Fighters over the Desert*' Christopher Shores & Hans Ring Spearman

'*Hurricane at War*' Chaz Bowyer Ian Allan

'*Chronology of The War at Sea*' J. Rohwer & G. Hummelchen Ian Allan

'*Aircraft Carrier*' Norman Polmar Macdonald

'*Fleet Air Arm at War*' Ray Sturtivant Ian Allan

'*War in a Stringbag*' Charles Lamb Cassell

'*Wings at Sea*' Gerard Woods Conway

'*The Gloster Gladiator*' Francis K. Mason Macdonald

'*These Eagles*' R.A.A.F. Public Relations Australian War Memorial

'*New Zealanders with the Royal Air Force*' Wg.Cdr. H.L. Thompson War History Branch, N.Z.

'*Jagdgeschwader 27*' Werner Girbig & Hans Ring Motorbuch Verlag

'*L'Aeronautica Italiana della 2ª Guerra Mondiale*' Gen. Guiseppe Santoro Esse

'*Il 23º Gruppo Caccia*' Nicola Malizia Bizzari

'*Inferno su Malta*' Nicola Malizia Mursia

'*Il Fiat CR 42*' Nicola Malizia Ateneo & Bizzari

'*Il Reggiane 2000*' Nicola Malizia Ateneo & Bizzari

'*Gli Stuka della R. Aeronautica*' A. Borgiotti & C. Gari Stem Mucchi

'*Le Medaglio d'Oro al Virtuti Militari*' Stato Maggiore

'*Regia Aeronautica: La guerra aerea nel Mediterraneo*' Angelo Emiliani, Guiseppe F. Ghergo & Achille Vigna Intergest

'*Flight*' *magazine for 1941* – various copies

'*Times of Malta*' – various copies.

426

INDEX

Personnel – I, Allied

Bendall, Sgt. J., 105 Sqn. 292
Benitz, Sgt. F.M., 104 Sqn. 314
Bibby, F/Sgt. J., 431 Flt., 69 Sqn. 69, 70, 409
Bibby, Lt. R.E., 830 Sqn. 257, 310
Bidgood, Flg.Off. E.C., Hurricane ferry pilot 86
Bird, Flt.Lt. S.R., 605 Sqn. 329, 330
Black, Lt.Cdr. A.F., 805 Sqn. 95
Blackburn, Plt.Off. C.A., 46, 126 Sqns. 230, 286
Blaize, F/Sgt. R. (French), Loire 130/He 115 pilot 75, 293
Blanchard, Plt.Off. M.C., 242 Sqn. 329, 358, 387
Bland, Sub Lt., 800X Sqn. 303
Blennerhassett, Flg.Off. J.W., 252 Sqn. 195
Bloxham, Flg.Off. J.R., 69 Sqn. 185, 243, 245
Bolton, Sgt. J.R., Wellington pilot 238
Bone, Sgt. D.T., 18 Sqn. 343
Booth, Sgt., 252 Sqn. 215
Boret, Plt.Off. F.J., Hurricane ferry pilot 86
Bowden, Sgt., 431 Flt. 71
Bowerman, Sgt. O.R., 418 Flt., 261 Sqn. 44, 47, *49*, 51, 53, 180, 376, 382
Bowie, Sgt. D., 272 Sqn. 318
Boyd, Capt. D., H.M.S. 'Illustrious' 114
Boyd, Sgt. J.L., 242 Sqn. 329
Boyd, Air Marshal O.T., Deputy C. in C., M.E. 89
Boyle, Plt.Off. J.M., 249 Sqn. 248, 255
Boys-Stones, Flg.Off. J., 431 Flt., 69 Sqn. 99, 164
Brabner, Lt. R.A., 805 Sqn. 95
Bradbury, Flt.Lt. H.F.R., 418 Flt., 261 Sqn. 45, 47, 51, 53, 89, 147, 148, 154, 163, 376, 382
Branch, Sgt., 249 Sqn. *218*, *345*
Brandt, Flt.Lt. S., 249 Sqn. 347, 358, *359*, 387
Brandwood, Sgt. F.B., 105 Sqn. 292
Branson, Sgt. R.A., 261, 185 Sqns. 190, 198, 206, 260, 381
Bridger, Plt.Off. J., Wellington pilot 180
Broadley, Flt.Lt. A.B., 105 Sqn. 273
Brokensha, Sub Lt. G.W., 803 Sqn. 58
Broom, Plt.Off. I.G., 107 Sqn. 332
Brown, Sgt. G., 69 Sqn. 175, 176
Brown, F/Sgt. K.C., 233 Sqn. 347
Brown, Wg.Cdr. M.H., Takali Wing Leader 324, 327, 387
Bruen, Lt. J.M., 803 Sqn. 58
Bryant, Sub Lt. R.F., 805 Sqn. 95
Buck, Sgt. D.W., 107 Sqn. 332
Buckley, Sgt. E., 272 Sqn. 318
Buckley, Plt.Off. J., 105 Sqn. 277
Burges, Sqn.Ldr. G., Ftr.Flt., Hal Far, 261, 69 Sqns. 2, *6*, 10, 11, 29, 35, 36, 37, 41, 51, 53, 54, 81, 89, *101*, 122, 125, 134, 197, 228, 369, 376, 382, 384, 403–406, 412
Burgess, Flg.Off. J.T., 431 Flt. 83

Burnett, Flt. Lt. N.W., 46 Sqn. 230, 234, 387
Burnett, F/Sgt., 233 Sqn. 59
Burston, Pty.Off.(A) L.E., 800 Sqn. 50, 84, 94
Burton, Sgt. H., 261, 185 Sqns. 190, 206, 381

Cahill, Gp.Capt. C.A., Luqa 226, 309
Callingham, Lt. G.R., 800 Sqn. 50, 51, 94
Camilleri, P/C C., Malta Constabulary 79
Cambell, Lt. N.K., 830 Sqn. 199
Campbell, L.A.C. D.A., 230 Sqn. 39
Campbell, Flt.Lt. G.L., 272 Sqn. 259, 267
Campbell, Sub Lt. S., 830 Sqn. 313, 327
Campbell, Sgt., 238 Sqn. 238
Carlisle, Pty.Off.(A) R., 807 Sqn. 201
Carnes, Lt.Cdr. C., R.N. Decyphering Officer 263
Carpenter, Flt.Lt. J.M.V., 46, 126 Sqns. 230, *231*, 246, 285, 286, 306, 324, 327, 336, 356
Carson, Sgt. R.R., 46, 126 Sqns. 230
Carter, Plt.Off. R.W.H., Hurricane ferry pilot 15, 17, 24
Carter, Sgt., 249 Sqn. 248, 288
Carver, Lt. E.S., 800 Sqn. 30, 50
Cashmore, Plt.Off. V., 113 Sqn. 302
Cassidy, Flt.Lt. E., 249 Sqn., M.N.F.U., 1435 Flt. 217, 251, 270, 273, 274, 282, 310, 326, *342*, *343*, *344*
Cathles, Sgt. N.A.C., 110 Sqn. 257
Cavan, Flg.Off. B.M., 261, 249 Sqns. 190, 209, 351, 381, 387
Chandler, Sgt. E.F., 82 Sqn. 241
Charney, Sqn.Ldr. F.R., 105 Sqn. 292
Christian, Lt. J.M., 803 Sqn. 31
Churchill, the Hon. Winston, British Prime Minister 134
Clark, Sgt. C., 69 Sqn. 284
Clarke, Flg.Off. D., 272 Sqn. 266
Clarke, Flg.Off. R.W., Hurricane ferry pilot 86
Clerke, Sqn.Ldr. R.F.H., 1 P.R.U. 333
Clifford, Alex, 'Daily Mail' Correspondent 39
Clisby, Sub Lt. W.H., 806 Sqn. 84, 95
Cockburn, Lt. R.C., 808 Sqn. 260
Coffin, Plt.Off. H.M., 126 Sqn. 290, 291, 323, 350, 352, 354, 356
Cole, Flt.Lt. E.S.T., Blenheim ferry pilot 15, 16, 18
Coles, L/A J., 800 Sqn. 30, 94
Collard, Wg.Cdr. R.C.M., 37 Sqn. 367
Collins, Plt.Off. W.P., Hurricane ferry pilot 15, 21, 22, 23, 24
Colville, Sgt. G.D., 40 Sqn. 321
Connolly, Lt. P.J., 800X Sqn. 213, 214, 215
Constable, Sub Lt. P., 808 Sqn. 298, 301
Cook, Wt.Off. F.W., Blenheim ferry pilot 16, 17, 24

Cooper, Flt.Lt. L.F., 233 Sqn. 12, 24, 59
Cooper, Sgt., 249 Sqn. 217
Copp, Sgt. W.E., 46, 126 Sqns. 230, 242, 243, 336, 352, 356
Corbishley, Flt.Lt. P., 69 Sqn. (attached) 128, 129, 139
Cordwell, Pty.Off.(A) V.H., 800 Sqn. 84
Cotton, Sub Lt. P., 830 Sqn. 285
Couch, Sub Lt. P.W.N., 808 Sqn. 297
Counter, Plt.Off. C.F., 261 Sqn. 133, 374, 375, 378
Courtney, Sqn.Ldr. R.N.H., 261 Sqn. 375
Cousens, Sgt. R.A., 185 Sqn. *247*, 248, 265, 334, 387
Coventry, L/A C., 807 Sqn. 312
Cover, Sgt. J.A., 82 Sqn. 245
Cox, Flg.Off. G.D., 230, 148 Sqns. 119
Coxon, Sub Lt. C.R.J., 830 Sqn. 289, 310, 325, 348
Crane, Sub Lt. V.B., 252 Sqn. 195
Crossey, Flg.Off. J.T., 249 Sqn. 217, *224*, 336, 354
Crossley, Sgt. E., 107 Sqn. 347, 355
Crossley, Sgt. H., 113 Sqn. 302
Cunningham, Adm. Sir Andrew, C. in C. Mediterranean Fleet 56, 60, 104, 202, 403, 410
Cunnington, Sgt. W.G., Hurricane ferry pilot 86, 87
Currie, Plt.Off. I.R., 261 Sqn. 130, 378
Cursham, Cdr. M., Cdr. Flying, H.M.S. 'Victorious' 213
Curtriss, Pty.Off.(A) W.E., 808 Sqn. 260

Davenport, Flg.Off. R.O., 272 Sqn. 266, 267
Davidson, Flg.Off. J.C., 252, 272 Sqns. 195, 202, 215, 259, 268, 273, 318
Davidson, Sqn.Ldr. R.T.P., 261 Sqn. 375
Davies, Plt.Off. J.H.M., 148 Sqn. 118, 119
Davies, Flg.Off. G.W.V., 233 Sqn. 12, *12*, 24, 58, 59
Davies, Sgt. L., 261 Sqn. 133, *133*, 138, 139, *140*, 149, 155, 158, *187*, 189, 203, 378
Davies, Sgt. M.P., 274 Sqn., attached 261 Sqn. 168, *187*, 380
Davies, Sgt., 249 Sqn. *345*
Davis, Flt.Lt. C.C.H., 249 Sqn. *218*, 248, 253, *345*, *349*
Davis, Cpl. J.G.M., Luqa 67
Dawson, Sub Lt. R.N., 830 Sqn. 183
Day, Sqn.Ldr. L.H., 38 Sqn. 312
Deacon, Sgt. A.H., 261 Sqn. 130, 131, 180, *181*, 185, 378
Deakin, Sgt. W.M., 272 Sqn. 258, 259
de Frias, N/A F.J.L., 803 Sqn. 30, 31, 46

De Gaulle, Gen. Charles, Free French Leader 64
De Moulin, Sgt. R.J.G., 272 Sqn. 266, 296
Dempsey, Sister, Imtarfa Hospital 153
Dennis, Plt.Off. D.F., 21 Sqn. 199
Dexter, Sgt. L.J., 261 Sqn. 133, *187*, 228, 378
De Wiart, Gen. Carton 180
Devine, Flg.Off. P.S., 431 Flt., 69 Sqn. 69, 70, 305, 409
Dickinson, Plt.Off. E., 126 Sqn. 248, 281
Dickson, Sgt., 1435 Flt. *342*
Dobbie, Gen. Sir William, Governor of Malta 14, 77, 134
Dodd, N/A F.W., 818 Sqn. 51
Dooley, N/A, F.P., 803 Sqn. 31
Douet, L/A P., 806 Sqn. 72
Doughty, Flg.Off. N.A.R., 261 Sqn. 190, 380
Douglas, Lt.Cdr. J. Sholto, 808 Sqn. 200, 201, 257, 260
Dowland, Wg.Cdr. J.N., 69 Sqn. 283, 321, 325, 333, 334, 368
Downey, Sqn.Ldr. E.R.G., 261 Sqn. 375
Downie, Plt.Off. N.C., 213 Sqn. 213
Drake, Sub Lt. R.G., F.A.A. observer 293
Dredge, Plt.Off. A.S., 261, 185 Sqns. 190, 198, *199*, 206, 255, 381
Drew, Flg.Off. R., 69 Sqn. 229, 240, 249, 284, 353
Drummond, Lt. D.R.H., 813 Sqn. 62
Drury, Sgt. J.B., 18 Sqn. 347
Dubber, Pty.Off.(A) R.E., 808 Sqn. 200
Dunlevie, Wg.Cdr. J.S., 107 Sqn. 367
Dupont, Sgt. J., 230 Sqn. 352, 353
Duvauchelle, F/Sgt. R. (French), Esc. 2HT, 230 Sqn. (attached), 69 Sqn. 27, 64, 117

Easton, Plt.Off. G.H., 40 Sqn. 347, 352
Eccleshall, L/A L.V., 800 Sqn. 50
Edmondson, Midspmn. D.S., 830 Sqn. 52
Edmunds, Flt.Lt. E.G., 18 Sqn. 338, 339, 347
Edwards, Wg.Cdr. H.I., 105 Sqn. 270, 284, 367, 420
Eliot, Flt.Lt. H.W., 261, 185 Sqns. 86, 88, 142, 147, 158, 206, *206*, *207*, 305, 377
Ellis, Sgt. R.J.F., 185 Sqn. 248, 260
Emery, F/Sgt. F.R., 46, 126 Sqns. 230, 354, 387
Etchells, F/Sgt. F.A., 249 Sqn. 217, 237, *251*, 323, 352, 354
Evans, Lt.Cdr. C.L.G., 806 Sqn. 57, 59, 60, 72, 75, 82, 84, 104, *113*, 385
Eyres, Lt. D.E.C., 800X Sqn., Rescue Flt. 305, 321, 365

Fairbairn, Flt.Lt. G.M., 82 Sqn. 223
Farries, Flg.Off. S.M., 228 Sqn. 80
Fell, Sub Lt. M.F., 800 Sqn. 30, 50

Handley, Plt.Off. C.W., Blenheim ferry pilot   16, 20

Hanson, Sgt. B.P.   69 Sqn.   243

Hanson, Sgt. H.L., 107 Sqn.   332

Hardie, Flt.Lt. E., A.S.R. launch commander 232

Hare, Lt.Cdr. G., 800X Sqn.   211, 212, 214

Hare, Sgt. M.T., Hurricane ferry pilot   246

Harrington, Flg.Off. E.J.F., 249 Sqn.   217, *218*, 220, 222, 232, *345*, 355

Harris, Gp.Capt. S.H.V., Luqa   309

Harrison, Sgt. J.H., 82 Sqn.   242

Harrison-Broadley, Sqn.Ldr. J., 82 Sqn.   241

Hart, Pty.Off.(A) R.F., 800 Sqn.   50, 82, 84

Harte, Wg.Cdr. F.A., 107 Sqn.   292, 310, 367

Hartill, L.A.C. W., 185 Sqn. groundcrew   *207*

Hartley, Flg.Off. P.W., Ftr.Flt., Hal Far   6, *7*, 10, 31, 41, 369, 370

Harvey, Sgt. R.V., 242 Sqn.   329

Hay, Lt. R.C., R.M., 808 Sqn.   178, 201, 258, 301

Hay, Plt.Off. W.B., 242 Sqn.   329

Hayes, Sgt. B., 185 Sqn.   *247*, 248, 352, 387

Haylock, Sgt. R.A., 272 Sqn.   303

Haynes, Lt. G.M., 828 Sqn.   368

Heard, Pty.Off.(A) W.J., 800 Sqn.   50

Heath, Plt.Off., Hurricane ferry pilot   131

Henley, Sgt. R.F.J., 107 Sqn.   354

Henley, Lt. R.S., 806 Sqn.   109, 126, 161, 202, 205

Hewitt, Air Chief Marshal Sir Edgar, Inspector General, R.A.F., M.E.   418

Hibbert, Sgt. L., Blenheim navigator   22

Hill, Plt.Off. F.C., 249 Sqn.   *218*, *219*, 248, 261

Hills, N/A, 800 Sqn.   50

Hirst, Flg.Off. P.S., 252 Sqn.   195, 211

Hitching, Sgt. J.T., 261 Sqn.   163, 379

Hodson, Sgt. C.G., 261, 185 Sqns.   130, 206, *206*, *207*, 378

Hogg, Sub Lt. G.A., 806 Sqn.   72, 75, 82, 84, 109, 121, 385

Holgate, Flg.Off. J.B., 252 Sqn.   195, 215

Hollingsworth, Sgt. A., 148 Sqn.   96

Holme, Sub Lt. K., 252 Sqn.   195

Holmes, Sub Lt. D.A.R., 830 Sqn.   243

Holmes, N/A, R.H., 800 Sqn.   50, 84, 94

Hood, Mr., Luqa Controller   30

Hopkins, Lt.Cdr. F.H.E., 830 Sqn.   348, 368

Hopkins, Sub Lt. R.D.B., 252 Sqn.   195

Hopkinson, Sgt. W.A., 107 Sqn.   325

Horgan, Flt.Lt. T.M., 431 Flt.   70

Horrox, Plt.Off. J.M., Hurricane ferry pilot 86

Horricks, Sgt. G.E., 249 Sqn.   346

Horsey, Sgt. J., 185 Sqn.   *247*

Horton, Flg.Off. P.W., Hurricane ferry pilot   86, 88

Howard, Pty.Off.(A) L.G.J., 808 Sqn.   200

Howe, Sgt. D.J., 605 Sqn.   329

Howell, Sgt. A., 605 Sqn.   329

Howie, Lt.Cdr. F.D., 830 Sqn.   9, 27, 138, 257, 271, 368

Hubbard, Sgt. B.F., 431 Flt.   83

Hughes, Flt.Lt. S.W.R., 230 Sqn.   352

Hulbert, Plt.Off. J.G.K., 249 Sqn.   217, 279

Humphries, Lt. G.R., 820 Sqn.   *50*, 51

Hunt, Lt.Cdr. J.G., 830 Sqn.   305, 327, 368

Hunt, Wg.Cdr. T.M., 110 Sqn.   253, 367

Hunton, Sgt. C.L., 185 Sqn.   *247*, 248, 315

Hurle-Hobbs, Sub Lt. B.H.St.A.H., 800, 800X Sqns.   50, 84, 321

Hutt, Plt.Off. D.F., 40 Sqn.   344

Hutt, Sgt. J.K., 69 Sqn.   252, 272, 336

Hyde, Sgt. R.J., 418 Flt., 261 Sqn.   45, 47, *48*, 51, 53, 63, *85*, 128, 188, 193, 377, 382, 384

Inman, Sgt. E.B., 82 Sqn.   223

Innes, Plt.Off. R.A., 261, 185 Sqns.   190, 194, 206, 271, 381

Izycki, Wg.Cdr. M., R.A.F. Takoradi, West Africa   131

Janvin, Lt. R., 431 Flt. (attached)   411

Jay, Flt.Lt. R.E., 252 Sqn.   195

Jeffries, Flt.Lt. C.G.St.D., 261, 185 Sqns.   190, 197, 206, *206*, *247*, 248, 249, 251, 252, 286, 305, 380

Jeffries, Flg.Off. C.H., 249 Sqn.   255

Jenkins, Sgt. C.F., 272 Sqn.   259

Jennings, Sgt. H.H., 261 Sqn.   178, 200, 380, 386

Jessop, Sgt. E.R., 261 Sqn.   178, *187*, 380

Jessop, Sgt. F.J., 261 Sqn.   163, 164, 379

Johnson, Pty.Off.(A) A.G., 807 Sqn.   200

Johnson, Plt.Off. D.S., Blenheim ferry pilot   15, 20

Johnston, Sgt. J.H., 46, 126 Sqns.   230, 234

Johnstone, Lt.Cdr. M., 810 Sqn.   93

Jolly, Sgt. A.W., 261, 185 Sqns.   *187*, 190, 197, 206, *206*, *207*, 231, 244, *247*, 249, 305, 358, 371, 381

Jonas, Wg.Cdr. R. Carter, Luqa   30, 37, 41, 76, 127, 150, 164, 172, 262, 370

Jones, Sgt. A.S., 228 Sqn.   165

Jones, Sgt. D.H., 242 Sqn.   328

Jones, N/A G.J., 800 Sqn.   84

Jones, L/A, 808 Sqn.   298

Jopling, Pty.Off.(A) A., 800, 800X Sqns.   84, 94, 145, 274, 284, 290, 303, 307, 308, *308*, 341

Jordan, Sgt. P.L., 261 Sqn.   *187*, 190, 202, 203, 374, 381

432

433

434

435

Thompson, Sqn.Ldr. J.R., 139 Sqn.   228
Thompson, Flt.Lt. P.D., 261, 185 Sqns.   190, 198, 206, *247*, 261, 265, 301, 358, 380
Thompson, Plt.Off. P.J.A., 261 Sqn.   190, 207, 381, 387
Thompson, L/A W.E.J., 830 Sqn.   170
Thornton, F/Sgt. P.S.G., 38 Sqn.   312
Thorpe, Sub Lt. M., 830 Sqn.   274
Thurston, Flg.Off. G.R., 10 R.A.A.F. Sqn.   202
Tillard, Lt. R.C., 808 Sqn.   83, 84, 94, 108, 178, 200, 385
Timms, Sgt. W.J., 418 Flt., 261 Sqn.   44, 47, 51, 53, 116, 117, 377, 382, 386, 406
Tipton, Plt.Off. J.E., 40 Sqn.   350, 360, 403, 412–413
Todd, Sgt. A.G., 261 Sqn.   133, 378
Tompkins, Mr., Luqa Controller   30
Touch, Sgt. D.F., 272 Sqn.   267, 273
Tranter, F/Sgt. J.H., 252 Sqn.   202
Tribe, L/A D.J., 806 Sqn.   60, 80, 110
Triggs, Sgt., 252 Sqn.   341
Tritton, Sub Lt. A.M., 800, 800X Sqns.   94, 249, *250*, 253, 285, 307, 321, 341
Trumble, Sqn.Ldr. A.J., 418 Flt., 261 Sqn.   45, 47, 51, 53, 96, 154, 365, 375, 382
Turner, Sub Lt. J.F., 807 Sqn.   298
Twist, Sgt. W.H., 110 Sqn.   252

Underwood, Sub Lt. J.F., 807 Sqn.   299, 312
Urry, Sub Lt. L.D., 808 Sqn.   297

Valachos, Plt.Off. P.J., 148 Sqn.   127
Vardy, Sgt. B.J., 261, 185 Sqns.   178, 206, *206*, *207*, *247*, 358, 380
Veitch, Plt.Off. P.J.B., 185 Sqn.   248, 305, 307, 387
Vella, Philip, Maltese civilian   121, 263, 424–425
Verity, Flg.Off. H., 252 Sqn.   195, 215
Vickers, Sgt. H., 18 Sqn.   324
Vincent–Jones, Lt. D., 806 Sqn.   60, 105, 109, 110, 111, *113*, 114, 136, 139, 159, 160, 365, 385
Virgin, Flg.Off. N.E.H., 252 Sqn.   195, 215

Waghorn, Sgt. P.H., 261 Sqn.   178, 180, 183, 380, 386
Walford, Lt., 431 Flt. (attached)   411
Walker, Flg.Off. B., Blenheim ferry pilot   15, 17, 24
Walker, Sqn.Ldr. D.R., 261 Sqn.   375
Walker, Sgt. G.A., 261 Sqn.   178, 200, 380
Walker, Sgt. J.H., 18 Sqn.   339
Walker, Flg.Off. J.R., Hurricane ferry pilot   86, 88
Walker, Sgt. N.McD., 46 Sqn.   230, 233, 236, 387
Walker, Sub Lt. R.F., 807 Sqn.   201, 299
Wallace, Sgt. W.H., 105 Sqn.   289

Wallis, Sgt. F.R., 252 Sqn.   341, 345
Walmsley, Sgt. B.C., 261, 185 Sqns.   190, 194, 206, 381
Walsh, Plt.Off. J.J., 261 Sqn.   130, 155, 158, 378, 386
Warburton, Flg.Off. A., 431 Flt., 69 Sqn.   69, 70, 75, 76, 80, 81, 82, 99, 117, *143*, 147, 165, 185, 240, 252, 256, *256*, 284, 294, 303, 384, 409, 410
Wardrop, Sub Lt. J.E.G., 807 Sqn.   298
Ware, Flt.Lt. E.M., 228 Sqn.   80
Warfield, Wg.Cdr. J., Takali   210
Warren, Sqn.Ldr. T.J.S., 107 Sqn.   293
Waters, Lt. D.W., 830 Sqn.   52
Waters, Flt.Lt. J., Ftr.Flt., Hal Far, 261 Sqn.   4, 7, *7*, 8, 26, 51, 53, 76, 96, 108, 115, 180, 370, 376, 382, 384
Watkins, Flt.Lt. T.J., 82 Sqn.   241
Watson, Flt.Lt. G., 261 Sqn.   134, 147, 148, 379, 386
Watson, Sqn.Ldr. M.L., 82 Sqn.   234
Watson, Lt. M.W., 808 Sqn.   297
Wavell, Gen. Sir Archibald, C. in C., M.E.   50, 93, 205
Welland, Sqn.Ldr. R.D., 69 Sqn.   228, 283, 368
Wells, Flg.Off. M.L., 69 Sqn.   305
Wells, Sgt. P.C., 69 Sqn.   354
Wells, Flg.Off. P.H.V., 249 Sqn.   217, 220, *224*, 268, 282, 294
Wells, Sqn.Ldr. R.J., 148 Sqn.   242
Wells, Sqn.Ldr. W.G., 242 Sqn.   329, 366
Welsh, Pty.Off.(A) W.G.T., 830 Sqn.   199
Westcott, Sgt. J.A., 185 Sqn.   248, 251
Westmacott, Sqn.Ldr. I.B., 261, 185 Sqns., 1435 Flt.   177, 178, 180, 183, 184, 185, 193, 198, 206, 207, 213, 268, 282, 312, *342*, 342, *343*, 356, 366, 380
White, Sgt. A.E., 69 Sqn.   175, 176
Whiteley, Sqn.Ldr. E.A., 431 Flt., 69 Sqn.   68, 69, *69*, 70, 71, 85, 87, 96, 183, 185, 211, 228, 368, 403, 404, 405, 409–412, 420
Whitford–Walders, Flg.Off. N., 107 Sqn.   310
Whitney, Plt.Off. D.M., 261 Sqn.   *162*, 163, *163*, 171, 181, 189, 194, 217, 379
Whittingham, Sqn.Ldr. C.D., 261 Sqn.   130, 133, 138, 150, 154, 155, 158, 161, 170, 193, 198, 208, 365, 375, 378
Whitworth, Lt. A.S., 830 Sqn.   272, 277
Wickham, Plt.Off. P.R.W., 112 Sqn.   56
Wigley, Plt.Off. P., 605 Sqn.   *328*, 329, *331*
Wigram, Lt. A.F., 830 Sqn.   327
Wild, Sqn.Ldr. F.W.L., 4 Ferry Pool   15
Wilkins, Sgt. F., 69 Sqn.   277
Wilkinson–Bell, Flt.Lt. J., Blenheim ferry pilot   15, 20
Williams, Flg.Off. E.J.A., 69 Sqn.   305

436

Personnel – II, Axis

a) Italians

Boetto, Cap. Armando	49ᵃ	38°	32°	B.T.	200
Bombardini, Serg. Alfredo	97ᵃ	9°	4°	C.T.	334
Bonfatti, Ten. Pietro	73ᵃ	9°	4°	C.T.	305, 315, 316, 334, 335
Bordin, Ten.Col. Giuseppe		31°	43°	B.T.	224, 393
Borghese, Ezio – see Viglione–Borghese					
Bosio, Sottoten. di Vasc. Carlo				(10th Light Flotilla)	264
Botti, Serg.Magg. Enrico		10°	4°	C.T.	253
Botto, Magg. Ernesto		9°	4°	C.T.	26
Bragadin, Sottoten. Vittorio	238ᵃ	96° Aut.		B.a'T	324
Brambilla, Magg. Bruno		17°	1°	C.T.	81, 180, 389, 392
Brambilla, Ten.Col. Nello		99°	43°	B.T.	200, 274, 393
Brandi, Ten. Raffaele	195ᵃ	90°	30°	B.T.	83
Bravin, Mar. Giovanni		16°	54°	C.T.	243
Brezzi, Ten.		96° Aut.		B.a'T	61, 65
Brigante Colonna, Sottoten. Carlo		23° Aut.		C.T.	258
Brini, Mar. Augusto		23° Aut.		C.T.	*175*
Brissolese, Sottoten.	208ᵃ	101° Aut.Tuff.			295
Bruttini, Av.Amleto	238ᵃ	96° Aut.		B.a'T	324
Buffa, Mar. Giovanni		171° Aut.		C.N.	306, 394
Buogo, Serg.		17°	1°	C.T.	235
Buri, Magg. Arduino			36°	A.S.	296, 298, 331
Buscaglia, Magg. Carlo Emanuele		132° Aut.		A.S.	*300*
Bussolin, Sottoten. Felice	73ᵃ	9°	4°	C.T.	314, 320
Cagna, Gen.Brig.A. Stefano					46
Calafiore, Sottoten.	376ᵃ	21°	51°	C.T.	339
Calistri, Cap. Pietro	72ᵃ, 377ᵃ	23° Aut.		C.T.	39, 255, 394
Campioni, Adm. Inigo					93
Cannarsa, Ten.Col. Eugenio		90°	30°	B.T.	392
Cannaviello, Ten.Col. Vittorio		34°	11°	B.T.	389
Cantele, Sottoten. Luigi	76ᵃ	7°	54°	C.T.	281
Capanni, Ten.Col. Nello		27°	8°	B.T.	46
Caponetti, Ten. Angelo	279ᵃ Aut.			A.S.	109
Carapezza, Sottoten. Enrico	200ᵃ	92°	39°	B.T.	34
Carmello, Mar. Giovanni		23° Aut.		C.T.	*81*
Carrozzo, Mar. Leonida		17°	1°	C.T.	81, 92
Castiglione, Cap. Alfredo	57ᵃ	32°	10°	B.T.	
Catani, Serg.Magg. Luigi	237ᵃ	96° Aut.		B.a'T	65
Cavalli, Sottoten. Franco	70ᵃ	23° Aut.		C.T.	66, 67
Ceoletta, Serg. Battista		10°	4°	C.T.	279
Cesolini, Ten. Arrigo		116°	37°	B.T.	332
Chellini, Sottoten.		17°	1°	C.T.	235
Chiodi, Cap. Antonio	75ᵃ	23° Aut.		C.T.	35, 41
Ciano, Ten.Col. Galeazzo		(Foreign Minister)			*90*
Cibin, Ten. Armando		7°	54°	C.T.	234, 246
Cimicci, Cap. Giuseppe		132° Aut.		A.S.	*300*
Cipriani, Ten.	283ᵃ	130° Aut.		A.S.	258
Contarini, Serg. Luigi	90ᵃ	10°	4°	C.T.	244, 253, 288
Corsini, Cap. Luigi	80ᵃ	17°	1°	C.T.	81
Cozzoli, Serg.				C.T.	261
Cumbat, Ten. Antonio		96° Aut.		B.a'T	61
Cupini, Col. Ranieri			10°	B.T.	242
Curcio, Sottoten. Umberto		17°	1°	C.T.	234, 393

Name					Pages
Cuscuna, Serg. Francesco		23°/156° Aut.		C.T.	283, 331
Daffarra, Mar.		6° Aut.		C.T.	172
D'Ajello, Cap.	163ª Aut.			C.T.	62
Dalle Nogure, Cap. Bernadino		31°	43°	B.T.	274
Dallari, Serg.Magg. Enrico	73ª	9°	4°	C.T.	305
Damiani, Mar. Rinaldo	97ª	9°	4°	C.T.	334
Deanna, Sottoten. Giuseppe	97ª	9°	4°	C.T.	327
De Benedetti, Sottoten. Neri	90ª	10°	4°	C.T.	244
Del Cerro, Sottoten. Gaio			30°	B.T.	95
Dell'Olio, Ten. Nicola	201ª	92°	39°	B.T.	62
De Mattia, Mar. Avellino	98ª	7°/10°	54°/4°	C.T.	246, 265, 281, 288
de Porto, Magg. Cesare		29°		B.T.	394
Deslex, Ten. Carlo	280ª	130° Aut.		A.S.	297
Di Giorgio, 1ᵉ Av. Francesca	237ª	96° Aut.		B.a'T	66, 67
Di Giorgio, Ten. Silvio	98ª	7°	54°	C.T.	261
d'Ippolito, Ten.Col. Pasquale		60°	41°	B.T.	389
Di Jorio, Ten.Col. Renato		55°		B.T.	310, 395
Di Trapani, Sottoten. Antonio	287ª Aut.			R.M.	57
Dobrilla, Sottoten. Diego	287ª Aut.			R.M.	145
Dollfus, Ten.	283ª	130° Aut.		A.S.	258
Donadio, Magg. Giuseppe		101° Aut.Tuff.		B.a'T	393
Donda, Ten. Silvano	196ª Aut.			R.M.	84
Draghelli, Ten.Col. Emilio		59°	41°	B.T.	389
Drago, Col. Carlo			36°	B.T.	390
Dusi, Serg. William		23ᶜ Aut.		C.T.	*68, 92, 255*
Erasi, Magg. Massimiliano	278ª Aut.			A.S.	393
Ercolani, Magg. Ercolano		96° Aut.		B.a'T	61, 390
Euria, Sottoten. Tealdo	170ª Aut.			R.M.	83
Facchini, Serg.Magg.		7°	54°	C.T.	234, 264
Fagnani, Col. Tarcisio			54°	C.T.	394
Falconi, Ten.Col. Tito		23° Aut.		C.T.	35, 64, 92, 180, *294*, 332, 393
Fargnoli, Cap. Ottorino		23° Aut.		C.T.	35
Fedrighi, Gen.					265
Ferrara, 1ᵉ Av.Am. Francesco			52°	B.T.	2
Ferrari, Ten. Adolfo	257ª	108°	36°	B.T.	72, 73
Ferretti, Sottoten. Duca Gabriele	86ª	7°	54°	C.T.	281, 302, 345, *346*
Ferri, Sottoten. Alfio	144ª Aut.			R.M.	83
Ferri, Ten. Pietro			36°	B.T.	37
Ferrulli, Mar. Leonardo	91ª	10°	4°	C.T.	252, 253
Festa, Cap. Valentino			54°	C.T.	287
Filippi, Sottoten. Felice	195ª	90°	30°	B.T.	31, *32*, 134
Filippi, Cap. Luigi		156° Aut.		C.T.	158, 392, 393
Finito, Serg.Magg. Natale		10°	4°	C.T.	253
Fiorentini, Mar. Diego	75ª	23° Aut.		C.T.	308, 347
Floreani, Sottoten. Ciro	194ª	90°	30°	B.T.	33
Focacci, Ten. Guido	258ª	109°	36°	A.S.	315
Folli, Ten.			54°	C.T.	259
Forte, Ten.Col. Ferri		33°	11°	B.T.	389
Francois, Ten.Col. Armando		6° Aut.		C.T.	2, 389

Frigerio, Sottoten. Jacopo	97ª	9º	4º	C.T.	304, 327, 334
Galati, Sottoten. Antonio	259ª	109º	36º	A.S.	349
Gallina, Serg.Magg. Ruggera	76ª	7º	54º	C.T.	265
Gandais, Serg.Magg. Arnaldo	79ª	6º	1º	C.T.	174
Gasperoni, Mar. Germano		23º Aut.		C.T.	92, 236, 331, 347
Gastaldi, Magg. Goffredo		109º	36º	A.S.	349
Gavani, Serg.Magg.	376ª	21º	51º	C.T.	326
Giacomelli, Cap. Giuliano		6º Aut.		C.T.	71
Giannoccarso, Sottoten.		7º	54º	C.T.	264
Giobbe, Cap. di Corv.		(10th. Light Flotilla)			264
Girandola, A.					72
Giuliani, Ten.Col. Mario		87º	30º	B.T.	392
Golino, Serg. Angelo	97ª	9º	4º	C.T.	334
Gostini, Cap. Saverio		7º	54º	C.T.	246, 264
Grancich, Serg. Guelfo				C.T.	312
Granzoto, Giuseppe	257ª	108º	36º	A.S.	75
Grossi, Cap. Giorgio	283ª	130º Aut.		A.S.	257, 258, 296
Guerci, Serg. Mario	73ª	9º	4º	C.T.	315, 320
Guiducci, Cap. Giovanni	90ª	10º	4º	C.T.	244
Gulla, Serg.Magg.	376ª	21º	51º	C.T.	326
Iacone, Serg.Magg. Ezio	70ªbis	23ºAut.Nucleo		C.T.	125
Ivaldi, Cap. Carlo	73ª	9º	4º	C.T.	305, 315
Labanti, Serg.Magg. Dante	96ª	9º	4º	C.T.	335
Lagi, Mar. Gino	79ª	6º	1º	C.T.	71
Lalatta, Col. Sergio			43º	B.T.	393
Lalli, Gen.D.A. Tedeschini	(Cdr. 2ª Squadra Aerea)				379
La Manna, Ten.Col. Gennaro		90º	30º	B.T.	380
Lanzarini, Serg. Abramo	72ª	17º	1º	C.T.	35, 81
Larismont Pergameni, Magg. Antonio	97ª	9º	4º	C.T.	315, 316, 334
Leotta, Col. Eugenio			4º	C.T.	304, 316, 394
Liberati, Sottoten. Francesco	98ª	7º	54º	C.T.	261
Liberi, Ten.Col. Roberto		30º	10º	B.T.	265, 393
Ligugnana, Sottoten.		17º	1º	C.T.	235
Lorenzoni, Ten. Lorenzo	74ª	23º Aut.		C.T.	95
Lubelli, Col. Arnaldo			11º	B.T.	2, 389, 392
Lucchini, Cap. Franco	90º	10º	4º	C.T.	244, 252, 253, 279, 287, 300
Lucchini, 1º Av. Giacomo	259ª	109º	36º	B.T.	*26*
Maccagni, Ten. Remo		33º	11º	B.T.	25
Magagnoli, Cap. Dante	278ª Aut.			A.S.	299
Magli, Mar.		17º	1º	C.T.	35
Magnaghi, Serg.Magg.	98ª	7º	54º	C.T.	265, 300
Magnani, Sottoten. Luigi Illica	192ª	87º	30º	B.T.	31
Magrini, Sottoten. Gianfranco			43º	B.T.	250
Maiorca, Magg. Paolo		52º	34º	B.T.	389
Majorana, Sottoten. Giuseppe	287ª Aut.			R.M.	299
Malvezzi, Ten. Fernando	236ª, 96ª	96º, 9º		B.aT	65, 67, 114
				C.T.	335, 390
Mantelli, Serg. Mario		23º Aut.		C.T.	302
Mantovani, Ten. Gian Paolo		7º	54º	C.T.	249
Marasco, Mar.		6º Aut.		C.T.	76

Name					Pages
Marcaccini, Sottoten. Sigfrido	198ª	94°	31°	B.M.	51
Marcantonio, 1e Av. Tomaso		116°	37°	B.T.	317
Marcucci, Ten.Col. Antonio		32°	10°	B.T.	393
Marini, Cap. Marino	282ª Aut.			A.S.	272, 296, 394
Marinone, Ten. Marco	70ª	23° Aut.		C.T.	228
Mariotti, Serg.			54°	C.T.	*239*
Martinoli, Serg. Teresio	73ª	9°	4°	C.T.	307, 314, 315, 320, *335*, 341
Martini, Sottoten. Gino		23° Aut.		C.T.	331
Marzocca, Serg. Raffaele	74ª	23° Aut.		C.T.	95, 96
Massini, Ten. Mario			10°	B.T.	253
Maurer, Ten.		7°	54°	C.T.	246, 250, 300
Mauri, Serg. Arnaldo		7°	54°	C.T.	246, *266*
Mazzini, Col. Umberto			34°	B.T.	2, 389
Mazzucco, Gen.D.A. Renato	(Cdr., Aeronautica Sicilia Pelona)				392
Melley, Cap. Franco	283ª	130° Aut.		A.S.	296
Mezzetti, Magg. Vezio		6° Aut.		C.T.	76, 108, 158, 172, 392
Migliavacca, Serg. Giardano	386ª	21°	51°	C.T.	115
Minelli, Serg. Gustavo	96ª	9°	4°	C.T.	311, 335
Miotto, Serg.Magg. Elio		10°	4°	C.T.	253
Moccagatta, Cap. di Freg.	(10th. Light Flotilla)				264
Molteni, Ten. Giulio	193ª	87°	30°	B.T.	98
Molinelli, Serg.Magg. Lamberto	88ª	6° Aut.		C.T.	11
Mondini, Cap. Bruno	386ª	21°	51°	C.T.	302
Monti, Ten. Ezio		23° Aut.		C.T.	80, 92
Morandi, Sottoten. Sergio		17°	1°	C.T.	96
Morelli, Sottoten. Vincenzo	258ª	109°	36°	A.S.	299
Morri, Serg. Aristodemo	163ª Aut.			C.T.	62
Moruzzi, Ten. Carlo		156° Aut.		C.T.	*175*
Mussolini, Benito					1, 105, 410
Nasoni, Ten. Mario		6° Aut.		C.T.	72
Natalucci, Ten. Carlo			43°	B.T.	250
Nioi, Cap. Olizio		17°	1°	C.T.	235
Nobili, Magg. Guido		157°	1°	C.T.	*40*, 389
Nogare, Cap. Bernadino Dalle (see Dalle Nogare)					
Novelli, Serg. Raffaello	97ª	9°	4°	C.T.	305, 334
Oblach, Sottoten. Giuseppe	73ª	9°	4°	C.T.	312
Oliva, Cap. Domenico	287ª Aut.			R.M.	30
Olivetti, Mar. Manlio	96ª	9°	4°	C.T.	311
Omiccioli, Serg. Walter		7°	54°	C.T.	246, 264, 281, 288
Palazzeschi, Ten. Antonio		6° Aut.		C.T.	117
Pandolfi, Ten. Bruno	283ª	130° Aut.		A.S.	257, 258
Paolazzi, Sottoten. Bruno	96ª	9°	4°	C.T.	311
Papini, Serg. Felice		156° Aut.		C.T.	*175*
Pardini, Serg. Pardino	70ª	23° Aut.		C.T.	89
Parmeggiani, Sottot. Amedeo	376ª	21°	51°	C.T.	339
Parodi, Serg.Magg. Egeo	96ª	9°	4°	C.T.	335
Pasqua, Sottoten. Andrea Della		9°	4°	C.T.	287
Patriarca, Mar. Vincenzo	356ª	21°	51°	C.T.	344
Paulello, Ten.Col. Marco Minio		9°	4°	C.T.	304, 316, 320, 394

Pederzoli, Ten. Wisdor		23º Aut.		C.T.	283
Perdoni, Serg. Luciano	84ª	10º	4º	C.T.	244
Persani, Mar.		6º Aut.		C.T.	123
Pesola, Ten. Giuseppe	79ª	6º Aut.		C.T.	2, 4, 80
Pezzi, Col. Enrico			41º	B.T.	2, 389
Piccinini, Ten. Col. Mario			1º	C.T.	389
Pieri, Ten. Giorgio		109º	36º	B.T.	75
Pinna, Ten. Mario		23º Aut.		C.T.	37
Pluda, Cap. Mario		9º	4º	C.T.	305, 315, 316, 325
Poli, Ten.Col. Renato			53º	B.T.	389
Pozzalini, Ten. Girogio	194ª	90º	30º	R.M.	234
Primatesta, Ten. Paolo	186ª	83º Aut.		R.M.	82
Querci, Sottoten. Alvaro	73ª	9º	4º	C.T.	315, 334
Reggiani, Ten. Sergio		99º	43º	B.T.	231
Reglieri, Col. Alfredo			1º	C.T.	392
Rigatti, Ten. Mario	75ª	23º Aut.		C.T.	54, *55*
Riosa, Ten. Giovanni	188ª	85º Aut.		R.M.	58
Romagna, Serg.Magg.		17º	1º	C.T.	235
Romagnoli, Ten.Col. Carlo		10º	4º	C.T.	239, 240, 253, 287, *287*, 288, 394
Romeo, Sottoten. Antonio		99º	43º	B.T.	274
Rossetti, Ten.Col. Luigi		53º	34º	B.T.	389
Rossi, Serg.Magg. Pasquale	73ª	9º	4º	C.T.	314, 334
Rossi, Serg.Magg.		17º	1º	C.T.	235
Rotolo, Cap. Alfonso	257ª	108º	36º	A.S.	299
Ruggeri, Sottoten. Luigi	257ª	108º	36º	A.S.	29
Ruspoli, Cap. Carlo		6º Aut.		C.T.	76
Saachi, Serg. Luigi		23º Aut.		C.T.	331, 347
Sala, Serg.Magg. Arnaldo		23º Aut.		C.T.	95, 96
Salvaneschi, Ten. Aldo	170ª Aut.			R.M.	84
Salvatore, Serg. Massimo	97ª	9º	4º	C.T.	327, 334
Sanguettoli, Serg. Giuseppe		23º Aut.		C.T.	187
Santinoni, Ten. Giovani	237ª	96º Aut.		B.a'T	390
Saracino, Serg. Giuseppe		23º Aut.		C.T.	331, 347
Sartirana, Ten.	72ª	17º	1º	C.T.	53
Savi, Magg. Ercole		33º	9º	B.T.	394
Scarabellotto, Cap. Valerio	192ª	87º	30º	B.T.	29
Scarlata, Col. Giuseppe			37º	B.T.	395
Scarpini, Mar. Elio		96º Aut.		B.a'T	65
Schiavetta, Ten.Col.			30º	B.T.	54
Sclavo, Serg. Alfredo	90ª	10º	4º	C.T.	244
Seidl, Col. Riccardo Zario			36º	A.S.	296, 299
Serra, Col. Antonio			30º	B.T.	31, 390
Serini, Ten. Pietro		23º Aut.		C.T.	300
Sguario, Ten. Mario	259ª	109º	36º	B.T.	26
Sigismondo, Mar.		16º	54º	C.T.	240
Silvestri, Ten.Col. Vincenzo		87º	30º	B.T.	390
Simionato, Mar. Otello		16º	54º	C.T.	243
Solaro, Ten. Claudio	70ª	23º Aut.		C.T.	89, 294, 302
Solaroli, Ten. Giorgio		23º Aut.	156º Aut.	C.T.	255, 258, *258*, *262*, 332

Soldati, Ten. Alberto		108°	36°	B.T.	75
Solimena, Ten. Francesco	216ª	53°	34°	B.T.	10
Soprana, Ten.	90ª	10°	4°	C.T.	244, 279
Spitzl, Serg. Bruno	96ª	9°	4°	C.T.	335
Spolverato, Magg.	18ª	27°	8°	B.T.	46
Stabile, Serg.Magg.	88ª	6° Aut.		C.T.	80, 172
Steppi, Serg. Roberto	84ª	10°	4°	C.T.	240, 243
Tabocchini, Ten.Col. Vincenzo		87°	30°	B.T.	390
Talamini, Ten.		17°	1°	C.T.	235
Tarantino, Serg. Manlio		23° Aut.		C.T.	41
Taroni, Serg.Magg. Luigi	96ª	9°	4°	C.T.	311, 325
Tempra, Ten. Francesco		109°	36°	B.T.	75
Tesei, Magg. Teseo	(Human torpedo pilot)				263, 264
Tessari, Ten. Luigi	97ª	9°	4°	C.T.	305
Tirapelle, Serg. Antonio	76ª	7°	54°	C.T.	234
Tomaselli, Ten.		6° Aut.		C.T.	80
Tomasino, Cap. Bartolomeo	258ª	109°	36°	A.S.	299
Torelli, Ten. Renato	204ª	41° Aut.		B.T.	28
Torreggiano, Sottoten. Marcelo	356ª	21°	51°	C.T.	256
Toscano, Ten. Francesco		116°	37°	B.T.	317
Toschi, Magg. Cesare		116°	37°	B.T.	332, 395
Tosi, Serg. Armando	238ª	96° Aut.		B.a'T	324
Tugnoli, Cap. Giorgio		3° Aut.		C.T.	200
Valotti, Serg. Luigi		24° Aut.		C.T.	298
Vanzan, Sottoten. Virgilio	90ª	10°	4°	C.T.	243, 244, 321, 327
Velardi, Gen.D.A. Vincenzo	(Cdr., 1ª Div. Aerea C.T.)				
Venanza, Ovidio					96
Vercelli, Ten. Livio			43°	B.T.	276
Verna, Cap. Giusellino	259ª	109°	36°	A.S.	299
Verrascina, Cap.		87°	30°	B.T.	54
Vesco, Ten.	('Maiale' pilot)				295
Viglione–Borghese, Cap. Ezio	96ª	9°	4°	C.T.	335
Vincenzi, Ten.Col. Ugo		109°	36°	B.T.	390
Vio, 1ᵉ Av. Gianpiero		96° Aut.		B.a'T	65
Visintini, Ten.	('Maiale' pilot)				295
Vittorio Emmanuel III	(King of Italy)				*294*
Volpe, Ten. Giuseppe		6° Aut.		C.T.	85
Weber, Sottoten. Marcello	193ª	87°	30°	B.T.	231, 232
Zagnoli, Ten. Pellegrino	233ª	59°	41°	B.T.	28
Zanandrea, Mar. Ettori		6° Aut.		C.T.	108
Zemella, Serg.Magg. Celso	70ª	23° Aut.		C.T.	35, *68*

b) German

Babinek, Lt. Wilfred, 3/NJG 2   358
Becker, Uffz. Heinrich, 9/St.G 1   197
Bernhard, Fw. Karl, 2(F)/123   158
Bergfleth, Oblt., 9/ZG 26   201
Böhmer, Lt. Hermann, 8/LG 1   135
Braun, Fw. Johannes, 4/St.G 1   159

Brauns, Lt. Wilhelm, 1/NJG 2   350
Bude, Fw. Otto, 4/KG 77   354

Diekwisch, Fw. Erwin, 9/St.G 1   155
Dobislav, Hptm. Max, III/JG 27   209
Dunkel, Lt. Horst, 7/LG 1   123

Places

445

447

Zante Island, Adriatic, 80, 175, 326
Zebbug, Malta, 36, 172
Zeitun, Malta, 81

Zonkor Point, Malta, 139, 279, 354, 424
Zuara, Libya, 249, 252, 272, 293, 307, 312, 316, 348, 355

I: Air Force Units

a) Royal Air Force and Fleet Air Arm

Squadrons:

1 Squadron, 16, 130, 169, 177, 190
3 Squadron, 190
17 Squadron, 163
18 Squadron, 310 (arrival on Malta), 312, 314, 320, 323, 325, 332, 338, 341, 343, 346, 347, 348, 352, 355, 360, 368, 423
19 Squadron, 47
21 Squadron, 15, 193 (arrival on Malta), 195, 199, 227, *261*, 360, 367, 423
22 Squadron, 68
32 Squadron, 47, 130, 190
33 Squadron, 14
37 Squadron, 83 (arrival on Malta), 86, 367, 423
38 Squadron, 130, 273 (arrival on Malta), 282, 292, 293, 313, 314, 367, 423
40 Squadron, 314 (arrival on Malta), 316, 321, 326, 336, 339, 341, 342, 344, 347, 350, 352, 358, 360, 368, 412, 423
41 Squadron, 88
43 Squadron, 47, 130, 163
46 Squadron, 44, *227*, 229 (arrival on Malta), *229*, 230, *231*, 231, 233, 234, 235, 240, 242, 243, 244, 245, 366, 384, 387, 423
55 Squadron, 283
56 Squadron, 178
60 Squadron, 16
64 Squadron, 47
66 Squadron, 47
69 Squadron, 117 (formation on Malta from 431 Flight), 134, *143*, 147, *149*, *154*, 164, 165, *174*, 175, *179*, 183, 185, 197, 211, 222, 228, 229, 240, 243, 245, 252, 253, 256, 257, 272, 275, 276, 283, 291, 294, 305, 313, 316, 321, 323, 325, 326, 333, 336, 341, 353, 354, 355, 363, 368, 384, 397, 400, 403, 404, 409, 412, 420, 423
70 Squadron, 155
73 Squadron, 88, 131, 132, 169
80 Squadron, 30, 115
82 Squadron, 210 (arrival on Malta), 223, 227, 230, 234, 241, 242, 245, 249, 367, 423
85 Squadron, 129, 130
104 Squadron, 313 (arrival on Malta), 314, 316, 321, 325, 326, 336, 339, 341, 344, 368, 423
105 Squadron, 254, 265, 270 (arrival on Malta), 272, 274, 277, 282, 284, 289, 291, 292, 309, 310, 323, 367, 423
107 Squadron, 284, 292 (arrival on Malta), 293, 300, 307, 309, 310, 312, 316, 320, 325, 332, 338, 341, 343, 347, 348, 353, 355, 360, 367, 423
110 Squadron, 247 (arrival on Malta), 251, 252, 253, 257, 270, 284, 367, 423
111 Squadron, 130
112 Squadron, 56, 206
113 Squadron, 300 (arrival of detachment on Malta), 302, 363, 366
125 Squadron, 333
126 Squadron, 246 (formation on Malta from 46 Squadron), 248, 249, 251, 254, 264, 270, 271, 275, 279, *279*, *280*, 281, *282*, 285, 290, 291, 306, 309, 314, 323, 324, 327, 336, *337*, 341, 346, 347, 349, 350, 354, 356, 360, 366, 384, 387, 423
127 Squadron, 217, 374
138 Squadron, 321 (arrival of detachment on Malta), 325
139 Squadron, 210 (arrival on Malta), 223, 228, 367, 400, 423
145 Squadron, 130
148 Squadron, 76 (formation on Malta), 86, 92, 96, 108, 118, 119, 134, 139, 154, 155, *156–157*, 163, 193, 205, 242, 249, 254, 367, 398, 400, 421, 423
151 Squadron, 130, 133
156 Squadron, 360
157 Squadron, 333
185 Squadron, 205 (formation on Malta), *206*, *207*, 208, *208*, 209, 213, 218, 229, 231, 244, *247*, 248, 249, 251, 252, 253, 260, 264, 265, 268, 270, *275*, 275, *276*, 281, 285, 286, 290, 294, 295, 301, 304, 305, 306, 307, 309, 310, 314, 315, *319*, *322*, *323*, 323, 326, 330, 334, 341, 342, 348, 352, 354, 358, *361*, 365, 371, 374, 384, 387, 423
200 Squadron, 238
202 Squadron, 7, 38, *38*, 50, 247, 397, 403
203 Squadron, 350
213 Squadron, 130, 169, 211, 213, *214*, 215, 219
219 Squadron, 290
221 Squadron, 305 (arrival of detachment on Malta), 309, 319, 341, 354, 368, 423
222 Squadron, 47, 230

from the M.N.F.U.), *342*, *343*, 344, *344*, 346, 355, 356, 366

Fighter Flight, Hal Far, 6 (formation on Malta), 7, 7, 37, *49*, 51, 134, 210, 365, 369, 374, 375, 384, 386, 403

Station Flight, Hal Far, 400, 403

Station Flight, Luqa, 400

Kalafrana Seaplane Rescue Flight, 277, 304, 305, 339, 358

Fulmar Flight, Hal Far, 400

Reserve Flight, Stradishall, 167

Other Units:

1 Photographic Reconnaissance Unit (1 P.R.U.), 25, 293, 333

No. 2 Group, Bomber Command, 193, 226, 241

3 Anti-Aircraft Co-operation Unit (3 A.A.C.U.), 6, 7, 7, *8*, 9, 37, 71, 154, 397

3 Bombing & Gunnery School, 44

4 Ferry Pilots' Pool, 15

7 Operational Training Unit (7 O.T.U.), 45

10 Maintenance Unit (10 M.U.), 12, 15

15 Operational Training Unit (15 O.T.U.), 238

20 Maintenance Unit (20 M.U.), 15

22 Operational Training Unit (22 O.T.U.), 316, *317*

27 Maintenance Unit (27 M.U.), 15

241 Air Ministry Experimental Station (241 A.M.E.S.), XI

242 Air Ministry Experimental Station (242 A.M.E.S.), XI

266 Wing, 327

Takali Wing, 360

Air Delivery Unit (A.D.U.), Takoradi, 374

Overseas Air Delivery Unit (O.A.D.U.), 283, 321, 331, 359

Headquarters, Malta (H.Q., Malta), 13, 14, 134, 141, 168, 183, 195, 211, 268, 293, 305, 362, 371, 372

Headquarters, Royal Air Force, Middle East (H.Q., R.A.F., M.E.), 14, 130, 238, 239, 303, 345

Pilots' Pool, Ismailia, 163

B.O.A.C., 340

b) *Regia Aeronautica*

Squadriglie (where individually specified):

10ᵃ Squadriglia (28°Gr., 8°St. B.T.), 391

18ᵃ Squadriglia (27°Gr., 8°St. B.T.), 46, *46*, 391

19ᵃ Squadriglia (28°Gr., 8°St. B.T.), 391

30ᵃ Squadriglia (76°Gr.Aut. O.A.), 390

49ᵃ Squadriglia (38°Gr., 32°St. B.T.), 30, 200, 391

50ᵃ Squadriglia (38°Gr., 32°St. B.T.), 391

52ᵃ Squadriglia (27°Gr., 8°St. B.T.), 391

55ᵃ Squadriglia (30°Gr., 10°St. B.T.), 393

56ᵃ Squadriglia (30°Gr., 10°St. B.T.), 229, 265, 393

57ᵃ Squadriglia (32°Gr., 10°St. B.T.), 195, 393

58ᵃ Squadriglia (32°Gr., 10°St. B.T.), 195, 242, 393

59ᵃ Squadriglia (33°Gr., 11°St. B.T.), *286*, 389, 394

60ᵃ Squadriglia (33°Gr., 11°St. B.T.), 8, *284*, 389, 394

62ᵃ Squadriglia (29°Gr., 9°St. B.T.), 394

63ᵃ Squadriglia (29°Gr., 9°St. B.T.), 394

65ᵃ Squadriglia (31°Gr., 43°St. B.T.), 224, 393

66ᵃ Squadriglia (31°Gr., 43°St. B.T.), 224, 393

67ᵃ Squadriglia (32°Gr., 10°St. B.T.), 234, 389

68ᵃ Squadriglia (34°Gr., 11°St. B.T.), *1*, 389

70ᵃ Squadriglia (23°Gr.Aut. C.T.), 35, 66, *92*, 95, 125, 228, 392

71ᵃ Squadriglia (17°Gr., 1°St. C.T.), 81, 389, 392

72ᵃ Squadriglia (17°Gr., 1°St. C.T.), 39, 53, 81, 99, *100*, 389, 392

73ᵃ Squadriglia (9°Gr., 4°St. C.T.), 25, 315, 325, 394

74ᵃ Squadriglia (23°Gr.Aut. C.T.), 37, 95, 96, 187, 236, *258*, 392

75ᵃ Squadriglia (23°Gr.Aut. C.T.), *34*, 41, 54, 81, 89, 92, *282*, 308, 347, 392

76ᵃ Squadriglia (7°Gr., 54°St. C.T.), 224, 265, 393

79ᵃ Squadriglia (6°Gr., 1°St. C.T.), 2, 71, 108, 174, *236*, 389, 392

80ᵃ Squadriglia (17°Gr., 1°St. C.T.), 81, *100*, 389, 392

81ᵃ Squadriglia (6°Gr., 1°St. C.T.), 2, *3*, 108, 389, 392

84ᵃ Squadriglia (10°Gr., 4°St. C.T.), 244, *309*, 394

86ᵃ Squadriglia (7°Gr., 54°St. C.T.), 224, *237*, 281, 302, 345, *346*, 393

88ᵃ Squadriglia (6°Gr., 1°St. C.T.), 2, 11, 27, 80, 108, 389, 392

90ᵃ Squadriglia (10°Gr., 4°St. C.T.), 244, 394

91ᵃ Squadriglia (10°Gr., 4°St. C.T.), 394

96ᵃ Squadriglia (9°Gr., 4°St. C.T.), 25, 325, 394

452

385ª Squadriglia (157ºGr., 1ºSt. C.T.), 389
386ª Squadriglia (21º/157ºGr., 51º/1ºSt. C.T.), 302, 389
601ª Squadriglia S.A.S., 27
612ª Squadriglia, 124, 211, 235, 244, 251, 277, 287, 395

Gruppi (where no squadriglie specified):

3º Gruppo Aut. C.T., 93, 94, 200, 391
6º Gruppo Aut. C.T. (later 1ºSt. C.T.), 2, *3*, 27, 39, 63, 64, 71, 72, 76, 80, 85, 95, 108, 123, 125, 171, 210, *236*, 239, 347, 389, 392
7º Gruppo (54ºSt. C.T.), 224, 233, 234, 235, *237*, 237, 244, 246, 249, 250, 253, 261, 264, 265, *266*, 280, 300, 302, 393, 395
9º Gruppo (4ºSt. C.T.), 25, 26, 29, 31, 35, 304, 305, 311, 312, 314, 315, 320, 321, 327, 334, 335, *335*, 341, *346*, 394
10º Gruppo (4ºSt. C.T.), 239, 240, 242, 243, 244, 249, 250, 252, 253, 260, 279, 280, 285, 287, *287*, 288, 300, *309*, 321, 327, 394
16º Gruppo (54ºSt. C.T.), 239, 240, 242, 243, 244, 250, 253, 280, 394, 395
17º Gruppo (1ºSt. C.T.), 35, 39, 53, 81, 96, 99, *100*, 180, 186, 210, 234, 235, 237, 239, 389, 392
19º Gruppo Aut.Com., 391
21º Gruppo (51ºSt. C.T.), 115, 256, 302, 326, 344
23º Gruppo Aut. C.T., *34*, 35, 37, 41, *43*, 53, 54, *55*, 63, 64, 65, *68*, 80, 81, *81*, 89, *91*, 92, *92*, 95, 96, 99, 108, 125, 134, 170, *173*, *175*, 180, 186, 187, 205, 210, 228, 235, *237*, 237, 239, 255, *255*, 257, 258, 282, *283*, 283, 292, *294*, 300, 302, *302*, *303*, 308, 314, 331, 332, 347, 362, 392, 393
24º Gruppo Aut. C.T., 296
27º Gruppo (8ºSt. B.T.), 46, *46*, 391
28º Gruppo (8ºSt. B.T.), 391
29º Gruppo (9ºSt. B.T.), 394, 395
30º Gruppo (10ºSt. B.T.), 210, 229, 265, 393, 395
31º Gruppo (43ºSt. B.T.), 274, 393
32º Gruppo (10ºSt. B.T.), 195, 210, 234, 242, 258, 284, 393, 395
33º Gruppo (11ºSt. B.T.), 8, 25, 284, *284*, *286*, 295, 389, 394, 395
34º Gruppo (11ºSt. B.T.), *1*, 34, 389
38º Gruppo (32ºSt. B.T.), 30, 391
41º Gruppo Aut. B.T., 28
51º Gruppo Aut. B.T., 257
52º Gruppo (34ºSt. B.T.), 2, 8, 27, 389
53º Gruppo (34ºSt. B.T.), *3*, 10, 389
55º Gruppo (37ºSt. B.T.), 310, 395
56º Gruppo (39ºSt. B.T.), 392
59º Gruppo (41ºSt. B.T.), 28, 60, 389
60º Gruppo (41ºSt. B.T.), 53, 389

76º Gruppo Aut. O.A., 390
83º Gruppo R.S.T., 390
84º Gruppo R.S.T., 392
85º Gruppo Aut. R.M., 224, 391
87º Gruppo (30ºSt. B.T.), 29, 31, *32*, 54, *54*, 98, 186, 194, 210, 284, 390, 392, 394
89º Gruppo (32ºSt. B.T.), 391
90º Gruppo (30ºSt. B.T.), 31, *32*, 33, *52*, 210, 390, 392, 394
92º Gruppo (39ºSt. B.T.), 34, 62, 392
93º Gruppo (31ºSt. B.T.), 391
94º Gruppo (31ºSt. B.T.), 391
96º Gruppo Aut. B.aᵀ., 58, *59*, 60, 61, *63*, *66*, 67, *67*, 75, 95, 105, 108, 390
97º Gruppo Aut. B.aᵀ., 95
99º Gruppo (43ºSt. B.T.), 200, 210, 231, 274, 393
101º Gruppo Aut.Tuff., 224, 258, *259*, 259, 274, 285, 335, 393
105º Gruppo Aut. B.T., 54, 75, *90*, *91*
108º Gruppo (36ºSt. B.T. later A.S.), 29, 72, 75, 296, 298, 331, 390
109º Gruppo (36ºSt. B.T. later A.S.), 26, *26*, 52, 64, 75, 296, 298, 348, 399
116º Gruppo (37ºSt. B.T.), 306, *306*, *307*, 317, 340, 395
130º Gruppo Aut. A.S., 296
131º Gruppo Aut. A.S., 224
132º Gruppo Aut. A.S., *300*
156º Gruppo Aut. C.T., 134, 138, 158, 159, 170, 393
157º Gruppo (1ºSt. C.T.), *40*, 389
171º Gruppo Aut. C.N., 306, 394

Stormi (where no gruppi specified):

1º Stormo C.T., 35, *40*, 65, 81, 85, *100*, 194, 210, *235*, *236*, *237*, 239, 389, 392, 394
4º Stormo C.T., 25, *237*, 239, 267, 304, *304*, *306*, *309*, *311*, 316, 320, 324, 326, *337*, 394
8º Stormo B.T., 46, *46*, 391
9º Stormo B.T., 284, *284*, *286*, 289, 315, 394, 395
10º Stormo B.T., 28, 195, 210, 229, 250, 251, 253, 258, 265, 276, 284, 393, 395
11º Stormo B.T., *1*, 2, 4, 5, 8, 11, 25, 28, 389
14º Stormo B.T., 28
15º Stormo B.T., 28, 33, 34
30º Stormo B.T., 28, 29, 31, *32*, 33, *52*, 54, *54*, *55*, 83, 95, 96, 98, 99, 210, 258, 276, 390, 392, 394
31º Stormo B.T., 391
32º Stormo B.T., 94, 108, 257, 391
33º Stormo B.T., 33
34º Stormo B.T., 2, *3*, 4, 5, 8, 10, 25, 28, 33, 38, *38*, 63, *71*, 75, 81, 89, 95, 389

453

35° Stormo B.M., 28, 33, 65, 82
36° Stormo B.T. later A.S., 26, *26*, 28, 29, 33, 37, 52, 60, 63, 72, 75, 83, 296, 299, 348, 390
37° Stormo B.T., 28, 306, *306*, *307*, 312, 313, 395
39° Stormo B.T., 34, 62, 392
40° Stormo B.T., 28
41° Stormo B.T., 2, 5, 9, 28, 33, *43*, 53, 60, 389
43° Stormo B.T., 200, 210, 223, 224, 250, 251, 253, 273, 274, 276, 285, 393
51° Stormo C.T., 145
54° Stormo C.T., 224, *237*, 239, *239*, 249, 251,

252, 258, 260, *266*, 287, 288, 315, 334, 335, 394, 395

Other formations:

1ª Divisione 'Aquila', 389
3ª Divisione 'Centauro', 10, 389
11ª Divisione 'Nibbio', 390
2ª Squadra Aerea, 1, 5, 9, 10, 25, 37, 75, 83, 85, 95, 98, 389
Aeronautica della Sicilia, 392
Aeronautica della Sardegna, 46, 391
Aeronautica dell'Egeo, 392

c) *Luftwaffe*

Staffeln (where specified):

4/LG 1, 136, 161, 162
5/LG 1, 121, 166, 205
6/LG 1, 121, 139
7/LG 1, 123, 151, 205
8/LG 1, 121, 126, 135
9/LG 1, 194
1/St.G 1, 126
2/St.G 1, 115, 126
3/St.G 1, 115
4/St.G 1, 159, 203
5/St.G 1, 159
6/St.G 1, 159
7/St.G 1, 163
8/St.G 1, 173
9/St.G 1, 155, 163, 173, 183, 197, 203
4/St.G 2, 115
5/St.G 2, 115
2/NJG 2, 352
3/NJG 2, 358
1/NJG 3, 155, 166, 186
5/KG 4, 188
7/JG 26, *144*, 145, *147*, 147, 149, 158, 160, 161, 162, 164, *164*, 166, 167, *169*, 171, 179, 180, 184, 188, 194, 195, 196, 198, 203, 209, 220, 225, 362
4/KG 26, 139, 198
5/KG 26, 141, *146*, 146, 170
6/KG 26, 188, 194
9/ZG 26, 201
7/KG 30, 186
8/KG 30, 198
9/KG 30, 197
Stab/JG 53, 358
4/KG 77, 354
5/KG 77, 354
1(F)/121, 106, 138, 145, 202
2(F)/123, 106, 158, 183, 202, 203
Seenotberichskommando X, 106

Gruppen (where Staffeln not specified):

II(K)/LG 1, 106, 119, 121, 141, 142, 145
III(K)/LG 1, 106, 126, 143, 145
I/St.G 1, *105*, 106, 109, 119, *122*, 123, 126, 145, 201
II/St.G 1, 159, 202
III/St.G 1, 155, 159, 163, 171, 186, 202
I/JG 2, 340
I/NJG 2, 340, 344, 347, 348, 350, 358
II/St.G 2, 106, 109, 115, 116, 126, 145, 205
II/JG 3, 339
II/KG 26, 106, 119, *142*, 174, 198
III/ZG 26, 106, *106*, 121, *121*, 126, 145, 158, 166, 176, 340, 350, 352
I/JG 27, 161, 162
II/JG 27, 339
III/JG 27, 196, 198, *199*, 207, 208, *208*, 209, 213, 339
I/KG 40, *166*
I/JG 53, 350, 351
II/JG 53, *340*, 354
III/JG 53, 339, 362
I/KG 54, 340
II/KG 77, 354, 356
KGr. 606, 340
KGr. 806, 340, 354, 356, 360
III/KGzbV 1, 313, 314, 316
KGr.zbV 9, 106, 119

Geschwadern (where no Staffeln or Gruppen specified):

Lehrgeschwader 1 (LG 1), *120*, 121, 150, *150*, 194
Stukageschwader 1 (St.G 1), 162, 163, 173
Jagdgeschwader 3 (JG 3), 171
Stukageschwader 3 (St.G 3), 145
Kampfgeschwader 26 (KG 26), 147

Jagdgeschwader 27 (JG 27), *225*, 362
Jagdgeschwader 53 (JG 53), 339, 350, 352, 356, 358, *359*, 362
Kampfgeschwader 77 (KG 77), 340

II: Naval Units and Ships

a) British

455

b) *Italian*

Maria, 325
Montello, 228
Neptunia, 243, 292
Nicolo Odero, 292
Nita, 274
Oceania, 243, 292
Panuco, 253
Pietro Barbaro, 285
Rialto, 309

Rina Corrado, 325
Sabaudia, 185
Sagitta, 325
San Marco, 325
Sparta, 249
Tembien, 241
Volturno, 339
Vulcania, 243, 292

c) German

Warship:

Battle Cruiser

Hipper, 104, 131

Cargo and Merchant Vessels

Duisburg, 138
Ingo, 138
Inza, 138
Preussen, 257
Reichenfels, 343
Wachtfels, 241

III: British Army Units

No. 2 Commando, 146
24th.Coy., Bomb Disposal Squad, R.E., 126
King's Own Malta Regiment, 269

Pioneer Corps, 146
Royal Artillery, 270
Royal Malta Artillery, 270

IV: British Naval/Air Operation Code-names

Operation 'Callboy', 312, 388
Operation 'Collar', 93
Operation 'Colossus', 141, 146, 147
Operation 'Crusader', 332
Operation 'Dunlop', 189, 190, 388
Operation 'Excess', 104, 108, 109, 116, 131
Operation 'Grab', 59
Operation 'Halberd', 293, 295
Operation 'Hurry', 47, *48–49, 50*, 388
Operation 'Perpetual', 328, 388
Operation 'Railway I', 244, *245*, 388
Operation 'Railway II', 246, 388
Operation 'Rocket', *227*, 229, 388

Operation 'Smash', 59
Operation 'Splice', 213, *214*, 388
Operation 'Status I', 290, 352, 388
Operation 'Status II', 290, 352, 388
Operation 'Substance', 256, 257, 260, 271, 388
Operation 'Tiger', 195, 197, 200, 205
Operation 'Tracer', 235, 388
Operation 'White', 88, 388
Operation 'Winch', 177, *177*, 190, 388

Other Codename

'Ultra', 263, 272, 280, 292

457

MEDITERRANEAN AREA